The Diaries of
Hans Christian Andersen

THE DIARIES OF

Hans Christian Andersen

Selected and translated by

Patricia L. Conroy and Sven H. Rossel

UNIVERSITY OF WASHINGTON PRESS

Seattle & London

To Erik Dal

Library of Congress Cataloging-in-Publication Data

Andersen, H. C. (Hans Christian). 1805–1875.
[Diaries. English. Selections]
The diaries of Hans Christian Andersen / selected and translated
by Patricia L. Conroy and Sven H. Rossel.
p.   cm.
ISBN 0-295-96845-1 (alk. paper)
1. Andersen, H. C. (Hans Christian), 1805–1875—Diaries.
2. Authors, Danish—19th century—Diaries.   I. Conroy, Patricia L.
II. Rossel, Sven Hakon.   III. Title.
PT8118.A6   1990.
839.8'18603—dc20

[B]   89-22463
                                                                          CIP

This book was published with the assistance of a grant from the
National Endowment for the Humanities.

The paper used in this publication meets the minimum requirements of
American National Standard for Information Sciences—Permanence of Paper
for Printed Library Materials, ANSI Z39.38-1984.

This one-volume translation is based on *H. C. Andersens Dagbøger 1825–75*,
the definitive twelve-volume crticial edition published by Det danske Sprog- og
Litteraturselskab (Copenhagen, 1971–76).

Title page illustration: *Pierrot* papercut by Hans Christian Andersen.

Contents

Illustrations

Translators' Preface

B Y 1825, HANS CHRISTIAN ANDERSEN was twenty years old and had already spent three years at the Latin school in Slagelse trying to fulfill everyone's expectations of him. Important men in Copenhagen and Odense—Titular Councillor Jonas Collin and Lieutenant Colonel Christian Høegh-Guldberg—had seen promise in the young man's imaginative but undisciplined and ungrammatical writings and had provided him with the opportunity to get an education. But the Latin school's stern principal, Simon Meisling, made this stipulation: Andersen was not to waste any more of his time scribbling; he was to concentrate on his studies.

Fearful that he might be abandoned by disappointed benefactors, Andersen studied earnestly, driving himself into such a state that he could hardly function and always did badly. As a relief from this diligence, however, he could not refuse himself a little recreational reading from time to time. In the autumn of 1825, he devoured works by Shakespeare, Smollett, Calderon, Schiller, Schlegel, Tieck, Oehlenschläger, Holberg, and Molbech, and read all he could in popular magazines filled with stories and poetry, such as *Monthly Roses*, *Miscellany*, *Ceres*, and Riise's *Magazine for Young People*. During school vacations he felt himself to be his own man, free to put pen to paper as he saw fit. That autumn he wrote at least five poems (some of these may have been written clandestinely during the school term), a story, and a historical novel set in a sixteenth-century Danish civil war. Meisling was furious.

Andersen was a compulsive writer who wrote reams of letters when it was forbidden him to write creatively. However, a new "safe" outlet for his craving may have been suggested to him by a fictional diary novella published in an issue of *Miscellany* in 1824. *Fragments of a Country Deacon's Diary* was so convincing that many readers believed the claim by the author, Steen Steensen Blicher, that he had merely found and edited the work. In the novella, the situation of the fictional diarist is strikingly similar to Andersen's own: he is the son of poor parents, and his intelligence has attracted the attention of a learned churchman, who has taken the boy into his home in order to provide him with an education and a start in life. The diarist's dependence on his benefactor, whom he is desperately anxious to please, must have found an echo in Andersen's heart. On September 16, 1825, he began his own diary.

Andersen's schoolboy diary of 1825–26 is a record of an exciting period in his life. Late September was an eventful time for him. His first entry, for example, expresses his joy at receiving a forgiving letter from Høegh-Guldberg, written after a long and censorious estrangement. A later entry reveals that he has just been invited to lodge with the Meislings instead of out in town—a development he saw as very promising. There was also talk at school that Meisling was considering a position in Elsinore, just north of Copenhagen, and Andersen was in an agony of suspense about whether he would be asked to accompany his principal. Indeed, the future was looking very bright for Andersen in late September, were it not for the exams that he must pass in order to escape the disgrace of *again* being held back in the third form! A few weeks later, the actual move into the Meisling household prompted Andersen to write another spate of entries, and in late November he happily reports the invitation he has received to spend the Christmas holidays in the capital, followed in December by his long account of the visit itself.

For the next thirty-five years nearly all of Andersen's diaries are reports of his travels, both at home and abroad. They were often begun on the very day of departure and continued uninterrupted until the last, routine stages of his journey. Like his schoolboy diary, these travel diaries record extraordinary times in his life. Travel was Andersen's lifeblood. It put him in touch with the great masterpieces of Western civilization—its monuments, its statuary, its paintings, its music, and, not least, its theater. In Paris, he could speak with Hugo, Lamartine, and Heine about life and art, as he never could with colleagues in the feud-ridden, claustrophobic Copenhagen of his day. The grandeur of the Alps and the exotic atmosphere of Constantinople exhilarated him, but also prompted in him on his return a renewed appreciation of the subtle beauty of Denmark.

In late August 1861, when Andersen was on the last leg of his journey home from a trip to Rome, word reached him that Jonas Collin, his benefactor and friend for thirty-nine years, had died. Saddened, he continued his journey to Copenhagen to attend the funeral. This time he did not cease writing his diary at the trip's end

but continued to make entries, reporting his impressions of a Copenhagen so familiar to him but now made alien by the absence of
his good friend. From this point on, Andersen made of his diary an
unbroken record of his life until the pen literally fell from his hand
during his final illness. In these entries, Andersen is in his worka-
day world, among the people who mean most to him. It is particularly in these entries that the reader learns of his irascibility, his small
vanities and petty tyrannies, as well as his capacity for friendship,
his honesty, and his kindness.

No reader can come away from Andersen's diaries without the
feeling of having met both a remarkable artist and a remarkable man.
In making our selections from his diaries, we, his translators, have
tried to allow Andersen to document himself in both these regards
for his English-speaking audience. We have naturally focused on those
periods in his life that seemed to us especially interesting, but w
have sought to fashion the excerpts so that they also include some
of his more ordinary experiences—after all, his life was not all agony
and ecstacy. His first diary, for example, shows the plight of a young
man forced to play schoolboy for his own good. The diary from his
trip to Rome in 1833–34 records the raw material that the young
artist will soon use to forge his breakthrough novel, *The Improvisatore*. Unfortunately, the few diaries that exist from 1835 to 1840 reflect little of Andersen's productivity—he wrote three novels and
numerous tales and singspiel—or his struggle for recognition. It is
not until his trip to Greece and Turkey in 1840–41 that we encounter
another treasure trove for those interested in the best of his travelogues, *A Poet's Bazaar*. Later travel diaries show Andersen enjoying
his acclaim abroad, visiting famous artists and nobility, and impatiently enduring the role of travel guide for Jonas Collin's grand-
sons. We decided to translate the diaries from his two trips to England in their entirety because of their special interest for the English-
speaking audience. The diaries of his last years are an interesting
document of his struggle with old age, when his health deteriorated
and failed. The diaries for this painful period show Andersen at his
most admirable, bearing not only the discomfort of his illness but
the gruesome medical treatment that was standard at that time. When
he became too weak to hold a pen, his friend Mrs. Melchior made
his entries for him, at first from dictation and then, when he fell
silent, in her own words until he died.

The language of Andersen's diaries poses problems for his translators. At its best, it is spontaneous and witty. But at times it can be

careless, awkward, and ambiguous. At other times—when he is re-
counting an audience with the king, for example—it can be stuffy.
In order to preserve for the twentieth-century reader the intimate
flavor of this document written by a man for himself, we have cho-
sen to eliminate the awkward aspects of his prose and to update his
mannerisms. We have also silently resolved unintentional ambigui-
ties and corrected mistaken references, as well as errors in spelling
and punctuation. We have used the conventional ellipses for spaces
left by Andersen where he had forgotten a name or quotation and
have extended these ellipses and placed them in brackets to indicate
missing lines at the tops and bottoms of pages where the paper has
worn away or where an entire page has been lost, as in the entry
for 25 July 1849. Bracketed words and phrases are provided by the
translators. Any asterisks or other marks are, of course, Andersen's
own. We have kept explanatory notes to a minimum, preferring to
refer the reader to the index. All titles have been translated into
English.

Many times during the course of this project, we have turned to
others for help. We owe a great debt of gratitude to Det danske
Sprog- og Litteraturselskab in Copenhagen for permission to use its
edition of the complete Andersen diaries. We are likewise indebted
to the Hans Christian Andersen Museum in Odense and its director
Niels Oxenvad and the Royal Library in Copenhagen for valuable
assistance with Andersen's drawings.

On numerous occasions we have been helped by librarians at the
Royal Library and the Special Collections of Suzzallo Library, University of Washington, as well as the library's Scandinavian special-
ist A. Gerald Anderson. For advice about textual matters, such as
ambiguity and lack of clarity, both Dr. Erik Dal, administrator of Det
danske Sprog- og Litteraturselskab and an outstanding Andersen
scholar himself, and Dr. Klaus Neiiendam, University of Copenhagen, have our heartfelt thanks. We have also benefitted from the
suggestions of Professors George A. Shipley and Farris F. Anderson,
University of Washington, concerning mistaken references. However, the responsibility for any infelicities in this translation is our
own.

A final note of gratitude must be extended to the University of
Washington for granting us a Graduate School Research Award in
1984.

Patricia L. Conroy

Introduction

IN HANS CHRISTIAN ANDERSEN's first autobiography (1832), one looks in vain for the well-known statement that opens his definitive autobiography, *The Fairy Tale of My Life* (1855): "My life is a beautiful fairy tale, rich and happy. . . . The story of my life will say to the world what it says to me: there is a loving God, who directs all things for the best." Andersen's public idealization of his own life and career was done in retrospect by an author who had by then become a renowned European celebrity; yet he never forgot to record with pedantic accuracy any criticism of himself or injustice done to him. In all of his various autobiographies, including a German version (1847), *Das Märchen meines Lebens ohne Dichtung*, and an American edition (1871), *The Story of My Life*, containing additional chapters covering the years 1855–67, Andersen consistently strove to present a generally positive and optimistic world view.

But the opening statement from Andersen's 1855 autobiography must be supplemented with another quotation from the book: "First you go through an awful lot, and then you become famous." Adversity certainly did prevail in his life until the decisive year 1835, when he published his first novel, *The Improvisatore*, as well as his first collection of stories, *Tales, Told for Children*; and the author—the first Scandinavian writer from the working class—never overcame his social traumas. Even after his artistic breakthrough, he often imagined that he was enduring hardships similar to those of his youth. This attitude partly explains his snobbery, his self-assertiveness, and his need to be appreciated.

Andersen's life never became a beautiful fairy tale, and he was well aware of this. Thus the glorification of his own fate and genius in the tale "The Ugly Duckling" is only partly valid. The magnificent white swan had not only been persecuted and ridiculed, but it ended up a domesticated bird taking its food from the hands of little children. Here Andersen deals with a subject also illuminated by the diaries, the relationship between the author and his audience—in other words, the proletarian who attempts to cut off all connections with his former life and who climbs socially, ending up the favorite author of the bourgeoisie, with access to the royal table. Yet even in this situation Andersen could not suppress the feeling that he was an outsider. It is precisely from this outsider's point of view that he wrote his scathing satire on the emperor's court in the tale "The Nightingale." He also launched frequent attacks on the arrogance and stupidity of the upper class in his diaries.

A critical reading of several of Andersen's other major tales and stories, such as "The Fir Tree," "The Shadow," "The Gardener and the Lord and Lady," and "Auntie Toothache" (one of his last tales and the tragic epilogue to his entire oeuvre), reveals that his world view was not as optimistic and harmonious as has been thought. In these works, he expresses a gloomy pessimism about the world and a strong skepticism about his own fate in general and his vocation as an artist in particular. If one turns to the diaries—it hardly matters which part of them—a similarly mixed impression is conveyed. Certainly, the author experiences moments of great happiness—the remark by Crown Prince Maximilian of Bavaria that "writers and kings can always meet and have access to one another" (July 12, 1861) must have thrilled him! But it did not take much for Andersen's mood to drop below zero; a rash remark or an unfriendly look immediately made him feel misunderstood and rejected.

A hectic social life, successful recitals, friendships with internationally known artists and writers, and visits with the royal courts all over Europe alternate with expressions of loneliness and dejection that hardly bear evidence of the direction of divine guidance that Andersen could not be without. It is this duality that creates such an astounding and gripping close-up of the author both at the height of his fame and in the darkest abyss of loneliness. Andersen's prima-donna behavior, obsessions, and constant hypochondria alternate with expressions of gratitude, a craving for intellectual stimulation, and a basic curiosity that is the hallmark of a true artist—an artist who is always searching for new impressions and inspirations. Andersen's egocentricity never prevented him from recording with minute precision details about people and places. His memory was fabulous.

Andersen's diaries were written for his own use without regard to later publication, but he foresaw that they would be read after his death: "If this diary will be read once, one will find it empty and indifferent. What happened within me and around me I don't put on paper out of consideration for myself and many others" (May 9,

1870). With this negative view of the entries (on the last day of 1871 Andersen wrote: ". . . my intention is to burn all these notes"), he immensely underestimated the value of his diaries. Apart from their biographical and cultural information, they originally served him as a huge storage room containing material from his numerous travels. For the period between 1836 and 1844, only entries from his travels exist; and they illustrate his talent for superb observation of both his environment and himself, done with the sensory precision of a painter. It is precisely these travel sections that provide examples of Andersen's linguistic virtuosity so exquisitely manifest in his tales and stories.

In contrast to the well-balanced, carefully composed autobiographies, the diaries are an inexhaustible collection of raw material, improvisations, moods, and concrete details written in the shorthand style of the moment. The artistic results of piecing these elements together can be found primarily in the travelogues and novels, but the genesis of many tales and stories can also be traced back to them. Not only the date but also the immediately preceding circumstances in connection with the commencing and concluding of a certain text are presented in Andersen's diaries. In addition, one can find his sources of inspiration, such as his stay in Naples during the almost unbearably hot summer of 1846, during which Andersen worked on the manuscript for his German autobiography. The entries from this stay contain many observations later used in the introduction to the story "The Shadow," with its portrayal of exotic Italian folk life.

With increasing frequency Andersen began to write down important historical events, such as the wars between Denmark and Germany in the 1840s and 1860s, and autobiographical information to be used primarily in his memoirs. After returning from his trip to Spain in 1863, he abandoned the previous, relatively brief, factual entries, the longest of which frequently consisted of lengthy, cataloguelike descriptions of visits to museums and art galleries abroad. (In Rome alone he visited and mentions approximately three hundred churches and twenty-five museums and galleries.) Beginning with his entries during the 1860s, it is possible to follow the author day by day in often sweeping descriptions covering the entire year— Andersen loved gossip—in his home country, particularly in Copenhagen, where he resided after 1866. These are period pictures bursting with details of Danish culture and history continuously displaying Andersen's sophisticated ability to catch a significant situation and hold onto it. From the point of view of literary history these entries show that Andersen was productive into his old age despite frequent complaints of lack of inspiration. In addition to his daily, extensive correspondence—seventeen letters in seven days, as he notes in one entry—he wrote tales and stories, poems, novels, and the last part of his autobiography.

Andersen's diaries have not been preserved in full, and an excellent supplement—as yet unpublished—would be his pocket calendars, in which he had begun in 1833 to write down daily events all year round. But as the entries in his diaries expanded in length, Andersen lost interest in his calendars, and from 1862 to 1872 they almost exclusively contain a record of his correspondence. In his diaries, pages are occasionally missing, and from the early travel diaries only fragments have been preserved. Andersen did not number the pages of his diaries, and at his death they consisted of a pile of loose, disordered sheets. These were not restored and bound in fascicles until 1925–29. The diaries from 1825 to 1863 stem from the manuscript collection of Edvard and Jonas Collin, Jr., and the rest belonged to the Melchior family. The originals, with one exception (entries from Slagelse from March 4 to April 11, 1826, which were purchased in 1956 by the Hans Christian Andersen Museum in Odense from a Swiss antiquarian bookdealer), are kept in the Andersen Archives at the Royal Library in Copenhagen. The earliest consist of loose pages; the later segments are generally notebooks in octavo or—after 1863—exercise books in small quarto.

A few excerpts from the diaries were included in Edvard Collin's book *H. C. Andersen and the Collin Family*, and some more were added in *The Last Years of H. C. Andersen: His Diaries 1868–75* by Jonas Collin, Jr.—containing, however, quite a number of misreadings. A scholarly and annotated edition did not appear until 1936, when H. G. Olrik published *H. C. Andersen's Diary from His Last Year in Slagelse 1825–26*, a work which in the following years was supplemented by several additional excerpts covering the author's travels to Rome, Paris, Norway, England, and Scotland.

No modern editor of Andersen's works has failed to use the diaries for references and background material. Various publishers of Andersen's travelogues, in particular, have undertaken comparative studies between the firsthand impressions of the diaries and the editing of the material that Andersen did later. But his diaries can be used far beyond this purpose as a source of information. Throughout the years they have not only served as a main authority for the popular biographical study of Andersen, but they have also provided valuable information about the literary milieu of his time and his relationship with domestic and foreign literature and criticism. In the complete, scholarly definitive edition of the diaries in twelve volumes (1971 to 1976), Andersen is finally presented as a whole figure, as the constantly unpredictable genius who is not being used by us but who now exerts his power over us.

Who, then, is the Hans Christian Andersen we encounter in these diaries? Even though they obviously can be read to a certain degree as preliminary studies to parts of his other works, they first and foremost constitute a unique self-analysis. Andersen apparently learned to comply with his environment—least successfully during his unhappy years from 1822 to 1827 at the schools in Slagelse and Elsinore, where the principal, Simon Meisling, displayed so little sympathy for the hypersensitive adolescent—but he always reserved the right to write down his differing opinions. And despite all his physical frailties—constant toothaches, abdominal pains, insomnia, respiratory problems, and digestive troubles, as well as his extreme emotional vulnerability—Andersen remained a keen observer and critic of music, theater, literature, and his fellow humans. Is it not then possible that it is this artistic professionalism rather than mere sexual fears that might explain the sublimation of sexual urges that the diaries give so many examples of? They do demonstrate that Andersen lacked neither impulse, desire, nor opportunity for sexual relations, although he never succumbed to the temptation. The numerous Greek letters and, in particular, crosses scattered around in the entries—signs of masturbation—speak their own language.

There was another high price Andersen had to pay for his poetic genius. He was born with the gift of a vivid imagination, but it did not always serve him. When it took over, he was seized by fears of becoming insane like his maternal grandfather. These fears were especially overwhelming during the spring of 1871: "God has given me the imagination to create literature but not to become a candidate for the insane asylum! What are those fixed ideas that so often haunt me?" (March 2)

Whereas Andersen's autobiographies are colored by being apologies for a writer who felt he had been unjustly treated by the Danish critics, the diaries present an unretouched portrait of an artist who with powerful memory was able to keep track of the many hundred people he associated with. They show his immersion in the narcissistic moods of youth and his longing for social advancement. They show his troubles in his old age with enemies, as well as well-intentioned friends. Psychologically he strips himself totally naked without disguising or rearranging facts, even though he is remarkably discreet about the women in his life. Hidden between trivial accounts of visits to the hairdresser's, financial worries, and other personal annoyances are valuable pieces of information which give us deeper insights into his psyche as well as putting us on the track of larger, unnoticed coherences in his writing.

To a certain degree, Andersen's personality never changed, or, rather, never developed. Not only his sexual but his social constraints followed him to his death, during his life and in his dreams, as he wrote as late as June 4, 1870: "Yesterday my dream was again about being dependent: I ran away from Meisling, was afraid of Old Collin because everyone was dissatisfied with me at the new school." He had become world famous and clearly enjoyed it, but his subconscious was dominated by a trauma that can be traced back to his years in Slagelse and Elsinore.

And with approaching death—Andersen thought of it daily—life's conclusion became at the same time something he dreaded and something he was longing for as a means of liberation: "I'm sitting here like a person sentenced to death, who daily awaits his execution, who is afraid of how embarrassing it would be and who nevertheless would like to see an end to it all" (September 14, 1873). Andersen kept a close watch on the state of his health. All the details of his physical deterioration are written down with clinical care. The later entries give both a shattering and gripping close-up of Andersen's nervous and sensitive nature, his feeling of being old and lonely, and his sense of everything's perishableness (balanced by that hope of immortality which he could not be without).

Andersen's diaries interest posterity for two main reasons. Through them we learn of his reading, visits to museums and theaters, and musical experiences. Revealing how deeply he was part of the European literary and cultural tradition, his diaries constitute a source of the greatest significance. Likewise, one can find information about Andersen's daily associates, what he learned and encountered, and what impact his environment had on him. Second, his diaries contain a poignant expression of human weakness as well as strength: nowhere does one come closer to the author than through these simple entries in which great and small philosophical speculations and impromptus are experienced and depicted side by side. Here one finds that strange mixture of precision, irony, and naïveté that is so characteristic of Andersen and his writing. His diaries present one of the strangest and most disparate artistic portraits in world literature.

Sven H. Rossel

The Diaries of
Hans Christian Andersen

The Early Years
1825–31

Hans Christian Andersen *was born April 2, 1805, in the small provincial town of Odense on the island of Funen. He was the son of a poor shoemaker and an almost illiterate mother, who after her husband's death in 1816 maintained herself as a washerwoman and died in 1833, an alcoholic in the Odense workhouse. When Andersen was about five years old, he was sent to the first of the three schools he attended in his hometown, acquiring only very basic reading and writing skills. Although Andersen never learned to spell properly, he became a voracious reader, devouring everything available—from the Danish classics to Shakespeare. When only seven, he was taken to the local theater by his parents. He began to collect playbills, and with these as his source of inspiration he would make up his own plays, even attempting to write an entire tragedy.*

Prominent people in Odense, including a Lieutenant Colonel Christian Høegh-Guldberg, began to take an interest in Andersen. Following his confirmation in 1819, they urged his mother to let him learn a trade. However, Andersen's fondness for the theater had steadily increased during these years— in 1818 when the Royal Theater visited Odense he was given a walk-on part—and he was determined to become an actor in Copenhagen. Neighbors and others who heard of this plan tried to dissuade him, but in the end his mother gave in, and on September 6, 1819, Andersen arrived in Copenhagen.

He knew no one in the capital, but armed with a letter of introduction from Mr. Iversen, a printer in Odense, he paid a visit to the Royal Theater's leading ballerina, Anna Margrethe Schall. The letter was of no use, since she had never heard of the printer, and she did not hesitate to show the boy the door when he began to improvise a song and dance based on Cinderella, *a play he had seen twice in Odense. Andersen now presented himself to the director of the Royal Theater, Colonel Frederik von Holstein, who had already been notified about his visit by C. Høegh-Guldberg. This visit turned out to be even more disappointing. Holstein advised Andersen to go back to Odense, but the thought of going home a failure made the boy decide to stay. Besides, since he would have to learn a trade if he returned to Odense, he might just as well do so in Copenhagen. Unfortunately, an apprentice-*

3

Stage of the Royal Theater in Copenhagen, 1821, the earliest drawing by Andersen

ship with a joiner lasted only half a day. As a last resort, Andersen decided to pay a visit to the Italian tenor Giuseppe Siboni, recently appointed head of the Royal Choir School.

This visit proved to be a turning point in Andersen's life. Siboni promised to give him voice training, and the prominent composer C. E. F. Weyse organized a collection to support him. But in the spring of 1820 Andersen's voice began to break, and after telling him that neither his appearance nor his manners were suitable for the stage, Siboni suggested that Andersen return home. The boy refused with the stubborn persistence that was such a dominant trait in his otherwise hypersensitive character. Instead, he wrote to a brother of C. Høegh-Guldberg in Copenhagen, the poet Frederik Høegh-Guldberg, and made a successful appeal for help. With the financial support of new benefactors, among whom were the Colbiørnsen family, Andersen was now admitted to the Royal Ballet School. The leading solo dancer, Carl Dahlén, also opened his home to Andersen. During the winter of 1820–21 he even received private lessons from an actor, Ferdinand Lindgreen, who ended up by dismissing him with the words: "You have a heart, and, by God, also a head, but you shouldn't go on wasting your time; you ought to

4

study." Andersen ignored Lindgreen's well-intended advice and entered the theater's singing school, managing to get various walk-on parts. Finally, however, in the spring of 1822 he was dismissed from the Royal Theater altogether.

Now Andersen decided that if he could not conquer the theater as an actor, he would do it as a dramatic writer. He had, in fact, already submitted a play to the theater in 1821, The Robbers of Vissenbjerg on Funen, which had been rejected with the comment that the management "desired to receive no more works which, like this one, betrayed such a lack of elementary education." Now his benefactors, Holstein and Høegh-Guldberg, joined Lindgreen in advising the boy that he needed more education. He did, indeed, take private lessons in Latin, but spent most of his time writing— much to the distress of Høegh-Guldberg, who actually broke off relations with him.

Andersen's next play, the tragedy Alfsol (published in his first book, Youthful Attempts, 1822) was first read aloud to F. C. Gutfeld and P. F. Wulff, Denmark's premier translator of Shakespeare. We do not know what Wulff thought of the play, but he did ask Andersen to visit him again, and on Andersen's behalf Gutfeld subsequently submitted the tragedy to the Royal Theater. Although Alfsol, too, failed to gain acceptance at the theater, the rejected manuscript was accompanied this time by a comment that the author might one day be able to produce something of value, if only he could be given an education. The theater's board of directors offered to send Andersen to a grammar school for the next three years. It was left to one of the board members, the extremely influential Jonas Collin, a senior government official, to take the necessary steps. He obtained royal funds and sent Andersen to a school in Slagelse whose principal, Simon Meisling, was a well-known classical scholar and translator. Andersen arrived there October 26, 1822, took a room with a widow, Mrs. Henneberg, and two days later started school in the second form.

For the Christmas holidays in 1822, Andersen went with the Meislings to Copenhagen, where he was invited for the first time to have dinner with the Collin family. Jonas Collin expressed great satisfaction with Andersen's grades and encouraged him to write every month to let him know about his progress in school. However, upon his return to Slagelse Andersen's relationship with his principal began to deteriorate. Meisling categorically forbade him to write creatively, and the man's quick temper and rough, ironic manner of speech made the boy constantly afraid of not passing his examination and falling into disgrace.

In the autumn of 1823 Andersen—despite his poor grades in Latin and

Greek—was promoted to the third form, and when his diaries open on Sep-
tember 16, 1825,[1] he had been stuck in this form for two years. During his
years in Slagelse Andersen wrote regularly to Jonas Collin, Mrs. Wulff,
and—after a reconciliation—also to Høegh-Guldberg, complaining about his
agonized relationship with Meisling and academic woes.

Friday, September 16 [1825]. Letter from Høegh-Guldberg. My God!
My God! How good You are! I can never be deserving of this—I
have a friend, a father; oh God, how I love him—Father! Divine
spirit on high, see my heart's delight; from above, behold with a
father's eye my bliss. So away, you Temptress who oppresses me,
who bends my soul into the dust, though it apprehends, perceives
God!—

> Thy will be done, oh Lord!
> My trust I put in Thee,
> In Thy rays have soared
> Both angel and humble bee.
> Thou steerest star and sun,
> Thou steerest mortal fate,
> Thy will by me is done,
> For Thou art wise and great.
> For strength from Thee I yearn,
> Teach me some part to earn
> Of all Thy blessedness.

Saturday, September 17. Listless and tired from reading—φ—studied—on account of listlessness, went to bed before 10 o'clock.
Sunday, September 18. No letter from Collin. Was with Mrs. Meisling; she hoped we would be going to Elsinore, wished me luck in
my exams. Was at Brinck-Seidelin's; he served me some sort of li-
queur, declaimed nonstop, showed me his study: "There on the sofa
I compose Anacreontic songs, here at the table elegies—'Oh, you
who've never loved, love now! You who have loved, love anew!'
See, here I have my diary; yes, you can be sure a lot about you is in
here; my wife is in Korsør; I'll be riding out now to meet her. Here
are pencil and paper; I'll compose the rest for your album on the
way." Forgive me, Almighty Father, these audacious thoughts which

1. Andersen's diary for his last years in Slagelse has been published by H. G.
Olrik, *H. C. Andersens Dagbog fra hans sidste Slagelse-Aar 1825–26* (*H. C. Andersen's
Diary from His Last Year in Slagelse 1825–26*), in *Anderseniana* 4 (1936): 1–150.

arise in my soul, but they alone buoy up my courage; otherwise I would sink in despair. I must carry out my work! I must paint for mankind the vision that stands before my soul in all its vividness and diversity; my soul knows that it can and will do this, and so You must not forsake me, for I wish to become Your priest; oh God, you must not forsake me if I sink in the dust. My spirit dwells with You—it renounces what is sinful; it is though Yours—what are my just desserts?

Monday, September 19. My God! My God! Thy will be done; just reward me for my effort this year, nothing more! (God only knows what fate has in store for me when this page is turned! Unlucky me! Did miserably in Latin. You won't be advanced into the fourth form! Out of school! To become an artisan or a corpse is your fate! God! God, are you really near! But all the same, "Praised be Thy name."— I did better in Latin grammar, maybe a "good," also a "good" in German.—I cannot comprehend Your will, Lord; oh, don't let me lose hope that You govern all things, give me courage to meet my fate; I can see what it will be, oh God! Farewell to all of my hopes and dreams; yes, they were only dreams! Oh, if I only had courage—Death, you are not so terrifying.—Why did the principal have to examine me in precisely what I had trouble with? Oh God, the man who earns his bread in the sweat of his brow is happier than the one who labors in the so-called higher spheres. He knows no better, for food and sustenance are his only concerns. His work goes automatically for him; for him a meaningless jest is a source of great joy, whereas the other man must struggle against a sea of difficulties and hindrances, is maligned and picked to pieces. Gifted with a greater sensitivity, his heart is crushed.—Oh, why have I gotten so far, why have I climbed so high? I no longer live in obscurity, and now I am falling. Oh madness, eat your way into my brain so that I can forget my own existence. Being, whose proper name I do not know, give my soul courage to tear itself loose; swell, oh Heart, so that you might burst!—Ha, you inflated fool! Give free rein to your desires in the short time that you have. Fate rules all—what must happen will happen anyway! My God, I could become great, respected by my fellow men, give joy; my path was already heading that way! I could become an angel; either an angel or a devil is what I'll become—it is hanging in the balance! My God, it is You who determines the despairing man's lot! Why is so many a family father snatched away, so many an able man and beloved youth; and I am left alive, I who desire death. Yes, send death to me, even if my future does not turn out to be dismal. Death is dearer to me; a life without hope is a hell—to see my fellows climb while I fall, to be torn away from the society of cultivated people; oh no, God, that is too cruel!

Tuesday, September 20. What could become of me, and what will become of me? My powerful fantasy will drive me into the insane asylum, my violent temperament will make a suicide of me! Before, the two of these together would have made a great writer! Oh God, do Your ways really prevail here on earth?—Forgive me, God; I am unfair to You who have helped me in so many ways. Oh, You are God, so forgive and go on helping me. (God, I swear by my eternal salvation never again within my heart to mistrust Your fatherly hand, if only I might this time be promoted to the fourth form *and to Elsinore.*)

Wednesday, September 21. I was quite lucky in religion and Bible history, I was the best of all. Got a letter from Collin. Mrs. Meisling comforted me by saying that I would probably be promoted to the fourth form. Hope fills my breast! My God, I am again relying on You! (Vithusen and Frendrup have left.)

Thursday, September 22. Studied Greek until 1 o'clock. After that invited to celebrate Ludvig's birthday at the principal's home. (I've given him 11 shillings' worth of macaroons and a bouquet.) The children are quite fond of me. The principal and Hjarup told about a lot of shenanigans from their schooldays—fights and practical jokes. A carefree spirit, but not to my liking.—Accompanied Pedersen home.— Oh God, whatever are these people all about; oh, whom can one trust! Oh God, Your will with me be done; Your great world is boisterous and diverse.

Friday, September 23. "Excellent" in Danish composition.—Told Mrs. Meisling about it; was there to see my new room.—Spent a little time with Emil.—Fell asleep with faith in God.

Saturday, September 24. Arithmetic test. The principal was sitting by Knudsen's window: "Who told you yesterday that you got an 'excellent' in Danish composition?" "Torst, because I asked him!" "Yes, but you aren't supposed to find out about that sort of thing."— Was at Pedersen's for French, happened to tell them my story. When the maid came with the lamp and I was about to light it, it went out. I, "Oh, there went the light!" "Hee, hee," said the maid, "but the door is standing open, too!"—Studied diligently my Danish grammar.

Sunday, September 25. ϕ Studied French all morning with Pedersen, wrote a letter today to Madam Henneberg to the effect that I was leaving her lodgings. Depression, a nasty downpour, gray and autumnlike outside. Foggy and raw, as in my soul; God, I wish I were dead! I may be happier than during my childhood, but then I was ignorant, then I had no fears about a future that was unknown to me. Oh God, my soul is cowardly, my head sluggish. If only I were free!

During the following week, Andersen was in a state of constant torment about whether he would be advanced to the fourth form. Fortunately, his exams in French, Danish, Greek, Hebrew, and mathematics all went reasonably well; and on Saturday, October 1, he was given the good news about his promotion by Meisling. During the ensuing two-week vacation, he went on a reading binge punctuated by spurts of work on his "novel"[2] and visits to the homes of friends in Slagelse and nearby Sorø.

Tuesday, October 4. Toothache.—Up at 5:30 and walked to Sorø, a friendly welcome; took a walk with Ingemann; he told me that once when he was recovering from an illness a gremlin came in to him that was stranger than anything he had ever seen before and bowed and grimaced at him and sat down by his bed.—He told about Catholics and how he had in Italy seen their reverence for the cross and how it was profaned: he had seen houses whose lower sections had almost been painted over with crosses so that nobody would urinate on the house, but when people really had to go they pissed in between the crosses, and if they accidently hit one of them they ran into a church and confessed and carried on.—Miss Heger was staying with them.—Because of her bad leg Mrs. Ingemann rode into the academy garden in a cart pulled by Ingemann and steered by me.—Read Mrs. Hegermann-Lindencrone's *Danish Stories.* "Saint Peter" is very good, full of life and character description. The tale about the old fisherman was of interest because of the historical characters Rantzau and Christian IV.—Leafed through Deichmann's *Poems.*—Ingemann and his wife praised my story and the short poem "The Soul." It is his idea that I was born to write novels in order to describe the lower class. At home read aloud for the Hennebergs.

2. A fragment of a "historical novel" is published in *Anderseniana* 3 (1935): 29–58. But according to his *Levnedsbog (The Story of My Life)*, pp. 132–33 (2d ed.), written in 1832 (publ. 1926, 1962), Andersen at this time had already begun to work with the themes that he later used in his unfinished novel, *Christian den Andens Dverg (The Dwarf of Christian II)*, published in *Anderseniana* 3 (1935): 59–111. Subsequent references in his diary to "my story" or "my novel" refer to this text.

Wednesday, October 5. Tired, so I stayed in bed until 9 o'clock and read the first part of Oehlenschläger's *A Journey Told in Letters to My Home.* Letter from Collin. Oh God, how good you are; I don't deserve it.—During the afternoon read *Aladdin* for the Fuglsangs; in the evening at dusk I went to see old Madam Dall. She had asked Mrs. Meisling to tell me that if I were to come over she had something to say to me, but by now she had forgotten what it was. The old lady was lying in bed; she pressed my hand with her cold, clammy fingers! "Thanks!" she said and had to catch her breath between every word, "Thanks for the poem for my birthday! What do you think, my dear boy, the minister has himself made a copy of it and sent it to Herman [Christian Fuglsang]. In it you say that you love me; yes, I love you too, and I pray the Lord for the best for you— that you might become a happy child!" God has already done so much for me, I said. I told her all about myself, recited "The Soul" and the one to my mother. She wept, and I was moved myself.— Read some issues of *Monthly Roses.*

Thursday, October 6. Worked on my novel. Read Oehlenschläger's *Journey,* Part I, and something in *Miscellany.* Was with Mrs. Meisling.—Am beginning to get bored.

Friday, October 7. Worked a little on my novel. Read the beginning of Part III of Oehlenschläger's *Island in the South Sea* for the Fuglsangs.—The less we have to do, the less time we seem to have; I can barely find the time to write in my album for pure idleness. Spent the evening with the Pedersens. (I read for him alone my novel, which entertained him, especially the burlesque parts.) Sara showed off by listing the titles of novels and asking if I had read them and by telling stories about her little sister.

Saturday, October 8. Read in *Monthly Roses* and *Miscellany.* Went at 5:30 to the Fuglsang's, read Part III of *South Sea*—it worked, and Mads Hansen amused me. Oehlenschläger certainly knows how to link together a lot of anecdotes and historical characters that make the book interesting. They greet us like old acquaintances—but you can surely tell that it was Oehlenschläger who wrote it.—Stayed all day at the Fuglsang's and ate there; we also managed to read some short poems and *The Roses of Mr. von Malherbes.* I was in fine fettle, picked walnuts for them on a shakey ladder and ate cherries. (Home by 10 o'clock.) Started on *The Expedition of Humphry Clinker* by Smollett.

Sunday, October 9. Read anecdotes.—Worked on my story.—Letter from Collin; he is very considerate.—Bored.—Wrote to Høegh-Guld-berg. Read some issues of *Monthly Roses*.

Monday, October 10. Bored!—Write and read.—Read my story to the Holsteins. The old squire fell asleep during the second chapter, but he was very tired because he had been awake all the night before. Read *Humphry Clinker*. I count *The Adventures of Roderick Random* a far better work.

Tuesday, October 11. Each morning I read what I have written to Miss Lange. Høegh-Guldberg crosses my mind—but it's my vacation! Read Riise's *Magazine for Young People*.—Started on Molbech's *Journey Through a Part of Germany, France, England and Italy in the Years 1819 and 1820*. With a map and geography book before me I'm also thinking of trying to pick up a little geographical knowledge. I'm bored, bored! Tired of it all. The town was illuminated because of Strande's wedding.

Wednesday, October 12. Read the journal *Ceres*; finished *Humphry Clinker*; read Riise's *Magazine* to Miss Lange during the afternoon. I entertained myself in the evening by cleaning up among my letters and putting them in order.—Wrote to Madam Dahlén and Balling.

Thursday, October 13. Now time is passing fairly quickly. Was called to lunch by Mrs. Meisling (beefsteak, and Pedersen and I split a bottle of Graves). Hviid came home, told nasty stories about Zeise and Gier. (We are all of us carnal. Oh God, keep me from suffering temptation myself!) Was at the Fuglsang's; read *Axel and Valborg* along with the singspiel *Freyja's Altar*. (Old Mrs. Dall) It was the birthday of Mrs. Fuglsang's brother (in Norway); for that reason we all had punch. A nice home.

Friday, October 14. Put my papers in order.—Read *Mr. Musard, or How Time Flies*. Read the last part of *Island in the South Sea*; the beginning good, the rest boring. Old Madam Dall gave me Tullin's prize-winning poem.—We all laughed at the awkward things in *Island*.

Saturday, October 15. Read Smollett's *The Adventures of Sir Launcelot Greaves*! Received schoolbooks from Copenhagen. Read Foersom's *1805 New Year's Gift for Play Lovers*.—Uneasy about whether I'll get any money tomorrow.

There is an eleven-day break in the diary entries, from October 16 to 26, when Andersen apparently got caught up in the new school term and preparation for his move from Mrs. Henneberg's to the Meislings'. During the first few weeks, he seemed pleased to be living in the Meisling household as

well as going to school there. But his pleasure evaporated when he discov-
ered he now had no refuge from Meisling's dissatisfaction with his school
performance.

Vacations were the only periods of happiness. Some were spent in Odense
with the Høegh-Guldbergs and the Iversens, whose granddaughter, Hen-
riette Hanck, was his good friend; some, in Sorø with the poet B. S. Inge-
mann and his wife; and some, in Copenhagen with Mrs. Jürgensen, the
widow of the royal watchmaker, and with the Wulff family, who resided in
a wing of Amalienborg, the royal palace. When he received an invitation
from Mrs. Wulff on November 22 to spend the Christmas holidays with her
family, Andersen was overjoyed and eagerly looked forward to spending a
few weeks in Copenhagen, away from the tensions of being both Meisling's
student and his boarder.

Saturday, December 10. Oh God, how my heart is oppressed! Oh
almighty God, be merciful! I am going in there now, and when I
come out again, then—I also got a "poor" in Greek! Oh God! For a
while the pain ceased, but, now, if I only had courage! Oh God,
how heavy at heart I am, and yet there is a consolation that often
insinuates itself, that I've done what I, with my abilities, could do.
Emil, Giesemann and I weren't tested in Latin grammar, since the
principal wanted to test us in this. Though he didn't say anything
when I was alone upstairs with him at 5 o'clock for tea. When I left,
I had an impulse to run over to him and ask if he was angry with
me, but I didn't dare. I had in mind writing about it to Collin, not
to the Titular Councillor, but to the man with a heart; it was my
only comfort, but, still, I put it off until Thursday.—Yes, the principal must be dissatisfied with me, and I can't perform any better. It
will end with my having to leave school. He'll probably regret he
said anything about taking me along with him to Elsinore. I can see
that he means well. Being strict is the only way to guide my confused spirit; now that I live in his house, he probably even regards
it as his duty. I ought to be grateful to him like the patient his doctor, but can't the patient be forgiven if he moans under the knife!—
"It won't help to grind away day and night at your studies," the
principal said. "It will dull your wits and make you beside yourself.
No, day-to-day diligence!" (But this is what I've been doing!) "Don't
think that this impetuosity of yours is genius; there is much to be
shorn away before you turn out to be anything. Even if he knew
everything, a person like you would get bad grades in the exams in
Copenhagen, just because of the way he was."—Oh God, oh God,

I've been like a child so fervently looking forward to Christmas; with what pleasure I've been contemplating seeing my friends, now that I've been promoted to the top class and in the two months it's taken gotten good grades. And now everything is ruined! I can't look forward to Christmas any more, and even in my most poverty-stricken childhood I was able to do that; then it was for me a simple, holy day of rejoicing; I was happy in that tiny room, oh, so happy; I'll never have such sustained happiness again! Oh glorious childhood, then I was not aware of all the good things God often has bestowed upon me, but I lacked nothing! My heart was pure, my trust was unfaltering and I didn't think about the future! Oh God, do not forsake your weak child!!!

Sunday, December 11. Got a letter (with two rix-dollars) from Professor Ørsted.—Wrote to Collin about how badly I did in Greek and Latin. (Mrs. Meisling is complaining about the governess and vice versa; I have to run with the hare and hunt with the hounds.) The principal does not speak with me much. Stayed up with the children and ate up there; in the evening, though, the principal sent a toddy down to me. I am fuzzy-headed and tired of studying.

Monday, December 12. [. . . .] wrong, too. [. . .] *I knew it!* Got a "good-minus" and was less worried.

Tuesday, December 13. My Danish essay inspired me with trust in God. It dealt with His providence, and I felt I was touched by it and took heart. Trust in Him irradiated my soul. I have studied hard; I can do no more. His will be done. (Mrs. Meisling and the governess reconciled.)

Wednesday, December 14. Father, now, in Your holy name—give my trust foundation—I have done what I could! Be a father to me now!—Got a "good" in French; it was far better than I had expected, but Qvortrup and especially Hansen helped me. With trust in God I went contented to bed. (Received an apple from the principal.)

Thursday, December 15. It went much better than I expected in history—I got a "very-good." The principal examined me and was quite satisfied. In the afternoon I got a "very good-minus" in Danish, "excellent" in composition, and the usual "fair" in Latin.—An impoverished schoolteacher came around begging, but didn't get anything; his tone pierced me to the heart, and I would have given him a shilling, but he was gone by the time I got there. The principal gave me an apple, but was so cold that I was somewhat dejected.— I had thought that I might write a rather cheerful letter to Høegh-

Guldberg and write him in the style of a diary about my trip to Copenhagen; now the exams have annihilated my good spirits.—Oh God, in You resides my trust; oh, do not forsake me!—I'm sluggish and tired from studying. If only I dared to get some rest!

Friday, December 16. Some fellows from the third form asked me out in the hall what I had gotten in Danish composition. "Excellent," I answered. "Yeah, he could certainly use it," said Pedersen. We had a bit of an argument; he has such grand ideas about his minuscule learning, and he's slow-witted, anyway.—I had to translate my German without reading aloud; that meant that I couldn't get an overview of the sentences, even though I otherwise [. . . .]

[Saturday, December 17 . . . .]
on the floor, holding each other by the arm. Giesemann drew a louse on the blackboard, played landlord with the inkpot and the inkhorns, picked his nose and spat, and did a few other vulgar things.— Got a "fair" in Latin grammar. If I had been a little better in my New Testament, then I probably would have gotten an "excellent" in religion, but ended up with a "very good." This afternoon we were switched around, but I got a "very good" as my final grade anyway.—The principal was quite friendly, gave me a toddy and some morning papers to go downstairs with and read; I gloated, thought about Copen(φ)hagen, read Holberg's *The Invisible Lovers* and his *Masquerades.*

Sunday, December 18. Woke up very early and couldn't study because I was thinking about the trip.—Started my letter to Høegh-Guldberg. Went to Torst about the subscription form for getting *Gefion.*—"We don't see anything of you anymore," Lucie said. "It's because the gate is locked so early, and then I don't feel right about going out."—"Are they also going to lock your noggin on you?" she asked!—(See the meeting on the boulevard.)[3]

Monday, December 19. Slept with Giesemann until around 3 o'clock. At 3:30 we drove off enveloped in the most wonderful fog imaginable; we rolled onward.—I almost didn't sleep at all and thus was out of bed at 2:30; at 3:30 we rolled out of town—as the saying goes, "Juno comes in a cloud," but in this case it could be said, "Everything comes in a cloud" because we were right in the middle of a cloud of fog. You might almost think we were traveling through the air, but the road reminded us that we were on the ground because

---

3. This statement perhaps refers to Andersen's entry of November 13 that he had been instructed by Meisling not to greet any townspeople on his walks.

we encountered pothole after pothole, so that I was afraid of breaking both arms and legs, or at least my neck. (Good heavens, if he didn't divide our expenses at all of the wayside inns by three, even though I thought I had been exempted—penny-pinching is penny-pinching!) The innkeeper of the Ordrup Inn showed us his book in which travelers have written their complaints, even in foreign languages.—At the Roskilde Inn we had by way of reading matter *Holger the Dane* and another old book that was missing both beginning and end.—By 9 o'clock we reached Copenhagen. The fog had let up; indeed, before the sun went down we even got to see a bit of it. Like Chilian in *Ulysses from Ithacia*, I would gladly have kissed the earth because I had arrived in the Vesterbro district in one piece, but the earth of Copenhagen doesn't look to be well scoured; now I rushed down to the Wulffs'; my welcome was hearty—it was like the way you[4] greeted me last summer; I can't express it any better. Wulff was at a party at the Oehlenschlägers', but I found Mrs. Wulff, the daughters and Wulff's sister at home. We talked about you, and Jette asked in particular about Petra and Stierna. I had to sing them a little song before I went to bed.—I have been given two rooms out toward the square, one to sleep in and the other, which is heated, where I'll read in the morning; the ceiling arches high above me, so I can really imagine that I am in a knight's castle.—I was given as a gift from Wulff the three volumes of Shakespeare's plays that he has translated. They are printed on fine paper and beautifully bound, as any work by Shakespeare deserves. I am alone in my room now; a thousand feelings are flowing through me—oh, what hasn't God done for me! It is going for me as it did for Aladdin, who says at the close of the work as he is looking out of a window of the palace:[5]

> [Down there I walked when just a lad
> Each Sunday, if I was but allowed,
> And gazed with wonder at the sultan's palace.]

Five or six years ago, I, too, was walking around on the streets down there, didn't know a soul here in town, and now I am gloating over my Shakespeare in the home of a kind and respected family.—Oh, God is good; one drop of the honey of happiness can get

4. Andersen wrote this part of his entry as a letter to Christian Høegh-Guldberg.
5. Apparently Andersen did not remember the exact quotation from Adam Gottlob Oehlenschläger's play *Aladdin* (1805), the final lines of which have been included here.

me to forget the bitterness. Oh, God will not forsake me—He has made me so happy!

Tuesday, December 20. Old habits are hard to break—I couldn't sleep any later than to 6 o'clock, even though I had been beaten black and blue all over by that prosaic coach. Finally, the servant came and laid a fire in my stove, and so I got up then and read some *Cymbeline.* After my morning tea, I made my first visit to Collin; he was pleased with me. "I can clearly see that you have been industrious," he said, "and that is what is most important."—Then we talked about *King Solomon and George Hatmaker,* but Mrs. Collin (who had lived in Korsør when married to Birckner and therefore knows the Korsørians) said that there was nothing in it that could be insulting to them. The subject matter was about like in Heiberg's *The Entrance.*—From here I went to the wife of Titular Privy Councillor Colbiørnsen; nobody was up yet, but Mrs. Colbiørnsen sent in some reading material to me, and so I read until they showed themselves. Just as when I arrived yesterday evening at the Wulffs', everybody here was talking about the Russian Czar's death and that war seemed imminent. Mrs. Colbiørnsen doesn't seem to me to have aged at all; Angelique is even more charming to me than last time; the same is true of Christiane; they invited me to dinner tomorrow.—Then I went to see Meisling; I had to run some errands. (I didn't get a chance to talk to Mrs. von der Maase.) From the Stock Exchange I went to see the Misses Falbe. (The Holsteins weren't at home; at Herbst's I met Captain Jenssen.) It got to be 3 o'clock before I arrived back at the Wulffs'. We ate at 4 o'clock; both Wulff and Mrs. Colbiørnsen had given me theater tickets, and I saw *Tancredo.* The parterre has been enlarged. I heard Miss Wulff, but I don't think much of her at all—when she sang, it was as if I had cotton in my ears. Her features are too delicate for the stage, and then she went around tugging at her train just like Dorthe in *High Life in the City.*—But Løffler, Cetti and Zinck made a marvelous trio.—Back at the Wulffs' I met Mrs. Saabye and her sister (a Miss Høyer). Wulff asked me to read the section of my novel that I've been working on during the vacation; I did so, and everyone expressed his enjoyment. He found it to be more lively than what you heard and less monumental, even though he has nothing against the monumental per se when it is a natural part of a work, but he did say: "When it's there, it seems effective, but if you take it away, then no one will miss it." (Today I met Werliin with glasses on: "Do you know why I am wearing them? It's so I can see Ida Wulff, who's said to live here!")

Wednesday, December 21. Wulff wasn't feeling well today. After tea I made my first excursion to see the lady-in-waiting. I was asked to come again in three-quarters of an hour because she was still in bed. Then I dashed off to Balling's; he gave me a hearty kiss and invited me to drop in often. After lunch I went over to Oehlenschläger's; it was one of the young ladies of the house that greeted me very warmly and whom I did not recognize.—I read my story, which Oehlenschläger praised: "It is very good—maybe a little too elaborate, and to depict a thing in so much detail is not what we call poetic. Indeed, it is almost as if I were to say: 'Andersen was sitting on the sofa reading; next to him sat Lotte Oehlenschläger and Miss Herbst. Johannes came home from school, and when he heard someone reading, he went very quietly over and sat down on a foot stool from which most of the color had been worn.' See, that isn't poetic! But there are many good things in your story, and it's clear that you're good at making use of a number of historical subjects and that you have observed well the people around you. The description of the castle is quite poetic and shows that you have a talent for it." Then I read him my little poem "The Soul." "That is marvelous!" he exclaimed. "I rate that higher than the story!" He read it through for himself once more. "You might make a few small changes, like 'on high' and 'stars in the sky'—that's so trite!"—Then I went to Ørsted's; it was the titular councillor's birthday, and I was invited over on Christmas Eve.—Meisling was sick, and so I had to go out by myself to shop; I walked to the Stock Exchange with Werliin— who was head over heels in love with Ida Wulff—in tow.—After that I was over at the Dahléns', where I had something to eat and some coffee.—From there I was off to see the wife of the titular privy councillor, where I was invited to dinner. A Groom-in-Waiting Colbiørnsen was there. People praised my little poems. After that, I sent off a letter to Rine Hundrup and looked in on Mrs. Krieger; the lady-in-waiting wasn't at home, and so I went on to Herbst's, where I met a Mr. Høyberg. I recited some things, and, in return, the Misses Herbst sang for me. When I got home, the Misses Stephansen were there, and I had to recite and read "The Soul." (Visited Madam Andersen—she was in bed, but spoke very cordially to me.)

Thursday, December 22. After teatime, I went to see the lady-in-waiting Mrs. Buchwald; she promised to extend my greetings to Her Royal Highness. I had tea there and received some money for a ticket. The Collins weren't able to get me one, and people were standing all the way out to the statue in the center of the square.—Then I was at Høegh-Guldberg's; we talked about Slagelse: "No, I don't want to hear anything about your poems. That way I won't praise you and thus encourage you, because now your studies must be your chief concern." He gave me his little poem "The Monster" as a present.—(Fuglsang wasn't at home.) Then I was at Madam Jürgensen's and read my poems. "God knows, I haven't heard anything by our Storm that was more beautiful than 'The Soul.' A person who can feel and write such things must also be able to write a tragedy. You say that Oehlenschläger liked your comic things better—he is afraid that in time you will become his rival!" "Oh heavens, how can I even dare to think such a thought!" "Who knows what will become of you; you are still very young. Think back to this moment in ten years' time, and see how things have turned out."—Then I began on my story, but was interrupted by a guest. (Meisling was irritable.) Had cabbage at Balling's and sat with him in the parquet, where I saw *King Solomon and George Hatmaker*. (The first work, *The Castle of the Uncle, or The Husband by Accident* was also quite entertaining.) But the other one was marvelous! The house was jam-packed. It was funny hearing "The Hunter's Chorus" sung by such plainly clad people. Frydendahl was marvelous gnawing on the drumstick of a goose, and the way Stage walked was superb. The line about the night cap, however, was somewhat coarse, as was having the ladies of Korsør sing, "We, we, we must, by jingo!!!" Ryge made a marvelous Jew.—After dinner I received some presents.—(Was at Nyerup's today.)

Friday, December 23. At Mrs. Buchwald's. She wasn't at all dismayed at the long speeches I put in the mouth of Magdalene in my story; she liked them. She greeted me from the princess. I had tea there.—At Herbst's, where I wished Miss M. Holstein a pleasant journey, I had to recite a few things for the ailing young lady, who gave me a horse that she had fashioned with her own hands out of wax. I gave it to Ida, who was delighted with it.—Was at Meisling's: "Haven't you inquired about a carriage for Tuesday?" "No." "But you must see to getting back to your Greek and Latin and starting work again." It seems to me, though, he's going too far—I'm only here for a few days. He knows that I want to go home, and yet he is always at me—a strange contrast to the reception I get everywhere else. I go to see him every day, and yet he has only a scowl for me. I would like to be sincerely fond of him, but I can't force my feelings.—Just got *Gefion*; there is a lot of crap in it. Oh, Thomsen has simply filched his story from Oehlenschläger.—Was at Dahléns', who got three pages for his album. Ate lunch at Urban Jürgensen's.— Here at home we didn't eat dinner because of the dance this evening. I've been invited plenty of places, but I don't really want to go; read to the young ladies and Christian along with making verses that rhymed on the words they gave me.—The carriages are rumbling outside; now the king is arriving. I'm going to go upstairs to see the cadets. At 8 o'clock Lotte Oehlenschläger and the others arrived; oh, if only I were dressed better!—I was just upstairs in the magnificent hall. People all dressed up there, in particular the military men, the king and the princes. The minister made a fine speech; the cadets performed marvelously—I was especially impressed by the sword dance. Oh, what figures, what grace! Oh God, who am I that I thought about dancing among them this evening!—The princes are in the parlor, but I've retreated to my room: I feel embarrassed. Then the guests arrived; the gilded halls shone with the sun-bright light from the chandeliers. I went down in my jacket, but when I saw Wulff speaking to his wife, I suspected that I shouldn't put in an appearance looking like that. I put the question directly to Mrs. Wulff: "Well, if you have a dress coat, it would be better." I put on my gray—yes, that was much better. Now the guests were streaming into the house, but all of them were in black. I was the only one in gray and didn't know whether to stand on my head or my heels. Only Oehlenschläger spoke to me. I felt very embarrassed; they probably take me for one of the servers, and Lotte Oehlenschläger has to see me like this! Oh, what torment! I rushed right back to my room, went to bed cursing my fate that I didn't have any dress clothes. The carriages were rumbling outside, and thoughts rumbled inside my head, and that is how I fell asleep. From 6 o'clock in the morning on, I had a nephew of the composer Kuhlau for a bedroom companion. φ

Saturday, December 24. Mrs. Belfour not at home, the same with Countess Frijs. Was at Ørsted's and helped them with the Christmas tree.—After lunch there, I went to Meisling's. Not at home. At Mrs. von der Maase's, guests.—At the Misses Falbes' was the Jew Hamm, who told about Mademoiselle Mars and Talma. "They never visit us! They are ignoring humble folk!" said Miss Mine. Was at Krieger's. For the rest of the day at the Wulffs'. "Indeed," said the commander, "we must please others with our inner selves; the outer won't do, and yet I got a pretty wife; you'll probably also get one."—

On Christmas Eve at Ørsted's, we took well-known songs and guessed what they were. The titular councillor was there.—Nearly didn't make it back into the academy.

Sunday, December 25. φ Was at Rine Hundrup's. Said goodbye to Mrs. Colbiørnsen, who had invited me to dinner—a fond farewell.— Countess Frijs was busy looking after the house. Meisling, not at home. Was at Mrs. von der Maase's (one rix-dollar), splendid, lovely rooms; she asked me to write her as often as I wished. Ate dinner at Dahlén's; Dahlén kissed me, praised my poems; the Kunzens were there. (On Saturday met Lord-in-Waiting Holstein, who praised my progress and industry.) Afterwards at the Ballings', where I ate again and got a note admitting me to [the music club] Euterpe. There I met Mr. . . . He told me that they were to have performed a work entitled *William Shakespeare* for the king's birthday celebration. He recounted part of it, and I was really galled that it had been Boye and not me who had written it. They'll have *The Magic Flute* for the birthday celebration. The Ballings got me a ride to Slagelse with Thrane on Wednesday.—When I left the Euterpe, a stupid man came up and asked my name. I told him. "You're not a member of the club." No, but I have a ticket from Ballings (the written note). Yes, but gentlemen can't get in on a lady's ticket. But it was to the management. Now the man understood that it was a management ticket, apologized abjectly, and I went on my way.—Here at home were Mrs. Saabye and Adler, who regaled us with all of *William Shakespeare*; oh, the idea was entirely like my own, and those sweet fairies, too.

Monday, December 26. (Visited Høegh-Guldberg's son yesterday.) Did not find Countess Frijs at home.—At 12 o'clock went and made my way up to Meisling's; he wasn't at home, but I found a note from him: "I have nothing to communicate to you upon your departure, only the sternest admonition that you not use your time for writing stories and poems—which you have served up here to this party's great amusement—after your arrival in Slagelse, but for your studies. I shall certainly speak face to face to you about how much you have disappointed me by wasting time in *that* way, when I trust you to read your assignments, and I will furnish you with various data that might possibly deflate you. I do not wish you to take part in any decoration of the children's Christmas tree, creches, masquerades or God knows what has been planned, since I can see that you put your time to bad enough use anyway. Meisling." Disconsolate, I read the letter several times. All my strength drained out of me. Pale and grim, I arrived at the Wulffs', who read my letter and sympathized with me. Then I went to Meisling, and since he was out I asked for paper and ink and wrote a note to him in which I told him that the poem had been written during a vacation and that I couldn't demonstrate greater diligence than I already had. I was depressed about it all day long. In the evening I read for the Wulffs Boye's *William Shakespeare*. The author has described him completely after my own heart. In the first act, William's lines echoed exactly my feelings: he has an intuitive feeling he will become a writer; he decides not to compose poetry. Oh, tears came to my eyes; in bed all my disconsolation was reawakened, but I fell asleep with faith in God and the certainty that I had worked according to my best abilities.

Tuesday, December 27. Visited Countess Frijs (two rix-dollars). At Mrs. Buchwald's, from the Princess (five rix-dollars). After that, looked in on Mrs. Gutfeld, who was concerned about my situation, asked me to take heart and not let myself be treated like a child, not to leave Slagelse but when I did happen to be in Copenhagen to come often and visit her home, where I would meet some nice young people. I gave her my word I would endure my fate like a man. Saw once again my benefactor's portrait. "Indeed, his passing was a great loss for many," she said with tears in her eyes; and I started to cry too.—On the street I met Meisling; he walked a ways with me, wished me a pleasant journey; when I tried to say something to him, he said: "We'll soon be seeing each other back at home."—Was at Balling's for dinner; he gave me a hearty kiss when I left and pressed four dollars into my hand. I gave the Misses Hornemann my regards and said goodbye to Collin and showed him Meisling's note. He was pleased with me. "As is said in *King Solomon*, 'Each land indeed has its plague,' " he remarked. "You must accept your fate." I then asked him please only to say something if ever there should be anything that displeased him, and he promised to do that.—At the Wulffs' we played parlor games; and when the card party broke up, we played guessing games. (Wulff guessed that we had Shakespeare's fantasy in mind.) We had toddies and sandwiches, and then said our farewells. Lying in bed, I prayed God not to forsake me.

Wednesday, December 28. I woke up early; the moon shone in on me through the window; already there were people out in the square making noise. I was afraid that it was late; so got up in order to find the servant who was to bring me tea, but I took a wrong turn and ended up in my stocking feet in the maids' room. As soon as I discovered my mistake, I dashed out. When I got tired of waiting, I went downstairs. Finally the servant came up. When the tea was finished, I departed from my beloved palace and went down to Mrs. Thrane's.—The lieutenant's dog ran off, and that was why we didn't leave before 10 o'clock. I spent one whole hour waiting outside by the statue, walking around and reading the first act of my *Emilia Galotti*.—The farmer who was driving for us, asked if he might turn in at an inn to get fresh horses. Here we were served crullers sprinkled with white sugar. He fooled the women into believing that he was off to enlist and that I was studying to be a minister. He joked around with them, but I was supposed to be a solemn personage.— A stepson of Principal Biørn came into The Prince and treated us to a bottle of wine; at our departure he thanked me for my pleasant company. (And I had hardly said three words!) Outside of Roskilde we happened upon a journeyman: "Why don't we let the poor guy ride along with us!" suggested the lieutenant. "Sure, if he'll give me something," answered the fellow who was driving. "I'll give you a———!" said the journeyman. "Just jump up in back on top of the luggage." He managed to get up, but fell right off again onto the ground: he was drunk. He did, however, finally make it up. The road was bad and he couldn't be bothered holding on, because he wanted to show us his scars and his military papers indicating he'd served under Napoléon—so the lieutenant had to hold onto him. "He's probably a scoundrel," I thought to myself, "maybe he'll stab the lieutenant in the chest!" The horses were unruly, so I was sitting between the devil and the deep blue sea. At last I screwed up my courage and asked if he didn't want to get off and have his mark refunded, because now we were going to turn off the road. He went along with this right away and then walked over to the ditch and lay down to sleep, even though the ground was wet and a damp fog blanketed the entire area.—While the lieutenant played cards, I went to bed, drank a toddy and ate some cake, but dreamt all night long about Meisling; in the dream, though, he turned out in the end to be good.—The lieutenant was toying with the maid, but she took to her heels.

Thursday, December 29. Now we are approaching Slagelse.—At the Crayfish Inn I was asked to recite my poem "The Soul" for another lieutenant. When we were alone, the fellow who had been driving said: "May I inquire, are you by any chance the lieutenant's servant?" "No, I've just hitched a ride with him to Slagelse." "Yes, I thought I could tell this morning that you couldn't be his servant," and then he told me about himself.—It first began to rain when we got to Slagelse; it was the heavens lamenting my arrival.—After I treated the lieutenant to some wine at the station, we parted; and he promised to write and send me the page to my poetry album. Back at home Ane told me Meisling had written his wife that he was angry with me, and Mrs. Meisling said her husband had written that by the third day after my arrival in the city I still hadn't come to fetch my books, that I wasn't doing any studying whatsoever.— A hell awaits me. I'm in despair! Oh, he is too hard, too hard!

Friday, December 30. Last evening, a lot of guests came. I danced almost every dance; then slept until 9:30.

Saturday, December 11. We ate our New Year's dinner already at 6 o'clock. I can tell that Meisling has forbidden her to allow me to play with the children, because we just sat and looked at each other; and at 8 o'clock we all went to our separate rooms.

New Year's Day. Sunday, January 1, 1826. God, will the entire year be like this day? Anxiety and despondency plague me; I wrote some bitter letters to the Collins and the Wulffs. Oh God, let this be my last New Year's Day!

The diary entries up to April 11, 1826, continue to be dominated by Andersen's descriptions of his problems at school, his anxieties about poor grades and the possibility that he might fail his examinations. From April 12, 1826, to August 4, 1830, however, there are no extant diary entries. We learn, though, from his several autobiographies that in May 1826 he moved to Elsinore with Meisling and continued his studies there, later referring to this period as the "darkest, bitterest time of my life." His tragic poem "The Dying Child" (1827) seems to have captured the tenor of his emotions in Elsinore. With Collin's permission, he moved to Copenhagen on April 18, 1827, to pursue his education through private tutoring. In October 1828 he passed his university entrance examination and one year later concluded his studies with the so-called second examination at the University of Copenhagen.

During this period, Andersen published his first works under his own name. In 1829 came A Walking Tour from Holmen Canal to the Eastern Point of Amager in the Years 1828 and 1829, *a witty account of his daily walk across Copenhagen to see his tutor, and the singspiel* Love in Saint Nicholas Church Tower, *the first of his works to be performed on stage. His first poetry collection,* Poems, *was published in 1830. This was followed in January 1831 by a second collection,* Fantasies and Sketches, *which contained all the love poems recording his short-lived infatuation with*

Riborg Voigt. They had met on Funen in the summer of 1830 when he was visiting her brother Christian, a schoolmate from Slagelse, and he never forgot her.

By 1831 Andersen had established quite a reputation for himself as a promising young writer. Unfortunately, the only record of these early years is in his autobiographies, in which he gives us a somewhat distorted account of this period, dwelling on the ridicule and persecution he was made to suffer. There were, to be sure, some attacks on him. He was particularly offended by Henrik Hertz's anonymously published Letters of a Ghost *(1830), which took him to task for his vulgar popularity and grammatical howlers. Then, as later, Andersen's response was to escape on a trip abroad, and he decided to leave Copenhagen for a six-week tour through the Harz Mountains to Leipzig and Dresden and, via Berlin and Hamburg, back to Copenhagen.*

From Copenhagen *the 16th of May [1831].* In the morning when I awoke, I listened every time a carriage drove by because I thought it might be a storm.—A swallow was chirping outside my window as if it wished to tell me something or another about my journey; but what it really was saying, I don't know. Christian, Læssøe, Lehmann and Hartmann accompanied me on board. We had almost a dead calm the whole way. We ate in the cabin. At sunset we could still see Møn, where the woods were green. I couldn't sleep. At 2 o'clock as we were passing Falster, I went up on deck; after that I saw the sun rise. Off the coast of Holstein, a Berliner wanted to entertain us with Berlin jokes (it was something about drinking schnaps). In the meantime a thick fog had settled, which did, however, let up.—During the night I lay stretched out on the long bench that served as three berths. The man who was lying by my head wanted me to move my head; and the man who was lying by my feet, asked me to do the same with my feet.—At 11:30 [May 17th] we arrived in Travemünde. Everything was green; two fields were yellow with flowers. It was a lovely approach. We couldn't see a thing because of the fog, but just as we glided in, we left it behind us, and my first river sailing began. It's strange to be on a great steamboat in a narrow waterway that twists itself in numerous loops. I was so exhausted when I went ashore that I hardly noticed that the tiny children could speak German. We arrived that night in Schönberg at an inn where the maid was angry because we wanted to have something to eat. The room was filled with wet clothes. I had to go out into the kitchen to placate her. However, she handed her apron over to Mr. Smith. I had a horrible toothache and had to get out of the carriage at every inn to get some alcohol liniment to use as a compress. Finally, I had to buy a small bottle with a bit in it and get some cotton for it. That helped somewhat.—The road was intolerable; many times we nearly tipped over. Once Iversen even jumped off.

Wednesday, May 18. At almost 5 o'clock in the morning we arrived in Hamburg via Wandsbek, where we saw the outside of the church and Schimmelmann's grave. Even though I hadn't slept in two nights, I didn't go to bed, but had a look at the Elbe, the harbor, the ramparts. Visited Freund in Hamburg and got lost in the city. At the *table d'hôte* I was addressed as Mr. Candidate. Iversen left us at 1 o'clock for Hanover.—I had another unbearable toothache.—Judge Advocate Aall and I had a room with a lovely view over the Alster. My teeth are monstrously painful. The nerves are in fact delicate tangents that imperceptible movements of air play upon, and that's why those teeth are playing the devil with me—first piano, then crescendo, all the melodies of pain at every shift in the weather. Even my corns are not unimportant instruments. *Richard's Roving Life* was playing at City Theater in the evening; and at Tivoli Theater, *Visit to the Madhouse,* a singspiel; but I didn't go anywhere because of my toothache and went to bed at 9 o'clock.

Thursday, May 19. I was awake before 5 o'clock and got up to begin on my letters. The weather was delightful, but my teeth not so good; hiked to Altona, where, at Freund's, I met a Dane, Hindenburg, who had been abroad. Freund was afraid that I wouldn't be able to make my money last until Berlin, and so he let me have four *louis d'or,* which I hope I don't have to use.—From there I walked to Ottensen, where I saw Klopstock's grave under a large tree. I crawled through a hole in the fence and wrote on the monument Riborg's, Mrs. Læssøe's and my own names. It was an impulse. Since Riborg is dead, her name belongs on a tombstone.—I walked home through Altona's Palmaille and had a glass of lemonade on the way. Today I was at the Alster Pavillion and had chocolate and a cake; it cost five shillings.—I've been in the Botanical Garden. Lehmann has departed for Dresden with his family; (I'm to meet him there at Count Hoffman von Hoffmannsegg's or Medical Director Kreysig's.) The gardener showed me around in the garden; it was much more beautiful than ours. The strawberries were in full bloom. In the greenhouses were flowers imported from abroad that were beautiful, or I should rather say extraordinary. Our native flowers are just as beautiful, even our wildflowers.—That little Hudtwalcker was here today to invite me tomorrow to his parents' country house outside of the city. Today I'm to eat at Dr. Albers' (he can speak Danish), and afterwards to City Theater, where *The Freeshooter* by Weber is playing. The theater is large and very elegant, four balconies high, white with gilding, a big, brilliant chandelier with a row of lights; the parterre (one *taler* and four shillings) comprises almost the entire floor and is so large that you could dance around the outside of the seats. Both men and women attended; people kept their hats on. The orchestra was quite good. A Mademoiselle Gned from Prague (?) gave a guest performance as Agathe. After her magnificent aria in the second act she received much applause, and so she made a curtsy, which destroyed the illusion completely. The sets were excellent: the head forester's room was hung with paintings, and in the wolf's glen there appeared will-o'-the-wisps that danced around. Red flames shot up from the ground; a big dragon spewing fire raced across the stage, but this I didn't care for. The wild hunter was staged better than at home—there were brilliant white transparencies cast against a blue backdrop; you might think it was clouds forming in those figures. Samiel looked like a red hussar.—Now I am at home sitting in my room, drinking a toddy and writing, as I think about home; and every so often I look out of the window over the Alster, where round about lamps have been lit. People are already saying I speak fluent German.

On May 21, Andersen left Hamburg for the Harz Mountains, where he made a walking tour from Goslar to Eisleben over the highest peak, Brocken, famous for its legends celebrated by Goethe in Faust. *From Eisleben he continued on to Leipzig, where he immediately looked up the prominent publisher Heinrich Brockhaus, who happened to have as house guest an acquaintance of his from Copenhagen—Oehlenschläger's daughter, Lotte. On the following day Andersen set out on his usual round of calls.*

Tuesday, May 31. The weather is cloudy today. Out on the sidewalk for as far as I can see from my window, there are farmers' wives sitting and selling butter. I stopped by Candidate Schumacher's; he wasn't at home. From there I went to see Dr. Hasper, an engaging man who received me very cordially and spoke of the many people here (over 1,000) who had come down with influenza. Afterwards I visited Titular Councillor Brandes, who thought he had seen me before and offered to help me in any way he could.—I am praised

Sketch from the entry of May 22 that describes
the trip from Lüneburg to Braunschweig

everywhere for my fluency in German. These dear people!—A bookseller Hoppe from Christiania has been at the hotel asking for me,
but they said there weren't any Danes here, only an Englishman.—
I ran across him later at Hôtel de Saxe; he reminded me a lot of
Høegh-Guldberg. His wife at home was the daughter of an actor at
the Royal Theater.—I had a magnificent dinner at Brockhaus's. I assumed he and my hostess were the children, sister and brother, of
old Brockhaus and waited a long while for one of the parents to
appear; when I later came to refer to my host as "brother," it provided amusement; a number of people have made the same mistake.—Was visited by Hoppe.—Was at the theater, where he was
sitting close behind me. The second part of *Guillaume Tell* had particularly spectacular numbers. The Hagen Brothers were in the parquet. The Brockhauses were in the same circle I was.—Lotte Oehlenschläger told about a German lady who had said that the four
temperaments were melancholy, epilepsy, geometry and diarrhea.—
The poor person who only had the last one!—Ate with Hoppe at the
Hôtel de Saxe; he recounted to me episodes in his life, and we parted
with sincere friendliness; it was with him that I had first been to

Gerhard's Garden, written my name in the visitors' book and seen the place where Poniatowski drowned and where he was pulled out again. There was a monument there hardly two feet high.—There are some people one can rub shoulders with for many years without feeling close to them; others, one has scarcely looked them in the eye before one has found a heart where one feels at home.—Oh, to travel, to travel, if one could only spend his life fluttering from one place to another! Indeed, I feel as if the world is my home, and I shall, I must, frolic in this home.

> How the storm lifts its voice on high!
> How the wave swells on the mighty sea!
> I think only of you—you're God's gift to me.
> You're in my heart; for you I sigh!
>
> On wide plains, with echoes of a stallion's cry,
> On high peaks, with chill clouds as crown,
> I see only you in each alien town.
> You're in my heart; for you I sigh! (Leipzig)
>
> Away, away from homely hearths I'll fly,
> To steep mountain slopes decked with trees,
> Far away, far away, my heart finds its ease.
> You're in my heart; for you I sigh!

Wednesday, June 1. Yesterday when I was walking with Hoppe to Poniatowski's memorial, we passed a house that had a trellis reaching up to the second story covered with beautiful moss roses whose blooms were hanging from among the green leaves. Today I was at Hoppe's; then visited Schumacher, with whom I went to Auerbach's Cellar and saw the window that Faust jumped out of.—There were several portraits of him hanging there. And on the wall were two paintings depicting scenes from the story (Faust riding on a cask). Later, we strolled in the Rosenthal Forest and were at the Pavillion.

Please remember with kind thoughts
Wilhelm Schumacher[6]

---

6. These lines were written by Wilhelm Schumacher himself.

1831

Thursday, June 2. At Brockhaus's for dinner; there I met a doctor from Braunschweig and a Captain Einsiedel of the cavalry; he asked me to give his greetings to von Schmidten, as well as to Ørsted, when I got home. Brockhaus promised to take several of my poems in order to publicize them.—Went with Lotte Oehlenschläger out to the cemetery and saw Gellert's grave there; lying on top was a simple flat stone with his name and year of death; encircling it was a wooden grate where many had written their names. We wrote ours, too.—I was otherwise in a droll mood and kept Lotte laughing. The graves were strangely decorated with flowers and ribbons; there was silver and gold lace on the ribbons and verses that had been printed on them. On one grave people had placed lemons that had been cut in sections—it looked like a compost heap. A body was being buried there. People flocked around; Lotte and I were foremost in the throng. It was a cabinetmaker. Long ribbons fluttered from the casket, and the apprentices sang beautifully in the fresh summer air. Afterwards, we walked back to town and saw Nicolai Church, where there were paintings by Oeser; in particular, I liked *Christ at the Well* and a hovering angel up in the dome. They were cleaning the church, and there was a man sitting high up, just like a plaster figurine, so that Lotte was miserable on his account. In a cubicle stood the old pulpit from which Luther had preached; I placed my hand on the spot where he must have placed his. The church is large, light and beautiful. I took my leave from Lotte, who hoped we would meet in Dresden. Was at Schumacher's and had coffee.—Said goodbye to Hoppe! At 8 o'clock we rolled out of town in company with a doctor from Leipzig and two young gentlemen from Frankfurt am Main, along with a little boy who was an unticketed passenger and sat in between. I was reminded of Heine's "Cupid, the Stowaway," and so we accordingly called him "Cupid." In Oschatz where we arrived the morning of *June 2 (Thursday),* the doctor asked me what my name might be; I said, "Andersen." "You are perhaps related to the famous poet Andersen." I said then that no Danish poet went by that name except me, whereupon he explained that he had read German translations of many things by me that he had liked.—As we approached Meissen, the countryside began to take on a romantic appearance. It wasn't Danish-looking, as it had been from Merseburg on; now there were mountains that looked very different from those of the Harz; they were a reddish-yellow color and covered with beech trees. Beneath them the Elbe, plied by barges, wound its way in picturesque curves. All along the shore lay villages and houses.—

We arrived in Meissen at 10 o'clock. The porcelain factory looked like a church and lay high up on a mountain. The entire trip was delightful: the Elbe with mountains on the one side and mountains with houses on the other.—We stopped in a village seven miles from Dresden; here I had my first strawberries of the year (one *groschen* for a cup). The postal employees were handsome fellows; had bright yellow uniforms with a blue collar and a trumpet on the back, with a long braid and a blue and white tassel.—Along the route were walkways lined with pear trees and acacia and, encircling house windows, cabbage roses in bloom.—At the city gates of Dresden I had to show my passport. I took a room at the Hôtel de Russie, where my toothache started up again. After the *table d'hôte* I paid a visit to Dahl, who received me very cordially, even though he didn't have any idea of who I was because Jette hadn't written him. There was *no* letter for me at the post office.—At 6 o'clock I went with Dahl, Aall and Faye to see Tieck, who conversed with me for a long time and, after we had tea, read the second part of Shakespeare's *Henry IV*. Really magnificent! One of his daughters is reasonably pretty; the other had a strange chicken-face.—Before going to Tieck's, I had otherwise been in the Catholic church: they were celebrating Corpus Christi, and during the morning there were processions in the streets.—The church was big and bright, with several chapels where people were kneeling. There was beautiful music, and the *castrati* sang like young girls. It had a strange effect on me.—In the aisles there were attendants in yellow robes and with big silver staves; in front of the altar stood three priests in white silk embroidered with gold and flowers. Choirboys in red robes covered by a fine, white tunic held candles and swung censers in many strange rituals. I saw some Bohemian farm girls, who dragged all their stuff along with them into the church, knelt in great haste and made the sign of the cross, and then hurried into the chapels.

Friday, June 3. Was on the Brühl Terraces and drank some chocolate; I had an awful toothache.—Visited Dahl, whom I accompanied to the Picture Gallery. Most magnificent of all was Raphael's *Sistine Madonna;* the more one looks at her, the more divine she becomes. After having seen her, all the others look hideous.—It is a childlike, ethereal face; it is to be worshipped, not loved! Now I find it quite natural that Catholics can kneel before a picture, if it is like this one; it's not pigment on canvas they worship—it's the *spirit* that is revealed corporeally to the corporeal eye. Correggio's *Holy Night* is delightful, especially the female figure shielding her eyes from the blinding light emanating from the Child. *The Madonna of Saint Sebastian* by Correggio had some lovely groups of angels. *Christ Blessing the Bread and Wine* by Carlo Dolci was the most beautiful rendering of Christ's head. A painting by Rubens depicting Doomsday—the angels took two of his wives; the devil took the third; he himself sat pondering where he would end up. *Noah Leading the Animals into the Ark,* painted by Bassano da Ponte, was funny—it showed a swine as the first animal to be led in, and it got the best place.—*Mary Magdalene* by Batoni was lovely, but somewhat worldly; she seemed to be flirting with her sanctity, and an old colonel remarked about her: "She was probably good for a few more years of service!"—I wrote my name in the book there. Spoke with Miss Schwerdgeburt, who couldn't quite place Jette.—At the *table d'hôte* a gentleman, Manuel, a "Polonaise" officer, asked to be remembered to Monsieur Fabricius in Copenhagen!—Went to visit Ebert, but didn't find him at home. Dropped in on Warnatz, the merchant who was my traveling companion from Hamburg to Braunschweig. Called on Dr. Förster, a very engaging man, whose facial expression resembled Otto's.—Took a walk on the Brühl Terraces and went to the Linckesche Resort (like the resort at Charlottenlund), where there was music; after having some lemonade, I was at the Royal Saxon Court Theater, where I saw *The Queen of Sixteen Years.* A Russian woman, Mademoiselle Gebhard, played Christine and did it quite admirably; her eyes were extremely expressive. After that, a ballet, *The Cooper,* thematically trivial, but with some quite lovely ensemble numbers; at the end Ballet Master Gärtner was given a curtain call by a few individual voices. The curtain was raised; all of the dancers stood there, but *he* really showed off. When the curtain was lowered, people laughed. Tieck was there and said a friendly hello. Together with two people from Frankfurt (an der Oder) we sailed home down the Elbe in a boat. It was a lovely evening. The bridge was mirrored in the water, and Dresden lay with its steeples and domes in the clear air. We walked across the Brühl Terraces, where there were a lot of strollers and the air was scented with jasmine. After I had me a steak, I fell asleep. Still no letters!

Saturday, June 4. I did a lot of running around. Got hot, but gave my stomach a chill with ice cream. Was on the Brühl Terraces and in the Catholic church. Ebert led me on a tour of the lovely library; the floor was like a mirror. He showed me some manuscripts and drawings by Dürer, among them a human figure made up of rectangles.—He was quite taken by my "Dying Child," which he insisted

From the valley of the Plauenscher Grund near Dresden (from the entry of June 4)

I make a copy of right then and there. From the windows there was a lovely view over the Elbe and the surrounding vineyards.—I visited Tieck. After the *table d'hôte* I went with the two fellows from

Frankfurt and the doctor from Leipzig to the valley of Plauenscher Grund. A small river wound its way alongside the highway between the steep mountainsides. There was a bridge and a mill there that made a pretty picture. Charcoal burners drove by; farmers came along with their carts drawn by oxen; and two shepherd boys, in their white straw hats with red hatbands, drove a herd of goats and sheep into the forest between the mountains. I met Mrs. Tieck there, along with her daughter and some ladies, and we drank coffee.—Today I've visited the Danish diplomat Coopmans, who was with Dahl and me yesterday at the gallery.—Was on the Brühl Terraces, where there was music playing. There I met Frøhlich, who was very eager to hear news from Copenhagen. We walked together in the Zwinger, a magnificent old building; later we were at a restaurant, where we met some local residents. Frøhlich discussed the recent troubles and said it was probably over now, but one of them answered: "It isn't evening yet!"

After a three-day side trip into Saxon Switzerland, Andersen left Dresden for Berlin on June 10. There he called on Adelbert von Chamisso, his first German translator and the author of the tale Peter Schlemihl's Strange Story *(1814), which later suggested the theme for Andersen's own "The Shadow." On June 24, he was back in Copenhagen and, just three months later, ready to publish an account of his German travels,* Rambles in the Romantic Regions of the Hartz Mountains, Saxon Switzerland, Etc., *the first of his many travelogues.*

The Great European Journey
1833–34

ANDERSEN'S FINANCIAL NEEDS *did not permit him to devote much time to his own work, forcing him to labor at translating and adapting French plays and writing libretti for Danish operas based on foreign novels and plays. Nonetheless, in the fall of 1831 he wrote to his close friend in Odense, Henriette Hanck, about his creative energies: "I have almost too many ideas so that now I'm really being extravagant with them and have in mind perhaps publishing a whole book entitled 'Ideas for Those Who Have None Themselves: A Needful Resource Book for These Lean Times'! This in itself is even a good idea!" In December 1831 he was able to publish a collection of poetry,* Vignettes of Danish Poets, *and one year later another volume of poems appeared,* The Twelve Months of the Year. *Criticism that his works were superficial and undisciplined so embittered him that he once again decided to leave the country. His mentor, Jonas Collin, was in favor of the idea and drafted an application for a travel stipend to the Royal Fund. Upon recommendation by the influenctial scientist Ørsted and such prominent poets as Heiberg, Ingemann, and Oehlenschläger, he was granted in April 1833 an award of 600 rix-dollars per year for two years.*

Despite the cavilling of critics, Andersen appealed to a faithful reading public, and during these years he won new friends who were to have great influence on his development: Mrs. Signe Læssøe, the composer J. P. E. Hartmann, and, in particular, various members of the Collin family (the second son, Edvard; the eldest daughter, Ingeborg Drewsen; and Louise, the youngest daughter, with whom he fell in love). Even though the Collin home was always open to him and he was treated almost as one of the family, his relationship with the family was not without its problems, for they never really came to understand him as an artist. Especially difficult was his relationship with Edvard, who had rejected his fervent wish for a more personal friendship even though he had become an invaluable business adviser to him. On New Year's Day of 1833, when he heard the announcement of Louise Collin's engagement to W. Lind, he had even greater reason to feel rejected. Both the Collins and Andersen himself must have felt relief when he left Denmark on April 22, 1833.

Although there exists only a brief diary fragment from a visit to the In-

gemanns in Sorø in 1832, the great European journey of 1833–34 is docu-
mented almost in its entirety. From Copenhagen Andersen traveled to Ham-
burg by way of Lübeck. South of Hanover, he encountered two groups of
emigrants on their way to America: "The women carried their children on
their backs. It was a pitiful sight on the black moor where the sandy fields
with a few sheaves of grain stood as symbols of their frail hopes on the other
side of the sea" (April 29). In Kassel he visited the composer Ludwig Spohr,
and from there he traveled via Frankfurt and Mainz to Paris, where he
arrived May 10.

Sunday, May 12 [1833]. Did a lot of trotting around all day long.
Went with Feddersen to see Cherubini and brought him Weyse's
Ambrosian Hymn. He lives very comfortably. His servant went around
with a cat on his shoulder. Cherubini was old, but looked quite ge-
nial. He didn't know Weyse, but asked after Professor Schall; after
a short conversation we parted. Feddersen was to depart on a trip
and had forgotten to retrieve his passport. We all ran around, and
the moment the coachman cracked his whip, Grevenkop-Castenskiold showed up with it! He had nearly left the letter of credit at
home. That evening, went with van Dockum, Jespersen, Sager, Bielke
and his Norwegian cousin to "Tivoli," where we met Dinesen. It
was really splendid there—decorated with red, white and blue lamps,
good music, a big orchestra, a roller coaster with boats. There was
also a theater that was quite nice; we saw an excerpt from a singspiel, but the actors and actresses were pretty awful—they couldn't
act and sang off-key. The Frenchmen there had a great time laughing and shouting "encore." It was quite funny, but you couldn't
hear a word.—Then we were presented with some fireworks that
produced a fine display. People danced in the woods along the illuminated paths. It was exceedingly orderly. We saw a Turk in his
national costume.—We drove in an omnibus to the Palais-Royal, and
from there van Dockum accompanied me home.—Was paid a visit
by Sager after I was in bed.

Monday, May 13. Went to see Lowenberg and got 200 *taler;* trotted
around in this interesting city and, when I got home, received a
letter from Jette Wulff, from that dear, kind-hearted sister. In the
streets there are portraits hanging that show a person on one side
and his counterpart on the other—for example, Napoléon and his
consort, Talma and Mademoiselle Mars.—This evening I went for
the first time here to the theater; I went to the Opéra-Comique. The
building is taller than ours. They played *The Magistrate,* which has

nice music, but a trivial plot; after that, *Priests' Meadow*, the music of which was by Hérold and really masterful. (It was his last work.) I didn't understand one bit of the whole piece, except in the last act, when the fisherman sang: "Il est mort!" (Clara resembled Mrs. Koch a little; she sang beautifully.) On the other hand, Madame Ponchard as the queen was too ordinary. In the last act there was a view, I think, of the Seine; evening was falling, and one by one the lights went on in the big building on the back cloth. I entered into a conversation with a young Frenchman and met a young man from Hamburg, who had made the trip here over Le Havre. Found my way home, and slept well.

Tuesday, May 14. No letter yet from Edvard. Went with Sager to the Palais de Justice. In the peristyles were shops; the lawyers were running around in black robes of the same cut as those you see in a comedy by Holberg. We were in a courtroom where a young lawyer very monotonously pleaded a case for some old folks. After that we went to the cathedral of Notre-Dame, which is located in the part of town that is built on an island in the Seine.—It is rather hemmed in on the sides. The pointed arches in the portal are embellished with statues of saints en masse. Inside it is big and light, despite the fact that the light must enter through stained glass windows. The large round ones looked exactly like huge kaleidoscopes. It was white inside. No one could be seen at prayer; no mass was being held. Up one of the side aisles of the chancel, there was a priest sitting and reading for some poor boys; one was sitting right in the middle of them, looking very crestfallen; he was probably in the doghouse. On the other side there was someone reading just for little girls; he looked a lot happier and smiled at them with pleasure.

Wednesday, May 15. This evening I was at the grand opera house, the Académie Royale de Musique, as it is called, a gigantic building painted white and red with gilding. Between the loges, arabesques and sphinxes are painted hovering over each other; there was absolutely no special decoration on the royal box. After the piece had begun, the queen arrived with a number of ladies. (What unusual luck I had!) She was somewhat blond and not beautiful. The music and acting were like at home, but the sets! Indeed, now for the first time, I have a conception of how these things *can* be!—They were performing *Gustavus III*. The costumes were relatively faithful, and the first interior, like a re-creation of the real thing. Everything kingly and grand. In the second act you were looking out a window—ships in the harbor, a clear, bright day, as in nature. But in the third act!

Oh, if only everybody could have been here to see it! The setting was the environs of Stockholm—the moon was mirrored in the water; light shone from windows in Stockholm; clouds drifted lightly through the air, where you could see up into God's great, blue heaven.— Snow was lying on the stage floor. There were no side scenes that you could see; one melded into the next; it was one continuous whole, a great unity, as in nature. The gallery in the fifth act was beautiful, with marble stairs adorned with carpets and flowers. But what was that compared to the magnificent ballroom! I counted thirty chandeliers and twenty candelabras. On the sides were galleries where people were sitting and looking at the masked guests, some four to five hundred of them, each one different. Particularly remarkable were a cock that crowed and a couple of Quakers who transformed themselves by turning around—it wasn't possible to see which side was really the back. Quite fine characterizations and magnificent dancing. It was almost midnight before it was over. I made my way home. Yesterday I had a visit from the chargé d'affaires, Koss, who brought me an entry card to the Chamber of Peers.

Thursday, May 16. Was in Notre-Dame; it's Ascension Day, but I couldn't find any sign of religious services. In Saint-Sulpice it wasn't any different; it looked rather grimy and can't be compared to Notre-Dame.—All of us Danes had dinner together. In the evening I went for a stroll alone in the Palais-Royal; it was like the streets at home when they are illuminated in somebody's honor. Water in the fountain played in the air, and people strolled among the green trees.

Friday, May 17. Was at police headquarters [. . .] to pick up my passport; afterwards I went for a walk in the Luxembourg Gardens while Dr. Jespersen was using my card up in the Chamber of Peers. Then I went up. I entered a gallery; beneath me a number of ordinary civilians, but with red ribbons in their buttonholes, were sitting in a circle and writing. Someone was holding a speech from the podium; I think it was about religion. There were some people sitting behind him, listening attentively. The niche in front of them was adorned with winged goddesses with real flags hanging by them. Painted on the ceiling were the symbols of justice. Now I have seen the opera-ballet *The Temptation.* In comparison to this, our theater is like a spiritually well-endowed individual who is shabbily dressed and doesn't know how to behave himself; however, in this ballet the externals are everything—the eye and the ear are beguiled; a fantasy world sails by on waves of music, but you do not yourself join in because there is nothing that draws your heart, that winged griffin of our being.—It was a mess trying to get a ticket. It went so slowly at the box office that the Parisians became impatient and chanted "bureau" and "police" and stamped and whistled. The overture had already begun by the time I got in with my ticket.—In the second act you could see the inside of a volcano. To the right was a stairway that stretched up endlessly high; the spirits, about four to five hundred of them, came down it; it and the whole stage were completely filled up. In the fourth act, a seraglio, a lovely fountain, everything voluptuously oriental; and then, at the end, as the clouds descended and parted, you could see all the holy spirits kneeling. The clouds rose and angels in white robes soared ever higher and higher; it all became an eternity that revealed itself more and more as the curtain fell.—The devils' sabbath itself nearly did me in because it was really eerie; the whole thing was rendered with a diabolical fantasy.

Saturday, May 18. Began to think about my *Agnete and the Merman;* strolled around the streets, and in the evening, at the Palais-Royal.

Sunday, May 19. Had tea at Brøndsted's; he presented me with his *Memoirs from Greece,* played for me a waltz he had composed; was very interesting. Was at Dinesen's, where Delong later showed up.

Monday, May 20. Today Troels Lund left; I ran into him at dinner at Desmeneuil's.—I took a walk to Place Louis XVI. A simple, white monument stood where he was killed;[1] a black banner was waving from it.—The Champs-Élysées looked very dusty, and so I turned back and crossed the beautiful Pont Louis XVI, which is adorned with huge statues of famous Frenchmen, such as Bayard, Colbert, etc. Started on *Agnete.*

Andersen stayed in Paris for a little over three months. Later, in his 1847 autobiography, he wrote about his literary activity during this period: "The idea for a literary work occupied my thoughts more and more, and as it became clearer to me, I began to hope I might win over my enemies with it. It was an old Danish folk ballad about Agnete and the merman. . . . I was free in my lyrical and dramatic adaptation of the ballad. Indeed, I dare say it all grew out of my heart, and every memory of our beech forests and the open sea came together in it." While he was working on Agnete, *however, his "enemies" continued to plague him. Enclosed in an anonymous letter that reached him in Paris on May 27—his first letter from Denmark in more*

1. Louis XVI, king of France, was executed here January 1, 1793. Later the square was renamed Place de la Concorde and Pont Louis XVI renamed Pont de la Concorde.

than a month—he was devastated to find a copy of the newspaper The Copenhagen Post *with a lampoon attacking him.*

*Andersen was equally devastated by not having heard from Edvard Collin
in response to a letter he had written to him from Hamburg. On June 11 he
wrote again: "Your silence has awakened in me a strange emotion I haven't
experienced before. It's a kind of anger which borders on love and sadness."
When Edvard finally wrote an apologetic letter, he responded: "My anger
with you, my deep sadness, should simply tell you of my great affection for
you! I have spent several sleepless nights because of you, but this is all
forgotten now. . . ."*

*Andersen had ample time to explore Paris together with the many Danes
who spent the summer of 1833 in the city. He visited cafés, churches, and
museums and went to the theater as often as he could afford it. There are
no diary entries from June 14 to August 14, but from his autobiography
and letters we know that around July 25 he met the German poet Heinrich
Heine, who had been a model for him in his youthful poetry. On August
14, the day before his departure from Paris, he called on another writer he
greatly admired, Victor Hugo. On the same day, he sent Edvard Collin the
first part of* Agnete and the Merman.

In the Jura Mountains

From Paris, Andersen traveled by way of Geneva and Lausanne to the Jura Mountains. He spent three weeks in Le Locle as the guest of the Swiss watchmaker Jules Houriet, whose sister, Mrs. Jürgensen, was one of Andersen's Copenhagen acquaintances. Here, he concluded the second part of Ag-nete and mailed the manuscript to Edvard Collin on September 11. Three days later he bade the hospitable Houriet family goodbye and set off for Brig, where he arrived September 16.

Tuesday, September 17. With this town everything is certainly be-ginning to look foreign! There's a convent with nuns here and a residence with Jesuits. This morning when I came out onto the street, I met a hermit, a so-called "forest brother," in a brown monk's gown; he smiled so dementedly at me! The old farmer women also smile nastily, as if I were an exotic animal, but many say hello with such respect that I don't know how to respond. (When we were driving yesterday, the soldier saluted everytime we passed an image of Christ. The clouds kissed Pissevache as they flew by.) I went into the Jesuit church; it is light and beautiful. A Jesuit was sitting in quiet contem-plation; a painting of Loyola hung on the wall; in the chancel a lamp was burning. I took a walk to a small village . . . near Brig. It had a big, beautiful church; the entrances were hung with crosses, and inside it was almost overloaded with ornaments and bad paintings. Met a Jesuit, who was young, handsome and forceful; he nodded to me. I had a look into the convent, but all I could see was a brightly colored easy chair on a stone balcony. Here, at last, there are beau-tiful women to be found! But they have these hideous little hats, like a baby's quilted bonnet with a broad ribbon around it.—Today I was terribly anxious about how little money I have left, but I took heart when I read at the dinner table about the daily mail delivery from Sesto Calende.—This is an awful hotel, and it is supposed to be the best in Brig.

Wednesday, September 18. Sketched the town gates and the Jesuit monastery.—Went for a short walk in a black jacket, vest and trou-sers. The farmers probably took me for a cleric, because they stood still and tipped their hats. All of a sudden an old fellow came toward me and fell on his knees; then I got really scared and turned back.— This is the first time anyone has knelt in front of me.—Was in the village again; a man was confessing aloud his sins before the picture of the Madonna. Went to the Jesuit church; two young Jesuits were cleaning it.—Around the residence there is a high wall with shoot-

Gateway at Brig (dated September 18, 1833)

ing holes, but in front of the holes the grapevines were peacefully twined.

Thursday, September 19. Couldn't sleep because of money worries. Shortly after I had gone to bed, the stagecoach conductor knocked on my door to tell me he had a full load of passengers, but he promised to squeeze me in.—Now I'm also worried about my baggage, since I can't myself check to see that it is loaded onto the coach. It is with a sickening feeling that I leave this side of the Alps—I almost said Europe. Well, in the name of God, now begins my journey out into the world. May the Lord let it go for me as best it can!

Thursday, September 19. The post coach was full. If a lady hadn't gotten off in Brig, there wouldn't have been any room for me. At 2 o'clock we drove out of town; it was very dark and still, like at the opera just before they strike up the overture. As we began to climb the mountain, we couldn't see a hand before our eyes; there was just the sound of rushing waterfalls. Soon white clouds passed low over the coach, like transparent marble slabs being closed over us. I was sitting in the compartment.—The road has been hewn into the cliffs and ascends very gradually. At dawn everything above us was enveloped in clouds; far below in the dark valley lay the wooden houses of the Swiss; we passed several waterfalls that plunged down through the firs.—At a way station—Napoléon has had several built—we had our coffee. We sat at tables with benches around a big fireplace where the burning fir crackled. On the wall there were thousands of names written. There were three officers from Prague; one of them in particular seemed very stupid—he was sitting next to me.—The weather turned bad; the valley was hidden by clouds and the mountaintops as well. You could only see the middle section of the slopes where we were driving. Waterfall after waterfall; then we came to the first gallery, a hollowed-out place in the rock through which the road runs, with only a deep, dark abyss on one side filled with fir trees that had grown to a monstrous height and stuck up like flimsy sticks out of the wall of the cliff. The conductor told us that he had this winter seen a bear walking right across the road and growling a little. Then we came to more galleries, built to allow the avalanches to pass over them into the abyss. Here the snow had piled so high this winter that they had driven *over* them. Farther on we came to a place where the road looked as if it had been cut away; now there lay a simple wooden bridge over it; an avalanche this spring had passed this way taking a part of the road with it down into the abyss.—Then we came to the hospice; the prior was working in his potato patch. It is a magnificent, large building. Nary a tree grew around it. Then we came to the old hospice, which lay in a valley. Everything was wild and desolate. The rocks looked metallic: they all had the color of verdigris; different mosses grew all around, and right in front of us was a massive glacier, looking as if it were made of green glass with snow on top. In Simplon it was bitter cold, but the tiled stove was very warm. In the outhouse there were two cupboards; I opened them up, and here I found jars of preserves—I thought I was back with the Meislings!—Now it was blowing very hard. We encountered children wrapped in sheepskins out herding cows.—The landscape got more and more desolate. At the gallery . . . the huge masses of stone gripped me; on one side a mighty

The Simplon Road across the Alps

waterfall plunged far down.—Everything was granite—it was like driving through the earth's backbone.—The weather cleared; then we arrived at the Italian border post, Isselle, and were inspected. The sky was, or rather became, quite overcast, but it was strange how mild the air was. A fig tree grew by the side of the road; chest-nuts were hanging out over our heads; corn and winegrapes, every-thing showed signs of a more fertile nature. At about 2 o'clock in the middle of the day we arrived in Domodossola, which lay in the midst of the mountains. The inn here was very Italian with spacious arched passageways and balconies. I bought a handful of grapes and then got back into the coach. An Englishman, a Russian, a French-man and an Italian with his vivacious wife had joined us; she recited poems and made eyes at us.—Now the winegrapes were hanging and forming arbors. The children herding cows were so beautiful. In the evening the mountains had an indigo-blue color. From within a church where there were lights burning, we heard children's voices singing. At 10 o'clock we arrived in Baveno, where I got a bad room and bad tea.

Friday, September 20. Up at 6 o'clock in order to make the steamer to Sesto Calende. Somebody said that I would have to hire a boat because the ship picked up its passengers in the middle of Lake Maggiore. I did so, but damnation! It cost eight francs! I nearly flew into a rage! I didn't have anybody who could go along with me, and everyone else who was going out to the ship had already gone. I arrived now at the Borromean Islands, which lay smiling out in the green lake.—I landed on Isola Bella where the Borromeo family, after which the islands are named, has its residence. In the garden were orange trees and laurel; Napoléon has carved "batallia" into a cedar tree. Everything smelled fragrant; everything was so peaceful. But the sky was not Italian, it was Danish; it's nice, though, in fragrant Italy to encounter a home sky.—A young girl gave me a beautiful red flower, *Salvia splendens.* In order to get to the palace I had to go through the small town. First we went through the arsenal and then the inhabited rooms, which looked quite princely decorated with lovely paintings. I was fascinated by an engraving of a sleeping ban-dit in which a woman is sitting thoughtfully and looking at his face, which mirrors his passions.—In the rooms below, the floors and walls had mosaics. There were two marble Venuses here (by Monti). The one sleeping was sensually beautiful. Above, an Aphrodite (cover-ing herself with her fishtail); there was a thin veil hanging there; I lifted it up, and there was a madame smiling suggestively at me.— Otherwise the lake and the islands are not at all as I had imagined: they are lovely, but we have the same peaceful tranquillity at home, just no mountains.—When we departed we could see the gigantic statue of Carlo Borromeo on the shore. A cleric from Milan was traveling with us; he entertained himself by speaking with me half in Latin, half in French. He was surprised that I had come such a long way and asked if I were a Calvinist. There were twelve German students; they said that I had a countryman in their group—it was a young man from Holstein, but he couldn't speak Danish. On the lake we met some fishermen; they sang beautifully, without screeching the way people do at home, and each one had his part. This seemed Italian rather than regional. The shore continued low and resembled the Danish coast.—In Sesto Calende there was trouble with the passports and baggage. People were sitting out on the street working.—I got a seat in a coach; we departed at around 4 o'clock and were already to be in Milan by 10 o'clock. I had gotten so sunburned during the last part of the ride on the steamship that I had to put my handkerchief between my head and my hat. The oppressive heat continued.—We galloped through fertile landscapes; the women called to us quite gaily. On a hillside there grew a large number of pines, and in Somma Lombardo there was a cypress as huge as our walnut trees.—The Alps looked like the glass mountains of the fairy tale, and now I had crossed them. Monte Rosa was completely covered with snow; the moon came out and was swimming in a clear blueness; the heavens were three times as high as ours at home.—At 10 o'clock we arrived in Milan. All of the rooms at Reichmann's were occupied; a poor young German from Osnabrück had to share a room with me.—Oh, I was so tired and hungry! A pretty Tyrolean girl made up my bed and chatted with me; she seemed a little wanton.—The motley assortment of things I had seen still floated before my eyes: the towns we had raced through that evening, the large convent in the moonlight, the girl who had sold me grapes and the musicians in the little town where the two lighthearted girls were playing with the cat.

Saturday, September 21. Bought myself boots. Went to see young Puerari; he said that on the same evening I arrived a coach was attacked by twelve heavily armed robbers and a woman robbed of all her gold and silver.—I don't quite like Milan, just as I didn't Paris: the streets are narrow and dark, and everything seems designed to create shade. Most doorways don't have wooden doors, but long curtains instead, like at the circus riders' in the Dyrehave Amusement Park at home.—Bought some souvenir pictures and went into the church. It is made of white marble, and they are still working on it. I was very impressed by it. It's somewhat grander than Notre-Dame. Almost all the windows had stained glass in them; because of this, everything lay in a half-darkness that made the vaulted roof doubly majestic. People were all around kneeling and genuflecting; I felt like an alien among them.—At the *table d'hôte* I met the young Russian I saw in Brig.—In the evening went to the Teatro alla Scala. They were doing a melodrama: *The Two Sergeants* with music by Luigi Ricci. It was about two men who had been sentenced to death; one was to be granted clemency, and now they were going to throw dice to see which of them it would be.—The recitatives were accompanied only by a violoncello; they were so dull that I can't blame the Italians for chattering through them. After that, *Giuditta, Queen of France*, a magnificent ballet without any particular sense to it; the way in which they did it was really unusual: every movement was measured—they looked like marionettes. Everything was heavily accentuated: the old king in silver brocade and with a golden crown resembled the king of diamonds, and he had a face like Pierrot. He carried on hilariously in his desperation.—The theater itself has six stories of loges, curtains of blue silk and a large chandelier. The muses are depicted on the ceiling.—The royal box is in the center and has a chandelier. Admission cost around two francs; you didn't get any reentry tickets at all, and you could come and go as you pleased.—I didn't feel like seeing the whole thing; found my way home through the sinister streets; two vagabonds were lying asleep on the stairs of the church. Before I went to the theater, I visited the church, which now stood almost completely darkened; on the high altar there burned several candles. All day long there has been an endless tolling of the bells.

Sunday, September 22. It was the feast day of an important saint. Everybody was flocking to the church. In one of the streets they were carrying white hangings with gold fringe and tassels from neighbor to neighbor.—I was at the hospital and several public squares where there stood stone statues of saints with big iron crosses. At the *table d'hôte* we had some music: a melancholy lady played the guitar; the clock chimed in; people babbled, so that you couldn't hear yourself think.—On the street today I saw two boys fighting; the mother of one of them came up and interfered in the fight, beating up on the other boy, so that now everyone sided with him and the mother was pushed away; she carried on like a chicken with her head cut off.

*True poetry is a divine inspiration; it is the gold in the mountain. Breeding and Upbringing are the clever miners who know how to purify and refine it. Often perfectly pure nuggets can be found; similarly, as well, a single song by a natural poet.—In other veins there are tin and baser metals; these can be worked so that they look like silver; they can dazzle the masses with their chased figures and engravings. *Letters of a Ghost* is that sort of goblet: it is polished to shine like silver and mirrors the flaws of everything it is held up to. It is a nice piece of work, only not of gold; but that sort of thing has its uses. Hertz is, so to speak, a kind of poetical tinsmith, a tinker, although I don't want to go so far as to say that he tried to pass off on Copenhageners his highly polished tinny piece as gold.—Hauch works exclusively in copper. Many do their work in simple potter's clay, such as most nonpoets, but they want to join the guild anyway. Molbech has used it to make chamber pots that he empties out on people with a certain poetic license. That is what happened to Ingemann, whose poetic soul and deep sensitivities Molbech tried in vain amid his youthful exploits to surpass.

Monday, September 23. Trotted around, but began to get bored. Dinesen and Neergaard arrived during dinner. We all went together to see. . . . This was the second time for me, but I didn't see the whole thing this time either—the others were too tired. Got a long letter from Edvard; there has been some sort of opposition to *Agnete.* I don't want any more to be the one who is forever and always accomodating others, to be treated like a child by someone younger, even a friend!—Such a tone as the one Edvard uses is asking for opposition, even though I love him dearly!

Tuesday, September 24. Was in the cathedral with the other two and a Pole. Beneath the chancel is the grave of St. Borromeo. The casket, walls and everything were overlaid with silver; there were real *piasters* spilling out of the cornucopia.—We climbed to the uppermost part of the church. It is a mountain of marble. We nearly got lost up on the roof among the spires and marble figures. They began to build it in 1386, and they were still up there working on it. We were up in the highest spire, from which we could see the Apennines and the Alps. Between them was a huge plain as fertile-green as a garden. We went out to the Amphitheater, which was built in the old style. They hold animal fights there. A little stream has been channeled through it, so that the entire center stage can be flooded and small sea battles can be staged. From the balcony there was a view of the Piazza d'Armi with Napoléon's victory arch (Porta Sempione), which hasn't been completed.

Wednesday, September 25. Was at the Viceroy's palace. He is the brother of the Austrian Emperor and looks quite a bit like him. We encountered him just as we were entering his palace. There was really nothing to be seen there—some tapestries, but not a single painting except for the ones on the ceiling.—The ballroom was large, with a gallery, but it had a stone floor. The concert hall was overloaded with chandeliers.—From there we went to the large exhibition of paintings [at the Brera Gallery]; there was a lot of awful stuff. An original painting *Mary's Betrothal* by Raphael consoled me.—A chimney with a cat, a lizard and a chimney sweep were quite amusing. Thorvaldsen's portrait.—We entered the archbishop's palace, where people were sitting in the lobby just like at one of our ministers' at home.—Willibald Alexis will be coming here soon; Dinesen and Neergaard ran into him and have conveyed me his regards; got a letter from Le Locle and Louis Jürgensen.—(I wonder if the farmer in Brig who knelt down before me could have known that the Ghost[2] has placed me in the ranks of the blessed?) Today we met our first monk in a brown cowl with bare feet; he was hardly twenty years old and beautiful. Sent Edvard a letter.

From Milan Andersen traveled to Genoa and via Pisa on to Florence. His diary entries record his enthusiasm about Italy. In Sestri Levante, he wrote on October 2: "If France is the country of reason, then Italy is the country of the imagination. (Germany and Denmark, of the heart.)—Here is all you could wish for in a landscape—the oranges hanging so yellow between the lush greenery; big, grass-green lemons greeted us with their fragrance.— Everything was like a painting. . . ."

Andersen spent three days in Florence eagerly visiting churches and art galleries, which he described in his diaries in great detail. Writing for his autobiography of 1871, he summed up his artistic experiences in Italy: "I never had an eye for sculpture; I had seen almost nothing at home; in Paris I had certainly seen many statues, but my eyes were closed to them; but here when visiting the magnificent galleries, the rich churches with their monuments and magnificence, I learned to understand the beauty of form— the spirit which reveals itself in form" (p. 154). On October 13 he departed from Florence, continuing his slow journey southward by stage coach. On October 18 he finally reached his goal—Rome.

Friday, October 18. Hungry and exhausted because of lack of sleep, we rolled toward Rome; when we saw it in the distance, our only

2. Reference to Henrik Hertz's satirical work *Letters of a Ghost (Gjenganger-Breve,* 1830), in which Andersen had been attacked.

Genoa (dated October 2, 1833)

thought was that now we could get something to eat. As we approached the city (we saw it from a hill first), the landscape became
a veritable desert with scattered somber ruins. The dome of St. Peter's Basilica greeted us from afar; we rolled through an extremely
long, dead street into the city, which appeared bright and friendly.—
The inn was second rate, and the coachman didn't want to drive us
any farther. Then a young Jew from home, Steensen-Leth, came and,
later, Bravo, who obtained for us some rented rooms, eight of them
for fourteen days; we decided to stay there (twelve *paoli* per day)—
At the post office I found a letter from Jette, Mrs. Læssøe, the Iversens and Høegh-Guldberg. Christensen had one from Edvard to me.
We were lucky enough to make it to Raphael's burial. There was a
skull kept at the Accademia that people claimed to be his. In order
to prove it, they opened the grave and found him all in one piece.
Then the body had to be reburied, and this took place this very
evening in the Pantheon. We got a ticket. It was a magnificent vault;
on a black platform stood a mahogany casket covered with a golden
drape; the priests sang the *Miserere.* The casket was opened, and
within it were placed the findings concerning the artist, which had
been read aloud; then it was sealed, while an invisible choir sang
beautifully. I saw Thorvaldsen with a candle in his hand, just like

all the other important personages.—The Danes gave me a warm welcome.

Saturday, October 19. Christensen said everybody had looked forward to seeing me, but that is probably just a Roman figure of speech. I paid a visit to Thorvaldsen; went first to his studio, then found his residence. He was very friendly, showed me his costly collection of paintings by living masters that he intends to donate to Denmark after his death. He showed me a bas-relief of Raphael that he is now working on for his own pleasure. The subject was sitting on some ruins where you could see the graces and Harmony sculpted; he was sketching from life, and Love was holding his drawing pad as she proffered him a poppy, as a figurative allusion to his early death.—The genius with a torch was looking sadly at him, and Victory held his wreath over his head. On another, with a shepherdess and a flock of cupids, there was one figure I couldn't make any sense of, so I asked about it. "Well, I hadn't really thought about it!" he answered.—Wrote to Edvard.—Stopped in at Küchler's and saw our library.—Was at the Caffè Greco and stopped in at Trattoria Lepre. All my countrymen here seem to be sincerely friendly.

Sunday, October 20. Paid a visit to Jensen's and afterwards to the Princess. She was very charming and beautiful. She regretted being forced to live in Piacenza, said that she never wanted to return to Denmark, asked me to spend the evening with her whenever I didn't have anything better to do. I walked around the Capitol Hill, where I had been the very first day I was here. Then strolled out past Castel San Angelo and saw St. Peter's Basilica for the first time. Other churches have been constructed so as to appear bigger; this one, on the other hand, smaller! The cathedral in Milan impressed me far more; it is colossal and magnificent. This one seemed to me so ordinary. It will have to be viewed several times.—We spent the evening at the Germans' tavern, but there were more of us Danes and Swedes than them. A wreath of flowers was hanging from the ceiling with candles in it. The artists were sitting around in their shirt sleeves and smocks. German, Swedish and Danish songs were sung in a hodgepodge; it was a pan-Scandinavia of the North. Bissen very cordially came over to give me his regards, said he was so glad I had come. An older painter from Hamburg kept looking at me and toasted with me at every opportunity.

Monday, October 21. Was at the Capitoline Hill, saw the ruins of the Imperial Palace, the old temples and the magnificent Colosseum. Went to the Lateran, where we saw in the cloister yard how tall

View of the Dome of St. Peter's from Monte Mario (dated January 26, 1834)

Christ was—approximately my height. Saw the Samaritan well, the gravestone where the soldiers threw dice for Christ's robe.—At the house of Pilate people crawled on their knees up a very long flight of stairs. One old lady was in a particular hurry; Steensen-Leth laughed, and the Italians said "Lutherani"!—We heard the papal band; the pope came, but since Dinesen had offended me with his manner toward me, I went home without seeing anything. Was at the theater; it was big and dirty, miserable decorations. *Two Houses in One*

House and an opera, *The Maniac of the Island of San Domingo*—I left after having seen one act of each. Today I saw Christensen working on an image of Thorvaldsen; and at Küchler's, a beautiful piece—a Roman scene.—Received a letter from Houriet.

Tuesday, October 22. Took a walk. A priest came to beg, later an old gypsy woman. While at home, a Franciscan came; he was quite jovial, showed us his woolen shirt and bare legs, asked if he might come again next week. He spoke German and was from Koblenz.— We were out at Monte Testaccio, a mound formed by potsherds; a cross stood on top of it. When it got dark, we went to an osteria on an island in the Tiber. It was quite literally a kitchen with boiled lobster, fried fish and vegetables. A lamp was burning in front of a picture of the Madonna which hung on the wall; various people sat eating at the tables; outside some children were singing beautifully by a picture of the Madonna.

Wednesday, October 23. We took a coach, drove first to Monte Testaccio, to another theater, then toured the Cloaca Maxima and ruins of the bridge where Cocles once stood, after that ascended to the Imperial Palace. A wretched building with a hare's foot on the door that one was supposed to ring with led in to the magnificent ruins. Garden plants were growing all around where once there had been

Monte Testacio near Rome (dated January 24, 1834)

splendid halls. Ivy with huge leaves hung from the ruins. We had a view of Soracte and the Apennines covered with snow. Afterwards we went to the Baths of Caracalla, which are larger ruins than the palace. Through the arches we saw the lovely, incomparably blue sky. All around grew grass and flowers.—After that we went to the tomb of the family of Scipio. The entrance was in a vineyard. We each got a candle; an old woman walked ahead of us and showed up the graves carved into the rock walls. I read "Scipio Africanus." At this point we drove from these catacombs out to Egeria's Grotto.

Egeria's Grotto outside Rome

The nymph was missing her arms and her head; there was only grass growing all around, but the spring burbled exuberantly. I sat on a rock and composed. A short distance away there was a grove. The pines look like open umbrellas and the cypresses, closed ones.— Drove then to Caracalla's huge circus, and close by lay Cecilia Metella's sepulchral monument, a magnificent ruin. We could see the old ruins; through the broken dome crowned with vines, the fresh, green plants and the blue sky—was it not ancient times, the present time and the far distant all in one?—Lots of lizards.—Then we set off for the church of S. Sebastiano, saw his grave and the marble figure with gilded arrows; this is where he suffered martyrdom. With lighted candles we descended into the catacombs—low, narrow passages through the earth all the way to Rome; indeed, in the old days, to Ostia.—By the light of the candles we could see through a fissure. The monk showed us the skeleton of a human body; fourteen popes and 170,000 martyrs lie interred here. Then we went to the basilica of S. Paolo, which is in ruins but is now being restored. The mosaic filling the half dome of the altar was like new. Lovely, huge granite pillars lay on the ground; a few are already standing upright.—A beautiful cloister with many roses.—Drove to the Cestius Pyramid and went inside the cemetery, where we found the grave of Goethe's son with the inscription:" . . . "We spent the evening with the princess, who did not seem very esthetically inclined. She started off by asking me whether I wouldn't get down to my reading right away since she had to leave at 7 o'clock. It lasted until 8:30. Thorvaldsen seemed delighted, praised the harmony, the beautiful verses and the central idea of the work; asked me to read it for him at my leisure. All the artists wanted the same thing and drank a toast to me.

Thursday, October 24. The weather was beautiful. At 9 o'clock we set off in two coaches for the countryside. (Bødtcher, Dinesen, Neergaard, Blunck, Küchler, Steensen-Leth, Fearnley, Zeuthen and myself) The sun was burning hot.—The entire Campagna is a big, desolate plain, but there is ruin after ruin and with each one is associated a historic name. Toward noon we reached the Alban Hills and were in Frascati; it was swarming with foreigners. We ate at a miserable osteria that had no ceiling, just big beams and a roof. Farmers and priests sat at long tables; a fire was burning in the fireplace, and awful, grotesque pictures were painted on the wall. Then we rented donkeys; I got the best one. Thus equipped, we rode into the mountains past the ruins of Cicero's villa and up to ancient Tusculum. In the thorns and nettles we found the stairs of an amphitheater. We went up to where the town once stood and rode along the cobbled streets. The road from there led through laurel and chestnut trees, deep sunken roads and sweeping panoramas of Rome. Toward evening the air became wonderfully tinged with colors—it was like seeing everything through a rainbow. We entered a small town, Monte Porzio, where there is an extraordinary well with a deep echo.—(In the evening there were fireworks in Frascati; a great multitude of children sang in front of the chapels.) When we rode home in the beautiful moonlight, we saw the Cenci castle, where Beatrice Cenci lived. It occurred to me to write about her life story. Through the bars I saw the moon in the dark blue sky between the cypresses.— We ate and slept well in Frascati.

Friday, October 25. On foot we set off up into the mountains. The gigantic Campagna lay before us. (Just yesterday we saw the sea.) In the woods we came via a little stream over a simple bridge. At each end there was an *N*, but this was no mystery—it was Napoléon's name. He had built it, and the Italians had put this *N* there. We passed an immense tree which had been hollowed out into a chapel. The crown had been clipped in the shape of a cross with a wreath around it, and inside the trunk there was a little compartment with a glass window and a Madonna inside. A few stone steps led up to it.—Then we came to Grottaferrata. We went into the cloister church, where there are four superb paintings by Domenichino, who had taken refuge here in the cloister on account of a murder and painted them out of gratitude. On one there was a German emperor visiting St. Nilo—trumpets are blaring and the herald orders them to be still because the emperor wishes to speak. In the foreground there are two figures conversing, and you can see the words on their lips.—Two dwarves are holding the horses.—A miracle by St. Bartholemew and St. Nilo, who is healing a leper. The expression on Nilo's face is absolutely superb, the Mother's pious hope, the two curious boys and the madman's gaze. (Finally came the Madonna in the tree.) Then we came to a lovely tree by a watercourse where girls were washing linen.—Soon we caught sight of the sea (as if gilded). Below us to the left lay the Alban Lake, perfectly calm. In Albano we took lodgings for the night, ate and then strolled by the grave of the Horatios, which lies close to the road. We found mignonette and wallflowers growing wild; the periwinkle bloomed and bore fruit, and between the green treetops we saw the dome of the beautiful church in Ariccia. Here in town you could read on every house: "Viva sangue di Gesù Christo!" The road up here was sunken and deep. On a slope an old beggar in a shabby cassock sat under a cross, with the sea for a backdrop.—We passed Genzano, where there is a feast of flowers in the month of June; the streets are covered with flower petals in the most beautiful designs; tapestries are woven from flowers with pictures of the flight of Mary and Joseph.—It's supposed to be incomparably beautiful. Toward evening we came to Nemi, which lies high atop a tree-covered cliff casting its reflection in placid Lake Nemi. It was evening before we headed for home.—We walked in a group to avoid assault, for it's unsafe here in the mountains. The moonlight was very lovely. We met farmers on their way back home, some of them with guns; they greeted us in a friendly fashion, but they probably weren't to be trusted. In Ariccia there was a handsome Italian who invited us to supper, but we contented ourselves with just wine and ate later in Albano, where Bødtcher, Steensen-Leth and I slept in one bed.

Saturday, October 26. We took some donkeys and then rode up to the cloister Palazzola on Monte Cavo, the highest point in the Alban Hills.—We rode close to the edge of the Alban Lake. The forest was varied. A huge cave, naturally overgrown with ivy inside, lay close to a large, ancient cloister. As soon as we got higher, the countryside began to look more autumnal.—At the cloister one of the monks opened the gate for us; the others were singing in the church. I was in a small cell; the garden was laid on the large foundation stones of Jupiter Stator's Temple and was enclosed by a hedge of poisonous laurel. A cloud hung like a curtain between the cloister and Rome; the Alban Lake and Lake Nemi gazed up at us like the two dark-blue eyes of a pretty girl. On our donkeys we descended through fog between the cliffs. In the small town up there Zeuthen was thrown. In the afternoon we drove home. It was soon evening with lovely moonlight. Everything was clear, except for the mountains with a heavy cover of clouds over them like a marble slab.—On the big, silent Campagna the lonely ruins of the huge aqueduct stood. (Near Albano, the grave of Ascanius.)—In the little valley in Campagna lay some ground fog. We went through it. It was as if an elfin maid had wrapped her cloak around me; it was a dank shroud. I pressed my lips together to avoid her kiss. As we drove past the Colosseum where the moonlight shone among the ruins, some people with red torches were walking around up there. The effect was splendid. A glass of toddy warmed me up again.

Sunday, October 27. Was in St. Peter's Basilica, where Canova's

Grave of Ascanius

papal monument impressed me far more than Thorvaldsen's. Walked
to the Villa Borghese. Carriage after carriage drove by with elegant
Roman women. Only the boulevards of Paris can display such life!
Country girls walked in clusters beating on tambourines. Shady, tree-
lined streets, lovely parks. I walked home in a foul mood.—Bødtcher
took a stroll with me in the evening and tried to cheer me up,
prophesied immortality for me even if I were to die now. We saw a
balloon burning in the sky. Today I got my hands on a *Copenhagen
Post* from 1827. I skimmed through it. It was as if I was looking
down from another world on all that childish nonsense and bickering. Everything seemed so trivial, so out of kilter: it started with an
agreement between Heiberg and Liunge that their journals would
never be at loggerheads.—On this page Y Z praised Nathan David's
poem; here proof is given for the validity of phrenology, for the fact
that Raphael's head, which I have just seen, is not Raphael's head;

Villa Borghese

here can be read a poem by Dahlgren for the Danish poet Miller, who has never been a poet; and here some sort of apology is offered for publishing my poem "The Dying Child"—now it is regarded as a literary pearl, and all this happened just five years ago.

Andersen's stay in Italy contributed greatly to his personal and artistic growth. The distance from familiar surroundings increased his independence from the critics at home, and his rich impressions of nature, folk life, and art clarified his vision and sharpened his perceptions. Every day he recorded his experiences in his diary, and excited by them he began work December 27 on what was to become his breakthrough novel, The Improvisatore.

In Rome Andersen frequented the Trattoria Lepre and the nearby Caffè Greco, where he picked up his mail and met with a number of compatriots: the poets Ludvig Bødtcher and Henrik Hertz (whom Andersen generously befriended despite Hertz's gratuitous attack on him in Letters of a Ghost), *the painters Albert Küchler and D. C. Blunck, and the sculptors Christen Christensen, H. W. Bissen, and Bertel Thorvaldsen. Andersen's friendship with Thorvaldsen was to last as long as they both lived. Thorvaldsen had immediately taken the newly arrived young author under his wing. He helped him find his way among Rome's many art treasures and comforted him following news of his mother's death and when he felt persecuted by his detractors at home.*

Monday, December 16. Today I bought myself a brazier. It is standing on one side of me, and the sun is shining from the other. It makes me feel better, but I am somewhat debilitated. If only there were a letter for me today!—There was a letter from Collin senior; it reported my mother's death. My first reaction was: Thanks be to God! Now there is an end to her sufferings, which I haven't been able to allay. But, even so, I cannot get used to the thought that I am so utterly alone without a single person who *must* love me because of the bond of blood!—I also received some critical commentary from Heiberg about my two singspiels—I am just an improvisator!—People are anxious about the criticism of my *Agnete,* and Reitzel doesn't dare risk one hundred rix-dollars on it. Now I'll have to publish it myself!

Tuesday, December 17. Got almost no sleep on account of a headache, wrote to Jette Wulff and Collin.—Hertz came quite amicably over to me this morning, told me not to let it get me down—the news of my mother's death. This evening the princess said to Zeuthen, who hadn't been there since I gave my reading: "Well, you haven't been here since I was so *naughty!*"

Wednesday, December 18. Rather depressed. Was at the Doria Palace, where I've been so many times in vain. The paintings hang in terrible lighting and are not well maintained. In the first gallery are watercolors by Poussin, Italian landscapes, two of them by Salvator Rosa. *A Turkish Woman on Horseback* by Castiglione. *St. Catherine's Betrothal* by Gaëtano. A portrait of Machiavelli by Bronzino. Titian's *Beautiful Woman,* who looks like a fresh, plump and healthy farmgirl, albeit a bit on in years. *The Deposition from the Cross* by Paolo Veronese—the colors are a trifle faded, and Christ seems to be more asleep than dead; perhaps it was his intent to portray His death as if it were a sleep.—*Cain and Abel* by Salvator Rosa—Cain is dark and powerful; Abel, on the other hand, has a feminine complexion, a fair, delicate skin tone. The altar fire is still burning and a storm is passing over the pasture, but the painting is badly hung. *The Deposition from the Cross* by Vasari—here the Mother is far younger than her Son; she looks like a girl of sixteen to eighteen years of age. All the figures have idealized faces. The *Pietà* by Annibale Carracci— here the dead Christ being removed from the cross looks like a youth of about twenty years.—*Endymion* by Rubens—a dog is asleep in the foreground; a lovely, little cupid is peeking out from among the green shrubs as the goddess approaches to kiss him. *Hagar and Ismael* by Caravaggio—an angel stops the sorrowing mother in the wilderness, where Ismael, half dead, has just cast himself upon the earth moaning for a drop of water. Rubens' wife by Rubens. *Jacob's Flight* by Bassano. *Icarus* by Albani. Holbein's wife. (In this gallery you can really get to know the wives of painters!) A lovely *Madonna* by Sassoferrato. *Portrait of a Franciscan* by Rubens—a strong, powerful head, full of good humor. Titian's wife painted as Mary Magdalene by Titian. *The Flight to Egypt* by Annibale Carracci, where you can see the Madonna walking with the Child and Joseph walking behind her, driving the ass.—*St. Rochus* by. . . . *The Flight to Egypt* by Claude Lorrain—the clear air, the fragrant trees, the fresh water, the movement on the bridge—everything is alive. *The Madonna and Child* by Francesco Francia—a superb piece in the old style with gilded halos around the heads. One of Olympus and Marsyas by Annibale Carracci. (He is teaching him to play a flute.) *The Usurers* by Quentin Massys—very characteristic; they are sitting with their money and their holy books open before them.—*The Four Elements* by Brueghel— well painted but tasteless composition, especially of the water, where the fish are literally leaping up onto land, seabirds flying all around; for fire there is Vulcan's forge; air is a mountain peak with all sorts of birds in the thousands; a naked woman is standing in the midst of them, and the birds are looking at her as if they were saying: "Why does she leave so early, what is her desire? How dare she roam in such diaphanous attire?"[3] Below them are glaciers and icebergs; the earth is covered with flowers. *A Farmer's Wedding* by Teniers appeals to me more.—In the evening Bødtcher read for us *Witchcraft, or False Alarm;* soon we will have heard half of Holberg's comedies. It is interesting to see how natural and enjoyable it is for my countrymen to sit in a circle and listen; a number of them don't know anything in particular about Holberg.—Blunck is in especially good spirits, and so is Bissen.

Thursday, December 19. Trotted around with Berg in the Piazza Navona, where there were whole mounds of lemons and oranges. The fountains there are superbly crafted; as everywhere in Rome, they are designed in imitation of nature.—Here is an obelisk resting on four boulders; on these sit river gods, and the water flows out from

3. Here Andersen quotes Ludvig Holberg's comic epic *Peder Paars* (1719–20), book 3, song 3, verse 173–74. The quotation in English is from Ludvig Holberg, *Peder Paars* (Lincoln: University of Nebraska Press, 1962), p. 130.

the rock which is below them and appears unattached. On one side, between the boulders, there is a horse, and on the other, a lion; they seem to be quenching their thirst with the water in the pool. It is the same way with the Fontana di Trevi, where the tritons hold the horses of Neptune, who is driving forth from among the scattered boulders from which the water is gushing out; the entire foundation of the palace consists of one waterfall after another. On Monte Cavallo there is an overflowing basin that has provided the inspiration for the fountain. By the Spanish Steps there is a big ship that is half submerged, and the water is spurting out from all over the wreck. People say that once the Tiber rose so high that it washed a boat all the way up to this spot and that this was the source of the idea. On the way to Porta Pia you can see Moses on the mountain raising his staff and water spouting out of it. With the smaller ones that are to be found splurting out of a housewall in almost any street, there is almost always some fine idea. For example, there is a really splendid one in the Corso, where the stone is in the shape of a man with a keg in his hands; the water is squirting out of the open bunghole. Sometimes you see a star on the wall; long beams have been carved out, and the centermost and biggest is the spurting water. Or two dragons spit water at each other, while larger volumes cascade down from overflowing vessels on the second story of the building. One of the finest is to be found in the square by the Jewish quarter: there are four young fauns, each holding a turtle trying to jump up into the water basin, thus providing support for it.

Friday, December 20. Went with Bødtcher, Bissen and Küchler to look in on the painter Overbeck, probably the greatest painter of our day. We saw two works—one finished and the other blocked out. The former depicted Christ on the Mount of Olives: the countryside is desolate; there is a thornbush right next to him; he seems to be humbly praying to God for strength in his hour of need. An exalted angel with a cross appears in the clouds before him. Down below are the sleeping figures of James, John and Peter with the sword; you can see by the exhaustion in their faces that they have struggled against the sleep that has overcome them. In the distant background the guard is approaching with a torch. The second piece is almost twelve feet on each side and only sketched in; it is *The Triumph of Religion in the Arts,* a painting full of spiritual and poetic feeling. It is an entire history of art with over a hundred figures, half of which are portraits. In the clouds is the Madonna sitting in the bright sunshine with the Child, who is pointing at a piece of parchment; she is holding a flaming pen. Adam and Eve, Noah with the dove, Moses, prophets, poets and saints are seated in the clouds. In the center of the work is a fountain, where the water is jetting out of a cross; the sun is shining on the gushing stream producing part of a rainbow. One group is focusing its attention on that, while less initiated and younger artists amuse themselves by looking at its reflection on the surface of the water below them. Raphael is standing like a king on one of the uppermost steps, gazing out into the distance; painters, poets, sculptors are all around him, also kings and popes who have been patrons of the arts. Standing foremost among them is the master builder of the cathedral of St. Stephen in Vienna showing his plan to several younger architects from different countries. He is resting his elbow on a Moor, by way of indicating that he has based his ideas on moorish building techniques. Capitals of columns and statues lie in the foreground, where the artists are studying sculpture. Lots of people came to see this piece. Overbeck is gaunt and emaciated, wears his hair like Raphael. The work will go to his hometown, Lübeck, but won't be finished for several years yet. He has converted to Catholicism out of sincere conviction.

Saturday, December 21. A letter from Neergaard in Naples! Bad weather, but not cold. Composed "Sweet the Scent of Christmas Boughs." Lent Bødtcher five *scudi*. Hertz quite the confidante this evening! Gossiped about the theater management and lechery.

Sunday, December 22. Got almost no sleep last night because there was a storm at 2 a.m. that shook the whole house. There was one bolt of lightning after the other, thunder crashed and the rain poured down. Several times this winter we've had bad thunder storms, but never with winds like last night.—A visit from Hertz; he was very affable, asked me to visit him soon, told about how he had read at the Caffè Greco a review of my *Agnete, Agneta und der Meermann*, in the *General News*, which is published in Augsburg. Later, I read it myself, and I'm so much the child that it has really put me in a good mood!

Monday, December 23. Lovely summer weather! Took a stroll in the garden of the French Academy. Boxwood has been planted as low shrubbery, and the walkways are lined with laurel. There are cypresses here and there, and in the center of a large stone basin is a small island with roses. You can see live oaks sticking up over the wall, so that wherever you look everything is green. There's a fine view over to Raphael's villa, which lies close to the pine forest of Villa Borghese; behind it are snow-covered mountains. Casts of the lions of the Capitoline Hill, the Vatican *Apollo,* etc. are to be found in the vestibule of the academy. There were a lot of English and French ladies there taking a stroll.

Tuesday, December 24. There weren't any locales available to us in the city because it was such a holy day and we wanted to sing. We got one, therefore, outside the city, in the large house on the grounds of Villa Borghese, close to the Amphitheater by the pine forest. Some of us went out there already this morning to set up for the party. Jensen and Christensen, along with me, tied wreaths; mine was the most attractive, and it was intended for the princess. I placed a garland of flowers around the entire table. We ate out there; at 3 o'clock I went home to freshen up and put on my dress suit.—By 6 o'clock we were all gathered; the princess, as a Catholic, didn't dare attend.—Plagemann had painted the coats of arms of the three Nordic nations; they hung decorated with oak leaves and laurel wreaths among large laurel garlands. All around the table I had arranged a flower garland, and on each plate was a wreath of ivy to wear; on the ladies' were roses. We started in by the Christmas tree; it was a magnificent, big laurel tree decorated with oranges and presents. As luck would have it, I got the best and most expensive present (six and one-half *scudi*), a silver cup with the inscription: "Christmas Eve in Rome 1833." In addition to that, a lovely change purse. My present in all its wrapping paper was the one that made the biggest hit for being the funniest. Byström got it, and everyone applauded me.— Hertz got a ring with an antique inset in it; Zeuthen, Thorvaldsen's medal, given by Thorvaldsen himself.—When we were eating, Bødtcher had promised to manage everything to perfection concerning my song, but he started it three notes too high; didn't want to admit his mistake, and so no one could sing along. That was the reason, when the toasts for the kings were proposed, there was such confusion that they sounded very feeble.—Then they did a dumb thing and sang it once more and drank toasts with champagne; the same thing happened with the toast to the princess. Blunck shouted: "May she live well!"—I thought he said: "We've got to yell!" Already at 11 o'clock Thorvaldsen and some of the older guests left; I went then along with them. When our first knocks didn't open the gates of Rome, I did some knocking. "Chi è?" they asked. "Amici!" we answered, and then a little wicket was opened and we squeezed through. It was lovely mild weather! "Well," said Thorvaldsen, "it is different from at home; my mantle is really getting too heavy for me!" Palin and Carlstedt wandered off. Fearnley talked to Thorvaldsen about seducing me, about my innocence. In the meantime bells were ringing continuously, and people were on their way to the church of S. Maria Maggiore. I left to go to bed.

Wednesday, December 25. Got almost no sleep because of the bells. Then went to St. Peter's Basilica; there were soldiers stationed there. The priests and cardinals walked in a procession; the pope was carried and fanned with the large tailfeathers from a white peacock; castrati sang. There were a lot of people there; I fell into conversation with a young abbot, who mistook me for a Frenchman. Was then at S. Maria Maggiore, where Christ's cradle was in a glass container which had been carried in a procession last night. Now there were two guardsmen standing watch there.—After dinner I was awfully bored; it certainly wasn't like Christmas at home. There has also been some trouble between the Swedes and the Danes last evening. Sonne, Petzholdt and several others were terribly drunk.— Stammann was much too familiar with Mrs. Jensen.

Thursday, December 26. Hanging around a lot with one's countrymen is not a good thing. They aren't interested in each other either— the tavern and meals are what brings them together. (Hertz told me that they drank a toast to me on Christmas Eve after I had left and that he had acknowledged it.—He had the misfortune, when he was on his way home in the evening and rubbing his hands together with pleasure, of dropping his present, the ring with the antique inset.) Today I made a visit to the princess. She was very amiable. (It was the first time that I have been there since I read aloud my *Agnete*). She very much regretted that she had not been able to participate in the Christmas tree party, but that as a Catholic she had to observe the customs, especially since the pope had mentioned that he would not be pleased.—The Danes asked whether we might not go for a drive. We went in three coaches; I was to go in the same one as Mrs. Jensen, and it was figured that I would pay half for her. (This is the second time I've had to be gallant like this; if only my wallet would permit it!) There is no real geniality among these countrymen of mine. The association with Hertz could perhaps be of greatest benefit to me, but—no! No!—We drove over Ponte Molle and down along the Tiber; had on the right the hill where Fidenae used to be. Here, a theater filled with several thousand people once collapsed. Now there is just a solitary vineyard!—In the mountainside to the left there was a cave with some sort of fresco; it's indeed said to be Nero's grave. The Campagna is a bit hilly here. The sun went down and the sky took on a special warmth, a lovely rosy-red tinge with brown clouds. To the other side it looked cold; the moon was shining from among olive-green clouds.—I've received a letter from my dear Mrs. Læssøe. I'm going to spend the evening enjoying it.

Friday, December 27. People are saying there was a complete eclipse of the moon last night. Suddenly everything turned dark, and the moon looked like a big mushroom.—Went for a stroll with Hertz to S. Pietro in Vincoli and saw the statue of Moses. There was almost no one in the church, but lovely music. Was up at S. Maria in Aracoeli. Portraits of nuns and monks were hanging between each pillar. The Christ Child was displayed in cloth-of-gold. It's taken around to the sick, and soldiers shoulder their arms in honor of it.—On the stairs people were selling pictures of it; I bought one for four *baiocci*. Was in the church of S. Maria degli Angeli—it is a veritable picture gallery. Began this evening on my novel *The Improvisatore*. Today, when we were strolling in the warm sunshine under the green pines and I was comparing Italy with back home, Hertz said: "God only knows how it will go for us when we get back home. There, it's much too different, indeed!"

Saturday, December 28. Today, was at S. Agostino's, where the *Madonna of Delivery* is in marble. Several years ago a small child was kneeling in front of it, when a voice came from the picture: "Why is there no lamp burning for me?" The child became frightened and ran to one of the priests, who heard the same voice. A lamp was brought then, and there were a lot of miracles—several sick people who called on her regained their health, and since then she has been inundated with gifts. She is almost hidden behind glittering diamonds, earrings and necklaces. Two big boxes are located above her head with enough rings in them to serve as stock for a young jeweler starting out in the business. Hanging on the walls all around are votive tablets depicting the misfortunes from which people have been freed with her help.—People showed the greatest devotion, and everyone kissed her feet. Everyday her oil and holy water are sold by the monks. The church is now among the richest. According to the *General News*, Kaspar Hauser has been killed. Koop was here and borrowed one *scudo*. He wanted to have more to begin with, but since I've heard that he doesn't pay anyone back, I lied my way out of it. When he finally asked for one *scudo*, I had to hand it over. *Adieu!*—Bad weather. Pouring rain.

Sunday, December 29. Lovely sunshine, but the streets really messy. Took a walk in the French Garden; the mountains were white with snow.—Went in the evening to the Alibert Theater, the largest in Rome where they hold the carnival masquerade. It is five balconies high and something like the French Opera. It was jam full, but we were served up a miserable performance of *The Barber of Seville:* the voices sounded as if they had been wrapped in sacking; wretched acting or, rather, none at all. A dreadful count, who looked like a shoemaker's apprentice in disguise—the only time he was convincing was when he played a drunken soldier. Figaro was a boisterous and lewd fellow. Basilio was dressed almost like a Jesuit, but had a Pierrot face. After the first act there was a tightrope walking act; a small young thing went right down from the askew line to the audience, which was wretchedly fearful; and then she sang along with the music—it sounded like when the old father has to sing in *Jean de France*—half sobbing and half bawling. The audience clapped for everything. There was also a ballet, balancing acts. A whole nine acts and all for one *paolo* (one Danish mark). At 9:30, when I left, there were still five acts to go. Around the moon there were summer-brown clouds. It was freezing.

Monday, December 30. Lovely weather. If only I would get a letter!—No, nothing.—Zeuthen is truly half mad!—He wants to be a philosopher by hook or by crook and has all of the quirks of one without possessing the intelligence.—He says impertinences to us all and, on top of everything, is so very goodnatured that you can't really be angry with him.—Bad weather.

Tuesday, December 31. Lovely sunshine. Sketched Raphael's villa. Went to see Vernet's atelier. There are two works here; one depicts a scene from the July Revolution. It is evening; you are in the middle of Paris, see its houses with the walls covered with names, sign after sign; in the windows candles are burning, and from the side streets the torches are shining. Across the middle of the street there is a barricade of rocks, trees and furniture. A crowd of people is engaged in activity in front of it—one is reading a newspaper and two others are listening to him; here, you can see a weeping woman; there, two officers of the Guard in civilian overcoats who are sneaking away, trying to conceal who they are. In the foreground Louis-Philippe is walking with some men, all dressed as civilians, into a building, from which the tricolored flag is waving. The entire work is full of life, but especially the street perspective and lighting disappointing. Otherwise, I rate the other painting far better. It is a group of Bedouins who have encamped under a fig tree. One of them is telling a story and the others are listening. Everyone is in a white robe, with characteristic, lively faces. A beautiful, brown boy is making coffee; the fire is really burning. Inside the tent a young girl is sitting and working; she is holding the piece of cloth she is cutting with her hand and one foot. A slave is standing with a fiery, white Arabian horse. They are all drinking coffee and have taken off their colorful shoes. In the background the herd of sheep is almost hidden in the lush grass. A lot of cattle are grazing; a caravan with camels is moving off in the direction of the forest-covered mountains as a horseman races across the plain. The entire work is painted with a remarkable boldness; the colors, freely applied, create the most splendid effect. On the white wall in the atelier was a carica-ture of Vernet sketched in charcoal, rather exceptional, probably by Vernet himself.—Went at 3:30 to the Jesuit church. The walls were covered with green hangings, the main altars decorated with can-dles. A *Te Deum* was being sung. There are three organs in the church—the one picked up where the other left off—and two differ-ent choirs at each end of the church echoed one another. It was an ocean of sound that roared about my ears. The people were kneel-ing. St. Loyola's statue was in silver brocade. The Christ Child was taken from the altar, and the monstrance set in its place. It was the feast day of St. Silvester. It was strange to hear the church bells ringing *Ave Maria* during the singing, mixing with the song.—This evening, had for the first time a long chat with my landlord; he praised my French, the dear man, showing how little he knows him-self.

Wednesday, January 1 [1834]. Had a fever all night long, and in the early hours of morning dreamt about a bat I was struggling with; the wings kept getting bigger and bigger; the moment I was about to get the best of it, I woke up.—Then went out to St. Peter's Basil-ica—the Sistine Chapel, where the pope was, and music; saw Ra-phael's loggias. Felt ill and waded home through the muddy streets. Lay the whole afternoon on the bed, dozed a little. There was an oppressive sirocco; it wasn't until the evening, when the weather turned cool, that I felt better. Saw the copperplate engravings at Küchler's, and my mood improved. What a strange creature—some-times everything weighs me down; at other times I take things too lightly. God, dear God, watch over me during the New Year! If only it might bring me luck, like the old one.

Thursday, January 2. Went to the Apollo Theater. It belongs to Tor-lonia; the name of the brothers is in gilt letters on the door in the oval foyer, which is decorated with castings of Canova's *Dancers.*

The theater is the most splendid in Rome—white and gilt, with glass inlaid in the columns. They were doing *The Normans in Paris;* and between the acts, the ballet *The Two Queens.* Magnificent costumes, quite good scenic decoration and beautiful dancers. The singer acted especially well; was almost more an actress than a singer. On the intermission ticket was printed a picture of Greeks swarming out of the wooden horse in Troy. In the first scene there was a little fountain with real water plants.—During the evening there was a hard frost, but there was lightning as well.—Petzholdt and I talked nonsense all through the comedy; I laughed as I haven't done for a long time.—When I went for a walk today with Bødtcher, he said that Hertz would probably like to take me by the ankles and fling me out of Italy, that he was malicious, that he was not well disposed toward me.—Hertz has composed a poem about Küchler's piece.

Friday, January 3. Sat by the palm tree by the church of S. Pietro in Vincoli; read *An Everyday Story.* Life in Rome now is also getting "everydayish."

Saturday, January 4. Was the entire morning at Küchler's being painted; saw a model who worked as a prostitute—she was beautiful *once.*—Went to the Argentina Theater, where the Chiarini Troupe give their performances, a tight wire act and pantomime. Seven or eight people do it all. A little girl danced really masterfully and with a daring and grace that was enthralling. She fell down twice, but was caught in midair and thrown back up on the wire, so that it looked like a game.—The pantomime players reminded me of old Casorti—they were whimsical and inventive. At the end there was an ascent along two wires from the theater floor to the fifth balcony. Four knights bore a lady up; she was standing on the tips of her toes on a pole entwined with flowers. When they had reached the middle, the two of them knelt while the two others did handstands. It was very crowded, and people were talking all through it. I was quite cross. It lasted until 12:30. The streets were empty, and the fountain at Trevi made a lot of noise.

Sunday, January 5. Beautiful weather. Felt good. Sketched the column by the church of S. Maria Maggiore; read *King Hart* and got a toy from Sonne and Bødtcher because it was Epiphany. Yesterday evening I could already see the beginnings of it—over by the Pantheon there were stalls with toys; the street was swarming with children and grown-ups who were blowing into small flutes. There were lights everywhere. Some people were carrying signs: tables for sale here for one *baiocco*—I bought one, but since carrying it was bothersome I gave it to a little boy who was walking along with a woman. The child stared at me, completely amazed; probably thought I was one of the three wise men standing next to the Christ Child this evening and handing out toys to the children who have been good.

Monday, January 6. Went, like yesterday, to Küchler's for a sitting, and while I was there a young model of about sixteen years of age came with her mother. Küchler said he wanted to see what her breasts looked like; the girl seemed to be a little bashful because I was there, but the mother said "Fiddle-faddle!" and loosened her dress and pulled it and her shift all the way down to her waist. There she stood then half naked, with somewhat dark skin, arms a bit too skinny, but beautiful, round breasts. As the mother exposed her, I could feel my whole body tremble. Küchler saw that I went pale and asked me if there was anything wrong with me.—After that we went to the Greek church, where they were celebrating a mass—Epiphany; there was no music, and it was boring. At dinner we drank a toast to the health of Father Collin, who has a birthday today. Sat again in the afternoon for Küchler. We've been having cold, gray, dull weather, but tomorrow the sun will shine, because the weather just has a case of the three-day flu. If only there's a letter today!— Indeed, there was a letter from Father and Edvard, the latter with admonitions and in such a harsh, didactic tone full of anger. He pronounced for me the death of my reputation—*Agnete* was a desperately ill-conceived, mongrelized, pedestrian work. It shook me profoundly to the core of my being; I was so overwhelmed that I was left numb, my belief in God and my fellow man destroyed. The letter drove me to despair. Bødtcher tried to comfort me. How could he!

Tuesday, January 7. What a night I've spent! I had a fever; I tossed and turned in my bed. How close I was to ending this cursed life! God forgive me my thoughts! May God forgive those who have wounded me so deeply. During the morning I spoke with Hertz; he was much more warmly forthcoming than before. For the first time he talked with me about my work, about his opinions; touched upon *Letters of a Ghost*, and—strangely enough—*he asked me not to take unfair criticism too seriously.*—Told me about Molbech's criticism, said that Molbech was crazy, that he was just the slave of whatever was fashionable at home; and he marveled at the fact that the subscribers to the *Monthly Journal for Literature* permitted such a person to write for them; he really arrogated to himself the direction of taste at home, he who had none himself. Declared he'd like to continue this topic with me, and when we met after dinner, he invited me on a walk. It was really a repetition of his poem "Nature and Art"—he held that the Romantic sphere in which I move has lured me to excesses; felt, on the other hand, that my descriptions of nature, in which my sensibilities revealed themselves in their own special way, were very good and had appealed to him most. He also thought it must be a comfort that all true artists had certainly experienced the same crises as I, but that their works had not even then become well known, whereas after this purgatory I would receive true recognition in the kingdom of art.

Wednesday, January 8. Last night I got a little more sleep, but my feelings have yet to regain their balance. I am ill. All the Danes think so too. I have just written a serious letter to Edvard; he must adjust his tone to that of a friend; I cannot tolerate his hectoring any longer if we are to remain friends. I don't want to distress Father, though, to whom I owe so much. Have therefore sent him the letter; then he can give it to Edvard if he wants. Maybe I'll lose both of them.—But Father is an intelligent man; he won't get angry with me. May God direct and guide everything for the best. After dinner I visited Thorvaldsen, who wanted a copy of "The Dying Child." He is now working on a new bas-relief, *Nemesis;* the constellations arched over her with Libra closest; two genii—Punishment, with a sword, and Reward, with flowers and fruit.—Thorvaldsen's hands were covered with clay. He saw my pallor, asked whether I was ill, and when I

Thorvaldsen's house in the Via Sistina

told about Molbech's harsh, unjust criticism, he put his hand on my shoulder and said: "For God's sake, don't ever let such things bother you; the less a person understands about art, the more judgmental he is. The wonderful thing about the artist is that the more deeply he goes in his art, he sees its complexity and is kinder to others. How Baggesen and Oehlenschläger fought each other! The one lacked the other's spiritual depth; the other, the wit of the first one. And they destroyed each other's peace of mind and perhaps many a work of art because of meaningless strife.—Feel your own strength; don't let yourself be led by the judgment of the masses; and go calmly on. Thank God I'm not dependent on anyone, can live where I want. I can certainly picture your situation—the misfortune of having to have an audience, and it must never realize that or else you are vulnerable to being manipulated by its foolish whims.—Now I have what I require to live, need no one, and that is my good fortune! God knows how great the world would then call me!" He then presented me with thirty pages of sketches of his bas-reliefs, shook my hand warmly, and asked that I take the injustice of the world as lightly as I possibly could!—Hertz declared to me that after hearing *Agnete* read aloud that he had trouble making sense of it; thought the lyrical passages quite successful, but felt that what they had called a "formal flaw" at home consisted of the fact that the ballad had suffered by being treated as a drama; that's how Oehlenschläger ruined "Aage and Else" in his *The Pale Knight*. I could have objected that "Axel and Valborg" had worked out well as a tragedy,[4] but it was not a typical ballad because of its immense length.—This evening Küchler visited me; I was still sick. The weather bad, like in Denmark. Rain was pouring down and the wind made the windows rattle.

Thursday, January 9. Today I sent off my letters to Father and Edvard (Jette and Louise). God only knows what they will lead to! But God will direct everything for the best. His is the inspiration for every bold deed. It is difficult to tear oneself away from old relationships that have become oppressive, but better late than never! I won't let Edvard dominate me any longer!—Today, when I was taking a walk, I saw one of the farmers driving the little carts with two wheels climb on board—it looked tricky. He put his foot on the lowest spoke of the wheel as it was turning and let it raise him upwards; when he was as high as he could go, he made a quick move and jumped

---

4. Reference to Adam Gottlob Oehlenschläger's tragedy *Axel and Valborg* (*Axel og Valborg*, 1810).

on board. That is just the way you have to climb up on Fortune's carriage, but most fall under the wheel before they make it up.— Hertz told stories about Molbech's brutishness; conversed at his place in the evening.—He was bitter about Paludan-Müller—"but that is a young man with talent!" he said. Thought over Edvard's behavior this evening. "The acrimony of enemies cuts like a whip, but that of friends, like a scorpion."

For weeks Andersen agonized over Edvard Collin's reaction to Agnete and the Merman; *his diary entry for January 31, for example, reads: "Well, today is the end of this month. Not since my time with the Meislings have I each morning been in the grip of such demoralizing emotions as I am at this time. Then I was crushed; now I am infuriated and hurt. My God, Edvard, what kind of people are you and the others? You are destroying me!" On most days, however, Andersen managed to distract himself in the churches and museums of Rome and on long walks in the city and through the countryside. Although he postponed his departure from Rome in order to participate in the riotous carnival festivities, it wasn't until he finally left for Naples that he has able to forget his woes.*

Sunday, February 16. My first excursion was to see Vogt; according to directions from Bødtcher, he was supposed to be living near the church of S. Giuseppe, but since there are two of them called the same name, I went to the wrong one first. A man that I spoke French to answered me that he didn't understand German. Then I tried my Italian, but he said that he couldn't understand and that in Naples one should speak Italian! In the meantime I found the right way, and I asked a well-dressed young man about the museum and the church. The man knew French and asked about whom I was looking for. So I said the Danish chargé d'affaires. "You're Danish," he said and entered into a conversation with me, accompanied me right to the place, said at parting that he was delighted to have made such an interesting acquaintance. But this seemed to me suspicious—so I told him I was staying at a completely different hotel, Villa di Roma. Vogt was quite a charming man, who received me with great kindness, offered to send his valet, who knew French, down with me to look for rooms, but that we absolutely mustn't pay him, because he would not accept anything. He was a nice fellow indeed! We ran around a lot and finally got something at 70 Via Speranzella for quite a good price—nine *carlin* per day for four people. I nearly didn't get hold of the others, so that the matter could be settled.—I heard some beautiful music in the palace square; went for a walk out to Chiaia, where all the best people took their walks. The pounding surf beat against the stones; Vesuvius belched a cloud of smoke from out of the crater. I went to Largo di Castello (?). Out on the quay several tramps were squatting; a man on crutches was delivering a speech in front of them, and people were standing all around listening. The whole square was like Dyrehave Amusement Park, with theater after theater, clowns and monkeys, loose women and painted signs. While I was sitting in my room at dusk, waiting for the others because we'd been invited out to Vogt's, I heard all of a sudden a strange sound in the air, like when several doors are slammed all at once, but with a supernatural power. I pricked up my ears; right away the sound came again. It's Vesuvius erupting, I thought and ran over to the square. It wasn't spewing any column of fire, but one side of the mountain was a river of fire flowing downward, and the crater was burning like a bonfire. All four of us went afterwards to Vogt's, from whose window we had the same view. The housekeeper was very gracious. Her daughter sang beautifully; Vogt's foster daughter, as well. I became acquainted there with a middle-aged English lady, who knew Danish. She took us up to the roof itself to see Vesuvius, which was overflowing with red lava.—I also got to know Mr. Mathiesen along with his older relative and daughter; he had a memorized spiel about Vesuvius and probably repeated "the revolution of the year 76" to me at least nine times, but meant by it the destruction of Pompeii. We didn't get anything to eat or drink, so we left and went to a café, where we were served some awful toddies; then wandered out onto the wharf, where it was very still. The lava was running down Vesuvius, and the sea was breaking heavily against the coast.

Monday, February 17. Moved over to Speranzella. We first discussed terms with the porter, and even though the terms had already been agreed upon, he did a lot of shoulder shrugging anyway about the money. Then went with Hertz to Vogt, who led us through the new Toledo Street, where the roadway has been excavated, so that buildings that had before been level with the street now lay high above the houses that have been built like pediments for them. People think that the inhabitants here will be buried alive in an earthquake. An immense bridge stretches over the seven-story tall buildings and is as high as the church roof, which looks as weathered as a cliffside. We were in a pharmacy owned by a physician, in whose garden an espaliered asparagus tree was growing. There was

Vesuvius

a well in the living room. Vogt accompanied us home and had a look at our rooms. I walked back with him, since he didn't have an umbrella, and he took me up to see Baron Brockenhuus, my neighbor. He was a nice old gentleman, who talked about the old days, when kings were demigods and not *people* like now. He had been invited to Princess Pignatelli-Ruffo's for dinner, and it had been from her that he had heard about my arrival.—-Since it was still raining, I accompanied Vogt home and then had to promise him that I would stay for dinner. Looked at pictures of Sicily and spoke French with the ladies at the table. By 8 o'clock I was back home in my room; felt tired, but so inexpressibly happy, thankful to God. Slept.

Tuesday, February 18. Lovely weather. Intended to go to the cave at Posillipo and, to be sure, walked eighteen miles without finding it, but it was a divine tour—through Chiaia, where I bought some drawings, walked by the sea pounding against the rocks.—It was the world's great pulse beat that I heard. The sea raised its great wings, coal black smoke arose from Vesuvius into the blue sky. There were ruins along the shore; Ischia was swimming like a bright cloud on the sea. All around were pines. I walked until I saw the sea to my left and then took a shortcut home through a small village.— Visited Vogt, and toward evening took a walk to the wharf. Such shades of colors on the mountains! Just as the sun went down, the red lava was glowing. Some boys played soldiers on the beach, and tramps in their brown hooded coats sat on the rocks watching them. I turned into a side street, where cloaked, white figures carrying candles were following an open coffin on a bed of state covered with red velvet and lace; the corpse was holding a golden chalice in its hand. With difficulty I found my way back through the narrow streets in the dark. Early to bed.

Wednesday, February 19. Paid a visit to General Mathiesen, who invited me for a drive. It was exactly the same way I'd gone on foot yesterday. The sea was like glass. Capri, which I'd thought was Ischia, lay like a floating cloud; after that we saw Procida and the quarantine station, strolled around the Villa Reale, heard the old stories about the year . . . and had a good dinner at his home, chatted with the ladies of the house and was invited together with Vogt's ladies to accompany them to the Carlino Theater to see some farces in the Neapolitan dialect. In the dusk of the evening I was surrounded by a bunch of pimps, who wished to recommend to me a *bella donna.* I've noticed that the climate is affecting my blood—I felt a raging passion, but resisted.—God only knows what Hertz was up to when I got home! The room was locked, and when I knocked on the door he came out and, speaking to me outside the door, apologized for the fact that I couldn't come in. He appeared to me disconcerted. The Carlino Theater is a small hall with two balconies of loges, but clean.—They were performing a farce, of which I understood not a word, except for what Mrs. Guillaumo told me about it

The temples in Paestum

in French. The young gentlemen looked over our ladies through their lorgnettes. The loge was so small that we were literally packed in there like sardines. On the ceiling was written: "Castigat ridendo mores." I had actually no idea of what the piece was about. There was someone who got a kick out of getting people mad at each other. When I finally got bored and had a bit of a toothache, I left and was pursued in the street where I live by somebody who asked if I wanted to have a *ragazza* or a *ragazzo*.

Thursday, February 20. Went for a walk around the Villa Reale and looked at the beautiful sea. Not all of the waves wash equally high along the shore, but the smaller ones contribute to giving the larger ones greater power.—The sky is so infinitely blue, not a cloud.— Naples is a paradise.—(The play I saw yesterday had this long title: *Marco Sciarra, the Fellow from Down by the Docks, or The Man Who Doesn't Mind His Own Business Is Looking for Trouble.*) As I was sitting this evening in the Caffè d'Italia, a young blond man who had been staring at me for a long time came over and asked if I wasn't Mr. Andersen from Copenhagen. It was Dr. Albers's brother-in-law, whom I first met in Dahl's home in Dresden on my first trip and

since then have seen in Copenhagen. He had sailed on a Danish
ship here to Naples and was staying to study the sea.—Afterwards
drove with General Mathiesen to the home of Swedish Consul
Fleischer, whose whole family could only speak Italian. I conversed
in French with a young Italian and Vogt's ladies. The floor was so
slippery that the tiles were like sheets of ice, and I could hardly
walk. Vogt's servant arrived with a letter costing twelve *carlin* (one
species). It was from my kind-hearted old Collin and from Edvard,
whose missive did not satisfy me, really—he didn't seem to know
anything at all about *my* letter! Father's was so endearing.—There
was dancing, and Vogt's daughter sang. Since I was bored, I went
home. During the morning I was at the museum. It is extremely
large, with rich holdings. I saw only the paintings, which occupy
several halls. Especially pleasing were: (1) a genius hovering in the
air with his harp, by Annibale Carracci; (2) Guido Reni's sleeping
child, by whose side were lying nails, a whip and a crown of thorns;
in front of him was a skull; in the entire background only one small,
green tree—a cypress—could be seen; (3) two laughing boys, by Parmigianino; (4) *Leo X*, by Raphael; (5) *Madonna with the Child*, by Ra-

phael; this one greatly resembled the *Madonna of Foligno*—the same lightness, the same grace. I saw a number of depictions of ruins, done, I believe, with burnt cork. There were temples in Paestum, the Colosseum in Rome, etc., etc.

Friday, February 21. Went to the café early and from there along by the sea out to Portici. The way there is so long that it seems never to end. The palace there is large and magnificent; it lies in the center of town. I was in the church; a young lady was confessing. On the street I was almost attacked by guides who wanted to take me up to Vesuvius, to Herculanum and Pompeii. They were literally chasing me, underbidding each other. Since I'll be seeing these later with the other Danes, I had to say, in order to get away, that I would come back tomorrow. Then they all asked me to write down their names, and I got away by scribbling something down, and so I walked around in a small side street that seems to have been constructed entirely of lava debris. Close by was a very low wall, and within it lay Herculanum. It was small—infinitely small rooms, with well-preserved paintwork, but the outer building, extensively renovated. There was a long row of columns. They were still excavating, and there was a guard.—Smoke swirled thickly up out of Vesuvius, and the lava gave off a cloud of steam. I arrived home exhausted; started a letter to the Collins. Ate and stretched out on the bed. At dusk I walked down to the sea. Vesuvius spewed great streams of lava; it blazed into the air; it was like tongues of fire flaring up. This is the most violent I have seen it. But I had no peace from the pimps—a boy ten or twelve years old pursued me down the length of the street, speaking of this *donna multa bella, eccellenza!* I got really randy, but still resisted the temptation anyway. If I'm still innocent when I get back home, I'll stay that way. Hertz was standing on the corner, looking through theater glasses at Vesuvius erupting lava. We walked together to the wharf, where there is a never-ending circus—half of the show was outside for free; the other half, inside for a price! There is beautiful moonlight; now I am sitting in my room, drinking for the first time Lacrimae Christi, which the porter fetched for me. It tastes like good red wine and has something of an acrid flavor. I can't really say it's very good.

Saturday, February 22. Took an early walk out to the cave at Posillipo; Virgil's grave is close by. The cave itself extends almost a mile through the mountain—a whole town lies on top of it. Daylight can't reach from the one end to the other; thus, there are a lot of lamps, but they are hung high, and so there is an eternal twilight in there. Some goats with bells around their necks were herded through—we were practically falling over them. My shadow got so long that I nearly fell over it. Past the town of Posillipo I went a long way through a forest with vines hanging in the trees and arrived at an abandoned church that people had built their houses against; I màde a sketch of it. After several hours of walking I reached the sea with its islands lying offshore before me. The beauty was exceptional, and the sun burned with the heat of summer. I hiked up the mountain, and felt very listless with the heat. When I came home to recover, then Berg and Zeuthen wanted us to set off in an hour to climb Vesuvius. I was opposed to it, since it wasn't what we had agreed on—that we should have one day's notice. What a fuss! Hertz was on my side and the excursion was postponed. In the evening I was harassed by the boy about visiting his *donna;* then he gave me her address, but I threw it away and walked down to the sea. The moon was shining on the dark blue water, and the waves breaking on the shore looked like a glimmering piece of embroidery. Fire was running in great streams down Vesuvius, but there was almost no smoke to be seen.— I walked out to the lighthouse and saw then in the moonlight a handsome frigate coursing under full sail into the harbor. Down there is a never-ending circus, shows and stunts. I went into the puppet theater for two *grana* (two Danish shillings); it looked awfully shabby. A lot of children were making noise and screeching; two musicians were sawing away at "With Ardor Fired," from *The Lady of the Lake!* Over the curtain you could read: "Castigat ridendo mores." It was awfully bad. A princess was besieged, and in the last act she came out onto the wall with two of her ladies concealed, like in the Punch and Judy shows at the Dyrehave Amusement Park at home, in a big pot that everybody whacked away at; finally it broke into pieces all over the stage, and they all went at each other. The children there became frightened and screamed. The musicians played "With Ardor Fired" presto, and an old man cried: "Brandy!" while the proprietress already began to call to people to see the next performance. Took a walk in the moonlight on the bridge; walked a bit in Toledo Street and afterwards home to sleep.

Sunday, February 23. Last night it was so stormy that my balcony doors sprang open and the blanket was nearly blown off me. Took a walk around the Villa Reale and watched the frothing of the waves far out. Paid a visit to Miss Mathiesen and strolled through Toledo

Street. Then walked along the narrow side streets, where the six-story buildings are almost touching at the top. My blood is churning. Huge sensuality and struggle with myself. If it really is a sin to satisfy this powerful urge, then let me fight it. I am still innocent, but my blood is burning. In my dreams I am boiling inside. The south will have its way! I am half sick.—Happy is the man who is married, engaged to be married! Oh, if only I were bound by strong bonds!—But I will, I will fight this weakness!—In the evening went to the San Carlo Theater; it is very impressive: a gilt bas-relief, a beautiful border on the curtain, namely a procession of cupids driving—first one with billy goats; next to it is one with serpents but he falls off; the swans that are drawing the next carriage are stretching their necks and seem to be trying to bite the driver.—There are tigers, doves and rabbits drawing wagons. The building has six balconies, was tastefully illuminated, an elegant audience—the whole orchestra section was occupied by officers in well-fitting uniforms. The ticket collector showed people to their seats and asked for a few *grana* for doing it. They were doing Bellini's opera *Norma*. Madame Malibran was Norma; she isn't pretty, but youthful, though.— Everybody applauded; one booed. Envy there, too.

Monday, February 24. Lovely weather, but windy. Paid a visit to Vogt and was asked to introduce the other Danes to the Swedish consul. Took a walk around the Villa Reale. Åberg and Carlstedt arrived last evening. At 1 o'clock Hertz, Zeuthen, Berg and the Frenchman Lennel, who always stresses the last syllable, took the road along the bay to Vesuvius. No one had made any arrangements. We nearly weren't able to get a carriage; the one we did get was very small, and when Zeuthen climbed in last and had no room, he got angry and was so naive as to say that he wanted to throw me out of the carriage. He was serious; the others called it a joke. But it is intolerable to travel with a lunatic.—San Giovanni, Portici and Resina meld into each other, so that you can't tell where the boundaries are. We were five in that tiny carriage. Hanging on behind were two ragged boys that here count as lackeys, and the driver allowed one up on the perch that he himself was sitting on. That was how we with one horse sped to Herculanum in Resina and paid about eight Danish shillings.—We climbed down through a house to the amphitheater that had been discovered during the digging of a cistern. The aisles have been cleared of ash and lava, but since everyone must carry a candle and can only see bits of it at a time, it is hard to get the idea of it. The stage is supposed to be even bigger than all of the San Carlo Theater. It was a labyrinth of dark corridors. Finally, we came to the cistern opening, where there was a deep well, but we only enjoyed the daylight in this cylinder for a short time—we were to proceed to deeper dark passageways. Here you could see the place where the orchestra had been, the separate locations for the different musicians.—We saw the dressing rooms. At one place there was a full imprint of a mask in the lava above us. We found sort of a monument to the Balbus family, who had figured prominently in those days—a statue of him astride a horse is in the museum here, along with busts of his daughters. We climbed the stairs to the loges on the various levels. The passageways were big and broad. They can't excavate either it or the town of Herculanum, since a new town is situated on top of it all. From there we exited to the new town and wandered along a side street to the excavated section of Herculanum that I saw the other day from above.—Entire rooms and chambers, but terribly small, are there still, even the frescos on the walls—rams, birds, a fight between a horse and lion, figures, etc., etc. A rather large square with a portico around it is located in the center; here there is supposed to have been a garden, and now a small one has been laid out. The street running through the town is terribly narrow, hardly wide enough for one carriage, and paved, like now, with ashlar of lava. When they were laying the pavement with it, they probably were thinking least of all that they would get a new outpouring of the stuff over their heads.—We saw the prison building; the windows on three different stories still had their iron bars. In the rooms were beautiful mosaic floors. I got five small cubelike pieces, but the guide said we had to hide them, even though, God knows, there were plenty of them lying around.— There was charcoal here and there sticking out of the lava—these had been wooden beams. Several places the red paint on the houses had turned yellow from the heat. What has been excavated is still just a little of what is there.—We went to a trattoria, where the first course was a great plate of fire that they put in front of us for the sake of the warmth.—We all got up on assback after having had to listen to a lot of nonsense from the ten or so guides who had in a group followed and harassed us all the way out of town. Each of us had to repeat to the guide at least twelve times what had been agreed upon. They were miserable mules we had gotten, miserable saddles. The beasts bolted off, so that Hertz screamed and everything was

dancing in front of my eyes. The path went past vineyards and isolated buildings. It was blowing a lot. The vegetation soon began to
thin out to dry, rushlike growth and small trees. The evening was
so infinitely beautiful; the sun set like a ball of fire; the sky was a
glimmering gold that shaded over into an ether-blue. The sea was
like indigo, and the islands were lying like pale blue clouds on it. It
was a magic world that had manifested itself. All around the bay
Naples faded more and more. The mountains were shining so splendidly with their white snow; they lay far off in the blue sky, and
close to us we could see all the red lava on Vesuvius. It was almost
dark by the time we had traveled over a lava field and along a narrow sunken road to reach the hermitage. Here we bought ourselves
two bottles of Lacrimae Christi that the guide was to carry. The wind
was so biting cold that I had to get off my donkey and walk. The
boy got up on him and I got his walking stick. Soon the donkeys
couldn't take us any further. We stood before the mountain itself,
whose rounded contours were covered with blocks of lava and ash.
We were now ascending a fairly steep grade, sinking up over our
knees into ash. With every other step we slid backward by one.
Large, loose rocks went sliding downward when we stepped on
them.—Zeuthen got mad every time there was a stone that rolled.
Hertz got tired right away and kept shouting that we mustn't run,
even though we were crawling along. He always had something he
wanted to say to me; the guide was always having to sit and wait.
It didn't help that he shouted "Courage!" Hertz said at last that if
we didn't walk slowly and take rests he was going to turn around
and not go with us. (Vanity!) Finally he sank down exhausted. I
gave him some wine; the Norwegian took him under the one arm;
I, under the other. I sang loudly to show how little it was tiring me.
The Frenchman and the guide were always in the lead and comforted us that we were almost at the top. An hour passed and we
were on some sort of plain under the cauldron. Here we caught a
sudden glimpse of the moon right over the crater. Coal-black smoke
swirled upward; then a ball of fire and gigantic, glowing boulders
rolled down onto the plain that we had to cross to get to the lavaflow. It cast a fiery glow; we couldn't see it for ourselves yet, but all
of the tourists standing on boulders close to it looked larger than life
in that lighting.—There was no path at all; we had to walk and crawl
between the huge pieces of lava. Hertz fell and hurt himself.—With
every eruption the moon was entirely hidden by the pitch-black
smoke. It was night then and we had to stand still, for it looked like

black chasms between the crags. After a while we could feel the heat coming up from underneath us. In order to see the new lavaflow we had to cross one that had been flowing the night before; only the outermost crust was black and hard, and red fire was burning in the cracks. We stepped out onto it; it burned our feet through the soles of our shoes. If the crust had broken, we would have sunk into a sea of fire. Then we saw the monstrous stream of fire pouring slowly, thick and red like porridge, down the mountain. The sulphur fumes were so strong; the fire was burning our feet, so that after two minutes we had to go back. All around we saw fissures of fire. There was a whooshing sound coming from the crater, like when all at once a flock of birds starts up from a forest.—The cone was unclimbable on account of the glowing rocks that were constantly raining down.—The descent was great fun. We tore off, had to break with our heels, fell from time to time in the soft ash. That fall through the air lasted ten minutes. In the meantime the wind had died down completely. We could see the bay in the moonlight. The donkeys were stumbling badly on the descent, and Berg fell off. The donkey stepped on him; it looked awful. When my donkey stumbled, I nearly ruptured myself on the pommel of my saddle. The lava looked like colossal, fallen stars.—We rode again over the black lavafield. I hung back from the others in order to watch that matchless play of nature.—At 10 o'clock we arrived in Resina. All the houses were closed; there was no wagon to be had; it was terribly cold; but the moonlight, like daylight. It's not that bright in cloudy weather in Denmark at noon! So we had to walk to Naples in the nighttime. The others pulled ahead of us, since Hertz had a bad leg from his fall. I stayed of course with him, and he was grateful; said he thought we were walking in the abandoned city in *Thousand and One Nights*. The houses that are painted white are spectacular in the moonlight; the smaller ones with flat roofs looked like fire-gutted buildings in Scandinavia. We talked about poetry and about food, because we were hungry, very hungry. Hertz asked me to tell what food I would like to have to eat that evening and sang with me the praises of soup and roast beef, but feared that the trattoria Villa di Milano was closed. We would then drink toddy, and should all else fail our servant would get hold of some bread and wine for us.—Reaching Naples, we were challenged by the sentry; I answered: *"Amici! Une promenade de Vesuvio, returnate a Napoli!"*—Then he was satisfied.—Great lines of waves broke in the moonlight like shining silver or, more precisely, like blue fire. Vesuvius erupted columns of fire. We could see the lava reflected in the calm sea like a broad, dark-red column of fire. Finally we found an open trattoria, ate, drank and went home to sleep.

Tuesday, February 25. Wrote letters to the Collins and Jette Wulff, which have now been sent off. I'm black and blue on my backside from the ride yesterday. Now I have to pay for it. I'm terribly tired.— All my limbs feel as if they've been broken on the rack; I'm sleepy and not up to much. Even so, I was up two or three hours earlier than the others. They are suffering like me. Paid a visit to Åberg and Carlstedt in the Hôtel de Resio. Went for a walk, ate and took a nap after dinner, but am very worn out, though. Took my usual walk in the evening to the barracks and the wharf to have a look at Vesuvius. Saw them giving a street show. Am now back at home, have bought pastries for one *carlin* and a bottle of Lacrimae Christi for about six Danish shillings, indulging myself, and soon will go to bed.—Hertz says I resemble a big giraffe, but begs me not to take offense! He says, as well, that it is a nice animal. I do really think he has a good nature!

Wednesday, February 26. Had hideous dreams about Ørsted last night. I'm still sore all over from the trip to Vesuvius. Went for a walk over the big bridge up to the summer palace, but since I didn't have authorization I couldn't get in. Visited my young painter from Hamburg and saw his seascapes from around Naples. Walked after dinner down to the bridge; there was a man sitting there in a shabby coat, reading aloud from *Orlando Furioso*; sailors and tramps were sitting and lying all around listening. A short way off an improvisator was standing on crutches; it looked as if some tramps were furnishing subjects and rhymes, and he sang and was applauded. When I was walking down one of the little side streets to Toledo Street, I saw some very tiny children who had decorated themselves with orange peels and vegetable tops. In a nearby street some indigent porters were playing with oranges that they rolled down the street in the gutter to see which one would go the farthest. On the way there I saw down by the lighthouse a signboard painted over with an entire story and with Jesus in the middle with the fires of purgatory beneath him. A man played his guitar and sang; the woman, in some sort of gypsy costume, pointed out the different scenes; and afterwards people gave them a *gran* and received in return an amulet, a copper piece and a little picture with the Madonna and Jesus on it. I paid, too, and he kissed the picture when he gave it to me. Spent the whole afternoon strolling along Toledo Street, looking at the motley crowds and being pursued by pimps. The boy with the white hat, who keeps trying to seduce me, couldn't praise his *donna* enough: "O, multa bella!" he said. She was only thirteen years old and had just this month given herself over to carnal pleasure. Finally I got tired of him and turned onto a side street; suddenly he darted ahead of me because it happened to be precisely the street where she lived. He showed me the house, begged me to just take a look at her and said I wouldn't be able to resist. "Exactly!" I thought and said: "No! No! No!" as I walked to the next street.— "Strada Nardona, numero trenta due!" he shouted, and I escaped.— Then went and had me a good supper with a glass of Malaga. Thought about Louise and the others at home. If they had seen me this evening, they would certainly be worried about me. Naples is more perilous than Paris, because you freeze there, but here your blood boils. God, lead me to what is best and most sensible. I don't regard this gratification as a sin, but I find it disgusting and dangerous to do it with such creatures, and an unforgivable sin, with an innocent.—I am at the point of saying with Hertz: happy the man who is married and doesn't commit lechery.

The indefatigable Andersen hardly had time to recuperate from the strenuous climb of Mount Vesuvius before he set off on a five-day excursion to see Pompeii and the Greek temples in Paestum. He continued by boat to Amalfi and visited the recently discovered Blue Grotto on Capri. It was with reluctance that he finally left Naples on March 20 in order to celebrate Easter in Rome.

On the first of April, Andersen began his journey home, which was to take more than four months. His first stop was in Florence, where he spent one week before traveling on to Venice, a city he did not really care for. On his first day there, he remarked in his diary (April 19): "Venice is a dead swan floating on the water." As was typical for this otherwise seasoned traveler, he was plagued by fears that his money would run out and that his passport might not contain the proper visas. But his journey proceeded without complications, and on April 30 he arrived safely in Munich, where he spent the entire month of May. Although he felt quite at ease in this city, he could not help but compare it to Rome and find it lacking. Indeed, he spent much of his spare time reading all the books he could find about Italy. Soon, however, he managed to make a number of acquaintances, among whom were Henry Feddersen, a fellow Danish traveler; Christian Andreas

Piazza del Trinità with Michelangelo's house, Florence (dated April 11, 1834)

Birch, the son of a Danish emigre and business secretary of Munich's Court Theater; the German author Johann Firmenich; and the philosopher Friedrich Wilhelm Schelling.

Wednesday, May 14. Today a letter simply has to come! It's raining and quite cold. I slept miserably last night, and there was a dog forever barking. My neighbor even got up and shushed at it.—Suffered terribly from a toothache. No letter. Feverish. Spent the whole afternoon and evening lying on the sofa.—Oh, I wish I were dead!

Life holds no joy for me. Her, the joys of youth, Italy! Everything is gone!—Oh, I'm sick, sick in mind and body! If only I could sleep, sleep really deeply, so that I might never awaken in this world.

Thursday, May 15. Bad toothache. Took a walk in the English Garden and read Immermann's *Merlin*, a strange production without substance. I don't understand what his purpose really was.—Feverish, listless and unhappy. While I was sitting on the sofa this evening, a Dane who had just arrived came up to me—Køppen. This was his second trip to Italy, and he wanted to travel to Greece, too. He had seen my name in the paper and looked me up. I talked myself back to health about Italy and didn't go to bed until almost 12 o'clock.

Friday, May 16. Took a walk in the English Garden. In the café I read a poem by Saphir about the waterfall, but it wasn't finished. I was amused because several days ago I found him ruminating by the waterfall. When I was there today, he was writing. It was probably the continuation of the poem. Then I went to the Glyptothek, but felt so faint on the way that my legs were shaking. I had to sit down outside for a quarter of an hour to recuperate a little—then went in. In the first gallery were Egyptian artifacts. Saw the Aeginetan marbles, which had been part of the frontispiece of a temple. All of the faces are the same—the same smile on *Minerva* as on *The Dying Trojan*. They all had the same features. In the fourth gallery there's an *Apollo Citharoedus. Minerva* and a marvelous *Sleeping Faun;* the hand and arm have been restored by Thorvaldsen. From there, in to see the sleeping figure, the beautiful kneeling *Torso.* A mask of Medusa, the mouth of which is superb. A bad copy of the *Medicean Venus.* In the next gallery are three paintings by Cornelius: (a) *Olympus,* (b) *Neptune* and (c) *Pluto.*—But most outstanding is and remains his *Scenes from the Iliad:* Cassandra with her hair blowing; Hecuba sunk in agony. In the other piece Briseis has a precarious seat on her horse—she's not even touching it.—A beautiful marble figure tying its sandals. There aren't many bronzes.—I ran into Køppen here in conversation with a Dane—it was the young Hudtwalcker from Hamburg. We walked together to the Art Association, where they said I'd already been introduced—they had read of my name. In the arcade I met a young artist I have spoken with only once before, and he asked me if he might introduce me into the Literary Club; I'd be able to get an admission card there. I was registered twice in the Art Association and have free admission for four weeks. There are two works there by old Reinhart in Rome: (1) *Villa Pam-*

philj and from there (2) *A View of St. Peter's Basilica;* the beautiful *Sea Storm off Trieste* was by Sander (who introduced me the first time). The second time I was introduced by Haeselich. (A hideous name!)— Went to the Schweigerische Folk Theater with Hudtwalcker and saw *The Evil Spirit Lumpazivagabundus*, which was really far better than the performance of *Lenore*, but it was still bad. The play was over at 6:30. It had gotten cold because there had been a thunder storm. Then I went to the Literary Club, where I found almost all the German and French papers. In the *London Fortnightly Review* I found the following article from Denmark: "Mr. Herts, the distinguished author of the 'Gjenganger Poem,' in which he so admirably imitated the style of Baggesen and of Several succesful dramatic effusions, is at this moment making the tour of Europe, on a stipend from the King of Denmark. A similar travelling stipend has been granted to Mr. Andersen another youthful poet of great promise, already favourably known as the author of a 'Pedestrian journey to Amager,' an extravaganza in Hoffmanns manner, and several other works in vers and prose, evincing much originality of genius."—This was undeniably from a Danish correspondent, and yet it pleased me down to the ground. Last year there was also supposed to be a survey of Danish literature in *Journal for the Elegant World*, in which it was said that my appearance on the scene gave it a new direction, which is nonsense, but shows, though, that people are noticing me. Childishly pleased and grateful, I felt myself to be a better person.

Saturday, May 17. Was at the Literary Club and read almost all of the papers. Felt ill again. My nerves have been extremely affected; I have a fever.—Now I am finished with Immermann's *The Tragedy in Tyrol*, in which Andreas Hofer is the hero. It's a fine work. I'd like to translate it, but I'm afraid people won't appreciate it.—Got a letter from Colonel Høegh-Guldberg in Odense.—He doesn't like Italy. Went for a walk with Feddersen and Hudtwalcker out to the Chinese Pagoda in the English Garden, where they were playing music. There was a terrible thunder storm; we had to stand with an umbrella under the tall trees. The rain poured down; bolts of lightening lit up everything all around; it was spectacular.

Sunday, May 18. It was Whitsunday. Was in the cathedral and heard music and song. It's not impressive after St. Peter's Basilica. Visited Birch and went for a short walk with him.—Went to the Jesuit Church, where all the soldiers were and a huge crowd of people. Beautiful instrumental music. The church is quite large, but nevertheless only like a nook of St. Peter's.—Went to the Literary Club and the Art

Association, where there were a few new works. After dinner, a walk. What a magnificent sight the Alps made! Nothing but waving lines, shimmerings of snow and the cloudy sky of northern climes. Feddersen dropped in. A windstorm with swirling hail showers.

Monday, May 19. Birch dropped in with an invitation to an expedition this afternoon.—He is an extremely well-spoken, entertaining man. After dinner we set off for a friendly, little country village on the edge of the English Garden. He treated me to coffee, and we talked about a thousand things. I was in high spirits, and I believe I was quite entertaining. At 6 o'clock I was to go to see *Robert the Devil.* Since I had gotten nr. 1 close to the orchestra, he switched with me and let me have his free seat. Promised me a letter of recommendation for Vienna, with which I should be able to get free admission to the Imperial Theater. He accompanied me to my seat; the house was packed.—A few numbers were omitted. Demoiselle Hasselt didn't sing quite in tune. Here I saw Demoiselle Vio again, the widow of Spitzeder, whom I heard in Berlin. Pellegrini was excellent. The dancing, bad. The way in which all of the lights in the priory hall were turned on all at once was superb. The set extremely beautiful.

Tuesday, May 20. Was at Birch's to bring him his ticket. He asked me to keep it until this evening; invited me to dinner and tomorrow to supper; gave me in addition two letters of recommendation, one to Deinhardstein, who is a government councillor, and one to Castelli. How I otherwise suffered that night—an infected tooth that almost drove me crazy! Paced the floor, brushed and rinsed my teeth, no sleep. It was a whole *Miserere* that the pain was playing on my nerve-pipes. Was at a barber's to get a haircut. His wife told me right away about all of her children, showed me the smallest one in a cradle and asked if it wasn't beautiful.—So I gave her a twenty-*pfennig* piece for the haircut, and she followed me down the stairs with endless expressions of gratitude. Her nine-year-old son had given me a very nice haircut.—Had dinner with Dr. Birch at the Goldener Hirsch, where he treated me to a fabulous dinner—two kinds of wine and champagne. Afterwards we went for a walk out in the English Garden and had coffee. He was very entertaining; told me about his unfortunate father, his relationship to Mariette L. In the evening I went to the theater on his ticket and saw Victor Hugo's *Mary Tudor,* which really interested me, and I might like to translate it.

Wednesday, May 21. Took a walk in the English Garden and read

Harro Harring's poems. They seem to echo Heine, and yet are supposed to be his own life story, as it is mine.—Still no letter from Collin; it's surprising. Wrote therefore to Father.—In the evening with Feddersen at Birch's, where I read *Agnete*. They were very pleased with it. When I told Birch how badly it had been received at home, he said that it appealed to him; in several places it had brought tears to his eyes, not on account of the story, but because of the work's great Danishness. He could hear the sound of the waves, see the Danish countryside and the green beech forests. It was such a thoroughly national work that for this reason alone it must be given a prominent position. I arrived home late in the evening after a good meal and dozed. (A visit today from Dr. Levy.)

From Munich Andersen traveled via Salzburg and Linz to Vienna, arriving there June 9. The very next day, he called on the author Joseph Sonnleithner, at whose home he later met the poet and dramatist Franz Grillparzer. From there he went to see Rabbi Isac Mannheimer, a former resident of Copenhagen; and then, with Birch's letter of introduction in hand, he looked up the playwright and assistant manager of the Burg Theater, Johann Deinhardstein, who graciously provided him with a free pass, which he put to use almost nightly. After an enjoyable, month-long stay, he left Vienna for Prague, which was a disappointment to him, and Dresden, which seemed pleasantly familiar but less impressive than on his first visit in 1831.

As he neared Denmark, Andersen grew more and more unhappy at the thought of returning home to friends who were in the habit of criticizing and correcting him. Not even the warm welcome he received in Berlin and the notice taken of him in newspapers there were enough to lighten his spirits.

Wednesday, July 23. Now we are heading toward that German Sodoma, Berlin! A very cold wind. We passed barren land and cultivated land. We drove through Beelitz; the company was very boring and my neighbor, ignorant and stupid. Toward noon we arrived in Potsdam, where nature has put on a little more finery. I saw Sanssouci and the famous windmill, which just now was going full blast. The lake and the beautiful hillside were a fine sight. The town itself is awfully pretty and made a more pleasing impression on me than Berlin did later. We stopped at Der Einsiedler, where the service was miserable and the others had so much to drivel on about that we didn't leave until 2 o'clock. In the meantime I saw the palace courtyard, with . . . figures, the tower with Atlas on it; heard the

Beethoven's grave in the cemetery at Währing near Vienna (dated June 30, 1834)

bellringing. When we were on our way, we saw people working on the new bridge over the Havel; a small three-master was at anchor there.—In the distance, by the shore, we saw Spandau. Birch trees had been planted in front of the fir trees. The highway was excellent. Everything went really quite well, if only the officer's wife hadn't made such a fuss. I was rather cranky, awfully tired and bored. Finally we passed Zehlendorf, which I recognized. We encountered a lot of vehicles, gardens and country houses along the road. Free entry through the town gate. On account of the unloading I stayed with the others in one of the first hotels we ran across—Der goldene Adler. There is a beautiful view from the second floor out toward the big square.—Oh, how tired I am!

Thursday, July 24. Up at 6:30 and already out and about an hour later. Visited Häring, who said that Heine couldn't write poetry or prose. Talked about Oehlenschläger's anger against him and that he hadn't written to him, etc. I received from him a page for my album, then trudged all the way down the dull, long Friedrich Street to Chamisso's, but he was out of town in his botanical garden. Then I went to see our chargé d'affaires, Løvenørn, who thought I was from Holstein and lent me a copy of *The Day*. God, what nonsense! Pettiness!!! Went to see the ambassador, who was in the country, and later to see Feddersen, who lived next to a whorehouse which had as its sign a white cross out on the sidewalk. Zeuthen had his residence right across the street and, giving a shout, appeared in his familiar yellow dressing gown.—Then I went to the Bildergallerie— how much awful stuff there was! Most appealing to me were: (1) Titian's painting of his daughter Lavinia, (2) Karel van Mander's portrait of Christian IV.—*Io and Zeus*, by Correggio, is really superb.—I was in the Hall of Statues, but enjoyed most the beautiful view outside with the tall fountain. Here in Berlin the market is being held right now. I trudged around on the hard, sharp stones looking at the stalls. At noon at dinner I ran into Zeuthen, then Feddersen and the jurist Fiedler, Bartholin and Dr. Hahn. I trudged home with Fiedler and Feddersen, got my passport and reserved a seat in the mail coach to save two *taler*. Visited Chamisso, who kissed me quite fondly. We took a walk in his lovely garden, and he showed me his most recently published collection of poems, which contained five never before published. Béranger, Victor Hugo and I were the only three poets he had translated.—He really wanted me to go with him tomorrow to the Society of Authors, but I prefer to go to the theater; must also mail my belongings.—He talked about that new author's *Faust*, about Goethe's *Faust*, which didn't correspond to the fragment.—Went with Fiedler for a walk and in the evening was at a great tavern, where we drank ale, which tasted fine but was strong.— Met Bindesbøll there.

Friday, July 25. A terribly hot morning.—Went for a walk along the street where the prostitutes are. A visit from Bindesbøll. Went to see Baron Løvenørn, who was very flattering. The river Spree was beautiful, clear water. There is a market being held here in Berlin— it resembles the Odense market.—Then we went to Gropius's Diorama, saw the monastery at Amalfi, the mountain Jungfrau, the monastery in Zurich, in Assisi, a morning scene, but more magnificent was the monastery courtyard, where we heard the bells ringing; the door to the church opened; candles were burning on the altar, etc.—Then it turned; we heard the sound of surf and then saw the endless blue sea off Sorrento; the moon was shining on the foam.

Cape Mysenium, Procida and Ischia lay large as life before me. I was in paradise! It was masterful! Indeed, we saw it two times.—Zeuthen, extremely asinine at dinner. In the evening I was at Chamisso's. He expressed his regrets that I couldn't spend that evening at the Society of Authors. He called to my attention the work of a German poet. (The man lives in St. Petersburg and his name is Trinius). There were some lovely things there.—Heine was a true poet, he said, but he has only one string; you are more fortunate—you have several. He then presented me with his newest poems, which would otherwise have cost me a *ducat* and I did want them, since there are things by me in it.—Thunderstorms. Went with Bartholin, Feddersen, Valentin and Fiedler to the theater, where we saw *The Evil Spirit Lumpazivagabundus.* I enjoyed it a lot, but when I got home I had a vexing problem—the servant hadn't seen to getting my trunk to the post depot. Heaven only knows how it will go tomorrow!

The next day Andersen took the post coach to Hamburg, where he was overwhelmed with invitations. Although delighted by all the kindness shown him, he wrote the following to Henriette Wulff just before he left Hamburg on his way to catch the boat to Copenhagen: "The poet is dead, slain in Italy! If there is still life in him when he reaches Scandinavia, I'm sure they will finish him off—I know my people!"

Andersen's reception in Copenhagen was much friendlier than he had anticipated. The Collin family welcomed him very warmly; the king granted him an audience; and the Wulffs invited him to come and live with them at Amalienborg Castle. He stayed with them until the end of August, when he moved into two rented rooms by Nyhavn Canal, where he remained for more than four years.

During the autumn of 1834, Andersen worked hard on his Italian novel The Improvisatore. *Since his publisher, C. A. Reitzel, was reluctant to give him an advance, he had trouble making ends meet and had to support himself by other means. He applied unsuccessfully for a position at the Royal Library and wrote several occasional poems for the papers. He even completed the libretto for an opera,* Little Kirsten, *but this profited him not at all, for it was not staged until 1846, when J. P. E. Hartmann finally set it to music.*

The Improvisatore *was published April 9, 1835, with this dedication: "To Councillor Collin and his excellent wife, in whom I found parents; to their children, in whom I found brothers and sisters; to the Home of Homes I bring, with a filial and fraternal heart, this, the best that I possess." The*

THE GREAT EUROPEAN JOURNEY

novel became a great success both with the critics and the general reading public, and it was translated that same year into German, ensuring Andersen a European reputation.

Even before he was finished writing his novel, Andersen had started a new project, as he informed Henriette Hanck in a letter written New Year's Day, 1835: "Now I have begun to write some 'fairy tales for children.' I want to win the coming generations, you see." On March 16, he wrote to his friend Henriette Wulff about the same project: "I have also written some fairy tales for children, of which Ørsted says that if The Improvisatore *will make me famous, my fairy tales will make me immortal, for they are the most perfect of all that I have written; but I myself do not think so." As it turned out, Ørsted was right.*

The European Celebrity
1835–46

DURING THE CREATIVE, BUSY YEARS *of 1835 to 1839, when he managed to publish three novels, six collections of tales, and six singspiel, Andersen seems to have found scant time for his diary, keeping it mainly as a record of his occasional summer travels. It is particularly unfortunate that there are no entries at all for 1835, the year in which he made his debut as both novelist and writer of tales. The only diary records from this period consist of a few pages from the beginning of a trip to Odense in the summer of 1836 and a complete record of his month-long stay in Sweden in 1837, as well as a second, two-week stay in 1839.*

Andersen's personal life at this time had its ups and downs. His visit to Sweden in 1837 was, as he later reported in his autobiography, one of the most enjoyable he had ever made anywhere. On his way to Stockholm along the Göta Canal, he met the Swedish novelist Fredrika Bremer, with whom he remained in lifelong correspondence. Each seems to have made a singular impression on the other. Miss Bremer wrote in a letter to a poet-friend E. G. Geijer: "A Mr. Andersen is here, of strange appearance, but straightforward, sensitive and warm-hearted, good, with a childlike piety, and the author of fine books!" Andersen, for his part, later recorded in his diary that his whole trip seemed to have been made for the purpose of making Miss Bremer's acquaintance.

A lone entry for December 11 of the same year, recording his disappointment at the news of Sophie Ørsted's engagement, strikes a more dismal note: "Now I'll never be married! There are no young girls around for me any more! Day by day I'm getting to be more and more a bachelor! Oh, just yesterday I could be counted among the young—this evening I am old! God bless you, my dear, beloved Sophie, you will never know how happy I could have been with you, if only I had the money!" Sophie may have been forever lost to him, but the following year his finances were greatly improved when King Frederik VI granted him an annual stipend of 400 rix-dollars.

It was inevitable that Andersen's prolific output during these years would meet with a mixed reception. His second semiautobiographical novel, O.T., featuring a brooding Byronic hero with a dark past, was published in April 1836 and did not excite his readers the way **The Improvisatore** *had done* *just six months before. The following year his third novel,* Only a Fiddler, *about a struggling violinist, was given an enthusiastic reception by his German audience, whereas Danish readers greeted it with a measure of indifference. Insult was added to injury when in 1838 Søren Kierkegaard ridiculed it in* From the Papers of a Person Still Alive, Published against His Will *(with the subtitle "On Andersen as a Novelist, with Constant Reference to His Most Recent Work,* Only a Fiddler"*), calling the main character no genius, but a sniveler who "suffers a little adversity, as a result of which he succumbs."*

Andersen's tales grew more and more popular, and in 1839 he essayed a collection of prose sketches entitled Picture Book without Pictures. *In the same year he met with his first and last success on the stage—*The Mulatto, *another self-projection in its rendition of the theme of the outcast. If Andersen had hoped this success would win him future favor with the theater censor Johan Ludvig Heiberg and his wife, Johanne Louise Heiberg, the leading actress of her day, he was to be disappointed. The following year, when he submitted his next play,* The Moorish Maid, *Heiberg played cat and mouse with him; and his wife, for whom the leading role had been written, refused to play the part. Depressed, he decided not to see this problem-ridden production through to its opening, but left the country on an extended journey to his beloved Italy and perhaps even the Orient.*

Saturday, October 31 [1840]. I left Copenhagen at 2 o'clock. It was a difficult departure. Yesterday evening my friends held a going-away party for me at Ferrini's, which was attended by Oehlenschläger, Privy Councillor H. C. Ørsted, Collin, Titular Councillor Lund and many of my younger friends. Oehlenschläger and Hillerup composed the songs. I didn't get much sleep during the night. Today I said goodbye to the Collins. They accompanied me out to the ship, *Christian the Eighth.* There was a strong wind with heavy seas driving in off the Baltic. Edvard Collin was the last one out there. I said goodbye; he pressed a kiss onto my mouth! Oh, it was as if my heart would burst! I could still see Ingeborg and Louise in the boat. Seasickness set in already off Amager. I was sharing a cabin with Späth, who was on his way home to his father, Lord-in-Waiting Späth, in Kiel. My seasickness got worse, and there were heavy seas—time was heavy, too. I was really suffering. Once we caught a wave that hit so hard that we all thought we had run aground.

Sunday, November 1. The first calm water we had was off Fehmarn, but it was almost 11 o'clock—near the Kiel Fjord—before I went up on deck. The Spanish dancers were on board; I told Dolorés that

Thorvaldsen had been inspired by their dancing when he did his bas-relief *Satyr and Nymph*. We landed a little before 1 o'clock. I took a room together with the young Lieutenant Trepka at the Stadt Kopenhagen; went with him up to see the duke's gentleman-in-waiting and then up to the palace to see the duke. I was too tired to call on Lord-in-Waiting Späth. Stayed at home and wrote letters to Father Collin, Edvard and Hartmann, along with a note on a calling card to Jette Wulff. Bünke, a fellow from Holstein who knew the Falbes, was at the *table d'hôte*. When I was in bed and Trepka was undressed, he received an invitation to a ball from the duke. Even though I would have been desperate if it had been for me, I was chagrined not to have been sent for, since I had paid a call. Slept quite well.

Monday, November 2. A little past 6 o'clock on a rather lovely morning, Trepka and I drove in a rented carriage to Neumünster. There we ate breakfast together with a Danish officer-engineer and the workers that are stationed here to work on the new railroad.—We still had highway for about a mile more, and then it turned into a series of moorland roads through desolate, unpopulated districts. It reminded me of the heath in Bulwer-Lytton's *Ernest Maltravers*. The houses without chimneys, where smoke billowed out of big, open doorways. Roads through towns led hundreds of years back in time. Everything was mire and muck. At 5 o'clock we arrived at the Breitenburg Castle, where we met a gentleman who knew Trepka. He said the count had sent his carriage to Kellinghusen after me and that the postmaster in Bramstedt had gotten orders to assist me from there to Kellinghusen in one of his best coaches. I was dismayed. In the manor courtyard His Excellency gave me a warm welcome. After washing up, I was called to dinner. There were several of us at the table; Mr. Timmermann, ... I've been given a handsome sitting room and a pleasant bedroom. While everyone was drinking coffee I read *A Comedy Out in the Open Air* and some tales; then went to my room. The count accompanied me.

Tuesday, November 3. Up at 8 o'clock. Pottered about with my clothes. After having tea and coffee in my room, I took a walk in the lovely manor park, which is transversed by a canal; from here, a view of Itzehoe. The manor chapel looks lovely out in the midst of the high trees. His Excellency took me into the chapel and upstairs to a sort of banquet hall, where portraits of all his forefathers are hanging. From the tower there is a sweeping view to the other side of Kellinghusen. (Yesterday we passed a forest; with its brown foliage it looked exactly like a copper forest. There was something so utterly magical about it that the big steers we encountered on the muddy road appeared to me to be enchanted people, for the one, of course, had to correspond to the other.) The postmaster, Lord-in-Waiting Krogh, came to dinner today with his three lovely daughters. The next oldest sat on my right at dinner; she tried to call attention to herself. The poet Lobedanz was at dinner. I read *The Moorish Maid* and told several of my tales. Went down early and worked on Louise's wedding song.

Wednesday, November 4. All the early morning long I can hear the count's eldest, mentally deranged brother pounding on a door. He is always doing it. One day, after he is dead and gone, people here will think they can hear pounding like this every night, and then they will tell the story of his life. Finished my letters to Jette Hanck and Christian Voigt. Drove with His Excellency and Mr. Timmermann to Itzehoe to visit His Excellency's brother, who lives there. Called on the Kroghs. A large gentlemen's dinner party; a Mr. Abel, who in all likelihood once had a fine tenor voice, sang. Hennings, whom I know from Nysø, was there, along with Trepka and Count Ahlefeldt; the count accompanied me to the table through the gallery of works he owned by Thorvaldsen. A toast was drunk to me. I read some tales to them. The poet Lobedanz wrote in my album. (He is married to a former maid here at the manor.) A small room here is painted with Indian themes—palms and flowers; on the divan have been placed fragrant shrubs and porcelain figures—Venus, Mercury—and birds in cages can be seen in the midst of the greenery.—After the others had left, we stayed on and chatted until 10:30. (In the meantime, there was a large fire in the vicinity!) The manor here was once captured by Wallenstein from its Scottish defenders. Wallenstein had all the men killed, and when the women refused to clean up the blood, as he had ordered, they were also killed. Willenscharen is a town nearby where Ansgar is supposed to have lived.— The count followed me to my room and wished me a fond farewell!—I packed my things.

Thursday, November 5. Up at 6 o'clock. Drove with four horses and a servant to Itzehoe. Timmermann went with me to Heiligenstedten (where Count Blome lives). The oldest church in the country is located here (half-sunken into the ground or, rather, the ground has grown up over it). It is from the time of Charlemagne.—When we were supposed to depart, the steamship made too sharp a maneuver, and we formed a bridge over the Stör. We were delayed over a half hour. Hennings accompanied me on board. The trip through the marshland is monotonous. The Stör does a lot of winding here, and the gables of the houses are painted grass-green. When we entered the Elbe on the steamship *The Stör*—made in Glasgow of cast iron and making its first trips this year—we kept for the most part to the Hanoverian coast, where we picked up passengers. We passed an English steamship and then a large vessel with people emigrating to America. We took a lady on board, whom we later let off further up the Elbe onto a ship that had come from America. A man who was the first mate came with a boat to meet her. She got a big smack (kiss). For a long time we had a boat behind us on a tow rope. Two men from Holstein on board (one, a Mr. Dal) recognized me and attached themselves to me. Then a merchant from Hamburg, who was delighted to see the author of *Only a Fiddler*. There was a painter along with us who said he knew me from Munich and asked me to pay a visit to the painter Kaulbach. The Blankenese district looked splendid. As I was going ashore at Altona, a stranger was introduced to me; he said he was happy to meet Denmark's greatest writer. I said I had to run, because they were leaving with my suitcase; and I darted off and got into a hansom but had to pay three solid marks, just as much as for the entire trip by steamship. I checked into the hotel Zum König von Schweden, but it wasn't the one I thought it was. That was at 4 o'clock. After having eaten, I went, half asleep, to call on Töpfer. He was out. Then I went to see the Holcks, who graciously received me. The youngest of the sons accompanied me home and got a copy of *The Moorish Maid*, and now I am sitting here, writing this and a letter to Gottlieb Collin. The weather has been exceptionally lovely today, just somewhat cold. I am very tired. The nodule on my gum is plaguing me and making me anxious; there is a little pus coming out of it. If only I don't get an infection! Today is Great Prayerday[1] here in Hamburg.

Friday, November 6. Paid a visit to Töpfer, who said that Gutzkow was distant and cold. I looked Gutzkow up; he was warm and friendly and said I had a distinguished name in Germany. There was an actor with him; they both expressed a wish to stage *The Moorish Maid* here. I brought a copy to him later. I drove on an omnibus to Altona and brought Marie Schumacher her handkerchief. It was a cold, boring visit. Dinner with our Danish ambassador at Count Holck's, where we were served oysters and champagne. They presented me with a

1. Great Prayerday is a Danish holiday, Store Bededag, that falls on the fourth Friday after Easter.

ticket to Liszt's concert, and I went with the ladies in through a backdoor in the Stadt London into a magnificent hall which had been full of people for an hour. There lay a Jewish girl, fat and bedizened, on a sofa—she looked like a walrus with a fan. The ladies were particularly enthusiastic. The merchants from Hamburg seemed to be hearing in the music the klink of gold pieces, and that's why they were sitting with a smile hovering about their lips. I was seeing Liszt face to face! How great men resemble mountains! They look best at a distance—then there is still an atmosphere about them. He looked as if he had been in the Orthopedic Institute to be straightened out. There was something so spiderlike, so demonic about him! And as he sat there at the piano, pale and with his face full of violent passion, he seemed to me like a devil trying to play his soul free! Every tone flowed from his heart and soul—he looked to me to be on the rack. He was [Hoffmann's] Klein Zaches—while he was playing, his face came alive; it was as if his divine soul was emerging from the demonic. The music sounded like tinkling drops of water. The ladies' eyes sparkled. At the end of the concert wreaths were tossed up on stage to him. (The bathing attendant at the hotel had brought most of them and asked people to throw them. If this had been for Miss Grahn, what a clamor there would have been in Copenhagen because it had all been prearranged—for we Copenhageners are good at seeing things in the worst light!)—In the hall I met Stammann, whom I know from Rome. He introduced me to his wife and asked me to visit him at his home. However, I followed the Holcks home for tea and mailed a letter to Gottlieb Collin with the wedding song.

Saturday, November 7. Said goodby to Töpfer and the Holcks after I had first been to the Hanoverian Post Office on the other side of town. I crossed the Elbe on the steamship and there met Leibrock, a bookseller from Braunschweig, who was on his way from St. Petersburg. Having read my name on my luggage, he asked whether I was the famous Danish author. In Harburg we ate together with a lady who said she was an actress and had played with Pallesen: "I play heroines' roles, and they are so demanding; I've just been in Lübeck, acting." She was traveling alone to Bremen, seemed poor and was probably at least thirty years old. She'll be playing the Maid of Orleans. In the express coach I happened upon a baron from Hanover who had done some traveling in Sicily. He knew Captain Brinckmann, and I asked him to convey my greetings. I slept badly, in snatches. The Lüneburg Heath wasn't to be recognized since the last time I was here. We traveled to Celle on a good highway; there

I transferred into a not-so-good coach and had to ride backwards. The baggage carts were more like canvas-covered camels.

Sunday, November 8. In Braunschweig at 8:30 in the morning. Vieweg and his wife were away. Their son-in-law, Westermann, and someone from the office came; they greatly regretted that no one was at home, and no one was sure when they would return from their trip to the resort. They took me to see the castle; it has been very beautifully constructed, but not quite finished. When I was here last, it was all just a pile of rubble. The old lion was standing outside the church. I was inside the church. Had a big meal at the *table d'hôte.* Already a little anxious about money. Sore penis and worried about it. The journey over Göttingen and Eisenach is somewhat uncertain because of the mail coach connections; therefore, I'll be traveling over Magdeburg and Leipzig tomorrow, God willing. In the evening, taken by Westermann to see his brother-in-law Rönckendorff, whose wife, Bertha Rönckendorff, is Vieweg's sister; the other sister, Blanka Westermann, was there; both of them, spirited young ladies. We drank tea and chatted. Bertha bears a great resemblance to Camilla Wedel from Funen. She got "The Danish Peasant Made a Petition"; Blanka, Lorck's "Gallopades for Pianoforte."

Monday, November 9. Met Rönckendorff and went into Vieweg's book store. Vieweg got back last night.—When I was at the mail depot waiting to leave, he came up to me. He was a very charming man. He introduced me to a Mr. de Marées (whose wife writes poetry), to her and their daughter, along with a lady who was on her way to Magdeburg. They were quite delighted to be traveling with a literary figure. Vieweg regretted that Jenssen was no poet at all, and you could see that especially in [his translation of] *Picture Book without Pictures!* (I took my lunch in an old wine cellar.)—In the coach was a nice, young lawyer, Dr. jur. Robert Degener from Blankenburg in the Harz. He was musically interested and knew Hartmann's name, so there in Halberstadt, where our luggage was inspected and where he left us, I presented him with "The Danish Peasant Made a Petition." He paid me a few compliments and knew me well as an author. Right across from me was sitting a famous painter—Jordan. The conversation went briskly; the coach, slowly! We passed through Halberstadt in the early morning hours.

Tuesday, November 10. Arrived in Magdeburg, an impressive city with fortifications. I had coffee in Stadt Petersburg (?) and went at 7 o'clock, with a touch of railroad fever, to the railroad to ride on a train for the first time in my life! I felt as if I were surrendering myself to my God. I was together with a man who had arrived the evening before with the Elbe steamer. (Yesterday, as we were leaving Braunschweig, I saw a steam engine for the first time, though only the smoke. It was coming from Wolfenbüttel and was on its way to Braunschweig. It looked like a rocket whizzing in a straight line along the ground.) Today I was trying it myself.—I had the feeling that the earth was rotating—close to me the grass and the fields were moving like a whirling spinning wheel; only the things farthest off seemed to preserve their customary composure. Now I can imagine the flight of migratory birds; this is how they must leave the towns behind them. It was as if one town lay close to the next. There is something quite magical about it. I felt like a magician who has hitched a dragon to his coach and now sweeps past mere mortals, who, as I looked at a side road, were creeping along in their vehicles as if they were snails. When the steam is let out, it sounds as if it were a demon groaning.—The signal whistle is abominable—it's like listening to a stuck pig.—I was alone with a man in one compartment that accommodates eight people. The thought occurred to me that he might be crazy and have a fit. I got all worked up about it. At Köthen we picked up four passengers; one of them was very talkative and had a voice like a woman with a frog in her throat. From 7 o'clock to a little over 10:30 we covered the whole way from Magdeburg via Halle to Leipzig—sixty miles and something. I took a room in the Stadt Rom—where I'm now writing this—up high with a view out over the railroad station. I've been watching the trains whisking off to Dresden and to Magdeburg.—At 12 o'clock a powerful thunderstorm struck right over the building. I went to the post office immediately and had myself put on the passenger list for Hof tomorrow afternoon. Called on Brockhaus; he is in Paris. His wife gave me a warm welcome, walked me to the door of my hotel and invited me to dinner tomorrow. In the entryway I got something in my one eye that hurt. I drank a shot of rum; it went right to my head. Wrote to Holst; began a letter to Edvard.

Before leaving Leipzig the following day, Andersen paid a visit to Felix Mendelssohn-Bartholdy and heard a rehearsal of one of Beethoven's symphonies. Late that afternoon he left for Munich via Augsburg, where he was introduced to the daguerreotype, one of the great inventions of the day. He then spent two weeks in Munich, where he was feted as the famous author of The Improvisatore *and* Only a Fiddler. *While there, he renewed his acquaintance with the philosopher Friedrich Wilhelm Schelling and met for the first time Wilhelm von Kaulbach, whose later, well-known painting* The Angel *was inspired by Andersen's tale of the same name, published in 1843. He felt, however, neglected by his countrymen in Munich, and after a quarrel with the poet H. P. Holst, with whom he had planned to travel to Rome, he set out on his own. His return to Rome on December 19 was a deep disappointment. The weather was unusually cold, and he was suffering from influenza and one of his painful toothaches. Of the people he had known from his earlier stay, only the painter Albert Küchler remained, and Andersen was lonely. He waited impatiently for Holst's belated arrival and letters from Denmark, and on January 8 he received a letter from Jonas Collin informing him that the premier of* The Moorish Maid *had been a fiasco. In his diary the next day Andersen reported he'd slept badly during the night, dreaming "his head was made of stone, and someone was whacking at it with an axe, but it wouldn't break." In the following days he sought distraction in the art treasures of Rome, but found it in recurring toothaches and persistent fever.*

Saturday, January 16 [1841]. Beautiful weather. Entered S. Marcello's, where colorful silken hangings have been suspended between the pillars. Went for a walk on Monte Pincio. Went into the church of S. Maria Maggiore and then into the convent of S. Susanna and the round church of S. Bernardo. They are both on Via Pia near the fountain with Moses. Wandered back to S. Marcello's, where the feast was over. The mail didn't come today, so I'll have to wait until tomorrow to see whether there is a letter from Holst. Went to the Fiano and saw a new play, *Claudina*, which was much too boring to be entertaining. I sat in the dress circle for one *paolo*. The chorus and dance were the most entertaining. Løffler is sick; Margherita is pouting; God knows what I have done to her. How lonely I am! At home by 5:30 every evening. I am tired of reading and constantly looking at the clock to see if it isn't past 9 o'clock, so that I can go to bed and sleep my way to a new day!—I'm not afraid of being assaulted any more. Every now and then I even think it might be a good thing if I were killed. I understand it well enough. I have nothing to live for any more. Even art is a bit of a problem for me. My need to be noticed is so great that the idea of sudden death intrigues me. Oh, I recognize my weakness! I can see my faults!—Oh God, give me a great idea soon or great joy or death! In eternal Rome, where so much blood has flowed, where so much death and agony and misfortune have afflicted so many, what is my sorrow here?—I recently saw in the Colosseum a gnat struggling in a spider web; that's how

I am struggling here, entrapped in the memories that my life's Parcae have spun for me.—How the stars are sparkling this evening! I have seen them just as bright in the North, but here they seem to be higher; and the more I look, the more the sky is filled with them out to infinity.

Sunday, January 17. Today the donkeys are to be blessed at S. Antonio's. Went out there, but the blessing hadn't begun yet; the church, on the other hand, had been decorated and strewn with greenery. Walked in the warm sunshine from there to the Holy Steps and the Lateran Church, where there was a procession through the Colosseum, across the Forum to the Marcello Theater, which is the Palace of the Orsinis. Went into the church of Maria sopra Minerva, where the city councilmen were walking in a procession. Just as they stepped outside, there was a fanfare blown for them on the stairs. Went into the church of S. Maria Magdalena; it was beautifully painted. The mail still hasn't come. Went to S. Antonio's. The pictures there are wretched, unimaginative. On one a devil is knocking on St. Anthony's door; on another there are two people who come and seem to be making fun of his halo. There was wretched organ music and bad singing. It was very crowded; the sun was shining in through the open door onto the altar candles and the great numbers of kneeling people, as others pushed their way between them. The air smelled like at a Danish market.—A monk was standing in the doorway to the cloister sprinkling holy water on the horses and donkeys. A man standing at his side was selling on behalf of the monastery pictures of the saint along with a little cross. I bought one of them for a half *paolo.* An old woman was leading a tiny, little donkey with a ribbon on its tail and a tinsel pig fastened to each shoulder; she took it right up to the door and curtseyed low and made the sign of the cross as she and the donkey received the holy water. Some boys teased the little donkey as she was leaving, so the soldiers had to help her. Visitors were standing up in their carriages; in one was the prince of Mecklenburg, the brother-in-law of our crown prince. The Bruns were there in a carriage. Went with Rothe into S. Eusebio's, where there is a fresco on the ceiling of the ascension of the saint, by Mengs. After their animals had been blessed, the farmers were drinking lustily in the osteria. Most of them are picturesque—alone the pointed hats and the fact that they ride sitting right over the back legs of the donkey make them distinctive. We went into the church of Maria Maggiore; the side chapels are the most lavish in Rome. The walls are made of the most costly kinds of marble—agate and black and green marble. Read *Rienzi, the Last of the Roman Tribunes.*

Monday, January 18. Went to St. Peter's, where they were celebrating the feast of St. Peter on the occasion of Christ's words; "I tell you, you are Peter, on this rock I will build my church." I felt so ill that I nearly turned back, but continued on out there anyway; took off my outer clothes and went into the church. The noble guard was there at attention, and the pope, shaded by peacock feathers, was carried to the outermost altar. The music was lovely and everything was quite festive. I had to bow deeply several times as I was standing there in the midst of all the kneeling people.—The way home was just as tiring. At the Caffè Greco there was a letter from Edvard. There were no expressions of displeasure, but no great applause, either. However, the letter did me good and put me in a good mood. Visited Meyer and went for a walk along the Corso, and at home wrote a letter to Jette and Edvard. Received a visit from Løffler, who is now feeling better, and read a little in *Faust.* That's how I spent the evening until 10 o'clock.

Tuesday, January 19. The weather not so good! Løffler is in bed with smallpox. When he got home from my place yesterday evening and looked at his body, the pocks had broken out. My big toe is swollen and painful. Today there is another letter for Holst. If nothing has come from him by Thursday, then I won't expect him. Went this morning to the church of S. Maria in Traspontina. It's St. Knud's Day! On his altar there were only four small candles burning and the lamp in front. I asked the monk why they didn't hold a bigger celebration for the Danish martyr, and he said: "Our monastery is poor; we can't do anything!" Headed toward home through a wilderness of streets and arrived thus in Chiesa Nuova, but it had been too long a walk for me, and I felt tired and worn out. But I had to go on, and so it passed.—Now it's rainy and gray; then, sunny and then, gray again. I am hobbling on my foot; my big toe is one big blister.—This evening I've finished the letter to Jette Collin and one to Hartmann. Took a walk on the Monte Pincio, where I saw blood this morning from a fistfight. Everything was fresh and green. The trees had buds on them.

Wednesday, January 20. My foot is better, but my sore throat is still with me. Went for a walk to the church of S. Andrea della Valle and took a look at the frescoes in the dome; went into the church of S. Carlo ai Catinari, with its lovely frescoes. Walked across Piazza Na-

Rome

vona, where the Wednesday market was in full swing, with clothes, pottery and odds and ends, etc. In the later afternoon went for a stroll on Monte Pincio. Called on Rørbye. In Caffè Greco happened upon Koop; I beat a hasty retreat so that he wouldn't try to borrow any money. Ate figs for my digestion. See what a meager day it's been! I'd like to record here what the lobby of the inn in La Storta looked like according to my notes: "La Storta is a real stable—the walls are hideously painted with landscapes like the ones you see in a magic lantern. Wooden tables and benches; the only light, that coming through the door; a large, square brazier; bunches of bracken hung up on account of the flies (so that they won't ruin the frescoes). Chickens and bottles. The view out toward the road—a gravel pit, a dung heap, turkeys, pack and coach wagons." Today at Lepre's I caught sight again of one of the travelers I ate with in La Storta—he's from Faenza and knows Marietta. This afternoon I was at the exhibition, which is being held in a lovely locale near the Porta del Popolo. Two works appealed to me: one by the Spaniard Espalter depicting Moses, whose dead body was being carried aloft by angels, and *Minerva among the Graces*, by Consoni from Rieti, whose style was probably somewhat French, somewhat modern—in a not-so-good sense of the word—but whose human figures nevertheless had a certain feminine quality that was appealing.

Thursday, January 21. Rain shower. (Throat better.) Accompanied Rothe over to the Piazza Navona to the church of S. Agnese. (Today they are blessing the sheep over in the church of S. Agnese fuori le Mura.) We climbed down into the subterranean church, in reality three small chapels. Here there was supposed to have been a bordello, where Agnes was led to be raped by the soldiers and in that way killed. She was naked, but her long hair, according to the legend, hung down over her, and she saw an angel of the Lord who was hovering over her, so that the soldiers didn't dare to touch her. Then she was led outside and burned. Down there over the main altar was a marble bas-relief of her with her long hair, standing naked, and two soldiers following her. On a fresco by the stairs you could see her with the angel. From there we went into the church of S. Carlo ai Catinari, where the four cardinal virtues have been painted in the dome by Domenichino: (1) truth, (2) virtue, (3) fortitude and (4) temperance. We went into a similar church and studied the ceremonies carried out by the priest. Then walked in continual rain to Palazzo Mattei, where there are a great many sarcophagi and magnificent busts set in the wall; on the breast of one of them there was a remarkable head of Medusa. Then went into the church of . . ., in which dome inscriptions from the Song of Songs were written. Delivered to the post office letters to Edvard Collin (and Jette) and to Hartmann. At the Caffè Greco I found a letter from Jette Hanck, a lovely, fond one. It informed me that *The Moorish Maid* had, according to *The Copenhagen Post*, been *"very well received."* Even though it couldn't be true, it put me in a good mood. Thöming stupid or shameless (his anecdote about Victor Hugo and me). Called on Mrs. Rørbye this afternoon. Spent a lot of time with Adam Müller. This evening at Grevenkop-Castenskiold's for tea.

Friday, January 22. Headache and dizziness. It is raw outside today with winds off the mountains. I went to the post office again today to see about a letter from Holst; but, as usual, nothing. I was feeling very sick, so that it was distressing for me to be walking. Was in the little church at Trivio, where there was a celebration. Today seems to be my most meager day.—If only it were the last one in my life! What do I have? What awaits me?—Oh, I feel it in all its bitterness— these friends of mine at home who send me these drops of poison because they live only in fear of my failings. They see my enemies pointing out my failings and are totally preoccupied with those!—I have faith in nothing but God, but I'm not pinning my hopes on Him! Oh, woe is me! My mind is like a fallen angel sinking into eternal nothingness! What does it have to cling to!—Wrote to Jette Hanck.

As it turned out, Andersen's tribulations were not over. On February 15 he received a letter from Mrs. Læssøe reporting that Heiberg had just published a satire ridiculing him. In reality, it was just a matter of a few lines in the comedy A Soul after Death, *but Andersen did not have an opportunity to read the work until his return to Denmark. The next day he took his revenge: "This morning I composed a satirical rhymed-letter to Heiberg that Holst [who had finally arrived on February 7] naturally found too mean. But it has put me into a good mood, and I've felt livelier and more content all day. The letter won't be sent home." The Roman carnival helped lift his spirits, but it was his two-week stay in Naples that banished his depression altogether. No doubt the news that reached him on his first day there—that the Danish king had granted him a travel stipendium of 600 rix-dollars to enable him to continue his travels—had something to do with his improved spirits. On March 15 he sailed from Naples on a French steamer bound for Greece.*

Saturday, March 20. The coast of Greece. At 5:15 the sun came up red and oblong.—I caught sight of the snow-covered mountain in Morea already yesterday afternoon. Antonio Laccetti, the Neapolitan from Vasto, is the one who resembles Lorenzen in Sorø so much. A precipitous wall of a cliff down to the sea; behind it the high, snow-covered mountain.

> From the blue, the shining seas,
> You hail me, oh land of Greece.
> Flames of sun on that snowy peak:
> It's Morea, Morea, my eyes seek;

Dolphins and fishes leaping on high
From the deep to the sky.

The young American's name is Anson G. Phelps, Jr., from New York. Cythera (Cerigo) looked desolate; there we passed two ships, the one closer to the island, French. On the point of Cape Ange there was a hermit's hut; it was impossible to make out any path from it up the mountain; there's a Greek hermit living there. Then the sea began to heave. During the evening I was very seasick.

Sunday, March 21. A miserable night. The ship was lying still, so I slept a little; got up and we could see Paros, Naxos, Delos, Tinos. The sun came up over Messenia; two ships sailed by. At that point we were off Ermoupolis on Siros. The tiny, white houses had the appearance of a whole city of tents, a camp. Otherwise, it looked like a miniature Naples. The bishop's residence overlooking every-thing else, a sort of St. Elmo. The captain advised me to go aboard the steamer *Lycurgus* from Alexandria, which was lying here under quarantine—it was supposed to be under quarantine for only two days in Piraeus. I went ashore and made my arrangements; sailed then in a small boat across the rough water to the ship. My baggage had been put into a boat that was attached by a rope to the infected ship and brought aboard. Then I sailed ashore again. The boat nearly capsized in the heavy seas. Wandered around in the town alone; small, narrow streets; sails stretched out over them; the houses only one or, at most, two stories high. Went up to the church; small, with frescoes. In a café—the only privy, a rock by the shore. Went to a barber and sat there with the other Greeks on the bench along the wall and was shaved. Found my fellow travelers in the Hôtel de la Grèce, where pepper plants were growing in boxes on the wooden balcony. Sore throat. Met here a man from St. Petersburg, who carped at the Greek people and the Orient in the worst way; he had been robbed by Albanians. (The first class lounge for ladies in an armed steamer is round, with a piano. Above deck is a spacious room for the captain; the lieutenants have their quarters next door. In first class, a large room with a dining table, two mirrors more than five feet wide; the walls inlaid and polished, and along these are the doors to the bedrooms—two built-in bunks, one above the other, with nice curtains.—By the rudder hangs an hourglass filled with sand, a bell on which the hours are struck and a rather large clock next to it. In the middle of the ship, the machinery; on the sides, rooms for the commissioner, the first mate, etc.—In the middle, a kitchen. Second class, a large dining room with bunks at each end and along the sides, small rooms with four or eight bunks.—They ring for breakfast at 9:30, dinner at 5:30, a superb, lavish service—fowl, fish, roast, fruit, coffee. The ship is cleaned every morning.)—On shore I gave the Persian an orange; he touched his turban with his chestnut brown fingers. I went out to the steamer along with him and the English marine officer who could speak Persian. We had three Greek rowers; the water was rough. We made it on board; it was more elegant here than on the *Leonidas*. (The barber's pleasure over the nice Americans.) Pain in my throat. This evening the Persian reciprocated by giving me an orange. The starry sky beautiful.

Monday, March 22. Slept right until early morning, when they cast anchor. I walked along the deck looking at Piraeus before me; the mountain formations beautiful. Pain in my throat. Wrote a letter to Køppen in Piraeus, but without mentioning my name. Began a letter to Holst. The American Schmol, from Pennsylvania, invited me to America. Began a letter to Father Collin. A boat with ladies aboard sailed past us. A visit from Køppen, who chatted for a good hour with me from a boat at a suitable distance. He and my countrymen have been expecting me for a long time. Knew about my arrival from the *General News*; had later heard from his sister, who was staying with Miss Linde, that it was, however, doubtful. She had been delighted with *The Moorish Maid*. Showed me the view over Piraeus to the Acropolis and the mountain Hymettos, the bay at Salamis. Counted about 120 houses in Piraeus. (It is especially the memory of the outstanding people, the great events that have happened here that make this place interesting. It's like stepping back into their times when you cross their stage.) At the inlet there is one wave-shaped mountain after the next, each a different shade. (The Persian's home is in Herat.) At sundown a signal shot was fired, and the flags on all the ships were lowered. A boat with red sails glided by. From Piraeus came the sound of singing, so gay in the still of the evening. How desolate and solitary these mountains look, not a tree, not a bush. Seabirds are circling the ship.

Tuesday, March 23. Thorough cleaning on board ship; it was uncomfortable on deck. Yesterday evening the Russian scraped his leg and screamed for the doctor until morning claiming that he was sick. I don't really like him—polished, and yet has Russian blood. He showed us his copper engravings; some were missing. They've been stolen, he said, by the officers on the other ship. I said it was possible that he had forgotten them, like today when he'd supposedly

thrown away *Correspondence and Memoirs from a Voyager in the Orient,*
which I had lent him; it was found in his bed. Very warm, later a
cold wind. A Greek boy brought us wine, put it on the ship stairs
and hurried away. Gave bread to the fish. Wrote in my diary and
part of a letter to Jette Wulff. I'm already bored. When I was eating
dinner, I was called up on deck. Køppen and Lorentzen (the architect) were in a boat and talked with me until I was fetched back to
the dinner table. The evening so endlessly beautiful—this transparent air, these clear stars, the shape of the mountain; all these things
were both a comfort and an inspiration for me. I sat on a cannon,
thinking about my *Ahasuerus;* prayed to God for strength and good
fortune. In my cabin, read through the letters from home; thought
especially about Louise.

Wednesday, March 24. At 9 o'clock some boats came for us and we
sailed ashore without visiting the quarantine station, without showing our passports. I didn't find Køppen at home and so left a visiting
card for him. Drove with my four Americans and one Russian to
Athens. Our baggage filled an entire second caleche; a hired servant
in Greek dress got up behind. The road, which several years before
had been a bog, was now a fine highway. We gave something to
the first of the Greek beggars. It was very dusty, but it was, to be
sure, classical dust. We passed through a small forest of olive trees
and into Athens. Imagine for yourself a town built in a hurry, as if
for a big market, and that the market is in full swing—and there you
have the new Athens. The Theseum was in fine condition. The
Acropolis looked different than I remember it from copper engravings. We drove to the Hôtel de Munich. I got a particularly good
room out to the street for three francs per day.—I did a little running
around in town, went to a barber and then hired a servant who led
me to the post office, where I mailed my letter to Holst. Called on
Hansen, who was not to be found, but I left a card. Went to see Dr.
Ross, who has a nice home; I was given a warm welcome and was
quite taken by him, similarly Dr. Ulrichs, who was living in the same
house with him. They laughed at Wilke's description of Greece, said
that for people who had lived in Germany, seven to eight years was
just a short time; but, in a city like Athens, endlessly long—it was
growing and growing. Ross accompanied me to our consul, Travers,
who was Dutch and spoke Danish with me; said that I would lose a
lot here by drawing money from Rolli; he promised to introduce me
to the king and to arrange everything for me as best he could. He
took my passport. Was in the café, which is large and splendid, as

good as any in Vienna or Berlin; there were French and German newspapers there. This evening they are doing Italian opera at the theater—one act from *Belisario,* one from *The Barber of Seville.* My penis is giving me trouble, and, heaven knows, it isn't my fault. Walked up to a ruin that a Greek told me was a temple for Ares. The tall, solitary palm trees and cypresses nearby, the picturesque costumes!—I don't understand it myself; I still don't have any idea about it all, but I'm happy. I can't really believe that *I* am in Greece, in Athens! The city is growing as I walk here!—The man from Berlin looked terribly down on this city, and now, says Ross, there's a well-bred man here from Chios, who has never seen a city before; he's surprised by its grandeur, can't imagine a more magnificent city, with these many conveniences with regard to transportation and accommodations. As I was sitting at home, the Queen's court chaplain, Lüth, from Holstein, stopped by. He had heard that I had come and wanted to extend a welcome; his wife, [formerly] Miss Fischer from Fredensborg, and her sister were eager to meet me. He took me home with him; there were children. A little later Hansen came and gave me a kiss. He looked well-to-do. Køppen came later, another kiss. Consul Travers, who wanted to announce my arrival, showed up. We drank a good Greek wine and talked a lot. The chaplain, Køppen and Hansen accompanied me home; we ate and drank champagne. Some Germans turned up. In bed by 11:30.

Thursday, March 25. Loud thunder, different from at home. The ancient, thundering Jupiter is still here in the city of Minerva. Rain is pouring down. Went into the café and later home to my letters. The rain stopped at 11 o'clock. I went for a walk out to the Theseum along Hermes Street (in the middle of which there's a tall palm tree). It's entirely of white marble, resembles in form those at Paestum, but they are only of travertine. It's splendidly well preserved because it has served as a church for later generations. A sarcophagus and a lot of broken bas-reliefs outside. There I met Dr. Ulrichs, who had found on the temple wall a Christian inscription, which he read for me. I let a Greek take me into the temple, which was filled with ancient objects that have been assembled there: a statue of Apollo, a lovely female figure, two sarcophagi and a lot of other things. I walked up toward the Acropolis; big Greek dogs were watching me. To get to one of the main streets, I had to traverse a labyrinth of demolished stone huts; new ones had been built among them. If you followed a path, it ended at one of these or among the ruins of four walls. Then I came to the Tower of Winds, which I already had

A street in Athens

a look at yesterday. Penis still bad; if only I haven't caught anything in the ship's loo! Had dinner with Court Chaplain Lüth, who is supposed to have been delighted about my arrival. Hansen was there and a diplomat—Pohland—from Saxony. It was a little difficult for me to find the place, but I did manage to.—Outside the ground is splitting. It's a well; such things are said to happen frequently here. Last year they slaked some lime in the middle of the street by the big café, and several people fell in and were burned, even some of those who had come to help. The chaplain presented me with a map of Piraeus and Athens. Hansen, the dear fellow, accompanied me home. He told me about how there were really no artisans here. There were farmers, soldiers and robbers, who now and then picked up a hammer, watched for a while and thus turned themselves into smiths or, for that matter, bricklayers. That's why a sort of Sunday school had been set up. Hansen was teaching the students there to draw, and they demonstrated remarkable comprehension, also in learning languages. He told about his pleasant journey with the king through the country, where they had no concept of inconvenience, even if they were going to spend the night under the open sky.

When they arrived at the spot, the tents had been raised, the tables set, champagne, etc., and afterwards there was dancing. In a country village people said that fourteen robbers had been there the day before. The king went after them with his few bodyguards, but they were gone. The next day the Greek farmers caught them, and they went running with the bloody head of one of the robbers to show to the king and queen. Last year a robber was executed in the olive forest near Athens. He didn't want to be beheaded, and the executioner had to struggle with him for two hours and was half dead before he got the upper hand. The German soldiers didn't interfere, but just saw to it that the robber didn't run away. The executioner was later murdered by Greeks.

Andersen spent one month in Greece, where the small colony of Danes and Germans did all they could to see that he enjoyed his stay there. He visited the Acropolis and made day trips to Kolonos and the monasteries of Daphne and Pentelikon. He was also introduced to the court of King Otto and was even invited to a party at the royal residence. On April 20 he left Athens with regret and sailed to Smyrna, where he set foot on Asian soil for the first time. From there he sailed through the Dardanelles and the Sea of Marmara to Constantinople. He went ashore April 25 and took a room in the European section of the city, Pera.

Thursday, April 29. Saw Scutari and Constantinople in beautiful sunshine from the tower in Pera. Hübsch's dragoman came and announced his master. Talked with Hübsch and his son, declined the invitation to Scutari. Talked with Jongh from Smyrna. Went with the hired servant over to Scutari. We went in a long gondola; it was thin, as if it had been made from chips of wood. You had to lie down in the bottom of the boat on some cushions. There was just room for two side by side. You didn't dare move for fear of capsizing, and the boatmen shouted to each other as they passed to avoid collisions. We had to steer considerably northward because of the northern current. We went into a Turkish café. Sitting there was a dwarf, a rich Turk who was said to have twelve wives. He had a beautiful little boy, his son, with him, and he was just as big as his father. We went to the cemetery, which was very extensive. The graves of dervishes have dervish turbans; there are green turbans on the graves of those who themselves, or one of whose forefathers, have been to the Prophet's grave. We walked so far that we could see the town Chalcedon and the Sea of Marmara. (In Scutari we saw

Turkish graves near Constantinople (dated April 28, 1841)

Ali Pasha's grave, which had something like a wire birdcage over it and fountains.) Carved in the burial stones by the graves there is one big hole or two small ones for water, so that dogs can quench their thirst—this is a blessing for the dead. Then we went to the monastery of the dervishes. Everybody had to take off their shoes or boots. Unfortunately, I had pants on with foot straps that couldn't be unfastened; the priests gave me a pair of slippers I could put on over my boots. An Englishman had the same problem, but I didn't want to make do like that. I got a knife and cut the straps. "This is a good person!" said the Turk to my servant. We entered a sort of square hall with galleries, heavily grated to keep women out. There was a niche, and on the wall around there hung framed pictures of what looked to be buildings with Turkish inscriptions. All around the side walls were tambourines and cymbals. There were a lot of dervishes lying on white and black hides, and all were dressed differently—a few were even in military jackets. There were children there. A strange song with shifting rhythms was sung by a few of them and then by them all. It was something with scales and runs, as if a musically gifted savage had heard an Italian singer for the first time and now in his own way was trying to imitate him. They knelt and bowed their heads straight out toward the ground like the idol on Ceylon. A censer was placed before the priest; they kissed his hand and lined themselves up. Two sat on the floor and sang, but it was a hollow howl, a snorting or a death rattle. Then they were joined by a man with his upper lip cut off and long, black hair. (They had all taken off their turbans and had white felt skullcaps on.) His cape was white, and on the back of it were sewn in red two horses with a man on each, with horrible workmanship. He took it off and stood there in a red smock; then he uncovered his arms up to the shoulder. His one arm was shriveled—it looked horrible. Then his body moved to the one side, then into obscene positions; finally all his limbs were moving as if they were driven by a steam engine. All the dancers were groaning and drawing in deep breaths. The sweat was dripping from their pale faces; at last they sank to the ground. I felt really discomforted. We sailed back, landing near the Tower of Leander. Had dinner and spent the evening at the Stürmers', where I met two Austrian officers from Syria; they will be making the trip to Vienna. Some say it's a dangerous undertaking; others think not!—A man sang "The Monk," by Meyerbeer, a lovely bass. Extremely charming ladies.

Friday, April 30. Sent a letter home with Stürmer to Mrs. Læssøe, enclosed a note to Jette Hanck; letter to Edvard with a note enclosed to Mrs. Colbiørnsen. At 10 o'clock, went to a party with our Consul Romani and his dragoman. We first took a walk down to Pera; there was a shoemaker's sign hanging in the main street with the name Lange on it. He was Danish and hadn't been home in nine years; was married to a girl from Galati in Wallachia and wanted to stay here forever. His father had lived on the corner of Amager Square and Købmager Street. He asked me to say hello to his brothers and sisters; he was doing fine. He treated us to wine. Then we sailed over to Constantinople. We saw the grave of Abdul-Hamid (the grandfather of the present sultan); it looks like one of our pretty gazebos at home. In the middle of the floor there was a very large casket heaped with precious shawls and covered with a turban. It was surrounded by small caskets for his children. After we had seen everything through the window, someone came and closed the curtains, and a black boy chased us away. "Christians must not see such things!" he said. We walked through several streets; there were a lot of people there. Here we met Rifaat Pasha, the Secretary of State; he was riding in the divan. All of them in blue officers' jackets buttoned over their chests (on horseback) and fezzes with the tassel spread out all around them. Then we walked to the Sublime Porte, where I had to take my boots off; and, thus, wearing wool socks with a pair of old yellow slippers someone had lent me, I padded down the mat-covered corridors, crowded with soldiers and some people who looked like petitioners, to arrive at [the office of] Ali Effendi (the Under Secretary of State), where we met Baron Testa. Ali laughed at the zeal of the Turk who had turned us away from the grave and apologized. (Turks with dispatches came and went; one dispatch arrived in a red silk case.) He asked if our language was related to German, asked about Sweden.—Then we went to see Safet Effendi (an interpreter), "Interprète de Sublime Porte." He was sitting trimming his beard; asked me to sit down with him on the sofa. The servant brought coffee and a pipe; I accepted the coffee.— Then we walked to Ahmed's Mosque with its six minarets—a lovely, airy hall, dark cypresses against the beautiful blue sky; on the dome, a gilded ornament. Here in the Hippodrome Square, an especially large obelisk of porphyry, a copper serpent that used to be a fountain, but is now filled with stones. A huge column that looked as if it had been chiseled of stone. We passed Sultan Mahmud's grave of white marble, light and airy, like a ballroom; gilded gratings over the window and around the garden. We met Ruet, the editor of the Turkish newspaper; he said that we had made the trip together on the French steamer. We saw the Column of Constantine, which has been damaged by fire. Then we walked to the bazaar, which today, now that I'm better oriented, doesn't bother me as much as it did last time. The arcades are as tall as our ordinary village churches, white but with a little paintwork in the arch. The booths were pressed up against the wall. Bought two pairs of shoes for three Danish rix-dollars, a handkerchief for two marks. Since it was a holiday for some, their booths were closed—and with only a rag that had been hung up or else some netting; that's how safe they are here from thieves. Then we sailed over to Pera. I went alone, with just the dragoman, into the dervishes' monastery there. This is far more elegant than the other one in Scutari. Soldiers were standing guard there. The women kept to the forecourt. We entered through a side door with our boots off and into the gallery, which is at floor level inside. Then a short prayer accompanied by soft, monotonous music—one and the same note on a drum, two notes on a flute. It sounded like the monotonous splashing of a spring. A beautiful view from the windows over to Scutari. The hall was airy. The dervishes took off their tunics and now stood in their brimless, high-crowned, white hats, in open green jackets and long green skirts that were extremely wide, looking like funnels on them when they whirled themselves around on the same spot with their arms stretched out and half raised. There were two in the middle; the others were turning around them and around themselves. A priest walked very quietly among the ones in the middle and those on the outside. Their faces were extremely pale. There was the sound of music and singing. They stopped suddenly and stood still for a moment; then they began to dance the same dance again. They looked just like lifeless dolls; they were portraying the course of the planets. Lovely, warm weather. As I was sitting at home, there was the sound of regimental music. I ran out, took a detour and saw all of the soldiers passing by. The Prussian officer who eats at the hotel here was among the

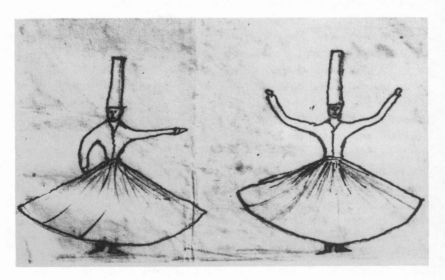

Whirling dervishes at Pera

officers and greeted me. The soldiers had dark blue trousers, jackets with a red border on the collar and fezzes; some had boots and some, slippers. They were playing something from *Guillaume Tell:* "I must toil like a coachman's nag." There were brown and coal-black soldiers mixed up together. (The soldiers have an hourglass at their post.) After dinner, a visit from a young, blond Russian fellow, Aderhas. He's from the Caucasus and staying here at the hotel, traveling to Egypt and then home over Copenhagen.—Feeling sensual.

Saturday, May 1. Sensuality is a thrilling tingling through the nerves as you release a drop of your vitality.—Walked to my barber's, an Armenian. The room was full of smoking Greeks, Turks and Armenians. Walked around in Pera, over to the tower. The mountains behind Constantinople had snow on them in the clear, warm sunshine. You can see Bulgarian farmers on the streets—one is dancing; another is playing the bagpipes. Walked down to the mosques by the quay. They are white inside, of marble, without ornament. Worshippers lie in straight rows praying and salaaming rhythmically in unison so that the colorful row makes a considerable impression in the white church. Walked out to the Scutari side. The nightingales were jugging, and the turtledoves were cooing in the high cypresses. The Sea of Marmara was like glass; the mountains in Asia seemed ethereal; in the clear air beyond lay a chain of snow-covered mountains. Ships with all their sails were lying at anchor like swans mirroring themselves in the water; the small boats were gliding like black snakes across the current. Happened in the street on all the foreign ambassadors, who are meeting to confer about the disturbances in Bulgaria; some of them had servants both fore and aft and secretaries on both sides. (Visited Hübsch and Romani. Mrs. Romani was lying on the sofa Turkish style with a turban on and raised herself into a sitting position on the sofa when I arrived and departed.)—Took a walk; went out and saw Mount Olympus covered with snow. At dinner, a young German who was only eating here to catch a glimpse of me; he had read my novels and my biography. The officer from Berlin in the service of the Turks told me several anecdotes about Mahmud, the father of the present sultan. His friend Ibrahim Agha has been given the nickname "The Black Hell": when Mahmud had the building where the Janissaries were set on fire, they had a priest with the Koran walk in front of them, certain that no one would dare shoot at a priest; but Ibrahim did and got his nickname. Mahmud sent him one of his most beautiful horses with a caparison studded with pearls and stirrups of pure gold and ordered his pashas to do the same. He converted what he got immediately into cash. Mahmud had otherwise had his oldest son killed, because he was afraid the Janissaries would have him proclaimed emperor. A sister of the slain prince has composed a lament which is supposed to be very poetic and has a lovely melody in a minor key: everything she sees is weeping—the flowers of the garden, the clouds and the waves of the Bosporus. The present emperor has recently demonstrated a powerful will and thus issued a decree that the Western Europeans appointed by him are to be obeyed in all things when they are acting in an official capacity, no objections to be tolerated. Marmier's biography[2] of me has been printed in a Smyrna newspaper. Today there were huge bouquets of flowers hanging over the entrances of most houses. The Sultan's mother is a Circassian; they are brought here as children, bought and given a good Turkish upbringing for the Seraglio and learn quite a bit. From the time of Suleiman the Magnificent the sons have always had to stay in the Seraglio, so that they can't stir up a rebellion. Mahmud traveled around with his sons. The women conspire. When Mahmud was buried, they positioned the casket where it is standing now and put a magnificent tent over it, and then a building was erected over it. Only Turks were allowed in, and they all were weeping—men with white beards—he was so beloved.—The French acting company in Smyrna comes from here. Bosco has been here recently. Had some Belgian beer.

Sunday, May 2. A visit from Lange, the shoemaker; his wife was sick with typhus when we were there. Walked down to the quay in Galata. What a throng of boats! Here my shoemaker sailed over to Constantinople. I walked around in the street where they make wooden chests of cypress; there's a lovely fragrance given off by the wood. Disturbances in Rumelia, Thessaly and Macedonia. People say it would be dangerous for me to take the Danube route. Visited by Lafontaine, who thought the same. I've a mind to travel home over Siros. Did a lot of walking around down in Pera. The buildings almost touch, and between them is a roof of vine leaves. Turks are lying with their long pipes inside the booth. Beggars of all nationalities. Encountered another corpse today, a Greek woman. An Asiatic sensuality is torturing me here. Oh, how I'm burning with longing!

Monday, May 3. Slept restlessly last night; anxious about the trip

---

2. A reference to an earlier published section in Xavier Marmier's *History of Literature in Denmark and Sweden* (*Histoire de la littérature en Danemark et en Suède*, 1839).

via the Danube; struggle and uncertainty. News has come today that the Austrian steamer *Stambul* has struck a rock in the Black Sea fifty-five miles east of Amasra. The passengers were rescued. Went to see Stürmer, who reassured me about the numerous bad rumors about the dangers of the journey. Thinking about taking the Danube route. The Emperor's name is Abdul-Mejid. My two traveling companions will be Lieutenant Colonel Philippovich and Major Trattner with the Corps of Engineers. The professor who came from Trabzon is a Mr. Fallmerayer. Made the acquaintance of the Turkish-dressed Achille Laurent. Invitation for this evening from Stürmer and for dinner tomorrow from Christides; I declined both. Mount Olympus with snow. Been down in Pera. Sent a letter with Christides to Ross in Athens. Persians are running around selling shawls; they have pointed, furry caps on. Circassians have round ones with wool on them, like the hair on a savage.—Tomorrow is Muhammad's [the Prophet's] birthday, and so this evening all the minarets are illuminated. Went out for a walk with the Russian Aderhas. The sun had set; the air, red in the west; but all the stars were twinkling in a southern sky. The moon was shining bright, and all the small minarets had a single garland of lamps; the larger ones, two; and the largest, three.—Lights were shining from Scutari and in Galata. The big warships there were lit up with lights in the mouths of all the cannons, three rows of them. At the corner of the Seraglio there was a flaming sword made up of lamps; between the Hagia Sophia and the nearest mosque, the minarets stretched upward like colossal flowers of fire on white stems. In the moonlight the white stripe of the minaret could be seen against the transparent sky. It was a lovely sight out over the cemetery—the coal-black cypresses and among these the scattered lights in the houses, but above the tops of the cypresses, the gleaming water with the illuminated ships; the entire city, where small and large minarets with garlands of lamps sticking up right out to the horizon; and now this stillness. Almost no one was out to see it. The evening was so mild; it was a fairy tale, the entire city. In the meantime, we took some paper lanterns and went for a walk in the moonlight and looked at all the illumination. (The painter Kretzschmer, who has painted the Sultan, is known to us at home through his painting *The Warrior with the Child*.) In the quiet evening we walked beneath the cypresses. At 9 o'clock cannon shots from all the ships and from the coast, so that the windows rattled. Shot after shot.

Tuesday, May 4. Woke up very early. Shot after shot in honor of

Muhammad [the Prophet]. Later music by the corps marching into Constantinople.—At 8 o'clock I went with Romani to Pera and rowed over to Constantinople in bright sunshine. Hübsch's dragoman walked in front of us (a Turk) and Romani's dragoman (an Armenian) behind. We walked past the walls of the Seraglio and between the entrance and the fountain; we were standing right across from the Hagia Sophia. Turks were reclining in the cafés all around. Women in particular filled the terrace of the Hagia Sophia. Platforms had been set up where women and Turks were reclining. Soldiers on horseback and on foot marched into the Seraglio and then back out again and positioned themselves in the street extending from the Seraglio to the mosque of the Sultan Ahmed. The Guard wore stiff neck bands and white collars with a scarf under the chin, and they all had white gloves. One regiment looked pitiable in its dress—they had their bare legs stuck into slippers.—The Prussian officer, Wendt, came and told me many things and wanted to introduce me into the foremost courtyards of the Seraglio. In the background lay the Sea of Marmara with the always snow-covered Olympus.—Where we were standing was where they used to throw the heads of executed prisoners to the dogs. The procession didn't begin until 11:30. Large numbers of beautiful horses with magnificent caparisons studded with precious gems were led by as music played. (A corps had ridden by earlier with a large drum, cymbals, etc.) Then came all the officers. Then the officials and the Grand Vizier. After that a column of horses with plumes and costly caparisons. Then came a column of pages of some sort wearing green peacock feathers, and in the midst of them (they were on foot) rode on horseback the young, nineteen-year-old Sultan in a jacket, a fez with a diamond and some kind of feather from a bird of paradise. He looked very pale. The soldiers shouted a "Long live the Emperor." Said goodbye at the Stürmers', where I was given a letter for his brother-in-law, Mr. Huszar, privy councillor in the Royal and Imperial Court and State Chancellery. (The name of my banker in Vienna is Simon G. Sina.) Anxious that something might be wrong with my passport. Oh, how good I am finding things to worry about! On the way to Pera, met my young American from the *Leonidas*. Today letters from Cairo and Constantinople report that two hundred people daily are dying of the plague. At 6:30, on board the *Ferdinand I*. Lovely weather. The first class lounge very handsome; many Turks were already on board. The moon hung big and round, though pale, over the Seraglio, while Scutari lay in bright sunlight. From between the black cypresses windows were glittering in the setting sun. Finally, it got to looking like thousands of fires; it was disappointing. All flags aloft on the Turkish ship. There was a hubbub in Pera, like a riot. Dolphins were cavorting among the ships. The sun was setting. Gondolas with Turkish officials in them were darting swiftly over the water. The rowers had powerful, naked arms sticking out of their wide, gauze-like knitted sleeves; it looked like part of a fairy tale. No one rows more beautifully than the Turks. Passport anxiety—that it hasn't been stamped with the proper visas.

Wednesday, May 5. We set sail at 4:30. (It's the anniversary of the day Napoléon died.) I was awakened by the motion. It was very foggy, but the fog had just lifted enough, so that you could see the whole coastline. It looked like a long road on both sides; and behind, low, forest-covered mountains. Gardens, towns, cemeteries alternated. Leafy trees, tall cypresses and flowering fruit trees. The sun broke through just once, and then the warships seemed like transparencies. Therapia, closed in by forest. Buyukdere, in a bay; this is where Medea was supposed to have been. Somebody showed me Hübsch's house. We came out into the Black Sea in cold fog and wind. The sea was calm; and by 12 o'clock, lovely weather. A little bird flew up to us and stayed on the deck. Down in our lounge there was a canary in a cage singing. Our captain is from Dalmatia and is called Florio. Sundown. I'm suffering from a strange apprehension.

Thursday, May 6. Once last night and all this morning we lay at anchor because of fog. This was repeated three more times. The sky above was almost clear, but fog all around, wet and cold. By the time the fog had lifted, we were far past Constanta. If we had sailed another half hour, we would have run aground; and this would have been the fourth steamer that has run into trouble: the *Seri Pervas* was Austrian; the *Neva,* Russian; and the *Stambul,* Austrian. At 10 o'clock we arrived in Constanta. A desolate, barren coast; there were a few houses lying by the open sea. The inn, clean and quite cozy. We went for a walk through the town. It was destroyed by the Russians in 1809, but it looks as if it had happened yesterday. A miserable café where Turks hung around. Here I saw this year's first stork. House beams bearing the roof or balcony, supported several places by a marble capital, stumps of columns. You can see traces of Trajan's Wall, which stretched from here to the Danube.—They burn cow dung here because there's no firewood to be found within a radius of many miles. A dead stork was lying by the sea; it had a

A Wallachian girl

melancholy effect on me—it had just reached the sea and then sunk down dead. The coaches, entirely of wood; at 4 o'clock our baggage was taken away on several such drawn by bullocks; they were driven by Wallachian farmers. A superb dinner. A wet, cold fog; the entire sea hidden from sight. Close to the dead stork there was a dead dog; I didn't make a note of it—the stork appealed to my imagination; the dog had perhaps been noble and faithful, and now went unnoticed. Rocks with petrified mussels. Suddenly the fog lifted. A Turk, abroad for the first time, asked if the Germans were mean to Turks;

The Pasha from Orsova (dated May 15, 1841)

he had put his passport in his suitcase, which had been sent off; and now he has to have it stamped with visas. We slept, the three of us—the Englishman, I and Trattner—on long couches, after we first had drunk a toddy. Since we came ashore, very happy.

Despite warnings about the dangers of the Danube route, Andersen's journey was without incident. He traveled through Wallachia, Bulgaria, and Serbia to Orsova, on the border of Hungary, where he and his fellow passengers were quarantined for ten days. On May 30 he arrived in Buda-

pest, where he was delighted to find his The Improvisatore *in a bookstore and later bought two copies. After a few days he continued his river voyage to Vienna, where he was bitterly disappointed to find only one letter, from his faithful friend Jette Wulff, and nothing from the Collins: "All the unpleasantness of home came back to me; I could feel this German-Danish atmosphere—I wish I had died in the Orient" (June 4). He spent three weeks in Vienna, renewing old acquaintanceships from the summer of 1834 and attending the theater as often as possible.*

Andersen's spirits were lifted when he arrived in Dresden on June 28 to find two letters from the Collins waiting for him: they were "very charming and delighted me so much that this evening turned out to be the happiest of my trip!" In Leipzig several days later, he smugly wrote Jonas Collin's son-in-law Adolph Drewsen: "My table is covered with calling cards from all the noted artists here in Leipzig. . . . Brockhaus has given a dinner in my honor and tonight I sat in his loge with Mrs. von Goethe." From Leipzig Andersen traveled to Hamburg and then to Kiel, where he made the crossing to his native Funen on July 13. After paying visits to Henriette Hanck and other friends in Odense, he went to Count Moltke-Hvitfeldt's country estate at Glorup, where his diary ends on July 17, the day of his arrival there.

During the months following his return to Copenhagen in the latter part of July, Andersen was busy working on a few tales and finishing A Poet's Bazaar, *the finest of his travel books. Indeed, a new installment of* Tales, Told for Children *appeared in December, in time for last-minute Christmas shoppers; and his travelogue was published in April 1842. Despite petty reviews, it became very popular with the reading public at home and abroad. Indeed, his works were so widely read in Germany that a publisher in Braunschweig found it worth his while to do a collected edition of them the following year.*

After his return from the Orient, Andersen found himself to be the happy recipient of invitations from the Danish aristocracy. Most of the summer of 1842 was spent visiting the country estates of Gisselfeld and Bregentved on Zealand and Glorup on Funen, and the only diary entries for the year— from June 30 to August 30—describe these visits. He seemed to enjoy the social whirl, and during his stay at Gisselfeld he was introduced to the ducal family of Augustenborg from Schleswig-Holstein, at whose home he was to become a frequent guest. But he also found time for some reading. He mentions enjoying Edward Bulwer-Lytton's Night and Morning *and* Zanoni *and Frederick Marryat's* Joseph Rushbrook. *He began work on "The Ugly Duckling" at Bregentved after a solitary stroll around the moat.*

Andersen's diary entries resume on January 30, 1843, when he was the

*guest of honor at a farewell diner given by Jonas Collin on the evening of
his departure for Paris. En route to Paris he stayed for two weeks with
Count Rantzau at Breitenburg Castle in Holstein and then spent several
days in Hamburg, where he met the artist Otto Speckter, who was later to
illustrate two German editions of a number of Andersen's tales. On March
3 he arrived in Brussels, where he visited the museum but did not like its
collection of paintings by Rubens: "I'm not fond of Rubens—these fat, blond
women with simple faces and faded clothes bore me." On March 8—ten
years after his first visit—he arrived in Paris and made his way to the Café
du Danemark to meet his compatriots, among them Theodor Collin, the
youngest of Collin's sons, who was later to become Andersen's personal
physician. He stayed in Paris for two months, where he discovered his name
was well known thanks to Xavier Marmier's biography of him in* History
of Literature in Denmark and Sweden *(1839).*

Monday, March 20 [1843]. Bad mood! Wrote to Mrs. Rowan that I
wasn't well and so couldn't attend the soirée. Met a Danish engineer
in the Café du Danemark. Wrote a letter to Holst and Mrs. Læssøe.
Went to see Alexandre Dumas in the Hôtel de Paris on the Rue de
Richelieu. He welcomed me with open arms, dressed in blue-striped
shirt and baggy trousers! The bed was in the same room and un-
made; the table, full of papers. We sat by the fireplace, and he was
extremely charming and natural. He related that the king of Sweden, who had been a general along with his father, had invited him
to Stockholm; he wanted to go there and then visit Copenhagen and
St. Petersburg. He offered to take me tomorrow at 8:30 up to the
Théâtre-Français and introduce me to Rachel. Then he presented me
with a ticket for two in the first gallery in the Théâtre des Variétés,
where they were performing *The Petty Secrets of Paris.* (There's a good
scene in this where the patrol is passing by and the man says: "My
poor wife, she's bored." He looks up, and close to her shadow on
the curtain can be seen the shadow of a man who is kissing her.
(The entryway to the Passage de l'Opéra, very authentic.) I think a
similar, original Danish work could be written.) *Marriage to the Beat
of a Drum,* from the time of the Revolution; the young girl sang quite
well; the last idea about the unhappy lover is funny. He says: "I
want to stay a bachelor forever, just like my father!" Lastly, *The Night
of the Mardi-gras,* a carnival skit. I took Theodor with me. We sat in
front of stage center; close to us was a lady; everybody was staring
at her; she was definitely an authoress or singer. Alexandre Dumas

talked about Thorvaldsen, whom he had visited in Rome. Gave me a note to Vernet. Talked about Liszt and Thalberg; he rated the latter higher.

Tuesday, March 21. Went to see Martin, whom I met at the customs office on Rue de Samson. He was very glad to see me and invited me home for a dinner. I read on a poster that Rachel will be performing tomorrow and not this evening; so hurried out to Theodor, had a letter in French written to Dumas and thus will now be able to hear Nissen in *Norma.* I'm tired—but healthy, thank God! Talked at length with Theodor!—At a restaurant on Rue de Richelieu, where Lehmann had taken us, but where I was dissatisfied. This evening at the Théâtre-Italien, where a whole row of Danes was sitting in front of me. Schiern said "ugh" the minute Miss Nissen stepped on stage; and no matter how beautifully she sang, so that the entire audience appreciated it, he grimaced and joined in the clapping as a joke!—She's a compatriot, so it's down in the dirt with her! That's how it was for Grahn: the great recognition that she had received had to be atomized! That cold, conceited bastard, Arnesen, wrote to the papers in Copenhagen, and the clique picked it up! The Danes are a clammy-cold people!—But back to *Norma!* Here, Grisi was great and enravishing. She was an outstanding performer in acting and song. She was at the center of everything! The duet in the second act between her and Nissen was called back for an encore, which they did. Grisi was given a curtain call, and she came out with Nissen.

Wednesday, March 22. Went out without a coat for the first time. Dropped in on Thalberg, who wasn't at home! Sent a letter to Mrs. Eisendecher in Oldenburg; finished letters to Holst, Mrs. Læssøe and Jette Wulff; bought cuffs and portrait photographs. In an excitable, irritated mood. Asked Jette to ask Adler if *Agnete* would be performed. This, of course, must be classified as a favor! Furious at Copenhagen; walked all over!—At 8:30 I went to see A. Dumas; I met him there in the street with his son, who is eighteen years old; he is himself thirty-six. We went first to the Palais-Royal, where he had to speak with Déjazet; then to the Théâtre-Français. I had to wait outside until he had seen whether Rachel was on stage or not. A stagehand called me. I was dressed in my best with my hair parted on the left, what we at home call "the king's side." Was backstage, where a small room had been partitioned off with a screen; there were three stools. Rachel, dressed as Phaedra, received us graciously! She is beautiful and has an extremely interesting face; none of her portraits looks like her. Her voice is very low, but beautiful. She asked us to sit down. I told her that in my fatherland she was known and loved and that her portrait hung in every home. She wouldn't believe this and said that when she did come to Copenhagen she would regard me as someone she knew. I answered that she would find so many friends there that she wouldn't need me. When I went up the stairs with Dumas, I said: "You will laugh, but my heart has been pounding as if I were a child because I was going to speak with Rachel!" He told her what I had said, and she exclaimed: "Artists do understand each other!"—Dumas was very animated when speaking to her; she laughed and looked very vivacious; then extended her hand in farewell and stood there like Phaedra before a jubilant audience. I wanted to stay, but Dumas said: "Now is just the time when they have short skirts on at the Porte-Saint-Martin; let's go there!" Arm in arm we walked down the Rue de Vivienne and the entire Boulevard. I was speaking horrible French. Dumas was saying, among other things, that Leuven-Brunswick who has written *The Postilion of Longjumeau*[3] and several other plays, is a natural son of the Swedish Count Horn. He told me that Rachel was the lover of one of Napoléon's sons.—We arrived at Porte-Saint-Martin. In the third act, in the middle of China, Dumas left me to speak with the director; and I stood there alone during singing and shouting, changing sets and hullabaloo. The ladies looked at me; I looked at them. An ordinary stagehand took one of the figurantes on his lap, and she put up with it, taking off her garland and arranging her long hair. She was namely one of the slain wives of the sultan. Between the acts a young man showed me the sea—how it and the starry sky were constructed.—Then we again set off for the Théâtre des Variétés, where Dumas left me after two good hours of conversation. At the Théâtre-Français he introduced Anaïs to me; we spoke with her. With her was a little girl; it was Elssler's daughter, he said. Had some wine. Sensual +.

Thursday, March 23. Headache. Went out to see the Danes at the Étoile du Nord. Got a letter there via Buntzen with an invitation for this evening to attend Countess Bocarmé's soirée. I went. The lady, who has estates in Belgium, was very gracious and grateful for the honor I was doing her. But it was really the unmarried Baroness von Bornstedt from Lucerne, a poetess, who accounted for my presence.

---

3. *The Postilion of Longjumeau* was in fact written by the two authors Adolphe de Leuven and Brunswick (pseudonym for Léon Lévy, called Lhérie).

That very day there had been a big argument, Buntzen told me, among the ladies about whether Balzac or I was the greater writer. Miss von Bornstedt had a request to make of me: I had to go into a little side room and listen to her poems. She called me the master and herself the disciple and asked me if she had talent, pressed my hands. She wanted me to go to Lucerne; I would have a comfortable room, where she would make everything pleasant for me and there I was to create. She had there an exiled Polish countess in whose house the Polish insurrection had begun. Her daughter, who is married, invited me to her Saturday soirées. Today it is Mid-Lent: masked people are running around in the streets; in the theaters there are costume balls. Didn't get home until almost 1 o'clock. Sent letters home: to Holst, Jette Boye, Gusta Collin and Father, to Jette Wulff and Mrs. Læssøe. At the café met the painters Lehmann, Friedlænder, etc.

Friday, March 24. Went out to see a Mr. Gathy in Rue de Paradis-Poissonière, nr. . . .—a man with a hunchback, who was delighted to see me. He wants to translate *The Improvisatore.* Visited Baroness Bornstedt, who wrote in my album and read many of her poems to me! I improvised a translation of her "The Spanish Woman." In honor of Bornemann's departure, we Danes ate a big dinner at a restaurant right across from the grand opera; we drank champagne and were in very high spirits, held speeches, lots of innuendos! Læssøe very quiet. I sat between Bornemann and Lehmann. When I got home, I found a calling card from Heinrich Heine. It was 10 o'clock, and I went to bed.

Saturday, March 25. Went to see Marmier. Accompanied Bornemann to the coach. He was traveling home over Brussels. Went home at 1 o'clock. Called on Rellstab from Berlin, but didn't find him at home. Schiern was here. Wrote a letter. A bit chilly, went for a walk. After having my hair done good and proper, I was picked up by Buntzen at 10 o'clock, and we walked to Countess Pfaffins's on Rue Sainte-Anne for the soirée. There I met Balzac, to whom I paid some compliments. He was a short, broad-shouldered, stocky fellow. I met the author Fanny Reybaud, who has written *The Waifs;* I told her that this story was the subject of *The Mulatto* and about the success this work had had. She asked me to come to her soirées and was very amiable. She went so far as to praise my French and said I was too modest. We talked about Danish literature, etc.—Then a pale, young Frenchman came up and began to jabber. I thought it was a story he was telling, but it was a discourse on God and religion, about revelations he had had, and he was serious! He had been leaning against an oak tree in some valley and saw a flame in which there was an inscription in French! He was very eloquent! The Greek Koreff and wife were there; he talked about Brøndsted, Koës and Oehlenschläger, whose German was supposed to have been far less good than mine when he had known him. His wife was sitting on the sofa with a brazier under her legs. I saw the flame and was confused as to whether the carpet was on fire or it was supposed to be a brazier. I battled with myself over whether I should warn her, but was levelheaded, thinking I'd first wait to see if the flame got any bigger, which it didn't. When I told Buntzen, he laughed, so that Miss Bornstedt absolutely had to know the reason why. She is too overemotional!—I had left her poems [The Legend of St. Catherine] at her place without realizing it; she had brought them along. I had to say some rubbish. Countess Pfaffins very amiable, extended an invitation for every Saturday. Went home at 1:30 at night.

Sunday, March 26. Visited Rellstab from Berlin, a fat, and, I dare say, stuck-up man, who welcomed me graciously, however, when he heard who I was. We talked together for about a quarter of an hour. Then I left to go out to see Heinrich Heine, who gave me the warmest of welcomes. He said that he had nearly forgotten his German, that he now had French joys and French sorrows, a French wife. The North seemed to him to be the mystical realm where the treasure of poetry lay buried; were he not so old, he would learn Danish. Our pixies and trolls interested him; that's why he had called his last book *Atta Troll.* (*Atta* means "father.") He thought that in Germany only lyrical poetry lived; mentioned Eichendorff, Uhland, Grün. I told him about Halm's *Son of the Wilderness;* about our newest literature. He had only seen my *Improvisatore,* and said it was well formed. "You are a true poet!" he said. He complained about how much he had been misunderstood, how ill-esteemed he was because of his book about Börne; he didn't think it so maliciously written. He asked me about Hauch and about Fredrika Bremer. He had been thinking of me when he wrote his *Rabbi from Bacherach.* It was in my style. He said that Kruse's translation of *The Improvisatore* was bad, that Kruse had died in the greatest misery here in a hospital; at the end he was so sick of everything that he didn't even have any appetite for men any more! He asked me to visit him often, was extremely charming. Trudged out to see Theodor.—In the evening at the Opéra Comique, where I saw *The Crown Diamonds,* which I found very boring. More interesting was Grétry's *Richard the Lion-*

Hearted, although I only saw two acts because I was tired. I was up on the third floor, which is to say the second balcony. Up on the ceiling you could see Paësiello, Paër, Grétry and Boïeldieu; in the foyer, d'Alayrac, Méhul, Boïeldieu and somebody with no name attached. At home, furious because the boy hadn't bought any cognac; ran out myself to buy some; found a letter from Saabye.

Monday, March 27. Not feeling well; went out to see Theodor; had a good time at Krieger's. (Wrote Italian notes for Theodor.) At home I found a letter from Gathy, who wanted to take me around to musical notables. Read in the newspaper that Admiral Wulff is dead. Cold weather; wanderlust. Dissatisfaction with home. No letters from there. A visit from Orla Lehmann. I've gotten a lot of pimples; I look sallow. Læssøe's narrow-mindedness, his talk about literature, which he places under his mathematical bushel!—If he isn't arrogant, then no one is!—and yet I find him interesting. Went to the Théâtre-Français and saw Rachel perform for the first time; it was in *Phaedra.* She must have a different costume for each time, because when I spoke with her she was dressed in white; this evening she was in sky blue with a red cape.—They all move with a certain rhythmic step—you can hear the lines of poetry. That is not so much the case with her; she is more natural, and it was precisely in these places she received the most applause. Miss Mars, with the lovely voice, performed, so that you felt that she is a great and talented woman. Rachel is—I won't say anything more—but something else. The Greek gods and heroes are dead for us, but if they were to step living into our world, then they would appear as Rachel renders them for us. This—the aura of what is past that conveys something divine—this is what Rachel has. She is herself the tragic muse, who reveals herself to us and embodies for us what she had the poet sing of. She is flesh of our flesh, at least of the Northerner's, but she is alive; she is life and soul. You get ice-cold shivers down your back, as if you were watching a sleepwalker who expressed your hidden, deepest feelings. A man seated behind me threw up, so that I nearly did the same because of the stench. An Englishman was sitting next to me; he told me that the poet Southey had died quite recently. The theater floor this evening had a white carpet. I was in the orchestra and could see right down into the lights. Rachel was given a curtain call. There was one hoot. She expressed her thanks, but not as I have seen it in other theaters where they smile ecstatically; she was as proud as a muse and modest as a young girl, serene, with lowered eyes. One hoot could be heard, like the one I heard directed at Malibran in

Naples. Envy hisses at anything great. From time to time she resembled Mrs. Nielsen and Mrs. Heiberg, for both are great practitioners of their art; but she had something they do not possess, and it isn't the French stage she performs on, but something all her own. Often she would begin her lines as if she were softly humming a melody. Her face was forever changing; she seemed to me like quite different people, a few times even like her own pictures. Sensual +.

Andersen continued frequenting museums, theaters, and the opera, although recurring attacks of stomach cramps and diarrhea did indeed keep him home several evenings dosing himself with rhubarb and Hoffmann's anodyne and barley gruel. Theodor departed for Rome on the first of April, leaving Andersen alone and, as it turned out, letterless on his birthday the following day.

Tuesday, April 4. A letter from Recke and Hoskier. The letter was ten whole days late. Walked in showery weather out to the Danish colony, where I chatted with Læssøe, who had brilliant things to say about *Ahasuerus.* Stopped in at Krarup's. Visited at home by Krieger. Felt on the whole quite good today. Went at 8:30 to a concert in the salon of Mr. Pleyel, where it was awfully elegant and brightly lighted. The knowledge that my boots had no heels and that I had on my worst pair of trousers made me ill at ease. Smartly dressed Frenchmen arrived. I gave one of the men a good looking over: his dress jacket wasn't as good as mine; the same went for the hat. I was feeling hemorrhoidal, awfully withdrawn into myself. A man came up and greeted me quite respectfully and familiarly. I've seen him before. Who is he? During the fifth number, I left. My thoughts had taken a different turn, and I was feeling good. Back home in my room, sick again. Fire burning hot in my veins; out—+.

Wednesday, April 5. Downpour! Suffering from last evening. + Went for a stroll in the Palais-Royal, where I ran into Læssøe! Visited Willmers; wandered around. Worked on *Ahasuerus.* Went to the grand opera with Krieger, Læssøe and the Norwegian to see *Charles VI;* Duprez and Mademoiselle Stoltz were performing. He looked exactly like a tailor's apprentice. Beautiful sets. In the third act a whole troop of horses came on stage; not over until almost 12 o'clock. +

Thursday, April 6. Constant rain. Visited Heine; recounted for him three of my tales. He offered to write a letter for me to Laube. We talked about Danish literature. "You're good at narrating!" he said. "Goethe could do it, but I can't!" He asked me to visit him often; I don't trust his face, though.—As I was walking across the Place de la Bourse today toward evening, a Frenchman stopped me and asked whether I might not be from Denmark: "You don't know me, but I know you, Andersen!" It was the dancer Dumalattre. I thought for a minute it was the fellow I had a letter for from Saabye, but he told me he was living at 8 Boulevard Montmartre. I speculated in vain about where he could know me from!—Bought wine; at home by 7:30 +.

Friday, April 7. A visit from County Magistrate Thygeson. Sent a letter to Ross in Athens. Bumped my knee getting into an omnibus to the Place de la Bastille. From there walked to Père-Lachaise in gray weather. Among the well-known graves to which chance led me were those of David, Le Sage and Suchet. A sweeping view over Paris; banks of fog glided over the vast city. It seems to me Rome is larger. The dead could have seen it from their graves by the light of the July illumination. I saw a grave with just the name Nina on it; I thought about the one who went mad. Fresh wreaths were hanging on the gravestone. Then I came to the graves of Masséna and Foy, large monuments. Suddenly I was standing before Börne's grave; a statue of him was on it; from there I looked out over Paris. The last grave I saw of a well-known personage was the monument over Casimir Périer; he resembles Napoléon in some ways. Walked back to the Boulevard and drove home at 12:30. Then went over to the Louvre; viewed the Dutch and Italian schools. Several works by van Dyck caught my eye, Domenichino, etc. Saw the new exhibit and found portraits of Mortier and Dumas. I arrived home very tired and lay down on the bed for a half hour. Then it was raining again. In the evening a champagne party for Læssøe at the Étoile du Nord; I arrived as early as 7 o'clock and was with Schiern until 8:00. We— Schiern, Krieger, Læssøe, Krarup and I—drank champagne; spoke in a bright and cheery way about the North and about traveling. Around eleven I walked home. The new moon was shining; the streetlamps were mirrored in the Seine. Near the Palais-Royal I had an absinthe and water and in the café saw Tousez from the Palais-Royal. I recognized him by his voice; the others were probably actors. I bought myself some cakes and am now imagining myself sitting at home.—Very sensual +.

Saturday, April 8. Was awakened this morning when I thought my name was being called. Very listless. Went out to pay a visit to Marmier. Called on Frijs, Sehestedt Juul and Delong. Letters of recommendation sent to me by Marmier. Wrote a letter to Ørsted and a note to Edvard. In the evening at the Théâtre des Variétés to see the Spanish dancers I described in *A Poet's Bazaar*. I had to stand in line for three-quarters of an hour, and the prices had been increased. I sat in the parterre. (1) *The Royal Hunt* boring; (2) the second act of *The Roe Deer*, in which Odry was playing John and which told the story of Charles Gris; (3) the dance "La Malaguena," danced by the Spaniards; (4) the second act of *The Rabble*, in which Odry was Picpus; finally (5) "La Rondella," a sort of Spanish evening with song and dance. I was so tired and strengthless that I could hardly hold myself together. A glass of toddy did me good, even though it tasted horribly of liquor.

Sunday, April 9. Was in the Notre-Dame! A visit from Willmers and the German Hagen; strolled in the evening on the boulevard, along the corridors of the Palais-Royal; had an offer of a prostitute; strolled home!—Now, at last, Theodor is in Rome. Today at almost 4 o'clock Læssøe left for Marseille on his way to Naples.

Monday, April 10. Went to see La Tour, who resides in the Tuileries; it was very elegant there, and royal servants took me to him. He had a medal, was very charming! There were paintings hanging on the wall! He asked me about Danish composers; I named Weyse, Kuhlau and Hartmann. He asked me to write in his album; showed me my biography in Marmier's *History of Literature in Denmark and Sweden*, asked me to visit him, etc.—Then I went out to see V. Hugo, where I had to wait a terribly long time. Finally he came in a dressing gown, invited me to partake of lunch and asked whether it wasn't very cold in Denmark now. I told him that it was only four days from here. He referred to his trip along the Rhine as a "promenade," said that he only knew French and Spanish, since he had spent his youth in Spain! He looked very aged and decrepit, compared to when I saw him ten years ago. He questioned me in detail about Danish literature; he only knew a few names through reading Marmier. A heavy hailstorm broke while I was riding home in the omnibus. At Hallavant's I got a letter from Theodor in Marseille and ran into Gotschalk and the fellow from Bergen, Nicolaysen. We three went to the Opéra-Comique and saw *Brother and Husband*, an opera in one act, and afterwards *The Ambassadress*, in which a Mademoiselle Lavoye was making her second debut. Flowers were thrown to her on stage, and she was given a curtain call. On the way home I was nearly run over.

Tuesday, April 11. Went out to the Arc de Triomphe with Gotschalk and Nicolaysen. On the way a powerful snowstorm struck.

No omnibuses came. Therefore the three of us clambered up onto a stagecoach on Champs-Élysées bound for Neuilly; the driver was from Switzerland and spoke German. With lantern in hand we climbed up the arch. Paris lay in a cloud of snow; the sun was shining on the outskirts of the city—a lovely panorama for us!—Then I left them to call on Alfred de Vigny—he is otherwise available only on Wednesday—at 6 Rue de Écuries d'Artois. He showed me his album, in which Rothe from Sorø had written a verse, and asked me if it was good. Requested that I write something the next time I came. We talked about Danish literature, etc. Large, old paintings were hanging on the wall. (This morning a visit from Ahlefeldt.) Music party at Thygeson's, where I encountered Swedish admirers and Miss Eisen.

Wednesday, April 12. Cold weather. Only a note from Collin. Flew into a rage! They don't have an ounce of consideration in them back at home. Ran out of Hallavant's because I didn't get what I wanted fast enough. Then went up to another place to eat and got something worse served even slower. At the grand opera the two first acts of *Fernando Cortez* and the ballet *Giselle,* in which the second act is especially poetic. Carlotta Grisi danced beautifully. Sent a letter home to Privy Councillor Collin.

Thursday, April 13. A pimple on my neck that is hurting. Buntzen lanced it. Went bathing in the Seine. With Buntzen; opened a letter to Theodor, wrote a few words to him; and sent a letter home to Gottlieb Collin and Bournonville. Bad mood. Went this evening to the Théâtre des Variétés to see *The Solemn Dunderpates,* in which old Lepeintre was superb in his baby bonnet and stroller. This parody is better than the one at the Palais-Royal. After that, *The Caravans of Mayeux,* in which Neuville was making his debut—a horribly hunchbacked vaudeville in five hunches. It was whistled off. I left during the last piece, *The Vendetta.* Very cold.

Good Friday, April 14. Liljenstolpe found me in bed; I had to turn him away. A very sore throat, which is quite swollen with two small abcesses. Went to a book club and read German newspapers. Really filthy mood. Sent a letter to Vieweg. Today is the last day of racing at Longchamps—there was nothing to be seen but coaches driving back and forth. Everyone was dressed in winter clothes.—Wandered around all evening; it was cold. I lit a fire in the stove and warmed myself up.

Saturday, April 15. The pimple on my neck is taking on the character of a boil. It hurts. At 4:30 I was at Alexandre Dumas's. He lay in bed writing. He asked me to excuse him for a moment; he wrote, muttering some of the words half aloud! "Voilà," he shouted and jumped out of bed, "'now the third act is finished!" It was a prose drama that he was working on for the Théâtre-Français. Then he wrote something from his tragedy *Caligula* in my album and furnished me with the address of Saint-Priest, a commission agent, in case I wanted to send him anything. Took an omnibus out to the Cirque Olympique, where I saw *The Pills of the Devil*, which surprised me with its special effects: for example, how they had put the things together that were blown into the air with the steam engine; the thin man who was inflated fat; the man in the rest home, where they started off with all their instruments and later he thinks he is crazy; the house that is turned around, the body with the rotating head. However, what surprised me most was the physical strength of the Bedouins. Went home at about twelve. Sensual mood. + The boil on my neck is plaguing me.

Andersen received numerous invitations to soirées and social gatherings, even from members of the French aristocracy. He particularly enjoyed his visit with the poet Alfred de Vigny, who presented him with his lyrical and dramatic works and bade him a hearty farewell: "Come back again soon to Paris and don't forget me!" On April 27, Andersen was thrilled to receive an invitation from Rachel to a soirée at her home, where he was chastened to note that although her shelves contained literary works from all over the world, even Sweden, there were none from Denmark. He was even more chastened when news of the opening of the stage version of Agnete and the Merman *reached him from Denmark.*

Saturday, April 29. At the Théâtre Palais-Royal in the evening and saw *Voyage between Heaven and Earth*. Schiern came and told me that the *Berlingske News* had said that *Agnete* had been hissed at. When I got home, I continued my letter to Jette Wulff: "May I never set eye on the home that only has eyes for my faults, but no heart for the great gifts God has given me. I hate whatever hates me; I curse whatever curses me!—From Denmark are always coming the chill draughts that turn me to stone! They spit upon me; they trample me into the dirt! I have, though, a poetical nature, such as God hasn't given them many of! But which I will pray to Him the moment I die that He never give that nation more of!—Oh what venom is flowing through my veins during these hours! When I was young, I could cry; now I can't! I can only be proud, hate, despise, give my soul to the evil powers to find a moment's comfort! Here, in this big, strange city, Europe's most famous and noble personalities fondly surround me, meet with me as a kindred spirit; and at home boys sit spitting at my heart's dearest creation! Indeed, even if I am judged after my death, as I have been while I lived, I will have my say: the Danes are evil, cold, satanic—a people well suited to the wet, moldy-green islands from where Tycho Brahe was exiled, where Leonora Ulfeldt was imprisoned, Ambrosius Stub was regarded as a jester by the nobility; and still many more will be ill treated like these, until this people's name will be legendary. But I am probably expressing myself characteristically for a playwright who has been booed off stage. My letter should be published and Copenhagen would have a good laugh! May I never see that place; may never a nature such as mine be born there again. I hate, I despise my home, as it hates and spits upon me!—Pray to God for me; pray that I find a quick death, never see the place where I have only suffered, where I am a stranger, a stranger as in no foreign place! But enough of this; much too much! I know you have had sisterly feeling for me in your heart; I think you can empathize with my feelings at this moment! But don't be sad! When you read this letter, a week will have gone by—I have a resilient nature—then my mind will be more calm; then I will hate—calmly—my home. Have never had a fever like now.—I am ill; my home has sent me a fever from its cold, wet forests, which the Danes gaze upon and believe they love; but I don't believe in love in the North, but in evil treachery. I can feel it in my own blood, and it's only in that way I know I am Danish!" Found an invitation from Lamartine.

Andersen did indeed allow himself to be distracted by the next days' visits to Heine, Lamartine, and Hugo and then by the travel arrangements and obligatory farewell calls of the following week. On May 8 he left Paris traveling by coach via Strasbourg to the Rhine, where he boarded a ship headed downriver. Interrupting his journey several times along the way to introduce himself to such German poets as Ferdinand Freiligrath and Ernst Moritz Arndt, he arrived three weeks later in Hamburg, where he met the celebrated Norwegian violinist Ole Bull. From there he traveled to Breitenburg Castle for a week's stay before boarding the ferry at Kiel, where, on June 14, he recorded the last of his diary entries, waiting for a storm to subside. He spent most of the summer of 1843 visiting the estates of his aristocratic friends on Zealand and Funen and working on the four tales that were to appear in November with the title New Tales.

1843

*Monument on a grave (drawing done two
weeks after Riborg Voigt's wedding in 1831)*

During the summer of 1843 Andersen fell out of love with an old flame
and in love with a new. During this diaryless period, he kept a terse record
of these events in his pocket calendar. While staying on Funen, he noted
that he had met a family, the Bøvings, and Mrs. Bøving happened to be the
former Riborg Voigt: "It's been thirteen years!" The first three weeks of
September are crowded with jottings that reflect his growing infatuation
with the "Swedish Nightingale," Jenny Lind. Within a week after recording

that he and she had both been dinner guests at the ballet master August Bournonville's, he wrote: "In the evening, with her at Bournonville's, they drank to her health and mine—in love!" Both these episodes are reflected in the collection of tales from 1843: the meeting with Riborg is wryly treated in "The Sweethearts," and "The Nightingale" conveys some of the feeling he had for Jenny Lind as a person and as an artist.

Andersen's diary for 1844 is, again, a record of his travels. It opens on May 23, the day he left Copenhagen on a ten-week trip to Germany. Stopping for a week or, in this case, two at Breitenburg, as was now his habit on excursions to the south, he traveled via Hamburg, Hanover, and Braunschweig to Weimar, where he was introduced to the Grand Duke Carl Friedrich of Saxony-Weimar-Eisenach and his son, the Hereditary Grand Duke Carl Alexander, with whom he later became warm friends. After visiting old acquaintances in Dresden, he traveled to Leipzig, where he had the pleasure of hearing Clara Schumann play three of his songs set to music by her husband Robert. In Berlin he called on Jacob Grimm without a letter of introduction and was humiliated to discover that the editor of German folk tales had no idea who he was.

After he arrived back in Copenhagen on August 3, there was a three-week period that he spent visiting Count Gebhard Moltke-Hvitfeldt at Glorup and kept no diary. On August 26 he received an invitation from King Christian VIII and his queen to visit them at a spa on the North Frisian island of Föhr. As he wrote the following day to Jonas Collin, he would go "despite the fact that my finances do not in any way permit me to make this trip."

Tuesday, August 27 [1844]. Traveled with Biering to Odense; met the Hancks here; visited several acquaintances; but concealed the fact that the queen had summoned me to Föhr in order to keep it from the newspapers. Rain and wind, so that several travelers stayed in Assens and didn't venture the trip over with us. It took us three hours to do the nine miles. I lay stretched out on a berth and avoided being seasick. At 10:30 we went ashore and rolled off toward Haderslev.

Wednesday, August 28. We passed through Åbenrå. The road runs close to the sea. Late in the morning we arrived in Flensburg. A steamer was leaving—it was the *Kamchatka,* with the Prince of Hesse on board, along with a prince from Glücksborg and the Russian Prince Suwarov, who was on his way from Föhr. In Flensburg people advised me not to leave right away, since I wouldn't arrive at high tide and would have to stay over in Dagebøl, where the inn was extremely bad. The roads were almost impassable. I stayed at the best hotel, run by Döll's widow. Visited the Rieffels, who were happily surprised; I was otherwise not very pleased with my expenses for this trip—indications are that it will end up costing more than fifty rix-dollars. Rieffel showed me the organ, which we got to by threading our way through the rooms of the house. The Reverend Asschenfeldt (a poet) was invited, along with another minister and a future son-in-law, Kuntze, a somewhat fat, rather unwashed young man with a loose collar. He forgot himself gaping at me; was awfully kind to me. I took a walk to the harbor in the rain. Ate dinner at the Rieffels' and presented Kuntze with *Picture Book without Pictures*. Went to bed at 6 o'clock in the evening and slept until 1 o'clock the next morning.

Thursday, August 29. At 2 o'clock in the morning exited Flensburg in lovely moonlight, but it was very cold in the open carriage; the desolate district, the thought of the gruesome roads that awaited me—everything foreshadowed something. It was so still; a single bird was chirping in the heather! The clouds raced by.—At daybreak we came to a country village with an inn; soon it was morning. The heather was flowering beautifully. Before dawn I saw a harbinger of bad road; several places boards had been put on the road for pedestrians to walk on. At one place in the road, there was a whole flood we had to go through. We passed through Stadum; here they didn't speak German well. Suddenly they opened a cupboard, which was a bed, and there lay a small child. "Well, you little rascal, my beautiful boy!" said a tailor there. Then I could hear they spoke Danish. "Yes, we all do here," they said, "but Frisian begins in the next village." We arrived there; people were not very polite, not a single hello; and if you said hello to them you got a brusk nod; no one took his hat off. We didn't go through Leck in order to avoid as much of the marsh as possible. Since the roads were now getting impassable, Oxholm had recently had to overnight at the last inn in the geest.[4] The marsh began. The road was liquefied earth; the horses sank in deep with each step, and so we had to drive up on the dikes which provided lee for the houses and which we expected to fall off of.—The pastures were under water, so that they looked just like lakes. It all seemed to me to resemble something Finnish. Entire fields of grain were standing in water after the rain. Horse beans were cultivated a lot.—The houses were all of brick, but moss-cov-

4. Geest: a Dutch word meaning a dry, loamy elevation in an otherwise marshy area.

Breitenburg

ered. If an artist were to paint these, he would have to have every color on his palette. Here they had chimneys and not, as at Breitenburg, large halls with an open fire. Everything looked more impoverished. At 12 o'clock arrived at Dagebøl, a miserable hole, unfriendly people.—The shore covered with plaited straw, so that it wouldn't be lapped away by the waves. I saw a man working on it; it's done two to three times a year. In the storm the day before yesterday the steamer with the princes on board had been close to running aground. Harms didn't venture ashore; the beating of the waves was too strong.—After a terribly long wait, I boarded the ferry *(The Springing Sheep)* at 3 o'clock, when the tide was in. We sailed across in one hour. The island looked friendly, the town clean! On the street I met Sally along with Wedel-Heinen, and he got me lodgings in the house where he was staying himself, the same rooms where von Holten had been staying. "Andersen! Mr. Andersen!" called two young ladies, "Mother, there's Andersen!" and a lady looked out of the garret. It was the duchess of Augustenborg and her daughters. It was embarrassing for me that I was still in my traveling suit.—I arrived at my lodgings tired, but was summoned that evening and so had to go. The king and the queen, very gracious. Kellermann played; I read "The Top and the Ball," "The Ugly Duckling." The king laughed a lot; and when I left, he said: "Thanks for coming this evening!" I was invited to visit the queen the next morning at 12 o'clock to read *Fortune's Flower*. Sally comforted me by saying that I would have my trip paid for. Went for a walk in the lovely moonlight.

Friday, August 30. Beautiful weather. Visited Rantzau. The houses in the street here all have only one ground floor and one garret that faces out to the street. The year a house was built—most of them are over a hundred years old—is marked in iron spikes. By the sea, a lane lined with young trees. At 12 o'clock at the queen's, where the duchess was with her daughters. We ate lunch, and I read the first act of *Fortune's Flower*, which was very well received. Nagel, from Altona, was there and very taken with *The Flower*. Summoned to dine; then it was canceled, because there wasn't enough room. Visited Miss Koren. Went to the resort salon and had dinner. Here I received another summons to dine; sat next to Levetzau, who lifted a glass with me. The king and queen sat right across from me and we conversed at length. In the evening, to tea; I wasn't in the mood; there seemed to me to be something stiff about it all. A man from Haderslev played the piano badly; the mayor of Oldesloe's daughter sang—thinly! I recounted "Thumbelina," "The Princess on the Pea" and "The Steadfast Tin Soldier," but felt dissatisfied. I arrived home in a bad mood.

Saturday, August 31. Met the duchess and the princesses on the Promenade. She invited me to walk with them, so I didn't get to make any visits; asked me again, though, to come to Augustenborg.—At 12 o'clock I boarded the steamer *Kiel* by invitation of the queen. We sailed to Oland, one of the largest of the North Sea isles. I was in the last boat, and we had about two miles to row. We reached the island, where I was being carried ashore by the sailors just as the king was coming back. I ran and jumped over the canals; reached the king in a sweat, and he told me not just to view the graveyard, but also to go into the houses; another boat would be coming.—I hurried to the end of the island, where the sea had torn away whole chunks of it during the high tides of the last storm. Here there was a gentle slope; rotten coffins were sticking out of it; all around there were human bones and skulls. All the bones that come loose are gathered up and buried further inland, until the sea reaches them again and washes them away. They are mostly sailors—this is how they can be buried in graves, but still be the prey of the sea. Most of the people here are widows. There are pretty girls among them; they marry for the most part men from Jutland, who come here to do the threshing; in that way they become *Danish* wives.—The whole island looks like an English park. There is only one kind of grass, one that can tolerate salt water. I hurried to the church; there was a little triumphal arch of flowers—even outside the house of God—for their king expects the best the island has to offer. Inside on the wall was a copper etching of the king. I went into one of the houses; here we saw the only male. The room was lined with tiles like a tile stove. On a shelf were lots of books for the winter. A wooden plaque was hanging in the front hall with an inscription in German: "Trust in God." We had some sheep's milk and then strolled off. The houses, reddish-green, stood close to each other, forming narrow, dark streets.—This is where the people have sat during storm tides, on the rooftops and in attics, until a boat ventured over with bread for them. The whole island has been under heavy waves. On the sandbanks off the outermost islands, wooden scaffolds like towers have been erected; a basket hangs from the top, full of bread and schnaps for castaways.—I shook hands with the women and girls; they thanked me for the honor. One of them questioned me about who the duchess was; they told us their minister had said something of the same sort to them. Then rowed back to the ship, where at the table I was seated next to Fensmark. He raised his glass in a toast to me, to bid me welcome home; and at the same moment the king was brought back on board, so we were lumped together. We made remarks about it. Zahrtmann drank with me a toast to Wulff; Dahlerup and I drank one to Buntzen.— After dinner we danced around the smokestack. It looked marvelous, like a well-choreographed ballet. Sailors were running between the dancers with the table boards; waiters, with plates! There was music playing; sailors sitting on the paddle boxes carried the bass, like a recitative. The pilot looked grimly at the sea and gaily at the dancers. I stood up in the gallery with Fangel, Krogh, etc. Schou was dancing with the smallest princess. Levetzau was a good dancer and very merry. He came and asked me for an impromptu verse for the royal couple. I came up with:

> Home from the sea a pearl we bring,
> A pearl full of memories and poetry;

A moving sight, it makes the heart ring;
On it, the royal visage filled with clemency.

Then a cheer was raised!—The king said that I should have a better look at the island; I could have a boat at my disposal. The queen spoke cordially with me; I told about how many impromptu verses had been produced at Bregentved, but there I was at ease, like at home: "But I should hope that you are at ease here with us, too!" she said. We talked about the trip, etc.—When the moon rose, I showed it to her. My impromptu about it was well received:

See, there we have a heart that's glowing,
In the waves baptized and blessed;
Here, blood through living hearts is flowing,
The hearts on Denmark's crest.

The king, the queen, the duchess, everyone very forthcoming with me.—We were set ashore on the Promenade, right up on the sand. Went for a walk with Dahlerup and Count Reventlow, from London. In the meanwhile, the king's boat had gotten stuck on a sand bar. Went to tea in the evening; I did "The Swineherd," and the king asked the ladies-in-waiting if it was true that they weren't for kissing. I read "The Nightingale," and the king said: "It is filled with a good spirit." Levetzau and Rantzau spoke about the deep thoughts in it.—Kellermann played beautifully. The queen asked me to sit with her and told me of a dream about the Day of Judgment and the angels, who proclaimed: "It is Advent!"—we talked about the Moltkes, etc.—I left at 12 o'clock; went for a walk.

Sunday, September 1. A little rain. Walked out to the church; on the tombstones in the cemetery: (1) the Holy City—Christ was leaving the city, spoke to a woman and her child; she was holding her husband by the hand; he was leading the children; the smallest was clinging to him.—(2) A man and woman were holding each other by the hand; she, the daughters; he, the sons. The clothes were different from the way they are now. The stone, over a hundred years old. Otherwise, on most of the stones there were ships. The church was completely full of people; a good sermon by Nielsen. Walked home and went at 1 o'clock for lunch with the queen. She ladled up for me porridge with cream. I showed them pages from my album, Retzsch's etching, and read "The Angel" and some short poems. Was again expressly invited to Augustenborg. Dinner at the royal table; the evening with the king and queen.

Monday, September 2. Matchless summer weather. Wrote to Father, Jette Collin and Henrik. Drove out to bathe; it was infinitely refreshing and salty; water was streaming from my eyes.—Was at the royal table; sat next to Christiani; went for a drive with the king and queen; received a poem from Christiani. In the evening told "Willie Winkie" and "The Angel."—A happy day. Lord, I give thanks unto Thee.

Tuesday, September 3. A morning call on Christiani, who wishes that the king would do something for me, that everyone is expecting it.—At 12 o'clock read the last act of *Fortune's Flower* to the queen; we talked about spiritual visions.—Paid visits. Dinner at the king's table; I'm there everyday. In the evening, there again. Improvised a poem in honor of the queen and, likewise, one on the ballad "Sir Peter Cast a Runic Spell."—This evening the moon rose so wrapped in haze and clouds, so red, so stormy-looking. The lighthouse could be seen below it; the waves were striking high up on the shore, and the water was spraying like champagne, like foaming sharks. Just now at the royal table, the king was telling me about how beautiful it had looked.

Wednesday, September 4. Visited the ladies-in-waiting. Received from Miss Krogh Biernatzki's *Collected Works*. Went for a walk with the district magistrate and heard about the islands in the North Sea: each house is built on a raised foundation ground; there are cows on Oland, sheep on the others. The water around them contains no fish; it is dirty-yellow. The water can spurt up against the windows. The people sit serenely inside spinning. They speak Frisian, related to English.—Their beds are like cupboards lined on the inside with plaited mats.—Ships have often been driven right up to one of these houses—with its lights shining it looks as if it were floating on the water. In a few places there is quicksand. The man who takes ships from here to Greenland, Holland, etc. is called the "commander." Whale tusks can be found all around; they look like large gateposts, green, weathered. If you examine them carefully, you see that they are flat on one side, crumbling on the inside. There are many of these by the gardens of Wyk; out by one field there is a whole hedge of them. The women wear a red fez under a scarf; unmarried girls, their uncovered, braided hair.—The water was turgid today; it was ebbtide, very salty. You undress, while the hired hand, on horseback with large boots on, pulls the bathhouse out into the water. If the tide rises too high, he comes back and hauls it up a bit. You are drawn up on the beach, and during the trip you get yourself dressed.—Jørgensen Jomtou has arrived. Visits from Ewald, Rantzau, Nagel and Levetzau.—At the royal table, asked by the queen to read a little in the evening.—Visited Westengaard. The houses here are quite Dutch, with a curved window that can be opened in the door—you can see it in paintings with Dutch women in them. The sitting room with glazed walls, green-painted windows and numerous cupboards in the walls; on the tile stove a free-standing brass compartment for putting the coffee kettle under and for decoration.—A ball in the salon. In the evening read to the king *Picture Book*, "The Emperor's New Clothes," "The Naughty Boy." Worn out.

Thursday, September 5. Thanks be to God for these twenty-five years! Visited Christiani and Rantzau; spoke about the meaning that this day had for me. At 1 o'clock read for the queen Thiele's biography of Thorvaldsen; talked about my own; asked her to read *Ahasuerus* when she got back to Copenhagen.—Strangely, forlornly happy. Composed a poem for Christiani.—Rantzau and Miss Rosen drank a toast to me at the royal table. A visit from Westengaard, who congratulated me. A poem from Christiani. Gave him a letter to Mrs. von Eisendecher. The evening, with the king; it was the 5th of September. The king came over to me, congratulated me about what I had gotten through and overcome; came over again later and asked about my first efforts, spoke of my recognition in Germany. I related a few typical incidents! He laughed; asked if I didn't have anything definite to live off of. I said that Frederik VI had given me 400 rix-dollars, and His Majesty had allowed me to retain this, for which I was grateful. "That's not much!" he said. "But I don't need so much!" I replied. He asked about my writings, what they brought in. I said twelve rix-dollars per signature. That's not much! We talked about life. I felt that here was an opportunity to ask for more, but it went against my more noble feelings. Then he said: "If I can ever be of any assistance to you in furthering your literary endeavors, just come to me!" I thanked him and said that at the moment there was nothing I needed. Rantzau, whom I accompanied home, said that the king had indeed been prompting me to make a request, but praised my noble feelings; promised, if the opportunity should arise, to put in a good word for me. I was a little dissatisfied with myself, but put my trust in God.

Andersen remained the guest of the royal couple until September 9, when he left Föhr to spend three weeks with Duke Christian August at Augusten-

borg Castle. During this visit he met Prince Frederik of Nør, the governor of Schleswig-Holstein, who, together with the duke, was to play an important role in the Schleswig-Holstein insurrection against Denmark in 1848.

Andersen's diary entries end on September 29, the day of his departure from Augustenborg. Upon reaching Copenhagen he busied himself with preparing the second installment of New Tales—*containing "The Fir Tree" and "The Snow Queen"—for publication in December 1844. A third installment appeared five months later, in April 1845. On October 31 of that year he set out on his third major European journey, and, as was his habit, he again began to keep his diary.*

October 31 [1845]. The last day of this tour in Copenhagen. Was with the king and queen. The whole day busy making visits. Said goodbye to the Collins at 1 o'clock; I didn't get to give my beloved Father Collin a kiss. Oh, I'm so worried I won't ever see him again!—God, as I roll out of the city this evening, how many hearses in the coming year will drive along this road with the names of dear ones shining from the coffins. Before, when I traveled abroad, I prayed: God, whatever Thy Will with me may be on this journey, let it be done. Now I say: God, whatever will happen to my friends during this long period?—I had a seat facing backward in the omnibus (nr. 15); Steinmann from the General Staff switched with me. Hofman-Bang was my neighbor. Professor Michaelis from Kiel came along. Jonna, Henrik, Gottlieb, Gusta, Viggo and Borgaard came to the post depot to say farewell. At midnight I was in Roskilde.

November 1. Over Ringsted and Slagelse to Korsør. Crossed the Great Belt in good weather. Very cold; leaves off the trees. Lange's theatrical company is in Nyborg; they were to have put on both *Mickey's Love Stories in Paris* and *A Comedy Out in the Open Air*. A carriage with four horses, a driver and servant were awaiting me. Arrived here at Glorup at 2 o'clock. His Excellency received me cordially. (Dr. Winther had already met me at Ørbæklunde.) Started a letter to Collin. In bed at 9:30.

November 2. Slept right up until 8 o'clock. Finished letters to Collin, Ørsted, van der Vliet; a short note to Borgaard. Will be sending this off in the mail this evening. Visited by the Langes from Ørbæklunde. Went up to Dr. Winther's, where I had some hot chocolate. Am comfortable in rooms no. 15 and 16, which face out on the garden. A fire in the tile stove, lovely sunshine. The water has been drained from the large pool, which is strewn with brown leaves.

Solitary and still. Winther and Biering were here for dinner with their wives. I have written a number of letters today.

November 3. Sent letters to Father Collin, to H. C. Ørsted, to Mary Howitt, van der Vliet, the hereditary grand duke of Weimar and a short note to Borgaard. There was frost last night. Took a walk in the garden. Later in the day, sunshine. A lovely fall day, with the leaves off the trees, but the sun is shining on the green grass, and the birds are chirping. You might almost think it was a spring day. The older man has moments like this in the fall, when his heart is still dreaming about spring. In the evening read *Agnete* aloud.

November 4. Soreness in my penis. Clear, freezing weather. Went for a walk. There is a strange mumbling in the forest. It has gotten old, but the springs and brooks are young; they are growing and babbling. There's a crackling noise with each gust of wind; it's the withered leaves falling. Started on Walter Scott's novel *St. Ronan's Well.*

November 5. His Excellency has driven to Odense today. I was alone in my room until 6:30, and it wasn't until then we had dinner. Had coffee with Winther in the morning; Mrs. Lindegaard and the Misses Ramshardt, who want to leave for Copenhagen on Tuesday, stopped in.—They stayed here at Glorup for dinner. Read through and corrected Petit's biography of me,[5] and worked on a letter to Zeise. It took the whole day.

November 6. A hard frost during the night. Already ice on the water for several days now. Constant soreness in my penis.—Walked for an hour. This evening I received my first letter from Father Collin.— How my day goes: up at 8 o'clock and drink coffee; putter around and write until 10 o'clock; then walk up along the long, tree-lined drive and out the gate to the path through the field to Hollufgaard; look at the strait and wander back; read, sew, put things in order; and lunch at 12 o'clock with a glass of port. Then a short rest and after that, as before, an hour's walk. It is the same route, and I take it a little farther out in the other direction. Read and write until around 4 o'clock, get dressed; and dinner is from 4:00 to 5:00. Now comes the most boring period, until 8 o'clock. I sit in my room; don't want to do anything, not to sleep either. One of the servants is playing a

5. A reference to "Des Dichters Lebensbild," published in Frederik Petit's translation of Andersen's *Fodreise fra Holmens Canal til Østpynten af Amager i Aarene 1828 og 1829* (1829) as *Abenteuer und Märchen einer Neujahrsnacht auf einer Fussreise nach Amack* (1846).

flute badly, practicing a piece; I'm reminded of the flute player at the quarantine station and have the same reaction. The wind is whistling outside; the fire in the tile stove is rumbling; the moon is shining in.—I don't want to think about home; I'll get homesick then!—Downstairs I conduct the entire conversation from 8 until 10 o'clock. Miss Lise's stomach growls. The only respite is when the servant calls His Excellency out, for the foreman is here now to talk with him. I look at the clock; it doesn't seem to be running at all; and when it finally does strike, each stroke falls as if marking time to a funeral march.—At 10 o'clock, upstairs; and a half hour later, in bed.

On November 10 Andersen left Glorup to spend ten days at Gråsten Castle as the guest of the duke of Augustenborg. He stopped for four days in Hamburg, where the artist Otto Speckter showed him the illustrations he had been working on for some of Andersen's tales. Andersen was particularly pleased with the one for "The Fir Tree" and promised to dedicate a volume of tales to Speckter. From Hamburg, he traveled via Oldenburg, where he visited his friends the Eisendechers and was invited several times to visit Grand Duke August, to Magdeburg and Berlin.

Friday, December 19. Up at 5:30. A porter took my baggage, and no one said anything to me about it. I blew up. Everything was all right, though. There was moonlight, ice on the ground. I sat completely alone through the first stations; rather used to the railroad. I didn't meet up with the man from Trier; his name was Hochmuth, I think. In Köthen we had to leave right away, so I couldn't get anything to eat or drink. None of my fellow travelers took any notice of me; none engaged me in conversation. We picked up an officer from Saxony and one with a Greek cap and eagle emblem. They called Jenny Lind "the divine."—Black ice and dreary. We were moving right along. At Grossbeeren there was a battle in 1813. Arrived at 1:15 in Berlin and took a room at the British Hotel; I sent a hired servant at once to Jenny Lind to announce that I had arrived and ask if she would get me a ticket. She sent word that I would get one, if any were available; but no one has come. Alone at the *table d'hôte.* I have a good room facing out over Unter den Linden.—The clock struck six; I went out then; it was raining and nasty. I arrived at the opera house; tickets for the parterre and balcony were still available. I went into the parterre. I had crude company there—soldiers and a drunken Frenchman. I stood by the door, listening to

Jenny; was actually inclined to be angry with her, but she melted me. She sings German the way I suppose I read my tales—where I come from shows through; but, as they say about me, this adds something interesting. The theater is splendidly magnificent, but I haven't looked at it; I was there only for Jenny's sake. I have heard her as if in a dream. I don't love her, I guess, the way everyone does.—I am not very happy, and yet it is pleasant here in this room. Today I feel so alone here in Berlin.

Saturday, December 20. Went to the post office, where I found a letter from Jette Hanck; then drove to 1 Hasenheidestrasse. Jenny was at a rehearsal; Mademoiselle Johansson had stayed at home to receive me. I was not pleased. Visited Kletke (8 Alte Jakobstrasse). He was just about to leave on a trip to Breslau. There I heard that Hitzig had suffered a stroke. Then went to see Baron Løvenørn (109 Leipzigerstrasse). He told about a theft here in the city. An officer had gone into a jeweler's shop and asked to see two costly pieces of jewelry for his bride. A little later, another officer from another regiment came; they knew each other. The first officer decided that the bride should choose which piece she wanted, took out a 200 rix-dollar bill and gave it to the jeweler as a deposit; asked his friend to stay there until he got back, as security for the jewelry. He left. A little later a police commissioner came: "You probably don't know me, but I'm a police commissioner sent by the police to inform you that there are some counterfeit bills going around;" and since he was a man exposed to this sort of thing, they wanted to warn him, in case he had any. "None, except for this one, that I just got this minute." "But it's false!" said the commissioner.—"False?" shouted the officer, and an argument began. "You will be so kind as to accompany me to the police station, but we'll take a cab to avoid a scandal." He took one; they drove away, but to their own home; and the jeweler had been swindled.—Visits all day. At home in the evening.

Sunday, December 21. Got a surprise early this morning when Holger Stampe stepped into my room. He had come here from Jena for Jenny's and my sake. Went to see Rauch, who pressed me into his arms, kissed me and said that my tales were immortal. Went to Olfers', where I have been invited on Friday evening.—Drove to see Jenny; she isn't receiving anyone, said the janitress. "Yes, me! Give her my card!' and then I didn't have one! "Tell her my name!"—Then she came to receive me herself; she looked as if she were flourishing even more than when she was in Copenhagen. We sat on the sofa and talked about the Collins. I ran into Count Wachtmeister, who has just been transferred to Brussels.—Visited Count Revent-low, who offered to convey my letters home. Was at Miss From-mann's, where I met Edmund's friend. . . . To the opera at the Tribune and saw Lachner's opera, *Catarina Cornaro;* the second act quite exciting. The sets magnificent. A young lady nodded to me and smiled from the first balcony. It was Gisela Arnim; she had rec-ognized me. Split my dress coat.

Monday, December 22. At Mrs. Zimmermann's, where I had my letter to the duke of Oldenburg translated. Received a visit at home from Engineer Jørgensen and from Baron Løvenørn. Drove out to see Alexander Humboldt, who said that I didn't need any letters of recommendation—my writings were my recommendation—and that the king wished to see me. We talked about Jenny Lind and differ-ent countries, about Oehlenschläger, about Ørsted, who has sent him a book about esthetics.—Went out to see Hosemann, a small, stocky, fat fellow, whose place was in a state of inspired chaos. Called on Minister Savigny; they both received me very cordially, invited me for Saturday evening. Later Countess Bismarck-Bohlen came, and she invited me for Thursday. Bettina has left, they said; and sud-denly the door opened, and in she waddled, slovenly, peculiar!—"You are looking better this year than last!" she said. "Go to your room," she said to her daughter, "you haven't gotten any prettier; he has!"—I said something, God knows what. "He's naive!" she said, gave me one finger and asked me not notice her disappear-ance.—Ate with Stampe at the Café Royal. Yesterday it said in the *Frankfurt Times* and *The Correspondent* that I was spending my second week in Oldenburg and giving pleasure with my costly tales at the Court and in private circles.—Ate with Holger Stampe at the Café Royal; the evening at Miss Frommann's, where the young Ulrich was, the poet Ungern-Sternberg, etc.—I read a number of tales. +

Tuesday, December 23. Somewhat indisposed. Visited Dr. Froriep; trudged out to see Stampe.—Sent a letter to the grand duke of Old-enburg.—Visited Dr. Häring—alias Willibald Alexis—who intro-duced me to his wife, an English woman. I had to translate for him a letter from Miss Bremer. Geibel is here. Not really in a good mood; feel a little lonely!—Jenny still hasn't sent a ticket. I've already been given one this evening by Miss Frommann from the princess of Prussia.—I'd written to Stampe that he could have the ticket Jenny was going to sent me; he has been here several times. No one has come. I was annoyed. Took a numbered seat and sat next to Miss

Frommann in front of the widow Mrs. Schinkel and a Tyrolean sculptress; behind me was a married couple. The young wife embarked on a conversation, asked me if I were a compatriot of Jenny Lind's. I said I was Danish. "Then do you know your famous countryman Andersen?" "Yes, somewhat!" I answered. Miss Frommann laughed silently. "I love his *Only a Fiddler* and *Picture Book.*"—"Indeed, you've seen his picture, haven't you?" "No!"—I could feel myself blushing. "God," she said, "it isn't you, is it?" I said yes, and she carried on about how lucky she was, etc. She was a daughter of the poetess Hohenhausen in Cassel; she was here with her husband Chief Councillor of State Rüdiger, from Minden in Westphalia. Jenny sang so beautifully that I wasn't angry with her.—No, no! She can't have forgotten me! Letter from Humboldt. Letter from the tailor Worch.

Wednesday, December 24. A visit form Dr. Meyn and Stampe; made an appointment at the lord chamberlain's. Sent a letter to Ross in Halle. Went out to see Jenny; no one at home; left a letter. This morning I composed for Mrs. Zimmermann a poem to her based on the copper etching *St. Catherine's Body Taken to Sinai by Angels!* Letter to Jørgensen that I didn't want to write a song for them. Visited Geibel. "I've written a poem against the Danes!" he said. "Indeed, two!" I said. He clasped my hand and said: "We'll stay friends, won't we!" He was very hearty. Visited Jacob Grimm, who talked with me about tales. Cornelius is in Italy. Was at Miss Frommann's and wrote for her a poem to Ulrich in a copy of my tales. Sent a letter to Mrs. Eisendecher. Haven't heard anything from Jenny. I'm feeling badly treated and sad!—She's not acting toward me like a sister here in Berlin; if I'd been a stranger to her here, then she could have told me what was wrong; and I would have done something about it!— She once filled my heart—I don't love her any more! In Berlin she has cut out the diseased flesh with a cold knife!—I wonder what she could be thinking about, since she is taking so little notice of me, I who came to Berlin mostly for her sake, I who could have spent a much more joyous Christmas Eve.—In Copenhagen I lived for her— what good did it do me? I have given a lot, and to someone the world calls the noblest and finest!—Now it is Christmas Eve! How happy it must be in a home where a man has a hearth! Now the Christmas tree is being lit. The wife is standing with the smallest child on her arm; it is stretching its hands out toward the many candles and is jumping up and down with joy on its mother's arm; the other children are clamoring and looking for what they might have gotten, and a circle of friends is sitting there.—The stranger abroad—his Christmas trees are the starry skies; his pictures, new cities, new faces!—He rushes along!—Under God's Christmas tree I raise my head and ask: "Father, what have I been granted?"—and maybe it'll be a coffin. Half sick, I went at 8 o'clock to Mrs. Zimmermann's. There was quite a commotion there, *à la* Madam Trumfmeier.[6] There I met a lady-in-waiting to the princess of Prussia, a composer, a painter. Two angels stood with flags around the Christmas tree. I received a beautifully bound book to write in and a lampshade. The ladies sang; I read a couple of tales. Was home at 11 o'clock. Everyone was asleep in the hotel. I went quietly to bed.

Thursday, December 25, Christmas Day. There is a veil over my thoughts, but they fly toward Jenny!—What have I done to her!—Is it out of caution for her reputation that she is taking so little notice of me? "I don't hate you, because I have never loved you," she once said. I didn't understand it; now I do. A visit from the young Ulrich. Drove out to see Reuscher at 8 Fliederstrasse, where I drank coffee. At home Professor Rauch had been by. A little indisposed from walking in the raw air. A letter from Jenny; she is very endearing. Dinner at Professor Weiss's, where they made a great fuss over me. Mrs. Weiss kept patting me on the hand. Horkel and Dr. Meyn, etc., were there.—The evening at Count Bismarck-Bohlen's, where I read two tales. Wilhelm Grimm was there; his personality appealed to me. He liked "The Fir Tree" a lot. There I met the Swedish ambassador, Count d'Ohsson!

Friday, December 26. A letter from Ross. Out to see Jenny, who had a Christmas tree; she gave me a bar of soap in the shape of a piece of cheese, Eau de Cologne; was so wonderful, patted me, called me a child. We drove together over to see Madam Birch-Pfeiffer, whom she said was like a mother to her. In the carriage she said that she probably wouldn't be going back to Sweden, that her situation there was frightful, that she would probably go to Hamburg and stay there with the Arnemanns, that she felt so at home in Germany. Madam Birch-Pfeiffer didn't know anything at all about my writings. Little by little she grew more amiable. Jenny said I was such a good person and a brother to her. When I got home, I found an invitation from the king for dinner at the palace. I had to send regrets to Rauch's, where I was to have eaten. At 3 o'clock, accompanied by a servant, I drove to the palace, where Lord Chamberlain von Meyerinck re-

6. A character from Johan Ludvig Heiberg's singspiel *April Fools* (*Aprilsnarrene*, 1826).

ceived me!—The king was very gracious; talked a lot about *Only a Fiddler;* said that when he was in Copenhagen he had at once asked about me. He wasn't familiar with my tales. The queen deplored our crown prince's illness, spoke warmly of their majesties, etc.—At the table I sat between Humboldt and the lord chamberlain. The king asked me about Bissen. After dinner he and the queen again talked with me for a long time, and the king requested that I call on him the next time I was in Berlin.—A von Norden and several gentlemen said hello to me!—In the evening went to Miss Frommann's, where there was a big party awaiting me. The Christmas tree was lit; I read some tales. At 9 o'clock I went to see Olfers, who also had a Christmas tree and where I met· Varnhagen von Ense, Rauch and the sculptor Tieck.

Saturday, December 27. A letter to Countess Moltke and a tale to the king of Prussia. Terrible downpour and slush.—In the *Prussian Times* it says that I am here and that I belong more to Germany than to my fatherland. Dinner at home. A letter from Father and Jonna; wrote several letters myself. The evening at Savigny's, where both the brothers Grimm were. I read "The Snow Queen" and "The Swineherd." There were several foreigners there. Young Savigny, who has been in Spain, promised me a letter of recommendation for there. Letters from Father Collin and Jonna.

Sunday, December 28. Rain and wind. It is foul weather. Summoned to the princess of Prussia's residence. In the vestibule, or where I waited, was a garden with vines, a statue, fresh water; in one of the other rooms—painted in Pompeian style—statues and books; the floors were as slick as ice. She received me extremely graciously; looks like her brother. We talked about Thorvaldsen. She has read that I have written about him, also my *Picture Book.* I read "The Fir Tree" and "The Ugly Duckling." She seemed delighted. Her son, who one day will be king, pressed my hand two times and then asked me to write my name in a book he brought. I wrote: "Gott segne die edlen Herzen!"—The princess said: "Indeed, we must meet once again before you leave." A playmate of the prince, along with the little princess, an officer and the teacher Curtius from Lübeck, were there. Had the wrong umbrella. I ran around and finally found mine at the Zimmermann's. Visited Weiss; a letter to Jenny; dinner at home. A visit at Miss Frommann's, where I made the acquaintance of a Frenchman Sougey Avisard, a friend of Bindesbøll's. The evening at Professor Weiss's, where I met Chamisso's two sons and two daughters. I was really fussed over.

Monday, December 29. Posed for a painter. Early in the morning the nature poet Worch, a tailor, came. In order to hear Jenny he had gone to the supervisor of the extras and been made one in *Norma*— a Roman soldier. He had stood quite close to her and been moved. One mustn't do that, and now he isn't allowed to go there any more. I offered him a rix-dollar for a ticket; he wouldn't take it. I gave him a copy of my tales; then he did accept the rix-dollar. He looked poverty-stricken. I saw from my window when he came that he went around into a side street and combed his hair. He told about his walking tour in the Harz. The man has sensitivity. I said I would visit him. "There are so many stairs—but you won't see a view like that anywhere else in Berlin; I can see the sun rise." Sat for a young painter. A visit from Dr. Horkel. Drove out to see Jenny, who was at a rehearsal. Drove to visit Reuscher, who put on an extremely elegant dinner. Present was the publisher Simion, who wanted to arrange for a collected edition of my writings with a portrait; I was to sit for an artist. Walked home and felt somewhat unwell from it. The evening at Mrs. Zimmermann's, where there was a big party— the young Reimerts, Titular Privy Councillor Matthes and Cornelius' sister. It was almost 1 o'clock when I got home.

Tuesday, December 30. Downpour. Sent letters to (a) Ørsted, Jette Hanck and Mrs. Balling; (b) Collin, Edvard, Jonna. Went to Reventlow's, where I met his wife and Mrs. Voss and accepted an invitation for Saturday evening. Visited Theodor Mügge, who was very charming. (On Thursday I'll be going with him to Mundt's.) We talked about all kinds of things. I've been troubled a bit by palpitations.—It's 2 o'clock and still no ticket from Jenny. If there's none this time, too, then I'll be angry!—This instant a ticket from Jenny came—no. 116 parquet right. Dinner at Savigny's—Mrs. Voss, Olfers, Mrs. . . . and the Minister of Foreign Affairs—a strange, dry physiognomy. I read "The Nightingale." He looked at me strangely; no one laughed. I had the uncomfortable feeling they didn't understand it. I chatted some and got into the worst mood, which stuck with me at the opera, where I sat behind Madam Birch-Pfeiffer.— Jenny's acting was gripping; her voice didn't really move me in this music. She was given a curtain call; the opera, booed. Chamisso wanted me to come along with him this evening, but I wasn't in the mood and ambled home.

Wednesday, December 31. Hardly out of bed this morning when Reuscher came. He is to oversee a collected edition of my writings. Simion wants to give me two *louis d'or* for each signature of my biography, which I will supply, and the same for my new novel. Right after that, Lieutenant Chamisso came, after that the poet . . . I couldn't get dressed. At 12:30 I went to see Olfers. He took me on a special tour of the museum—superb, painted clay busts of, among others, Machiavelli; altar tablets. A *Venus [. . .]*, an *Apollo Musagetes*. I saw the coin cabinet and the vase collection. Visited Miss Frommann. Letter to Humboldt. Dinner here at home. Went at 6 o'clock out to Jenny's, where a Christmas tree was lit in my honor. Jenny sang a couple of songs; we talked jovially. She asked me about *The New Lying-in Room* and said that she believed and didn't believe that I had written it, because I was a child and it was malicious.— As we were sitting and eating ice cream, there was a sound as if a note had been struck on the piano, but stronger. "What was that!" we both said.—But the piano wasn't vibrating; it couldn't have come from there. "What note was it?" I asked. "It was a C!" "My God, Collin!" I cried and I was overwhelmed by a dread that brought tears to my eyes. I said the name to Jenny and told her that I had always been afraid of visions and had therefore only wanted to hear from my loved ones by means of tones when they died!—Jenny also became frightened. I was depressed.—Jenny was to go to a ball given by the English ambassador, Count Westmoreland. (The story about it untrue.) I helped to pick ribbons. Received a ticket to the Tribune on Friday, a promise of her picture; she wrote a few words for me from Rückert's poem to Alexander Beaulieu-Marconnay. Went to Miss Frommann's; was listless. There was a big party there and tableaus! I received a beautiful drawing as a frontispiece for my tales. I got home at 12:30! Thank Thee, oh dear God, for the old year! May the curtain rise on a new, happy one! Thy will be done!

Thursday, January 1 [1846]. The curtain is rising on the New Year, on "The Tale of My Life's Journey"! God, Thou art composing it; Thy will is for the best. The weather is gray and wet. I went to see Theodor Mügge. He led me over to the actress Miss Hagn; she had received a letter from a pseudonymous Danish translator of *King René's Daughter,* inquiring whether she was interested in it. I said that Hertz himself had translated it and that I would write to him. She told about Nielsen, that he had appeared in *Cabal and Love* in Munich and was so flustered at having to speak German that instead of saying, "Louise, you look pale," he said, "Louise, you look stale!" The whole theater burst into laughter; she scarcely knew what she should do.—She knew that Mrs. Heiberg was an excellent, famous artist. We drove to see Mundt; he had left for Stettin. At home

I was surprised by a visit from the wife of Minister Savigny. The servant announced her arrival; the stately carriage was waiting outside. She sat in the sofa with me for a quarter of an hour, said that she and her husband, "we old folks were really looking forward to another visit from you!" She was very convivial and nice. Dinner at old Professor Horkel's. There I saw both the brothers Grimm; Wilhelm is always teasing me. Weiss and his wife.—When I came home this evening, I found a letter from Humboldt to the effect that the king had ordered him to write me if it was convenient for me, with regard to my trip, to come to Potsdam, then he wanted to invite me. I was pleased about it. The evening with Professor Bekker, who says nothing in seven languages. Here I met a Countess Ahlefeldt, who couldn't speak Danish. Curtius was there.

During Andersen's stay in Berlin, several publishing houses were negotiating with him for the right to publish a new edition of his collected works in German. It was finally granted to the Danish-born Carl B. Lorck of Leipzig, and it was for this edition that Vilhelm Pedersen was later to do his famous fairy tale illustrations.

On January 6, the day before he left Berlin, Andersen was dubbed a knight of the Red Eagle by the king of Prussia, Friedrich Wilhelm IV—it was his first decoration. Indeed, his entire trip southward through Germany was a triumphal march. In Oldenburg he read his tales aloud for the grand duke, and he was almost the daily guest of his dear friend Hereditary Grand Duke Carl Alexander in Weimar. In Leipzig he was feted by the publisher Brockhaus and praised lavishly by Mendelssohn-Bartholdy, as he smugly informed Edvard Collin in his letter of February 14: ". . . when Mendelssohn-Bartholdy heard me read for the first time, he rushed joyfully up to me and said, 'But you read fabulously; no one reads fairy tales like you!' And I'd done it in German!—Well, my dear boy, it seems you don't really know what you have in me!" In Dresden in late February, he was summoned to the court of King Friedrich August II of Saxony to read his tales; and while in Vienna in March, the Archduchess Sophie asked him to visit her and to bring along some tales suitable for her son, the future Emperor Franz Joseph.

Andersen arrived in Rome on March 31 and remained there for the entire month of April, pleased to be the center of attention of the Scandinavian and German colonies there. But, even so, he reported later in his autobiography that he did not feel entirely at home: ". . . Rome is not the Rome of thirteen years ago, when I was here for the first time. It is as if everything has been modernized, even the ruins—the grass and bushes have been removed, and

The River Tiber in Rome

everything has been tidied up; the folk life seems less evident." On the first
of May he left Rome for Naples, where he stayed for almost two months. He
busied himself with sightseeing and his autobiography The True Story of
My Life, which Lorck wished to use as an introduction to his new edition
of Andersen's collected works.

When a protracted heat wave began, with temperatures reaching as high
as 100 degrees Fahrenheit, Andersen spent most of his time indoors. On
June 9, he began on a new tale he called "The Story of My Shadow," in
which he recorded his impressions of Naples in the grip of this enervating
heat. His impressions also spilled over into his diary from this period.

Tuesday, June 16. Went bathing. Received a letter form Ørsted and
his wife. It is oppressively hot. Took the singer Gnosspelius to see
Miss Fjeldsted. There is a frightful din in the streets, an eternal ringing of cowbells, goats with smaller bells, a screaming and screeching; and then I live right across from someone who practices figured
bass or tunes piano for the whole town. It's a grabbing, roaring,

screaming, rending maelstrom for the ears; blacksmiths hammer, wagons roll, boys scream and people who are talking quietly about household affairs seem to be having a fight. Trouble with my passport, which Ferrari didn't want to have stamped with a visa for Genoa, because it was "throwing money away!" he said. The steamer officials declared it was necessary. I was annoyed by Ferrari's highhanded interference.—A little upset, terribly hot. Drove to S. Severo's, where there was a superb marble Christ figure with a marble veil over it; you thought you could see every feature through the stone. A marble figure in a fishnet—that was supposed to be the prince himself. A second figure, his consort portrayed as Modesty, also with veil.

Wednesday, June 17. Went to Rothschild's, waited an hour there for the cashier and got what remained of my letter of credit—300 marks sterling. I took eighteen *napoléons d'or.* Already felt faint with the heat; drove home, wrote a letter to little Augusta Bournonville in Paris, which I gave to Miss Fjeldsted, who is leaving today at 3 o'clock with the *Polyphemus.* Said goodbye to her and went up to rest. Stomach upset, my body limp, the heat intolerable. A messenger from the Prussian ambassador inquiring about the state of my health. It isn't possible to get a little sleep because of the noise. My neighbor is especially bothersome—those repetitive finger exercises, that eternal playing of scales. It was like being mentally tickled on the same spot from morning to evening.—Dinner at Vogt's; old Brockenhuus was talking nonsense there—saying that there is cholera here in Naples! Indeed, that's a fine state of affairs! Now we'll have to stay in quarantine! We ate extraordinarily well. Afterward I read without strain "The Ugly Duckling," but dreaded reading one more, because I could feel my strength was taxed to the utmost. They asked me to and I read the shortest, but was very fatigued, had to have some vinegar to inhale. Was given a few drops; and when we left, I was about to collapse before we reached the carriage. Thomsen supported me by the arm; as soon as I was seated and under way, I felt better. At home that decent fellow brought me some ice cream, sat and chatted with me.—The air, heavy and warm.

Thursday, June 18. Slept in front of the open balcony doors with a sheet over me, but it was no better than just bearable. Slept less than restfully.—This morning bathed with Herbst. A heavy heat lay over the mountains; it is like being in a new sphere of air.—Vogt said yesterday that during his long stay in Naples it had never happened that it had been as hot as it is now in June. It's seventy-nine degrees.—Dinner at the Prussian ambassador's. The new pope [Pius IX] has already been elected. It is a Cardinal Ferretti, who isn't old and is considered to have character. Moltke-Hvitfeldt and Bergman ate with us. Then I was asked to come and read just one tale. I excused myself because of my listlessness, but the request was wrapped in so many compliments: "You yourself are the reason people are plaguing you! Why did you read the way you did last time?" After dinner, somewhat limp. Moltke-Hvitfeldt went for a drive with me. At 6 o'clock was the procession to the four altars—two on Via Toledo, one at S. Carlo and one on Largo del Castello. We were still able to see some of the spectacle at Largo—there were fusillades and there was music. It was beautiful to see how the balconies and roofs were filled with people. Drove with Moltke-Hvitfeldt across Capodimonte. Vesuvius was spewing fire; the reflection lay across the water.

Friday, June 19. Bathed. Sent my autobiography to Lorck. Felt exhausted from the writing. The heat, the same. I have a burning sensation in my rear end; it's making me a little uneasy because of my

Tasso's home at Sorrento (dated March 7, 1834)

departure. I've lost over fifty rix-dollars for the steamer if I don't leave on schedule. Took a carriage and drove past the Villa Reale, out to Queen Giovanna's Palace. Got home at 9 o'clock. Tomorrow Læssøe will be leaving for Sorrento.—The heat is very debilitating.— Yesterday Thomsen was at Largo to find Conradin's grave in a church which is in a cellar. There was supposed to be a knight carved out of stone, but no one knew anything about it. You could read: "Hic jacet . . ." What remained, the most important part, was plastered over. Miss Løvmann has said in a letter to Mrs. Vogt that Jonna and Henrik Stampe have celebrated their wedding. The lowest bishop in Naples gets more per year than Denmark's highest bishop. In the evening someone walks along the street here with a swinging lantern and gathers everything up in his basket. The nights, very dark; the stars, dull. Today half decided to give up on Spain or, rather, gotten used to the idea of letting it be and heading into Switzerland. This evening when I was driving past Castel dell'Ovo, I saw eight flames on the water; it looked like fairies playing. Most painters render Italy's air as if it were a piece of blue cloth. They forget the delicate nuances, the progression from the horizon to the intense blue above. Claude Lorrain has seen and portrayed Italy. Right across from me lives a family. The wife is hunchbacked and hunchbellied. She is sitting thinly dressed, with a wide, hairless part in her hair; her handkerchief lies folded on the chair in front of her. There stands her serious husband, like a real man below the belt and like one above, too, but without any clothes on there. He is very serious. The maid is sitting on the third balcony sewing. The husband is getting his exercise walking from his wife to the next balcony and back again, but every time he reaches the maid, he says "pussycat" and pokes her with his finger. Then he goes back to standing and talking seriously with his old hunchbellied wife. He doesn't realize that he has an observer right across from him.

On June 23 Andersen left Naples on a ship bound for Marseille, where he met Ole Bull. The Norwegian violinist had just returned from a trip to the United States and could tell Andersen about his great popularity on the other side of the Atlantic and about the inexpensive American editions of his works that reached thousands of people. Because of the oppressive heat in southern France and the passport difficulties he encountered there, he abandoned his plan to continue to Spain, deciding instead to head at a leisurely pace for home over France, Switzerland, and Germany. As a fitting close to this triumphal journey, he received in Oldenburg a letter from Jonas Collin, informing him that the had been awarded the Order of the Dannebrog by the Danish king. He wrote his last diary entry of the trip a week later, on October 5, the day he left Oldenburg on his way to Copenhagen via Hamburg and Kiel.

In England
1847

W HEN THE DANISH KING CHRISTIAN *VIII suggested to him in 1847 that he visit England, Andersen was already a celebrated author there—Mary Howitt's translations of* The Improvisa-*tore,* O. T., *and* Only a Fiddler *had been published by Richard Bentley in 1845, followed by four volumes of his tales in 1846. Indeed, Andersen replied that he had already been planning such a trip! William Jerdan, the publisher of the influential* Literary Gazette *and one of his most fervent British admirers, had made this suggestion in November 1846 and several months later had written him, by way of encouragement, of Charles Dickens's interest in meeting him.*

Andersen began his diary for the journey on May 13, the day of his departure from Copenhagen. He traveled first to Germany, stopping several days in Hamburg and Oldenburg. From there he went on to Utrecht and Amsterdam, where he was enthusiastically greeted by everyone he met, and to The Hague, where a formal dinner was given in his honor by Holland's leading artists and writers. On June 22 he left Rotterdam for London, arriving there just a few days before the publication of the English translation of his autobiography, The True Story of My Life.

Wednesday, June 23 [1847]. At 7 o'clock I was on deck and saw England's east coast.—Our ship was sailing slowly; we didn't arrive in London until 5 o'clock.—The Thames bears witness to the fact that England rules the ocean. From here its servants sally forth, whole hosts of ships. Every minute a courier (steamer) arrives; the others have decked out their stovepipe hats: that one over there had a long smoke-crepe with a red fire-flower peeking out.—The long white wake trails behind them.—The coast, probably fifteen to twenty miles wide. The ships come running under full sail, pluming themselves like swans. Thousands of fishboats, like a teeming marketplace, like a brood of chicks, like confetti. Steamer after steamer, like rockets in a great fireworks display.—At Gravesend it looked like a big marsh fire, and it was the smoke from the steamers!—The pleasure yachts of rich, young gentlemen. A splendid thunderstorm; lightning struck several times to the north, and a railroad train raced along with its blue smoke against the black clouds—these things appealed to me more than the massive, sooty buildings on the other side of the Thames. "They know you're here and bid you welcome!" an Englishman said to me. Indeed, I thought, the Lord knows—he's the one making it thunder. (Once, in our age of greatness, Denmark's king was England's; but it's just as well things turned out as they did—after all, languages form the boundaries between countries.)— At the customhouse a man waved at me. It's Beckwith, I thought; and it was him, but I didn't wave back. The Englishmen aboard had warned me not to trust anyone when I went ashore, not to take up with anyone. I was the first one of all to tread upon English ground. Beckwith showed me the letter he had from me. I was the last one into the customhouse because they had forgotten to put me on the passenger list.—Drove to the Sablonière Hotel, got a room facing on the courtyard; the windows had so much soot on them that my sleeves were blackened. The sun is shining in on the bed to show that there is a sun here.—Beckwith had been waiting for me since 8 o'clock this morning; I was very embarrassed about it. Drank some stout and went to bed.

Thursday, June 24. Sunshine, clouds. Drove out to see Reventlow, who received me very cordially and discoursed at length about England and the English: they do not pay compliments; they say what they mean. Talked about Koss, who had sent dispatches home with anecdotes about the court, things that had not the least importance. He said that it was all a matter of etiquette; it wasn't, as in Germany, that artists and royalty associated with one another.—Gave me a letter from Lorck.—Drove home in an omnibus. Drove out to Marlborough House; was admitted to a royal chamber. The hereditary grand duke came, embraced me and kissed me. We sat together; he said to me that he felt restricted here. It wasn't possible for him to meet with literary figures; you didn't even dare mention that you wanted to see Lady Blessington. Everything was cliques. Dickens had written in *Punch*, and therefore you couldn't talk with him. They'll die from etiquette, he said. The queen herself was bound by it—two breakfasts and dinner in the evening at 8 o'clock.—They were outside in the lovely parks, but the queen had to be home by 8 o'clock.— Because of etiquette, she couldn't enjoy herself the way one does in Germany.—"But she is queen!" I said, "she can say, 'I want to!' "—

Page from Andersen's diary

"Yes, I said the same thing; 'You must surely be able to see whomever you wish!' "—'It wouldn't do; people all over England would
take exception," she said. "This is the land of freedom, where you
die from etiquette. Oh, then let me sing the praises of my little Ettersburg!"—How difficult it is to judge a country as a stranger there
for just a short time. You can see this best by reading the descriptions and impressions of others of one's own country!—There you
find written down what given individuals have to tell, construed
from their own points of view. There you find what the author has
seen through the jouncing eyeglasses of his own travels, so to speak.
He describes landscapes as seen fleetingly from a train window, and
not even as accurately as that.—He asked me to visit him between
12 and 2 o'clock as frequently as I could and gave me his hand and
extended a greeting to Jenny Lind. No letter from her. They thought
that my letter yesterday must have gone astray, because the street
number was lacking. Went to the Royal Italian Opera House. Did a
lot of running around; finally managed to send off a card and, later,
a new letter. At home I found a letter from her with the warmest of
welcomes. Plodded around the streets and oriented myself to some
degree in the immediate neighborhood; had two spells of limpness
and exhaustion. Was at Trafalgar Square, where Nelson's statue stands
on a pillar with two fountains. The first thing I saw when I went
out today was a window with my own picture in it from *Howitt's
Journal*; bought a copy later.—Music in the streets and a little girl
was dancing. A puppet theater.—Here is the liveliness of Naples,
but without its tumult. It more closely resembles Paris in a more
concentrated form.—("Don't worry about your letter of credit," Reventlow said today, "I'll advance you anything.")

Friday, June 25. Drove this morning out to Hambro's, a terribly
long drive. Met Bang, whose wife is away in Odense. He had received my letter of credit and let me have five pounds. When I got
home, I thought I'd been given too little and wrote a letter about it.
Went to the bank, a magnificent building with a statue of Victoria in
the middle of it. Drove out to see Jenny Lind, who lives infinitely
far out. The carriage pulled up and Mademoiselle Johansson came
out and called "welcome"; after her, Jenny Lind. She has the whole
house, which is extremely comfortable—a lovely little garden with
mown grass, flowers and shady paths. She invited me to eat with
her whenever I wished, even today; but since it was so early, I didn't
accept. She said that she would see to it that I got a ticket to the
opera, since it would otherwise be ridiculously expensive—thirty to

HANS CHRISTIAN ANDERSEN

THE DANISH POET.

FROM AN ORIGINAL PORTRAIT BY CARL HARTMANN.

Portrait (etching published in Howitt's Journal, June 26, 1847)

fifty Danish rix-dollars.—She found 150 pounds for my novel too beggarly; here you must demand an exaggerated price for everything. She had a little dog she had bought and was playing with.

"That was nice!" she said when I told her that the Dutch had drunk a toast to Collin.—Went over to see Reventlow, who again held forth at length on the power of the aristocracy—no one dared to drive on his closed-off street, except for those who had an errand there. A cow that had slipped in one place had caused a stir and attracted a whole crowd of people. That street is protected by barriers.—Mrs. Reventlow had said of Jenny Lind that she was a virtuous young lady; you could tell that by looking at her. I talked with Countess Reventlow, who was very friendly. Arrived home tired and hungry. A visit from Grímur Thomsen, who is here in London; he didn't find me in. A letter to Prince Albert.

Saturday, June 26. Drove to call on Grímur Thomsen without finding him in. After that I saw Hambro, who said that I could have as much money as I wanted; invited me out in the country tomorrow to stay with him, but I can't go. Read Danish newspapers. He told about Baggesen, that he had been in debtors' prison in Paris. You risk your life here driving among the carriages.—Was in the bank with the statue of Victoria in it. This morning a letter came from the hereditary grand duchess. Spoke with her and with Ziegesar. Drove out to see Reventlow; went in vain with him to call on Lady Morgan. Felt indisposed and anxious about the big world I shall now venture into. Drove with Reventlow and his eldest daughter to Lord Palmerston's; the highest of the nobility were here. Mrs. Palmerston somewhat resembles Madam Hanck and Mrs. von Holten. Talked with Ziegesar; I was presented to the one lady after the other. Each one knew almost all of my writings. The hereditary grand duchess introduced me to the duchess of Suffolk; she was delighted with *The Improvisatore,* the *first* book about Italy! The hereditary grand duke shook my hand. It was so hot there; I could hardly manage standing on my feet and had to go out for some air. People say that the aristocracy in England excludes all artists from their circle; I can't say that—I found the friendliest people, the heartiest reception. They say that Dickens and D'Israeli are excluded from these circles; they acknowledged me, they accepted me. Whether it was the influence of the Danish ambassador—he introduced me—that was responsible for this, I don't know.—Was introduced to the duchess of Sutherland, who is supposed to be the richest lady in England. The son of Duke Bernhard of Weimar was there. Bunsen and his wife welcomed me in a most friendly way. English ladies overwhelmed me with enthusiasm for "The Ugly Duckling," "The Top and the Ball," *The Improvisatore.*—Their toilettes expensive and tasteful. One lady was in red satin with black lace, all dressed to dance the "Cachu-cha"! Diamonds glittered and huge bouquets in people's hands caught the eye. We were standing crowded against each other, and I was dragged through the most densely packed groups. The duke of Cambridge asked about the king of Denmark.

Sunday June 27. A little more quiet in the city. Ate breakfast at Lyell's, whose ladies will now be traveling to Scotland. His most recent geographical work, translated into Spanish. Dinner at the Reventlows' with Hartmann. Sent letters to Ørsted and Baroness Pechlin. To Edvard, Jette and Augusta.—Leicester Square is not a fashionable quarter; that sort of thing is always noticed in high society. A visit from Count Barck. Was at the hereditary grand duke's.

Monday, June 28. Sat for the painter Møller. Out to see Hambro, who discovered that it wasn't today but next week that I'm to go to visit Lord Castlereagh. Came with his own carriage and took me out to the country. It was as if London had sunk into the ground—refreshing nature, velvet green grass, beautiful sunlight, everything of princely dimensions. Most people could speak Danish. Cows and horses ornamented the meadows. The railroad train rushed beneath the precincts of the city.—A bluish vapor lay over London. Departed by carriage at 10 o'clock; was at the Reventlows at 11 o'clock and drove to Lady Poulett's—terribly hot, packed with people on the steps, in the rooms; the dancers had something like a tabletop to move around on. Spoke with Lady Palmerston, Lady Stanley, etc. Lots of beautiful roses, baskets on the walls filled with roses and periwinkle, a table looking as if entirely covered with roses. I was about to faint a couple of times from heat and exhaustion. This is supposed to be a pleasure! I couldn't get away until 2:30. On Sunday I was at Lady Morgan's—small rococo rooms, an old, lively, heavily made-up woman, a balcony looking out on the courtyard overloaded with flowers. She owned *The Night* drawn by Thorvaldsen. She said she would invite all of London's famous authors in my honor. In the greatest haste she had, said Reventlow, managed to gather together and read around in a number of my writings. Letter to Lorck.

Tuesday, June 29. An invitation from President Laurie to dinner on Wednesday. Turned it down. Drove out to Bielke's; found there a letter from Lady Morgan with an invitation for Wednesday evening from Lady Duff-Gordon, a daughter of Miss Austin, the author. Somewhat indisposed.—"Where do you live?" and if you respond with an unfashionable neighborhood, then you're finished. "I live in Peter Madsen's Alley"[1]—that's like saying Leicester Square, even though it's next to the elite quarter. Indeed, a few years ago it was a part of it; and it is a large square with trees, a lawn and a statue of Leicester. Visited Miss Grahn, who didn't look as if she were doing well. She asked right away about Miss Nielsen's virtue, whether she had been with other men than the prince, and I said that people had taken exception to it. She asked me to say to Miss Nielsen that it was all right; you should do what you wanted. She said that H.'s wife has a baby. Then she started to ask: "What kind of a man is it that J. L. has taken up with? There is a lot of talk about it; it's really ruining her reputation." Somebody, I answered, who is taking care of her affairs!—"Yes, but he's not taking care of her affairs at night; it must be strange, indeed! He's actually sleeping there!—Don't trust anyone, A.!" I found it contemptible, but typical, in that she said "bravo" to Miss Nielsen, that it was all right; but found a fantasy reprehensible!—"How is my old lover doing!—He's gotten so disgustingly fat!" There was something so crude in everything she said; I don't think a woman of the streets would have spoken any differently. Either that or it was a frivolous French conversation in sober Danish.—I've never talked like that with a woman, as I did with her—that's a fine thing! Her mother was sitting and shaking her head dumbly, saying: "Goodness gracious!"—That dotard! "Do come tomorrow; it's my birthday." At home a visit from Reventlow and little Christian; someone had admitted him into the salon. I came down, having jumped up from a sound sleep. While I was eating, Viscount Mahon came; I was nonplussed, apologized; and when I apologized for a second time, he sprang up, exclaiming: "I'm disturbing you; I'll come some other time!" And then he took off. I was surprised and distressed; thought I'd handled myself clumsily, and this was just the fellow who might write home about it to Wynn. A maid came with a letter from Lucile Grahn, asking me if I wouldn't come to her loge this evening.—When I visited Barck today, he gave me an entry ticket to the stalls in Her Majesty's Theatre. (A writer has said that he saw a man standing from morning to evening on the same spot—he was waiting to cross the street. This is an exaggeration, but illustrative, nonetheless. Almost everyone must wait for a few seconds to be able to cross where two main streets intersect; however, these intersections are not, as in some cities, infrequent, but infinitely numerous. It is the quantity of them that is

1. A street in Copenhagen known for its prostitutes.

astonishing.) Went to the theater and saw *The Elixir of Love* with Lablache and son. The tenor, Gardoni, appealed to me the most. "People say that I should take up with him," said Miss Grahn, "and I don't even know him!"—I was in her loge for all of the second act and the interlude; she was there alone with her mother. "Don't ever marry!" she said, "it's just crazy!"—She talked about Hornemann— he shouldn't get married; he should keep his name in mind! She was witty. She told about who was keeping the various danseuses; said that Taglioni had asked her straight away whether she had any children. "Not that it matters!" Taglioni had said!—Went down to my seat and saw the rest.—At home and in bed by 1:30.

Wednesday, June 30. The painter Møller came and sketched me. A visit from Lange, the master tailor from Odense.—Then Mary How- itt came with her daughter, just when I was going to drive out to see her. She welcomed me very cordially, showed me my biography dedicated to Jenny Lind; said I should get some money for it from her, several pounds. Offered me ten pounds per signature of my new writings.—Asked me to stay with her; seemed exceedingly self- less and friendly.—Drove to see Hambro, who promised to take care of the matter and get more out of it. He said he had gotten a letter from his son in Scotland, who had written that Andersen is more world famous than Thorvaldsen: "If he comes to Scotland, I won't have space in my house for all the people who will want to see him." Invited me to spend Sunday with him and stay overnight; told me again not to worry about my letter of credit!—Visited Miss Grahn, whose birthday it is today.—Went out to Westminster; went into the Poet's Corner; the first grave I stopped at was Shake- speare's; I became agitated; my thoughts wandered chaotically; I leaned against the grave. To the left of his grave lies Thomson; and Southey, to the right. At his feet lie Garrick and Sheridan and Sam- uel Johnson. I ran through the other parts of the Abbey; then went to Westminster Bridge; they are working on Westminster Hall. Steamers came and went; it was full of life. It is hot in the sun.— This evening a visit from Grímur Thomsen, who lent me two sov- ereigns. He related that in Paris he and Brock were asked to submit my biography to the *Revue of Two Worlds*, but they didn't have a copy. Went to a party given by Lady Duff-Gordon, a daughter of Miss Austin, where I was presented by Lady Morgan. There were rococo rooms and a lot of people who spoke German; met a young Herder from Weimar. The bishop's daughter said that people had been awaiting my arrival with trepidation; she had felt anxiety and happy anticipation about meeting me. I said that my heart had also been pounding because of all the honor shown me. An old friend of Walter Scott promised me one of his letters. I had to speak English. Lady Stanley spoke Italian with me. Got into a bad mood because I was no linguist and went home. There were no carriages to be found; a servant went after one.

Thursday, July 1. While I was sitting for Møller, Beckwith came. I was missing some laundry and was desperate. Had to go with him to see Bentley, who was very charming and whose personality appealed to me a great deal. He went right along with the idea that it might be best for Hambro to serve as an intermediary in my affairs. Invited me for a ride in the country next week.—Went out to Reventlow's, where I was to dine with a large party of guests, and begged off because Jenny Lind had promised me a ticket for the opera. He excused me. I came home and waited; and then Jenny Lind's secretary came and said it was impossible to get a ticket for this evening.—So I went to the Haymarket Theatre and saw *The School for Scandal* and *The Jacobite*. The theater is three stories high, small, the benches (only two) stacked in the pit stalls (five shillings). The acting is better in Copenhagen. Sent a letter to Father.

Friday, July 2. Sat all morning for Møller. Wrote to Mary Howitt. Drove in an omnibus out to Old Brompton and made my way to Jenny Lind's. She didn't want to accept Hambro's invitation. A caricature of her was lying on the table: in it the director was strewing gold on the tail of a nightingale. She invited me over for dinner tomorrow. Drove to Wilton Terrace; met Grímur Thomsen. We took a carriage and drove to Westminster; visited the Poet's Corner. There was something magnificent about the Abbey—it's a shame that a little church has been set up inside of it, but it's for the comfort of the English. It's a big nation, and in our times perhaps the only truly religious one. There is a respect for proper behavior; there is morality. We won't talk about the excrescences and excretions that there are in every large city. Everyone is courteous. The police on the street give directions in the most attentive fashion; in every store you receive the friendliest answers to your questions.—There is an honesty in this people; you feel at your ease.—And what is that talk about the eternally gray air, the London fog? Yes, considerable amounts of the latter are probably to be found in certain areas, but most of the city isn't any more bothered by it than is Paris—I've seen more clear, sunny days and bright, starry evenings here.— Walked from Westminster to the bridge that is sagging; saw the lively steamer traffic. Was in a small restaurant and had lunch. Drove to St. Paul's; it looks more impressive from the outside than it does inside—I felt that one should go to Italy to see churches. It's small in comparison to St. Peter's Basilica, doesn't have the solemnity of Maria Maggiore and Maria degli Angeli. It impressed me like a grand Pantheon. The monument for Nelson—the figure of a youth is leaning up against the monument with his arm out over Copenhagen, supporting himself on it; and, as a Dane, I had the feeling he wanted to rub out the word Copenhagen on the memorial inscription, which reads: "Copenhagen, Nile, Trafalgar." (?) (Visited the editor of *The Times*.) On all of the statues in the church there was a layer of dust or, more accurately, coal dust, that gave the statues a peculiar, silk-like coating.—Ambled over to a coffee house; there I met Marshall from Weimar; accompanied him home and had tea with him. Was nervous and unwell; my tongue entirely white; my head aching. Went out for a bit and looked at the illuminated shops. How many gas flames are burning? Well, ask about the number of stars in the sky! People drive around with huge crates made up of stretched out placards. Who reads these? I don't understand it. Everything rushes busily by. The street sweepers just stand there. (Dickens has described one such.)[2] I saw an Arab, a son of the desert, a street sweeper in London. Omnibus follows omnibus; cab after cab, equipages—with a speed as if an important event had taken place in one or another part of the city, and everyone had to get there. Musicians, a whole chorus of them, are standing on the sidewalk performing. Who listens to them? Everyone bustles by. A little Scottish boy in a plaid is blowing on his bagpipes. (Saw my own face on one of the grave monuments in Westminster; there was one English family looking at me intently.)—London is the city of cities, with all due respect to Rome. These two cities fascinate me—London is the busy day; Rome, the great, silent night. The people, so friendly; even the police on the street, a remarkably mannerly, amiable police!—Thorvaldsen has created two immortal bas-reliefs, *The Night* and *The Day*. The former has strangely fascinated me with its serenity, its grandeur; on the other hand, I can only call *The Day* pretty. It doesn't seem to me to capture the essential quality. Yes, but how should it have been done, you may ask. Well, I don't know—inspiration must be the guide. *The Day* is bustling activity; it is the whirling bobbin. Two cities com-

2. Here Andersen is mistaken. The work he really means is William Makepeace Thackeray's short story "Miss Shum's Husband," in *The Memoirs of Mr. Charles J. Yellowplush* (1856).

prise for me the world's bas-relief of night and day—it is Rome and London. Rome with its grandeur; its life is just dreams—the carnival is a joyful, fantastic dream; even Pope Pius IX is just a grand idea in a dream.

Saturday, July 3. Drove to see Reventlow; no one at home. Called on Hambro, who invited me on a trip with him to Scotland. Drove out to see Jenny Lind; ate dinner with her at 3:30.—At the opera; a ticket from her to a pit stall. The duke of Weimar saw me, nodded slightly; I did likewise. The queen was there; resembles somewhat Jane Holck (Danneskiold). Prince Albert. I got sick and had to leave my seat in the third act. The duke saw it. I sort of gave an indication by fanning myself because of the heat. One of the ladies-in-waiting pointed me out to the others. Jenny Lind was the same as always, but in these surroundings her performance wasn't as much to my liking as in Copenhagen and Weimar, even in Berlin. For me, to my ear, the Italian language was like a foreign dress on her. She sang a lovely finale and received a curtain call and flowers. I had yet this evening to go to Lord Palmerston's; made my excuses there. Sent letters to Vliet and Kneppelhout.

Sunday, July 4. A visit from Beckwith; he is always saying that he is a poor man. It bothers me that it's going badly for him. He digs in and is so piteous. Sat for the painter. Bushby's visit.—Hartmann brought me Charles Boner, a charming man. Lunch at Reventlow's. Drove with Hambro out to his country house. Hoskier from Algiers, Bielke, Hansen and a neighbor came to dinner. Here it's very luxurious and lovely. Read "The Ugly Duckling"; in bed by 11 o'clock.

Monday, July 5. Went for a stroll in the early morning. Hot in the sun—London covered by fog. Already summer. The many trees all around in the green out-of-doors gives the whole place the appearance of a large English garden. Hambro told us that he left Copenhagen because, as a Jew, he wasn't eligible for office. Karl Johan had embraced him once. We drove out into a murderous heat, so that I grew faint. Passed Newgate where they hang thieves.—No mail yet. Took a carriage home, when I was too faint to take the omnibus. Rays of sunlight shone in on the floor through the fog, as through a colored glass, a brownish-yellow beam.—Spent some time with Miss Grahn, who presented me with her portrait—one for me, one for Collin. "Is Miss Nielsen faithful to the prince?" she began. Told about Grisi and Perrot's little girl, about Miss F. and Bournonville. It was a lewd conversation. "Hornemann is horny!" she said.—Terrible heat.—Dinner at Lord Castlereagh's. His father spoke German.

I sat between him and a young member of Parliament who could speak only English, an extremely charming man. I asked him if the average man knew Shakespeare, and he told about how an actor in the theater had forgotten his line and a voice from the gallery, where you pay six pence for a ticket, shouted it to him. I spoke some English; Lady Castlereagh's sister spoke German and was very congenial; we ended by venturing onto the subject of religion.—It was 11:30 before I left, and I was glad I had made my excuses for the ball.

Tuesday, July 6. Sat for Møller. At 10 o'clock Grímur Thomsen came and wanted me to go along with him to the editor of *The Times*, who had invited us to lunch. I hadn't gotten his card. The man I thought was begging yesterday was an Irishman who just wanted to talk with me, and I had repulsed him so coldly. Today I got a letter from him. A letter from Collin to the effect that he has been made titular privy councillor and H. P. Holst had been knighted.—A letter from Miss Bremer and from a young lady in Danzig who was completely captivated by my writings.—A letter from Donner. At 2 o'clock Jerdan came; we drove out to call on Lady Blessington, who lives elegantly and comfortably. She pressed my hand, said that my *A Poet's Bazaar* contains a literary treasure such as is not to be found in many books taken together, that she has mentioned it in her last novel.— She was familiar with *Only a Fiddler.* Her daughter's husband, who has a great talent for painting and sculpture, opened his studio to us. We walked out onto a large balcony entwined with ivy and vines; a black bird from Tasmania, two white parrots were swinging out there. The black bird had to warble for me. Down below were roses and a lovely lawn, two magnificent weeping willows, a meadow where a cow was grazing. We were really out in the country. Lady Blessington walked with me in the garden and told me about an idea for a book; asked me if I wanted to develop it—about the poor man who had hope and a rich one who had the means but no hope; he was unhappy; the poor man happy.—She showed me a suite of rooms; Napoléon's bust and portrait, a bust of Byron, Bulwer-Lytton's portrait were scattered around; at last we entered her work room; here there were several books about Anne Boleyn lying open. We talked about Jenny Lind, whom she esteemed, and she had tears in her eyes. Her nieces gave me some roses. Was invited a week from Friday together with Bulwer-Lytton. She is somewhat corpulent, though not much.—A letter to Lucile Grahn. Drove out to Lord Stanley's; the lady's sister speaks German; her sister's husband, Lord

Hamilton, sat on the other side of me at dinner and spoke good German.—Several members of Parliament were there. How strange it is on earth—many people in Scandinavia are now going to bed, and here we are just starting dinner. I said to the young lady that I had visited Lady Blessington. "Her!" she lisped. The authoress that they read at home in Denmark isn't mentioned, and *I* am read. My books, copies of three different ones, were lying on the table. At 11 o'clock I wanted to leave; I was indisposed. They said I mustn't go; I made my excuses and, in return for accepting an invitation for next Sunday, left. Nervous. A gentleman on the street very politely gave me directions! This is a remarkably polite nation, how different from the individual people you often meet abroad. It called to mind my insufferable Englishman in *A Poet's Bazaar*.—Drove home for the first time in one of those small cabriolets, where the coachman stands on the back and drives the horses. It's bright and starry with lightning out on the horizon. Barck dropped in today and again wanted to give me a ticket to the opera; he always has two. Oranges and omnibuses are the only inexpensive things in London.—Hamilton related that when he was in Oxford people there were aware I was in London.—Leicester Square is a place for ladies of the street, I can see. The Big Dipper is hanging this evening over the green spot where Leicester's statue stands. Boner came to see me after 12 o'clock.

Wednesday, July 7. Went with Boner to Taylor's, where we ate lunch with Spohr. Was given my *Picture Book* in English. Felt all right, but was so tired afterwards that I lay down for the whole day; Boner stayed with me, read a couple of his poems.—Letter after letter, a whole basketful. +

Thursday, July 8. Went to Hambro and got some money.—Trouble with Mary Howitt. Mr. Bird here yesterday and spoke on her behalf. Dinner at Reventlow's; spoke English with the woman next to me. Very tired, I drove home with Hambro. Letters to Edvard, Ingeborg, Jørgen Koch and Mrs. Balling. Dutch newspapers to Father. Found a letter from M. Howitt that annoyed me: I *had* to come tomorrow! Wrote that I couldn't.

Friday, July 9. Lunch at Bentley's; drove with him, Morgan and Taylor out to his country place, which is more than eighteen miles away. Lovely nature. The trees are grouped beautifully on the lawn.— It was the first time I was on my own with three people who could speak only English. Was warmly welcomed out there by Bentley's oldest daughter, wife and sons and nephews; one of these very handsome. Mistress Bentley sat the whole time at the lunch table talking to herself. It was probably her thoughts she was speaking aloud. We walked in the garden, which was on the edge of a park and separated only by a thin iron pole from the park of a count. A blue cast lay over the landscape. Bentley's country place is in the town of Seven Oaks. A large dinner for my sake. Once the ladies had left, Taylor kept proposing my toast to great acclamation—to my childlike spirit, my religiosity, my fervor, etc.—I was moved, saying: "I can not speake Englisch, bat I hope I scal in a neuw Worck give the Sentimens of my Heart! I thank you!" It was so marvelously old-fashioned there. Everything was rococo in the dining room: the mantel of the fireplace of wood, the polished wooden walls, the old cabinets, the porcelain vases. There was a portrait of the knight Sir Ruprecht as a youth and as a young man. After dinner there were a number of ladies upstairs: three Misses Philips who had an aunt in Copenhagen and Mrs. Bornemann, the mother of Mrs. Raben-Levetzau. I had to sing "The Danish Peasant Made a Petition," and "Denmark, Lovely Mead and Meadow."

Saturday, July 10. After breakfast, walked to the big park; roses and periwinkle growing up almost all the houses.—Went into the shop of a second-hand art dealer, who had great dramatic talent. Every conceivable thing was there, from old chairs you couldn't fall asleep in because the back would collapse to Sanskrit documents, books (This store is a veritable home for wayward books!), a mummy's mask, porcelain figures.—I stayed for dinner, and now, in three carriages, Bentley with me, we drove to the railroad in a town half the way from Dover—it was the first railroad in England. I was to ride on it; Taylor was my guide. It was a very fast train. (Bentley's little daughter took me familiarly by the arm at the railroad station.) We were flying along so it looked as if the heads and hats of people in the trains we passed were literally all run together. Picket fences turned into rushing fans.—At Greenwich different trains came from side tracks, so that it was a miracle we didn't collide.—Finally we drove above houses and roofs into London. At home I found a good fifty letters and notes. A letter from Edvard. Reventlow picked me up at 11:30, and I drove to see Lord Palmerston. He and his wife very friendly. Talked with the poet D'Israeli, who looks Jewish. Spoke Danish with the Portuguese minister's wife, the former Miss Jordan.—Home again at 1:30. (Two long, dark tunnels along the railroad. There I read in *The Morning Chronicle* that *Rambles in the Hartz Mountains* had been published in English, which was extremely vexing to me.) At home I found my biography in English, and in *The*

Athenaeum I saw myself named as a collaborator with several newspapers.

Sunday, July 11. Breakfast at Horner's, where I met the young Puggaard. Everybody was exceedingly charming to me. Then, hot and bothered, drove out to Mary Howitt's in Clapton. It was, I dare say, nine miles. The omnibuses are very cheap—a half shilling for that long trip. She lived very luxuriously; there were paintings, statues and a charming garden. They received me extremely nicely. We ate dinner early and then sat in the little garden. I finally became listless from the heat and the conversation. They wanted me to lie on the sofa. The daughter was very cordial, the oldest son also nice. The husband distant, despite his cordiality. I was very listless; wasn't happy about driving that long way home. They invited me to stay; I vacillated and—decided to go home. Visited Freiligrath; my portrait was hanging on the wall. Hartmann came; then left at 8 o'clock. The heat oppressive; the omnibus was constantly stopping. I felt very nervous, about to faint, so alone. I was about to leap out of the carriage and into a house, saying I was sick. Sweat was pouring out of all my pores; it was awful—never!—Finally we were at the bank, and at last, home.

Monday, July 12. Slept until 9 o'clock. Then Boner came and was beside himself because I had forgotten that we were supposed to eat breakfast with Lockhart, Scott's son-in-law. I still hadn't shaved. Sweat was running down his back, he said. We went in a gig.—Got a letter from Gravesend from the hereditary grand duke of Weimar; we hadn't said goodbye to each other, and so he was writing before he left the country. How warmhearted!—We arrived at Lockhart's. He was a fine, elegant, Byronic-looking Englishman. A cool reception. Then he finally figured out who I was—Boner had written my name unclearly—and he was very charming. His daughter, a beautiful, fine, lively girl, like her grandfather, was very friendly to me. Lockhart fetched Walter Scott's diaries for me. The last line in them was: "Slept well last night, but tomorrow . . ."—and it ended.—Indeed, "tomorrow I will be with God," could be added!—They showed me the oil painting most like him. It was the painted eyes that attracted me most. There was a sketch that showed best, said Lockhart, how he sat with the one leg over the other, his hand on the neck of his dog.—Promised me letters of recommendation to Scotland and a holograph by Walter Scott.—Drove to a bookseller's by Covent Garden who has had all of my Danish works ordered from Copenhagen. They were listed in Danish in *The Athenaeum*. I'm probably the first Danish author who has had this happen. He said they were selling well; several Britishers were learning Danish. Sent my biography to Miss Lockhart.—(There with her in the breakfast room was a screen on which I found among the numerous pictures on it portraits of three countrymen—Ingemann, Oehlenschläger and Thorvaldsen.) Sent a letter to the king and to the student Zahrtmann. Reventlow offered me a ride to Anthony Rothschild's. There was a princely splendor to everything there—marble stairs, flowers and a fountain in the room, a magnificent fireplace in the dining room, carved wooden paneling, rococo silver on display, a really exquisite dinner. The young Rothschild, an authentic, simple Jewish face, round and fat. The baroness quite lovely. The mother, an interesting face; her sister, Madam Montefiore, resembles her brother in Naples. I had promised him a copy of *Picture Book without Pictures*, with the part about her mother in Frankfurt. The pope's chamberlain belittled Thorvaldsen's monument in St. Peter's Basilica. It hurt me, even though I agreed with him.—Drove to Haymarket; walked home. (A tale occurred to me when I thought about "refinement" at home; I could call it: "It's Got To Be Big!")

Tuesday, July 13. Sat for Møller. A visit from Norton Shaw, who speaks good Danish. He said that I wasn't known only in fashionable circles, but also among the people of England. He got one of the Dutch papers mentioning me and promised to take me to see the editor of *Punch*. Then Charles Boner arrived. I got from Mrs. Taylor her translations of Auerbach and of my *Picture Book*. Oppressive heat like in one of Venice's lead chambers, so I went to the Panorama and saw Cairo—the weather was right for it—the Nile, the pyramids, a procession of pilgrims on their way to Mecca. Everything all around sere; the only green was in the gardens near the city.—The balloon from the other day crashed with all the people in it. No one was injured. (There must be such a thing as immortality! When a true artist, a master, makes even a flawed picture and rips it up, then we gather the pieces together and keep them. God's images of Himself—should He rip them up and throw them away? No!—A Shakespeare, a Napoléon, a Socrates tossed into a corner! No, they must live, live eternally! And what about less gifted individuals? Why were they so poorly endowed? Love and justice must dwell in the most perfect of beings. The less gifted cannot be rubbed out like a wrong number. There must be eternal life, because there is an eternal God.) Dinner at Bushby's. His wife has translated several of my poems, precisely the ones I've rejected. Titular Councillor Francke was there. I was fussed over a lot. The young ladies fanned me. I was allowed to leave the table with the ladies. They were clinging to me, plaguing me; I was peered at like a strange animal. A letter from Lockhart with recommendations for Scotland and Walter Scott's holograph.

Wednesday, July 14. Boner and Barck came at 9 o'clock. We went to Hungersford Bridge; fruit stalls all around; thousands of pineapples come by steamer from America. We waited in the heavy heat of the sun on some sort of floating bridge, swaying over the Thames, where ships and boats were making haste. It was low water; the wet, slimy banks of the Thames extended for a long way. One steamer after the other came and went. At last ours came. We drew under Westminster Bridge; the House of Lords looked grand. Then we traveled on the railroad, rushing past houses and gardens. Wherever there was a little strip of earth available along the tracks, it had been planted with flowers. Everything is comfortable and in good taste in England. We flew along; Mrs. Montgomery was there where we got off in order to see me. We got on an omnibus. I sat on top for the first time. (Barck, Boner, Taylor, Mrs. Taylor, his sister and Mrs. Spohr's sister.) Magnificent big trees along the road, picturesque churches with grain fields and gardens around them. God's blessing and then God's work; bread and the word.—Hampton Court, a large reddish palace; Tiberius and Caligula—the first two faces at the gate. We went into Cardinal Wolsey's dining hall; the sun shone through the multicolored windows where Anne Boleyn's name was written. Henry VIII's picture was on one window. A magnificent, Gothic arched ceiling with gilding, banners hanging down. The palace was built by Cardinal Wolsey. The large facade out to the garden—330 feet. Splendid stairs and colonnades. A large picture gallery; there was a picture of Christian IV hanging there. Barck was also happy to see a picture of this ancestor of his. It made me feel faint to walk through these long halls; we found a way downstairs with me, half unconscious, leaning on Barck. Then we visited Lady Montgomery. It was remarkable how she was able to understand my English, indeed, almost better than I did myself. How polite the English are, and how nice their compliments sound, not like empty words. They are pleased when they see someone making the effort to speak their language. She told me that at the palace there was a special sort of spider which wasn't to be found anywhere else, and people called it "Wolsey's Ghost."—Ate lunch and then left for the inn to find the others. We went for a walk in the garden, which is three English miles in circumference. We lay on the grass by a little stream with yellow and white water lilies; the latter were unbelievably large—the whole floating cluster of flowers like the loveliest poem. Drove in an omnibus in the burning hot sun to Richmond. An incomparably lovely view from Richmond Hill over the Thames (a long rush-covered island).—We rowed on the Thames. The water lapped up onto the fine greensward; they flowed into each other. Weeping willows hung down into it; ivy grew up the buildings as luxuriantly as a drapery.—A couple of Italians with a zither were begging. The organ grinder was playing *Annen-Polka* by Strauss.— Thomson has made this place famous in his *The Seasons*. In the garden you can see where Jeanie Deans (in *The Heart of Midlothian*) spoke with the queen.—The air was heavy with heat and humidity.—We drove in an omnibus to see Taylor's family. The sun was like blood.— There was a large party. I was embarrassed about looking so grimy. Met the poet J. P. Simpson, the author of *Gisella*, whom I liked very much.—Drove home with Barck and Boner. The shops illuminated; the streets endless; omnibuses—4,000, people say. Everything, was bustling.

Thursday, July 15. Hambro dealt with my financial affairs. He drove me over to Taylor's, where I had breakfast with Spohr. Visited Boner, who is like a brother to an ailing brother. Went for a drive with the composer Benedict; saw Wellington's statue. Terribly hot. Dinner at His Excellency Dr. Bunsen's. Everything new and grand; a beautiful portrait of the king of Prussia, a gift to Bunsen from him. Met the editor . . . whose face I didn't like. Read four tales. Bunsen said he never wanted to forget this pleasure, etc.—I was so exhausted that out on the street I had to hold onto the grating in order not to collapse from weakness. Before I went to Bunsen's, I received from Jenny Lind a ticket to the opera *The Daughter of the Regiment*, but I had to turn it down. Earlier, was out at Miss . . . from East India. There were East Indian fairies, a Greek antique from the Himalayas. She was a delicate, slightly too thin, pretty girl. She and her older sister were extremely friendly to me and passionately fond of my writings.

Friday, July 16. Went for a short drive out to Bielke's. Letter from Nieuwenhuis. Drove with Boner over to see the bookseller Murray. Saw there in his room an excellent portrait of Byron; the nose on it seems longer, or different, than the one on the statue Thorvaldsen has done. There were also portraits of Lockhart, Walter Scott, Thomas Moore and Campbell. Borrowed there *The Quarterly Review*, no. 150

(March, 1845), in which there is an extremely complimentary review of *The Improvisatore*, and no one at home has mentioned it!—"*The Improvisatore* is a Danish work, composed in the Danish language, the language in which Hamlet spoke and thought, that melancholy prince of Denmark."—A friend has said that *Corinne* was the grandmother of *The Improvisatore*. Perhaps there are similarities, but *The Improvisatore* is a more lovable companion.—"We shall not see many more life-drawn pictures of the real Venice—the Venice of Shakespeare's, Otway's, Schiller's, Radcliffe's art—and Byron's and Andersen's," etc.—Drove with Jerdan out to Lady Blessington's for dinner. At the table I was seated next to the secretary of the General Post Office and the lady's daughter (?). Wellington's son was sitting one over. The servants, as in other grand houses, were wearing powder in their own hair. Napoleon's portrait was especially illuminated.—I was just sitting and writing in *The True Story of My Life* when Dickens came. We shook hands, looked into each other's eyes, spoke, understood each other; and on the veranda tears came to my eyes as we were talking. At the table Count d'Orsay suggested that I drink a glass with him and Dickens, Wellington, too.—After dinner Dickens arranged for us to gather at his home on the first of August.—How strange it is in London to see a *Berlingske News* with long articles about every little barnstormer that performs in the provinces, about great performing artists that are known by so few, about personalities that are only known in the corners where they are active. Petty judgments about books.—Drove home with Jerdan.

Saturday, July 17. Thunder, downpour. Drove to Boner's at 8:30 and from there to see Longman, the bookseller. Once in Copenhagen I met the youngest of the brothers at Reitzel's. Discussed Mary Howitt; got a copy of my *True Story*. Was sick at the table. The lady of the house sang English and Irish songs for me. Lovely children.— Drove Boner home. He'll be leaving tomorrow; kissed him goodbye and promised him a letter soon.—At home, a letter from Mrs. Serre; she's here in London with her husband. In *The Literary Gazette*, a splendid review of me and *True Story*. Paid my bill at the hotel and drove with all my baggage out to Hambro's place in the country to get some rest and fresh air. Yesterday sent my regrets to Lady Duff-Gordon. In the evening, quite lively and well. Talked with Hambro and Hoskier.

Sunday, July 18. Beautifully fresh and green. Wrote letters and in my diary. As the day wore on, young Hansen arrived, and Hunt came to dinner with his wife and brother.—Went for a walk and felt more vigorous than in the city. Hambro told about a man who thought everything pointed to God, except for the fact that cherries, which were so small, grew on trees and pumpkins, which were so big, grew along the ground. But then the man fell asleep under a cherry tree, and a cherry fell onto his face and woke him up. "Well, it was a good thing it wasn't a pumpkin growing on the tree!" he said. Hambro related that when he was a young man he had been standing in the doorway where he lived with nothing to do, when he saw someone running very fast down the street. He followed and the man ran up one street and down the next, came back again and went into a pastry shop. That's what he did with his time! My idleness was just as productive.

Monday, July 19. Hambro drove into town; I'm the king of the castle! Wandered around outside in nature. Wrote the first chapter of the second part of my novel! Below the highway, the railroad trains rush by.

Tuesday, July 20. This morning Møller came out here to finish my portrait. It embarrassed me that I couldn't serve him anything. Worked on my novel.

Wednesday, July 21. Slight toothache. Wrote letters. Yesterday I saw for the first time the dome of St. Paul's in the London fog; today it can't be seen. Yesterday Hoskier went to Bristol; his wife will be arriving from Copenhagen on Friday. Hambro told about the one cheese mite who said to another who'd been curious when he'd looked out of a window and seen a field: "This is the world! And that's a cow, that animal eating over there—that's what fields are for. And the girl milks the cow and makes cheese from the milk, so that we can have something to live from! Everything exists for our sake!" This evening went for a walk down in the meadow and saw London illuminated. It was as if hundreds of torches had been lit. Moonlight.

Thursday, July 22. Am beginning to feel like going into town. "Just give your laundry to the maid, if you have any!" said Hambro. I gave it to her, and today I got the bill. Hoskier arrived; wrote letters. Went for a walk. Bad mood because people at home in Denmark don't make enough of me.—Beautiful sunset. Toothache.

Friday, July 23. Gave a tip of a half pound for six days; wasn't happy about it myself. Drove with Hambro and shared the cost of a small carriage.—Got my old room at the Sablonière Hotel. Drove out to Jenny Lind's. She invited me along for dinner on Monday; she was going to go to Parliament. Teased me a little that I was a child because I cared about being praised in the papers. Arrived early at Reventlow's; delivered letters to be sent to Mrs. von der Maase and Madam Hanck, to Jette Wulff, from whom I received a letter yesterday, and to Louise Lind and Edvard—*The Literary Gazette* and my portrait photograph were sent along home. Sent home with Hambro a package of books and three photographs of Miss Grahn.—Reventlow didn't get me a ticket to the close of Parliament. Ambled out in that direction and ran into Mr. Hunt, who took me up into a building right across from Whitehall, where I saw the procession. (Charles I stepped out onto the scaffold from a window in the wing I was in.)—Many ambassadorial carriages came, like the way we at home drive past the Supreme Court Building; heralds and halberdiers, like the Papal Swiss Guard. Finally Queen Victoria arrived in a tremendously large, old-fashioned carriage with colossal figures on it and gilding all over. She was in white satin. Prince Albert and a few others in the carriage. Far ahead of them the crown and scepter were driven in a carriage of their own.—The pages were in one carriage. There were eight white horses drawing the Queen's. People shouted hurrah. I was so nervous that I could hardly stand, threw myself into a carriage, came home, ate, drank beer and got the worst toothache. While I was lying on the sofa, the famous tragedian Macready came; I didn't recognize him, was out of my head with pain, got him on his way again in a hurry and then I first realized who he was. I was really upset; tried to take a little walk but was quite disoriented by my feverish toothache. Tired of London. Want to travel. An invitation to Lady Morgan's for this evening; turned it down.

Saturday, July 24. Drove to Macready's, but didn't find him at home. Went to see Hoskier, whose wife and children I met. Letter from Mrs. Serre, who is here and is on her way to Scotland with Prince Saleb from Java.—A letter from Mary Howitt to Hambro, in which she said she was offended and intended to give up on doing any more translating! Wrote her a few friendly words; disheartened.— Wrote letters. Decided on the trip to Scotland.

Sunday, July 25. Now I am tired of London!—Yesterday received an invitation to join the Athenaeum Club as "the famous traveler." Was out at Grímur Thomsen's yesterday, likewise visited . . . , who took a walk with me and showed me the garden where the "red rose" was plucked.[3] Drove today to see Reventlow and Bang. Didn't

3. Andersen probably visited the Temple Gardens, which Shakespeare used as a setting for the symbolic plucking of the red and white roses which opened "the Wars of the Roses" (see *Henry VI, Part I*, act 2, sc. 4).

know what to do with myself. Was at the hanging bridge; all the shops were closed.—Yesterday a neatly dressed man was standing with some children—five of them, each one smaller than the next—all of them in mourning and holding bunches of matchsticks. Was it planned to attract attention? I don't think so. People looked at them and went on. The men who go around sweeping the streets from curb to curb and expect a penny tip. A visit from Barck. Wrote letters. Inert. Walked along the streets and found a lot to see, when I looked at individual things. There are iron gratings out by the sidewalk; under these are the basements. The common people were standing around on the street in groups chatting. You can see dire poverty.—Went home; had the feeling in my bones that I would go crazy.

Monday, July 26. Went to the barber and had my hair done. Then went over to the Athenaeum, where they have admitted me for two months. It is the premier club in London. A magnificent building on Waterloo Square. Everything princely—the library, the reading room, the balconies. They took me down into the kitchen to see the elegant things there—the wine cellar and the coffee bar. Read in *The Examiner* criticism of my autobiography: "Childhood written by a man, manhood written by a child."—Decided to try eating there; and for one pork chop and half a glass of seltzer, paid three shillings; but the meal was served on silver. The waiters wore silken stockings—I consumed them right along with the meal (according to Jenny Lind).—Drove out to Jerdan's; he's married, has lovely children; his wife received me very graciously. I felt quite well. Visited Lord Willoughby d'Eresby, who had sent me a ticket to Parliament. He received me very warmly, invited me to Scotland. Ran into . . . on the street, who persuaded me to stop by his house—one window faced out on Piccadilly and lively London; another onto Green Park, so green, so countrylike. It was like witchcraft—two opposites. Drove out to see Jenny Lind. She didn't quite like Rachel; thought her brilliant, but not truthful—her Joan of Arc, no Joan of Arc. We talked about how to return to nature. Felt ill. Jenny had me lie on the sofa, ordered her carriage readied and her servant to accompany me home. (Young Hjortsberg, her foster-brother, showed up.) Uneasy about what she told me about. . . , who was all for marrying a rich girl: "Don't trust him," she said, "it will turn out that he wants to borrow money."

Tuesday, July 27. Slept badly; went out early. Drove to Taylor's (cost three shillings); no one at home. Was at Hambro's. Not a word about me in the Danish papers, a lot about Oehlenschläger's stay in Sweden—"What a fragile thing is mankind!" Hambro invited me to travel gratis with him to Edinburgh.—Sent letters to the hereditary grand duke of Weimar, Lorck, Hartmann and Moltke-Hvitfeldt at Glorup. On the streets, especially in the city, there are men walking around with cardboard signs in front and behind with names on them of candidates to be elected—Rothschild, etc. People rushed to the polls to cast their votes. Don't really want to go out—in despair about invitations.—Now I'm sighing I wish I were in Germany, and I have to go to Scotland—to break an arm and a leg, probably.—I've always said and written: "Everything always turns out for the best!"[4] A friendly letter from Mary Howitt. Went for dinner with the sculptor Lough, a congenial man. His efforts to acquaint our age with sculpture and nature; everything about him has to do with nature and the heart. A lovely, sleeping child—it seemed to be breathing; you wanted to kiss it! He is to marble what Retzsch is to delineation. His Shakespeare series (a shame that I didn't see *Hamlet*): *Ophelia* in her madness; *Lady Macbeth* with the lamp, sleepwalking, raising her finger as the clock strikes one; *Ariel* leaping forth; *Titania*; but especially little *Puck* with his hair sticking up like a flame, his robe drawn tight around him, a little fox peeking out from between his legs—he was holding a theater placard in his hand. I said that I wanted to write a poem about Puck, and he promised to send a casting of the Puck statue to me in Denmark. I was seated next to his wife at the dinner table. The ladies drank a toast to me. I talked a lot of English, and the ladies understood me best. This was one of the places where I enjoyed myself.

Wednesday, July 28. Posed for the sculptor Durham. He has also done a bust of Jenny Lind. We two as matching pieces.—Drove with Hambro out to see Jenny Lind; she wasn't at home to visitors, but she came and was extremely charming to the old man, who was delighted and wanted to kiss her hand; but most of the conversation was about money! Later, drove with him over to see Thalberg, who accompanied us out to Hambro's country house, where we ate dinner. Thalberg told about Melbye's genius and affectation. We became extremely good friends. He told me he'd been awash in tears when the little abbess in *The Improvisatore* entered a convent; told about the conspiracy against the pope [Pius IX] that had been dis-

4. This is not a direct quotation but expresses the underlying theme in *The Fairy Tale of My Life.* Andersen uses the expression several times in his letters.

covered. Played beautifully for us, and I was the one that he kept turning to. We drove together to London. He told about *Don Giovanni*, which had been booed off stage the first time it was performed, and *The Barber of Seville*, booed at its premier (in Rome)—the people's war against anything out of the ordinary. I drove him home.

Thursday, July 29. Switched my session with the sculptor to today. Wanted to write to Dasent and discovered then that it was precisely this morning that I was to have lunch with him; was in a panic. The hour had struck. I left. No omnibuses came by the bank; usually there are hundreds of them. When I at last boarded one, it drove very slowly; the streets were crowded. And finally it drove by the street, and there I ran into the wrong house, and I still was the first one to arrive! Was there with Grímur Thomsen and Bielke. Then drove to the sculptor and then home, where I lay down as if demolished. I should have been at Hunt's on Portland Place to see the election, I think, of Colchrane. Yesterday I saw a tribune with flowers and flags set up by Drury Lane; people were acting as if they were crazy. Men were running around with banners advertising the names of different candidates. Today I have even seen carriages turned out for the candidates. People have their names in large letters on their hats.—This evening it was posted who's been elected—on top of the list: Evans, Russell, Colchrane and Rothschild. A ticket from Jenny Lind to the pit stalls and saw Verdi's new opera, *The Brigands*—bad music, tedious. Jenny Lind sang beautifully, but she didn't make the impression on me that she has in other works.—Her costume in the first act lovely. Lablache was not at all suitable as the old Moor, especially when he emerges from the tower emaciated. Finally, the "Dance of the Goddesses," in which I saw Taglioni for the first time. She made no impression on me at all; she is a lovely, older woman. Cerrito (who is married to Saint-Léon) danced superbly a sort of flying dance.—Taglioni was indeed once outstanding—"Fuimus Troes!"[5] If Count Barck hadn't come, I might nearly have died of weariness. Then I saw some more, but left before the ballet was over.

Friday, July 30. Drove over and posed for the sculptor, and from there to Bielke's. Read the Danish papers, in which the story about The Hague has just appeared, probably based on the newspaper

---

5. "We were Trojans" (i.e., while Troy still existed), meaning "it belongs to the past" or "it is all over." Quotation from Virgil's *Aeneid*, 2.325.

mailed home. No letters yet. Came home tired and lay down for a rest. Visited the bookseller Longman (39 Paternoster Row); he said that Miss Lockhart has gotten engaged to a Hope and is going to Scotland and not to Spain. Took an omnibus; there was a traffic jam; more carriages kept on coming. Everything was standing stock still; even the small cabs couldn't slip through. Otherwise, it's marvelous how these people know how to drive—it all goes as planned. Dinner at the Hunts' with Hoskier's family and Hambro. Spoke English quite dauntlessly: "I can speak it better than I can understand it!" That means that I say only what I know how to, but I hear more than I know. At 10:30 I went home. The driver didn't know his way around; took off along a street going the wrong way; I had to show him the way to Leicester Square.

Saturday, July 31. Just as I was about to drive out to see Mary Howitt, I got a letter from Dickens that he wanted to call on me at 2 o'clock. I was in a great panic about not being able to stay at home. Drove out to Hambro's; sent from there a short letter to Dickens; took the omnibus to Clapton. A friendly welcome. Her husband was more appealing to me—he was extremely friendly. They seemed to be very congenial people. At 2 o'clock we ate, rather modestly. Then drove in a one-horse carriage—three outside and five inside—to the beautifully situated country home of an old lady. We crossed over a bridge where we saw all of London below us like an ocean of stone.— In one town, passed close by where Cromwell once lived; right across the way is the house of his mistress, an actress. Outside, under a big beech tree, we found a bunch of happy children with wreaths of beech or ivy on their heads. They were singing and jumping. They knew my tales and shook my hand. There were beautiful hills and places with trees and lovely deep shadows. I sat up in a sunny-hot gazebo making picture cutouts. A deaf authoress who wrote in a political vein and several poets whose names I didn't recognize were there. I got very nervous and had to lie down on the sofa. Was fearful and profoundly exhausted. Our carriage was the last to come— those were agonizing, painful hours. Finally we drove away, and at the bridge, saw below us London with all her lamps—it was a festival of lights. You could see along one street the entire curving, flickering contour of the gas lamps—it was a sea with thousands of fire boats.—I felt rather well when we got home. Read two tales.

Sunday, August 1. Slept last night with the windows open without realizing it. Froze a bit and was under the weather in the early morning. Got a book for "little Viggo." Promised to write from Scotland. Left there at about 10 o'clock; not feeling very well. Came home and was surprised to find from Dickens all of his works beautifully bound and inscribed inside: "To H. C. A. from his friend and admirer C. D." I was ecstatic! Drove over to say goodbye to Hoskier, who invited me to stay with him if I'm ever in Algiers. Had a letter to Dickens translated.—Wrote in Mrs. Hoskier's album.—Went over to see Sigismund Thalberg; he told about how he had once, at Prince Dietrichstein's, been astonished to hear Prokesh von Osten say that the time would come when Robespierre would be exalted as a martyr: his idea had been a great one. Thalberg had come to the same conviction through reading Lamartine's *History of Girondists*. (The pretty girl I saw at the theater the other evening was Lablache's daughter.) He asked me to give his regards to the Tuteins and Liliencron. (Yesterday, out at Clapton, I saw a cemetery; sunflowers had been planted on the graves, and they were facing the sun. These flowers had sprung up from the dust of the dead, and they were pointing toward light and life, just as if they were pointing toward their departed spirits.) I am anxious about this lassitude, this buzzing in my spine. I'll probably get spinal consumption or go crazy! Jenny Lind is ill; she was probably at Lumley's dancing and caught cold.—Clausen-Schütz has come from Manchester to give me his regards.—That strange staring gaze of the poor. They don't dare to beg, but their hunger can be seen on their faces. They stand outside of a pastry shop and stare fixedly at the stranger inside. Often they wear a sign on their chest: "Have not eaten in two days."—In my neighborhood there are only a few to be seen; and in the rich neighborhoods, none at all.—The poor pariah is forbidden there.—The police force must be incredibly large, but what a monotonous life to have only one's beat to move around in—like a pendulum, back and forth.—Dinner at Lady Duff-Gordon's; also there was the writer Mistress Norton, who is divorced from her husband. With her is living Countess d'Orsay, the daughter of Lady Blessington; she came there shortly after her wedding, following an illegal relationship between her husband and her mother. D'Orsay stayed with Lady Blessington. I said that there'd been tears in her eyes when she'd been talking about Jenny Lind as the sleepwalker. "No, that's outrageous!" cried Lady Duff-Gordon. "Lady Blessington, moved by Jenny Lind's virtue! She is despicable!"—(Jenny Lind was offended that I had been there; said all her men were deserting her.)—Mistress Norton has had exactly the same idea as I for "The Little Mermaid" and had written half of it when mine appeared. She abandoned it. An incomparably beautiful profile. Drove home in her carriage. I was promised holographs of Thomas Moore and Byron. Wrote to Dickens.

Monday, August 2. Drove over to sit for the sculptor. My bust, the image of my soul. Received a letter from Professor Meyer with an invitation to visit Prince Albert on the Isle of Wight. Panicked about it; drove out to Reventlow's and wrote a letter with my regrets. In unusually good health. Thank God! Dragged the big package of books to the Strand and took the omnibus out to see Hambro, who is sick, and dropped it off. Invitation from the Bunsens; turned it down. Wandered through some shops; at home, sat and packed.

Tuesday, August 3. Early this morning, . . . came and wanted to visit with me. I had to get rid of him because I was to go out to the country with Bentley. A letter from Clausen-Schütz, which there was no time to answer. Got no letter from Denmark today either. (I guess today is Louise Lind's birthday.) Lunch at Bentley's; spoke a lot of English. Departed around 1 o'clock; passed Bedlam. Then the road started to look somewhat like the outer end of the boulevard in Paris. One of my testicles is sore. In the country they were harvesting the wheat with a sickle.—Beautiful, Gothic-style buildings, wooden ornamentation, roses on the wall, weeping willows by the water. England resembles Denmark, but in grand style. Halfway there, we had another round of our rum and sodas. Looked around the rooms; there was a mangle that could be turned with one hand. On the wall there hung: "Vote for N."—Went over to the churchyard; looked in through the windows; below, a hop garden and a wheat field. Friendly reception. This evening, a Mr. Cole, who kept talking about Jenny Lind; he wrote poetry; gave me one set to music.

Wednesday, August 4. Drove over to Knole House, the grounds of which are adjacent to the garden here. It belongs to Lord Amherst; a building similar to Abbotsford,[6] but larger! Two courtyards, thick ivy up the wall, a large hall with modern and classical statuary, paintings. In all of the rooms, portraits and historical pieces. Queen Elizabeth portrayed as a whitewashed old hag dressed like a butterfly—extremely tasteless. Saw a gruesome picture of *Ugolino in Prison*, starving with his sons; he is half mad; the one son entirely contorted. A figure from the *Laocoön Group*—the eldest strikes himself on the forehead and seems to understand their misery. Henry VIII,

---

6. The residence in southern Scotland of Sir Walter Scott, one of Andersen's favorite authors.

with his beefy face, bestial. In the vestibule his and Anne Boleyn's names were on the body of the tile stove. Saw the bedroom of James I, with his gold and silk brocade bed and the surfeit of heavy silverware everywhere. Old, kingly chairs, uncomfortable to sit on. Beautiful view of the garden. A gallery of poets' portraits, among them the poet Count Dorset. (His family once lived here.) Walter Scott, the most recent portrait. Very tired; drove home through the beautiful park. The painter Forrester, called Crowquill, came; a very humorous man. After dinner he rendered, *à la* Mathews, a scene from a postcoach with a lady they wanted to sing and after her an old man who also wanted to deliver a song. He went outside the door and made an omelette—you could hear it hit the pan and sizzle; the cat was shooed away; he chased a fly off, etc. Went to bed early, but didn't sleep well.

Thursday, August 5. Wrote a little verse to Crowquill when he asked for my autograph. He took the train into the city. I walked around in the small town, where there are a number of shops and a picturesque church. Diarrhea.—It is strange to hear Mistress Bentley talking aloud to herself when we are all sitting at the table. She says her thoughts out loud. Drove with Bentley's two older sisters and his daughter over to the village of Chevening, which belongs to Earl Mahon. In the church there, a magnificent monument to Lady Stanhope, born Mansfield, who died in childbirth; she is in marble, lying with her dead child at her breast—by the famous deceased sculptor Chantrey. Wrote my name in the book lying in the chapel for travelers to write their names in.—The weather turned to rain on the way home. Picturesque houses, with Gothic or Saxon, whatever that is, gables. One house was so overgrown with ivy that even the chimney was hidden—it was literally a green-house.—(Red on top, like a field of ripe wheat, as people say to redheads.)—Read the beginning of *Gisella* and could understand it. It's the first English book that has been comprehensible to me. Bentley gave it to me.— His daughter and nephew are taking great pains to teach me English. Paid a call to Mrs. Bornemann's sister. Diarrhea all day long. They took good care of me. Went to bed early.

Friday, August 6. Slept badly. Up before 8 o'clock; ate breakfast and drove with Bentley to London. Fog lay on the hills as it does in mountainous regions. The clouds were constantly threatening with rain, but the blue sky broke through. There was an election in Bromley with two candidates—Hodges and Bodkin. We encountered supporters of one of them with waving banners, dark blue with orange;

there was music and a crowd, too. In the middle of town we saw light blue banners. The balloting was on the square. There, too, were market stalls, and they were putting up a theater. A quaking old man in poor health came to the inn on a two-wheeled cart to cast his vote. We came across entire houses on wheels—these are the homes of peddlers with their wives and children. A little boy and his father were riding; the house had a chimney, everything inside. Arrived in town at 12 o'clock; ate lunch and then drove out to Hambro's. We won't be leaving tomorrow morning—he has an intestinal bug—but on Monday or Tuesday. Unhappy about it, because it costs time and money to stay here.—Drove in to Bielke's; no letters. Sent a letter to Father Collin and a few words to Edvard. Somewhat listless. Saw pictures of me in bookstores. Bored at home. Definitely mysterious goings-on right across the way; it looked strange—I stared and the curtains were closed.

Saturday, August 7. Got a letter today from Mrs. Eisendecher and Alexander Beaulieu-Marconnay, later in the day a letter from Ingeborg, a few words from Father and a letter from Zeise and Falkenstein. Went and wandered about.—This morning ate lunch with Hambro, who now promises that we shall leave on Tuesday. Time passes, and it is costing me one pound per day at the hotel, so nothing has been gained with a free trip.—A calling card from Mrs. Hellesen and Augusta Müller.—Went over to Covent Garden to hear Grisi in *Lucrezia Borgia,* but since it cost a sovereign, I gave it up and walked home; ate oysters and drank stout.

Sunday, August 8. Drove over to Gusta Müller's, but she was in Richmond. Was at Bang's and read the Danish newspapers. Sent a letter to Lorck. Sundays are terribly boring in London. Went over to Mrs. Willich's (25 Suffolk Street, Pall Mall), where Clausen-Schütz said I was ardently admired. Found a middle-aged lady in velvet and with a gold chain. She and her married daughter literally swooned for me and Jenny Lind. The mother sat looking at me, lost in adoration; and once she grabbed my hand and wanted to kiss it. I was taken aback and kissed hers. "I must kiss that precious hand!" she said. I presented her with Møller's picture portrait of me; she thought it terrible, without spirit and soul; she only wanted it because I had given it to her. At my departure she again wanted to kiss my hand, looked at me with adoring eyes. Did not visit Jenny Lind to say goodbye, despite the fact I could have. What a mystery I am to myself! Wrote her goodbye. Did not receive Barck, who is traveling to Wight. Thunderstorm. I sat by the open window facing out on the courtyard. Two young women in the rear premises of the neighboring building kept looking at me, and when I lifted my leg up high onto a chair, they nodded. One of them dressed herself by the window, spread out her shawl so that I would recognize it, took her hat and went out—well, let her look and be damned!

Monday, August 9. Drove out to Bielke's and from there in an omnibus to Hambro's. Got twenty pounds. The trip set for tomorrow morning. Sent letters to Father, Jette, Ingeborg and Lohmeyer. Felt better than usual. Mrs. Willich said that Jenny Lind had many enemies, such as the author Planché (the author of *Oberon*) and many young ladies who sang—they paled when you praised Jenny Lind: "She doesn't sing; she shrieks!"—When I'm dead, this sea will flow eternally through the streets; always these waves—omnibuses, cabs, carriages, men wandering around with signs in front and behind, signs on poles, huge, rolling crates with signs on them about the air balloon that makes ascents night and day, Bushmen, dances in the park, Vauxhall, a waxworks museum with Jenny Lind, beggars with lists on the front of them: "Ladies and Gentlemen, etc."—Today, when I was walking along Henrietta Street, a man came rushing out of the German bookstore. It was the German minister in London . . . ; he had recognized me from my picture and simply had to talk to me. He invited me to visit him. My picture was hanging next to Jenny Lind's a number of places; people standing in groups staring at them. Tomorrow on the train, perhaps an accident! Thy will be done, oh Lord! And forgive my lament later!

Tuesday, August 10. Got a drunk driver who kept yelling "ahoy!"— Hambro had the beginnings of gout in his foot and looked bad. We drove off, I with little Hoskier on my lap. Waited at the railroad station a half hour; took the express train. Before you used to say "over hill, through dale," but now it's "through hill, over dale."— We were racing along like wild huntsmen, one long, dark tunnel after the other; one had three peek holes.—An idea for a railroad tale, "Railroad Puck"—the souls of those individuals who refused to acknowledge that people were getting closer together and understanding each other better were put into flasks and harnessed to a railroad train. How England is like Denmark, especially Funen; after . . . it looked mountainous.—Brickworks where fire was shooting out of the smokestack. Halfway there I was half dead from having to hold my water, because I couldn't get out.—When we got to York at 5 o'clock, a man spoke to me. It was Wellington's eldest son. I didn't recognize him right away and ran away from him, but turned back and excused myself; was introduced to two ladies. Drove to the Black Swan in York; after dinner, went to the cathedral, which is magnificent, like a cutout; in style the way the cathedral in Cologne will turn out. A number of ecclesiastical buildings, Jenny Lind's picture.—Rainy day. We passed endless numbers of trains; they rushed by like rockets; we met one in a tunnel. Here sits a mountain nymph; storks are flying along with us and some swallows. A couple of ruins.

Wednesday, August 11. Hambro sick early this morning. I didn't think we would be leaving; I felt ill!—At 9 o'clock we drove to Newcastle, which lay in a hollow in smoke and mist. Here we had to take an omnibus and came to another railroad where everything was crowded and disorderly. Today a big express train was leaving. All the first class cars were taken; so we had to travel in a second class car, which is made of wood and very shabby, like third class in Germany. The railroad tracks in bad shape; we drove, but carefully, over several deep valleys—it was very hard to sit in there. We saw the sea. At Berwick, even greater crowds and disorder. Got up on top of an omnibus that was about to capsize; rolled over the river, which forms the border there between Scotland and England; and got into a good first class car. Since we left York, not a single meal all day. On the way from there, a cake that Emil Hoskier said cost three pence. I put the coins on the table and left; later, pangs of conscience about not having asked the woman herself, because it might have cost more. The countryside began to look mountainous; the entire coast lined with small boats. Edinburgh lay brightly illuminated. We arrived at the station. I immediately caught sight of young Hambro, who was looking for us. A hearty welcome. His carriage was waiting with a driver. Hambro and I dragged our own bags to the carriage and then drove to Lixmount in Trinity.[7] It was around 10 o'clock. A rich house. There were letters to me there from Bielke, Jette Wulff, Jørgen Koch, Mrs. von der Maase, Baroness Pechlin.—I got a superb bed; read and reread my letters; was full of them and the thought that I was in Scotland, the land of Walter Scott.—Happy and rejoicing in God.

Thursday, August 12. After breakfast drove with young Hambro on the train to Edinburgh in ten minutes. Before reaching town, a tunnel—it's three-quarters of a mile (English). Most people got off, because they're afraid of it because they think it might collapse. Ham-

---

7. Lixmount was the residence of Carl Joachim Hambro in the suburb of Trinity.

bro told me about it, but we drove through. First went over to see Miss Rigby, who has written about Copenhagen. She had recently read my autobiography and especially liked the part about my childhood, which made everyone think of his own. Then drove to see Professor Wilson, who seemed a jovial man. Hambro wanted to invite him to the dinner party to be held for me. Lord Robertson was in the country. Drove up into the old part of Edinburgh, where I saw Scottish soldiers with bare knees.—Narrow alleys or passages. Delivered some letters. In Scotland I'm called the "Danish Walter Scott." Saw Walter Scott's monument; it seemed with regard to his figure somewhat too tall.—Drove home on the train; sent a letter to Mrs. Serre. Went for a walk with the young Hambro, who is a religious, educated man. We went down to the fishing village; the women looked like the fishermen's wives from Skovshoved.[8] Sea and sky, gray.—After dinner, home worship; the tutor read a chapter from the Bible; after that they all knelt and recited a prayer.

Friday, August 13. Sunny day. Sailed by steamer over to Kirkcaldy; passed a small island where the lighthouse was. We walked out to a ruin, Ravenscraig—at first Hambro was sure it was Ravenswood,[9] but one of the fishermen's wives said there was no shifting sand there. The doctor said it was an imaginary name made up by Walter Scott—the real place lay higher up. The Ashton family was also imaginary; the real family still lived and was named Stair. We walked through a garden to the ruin, where there were dark prison cells. It lay by a jutting cliff; the tide was out; a small oak grove close by and thick ivy growing up the cliff, as if it were a tombstone. I wrote a poem about Scotland's Romeo and Juliet (Lucy and Edgar). Ate at the inn. Edinburgh lay in a lovely light when we sailed home. A blind musician who played Scottish songs on his violin. This morning we drove by omnibus to Lord Jeffrey's; his house was quite a fortified castle. Ivy rooted on the one side of the wall hung like a thick carpet out over the other side. A fire on the hearth; all the grandchildren came; I had to inscribe a collection of my tales and *True Story.* Went along up into the park and looked at Edinburgh, which in its setting somewhat resembles Athens.—Letter from Boner.

Saturday, August 14. Drove to town on the railroad. Saw a manuscript collection that had belonged to Mary Stuart, Knox, etc., and

8. Fishermen's wives from Skovshoved, a fishing village north of Copenhagen, sold fresh fish daily by one of the canals in the center of Copenhagen.

9. The setting for Sir Walter Scott's novel *The Bride of Lammermoor* (1832), which Andersen dramatized in his opera libretto *Bruden fra Lammermoor* (1832).

with each one had been placed all the portraits and pictures belonging to the same person. Was at the gallery; *Judith*—the girl most interesting, the way she gazed up at Judith with a look full of awe and admiration. The statues all plaster copies. Drove early this morning to Leith, the harbor for Edinburgh; I was very on edge. Saw the old town; off from the main street, which is on a ridge, run narrow, black streets lined with six-story buildings, grimy and dark, constructed out of massive stones, like in the most wretched towns of Italy. Misery and poverty looked down from the windows; rags hanging; windows without panes, Latin inscriptions. In one of these streets we saw the first hotel in Edinburgh, where King . . . once stayed, where Samuel Johnson resided. It was like a wretched stable, dark and prisonlike. Knox's ramshackle house was on the main street; on the corner he himself had been hewn in miniature preaching from a pulpit. On the most beautiful street of the new town, a monument to Walter Scott—his dog Maida lies at his side; characters from his writings have been placed in the tower above him: Meg Merrilies, the Last Minstrel, etc.—In the valley down below the railroad train rushes between the new and the old Edinburgh. Bought copies of my tales and *True Story*. In the evening we flew a balloon from the garden. Very tired.

Sunday, August 15. Received this evening a map of Scotland. Young Hambro is matchless in his attentiveness to me and in discerning my every wish and fulfilling it.—Excused from going to church because my stomach was upset. I should be in the Scottish church, where several wished me to go; am sitting now writing letters.—A quiet day—bells are ringing; the sun is shining. Took a walk down to the wharf and watched the bathers. There were women walking there, looking. A young man swam so far out that I got anxious about him. A letter from M. Howitt.

Monday, August 16. Sent letters to Jette Collin, Jette Wulff and Jørgen Koch, Bielke, Mary Howitt, Madam Du Puget—Jenny Lind. Drove up to Heriot's Hospital from which there is a stupendous view of Edinburgh, the Castle, etc.—A goldsmith, when he lost his only son, used all his money to build this for poor boys. When we wrote our names in the book the porter had, he asked Hoskier: "Is it the Danish author? Is it that old man with white hair?" and pointed at Hambro. Hoskier indicated me. "So young!" he cried, "I've read him and the boys here read him! It's extraordinary to see such a man! Usually they're always old and dead!"—Then I shook hands with the man and felt highly flattered: at least, I thought, I'm read and recognized here in a Scottish orphanage. Drove up to the Castle, huge view. Drove to Holyrood House, which lies on the outskirts of town near the mountain [Salisbury Crags]. Saw a long banqueting hall with bad portraits. Saw a lot of boring rooms in which Charles X has resided. Went up to Mary Stuart's bedroom; on the upholstery by the bed had been woven Phaethon's Fall, as if it were a prophecy of her own. In a nearby room Rizzio had been dragged in and murdered—they showed you the blood spots on the floor. The murderers had entered the Queen's bedroom through a low door. There was a turret room on each side. Was in the church, which is now a lovely ruin. Ivy grew up the wall around the beautiful window. Saw the room where Mary Stuart made confession. Many tombstones lying there. Picked a flower.—Very tired. Walked to the "Heart of Midlothian," a somber building on the righthand side of the street. We arrived exhausted at Black's. He gave me his guidebook. Hambro wanted to buy a dagger for me, but since it cost thirty rix-dollars, I stopped him and chose a cap, a paper knife and a book of Scottish melodies. Big dinner party at home for my sake; the poetess Miss Crowe was there and was my partner at the table; she read aloud in English "The Ugly Duckling" and "The Top and the Ball." (A thorn from a thistle in my penis.)

Tuesday, August 17. Sent a letter to Bentley and Jerdan. Drove down to the big wharf and breathed the sea air. It was windy today. The gulls flew gracefully and dove into the water. Received from Hambro a miniature of the Walter Scott monument.—I was lying on the bed resting, when Lord Jeffrey came with his whole family, (. . .) and wished to give me his regards! The young lady said she would never forget me. Jeffrey asked me to come back soon to Scotland, since he didn't have so many years left to him.—Dinner at Doctor Simpson's, where Miss Crowe and another poetess drank ether. I had the feeling of being with two crazy people: they were laughing with gaping, lifeless eyes. There is something eerie about it. I think it is splendid for operations, but not for tempting God. A lady sang Scottish songs beautifully. I sang. Drove home late in the evening.

Wednesday, August 18. Drove with young Hambro to town; he presented me with a plaid costing twenty-eight shillings. (Later, available in Stirling for eighteen shillings.) Went to see the bookseller Watson, to whom I had to give several of my autographs. He promised me some, which I later drove in to get. Went to see the doctor's assistant and looked at daguerreotypes he had taken on a trip to

Palestine. Said goodbye at Doctor Simpson's, where I had to sign numerous album pages; on one to Miss Ross:

> When Scotland's skalds their songs composed,
> The Scottish thistle became a rose.

Drove home and rested and afterwards to dinner at Miss Rigby's. Wilson came in the evening with the two poetesses and some Germans. The carriage came for me as early as 9:30 and I left, even though they weren't happy about it and pleaded at length with me; but we were leaving at 6 o'clock the next morning. Drove with a groom. At home I found books from Mistress Crowe, a letter from the Duke of Weimar and Gebhard Moltke-Hvitfeldt. The doctor was there and brought news that, according to telegraph reports, Louis-Philippe had been killed. It made a deep impression on me. Now, of course, I can't go to Loch Laggan; invited to be a guest on their trip to the Highlands.

Thursday, August 19. Slept restlessly. Up at 5 o'clock. Drove down to the shore at 6 o'clock. Shifting fog banks; when we got out on the fjord unrelenting fog, cold and thick. Once we caught sight of a jutting crag near us in the fog. A blind man was playing the violin, performing Scottish songs, half in recitative, and fiddling in between the short verses. As we approached Stirling, the fjord, or river, as it must be called here, bowed sharply. The town, with its castle, was extremely picturesque. Took rooms at The Golden Lion. Drove out to where people go bathing. . . . Twice on this little road Hambro had to pay tolls of three shillings for two carriages! View of the town and castle. Very warm. Mrs. Hambro not well. I decided to forego the trip to Loch Laggan. Wrote to Professor Meyer about what he would advise me to do and said I would await his answer in Glasgow. An old bridge where Scots have probably met and fought.— Early to bed.

Friday, August 20. Sent a letter to Dr. Moir in Musselburgh. Walked up to Stirling Castle; magnificent view of the valley where the battle between Edward II and Robert the Bruce took place. On the other side, the mountains. Near the castle and the church, Mary Stuart's residence. Now it seems a sort of barracks, small and narrow, an old house with projecting statues, half of them with their heads broken, stone cannons. Down the street, Darnley's house. The Scots love to talk about their history—here, a shoemaker came out in his apron and told Darnley's story. Drove out to the hill where the battle took place between Edward and the Bruce. People have broken so much off the stone where the king set his standard that an iron grating has been put over it. Drove over to the house where James III took refuge, sent for a priest, confessed; and when the priest heard it was the king, he stabbed him with a knife. A woman showed us the corner in her small room, where the murder took place—her bed was standing right next to it. A fire in the fireplace (it's a smithy now). Cold weather.—At 2:30 we drove from Stirling; most of the way the landscape looked Danish. The linden trees were in bloom, and they've long since finished blooming in England. The oats quite green. (Louis-Philippe not killed, as the newspapers have been saying.) Came to a small, attractive inn with rugs on the floor and a stuffed fox over the fireplace. Then the mountains began. After a drive of two and a half hours, we arrived in the town Callander, where we took rooms at a hotel. A river winds in many curves outside of my window. An old, arched bridge leads over it; close by, a small hill that looked like one of our barrows. All the boys here have skirts of Scottish cloth and bare legs, small Scottish horses. In the background, a high mountain ridge. We were running around in our plaids. Fergusson, Duncan, Cowan are the usual names you see. All kinds of trade in small shops. Roofs with gray tiles. The wind is blowing cold. Many gentlemen out fishing.

Saturday, August 21. Up at 6 o'clock. At 7 o'clock drove into the mountains. They rose higher and higher. The heather began, isolated stone houses. Went along a river into a forest of young oaks. A small lake; now the mountains rose up. We were afraid of arriving too late at the steamer on Loch Katrine. It was very small and full of little white gnats that soon started biting. We came out into the narrow lake; deep, dark water, brownish green mountains. If the heaths of Jutland look like a sea in dead calm, then this is the heath in a storm—large mountain-waves, but all of them green with forests and grass. To the right we had a forest-covered island. It was Ellen's, the Lady of the Lake.[10] When we reached the end of the lake, a small, paltry inn with the beds side by side. A lot of wooden carts had stopped outside. Once there was only a mountain path over to Loch Lomond; now a road has been cut, but the kind of road they used to make several hundred years ago. The driver walked

10. According to tradition the home of Ellen, the heroine of Sir Walter Scott's epic poem *The Lady of the Lake* (1810).

alongside the horse; and when there was a hill, we careened down it at a mad pace. The carriage bumped along. Not a house in sight, not a person. Dark, still mountains shrouded in fog. Half way there we saw a hut for hunters and, once, a shepherd wrapped in his plaid. Ben Lomond was looking down at us. When we got near the lake, we had to get out of the carriage and walk down the mountain, where the road ran almost straight down. Here there was a rather friendly inn. Soon the steamer came; it was larger than the other one. I had forgotten my palmwood walking stick. Charles had taken it earlier so that the neapolitan palm could see Loch Lomond. "Look!" he shouted and held the stick up. Now it's been left behind. I must write a tale about the palmwood walking stick. A verse by Walter Scott[11] was written on the ship:

> Land of brown heath and shaggy wood,
> Land of the mountain and the flood.

It was terribly cramped on board. I encountered young Puggaard, who wanted to go up into the mountains and to Inverness. The rain began. We went all the way up to the end of the lake—just as if it were a river—where we set people ashore at Fort William. A local conveyance was waiting. We had to stay there for a few hours until omnibuses from all over arrived. The rain was pouring down. We were packed into the long, narrow cabin. A fat Scot almost sat down on my lap and blocked the door so that we couldn't get any more people in. As many as possible were sent into the lady's compartment.—All around the mountains in clouds and mist. We sailed back. Puggaard was set ashore at the inn we had come from. Passed Rob Roy's cave; rocks from the cliff had fallen down. A family came on board. A young man came and said there was a lady who knew me from my picture, if I might not be Hans Christian Andersen. She came and shook my hand. She was a Hamilton. I asked her for a flower; she gave me the best ones from her bouquet of wild flowers. She had come from Ben Lomond. Her husband, father and whole family flocked around me. I was now the object of the entire party's attention. Everyone looked at me in a friendly way. It amused Hambro. The family invited me to accompany them and to stay overnight with them. They gave me a note for the brother of the poet Tanahill. I had to reciprocate with a couple of calling cards and wrote a few

11. A quotation from Sir Walter Scott's epic poem *The Lay of the Last Minstrel* (1805).

words on them; I wrote: "Land of brown heath, etc."—Large waves rolled across the lake; it was stormy; clouds and fog covering the mountains. The lake widened, many islands. We arrived in Balloch, where Hambro hired a whole omnibus, and were another hour driving to Dumbarton. Mrs. Hambro has been suffering from a nervous ailment for a few years. She has endured this trying day nicely, and we must hope she is well. Hambro wonderful to me. When my umbrella broke, he asked me to take one of his as a keepsake, and he gave me his best! He has sought to fulfill my every wish, provide every comfort for me. People wilder here; mobbed as in Italy—they're Celts. It is terribly expensive to travel—every other minute a two shilling toll for our carriage.—We stayed at the King's Arms (along the way saw the Smollett monument).

Sunday, August 22. The way they were running around and making noise in the hotel, it was impossible to fall asleep yesterday evening: one had squeaking boots, another was rumbling around upstairs. Asleep by midnight and then awake again because of a storm. It came in long gusts, so that I thought I was hearing the sea. Everything was creaking. The window sashes that you push up and down were rattling. The house was creaking like an old cupboard. A sick cat kept on meowing. I jumped out of bed to find out what was really going on.—(Yesterday we sailed on Loch Lomond on the *Water Witch.)* Here in town there is a fearful silence; it's Sunday!—No one on the street; doors closed; curtains closed in most houses. They are reading the Bible or getting drunk. Scotland is the only country where there is no train service on Sundays.

Monday, August 23. Got up early with the thought that the Hambros were leaving at 8 o'clock; I would then leave at 8:30. They stayed until 11 o'clock. I accompanied them on board and was really sad at parting. They asked me to stay with them when I returned to London. Wandered around a little.—(This morning I was with Hambro in a book store. Hambro asked the man if he had any works by Hans Christian Andersen; and he said yes; and when Hambro inquired about the picture portrait, the man took out the issue of *Howitt's Journal* it was in. When Hambro asked whether it was a good likeness and pointed at me, the man got very red; his face lit up and he grasped my hand: "I'm very happy to see you!" he said.)—At 12:30 I sailed by steamer from Dumbarton. We encountered one steamer after the next out on the Clyde. The castle looked picturesque; Ben Lomond jutted up into the sky. The sunshine was warm and bright, but the air cold. Upright barrels on poles. On board, when I spoke to a young man from Dumbarton, he asked if I weren't Andersen; he had recognized me from my picture portrait. Arrived in Glasgow and drove by minibus to The Star. The service here incredibly bad. Drove (two shillings) to see Mistress Cowan, who wasn't at home. There was no letter from Loch Laggan. I fell into a bad mood; all of Glasgow looked bad to me because of it.—The streets rather attractive; walked along an alley.

Tuesday, August 24. Up at 6:30. An hour later walked to the post office, but there was no letter from Meyer. Desperate, and in a morbid frame of mind gave up the trip to Loch Laggan. Wrote my regrets to Meyer. My walking stick sent from Inversnaid; young Puggaard had taken care of it splendidly. A card from Mrs. Cowan inviting me to come, but I put myself onto the train (twelve shillings for a first class seat) and rode to Edinburgh; two long, dark tunnels. Took a room at the North British Hotel. At the *table d'hôte,* a man who asked whether he might not have seen me or a picture of me before; they all drank toasts to me. Sent letters to young Hambro, to Bielke and to Richardson. Gave up going to Abbotsford; I'll head for London tomorrow.—A strange restlessness—I have enough money, but no desire to travel any more. I'm longing for home and work. When you must make a decision, there are times when you feel as if you are in a magic circle. You are conscious of one thing: "I can; I will do it," but you are held by invisible bonds; you are faced with a struggle. You are at the outer limits of your freedom, the limits set by God.—The view from my window this evening is tremendous. The buildings in the old town, from eight to twelve stories high. Lights are shining from the windows, one on top of the other; gas lamps glow in the street; and lights shine through the glass roofs deep beneath me where the train tracks run; above them rises the steam; the rows of lamps look like garlands. Under the windows a little boy is dancing and singing and declaming, accompanied by a tambourine. Skirted Scots walk solemnly up and down— policemen. A steam whistle blows.

Wednesday, August 25. Up early. Still uncertain whether I should travel to York or to Abbotsford. Wandered aimlessly around the streets. Took the train. Hesse from Altona was in the same car; he and his brother have been in Glasgow in the same hotel as I; said the Edinburgh papers are reporting that I received an invitation from Prince Albert and went to Loch Laggan. It put me into an extremely bad mood. Drove by Berwick on the omnibus over the river that separates Scotland and England. Saw them working on the Herculean bridge at Newcastle. There at the station, encountered Barden-fleth, who was there buying horses. In York, stayed at The Black Swan. Bad mood. Feverish and uncertain whether I should return to Scotland.

Thursday, August 26. Same bad frame of mind; feverish morning; sensual, sick thoughts; unhappy, really desperate.—Left at 9:50. In the car, a gentleman and a lady I traveled with yesterday. They recognized me; said the Scottish newspapers had been full of me and my visit to the queen; I started sweating and agonizing. We parted in Sheffield, and he wrote his name for me; it was the poet Hogg, and he asked me to visit him. I had bought *Punch;* the lady showed me there was something about me in it concerning my invitation to Scotland. I was so desperate I wouldn't have minded if there were a train accident. How detestably egotistical! How our fate hangs suspended from fine threads! Only rarely, like gold in the hills, does a vein surface so that the eye can see it. We go out through the front door and are for a moment uncertain whether we should turn to the right or the left, and whatever we spontaneously choose will lead some of us to our death, others to the great events in our lives. Never before have I traveled with such nonchalance on the railroad. I arrived in London at 7:30. At the Sablonière Hotel I was received with near jubilation, and they insisted I take a room with a sitting room for five shillings per day.

Friday, August 27. Went out early to see Bielke, who tried to put everything aright for me; I was so upset that I cried. Reventlow comforted me; read to me a greeting from the king, who was pleased about the recognition I was receiving. Drove out to Hambro's; sent letters to Mrs. Zahrtmann, Father Collin, Drewsen, and Jette Wulff. Ate dinner at Reventlow's. Arrived home tired. Letters from Lorck, Edvard and Jette, Father.

Saturday, August 28. Drove out to see Jerdan and said goodbye to him, his wife and children; I was really moved. Drove to Hambro's and got the remainder of my letter of credit. Letters from young Hambro, Norton Shaw and Miss Crowe. Visits from Grímur Thomsen and Jerdan, who brought me his review of Jenny Lind's and my busts. Dinner with Reventlow; he asked me to take some dispatches to Frankfurt and then gave me a passport without a Prussian visa stamped in it—I was anxious about it. When I got home, I received a letter from Professor Meyer; he didn't go along to Loch Laggan, but is on Wight. That's why he hadn't responded before now; he advised me to abandon the trip, since the weather was bad in Scotland, and asked me not to risk my health; I was sure to get a letter from the prince.

Sunday, August 29. Slept restlessly. Awoke at 4 o'clock; up at 6:30; off by 8:30. The rain was pouring down. First sent letters to the Milnes and Mary Howitt; yesterday one to Edvard that they shouldn't be afraid for me regarding the big accident on the Thames that morning (yesterday): one of the small steamers, *Cricket*, crowded with people, exploded. One hundred were killed, many injured.—I could have been there, since I still haven't seen the tunnel and I was planning to go out there on one of the steamers. It could have happened to me.—Drove on the train to Tunbridge. The rain turned into fog, and it lifted. Bentley's carriage was waiting. The hops were hanging nicely. Now it was getting warm. What a difference between here and Scotland! You can really feel the degrees when you race 100 miles in one day on the railroad. Rumor now has it that Jenny Lind is married to Daquin—it's just talk. Lovely sunshine. Wrote to Hambro and Dickens.—Rain. This evening at around 10 o'clock everybody came into the living room. I got a pillow to kneel on; they all knelt with their faces hidden. Miss Bentley read aloud from a religious book; afterwards everyone recited the Lord's Prayer, and then there was some more reading.—Lovely moonlight; very tired; had the plans changed about going to see the poet . . .'s house tomorrow.

Monday, August 30. Inscribed the pages from several albums:

> When language closed the door now and then,
> Your eye was the key to open it again.
>
> In foreign tongues the song passes by you and me,
> But listen to the heart beating sweet the melody.

Left Seven Oaks at 1 o'clock; gave five half-crowns as a tip, four to the driver, which is to say around nine Danish rix-dollars. I've certainly been an English gentleman.—Bentley's son and nephew accompanied me to Tunbridge. The train took me by surprise. I managed to get on; was anxious about my luggage, which I thought was in the wrong car. Saw the sea; arrived at the Royal Oak; got a bad room with a good view. The whole hotel was full. Yesterday I wrote to Dickens, who lives in . . . with his family, that I was coming; and I found a letter from him at the hotel that they were expecting me for dinner, which they took at 5 o'clock. I rushed to get a carriage to take me there and back (six shillings); drove from Ramsgate to Broadstairs, which is said to be two and a half English miles away. It didn't seem so far. It was a nice little town, close to the sea. I arrived; they were seated at the table, because they thought I wasn't coming. Mrs. Dickens looked older, as a woman, than Dickens did, as a man. They welcomed me very warmly; I was so happy there that I only later discovered that we were sitting right by the ocean— the waves were rolling under our windows. Dickens was amiability itself. After the meal, along with the apples and pears, the children came in, all five. The sixth, the oldest, wasn't at home. They all kissed me, and the smallest kissed his spread-out hand. They were sweet, but plainly clad. Mrs. Dickens asked me for a holograph of Jenny Lind, and she shall have the letter I got from Jenny in London, which is as follows:

Old Brompton
Clairville Cottage
24 June 1847

My dear Brother!
  Welcome to England!
I'll be at home tomorrow from 12 o'clock to 3 and am looking forward to having a chat with you, dear Brother.
  Adieu until we meet.

Your sisterly friend,
Jenny Lind

Dickens promised to write to me regularly. He now wants to learn German and maybe later Danish. We were sitting in a dining room near the sea. It was ebb tide; the lighthouse lit up out on the sandbank, where many ships run aground. An Italian came and was playing outside; a beautiful, brown head. Dickens spoke fluent Italian to him.—I told him about Jette Wulff. After dinner I met there a lady who knew Count Barck and Bielke. Drove home at 9 o'clock. A bad hotel, the Royal Oak—bad service, dirty.

Tuesday, August 31. Awoke early. Up at 7 o'clock. Waited for the barber, annoyed.—A very bad hotel. I was cheated every which way.

I exchanged some sovereigns, and they came and said that there had been a *napoléon d'or* among the coins I had given them—which is impossible, since I didn't have any. That's how I lost five francs.— Dickens and . . . were standing on the wharf waiting for me. He had walked from Broadstairs in order to say goodbye to me, dressed in a green Scottish dress coat and colorful shirt—exceedingly, elegantly English. He was the last to shake my hand in England; promised when he received a letter from me to write about how things were going in England. After I came on board, there was still a lot of bother before the ship could clear the harbor. (At the hotel before I left, a letter from Lohmeyer in Copenhagen. The letter I received from him on Funen was the last I got in Denmark, and it irritated me and dampened my eagerness to set off for England. This letter was "Danishly" patronizing: said that a poet couldn't himself judge his own work and that *Rambles in the Hartz Mountains* was just as good as *A Poet's Bazaar*, etc. He wanted to get some money for his translation.) As the ship was gliding out of the harbor, I could see Dickens on the outermost point. I had thought him long gone. He was waving his hat and finally raised one hand up toward heaven; did it perhaps mean that we won't see each other until up there?— Beautiful weather. The crossing took four and a half hours. A man came up to me; he had recognized me. I saw the coastline by Calais and Dover. England disappeared, Dunkerque. When we reached the Ostende shore, a lot of flags were waving from the bathhouse. I stepped ashore, and the king of Belgium, the queen and two princes came straight toward me. I could see from how people were acting that it had to be the king. I recognized his face, greeted him; and he regarded me very cordially and greeted me. Entered a church, where there was beautiful music; worshipped in silence. At 7:30 the train left for Ghent, where I stayed at the. . . . We traveled here through the dark of evening. Huge embers fell from the locomotive to the ground; colorful lanterns were shining. There was no time to record a single word.

From Ghent Andersen traveled via Frankfurt and Eisenach to Weimar to visit his good friend, Hereditary Grand Duke Carl Alexander. After a week in Leipzig, where he looked up the Danish composer Niels W. Gade and discussed the second German edition of his works with Lorck, he headed for home along his customary route via Hamburg and Kiel, where he wrote his last diary entry of the trip on September 22. During the fall of 1847, he wrote five tales published first in English with the title A Christmas Greeting to My English Friends *and a special dedication to Dickens. (The Danish edition appeared the following spring.) His epic-dramatic poem* Ahasuerus, *which had occupied him since 1840, appeared in Copenhagen bookstores in time for the Christmas book season.*

Between the Wars
1848–64

IN OCTOBER *1848 Andersen moved into the boardinghouse of Mrs Anholm at 67 Nyhavn Canal, where he—with brief interruptions—stayed until 1867. The year 1848 was a crucial one in Danish history. On January 20, King Christian VIII died, and the nation was occupied with the succession of Frederik VII when the February Revolution broke out in Paris. In accord with the ideas of the revolution, there was a growing demand in Denmark for a free constitution and, in the pro-German duchies of Schleswig-Holstein, for independence from Denmark. On March 23 there was an armed uprising in the duchies, led by two of Andersen's former acquaintances, Prince Frederik of Nør and Duke Christian August of Augustenborg. Prince Frederik launched a surprise attack on the Danish garrison in Rendsburg, while the duke of Augustenborg was in Berlin negotiating for Prussian military intervention on behalf of the insurrectionists. After the Battle of Schleswig on April 23, German troops occupied the southern part of Jutland. On May 11, when Andersen began his diary for his six-week vacation from the city, he was on his way to Funen to visit the Moltke-Hvitfeldts at Glorup, which was not very far from the action.*

Thursday, May 11 [1848]. On the train to Roskilde at 10 o'clock in the evening. From the train station I could see the city lying in a quiet torpor, as if asleep. Lovely weather, star-bright. The Roskilde steeples jutting up into the sky; I thought of Christian VIII resting in peace there and the war we are facing.—In the coach there was a bookseller (Gudmundsson?) from Schleswig, born in Iceland. He mentioned a student at Uppsala to whom Jenny Lind had been engaged; told about his flight from Schleswig—stacks of bodies, especially those of Prussians, at Dannevirke. We encountered some bad inns: in Ringsted the whole place was asleep and closed down, and we stood in the wind and draught in the vestibule.

Friday, May 12. In Korsør we encountered a part of the Horse Guards. On the steamer we met Laurids Skau, who had some dispatches to take to Middelfart. He related how people had moved out into the fields because of the bombardment. Heard in Nyborg there were forty men stationed at Glorup, that all of Funen was heavily occupied by troops. A new highway passing close to Holckenhavn—two miles shorter to Glorup. At Frørup we saw some troops holding exercises. Ministers' wives and young girls were out watching them. Met His Excellency, who had driven for a visit to Holckenhavn. At the estate I met Lieutenant Colonel Nielsen, Major Blom, Linstow, Hohlenberg, Testman (a volunteer, married to Hohlenberg's sister), Petersen (who was to have been a carpenter), the son of Count "Lottery Agent" Moltke, Principal Borgen's son, Lieutenant Olsen, etc. After having heard all about their marches through the sands of West Jutland, went to bed early. Presented Dr. Bricka with *Agnete.*

Saturday, May 13. Wrote a letter to Edvard Collin. Visited Dr. [Winther], who has a Lieutenant Bentzen staying with him. Heard a good deal about the battle: the men shot in the chest or head had lain as if they were asleep; those shot in the abdomen had almost been unrecognizable because their faces were so convulsively distorted with pain. One had lain literally "biting the dust" with his teeth; his hands had clutched at the turf. Young Dons had gotten a lump on his back from a blow from a gun butt, and when he'd reached the others and an officer had given him his horse to hold, he had fainted. Maneuvers out on the manor field. Dinner today at 3 o'clock; General Hedemann here—he is a handsome man with a kind and intelligent face. For the moment he has his headquarters in Odense, where he is living at the castle. He invited me to visit him when I was in Odense. (I've forgotten to note that when I arrived here at Glorup the day before yesterday I—in the company of Dr. Winther and his brother-in-law—ran into our Dr. Kayser from Odense, who wished to pay a visit to His Excellency. He kindly asked me to stay with him when I came to Odense.) Volunteer Testman, married to Hohlenberg's sister, a Norwegian by birth, is a well-educated, pleasant person; he was nearly shot like Lundbye. When the rifle fell, the shot brushed his eye; he fainted; and when he came to, he heard the others laughing because he had shouted: "This is indeed a paltry death! I'm Volunteer Testman with the Third Battalion!" Lundbye, the officers told me, had been standing dejectedly leaning on his rifle; some farmers were passing by close to where the other rifles were propped up in front of him and happened to knock them over. They heard the shot and saw Lundbye fall to the ground, shot from below upward through the chin, his mouth torn and a piece of flesh with beard on it shot away. He emitted a few weak sighs; was wrapped in the Danish flag and buried. Lieutenant Høst, who is staying here, wept.—Lieutenant Dreyer with the light infantry is the one who told me about this.—The wounded in the camp hospitals stink horribly—the ones shot in the abdomen have feces draining out of their sides.—Talked quite a bit this evening with Captain Blom, who spoke very *openly*. Read two tales.

Sunday, May 14. Lovely weather. The forest, peaceful and beautiful. I feel so wonderfully free from the pressures of Copenhagen, feel myself to be a better person and the people around me, as well, feel free to express a greater sense of enthusiasm. Everyone is asking the crucial question: "When are the Swedes coming?"—Received from His Excellency the first strawberries. General Hedemann told us yesterday that the Prussian officers over at Snoghøj sent a man to the Misses Riegels with a white flag and some flowers from the ladies' garden, so that they could enjoy some of their own beautiful flowers; they enclosed a poem.—Visited Major Blom and the volunteers. A Volunteer Hansen came to dinner, the nephew of Privy Councillor Koch; he had lain with a fever in the camp hospital at Augustenborg in the duchess's bed (the dowager duchess's). There they were served asparagus and capon. Read tales in the evening.

Monday, May 15. Grímur Thomsen's birthday; sent a letter to him and a short note to Edvard. Major Blom told about the flight from Flensburg. After the battle our boys lay in a wet field and arrived after a march in Flensburg, where they rested. Toward evening they sounded the march for the fresh troops who hadn't been under fire, an order that had been decided upon earlier. Someplace else the signal was given to others to fall in, and just then some refugees arrived; those of our boys who were awake heard the last ones shout that the Prussians were coming. The local residents, who wanted our boys out of town to prevent a new attack, urged them to flee to get rid of them; and then everything went extremely fast, on horseback and by wagon. The powder kegs were dancing around striking sparks; they could have exploded. In the meantime, the Third Battalion was quietly marching down the sidewalk out of town, but the refugees didn't see that.—Today Major Blom left us because he has received command of his own battalion. Rumor has it that General Høegh-Guldberg, who lost his commission, has gone crazy and believes he is Karl XII.

Tuesday, May 16. Very warm.—They are shooting around here with live cartridges, so you hardly know where you can go. Called on

Miss Ipsen. Went for a drive with His Excellency through Svindinge and Langå. Biering's daughter is being baptized in church today. The thrushes and nightingales are warbling. A strange, dense fog. The moon red.

Wednesday, May 17. Went for a walk; read *The Heart of Midlothian.* Very warm. Nothing new from the camp.

Thursday, May 18. The others drove to Hvedholm; I chose to stay at home. All the officers of the Third Battalion were here and drank tea around the big stone table in the tree-lined drive. I particularly liked a fellow named Tvermoes. They told about their overnight stay on the street of a village in Schleswig; in wind and rain the entire battalion stretched out by the houses with their packs under their heads. Squeezed together into a small room—Linstow was sitting on a trunk with a heavy brass fittings that pressed into his flesh while he slept.—Later the lieutenant colonel (Nielsen) held a toddy party.

Friday, May 19. Great Prayerday. Drove with the ladies to church in Svindinge, where the young Riis was preaching (a son of my religion teacher in Slagelse). He touched upon the war and the enemy in Jutland. One soldier in particular wept.—A big dinner party here at home. Worked quite a bit on my novel. A visit from the two volunteers Testman and Hansen.

Saturday, May 20. Worked on the novel. Rainy weather; everything good and fresh. Have been reading aloud each evening.—X told about a lady who had been particularly interested in him and, when they parted, given him a piece of cheese, which he put in his suitcase and forgot. "What is it here that stinks?" he asked the porter, etc.

Sunday, May 21. Went up to the doctor's and had coffee; Lieutenant Bentzen was there, a charming person. Here for dinner were three officers from Mullerup, where fifty enlisted men were stationed. They're in the light infantry. The one officer was once a noncommissioned officer and is a very charming person. The Sørensen who graduated with me and took my book without paying for it was also there—he now manages the cash box.—Went for a walk and read *Rob Roy.* In the evening read aloud from my novel.

Monday, May 22. Letters from Edvard Collin and Richard Bentley. Sent a letter to Jette Wulff.—Presented some soldiers in the drive with a couple of printed poems.—It's been especially lovely weather. While they were doing drills along the road, I made great progress on my novel; later in the day a title for it occurred to me—*The Two Baronesses.* Today is a great day for ushering a novel into the world!

In the meantime, the Danish government made a successful appeal for help from England and Russia, both of whom had reason to fear an increased German presence in the Baltic. By May 25 Norway and Sweden had sent troops to Funen, and the German evacuation of Jutland began. An armistice was established on September 1 that lasted until spring of the following year.

Andersen was clearly excited by the dramatic events of the war. As time wore on, however, he was torn by the conflict between his heartfelt patriotism and his friendship for his admirers in Germany. It was especially painful for him to break off correspondence with his dear friend in Weimar, the Hereditary Grand Duke Carl Alexander. Indeed, his three-month visit to Sweden in the summer of 1849 can be seen as his attempt to distance himself, at least physically, from the war. He began his diary on May 17, the day of his departure for Stockholm via Gothenburg and the Göta Canal. His reception in Sweden was gratifying: he was recognized everywhere he went, honored with a dinner given by the Literary Association in Stockholm, and even received by King Oscar I and the royal family. On his return he stopped for a few days at the town of Vadstena to view the medieval monastery founded by St. Birgitta.

Wednesday, July 25 [1849].[. . . .]
the doctor at the insane asylum and a former military man who quoted poetry and was completely taken by Oehlenschläger, who had once read for him from *The Robber Stronghold*. He said that Oehlenschläger was the greatest writer in the world. This was more than I could take, and so I answered that Shakespeare was greater, something he wouldn't go along with, even though I said that Oehlenschläger was the greatest in Scandinavia. He said he couldn't be any less than that and that many people had been immortalized by having had one of his works dedicated to them. To the others he remarked: "There you have it—a prophet isn't respected in his own land!" Then I got mad and said how much regard I had for this great writer but couldn't praise his weaker things, and pointed out Shakespeare's humor; and then this other fellow mentioned *Freyja's Altar*. After coffee we went over to the convent church. The spires are gone; the three-story-high roof was converted to a one-story one during the reign of Gustav III, when everything Catholic was despised. It was so old, they said, and dilapidated, but old folks claimed that they had had to saw the beams over in order to get it to collapse. The church arches splendid; the pillars slender, as in many Swedish churches. Just inside the door is a burial stone covering the grave of

Bo Jonsson Grip, a great sinner. On it have been carved fourteen rings as symbols for the fourteen estates he gave in order to be buried fourteen feet inside the church. In front of the altar is Prince Magnus's elevated grave; in the cellar below the coffin hangs suspended from chains.—This insane prince has the most prominent place here in the church close to where all of Sweden's insane now live.—The altarpiece, a wood carving depicting the ascension of Mary, is still in place in this Lutheran church. It was taken from the Red Church (The cathedral is called the "Blue Church."); magnificently carved and bestowed by a pope. The old, original altarpiece—of St. Birgitta sitting between two cardinals, superbly painted—is below, stuck in a corner, badly damaged; the painted heads have been cut away. A bas-relief cut in stone—Christ bearing the cross between two soldiers, with the help of Simon of Cyrene—well executed by a Swedish sculptor Silfverling. His gravestone (1693) is outside. If these gravestones could open up and queens, heros, nuns, monks rise up to see this living dance of death! Queen Filippa's grave, just a stone set into the floor, flat like the others. Queen Katarina Stenbock's father and mother—they could rise up and tell their daughter's story!—In the sacristy, two good Italian paintings of the life of Christ. St. Birgitta's coffin of red velvet, set into a wooden casket; here rest hers and her daughter's skull and bones. Birgitta's are smaller. Her daughter, St. Katharina, was the convent's first abbess. Some say her bones are false and the real ones deposited in a convent in Poland. They are very large, like a man's. A painting of her death, painted in Rome.—In the church, Jens Eriksen, a Danish nobleman—the bailiff in Västerås, who in his cruelty often hitched women to the plow.—Echoes of poverty! Then we entered the convent, which is now an insane asylum. It was extremely gruesome. We entered, encountering the minister who, when he was told my name, asked the doctor maliciously: "Will he be staying here permanently?"— Saw a nun's cell. The light came through an opening in the wall which was more like a crack. Here, in this cold cell, stood the daughters of the first families of the realm. Down in the cellar there was a cell with a well in it for use by the convent.—Birgitta's cell— in the first of the small chambers stands the elaborately carved casket in which Birgitta was borne here from Rome on pious hands to the ringing of bells in all the towns they went through. In the tile floor in her little cell—with its pair of four-paned windows—is engraved a rosary upon which the nuns knelt reciting designated numbers of paternosters. No fireplace, cold, lonely. Walked to the insane asylum they are constructing for the patients that recover. Went to where the better class of patient was and encountered there a Consul Aller from Elsinore. Saw the women's ward; one ran to the window. In the evening, had tea with the dean.—Around 1526 Gustav Vasa found an opportunity to oppose the Catholic clergy. Michel Shopkeeper was a rich merchant in Vadstena whose lovely young daughter made an impression on a handsome young man who was called Silent Olof because his feelings of love made him so silent and lonely. He struggled against his love for a long time, but at last he told her. She became frightened, but soon she loved him, too. Olof proposed. The shopkeeper was furious, and when she remained true to Olof, her father sent her into the convent at Vadstena. (See *Ancient Swedish Ballads* by Geijer and Afzelius.)[1]

> But the silent Sir Olof bold,
> He was so sore distressed;
> They're casting there the blackest earth
> All on fair Agda's breast.

It went like this: one night, in stormy weather, Olof abducted the nun and in a small boat crossed Lake Vättern to the province of Västergötland. The next morning she was discovered to be missing. Bishop Hans Brask of Linköping anathematized them. Word of this reached them at the home of one of Olof's childhood friends at the lovely estate of Hallekis just as they were about to be married by a father from the cloister in Husaby. The message arrived at the wedding, and it was read up instead of the vows.—Everyone shrank back, even Olof's childhood friend. Olof asked in vain for a horse and a wagon, but they chased him away with stones and clubs; so he carried his bride. In Gullkroken in Västergötland they stayed with an upstanding old couple, whose young daughters came to love them dearly. (The wife was named Mother Sigbrit.) On Christmas Eve the husband, Torsten Haraldson, invited the neighbors for Christmas porridge; the parish priest entered the room and recognized Olof and the nun. Their Christmas spirit was extinguished, and the lovers were chased out into the cold night. It was there, then, that she advised Olof to turn to King Gustav. He was at Vadstena; here they were recognized and received with abuse. It was with difficulty that

1. "Sir Carl or the Bridestealing" ("Herr Carl eller klosterrofvet"), in Erik Gustaf Geijer and Arvid August Afzelius, *Svenska folk-visor från forntiden (Ancient Swedish Ballads)*, no. 26, 1814–16.

they got in to see the king, who wished to see everyone. He was moved by their misfortune and wanted to humiliate the bishop; he sent his chancellor Laurentius Andreæ to the shopkeeper, who was furious; but Laurentius threatened him that his head would roll—this was his own idea—if he didn't take the two of them amicably into his home. The shopkeeper was frightened and received them well. The king had them marry in the convent church; the nuns were commanded to attend. The king led her to the altar, and the shopkeeper gave them a lavish wedding party at which all the knights danced.

Andersen wrote the last entry of his trip to Sweden in Gothenburg on August 11, and several days later he was back in Copenhagen. He resumed his diary a month later to record the return of Danish troops to the city and a short visit to Funen. That autumn he was kept busy with the premier of his comedy More than Pearls and Gold *and the publication of a collected edition of his tales illustrated by Vilhelm Pedersen.*

In 1850 Andersen resumed his diary for his summertime tour of Denmark from May 17 to August 21, which took him to Sorø for a stay with the Ingemanns, to Silkeborg to see the Drewsens, and to Glorup to pay his usual visit to the Moltke-Hvitfeldts. His entries from Glorup reflect how he was made to suffer during the war years because of his past enthusiasm for Germany.

Thursday, June 20 [1850]. Today, a big review outside; met Lieutenants Knudsen and Popp, etc. Lunch, at which du Plat didn't speak to me. Remember that!—Lovely weather, but cold in the morning. The Hvidkilde-Baron has brought rumors to Nyborg that Copenhagen has received extremely bad news! That gasbag, when he doesn't really know anything, he should keep his mouth shut!—It's appalling to hear the vacuity of the aristocratic world—to talk confidently and cavalierly about everything! Ignorance! Stupidity! "Bracken is a primitive plant." "What do you mean with your primitives!"—"The first plants nature produced." "No, my good man, they aren't that old! Now you're imagining things! The world is, indeed, many hundreds of years old!"—What arrogant idiocy covered with a coat of arms!—"As long as you are truly Danish, Andersen!" says Miss Ipsen. "Isn't that a handkerchief from Schleswig-Holstein that you have there!" says Countess Sophie Scheel. "Your Grace, that is the Danish flag with the North Star." "You're certainly not writing to

Sketch for decoration of a tent in Glorup Park
at the celebration for demobilized soldiers, 1851

the Duke of Weimar, are you?"—It goes on and on like that!—Never have I felt myself to be more Danish than during this war, and they're talking like that to *me*, while many *non-Danes* play the role of Danish gentleman! I get irritated at all that nonsense!—Worked on my folk comedy.

Friday, June 21. Awakened by Count Siegfried Scheel, who had to drive to Hvedholm. Very hot. The fish down in the muddy pond are hovering in schools, sunning themselves. Travel fever!—Drove to Hesselager; was down in the old jailhouse and up on the hill with a view over the Great Belt. A brook murmered among the beeches at the foot of the hill. Beautiful weather. Awfully thin drivel from Countess Scheel—such arrogance, superficiality, bombast, that I won't have to put up with when I get home.

Saturday, June 22. Count Scheel, the lord-in-waiting, arrived this morning. Went for a walk with Captain Høhling, who spoke with interest about my life as an artist. Unwelcome political news. Read about Baggesen's meeting with and love for Sophie Haller; I got sad myself—a time like that will never come for me. In that mood I wrote the romance "Rest well———." (Dreamt last night about the Duke of Augustenborg; I saw his picture yesterday, along with Gülich's and the prince of Nør's, pasted up on an outhouse in Hesselager.) A strange, heavy fog all morning long. Wrote a letter to Jenny Lind.

Copied my poem "Poetry" for Jenny Lind. Letter to Høst, the bookseller. Drove in lovely weather out to the big rock on Hesselager Field. Unusually lovely weather.

Monday June 24. After dinner drove to the market at Frørup Spring; it's held right out on the highway. Booth after booth, jammed with people; we could hardly get through. Our horses nearly upended several booths. There was coffee brewing; smoke from the peat and the smell of bad tobacco fouled the air.—There were tables with platters of roast eel in all that dust.—We walked to the spring; in the trees around it were hanging slender little candles and a piece of a blue silk scarf. The water was dished up in a scullery ladle. The women washed themselves three times in the water. "It is good for a lot of things!" said one. There was a hideous vagabond standing by the spring; I had the feeling he might know who I was and could say something embarrassing to me—as if I were a pariah mixing with a higher caste.—I felt nervous in the crowd, and we went over a fence, a dug-up potato field, over a collapsed well, and into the mill, where they stood around in groups on the dunghill. The mayor from Svendborg and Pastor Chievitz were here for dinner.—A letter from Captain Christian Wulff.

Tuesday, June 25. A big dinner party—twenty-four people, excellent food and drink. After dinner we walked through the garden to the woods. Mr. Lindegaard was boorishly witty at my expense—talked about my courage with bulls and the like and later, at home, about my having made the cloth flowers in the chandelier. I gave him the cold shoulder then, but felt uncomfortable about it. Afterward, when all of us who hang our hats here, were sitting alone, Countess Scheel came with some drivel—that I was supposed to have said I didn't have the heart for war, but that I'd go along as a troubadour! I was angry to have such nonsense pinned on me and objected to such "unnatural talk."—"You aren't really good-natured!" said Captain Høhling when we went upstairs.—I was irritated; sat in my shirt sleeves by the open window; felt almost like leaving at once. My blood was boiling. Top-sergeant Ruben was made a lieutenant today.

Wednesday, June 26. Went out to pick forget-me-nots for Miss Raben and Countess Moltke; visited each one, spending a long time with the latter talking about the times. After dinner, went for a drive along the highway through the woods. Little Harald Biering's birthday. I am looking at the long, tree-lined drives and at the fish hovering motionless in the pond outside: an image of the life here—monotonous, like the driveway; inert, like the fish in that sleep-inducing sunshine in the midst of luxuriant grass and flowering bushes.

Thursday, June 27. The Day of the Seven Sleepers of Ephesus. A little rain in the morning hours. Scheel came back from Hvedholm at 12 o'clock last night. Fencing with bayonets in the yard.—Off and on worked on *In Sweden.*

Friday, June 28. While the men of the house were at Ravnholt, many guests arrived, among them Laub with his sweetheart; along with her was Pastor Nielsen from Frørup; the pastor's wife is the oldest daughter of the Fuglsangs from Slagelse. We talked about the old days; I haven't spoken to her for around twenty-five years.

Saturday, June 29. Showers. Everyday recently we've had bouquets of waterlilies. Høhling has brought them the past two days. Count Carl came from Zealand for dinner.—Read aloud this evening. (Worked on "The Sæter Valley.")

Sunday, June 30. Showers. The elder trees have already been blooming for the past couple of days. Last night the acacias came into flower.

Monday, July 1. Showers. Toothache and an abscess. Diarrhea. I took a dose of Chinese rhubarb; stayed in my room all day; ate a little capon and some strawberries. Severe diarrhea, so that I was really worried. Lay all day on the sofa. Bentzen came to say goodbye to me! Had to go to bed and take thin gruel; started to perspire profusely. Received today the next installment of Oehlenschläger's *Memoirs.* Melancholy; my progress as a writer is a thing of the past.

Tuesday, July 2. + Slept feverishly. Downpour after downpour today. Went downstairs again for breakfast, dinner, etc., but felt weak. Went for a short walk. Read Oehlenschläger's *Memoirs.*

Wednesday, July 3. Went up to Dr. Winther's; had my abscess lanced. It helped with the swelling.—Everybody wanted to go on a drive to Egeskov at 2 o'clock. I went along, but Countess Scheel dropped her umbrella outside the gate, and we stopped. I took the opportunity to get off, saying that the wind was too strong for my teeth. At home I had coffee with Miss Ipsen, the Scheels' governess and the housekeeper. Wind and rain. Foul mood. Letter from Jette Wulff and the Scotsman Hamilton.

Thursday, July 4. Wrote to Jette Wulff and enclosed letters recommending Hamilton to Nygren in Motala, to Beskow, Miss Bremer, Böttiger in Uppsala.—Titular Councillor Bentzen and family came to dinner. A furious downpour while I was entertaining little Marie and Captain Høst.—Saw in *Berlingske News* that Bøgh's *"More than Enough"* or: *Willie Winkie* has been published; got very depressed again.

Friday, July 5. Stockfleth said goodbye this morning! Went with the Scheel brothers over to Svindinge, where the regiment had been drawn up, ready to be moved. Spoke with Stockfleth, Boesen, Engelbrecht and Cramer, a junior officer who is a student at the university and appears very bright. I was very sad when they turned onto the road and disappeared behind the hedges. Who knows, I thought, if most of them aren't going to their death; we'll never meet again.—Tomorrow is the sixth of July; felt sentimental—and suffered because of Bøgh's book. Why must it always be me—now that there are so many people who could be viewed as much more suitable targets—that is picked on as the one to be mocked and laughed at.—At the breakfast table, Høhling let us read a military dispatch about the arrival of the Russian fleet off the coast of Schleswig. I walked up the road; dark and somber mood. As I was ambling back, a servant rushed up, saying they were all looking for me, there was wonderful news—peace had been declared! Tears sprang to my eyes; I ran in to His Excellency; saw the announcement on the leaflet sent us from Nyborg by the merchant Suhr. It isn't official; I don't dare give myself over to my joy. Instead, my thoughts were with the duke of Weimar, with those who died for us at Fredericia. Tomorrow is the sixth of July. Will that day bring us the official word? Oh my God, my heart is filled with joy!—In the evening, composed verses to the rhymes supplied to me; drew pictures for little Marie to cheer her up after Captain Høst's departure.—The newspapers arrived confirming what the leaflet had said— the king has announced at the Riflemen's Association that peace has been concluded.—+

A few weeks later, hostilities were resumed, and Danish forces scored a decisive victory at Isted on July 25. Andersen left Glorup in early August, taking a round-about route back to Copenhagen, and made the last entry in his diary on August 21, the day before his arrival back home. The Danes were again victorious against Schleswig-Holstein after the attack on Fred-

*eriksstad in October, and Andersen's next entries, beginning on February
2, 1851, record the entry into Copenhagen of the victorious troops.*

Sunday, February 9 [1851]. Went up to Tuteins just as they arrived—it was Ræder's battalion, most of them natives of Schleswig.—Today, all of the guilds joined in; they had taken up positions
on Old Square by the triumphal arch and then walked through it
greeting one another. Several of them had choirs. There came the
shoemakers with their double eagle, the tailors with lions holding
scissors.—In the old days we knew of these things only from the
theater, from *Hans Sachs!* Life has been rekindled in people; the old
despondency is gone. They're on the move; they get together; they
have been restored to an awareness of themselves and a sense of
brotherhood. Reitzel told me he burst into tears at the book fair in
Leipzig when he saw that the booksellers also had their banner. To
be sure, it moves many an ordinary man to see the importance to
the nation that his occupation has. How good this celebration will
be for the soldier! He will see he's appreciated and occupies a place
of honor after having done his duty so well.—When I got to the
Riding Academy today, I felt nervous and indisposed. After a while
it went away. The speeches weren't much. Ræder spoke for an eternity.—(Yesterday Congressman Hjerrild spoke; it was nothing
everyone didn't already know: "You are from Jutland; I am from
Jutland; the enemy was once up in Jutland, and we suffered greatly,
and you have suffered, and now we are here; some of you are from
one town, and others from another town, and I'm from still another!")—Everyday the queen and the princesses toss down to the
soldiers lovely bouquets and wreaths that they *grab* for. Four poor
souls had to stay outside to keep watch over the weapons—they
didn't get a thing. Today I went over to talk their comrades into
relieving them.—It was a fellow from Schleswig that I spoke to, who
wanted to go to Tivoli more than anything else.—"But it's closed
now!" I said. "They'll open up for us!" he said.—I got several seats
for *Marriage to the Beat of a Drum* this evening at the Casino; a native
of Funen got mine. I arrived with several soldiers just as Ræder
showed up; they were walking sociably with me, but stopped at
Ræder's arrival. I shook hands with him and we talked, but now the
soldiers were extremely reticent and embarrassed when I went to
take them in, but I really wanted them to go, and they were very
grateful.—When I came up to my seat, a fellow with a nice face

stood in back of it; he was a native of Funen, from around Odense, and was going to spend a year in Copenhagen. He hadn't gotten a ticket to the Casino today and was standing out on the street talking to a friend about how they weren't going to get in when a gentleman passed by; he looked at them for a moment and asked: "Didn't you get tickets to the Casino? Just come along with me; I dare say we'll get some!" Then the man bought tickets for them, and when they went to thank him he was gone. I asked whether he had been reading any newspapers during the campaign, and he said he and some of his friends had subscribed to *Dannevirke*. "Often there are nice songs in it," I said, "and they're composed by the minister who spoke today; he is the father of one of your lieutenants—Grundtvig!" He was glad to hear that, and then I took out a copy of Boisen's collection of war songs and said that here he had all the songs from the war and it was his to keep—and then I disappeared, too.— In the book I had written "To the brave, dear soldier—a souvenir from H. C. Andersen." Ræder spoke and a cheer was raised for the people of Copenhagen.—(Wrote a poem.)

Monday, February 10. Wrote a fair copy of "The Soldier Comes Home" and took it with me in my pocket to the Riding Academy.— I felt ill and didn't at all want to go to the Riding Academy, went home, but went out again right away. I saw the infantry on the King's New Square. (Lieutenant Boye should have been with them, but lies sick in Flensburg.) The hussars came. I saw Holger Stampe; he recognized me. Today everyone was on the balcony of the Riding Academy while 1,600 men were being served down below and there were tables even set up along all the riding paths!—The rows of red hussar uniforms looked great. The king was at this banquet, just as he was at the one for the guard. A lot of speeches. There's a story that an officer said to an enlisted man: "You should get up and give a speech, too; you're so good at it!" "It wouldn't be proper here," he answered. "Wouldn't it be a fine thing if an enlisted man gave a speech!" "Yes, but then it should indeed be a hussar!"—They are very modest: if they themselves didn't see much action, they point out the bravest and put the wreaths on these men. It was almost 4 o'clock when I read my poem to Pastor Boye; he liked it a lot, and so I went to Ploug, who vowed he would publish it in *The Fatherland* already this evening. I decided to give 1,200 copies to the soldiers. Wanscher donated the paper, and I'll pay for the printing, but I won't be able to get them by tomorrow. Went to the Casino and got seats for some soldiers. One soldier I'd shown the way there got my seat. (At the Royal Theater Miss Lumbye made her debut as Celestine in *Statesman and Citizen;* she showed talent. After the third act I left for the Casino to tell her father it had gone well. He was in the middle of conducting the overture to *A Midsummer Night's Dream* and looked questioningly at me.)

Tuesday, February 11. Today the defenders of Frederiksstad arrived. I was at Reitzel's, and he presented me with thirty songbooks (two kinds—one with melodies) to give to people. All of my pockets were full. I gave them to almost all of the invalids and then to the men pointed out by the painter Simonsen as the bravest, to young boys and otherwise at my discretion. Mrs. Drewsen had gotten two to give out; she gave the one to someone from around Horsens— Iversen, who was a graduate of the teachers' seminary; and since he had read my work, I was called over—he got the last book I had. A pitiable wounded man with an iron ring around his head got Boisen's songbook. There were several who wanted to have one, but I didn't have any more. It was a great pleasure to hand these books out. Someone said that at Frederiksstad one corner of the ramparts was under especially heavy fire; it was lit up by the burning city, and all the soldiers who ascended it were shot down. But then the last of them held their knapsacks in front of them and did their shooting from in between them.—Some had stood at their posts in water up to their waists.—None of the speakers remembered that today was the 11th of February, the anniversary of the Siege of Copenhagen.[2] I finally told a member of the committee, the needlemaker Hjorth; and he asked me if I wouldn't get up and improvise a toast. But I didn't dare, and I even had my grayish brown pants on! The Dutch ambassador, Martini, had eight soldiers billeted in the house he was living in; he asked them to invite eight more of their comrades, held a dinner party and dance for them and for dessert gave them a plate of silver dollars, which is to say, sixteen new silver dollars; but he hadn't been able to get enough with Frederik VII on them and had to use some with Christian VIII. Hartmann gave the soldiers billeted with him two bowls of punch.—This evening there was no performance at the Casino.

Wednesday, February 12. The Eighth Battalion of the Line arrived. The weather was wet, and there were fewer wreaths and people on the streets, but at the Riding Academy there lay by each place set-

---

2. After having carried on a siege of Copenhagen since August 1658, the Swedish King Karl X attacked the city on February 11, 1659, and suffered a crushing defeat.

ting a song by Hertz, one by an anonymous poet, H. P. Holst's "Sleep Sweetly in Schleswig's Earth," which has been sung in the Royal Garden, and my poem "The Soldier Comes Home." I'd brought it to the Riding Academy at 9 o'clock and handed out 2,000 copies. Watched from Tutein's windows; threw a wreath with my poem down aimed at the commanding officer; an enlisted man got it.—They forgot to hand out tickets to the Casino. The soldiers didn't come; I told a few of them on the street that they could just go in.

Thursday, February 13. Lovely, sunny weather! Flags are waving; people and soldiers are strolling around in large groups. At one o'clock some of the artillery arrived—the Schultz Battery, which went straight out to the barracks in Christian's Harbor. Here the decorations were especially lavish with wreaths, garlands and flags. An immense royal standard was stretched almost entirely across one of the streets. The Knippel Bridge was converted into two triumphal arches with trophies, Danish flags, shields with the names of heroes on them! The guard rails of the bridge were all lined with pikes and greenery on both sides; and there were vessels on both sides of the bridge, each one draped with countless numbers of flags. With its singularity and the surroundings, it was a more beautiful sight than even the triumphal arch on Old Square. (The fountain with the golden apples is turned on everyday.)[3] Outside of the wholesaler Heering's house there are a lot of flags hanging from the roof to the bulwark of the canal; the street has been decorated all the way to Amager Gate. I felt so good on this day.—(Saw *King Lear* at the Royal Theater.)

Friday, February 14. Lovely sunshine, but no soldiers. Flags and wreaths all over.

Saturday, February 15. Wet, foggy weather. Stood on Højbro Square and watched the troops. It was the Fourth Battalion of the Line, the last of the infantry to arrive. It took a long time before they got into the Riding Academy. I felt dizzy; spoke with a couple of soldiers but almost couldn't stand, and since I was freezing, I went upstairs and soon afterwards home.—Ancker's residence, formerly Holten's is nicely decorated; at the Lagerheims', coats of arms—Swedish, Norwegian and in the middle, the Danish flag, fluttering Swedish streamers.—A plaster statue of Mars is standing in front of Charlottenborg Palace, by the large, open balcony, against the red background. The Russian ambassador is flying big Russian and Danish

3. On special occasions, such as royal anniversaries, golden apples were placed on the spout of the fountain on Gammeltorv (Old Square) in Copenhagen, and the flow of water made them roll and bounce.

flags, and Salomonsen, the Danish coat of arms up on his balcony. A Scandinavian celebration at the Phønix for the officers from Frederiksstad—Ploug forgot to send me a ticket; came to pick me up, but I had left. *Wrote the poem to Collin.*

Sunday, February 16. Beautiful, sunny weather. At 12 o'clock walked from Holmen to the Riding Academy. The regular naval crew left a little before 12 o'clock, so I came just as they passed by. Inside the academy long red and white streamers had been added and hung magnificently like garlands from the ceiling, and an immense swallow-tailed royal standard was suspended over the three palms. At the end of the hall the Danish coat of arms had been placed with two large anchors. The king was there and greeted the seamen. These men had an appearance of an entirely different sort—they looked smart, Copenhagen-jaunty; they were well groomed with their hair combed to one side.—They didn't look sociable, as if you could approach them, the way the common soldiers did. I spoke with one of them anyway and said: "See what lovely sunshine our navy has for its celebration!"—"We always have good weather!" he shot back offensively, and I retreated! Then little Kolberg came and said that he had one thing on his mind—if only His Majesty would make me a professor. I said that at one time I would have appreciated it very much but that now everybody was one! "Touché!" he replied. Then Høedt came and was angry because Old Collin hadn't greeted him courteously enough, he said. A little later I saw Goldschmidt; I said some friendly words to him about what he had written about the soldiers in the last issue of *North and South,* but he said angrily: "But it is very rude of you when one does you the courtesy of inviting you one evening to his home because one has respect for your talent, and you don't come, don't send your regrets and don't make an apology later. I am no longer your friend." "I'm really sorry that you have taken it that way!" I replied. "I didn't think my not coming was anything to take offense at—I do it so often to my friends! You'll have to take me as I am! But if I have been impolite, then I ask you for your forgiveness and assure you that it grieves me terribly much; I didn't give it a thought, and you've certainly distressed me greatly, so that if I've offended you, you have now wounded me, and so let the one balance the other out!"—"I'll tell you why you didn't come!" he said. "It's a characteristic trait of yours that I'll store away and write some day in your biography, which I'll probably come to write—your vanity couldn't stand your being together with someone else who was to be feted!" "What you are saying now," I answered, "shows that you don't know me at all!" We parted from each other in a calmer frame of mind, however, but I left the Riding Academy dejected, distressed. There was something so coarse, so rude in his behavior—I now understood that little attack against me yesterday in *North and South*. I went straight over to his mother and sister's to make my apologies. I left and came right back again with two calling cards. The story is that last Wednesday, when I was handed a special written invitation from Goldschmidt to come to his house to celebrate Ole Bull's birthday, *Ole* had said, "I'll be there on Saturday!"—"Then bring your violin along," said Goldschmidt, "and play for us! You'll come too, won't you?" he said to me. I said yes, but I'd already by then decided not to go, that I would just not show up, as I so often do with other people, and then, when I next see them, make my apologies. I didn't go and went to the Casino.— This evening there were no soldiers there. I looked at how the pergola had been decorated: three big swallow-tailed flags hanging from the ceiling like a canopy, small Danish flags hanging like banners from poles with wreaths on them and smaller pennants all over. Over the entrance, the Danish coat of arms.

Monday, February 17. Gray weather. The Dinesen Battery arrived at 11 o'clock; I saw the last of them; they drove straight out to Amager. Depressed and wanted to go to see Mrs. Goldschmidt—she and her daughter have always been courteous to me; they are the last ones I would wish to have insulted. But Fenger and all the Collins advise me not to do it, because *those* people wouldn't recognize my good intentions, but only think that I was courting Goldschmidt's favor. So I gave up the idea.—During the festivities the golden apples have been bouncing around on the square.—A soldier said about a picture of Victoria that it was on display because she had sent them woolen blankets. A soldier who had fought at Frederiksstad had several bullets hit his cloak. "Oh, these are the king's clothes!" he said, but when a bullet hit his butter box, he got mad: "Now this is going too far! I can't afford this!" (Last Thursday I got the idea to raise funds for the wounded and the dependents of the soldiers who died by publishing the poems and songs I've composed during the war years. Reitzel was willing to take care of the whole thing, and now the book will be coming out tomorrow; yesterday I read the final proofs.) While dining at the Swedish ambassador's, I felt dizzy and didn't go to the Casino, where the sailors will be this evening.— A soldier came to where I live and asked for a vest; he got my green winter vest.—The widow has been here to get some trousers for her son, who is a soldier.—Today I received from Sweden *Tales of a Mermaid* dedicated to me.—My sorrows and joys go hand in hand.

Tuesday, February 18. Saw the Glahn Battery from Mrs. Hanck's window. It was beautiful to see—even the poorest street urchins gather up the bouquets and give them right away to the soldiers or push forward to decorate their horses. They say a boy has been trampled to death. From the police I hear that there have been no disorders at all during the festivities.—The Knippel Bridge has been decorated magnificently.—(Today is Old Collin's fiftieth anniversary in office; a portrait of him by Hansen has been hung in the Thorvaldsen Museum. The dinner party was at Gottlieb Collin's. In the evening I went to the theater to see *King Lear*. My *Patriotic Poems and Songs from The War* is out.

Wednesday, February 19. Today the Mossin Battery will be arriving—that means Camillo Buntzen. There was awful rain and sleet. I got desperate and took shelter with the Wanschers, where I took some Hoffmann's anodyne. Felt ill all day in that raw, wet weather. At the Casino—*Off on a Spree* (premier performance).

Thursday, February 20. Today, the last day of the festivities. The artillery were entertained at the Riding Academy. They marched there in sunshine from Christian's Harbor. All of the guilds were present with their banners. I was standing up on the balcony of the Court Theater.—The colorful banners, the crowds of people streaming past. Inside the Riding Academy the king gave several good speeches. Nielsen said that they had plowed the fields of Schleswig, not with straight furrows, as with a plow, but they didn't do it so that grain might grow there, but that laurels might flourish. There was a lot of life and good cheer.—In the evening I went to the Casino and procured seats for a couple of officers; then went to see *The Toreador*.

Friday, February 21. Unreasonably bad mood! No joy about the future. The wreaths and garlands have been taken down; there are a few places where they are still hanging like flowers after a ball. (I ate at the Kochs' and in the evening saw Hertz's new piece, *Sheik Hassan*.

Andersen's high spirits gave way to gloom. He was exhausted not only by the excitement of welcoming the soldiers home but also by the feverish pace he had set himself as author during the war years: he finished his novel The Two Baronesses, *which appeared both in Danish and in English translation in the fall of 1848, and completed by war's end no fewer than three fairy-tale plays, two comedies, one opera libretto, the travelogue* In

Sweden, *and a great number of patriotic poems. Moreover, the death of two dear friends—Mrs. Emma Hartmann and Hans Christian Ørsted—just two short weeks after the homecoming festivities did nothing to lift his spirits.*

On May 24, 1851, Andersen left Copenhagen and began the diary of his first postwar trip. He had decided to take Jonas Collin's eldest grandson, Viggo Drewsen, with him to Paris, and his route was a leisurely one allowing him to make his customary stop at Glorup and to visit friends in Germany that he had not seen since the beginning of the war. Unfortunately, the trip was not a pleasant one—in Prague he came down with a persistent and excruciating toothache, and he and the twenty-one-year-old Viggo were not getting along well. They headed back to Dresden, where Viggo left for home and Andersen followed along at a more dignified pace, arriving back in Copenhagen on September 10.

The winter months were eventful for Andersen. In October he was named titular professor, and two months later his fairy-tale comedy Mother Elderberry *had its premier. Early April of 1852 saw the publication of the first installment of* Stories, *containing seven stories he had been working on that winter.*

On May 16 Andersen began to keep the diary of his nine-week trip to Milan. He headed first via Lübeck and Magdeburg to Weimar.

Wednesday, May 19 [1852]. Got a wake-up call at 5 o'clock but slept on and had horrible dreams.—Sent a letter this morning to Zeise in Altona. Walked on the ramparts, where the wild chestnut trees are in full bloom; the lilacs, in their first flowering. Don't feel well.— Felt better when I rode at 12 o'clock from Magdeburg over Halle to Weimar, where Lord Chamberlain Beaulieu-Marconnay and wife, along with a cousin who had been wounded at Skanderborg, met me at the train. We drove in; my things came along later. At the Beaulieu-Marconnays', got two rooms next door to the officer. Went to bed around 10 o'clock. Heavy wind and hail. Got up to check the windows. Woke up again in the early morning hours because the finger I stuck on a needle yesterday was hurting.

Thursday, May 20. Up at 8 o'clock and down to the breakfast table. My neighbor, Beaulieu-Marconnay, was an officer in the war against us Danes, but seems to be a high-minded man. He has published a volume of poetry. One that he read about a Danish and a German soldier was composed in a conciliatory spirit.—At 11:30 I went to see the hereditary grand duke; he was at his mother's. I was taken to his room, where there was a fire in the stove. I felt nervous. He arrived, embraced and kissed me fondly. We talked about the war years, and I explained the good cause of the Danes.—Tomorrow he will be traveling to Berlin to his oldest sister's silver wedding anniversary.—Visited Baron Maltitz and Schöll. Very tired and hungry. When the others drove to Belvedere after dinner, I stayed home to rest and started on *Master Humphrey's Clock*.—In the evening, read from *In Sweden* and translated from *Stories*.—Don't feel quite at home.

Friday, May 21. Beautiful weather. Went to see Eckermann, who lives entirely for his son, a painter. He told me about Liszt, who is here living with Princess Sayn-Wittgenstein; and it's an open secret. He is doing a great deal of damage to the theater; won't do Mozart— whom he says is old-hat—but Wagner and other sensation-mongers.—Went to see Chancellor Müller's widow, who spoke about the deaths of her husband and son.—Her little grandson recognized me.—This evening was at the theater, in the first balcony, and saw *The Stories of the Queen of Navarra*, which we call in Danish *Dronning Marguerites Noveller*. It was very badly acted. What a difference between this Margaret and Mrs. Heiberg's!—I went home after the second act.

Saturday, May 22. Visited Dr. Froriep, whose wife I met the first time. Went over to see von Schober, who has a lovely home; from there to see Mrs. Schwendler, who lives in Wieland's old house. It was there in the sitting room that Wieland wrote his *Oberon*, and he died in that same room. Outside, on the street side of the house, facing toward the theater, a small garden; there, under the plum tree, he once sat reading in a manuscript by Schlegel—a page blew away, and Schlegel was never able to forgive him for that.—Heard about Princess Sayn-Wittgenstein that her father was the manager of the Sayn-Wittgenstein estates. The prince married her; she took her daughter and ran off after Liszt. Now they are living together, and there is a lot of talk about it. Her daughter is now about fifteen years old, a nice, quiet girl; lives with her but doesn't get out to socialize at all.—At the theater, saw Dr. Lederer's *Household Disorders*, somewhat long-winded but otherwise quite entertaining, and *A Tiger from Bengal*, an overdone farce.—Letter to London to Bentley and Arthur Smith.

Sunday, May 23. The same magnificent weather. Letter to Mrs. Serre. Went with Beaulieu-Marconnay to see the castle interior, which is quite magnificent. The Goethe Room has now been completed; the last time I saw it, it was still being worked on. Herder's is all finished. Most inspired is the painting of the arabesques in Wieland's Room; the best thing in Schiller's Room, the verse by the poet himself.—Was in the throne room, which is decorated with red velvet.—Tired.—Visited the governess, the little Fritsch; she's a "Your Excellency!" One of the first things she said was: "How have you treated those poor Holsteiners!" and I got furious at her.—Went to dine at the grand duke's; the grand duchess very cordial and kind.— "Difficult days have intervened since we last met!" she said. We talked about the death of Queen Marie. Was introduced to Prince Bernhard of Weimar, who has recently lost his wife and come from Batavia.—Was seated at the table between the governess and Princess Anna of Sachsen-Weimar.—At the theater the opera *Martha*, with music by Flotow, was really put on by Beaulieu-Marconnay for my sake—I haven't heard it before.—Lively music. "The Last Rose of Summer," which is the main theme of the work, is lovely. Lieutenant Beaulieu-Marconnay was seriously disabled—he had his head split open in the war with Denmark. Here at home today he nearly collapsed in a faint; he has complained about pain. He is lying in the room outside of mine; I'm completely shut in by him, and the thought occurred to me that he might go berserk during the night and come to murder me. I can't lock my door. Was a little slow to fall asleep.

Monday, May 24. Burning hot sun. Visited Mrs. von Gross, who was exactly the same as always and received me with pleasure. Her little girl has become a grown woman. Went to see Mrs. Maria Melos, who is Freiligrath's mother-in-law. One of her daughters lay in bed with typhoid fever, and she wasn't satisfied until I went in to see her; it bothered me to have to do it. I went home on account of the heat. Thunder and rain. Toward evening took a walk through the palace garden to Goethe's summerhouse; strolled along the river and thought about the great men who have passed away. There was loud thunder. Lovely, multicolored peacocks sat above my head in the branches of an acacia tree.

Tuesday, May 25. Visited Madam Kirms; she was overjoyed at my visit. I found the seltzer water and dates refreshing; received some flowers. Went to see Liszt, who lives outside of town. The heat was murderous. He was happy to see me; invited me to dinner, but I had to decline and then accepted an invitation for Thursday.—He wanted to stage Hartmann's *The Raven*; presented me with his book *Lohengrin and Tannhäuser by Richard Wagner* in French; was extremely pleasant.—Dinner at Mrs. Schwendler's; I was the only gentleman;

1852

Scene from The Raven

Mrs. Chancellor Müller, Mrs. Councillor Schöll, Countess Egloff-stein, etc. were there.—I read from *In Sweden*. Mrs. Schwendler told an anecdote about Jean Paul: he was so poor when he was young that he had to earn the paper for writing his first work by making copies of the village newspaper for the farmers in the country ham-let where he lived.—It was Gleim, who first noticed him and told Mrs. Schwendler about the young man and sent him five hundred *taler,* invited him to stay with him.—Toward the end of his life Jean

231

Paul was blind and had to dictate his last book.—When I got home, the Beaulieu-Marconnays were at Ettersburg. I went for a walk in the palace garden. More thunderstorms.

Wednesday, May 26. Sent a letter to Mrs. Drewsen and included in it a few words to Mathilde Ørsted. Letter to Lorck. Received a few words from Father Collin. When I walked home, I took another route through the streets and nearly collapsed in the murderous heat of the sun. Now I'm stretched out, and the Beaulieu-Marconnay's cousin is reading his poems to me.—I had coffee with Maria Melos, Freiligrath's mother-in-law, an ailing daughter, a married one from. . . . I read from *In Sweden* and wrote in three albums.—This evening, at the theater. A terrible storm. We could hear it in the theater, and Cousin Beaulieu-Marconnay claimed that it was part of the performance. I went outside, and rain and hail were beating down. The street was awash; bolt after bolt of lightning.—There was a performance of *The Consequences of Education* from the French; it was awfully trivial. Afterwards, *The Transformed Prince;* entertaining.—Schober accompanied me home. When I seemed sleepy, Beaulieu-Marconnay ordered me to go to bed; I was displeased by his manner. Up in my room Cousin made excuses for him and told about what was bothering him—immediately after his mother's death his father had married a vulgar young person, etc.

Thursday, May 27. Horribly hot. Letter to Mrs. Serre. Presented the young maid at Madam Kirms' with the music to *Willie Winkie.*—Paid a visit to Count von Beust and Sauppe.—Dinner at Liszt's. Princess Sayn-Wittgenstein resembles him somewhat, isn't very young but very animated, received me especially vivaciously. An Englishman with his wife was there to dinner. The princess accompanied me to the table. Afterwards I read "The Nightingale" and "The Ugly Duckling." She applauded and was very attentive at each humorous touch. When we had coffee, she smoked a cigar and asked me if I didn't find it strange to see a lady doing that sort of thing. Her daughter, Princess (Marie?), appeared to be a friendly little Mignon.— They (Liszt and the princess) asked me to think of their house as my home; wanted me to dine there tomorrow. I asked them rather to make it for Saturday.—Heavy rain and then clearing. Got home after 6 o'clock. Rested for a good half hour and then at 8 o'clock had to go to the grand duchess's. Among the guests were a Prince of Hohenzollern in Russian service, Baron Maltitz and wife, Vitzthum and wife, and Schöll. Schöll saw me to my door when we got home at 10:30.—Beaulieu-Marconnay annoyed because I wanted to see the

Liszts again. He is not a pleasant man, that Beaulieu-Marconnay. I don't feel comfortable with him.—Very tired. Couldn't fall asleep.

Friday, May 28. Visited Mrs. von Gross; read to her. She translated "On the Last Day." Dinner at the Baron Maltitz'. He told a good deal about Miss von Bornstedt. At home at the Beaulieu-Marconnays' there was an engagement. The youngest sister of Mrs. Beaulieu-Marconnay became engaged to her husband's gentleman-in-waiting. Beaulieu-Marconnay was cordial today; came up to my room; told me about his father's marriages, his grief.—Got *Mother Elderberry* from Lorck; read it at home this evening. Heard that Serre is going around with some compulsive idea. No longer inclined to go to Dresden, but hadn't yet decided. Mrs. von Bardeleben, I hear, has died.

Saturday, May 29. Decided to give up on the Serres. Wrote to Mrs. Drewsen that next Saturday or Sunday Viggo should set off from home, so that we could meet in Dresden next Monday or Tuesday. Spent the morning with Mrs. von Gross; a big party held for me. The hereditary grand duke and his spouse were there. I read from *In Sweden, Stories* and two scenes from *Mother Elderberry.* Dinner at 3 o'clock at Princess Sayn-Wittgenstein's. (Liszt paid a visit to me this morning.) At the party was the French ambassador Talleyrand, a relative of the renowned Talleyrand, as well as Mrs. Schwendler with her daughter; she told about when she first arrived in Weimar, the evening at court with Wieland, Herder and Musäus.—The princess bought in Holland a beautiful picture by Scheffer—*The Three Wise Men,* one of which was a portrait of Liszt. She explained to me, in reference to my comparison of Liszt and Thalberg in *A Poet's Bazaar,* that the latter had learned everything he knew, which was indeed quite considerable, that he was a master of everything that could be learned, but that Liszt had genius.—I had to read again; she wanted "The Nightingale," but I read "The Swineherd" and had the feeling that she felt slighted by my choice. I was in a rush to get to the theater for *Tannhäuser.* Talleyrand offered to drive me and Mrs. Schwendler, but I wanted to go home first. They detained me because of the heavy storm that had just struck. I ran—the rain was pouring down, and one bolt of lightning flashed after the other—and arrived home soaking wet.—It was a full house for *Tannhäuser.* The text, good; the performance on the whole better than expected. The music competent with regard to idea but lacking in melody. What Carl Maria von Weber or Mozart couldn't have done with it!

Sunday, May 30. Whitsuntide. My neighbor, Beaulieu-Marconnay, left this morning for Eisenach. Returned *Mother Elderberry* to Lorck with a letter. The air has turned cool.—Went for a walk in the palace garden. The peacocks opened their tails into wheels. Dinner at Privy Councillor Schöll's. An American family was there; a Mrs. Robinson here from Germany, born von Jacob (in Halle), who when young edited *Folksongs of the Serbs*. I had to write in the albums of their son and daughter. They told me how widely read and respected I was in New York. Downpour. At 9 o'clock in the evening the empress of Russia arrived.

Monday, May 31. Very cold. General von Staff, Mrs. Beaulieu-Marconnay's father, arrived, and there was a lot of shifting around. I was given another room. A letter from Mrs. Serre that she will be awaiting me on Wednesday. Wrote a letter back that I might not be coming at all. A visit from Liszt.—He and the princess seem to me like fiery spirits blazing, burning—they can instantly warm you up, but if you draw close you get burned.—It's like looking at a picture portrait to see those two fiery beings and know their story, and between them this tranquil Mignon, such as she appears to be, and the elderly English governess, who probably perseveres in order to provide good guidance for the young princess.—Visited Marshall. A sick horse was led by; it had recently fallen. Marshall recited a poem by Goethe about the horse, the noblest of creatures whose hands had been compressed into horn; it had no language—only its eyes could speak. Visited Schöll.—At the theater, *Alessandro Stradella*.

On June 10, Andersen left Weimar for Leipzig, where he met Viggo Drewsen, whose departure from Copenhagen had been delayed by almost a week. A week later Andersen again ran into the Robinsons in Munich and an acquaintance of theirs from Boston who said Andersen was so widely read in America that his novels were sold on the trains. From Munich he and Viggo traveled to Milan, where they stayed for a few days before returning to Denmark over Zurich and Frankfurt. He made his last diary entry of the trip on July 20 in Hamburg, just before setting out on the last leg of the trip home.

Between his return from Milan in July 1852 and his departure on his next tour abroad in May 1854, there are no diary records. It was a relatively quiet period for him: in November 1852 the second installment of Stories appeared; two months later his one act opera The Water Sprite had its premier; and during the following November his Danish publishers distributed to booksellers the first two volumes of his collected works.

The diary for Andersen's two-month trip in 1854 begins on May 5, when he left Copenhagen with Viggo's younger brother Einar in tow, bound ultimately for Trieste and Venice. Unfortunately, much of the trip was marred for Andersen by his companion's flashes of bad temper. He did, however, enjoy seeing many of his old friends again: he had dinner with the now married Jenny Lind in Vienna, met with King Maximilian II in Munich and Liszt in Weimar and spent two days with Carl Alexander, now a grand duke, at Wilhelmsthal, where he made his last diary entry of the journey on July 1.

In late June 1855, two months after the publication of his collected stories illustrated by Vilhelm Pedersen, Andersen left Denmark on a three-month trip to Germany and Switzerland. A week later the first Danish version of his autobiography, The Fairy Tale of My Life *appeared in the bookstalls of Copenhagen. In early August he was joined by another grandson of Jonas Collin, Edgar, in Munich; and three weeks later they climbed the Rigi-Kulm in Switzerland. In Zurich the next day, he called on the composer Richard Wagner before heading northward for Friedrichshafen and Ulm.*

Sunday, August 26 [1855]. Up and off by 6 o'clock. At the start, not feeling quite well but better later. The entire countryside like an orchard. We ate lunch in Ulm; then traveled over Stuttgart to Heilbronn. Bad weather; alternating heat and cold; I often felt a draft. Took a room at the Zum Falken in Heilbronn; got an excellent room with adjoining bedroom. Very pleased with the suite but tired, so that we decided to stay on here the following day. In bed before 8 o'clock.

Monday, August 27. Bad diarrhea this morning; three bouts one after the other. I was worried; lay on the sofa wrapped in blankets; drank a decoction of rice. By 12 o'clock it was better. The innkeeper came and interrogated me so inquisitorially about the state of my health that I got the feeling that he took me for a contagious guest. Ate only soup and fish. Walked with Edgar out onto the square where we're staying. Right across from us is the house where Kätchen of Heilbronn lived, the town hall with its movable figures that sound trumpets and turn an hourglass when the clock strikes. The church rather singularly constructed. Diarrhea again in the evening; very worried. Went straight to bed.

Tuesday, August 28. Lay sleepless in a terrible sweat all night. Everything was awash. I heard each time the clock struck. Up at 4 o'clock; Edgar helped me. The sheets had turned blue-green because of the blanket; the whole bed blackened. I myself was blue, my nails green. I have never seen such a wet bed—it was as if it had been drenched with pitchers of water. Drove down to the steamship in a very feeble state. Cold, heavy fog. Got Edgar's chenille blanket, too. So thirsty that my lips stuck to my gums. Drank a lot. The entire river tour very beautiful. Many ruins, such as Götz von Berlichingen's castle. We reached Heidelberg by 12:30 and at the Prinz Carl got a good room facing out toward the ruins. At the *table d'hôte*, a lawyer (Cornelius?) from Schleswig-Holstein sat next to me, and he was very anti-Danish. "The lawyers and churchmen are to blame for it!" I said.—He thought at first that I was Bishop Martensen.—Walked with Edgar up to the castle ruins. There, drank seltzer water and listened to music. My hands, thighs and legs have turned quite red from all the sweating. Early to bed. Letter from Augusta Collin.

Wednesday, August 29. Itching and rash on my thighs and hands. Wrote a letter to Augusta Collin. Up at the ruins we met Baron Dirckinck-Holmfeld. Ate and wandered around. Hot weather.

Thursday, August 30. From Heidelberg to Frankfurt. There was a fair. We sought accommodations at the Weidenbusch; got a bad room under the eaves. Moved later down to the second floor, where we had furniture upholstered in velvet. Paid a visit to Ambassador von Bülow, who was just about to leave on a trip out to the country. Drove to see Mrs. von Eisendecher, with whom we toured the city. It had turned cold. Saw the railroad bridge and the great bridge. She drove us over to Johan Bülow's, where Miss Riegels and her mother were staying.

Friday, August 31. Got a letter and three hundred rix-dollars yesterday from Father Collin, a letter from Gusta Collin and one from Christian Voigt. Today, walked up to the Imperial Hall. There were two Danes there—a man from Middelfart and the bookseller Iversen from Copenhagen. He came over and thanked me for *The Fairy Tale of My Life*, which he had read in Norway. I said I thought I would derive nothing but pleasure from this book, that's what all the letters from home had been saying. "You have a ferocious attack in store for you!" he said. "Levin stopped by and told me that he had been asked to get cracking on a review of it and he had already finished three sheets!"—I was surprised and upset; said—since I was being treated so unfairly—it would be a disgrace for my homeland to persist in attacking me like this! He thought I must indeed be used to it.—All my happiness was gone now. I went home quite upset.—It was torture for me to go to Mrs. Eisendecher's, where I felt half ill. Agonized, I wrote home to Father Collin and Mathilde Ørsted. A visit from Colonel Bülow.—In the evening I saw the illusionist Robin with Edgar and Mrs. Eisendecher in the hotel where we were staying.

Saturday, September 1. Traveled from Frankfurt to Cassel, a strange, insipid town—large and yet small, populated, yet empty. I was bothered by the itching on my hands and legs. My mood is totally shattered. Took a room at the König von Preussen. At the *table d'hôte* I met Emil Devrient, who was here acting in three guest roles. Went to the theater, which is old and hideous. Saw *Sullivan* and *The Lawsuit.*—Visited Spohr.

Sunday, September 2. At 11:30 I said goodbye to Edgar, who was traveling by stagecoach to Göttingen and from there by train. I was physically and spiritually ill; it was painful for me to swallow! The itching was bothering me, and I was in a bad mood! With tears in my eyes I said farewell to dear Edgar, who was also in a solemn mood.—By train to Eisenach, where I took a room in the Halbmond and sent a letter to Beaulieu-Marconnay at Wilhelmsthal that I had arrived.—Pain in my chest.

Monday, September 3. Still no letter from Beaulieu-Marconnay by 10 o'clock this morning. I went to the palace; heard that he was in Weimar and that my letter had been sent there. There was a train at 11 o'clock; I decided to take it. Encountered in the train compartment a lady who was reading her jotted-down thoughts aloud and eating fried bratwurst. Arrived at 1:45 in Weimar and drove over to Beaulieu-Marconnay's, where I was received with pleasure and got my room. After dinner paid a visit to Mrs. Gross, who said that there was cholera in Erfurt. Cold weather.

Tuesday, September 4. Letters to Mrs. Serre and Christian Voigt. Several literary types were here for dinner. Took a walk to the cemetery to see the Royal Crypt.—This evening, Schober.

Wednesday, September 5. By this morning, I think, Edgar will be in Copenhagen. Roamed aimlessly. Read in *Stories and Pictures from the Folk Life of Switzerland* by Jeremias Gotthelf.—Bad mood. Large party here this evening, at which I had to read. Sent a letter to Lorck this morning.

Thursday, September 6. (Today, then, it's been thirty-seven years since I first arrived in Copenhagen.) Got warm, cordial letters from Father Collin, from Ingeborg Drewsen, Louise Lind and Edvard. They put me in a good mood. Wrote a letter right back to Father Collin.— At home. Later Liszt came. We discussed *The Raven;* I showed him several of the most beautiful places. He leafed through it and said it was laudable; decided to put it on stage. Then *Little Kirsten* was discussed; he looked through it; thought it fresher, and then he preferred it. It hasn't been translated; I offered to produce one with Beaulieu-Marconnay's help. We started on it that very evening. I was in a good mood. Walked out into the garden and along the main road, happy and thankful to God. Mr. and Mrs. von Gross were here this evening.

Friday, September 7. Somewhat worried about my stomach. Cholera is rampant in Erfurt and now in Halle, too. Sent a letter to Thora Hartmann and Mrs. Balling. Very cold. Read Auerbach's most recent *Village Stories from the Black Forest.*—Bored at home here. Visited the cemetery and froze.

Saturday, September 8. Letter from Mathilde Ørsted. Beautiful, cold weather; froze. Called on Maltitz, who was suffering on account of the trends of the times. Translated, with Beaulieu-Marconnay, most of *Little Kirsten*, which will be called *Little Karin.*—A visit from Schöll. Spent the evening at Mrs. von Gross's, where I read aloud. Lovely starry sky when we went home.

Sunday, September 9. Letter from Thorald Læssøe in Brunnen. Finished, with Beaulieu-Marconnay, the translation of *Little Kirsten.* Visited Liszt, who gave his most fervent promise that he would tend to the music and the staging of the work. There was something about this in the Weimar Sunday paper. Sent a letter to Mrs. Serre. Visited Schober.

Monday, September 10. Letter from Father Collin with a letter enclosed from Jette Wulff, who will now be traveling to the West Indies. Letter from Miss Du Puget in Paris; she wishes to translate some of my works.—Very cold. I have my winter clothes on and sleep with a down comforter. Not in a good mood. Sent letters to Father Collin, Hartmann, Edvard Collin and Louise Lind. Got a letter from Lorck with old letters enclosed from Clara Heinke in Breslau and Claudine Decken near Dresden. This evening read aloud at home here for Maltitz, Mrs. Gross and Schober.

Tuesday, September 11. Letter from Beaulieu-Marconnay about coming for a day to see the Grand Duchess at Wilhelmsthal. A nice letter came from Edgar. The air warmer, but I was extremely nervous, so it was an effort to walk home from the post office. Sent a letter to Beaulieu-Marconnay that I would be coming tomorrow to Wilhelmsthal. Letter from Edgar, so full of warmth and gratitude. The whole thing about Levin's review evaporated into nothing. Sales of the book good. Wrote to Edgar and Hartmann. At home alone at the tea table with Mrs. Beaulieu-Marconnay.

From Weimar Andersen left for Copenhagen via Glorup, finishing his diary for the trip on September 30, the day he arrived home. After an uneventful winter, he began his diary on April 30, the day he set off on a month-long visit to the estates of Basnæs and Holsteinborg, where he managed to get some work done on his new novel, To Be, or Not To Be?

Wednesday, April 30 [1856]. Up at 5 o'clock. Rain that turned to snow. Drove for the first time on the tracks to Korsør that were just opened on Saturday. I went first class; sat alone in the car; felt a little indisposed for a short while. Snow was falling outside. It was growing more and more winterish. We stopped at Roskilde for ten minutes and at Ringsted for a quarter of an hour. Here the garlands were still green from last Saturday, when the king made the maiden run. (The route was first opened to the public on Sunday.) In the woods, a single tree coming into leaf; the willow trees looked as if they had been brushed with green.—When we arrived at the station in Slagelse at 9:45, there was no carriage for me and great confusion. Drove into town and happened upon the coachman from Basnæs; left immediately. Nothing but deep mire the whole way; froze, shivering with the cold.—Friendly reception. Miss Brandis was here. Got a room with a view of the water. A fire in the stove. This evening, a dance in the barn, an annual ball the lady of Basnæs holds for her people. The barn was decorated with greenery and there were eight musicians.—They were going to dance hand in hand down to the barn from the manor house over the drawbridge, the way they used to in the old days, but the weather was too wet.—I went down for a short while and afterwards to bed by 10 o'clock.

Thursday, May 1. Dreamt that I was writing and the letters set the paper on fire.—Rheumatic pains in my chest and stomach. Letter to Father Collin. Went for a walk in the garden, where there is snow on the ground and the violets are in bloom. Gray weather. Saw several steamships far off shore. Read a good deal of Auerbach's *Grandpa's Little Treasure Chest.*—Count Adam Moltke-Hvitfeldt of Glorup arrived at tea time and will be staying for a few days.

Friday, May 2. Gray. Rain. A fire in the stove every day. Started on Bulwer-Lytton's *The Last of the Barons.* Worked on my novel. A sty on my eye.

Saturday, May 3. Cloudy and rainy, although I did take a short walk. Violets and primroses in bloom giving off a strong scent; the latter smell like hops. Went down to get a taste of the Great Belt. Sent a letter to Jonna.

Sunday, May 4. Letter to Ingemann.—Rainy weather. Count Adam Moltke-Hvitfeldt left today; he's going to Paris. We drove over to Borreby. In the summer the road there can be driven in fifteen minutes; it took us forty-five minutes because of the mire. The manor house is old, with towers, bridges and moats. My eye hurt a bit. It was 11:30 before we got back home. (A compress tonight.)

Monday, May 5. My eye bad. I am dreaming a lot every night here at Basnæs—pleasantly and in great detail. Last night I thought I was in Constantinople; saw and recognized many things that have been as if erased from my memory. Suddenly I was in Japan—strange flowers. A quiet, moorish arcade—I knew I was risking my life by walking there, but I was quite safe because I also knew that if they came and killed me I would wake up at Basnæs—it was all just a dream.—Lord-in-Waiting Scavenius arrived today. I am sitting with half a boiled egg on my eye; can't get out at all, can't read and have difficulty writing.

Tuesday, May 6. The sty bigger.—Sent a letter to Edvard Collin and after that one to Baroness Stampe on Nysø saying that I didn't think I could fulfill their wish that I visit them at this time.—Sat inside yesterday and today with a compress on my eye; didn't go downstairs at all in the evening, but stayed in my armchair. The lighthouse on the island winked across the water at me.

Wednesday, May 7. Walked a little in the garden, but my eye was hot. Worked a bit on my novel. Letter from Jonna Stampe.—A slight stomach ache.

Thursday, May 8. Sent a letter to Ingeborg Drewsen and enclosed letters to Drewsen and Wanscher in Naples.—Letter from Mrs. Drewsen and from Drewsen in Rome; letter from Miss Bremer and from Ingemann and Edvard Collin. Lord-in-Waiting Scavenius left today in the afternoon. The weather is windy; the sea is churning. Just the other day Hjalmar was on board the steamer to Kiel that ran aground.

Friday, May 9. Walked a little in the garden; picked my first beech branch of the year. Sent a letter to Mosenthal in Vienna and one to Jonna with her father's letter enclosed.—Miss Brandis and Countess Moltke left today.

Saturday, May 10. Beautiful weather!—Sent a letter to Countess Holstein at Holsteinborg and to Mathilde Ørsted in Copenhagen. Yesterday I sent four marks to the post office in Skelskør to pay for the letter to Vienna and buy stamps with the money left over. I received a receipt: twenty-two shillings for the letter, twenty-four shillings for six stamps and then two shillings in change—altogether forty-eight shillings. But four marks is equal to sixty-four shillings; therefore, they had made a mistake. I wrote them about it and asked for the rest of the money in stamps, and I received four stamps and an apology for having mistaken my four-mark piece for a three-mark, but it never was a four-mark piece. It was a three-mark piece and a separate one-mark piece. I was going to write them again and set them straight, but Mrs. Scavenius pointed out that since the post office had gotten what was coming to it and I, what was coming to me, it wasn't worth quibbling about the details; the man wouldn't understand why, and it would just provide juicy gossip for that little town, where I was already a topic of conversation. I was upset, just like always at that sort of thing. It is indeed a terrible nervous disorder! I wanted to drive into town and explain to the man that he was wrong again, for I was truly distressed by this, as I've been by all the gossip this winter.

Whitsunday. Sunday, May 11. Strange that I can't combat this pathological self-righteousness—I am entirely in the right, and everything has been straightened out, but the problem lies in the way the man went about it. When I go to Skelskør before leaving the district, I hope to tell him so—writing may seem some sort of game to him, but my Whitsunday morning has nonetheless been ruined by it.—Sent a letter to Thora Hartmann.—Got a lovely letter from Countess Holstein at Holsteinborg. Letter from Augusta Collin that Hjalmar has become engaged to a young girl Jutta Sauerbrey, the daughter of a captain of the horse who has passed away.—This evening we had a visit from Wiehe's brother, who owns the mill, and Wiehe's sister, along with the widow Mrs. Fabricius and her daughters. I gave a reading.

Monday, May 12. Letter to Augusta Collin. Wrote to the postmaster that it wasn't a four-mark piece, as he believed, but a three-mark piece and a separate one-mark, that I'd sent. If the latter were missing, then it must have fallen out and I would then replace it.—Now, in a good mood because I had behaved honorably, even though it might be said to the point of the ridiculous. Beautiful warm weather. At the dinner table a letter arrived from Baroness Stampe inviting me to come there, a letter from Father Collin and one from Mrs. Serre, but from the postmaster, no message or stamps. Got annoyed and fretful. At that very moment the postmaster's factotum came with the letter and stamps that someone had forgotten to put into the mail pouch. Everything was all right—there was a quittance for what had been received. A little before Mrs. Scavenius had asked me to make up my mind fast to accompany Titular Councillor Neergaard to Førslevgaard, where there was a children's party. I decided, and I was ready in a quarter of an hour!—The weather had suddenly turned summerlike, but the road there was long, probably seventeen miles. We arrived there a little past 6 o'clock. There were only small children at the party. I was given a cold room with a bad bed—that was annoying. Later in the evening things improved a little—a young governess who had seen me at Miss Zahle's was there; so was Reverend Barfoed and Flindt from Næstved. At 11:30 I went to bed. The sheets were clammy; the bed, soft. Slept badly.

Tuesday, May 13. Headache and soreness in my arms and legs. Summer weather! We drove from there at 10:30. They invited me to come again. On the road one of the horses got the blind staggers! By 1 o'clock we were at Basnæs, where things were more pleasant and comfortable for me.—Reverend Holm (?) was here this evening. Letter from Jonna Stampe.

Wednesday, May 14. Last night I dreamt I ate a piece of a playing card, which tasted bitter, and all at once my mouth was stuffed full of card pieces, which I pulled out. I woke up and had exactly the same taste in my mouth. My lips were burning; I felt sick. Thought I had been poisoned; got up and rinsed my mouth.—This morning I still felt a little sick. There was thunder last night. It's raining, but everything has burst freshly into leaf. The woods green; the blackthorn in bloom. A nightingale sat on a dry branch and sang.—Translated at Miss Schumacher's a letter to Weimar, to the grand duke; one of these days it will get sent off.—Felt better later in the day. Letter from Mrs. Wanscher with a letter enclosed from Wanscher in Rome. Letters from Edgar Collin and Mathilde Ørsted.—The Moltkes from Espe were here for dinner.

Thursday, May 15. Sent a letter to Jette Wulff in America and a few words to Mrs. Koch.—At 2:30 I traveled with Mrs. Scavenius over to Holsteinborg. The countess, née Mimi Zahrtmann, gave me a warm welcome. The widowed countess was there on a visit. Here for dinner: Valdemar Fiedler, who is a district judge, terribly old and toothless; Steenbuch, a doctor—a fellow I graduated with—oldish and grayhaired, had a grown daughter with him. We dined royally. I got an extremely elegant bedroom and a small room facing out on a large courtyard reminiscent of Kronborg on a smaller scale. Wanda Zahrtmann and her governess Miss Saxtorph were here.—Retired before 10 o'clock. Letter from Thora Hartmann.

Friday, May 16. I first got some sleep late in the night and then only in small portions.—Sent a letter to Edgar Collin and Mrs. Wanscher, Mrs. Ingeborg Drewsen and the duke of Weimar. After dinner, took a drive with both countesses to Fuirendal and back through the forest. Read aloud in the evening from *The Fairy Tale of My Life.*

Saturday, May 17. Worked on the novel. Took a walk with the old countess in the garden, which extends down to the shore. Tree-covered islands out in the water; the young beech forest lit up by the sun. The names of the children are Ulrik Adolph and Bodild.

Sunday, May 18. The count arrived late last evening from Copenhagen, but will be leaving early tomorrow. Viewed with him and the countess the tower, the library and the whole house. Rain this morning, sunshine later in the day. Sent letters to Mrs. Louise Lind, née Collin, and Mrs. Balling.—Gave a reading from *The Fairy Tale of My Life.* Promised to stay over here through Sunday. Letter from Mrs. Drewsen and from Drewsen in Rome.

Monday, May 19. During the night I kept hearing a regular sound, like from a tower clock! I asked the servant; he said it was ghosts. A nursemaid here heard it too and said it sounded like someone limping out in the hallway. Sent letters to Jette Collin and Mrs. Drewsen, along with one to the elder Baroness Stampe to say I was postponing my visit to Nysø. In the newspaper I see that R. Bay has died.

Tuesday, May 20. Didn't win in the lottery! No letters!

Wednesday, May 21. Today the queen left on a trip abroad on the ship *Obotrit* of Mecklenburg.

Thursday, May 22. Finished *Letters in Opposition to Materialism* by F. Fabri. They have enlightened me, but haven't clearly eradicated every materialistic argument. Even with greater experience, I stand none the wiser between the spiritual and the material, but the intangible in me is drawn to the intangible. Letter from Jette Collin.—Wrote a letter back to her.—The farmers were holding a ball; I was with both countesses and viewed this revelry. I had to cut out a cross for the old countess; she gave me one in return with a verse in German. Late in the evening, when the people had left, she came herself to my door and brought me some arrowroot.

Friday, May 23. Rainy weather. Wrote letters to Ingemann in Sorø and His Excellency Collin in Copenhagen. The entire structure of the new novel revealed itself to me: a struggle for the only comfort human knowledge can attain.

Saturday, May 24. Lovely, warm, sunny weather. Grateful to God for the novel. The old countess sent for me, spoke to me confidentially and read me a letter from her son on the anniversary of his father's death. We read two lovely hymns by Kingo: "The Sun Now Rises in the Eastern Sky" and "Fare, World, Fare Well."—I feel happy.—At the dinner table I got some tough cartilage caught in my throat. I had a lot of trouble before I got it down; they were just about to send for the doctor.

On June 1, Andersen returned to Copenhagen via Sorø, where he had spent several days with the Ingemanns. One week later he left on a two-month trip to Germany, traveling via Dresden to the Serre's estate Maxen, where he was a guest along with the German author Karl Gutzkow.

Friday, June 13. Bad stomach. Drank some port. Better! Drove with Mrs. Serre, Siegwald Dahl and little Arthur Falkenstein to Maxen, where Minna, Margrethe, Mrs. von Berge and the old Baron Albedyll welcomed me so cordially, but one of the dogs, Lola, jumped up and bit me in the back of the thigh. I was aghast! There wasn't any blood to be seen, just tooth marks! Was given some salted alcohol to bathe it with. Read aloud for them. Thunderstorm.

Saturday, June 14. The major came today. It's very warm. Took a walk to my tree; ate and lazed around. Read Mrs. Zöllner's book

From Maxen in Saxony

Christian Wohlgemuth. It's of course me and my life that she's described to a "t."—The dog after me again. Thunderstorm.

Sunday, June 15. Wrote letters and went for a walk. Cloudy weather.
Titular Councillor Grimm, wife, children and mother-in-law, Baroness Bistram, came to dinner. He has been tutor to the heir to the
throne and a companion for him on his travels. There was something formal about them, cold—but they did thaw. Mrs. Grimm had
no praise for Jenny Lind; she herself sang with polish, but without
soul.—The mother-in-law talked a lot about Prince Frederik, when
he was in Russia.—The wife of the poet Ungern-Sternberg was there.
Her husband hates music and clears out when he hears any. "But
how eccentric!" people said.—Late in the evening, after they had
left, Gutzkow arrived on foot.

Monday, June 16. A thunderstorm last night, heavy overcast this
morning. Sent a letter to Beaulieu-Marconnay in Weimar and to Jette
Collin and Mathilde Ørsted. At 5 o'clock this afternoon, Mrs. Falkenstein left for Copenhagen with her children. Went for a walk
with Gutzkow, who told me about how he had staged the second
part of *Faust*.

Tuesday, June 17. Warm sunshine! The widowed Mrs. Zöllner came
out here for dinner. I don't feel really free and easy in Gutzkow's
company. At church today there was a wedding. They were farming
people, but dressed like a young lady and a professor. The church
jammed full of people. A big wagon with musicians drove first; next
the wedding party, whose wagon was decked with wreaths and poetry, handwritten and printed. The horses drawing the other wagons had red ribbons on their tails.—Gutzkow is cold, cautious, pedantic, not very charming. "Those who are only half acquainted with
Germany have such a poor knowledge of its literature!" he said when
I'd honestly confessed that I only knew three or four of the over
forty women writers in Dresden. He was so tactless as to ask whether
I had ever been in love—one couldn't tell from my books, where
love came in like a fairy; I was myself a sort of half-man!

Wednesday, June 18. Thunderstorm last night. Slept badly! My pillow too soft. Irked by Gutzkow. This morning the dog was downstairs again and right out of her bed after me. I don't feel comfortable here; would like to leave!—Letter written the 12th from Drewsen
and Wanscher in Naples. At the dinner table Gutzkow tried to pick
a quarrel with me about "Under the Willow Tree"—it was sentimental, forced; Christian was stupid; I had no understanding of children! I defended myself and said he hadn't understood the work or

read it deeply enough. Serre, Mrs. Serre and Mrs. Zöllner vehemently took my part against him. I tried to seem calm and took it seemingly well, but didn't fall asleep right away. The rain was pouring down. Today, translated *The Bird in the Pear Tree* directly from the manuscript.

Thursday, June 19. Mrs. Serre was crying, said she'd like to thrash Gutzkow, who was now chasing her dearest friends away. Serre came and spoke to me in an effort to restore harmony, asked me by all means not to be angry with them. Gutzkow paid me a visit. Everything was fine and dandy. The minister's wife was here with her daughter and the commission agent's young sister. I read aloud. Everything was sunny.

From Maxen Andersen proceeded to Weimar, Leipzig, and Dresden before returning to the Serres' two weeks later for a second, much longer visit. On July 30 he traveled home at a leisurely pace, visiting friends at Glorup, Basnæs and Sorø, where he made the last entry in his diary on September 5, the day before he arrived back in Copenhagen.

In the spring of 1857 Andersen had plenty to do. He was readying the manuscript of his novel To Be, or Not To Be? *for publication that May, and he was also busy with preparations for his second trip to England, this time at the invitation of Charles Dickens, with whom he had been corresponding for ten years. He was to stay with the Dickens family at Gad's Hill in Kent and at their London residence in Tavistock Square as well. He began his diary on May 30, when he left Copenhagen for London via Brussels and Calais.*

Wednesday, June 10 [1857]. Drove out to the station at 7 o'clock; didn't depart until shortly before 8:00; was in a more cheerful mood regardless of the fact that I had spent considerably more than I had intended—I'd wanted to get to London for eighty-five rix-dollars, and I'll end up using over one hundred. No matter! En route, in Brussels, I read in an illustrated London paper that *To Be, or Not To Be?* was out. We arrived late in Calais, at 4 o'clock. Staying at the Station Hotel, close to the harbor. Walked to the center of town and got a letter poste restante. I thought it was from Jonna, but it was from Mrs. Malle Drewsen. Called on Minet's parents, who live on Rue Royal. They served me wine and cake.—Went to bed at 9 o'clock in order to get up at 2 o'clock.

Thursday, June 11. As soon as I came on board at three o'clock, I had a bout of diarrhea; it worried me. The weather was beautiful. I broke into a sweat—I had to stay below, got seasick. A Dane from Manchester greeted me. I came up on deck when we were in the harbor and didn't dare go with the first train until I knew what my stomach would do, but my baggage was taken straight away to the train and I had to go along with it. Everything went well. I arrived in London; inquired about the North Kent railroad, and it was nearby. I was indeed afraid that my letter had not reached Dickens, but at Higham (it's only a few houses) the stationmaster asked if *I* were on my way to the Dickenses'; it was a mile and a half from there. He took my trunk and all my baggage on his back, and we trudged in the cold weather into the country and arrived at the Dickenses' lovely country home a little past 10 o'clock. He welcomed me cordially. Then I ate breakfast with him and Mrs. Dickens; afterwards went for a walk with Dickens in the garden and conversed. He had received *To Be, or Not To Be?* from Bentley; it's dedicated to him.—His country home lies on the main road from London. This is the exact spot Shakespeare used as a setting for *Henry IV*. The lady I met at the Dickenses' when I left England is still here in their home with them and is supposed to be one of the most wealthy and charitable ladies in England. I told Dickens the names of the fingers, and "Guldbrand"[4] was particularly interesting to him. We had an especially good dinner; toward evening the two oldest sons came home. The oldest has spent some time in Leipzig and speaks good German. There is a lady here who also speaks that language. Of Dickens's daughters, Mary is like her mother, Kate very like the portrait of her father in the early editions. The oldest son is called Charles.— I went to bed at 9:30; found it a little cold.

Friday, June 12. No one came to pick up my clothes this morning, so at 8 o'clock I got up, called the maid. There is no barber to be found here, but the way around that problem is that I can drive in the morning with the oldest son to a station about fourteen miles away and find one there. Dickens and his daughters went to London today. Drove with Mrs. Dickens and the three ladies to Rochester; here I got a chance to go to a barber; saw the town, the beautiful ruins of the castle and the magnificent cathedral; Scottish children were dancing in the street. When we got home, I was a great success after dinner with my cutouts. Dickens came home in the evening. Mrs. Dickens has invited me to go with her to the big concert

---

4. The name for the ring finger in a children's counting-out rhyme (meaning literally "golden flash").

at the Crystal Palace on Monday and in the evening to see Ristori at the theater.

Saturday, June 13. Today must be the day of the comet. Sent a letter to Ingeborg Drewsen and enclosed one to Mrs. Scavenius. Letters to London to our embassy and to Hambro. Beautiful weather, but cool.—Led the ladies up to the monument, from which there is a sweeping view. The smallest of the children held my hand and danced around and asked about what every little thing was called in Danish. Then told me what it was in English, and when the two languages were like each other, he chortled, "I understand Danish, it's so similar!"—We lay in the grass; the air was warm, the wind cold. I made little bouquets. After dinner today Miss Burdett-Coutts left us and invited me to dine with her on Tuesday; I could overnight at her house. I was talking a great deal this evening, and they understood me well.

Sunday, June 14. Got a letter from Count Reventlow-Criminil in London. Walked with Dickens to the little church in Higham; it was over two miles. The singing sounded soft and sweet; there were readings from both the Old and the New Testament ("Sun, stand thou still upon Gibeon" and about the rich man and the poor man). I understood everything from the Bible and the hymns, but not the minister's sermon. The minister's daughter found the hymns for me. I was very tired from walking the two miles back home. I finally had a bowel movement today, the fourth day, actually. There is a cold east wind. The names of Dickens' children are: Charles Dickens, Walter Landor, Francis Jeffrey, Alfred Tennyson, Sydney Smith, Henry Fielding, Edward Bulwer Lytton.—Forster (Editor of *The Examiner*) here to dinner with his wife.

Monday, June 15. Early to Strood and with the train to London. Dickens and Charles accompanied me. We went to Dickens's house, Tavistock House, which is handsomely furnished. Over the doors in the hall, Thorvaldsen's *Night* and *Day*. My portrait, which I had enclosed in a letter, was on the mantlepiece. From my room, a view over some small gardens. There wasn't any time to get a shave; I went around all day long with a long beard. We drove at once to the Crystal Palace, the new one that was built in Sydenham Park. It was the Händel festival, really a kind of rehearsal for the coming centennial celebration. The *Messiah* was performed—two thousand voices with music, over ten thousand people in the audience. Clara Novello sang solo and began with "God Save the Queen." One of the directors, in whose house we had left our coats, took us to a good place in the gallery, right across from the Queen's box. The Crystal Palace looks like a fairy city with vast, floating streets. There was a large marble basin there with red, white and blue lotus; vines climbed up the pillars; statues and flowering trees all around; the figures of savages under their native trees. I saw a gigantic tree trunk, too. There were Pompeian rooms, French galleries, everything in a fantastic combination, like an arabesque, and the sun was shining on the glass roof. An awning was stretched out inside to protect against the sun's rays. The wind was whistling outside, and when the singing and music sounded, my head began to spin; I was on the verge of bursting into tears. Outside the fountains were playing; it was as if we were walking in Undine's garden. Rainbows shimmered; there must have been over a hundred fountains. Only the Blue Grotto has exercised such a magic power. Entrance to the concert, two guineas, close to twenty rix-dollars, then.—We dined at the director. . . ; a vivacious governess from Württemberg lavished attention on me. She and the family spoke German; there were several there who knew me, and the husband gave me the name: "Father of All Children."—We didn't get back to town until half past eight; at the Lyceum Theatre the performance had already begun: *Camma*, a tragedy by Montanelli, bad in the manner of Racine/Corneille, a sort of Norma-Medea. Madam Ristori was Camma; has a good face for the theater; her expressions almost too pronounced, the transitions so quick. I thought about: "Won't these small children go down into the garden and take some apples, pears and cherries!" The last scene was best, when she has taken the poison and the priests' harps are playing and she thinks she sees her father, mother and husband—it was so deeply moving. It wasn't a full house; Kemble's sister, with thick coal-black hair, a granddaughter of Mistress Siddons, was sitting in the parquet.[5] I was so infinitely tired that I shouldn't pronounce judgment on Ristori. We met today the astronomer Adams, who told us that the comet didn't come, but a new planet has been discovered.

Tuesday, June 16. Walked arm in arm with Dickens to the office of *Household Words*, from there in a carriage to see Mistress Bushby, Reventlow-Criminil, Bentley and Hambro. From here I took the omnibus to Piccadilly; was again at Reventlow-Criminil's and made it to Tavistock House and left there at 6 o'clock with Walter Dickens

5. Here Andersen is mistaken. The famous actress Sarah Siddons (1755–1831) was Charles Kemble's sister, and "Kemble's sister" was, in fact, his daughter Fanny (1809–93).

to drive over to see Miss Burdett-Coutts, who is said to be immoderately rich—doorman, servants in princely livery, the corridors carpeted. I got the best bedroom I've ever had with a bathroom and a toilet, fire in the fireplace, view out over Piccadilly and the garden in front. Beautiful paintings and statues downstairs. At dinner there were several strangers, for instance, the marriage couple I met ten years ago at the train station in Ghent. A Mr. Grassett spoke German with me. During the evening others arrived. I was infinitely tired and went to bed at 12 o'clock. Happy and grateful to God. The fire was still burning brightly in the fireplace as I lay in bed.

Wednesday, June 17. Noisy outside the whole night, like at home when there is a fire. In the morning I went to see Reventlow-Criminil, who took me over to see Christian Moltke. Then went to Bentley, who paid me forty pounds for my novel. Received an invitation from Miss Bushby that I couldn't accept. Several guests came to lunch at Miss Burdett-Coutts's, for instance, Admiral Napier, who took a seat next to me and inquired after the king and "madam," as well as the Misses Holstein. At 2 o'clock Miss Burdett-Coutts drove us out to her garden. Mary Howitt lives close by in a small house. Rhododendrons taller than I are growing like trees in the garden; cedar trees and rare plants. It was a lovely garden, and from the vegetable garden, a sweeping panorama of London. Greenhouses, abounding with rare flowers, grapes and pineapples. We drank tea, but since time was getting on Mr. Grassett took Walter and me in his carriage, and we raced to Piccadilly. Rushed into a cab, but too late to get the train—it had gone. Walter was hungry, I not, but invited him then up to eat at a restaurant. After an hour and fifteen minutes we left and by 8:30 reached Higham, where a farmer boy carried my baggage up to Gad's Hill (which is the setting for Falstaff and the king in Shakespeare's *Henry IV, Part II*). I found a letter from Jette Wulff and went to bed tired.

Thursday, June 18. Wrote letters to Jette Wulff, Mathilde Ørsted and Count Reventlow-Criminil, which will be mailed tomorrow. Strolled around. The elders are in bloom. The hay is fragrant, but there is always a cold wind from the east. Dickens went into city after lunch. Today I received a second letter from Hald in Manchester with an invitation.

Friday, June 19. Drove with Charles to Strood to get a shave. We came just as the train rushed by and reached the station one minute before its departure. Along the route I saw names scratched into the embankment—Immortality, when are you not earthly? The little baby, which is to say Edward, met us outside of the city with Walter; he had taken the long way. In a few weeks Walter will be traveling to India; he is to be an officer in Calcutta and will be gone for seven years. Sent off my letters from yesterday. Drove with Mrs. Dickens on a lovely ride past Darnley's park and castle. (This is a descendant of the Earl of Leicester.) Queen Elizabeth has paid a visit here. After that we came to Gravesend, which was very pretty, as though it were a part of London's West End. In the evening Mary and Miss Hogarth played pieces from *Lucia di Lammermoor;* yesterday all of *Don Giovanni.* Dickens came home, and we talked a lot together about Danish folk legends. It was difficult for me to express myself.

Saturday, June 20. Thunder and lightening last night. I drove with Dickens, who was headed for the city, and left him in Strood to get a shave. It was low tide; the sun-warmed foreshore glistened. It was the first warm summer morning here in England. Dickens told me that Shakespeare had set the scene here at Gad's Hill because many pilgrims came here in those days, since it's halfway between London and Dover. In the second scene of the first act of *Henry IV, Part I,* the prince says: "But, my lads, my lads, tomorrow morning, by four o'clock, early at Gadshill! There are pilgrims going to Canterbury with rich offerings, and traders riding to London with fat purses. I have vizards for you all; you have horses for yourselves. Gadshill lies tonight in Rochester. &"—Two friends of Charles came out here in the afternoon. We played cricket on the lawn; I took a blow from the ball on one finger, so that it turned blue and the skin was broken. Diarrhea!

Sunday, June 21. Letter from Miss Bushby and from Bentley. Wrote letters to Bentley, Count Reventlow-Criminil, Jette Collin and Mrs. Balling; they'll be sent off tomorrow. It's going better with my stomach. The weather is delightfully warm; I'm wearing summer trousers. Yesterday I read without trouble a story in English by W. Irving. Very warm, but it soon turned to rain. Albert Smith, the author of *The Ascent of Mont Blanc,* is here today on a visit; he seems lively and loquacious. In the evening, music by Miss Hogarth and Mary. I was very tired. Yesterday Dickens asked me so nicely not to depart before I had seen the performance they were giving for Jerrold's widow; said he, his wife and daughters were so happy to have me with them. I was very moved; he embraced me, I kissed him on the forehead.

Monday, June 22. This morning Charles and his two visiting friends drove into the city. Miss Hogarth said that there was plenty of room for me, since they had two carriages and they were taking the larger one. And so I went with them, but I understood well it wasn't what Charles wished—he was not exactly pleasant and I returned in a very bad mood, which I couldn't conceal. This is the first disagreeable day in England. Jenny Lind stayed one summer here in one of the houses; one is standing empty, "to be let." I imagine to myself that it is the one. The nightingale is not in her cage. Her friend, the little sparrow is cheeping outside, remembers the song, remembers her—it is a sorrowful morning; the fog lies on the fields; bushes and trees are dripping with water; on every leaf all around is a tear, in my eyes as well.—Dickens's family so extremely amiable, and he himself as always. At 7 o'clock we walked up to the top of the hill to the monument. Dickens hadn't been there before and was delighted. A shepherd was shearing his sheep up there; the sun was setting, mirroring itself in the Thames. A ship was gliding like a shadow over the golden river bottom. The evening still; the grasshoppers chirping. Since his return Charles has been very nice; he must have his moods.

Tuesday, June 23. Drove to Rochester. On the way, the mailcoach went by. There were letters to me from Count Reventlow-Criminil, Lorck, Koren, Albert Smith, Jonna, Mrs. Ingeborg Drewsen.—Six letters in all. I was very happy. A cold, rainlike mist was falling, but when I drove home it was very warm. Took a walk up to the hill and started to write letters. I have a cut on my upper lip, and it's a little swollen.—Otherwise very happy, as it happens. Gad's Hill begins twenty-six miles from London—there, where the "three misbegotten knaves in Kendal green"—"for it was so dark, Hal, that thou couldst not see thy hand",—"and the 'eleven in buckram suits' proved too powerful for the skill of poor old Jack."—After dinner Dickens arrived here with Mr. Evans, the father of Charles's friends. We had heavy fog, wet and cold.

Wednesday, June 24. Beautiful, very warm. Drove to Rochester, got a shave and bought three newspapers. In one of these, *Lloyd's Weekly London Newspaper*, was a most enthusiastic review of *To Be, or Not To Be?*. Sent letters to Wiedemann in Leipzig. Afterwards, when I got home, wrote letters to Jonna, Father Collin, Koren and to Hald in Manchester. They'll be sent off tomorrow. Took a walk with old Evans up the hill. Music in the evening.

Thursday, June 25. Drove into London at 8 o'clock with Charles, who was very amiable. Called on Bentley, Reventlow-Criminil and Miss Bushby. Heard there that there was a critical review of *To Be, or Not To Be?* in the *The Athenaeum*. In *The Times* my stay here and the book mentioned favorably. Sent my letters off. These carriage rides very expensive, already half a sovereign. It's hot here, and I'm lonely. Went into a less than elegant eating place, and paid four shillings for a cutlet and soda water. Wandered around; went to the House of Parliament and Westminster. There at the bridge, young Wallich and Mr. Wesley came along. I walked a short way with them; then drove home tired to Tavistock House. Drank sherry and soda water and retired at half past nine. My letters are on their way home, along with a newspaper for Bille.

Friday, June 26. Slept excellently. Very warm. A letter from Jerdan. Before I left the house this morning, Dickens came; I told him my plans regarding my stay and departure. Went to Bentley's with my luggage. Saw the queen on horseback and the entire court, which was on its way from awarding the Victoria Cross to the soldiers. It was so hot from the sun that I was close to fainting. Was at Reventlow-Criminil's; didn't find Miss Burdett-Coutts in; lunched well at the Wellington, on the corner of St. James Street and Piccadilly. Suffering from the heat. Visited Westminster Abbey. Bentley drove me over to the House of Lords, a magnificent building with statues, bosses, scrollwork worthy of mighty England. Through a Gothic hall we ascended up to the interior; here I saw Victoria's room, with a full statue of her; saw the throne and after that one of the debates, at which the Duke of Argyll (red haired), the Lord Mayor (?) and Lord Granville presided. A man, in black and with a wig, kept repeating: "La reine (would?)." The same gentleman came to me later and was one of my admirers. I'm supposed to have delivered a letter from Worsaae the last time I was here to the gentleman who showed us around.—We were out on the balcony, looking over the Thames to the residence of the Bishop of Canterbury (?). I was half sick from the lack of air inside there; got some ice, but a couple of times I thought I was going to faint. Magnificent stained glass windows.— Drove with Bentley out to St. John's Wood, which lies just outside London. The air isn't so fresh as at Gad's Hill. Was very warmly welcomed. The youngest daughter is now a grown girl. I saw four sons and two daughters; his wife was quite well and talked sensibly. They all received me so cordially; made me so comfortable. Sat on the balcony and looked out at the lights of London in the evening. Miss Bentley played "The Gallant Soldier."

Saturday, June 27. I slept as good as not at all last night. Drove into the city with one of the sons, who was engaged. He accompanied me out to the station. It was an hour too early; the train wasn't scheduled to leave until 2 o'clock. He stayed with me until the last minute; bought me refreshments. I bought *The Athenaeum;* in it was a harsh review of my new book that said it was "a dangerous book." It upset me. The young Bentley comforted me, said that it was untrue and that my book was at the moment one of the most widely bought and read and that people could then make up their own minds. The heat was murderous. Shut up in the carriage I was close to being sick; the perspiration poured off me; better when we started to move. At Gravesend I saw Walter Dickens; at Higham he and the little Evans came; neither of them showed any particular attentiveness or interest in helping me by taking a little of my baggage. They walked ahead. Finally I got a porter to carry it and arrived dripping with sweat at Gad's Hill Place. After dinner, tired, read *The Athenaeum,* upset, fell asleep and was called for tea at 8 o'clock. I was heavy in the head, tired, confused, had the feeling that no one had any sympathy for me, so I said to Mrs. Dickens and Miss Hogarth that I was very tired and went to bed at 9 o'clock.

Saturday, June 28. Slept restlessly, dreaming. The review in *The Athenaeum* lay upon my heart like a vampire. I'm still sitting this morning heavy at heart.—Letter from Mrs. Scavenius. Today in *The Examiner* another not so very good review of *To Be.* They don't seem to have understood the book. I'm not content, cannot be so and feel myself a stranger among strangers. If only Dickens were here!—To exist without being able to express oneself, always fixing one's thoughts on the same dark point without being able to erase it. Lord God, it must be Thy will that I endure this!—Let me bear in mind that I must be friendly and kind to strangers. The forsaken are sent to me by God so that when we meet I can try to help them forget it's an alien land they're in, a language foreign to me they speak. Lord, teach me to be as Thou art—loving. After lunch I talked to Mrs. Dickens about my mood. She read the two newspapers, said it was "stupid" and that her husband never read what the papers said about him. ("Without his knowledge or consent, M. Andersen may deceive some young intelligence, some susceptible heart. In one word, the book is dangerous.") When Dickens came home, he heard about it from his wife and said at the dinner table: "You should never read anything in the newspapers except what you yourself have written; I haven't read criticism of me in twenty-four years!"—He had brought along with him a Mr. Shirley Brooks, one of the foremost contributors to *Punch,* the one who had produced that article about me. Later

Dickens put his arms around me, saying, "Don't ever let yourself be upset by the newspapers; they're forgotten in a week and your book will live on! God has given you so very much; follow your own lead and give what you have in you; go your own way; you're above all those petty things!"—And when we were walking on the road, he wrote with his foot in the sand. "That's criticism," he said and rubbed it out, "and it's gone just like that!"—"A work which is good survives on its own merits. You've experienced it before; see what the verdict is!" We lay up by the monument all evening. A mist was rising from the sea; the sun shone on the windows in Rochester. We drank mixed wine up there. Later there was lightning.—The visitor gave me two issues of *The Times* from a long time ago. When I went to bed, Dickens said he hoped everything had now been forgotten and that I would sleep well. When I was asked at dinner how long I was staying in England, I answered, "Long for Mr. Dickens, short for me!"

Monday, June 29. Today at eleven by train from Higham to London. We read in *The Times* en route that at 10 o'clock yesterday evening a big accident had taken place on the same tracks: a train had been standing still when the train from Strood came and ran into it. Fourteen people were killed, forty injured. We passed the place two stations from London. At London Bridge I left the family, then took a cab. The coachman drove me into one of the poor quarters in such a way that I believed he meant me harm, but I got home safe. Miss Hogarth is not at all attentive; her sons aren't either. There is on the whole a great difference between the entire family and Dickens and his wife. Not in a good mood. At 4 o'clock arrived out at the Bentleys'. Here, the sons are especially attentive. Big dinner. A friend of Kean . . . was here, a woman novelist Julia Pardoe, who has written about Constantinople. A young Mr. Bentley and wife, very attentive. It was after 12 o'clock when I got to bed.

Tuesday, June 30. My stomach bad. Wish to leave England. I'm not really happy with my visit.—I stayed in the country until nearly half past two; ate lunch; wrote a letter to Einar about the plan to go to Paris, which I've since shelved after counting my money.—The good people out at Bentley's did everything to please me. Drove in with the youngest. Saw an issue of *The Literary Gazette* that wished I'd written fairy tales and not *To Be*. Returned home to the Dickenses'; they were already at the dinner table. The aunt quite nice; Dickens marvelous, as usual. He's supposed to give a reading of his *Christmas Carol,* and therefore they were eating early. Asked if I would like to hear it, but I preferred to see him act. Took a very long walk to Piccadilly. Today a visit from Lyell's wife.—At 10:45 this evening the ladies came home. Dickens had created a furor. Mrs. Dickens tired; the daughters without a thought for me; the aunt even less. Went to bed in a bad mood.

Wednesday, July 1. Too little sugar in the tea. Mrs. Dickens cordial and pleasant. The young Evans came and picked me up at 11:30. It thundered and rained. We drove to *The Times*'s printing shop; in one of London's narrow, dirty streets down by the Thames lay the place from which the queen (nymph?) of the newspapers goes out into the world, more than 50,000 copies. A queen flower with more than 50,000 petals, whose fragrance and light reaches all of the countries in the world, from Stockholm to Hindustan. To see such a flower come into bloom, to hear it unfold and come into being in a minute; that is what's amazing. It was as if I was standing in the middle of a roaring waterfall when the big machines were sent into motion. The gallery I was standing on shook; I got nervous, dizzy. The big, white sheets moved fast as lightning and absorbed the impression of the words and fell from hand to hand.—Everything has been organized with full military discipline; each section, each article has its office, each individual stage from the white paper to finished printed copy, its floor. It is like one great body. Mr. Bloodless is a terrifying, powerful monster here.—Mr. MacDonald himself showed us around. Drove home with Evans; drank soda water; saw his father's big printing shop, the engraving of bank notes for Brazil; saw them printing *Punch;* I was given one copy (of 40,000) and one of *Household Words* (also 40,000) just as I saw it brought to life. Drove to Lyell's and paid a visit; afterwards, in the pouring rain, to see Count Reventlow-Criminil and delivered letters to Hambro and to Father Collin, Louise and Einar. Read in the newspaper that old Molbech is dead; met a nephew of the minister in Lyngby, Peter Rørdam, likewise, the Swedish chargé d'affaires. In the evening at the Princess Theatre and saw Shakespeare's *Tempest,* produced by Charles Kean, the son of the famous Kean. It was staged with the fantasy of Shakespeare. Caliban was excellent; Ariel, a lovely figure; Miranda sentimental, bloodless and yet captivating; the rest, only cardboard figures. The king and the whole Neapolitan court appeared just as they were coming from a shipwreck in gold and ermine and with crowns on. The borders weren't hanging right, and little mistakes occurred. In the first act, ocean right up to the footlights; a big ship is tossed around right out toward the audience. The masts are cut.

It sinks, and this is accomplished by inflating the whole vessel with air, which is now let out. The first appearance of Ariel is as a star falling from the sky, and just as it touches the grass it bursts into flame and Ariel can be seen within it. (He sweeps across the stage without a rope.)—A desolate, wintery landscape is transformed into the most lush piece of nature—trees burst into leaf; nymphs dance on the turbulent, rushing waterfall. In one of the acts the entire backdrop moves by so that the landscape changes. Juno in her coach drawn by peacocks, the sky full of hovering genies and finally Prospero on the ship, which sails away—it fills the entire stage and then glides off to the side revealing the whole backdrop, which is the outstretched ocean. The moon shines on the water, and high in the air a radiant Ariel hovers casting the colors of the rainbow down upon the water; he waves farewell to Prospero.—The whole thing is extraordinarily magnificent, but Shakespeare himself is lost in the scenery. The performance lasted from 7 o'clock to one. The intermissions were tediously long. The gallery made noise, whistled and shouted jests. It was over at 1 o'clock; I got to bed by 2 o'clock. My blood hot!

Thursday, July 2. The maid called me already at 7:30. I got up very tired! Went out, but returned soon and rested until almost 12 o'clock. It didn't look as if we were going to have lunch today. So I went out and had mine on Oxford Street. Visited Bentley and was at the barber's for a haircut. The weather cloudy and not at all warm.— Mrs. Dickens's mother and sister were here for dinner. Little Kate cutting; the aunt is definitely tired of me. At Her Majesty's Theatre with Mrs. Dickens and her mother and heard Verdi's *La Traviata*— the same theme as the young Dumas's *The Lady of the Camellias*. Mademoiselle Piccolomini an exceptional singer, who also could act. Giuglini an exceptional tenor and Beneventano bass. In the box we were visited by Collins's brother and, later, Lumley, who related that Jenny Lind had talked a lot about me when she was here.— When we drove home at night, the coachman didn't know the way. We went from one square to another—here one was locked up, and there in the other there was no one to be seen. Finally, late at night, we found our way home.

Friday, July 3. My stomach not good. Went out (letter to Mrs. Serre) and felt poorly. Didn't find Reventlow-Criminil at home. Was nervous and ill, but a little better after leaving the hairdresser's. Drank soda water and ate a little bread; felt well then and walked home by Oxford Street and Russell Place—that's to say, walked from the passage off Piccadilly home to Tavistock House. When Dickens is present, they are all very cordial to me. Dickens related that the railroad company will have to make a disbursement of 70,000 pounds to the next of kin of those killed.—This evening, a little after 9 o'clock, I was the first to arrive at Miss Bushby's. It was an assemblage that paid me compliments about my book. I didn't believe a single one— on the table lay *The Athenaeum* with a different opinion. Met a Dane there who's a resident and married to Wallich's daughter.—A gentleman did recitations in the manner of the most famous actors; Kean, whom I've seen in *The Tempest*, was especially easy to recognize. There was singing and dancing. I talked English the whole time. The coachman did a good job finding his way home. They were all at rehearsal. Last night it lasted from 12 o'clock to 4 o'clock in the morning, since it can't start until after the performance is over at 12 o'clock at night.

Saturday, July 4. Rainy weather. Walked to the passage by Piccadilly. Visited Bentley, who showed me a copy of *The Saturday Review* in which Dickens's *Little Dorrit* was dealt with most severely. "You see, you're not the only one!" said Bentley. I don't know, but my mood improved. What is criticism—often only born of the passion of friendship or envy; often stupidity, often the product of haste. Dickens told me an able contemporary of Shakespeare, William Kempe, had said about *Macbeth* that it was one of the stupidest pieces of junk imaginable. Went to the British Museum; saw relics from Nineveh, sphinxes with beards, Greek antiquities, walruses, lovely birds, flamingos, red and white, mastodons. Today I walked the whole way there and back from Tavistock Square. The way from here is Russell Place, Museum, Oxford Street, New Burlington Street and down through the passage. This evening at the Gallery of Illustration on Regent Street and saw Wilkie Collins's drama *The Frozen Deep* performed for the queen. She had wished to see it, Dickens said, but it wasn't customary in England for the queen to enter a private house. She could not, therefore, go to him; and his daughters, who hadn't been presented at court, could not, therefore, act in a play at Buckingham Palace. This was, then, a compromise for the performance held for Jerrold's widow. The queen did not wish a large audience, since it would otherwise get so hot. She knew I was there, Dickens said. Corridors and stairs beautifully decorated with flowers. The queen arrived at 9 o'clock with the king of Belgium, Prince Albert, the prince of Prussia and princes and princesses. Dickens recited a prologue (in a fog). The set in the second act with snow falling through the air very beautifully. The curtain between the acts was a turbulent sea with a lighthouse which was illuminated. In the last act a shot was fired from the little ship on the superbly painted backdrop. The play was well acted. The author performed the part of the happy lover; Dickens, on the other hand, the unhappy lover, which is the main part, and showed himself to be a quite remarkable actor, so free from all the mannerisms that are practiced in England and France particularly in tragic roles. It was so true, so natural, as we at home might see Wiehe render the part. The death scene so moving that I burst into tears. After that, a French farce *After Midnight*. In this Dickens was so full of humor and fun that it was a fresh revelation. Mark Lemon, the editor of *Punch*, acted the other part with so much humor and veracity that it was a joy. After the performance I drove over to the office of *Household Words*, where the actors, actresses, the whole company, gathered for a lively, enjoyable supper—we drank champagne. Collins's mother gave me a bouquet made of the parsley garnish on the ham, and Lemon said she was a coquette, called her the mama of the play. I arrived at Tavistock House after 2 o'clock. (Not really in a good mood at all the entire evening.)

Sunday, July 5. Drove at 1 o'clock with Mrs. Dickens to the railway and arrived in Higham at 2:30. Waited there until the carriage returned, and when I was at last at Gad's Hill, I met Bentley and Wilkie Collins, who were already there. Big dinner party. In the evening walked with all of them up on the hill—to "Andersen's monument," as Dickens calls it, because I was the first to take them up there and it is my favorite place.—Found letters from Father Collin, Jette Wulff and Anna in Ålborg, along with a letter from Holland to the author of *Only a Fiddler*. At home it had been taken to mean that I was a musician with one of the regiments.

Monday, July 6. Felt ill; went, however, from Higham to London, but expected, especially during the first part of the trip, that I might have to leave the coach at one of the stations. It was very embarrassing. Made it to London. The fellow who was driving didn't know where New Burlington Street was. I showed him the way, and after lunch drove with Bentley out to St. John's Wood, where I'm writing this in veritable fall weather. The sons and daughters extremely charming, more approachable and sympathetic than Dickens' children. In the evening a nephew was here with his wife. They made music and I sang Danish tunes.

Tuesday, July 7. Early in the morning dreamt I'd won in the lottery;

the drawing was yesterday. The weather cold, a little better than yesterday. Stayed out here all day long; in the evening took a walk with the sons across the meadows to Kilburn. The youngest son suggested to me that he travel with me from here over Dresden to Copenhagen. The sister said it would be good for him, since he was so nervous; asked me to suggest it to their father. I wasn't quite happy about the inconvenience this trip would involve.

Wednesday, July 8. Old Bentley was not in favor of his son's trip and it was abandoned. Drove by omnibus in to the bank—four English miles for six pence. Hambro invited me to stay with him on my next visit to England. Drove to Reventlow-Criminil's; left off letters for Jette Wulff and Mrs. Balling. Heard that there was a letter for me at Tavistock House; drove there. The letter was from Mrs. Balling. Drove by omnibus out to St. John's Wood, where I arrived for lunch at 1:30. Tired and took a rest. Drove after dinner through Regents Park to the Lyceum and saw Ristori in *Macbeth.* In the final scene she was quite remarkable—gesture, voice, everything gripping. Macbeth was well played in the Italian manner. Two ladies in crinolines took up three seats. Over at 11:30. Drove home in lovely moonlight.

Tuesday, July 9. Very tired. Didn't quite have the strength to get myself to the harbor. Wrote in Miss Pardoe's copy of *To Be, or Not To Be?:*

> With the eye of genius you saw the East,
> And what you saw, you expressed so true.
> With the eye of genius you'll grasp not least
> These Northern pictures I'm painting for you.
>
> ———
>
> "Often in a wooden house a golden room we find."[6]
>
> (Longfellow)

Drove by omnibus with Bentley's daughters to see Miss Pardoe, who presented me with her book *The City of the Sultan* in three volumes. Bentley's daughters wanted to walk home; advised me to drive. It was so expensive, they said, always to drive; therefore, they were going to walk. I took a carriage, but it pained me to see that they

6. A quotation from Henry W. Longfellow's poem "Art and Tact" in the collection *The Belfry of Bruges and Other Poems,* 1846.

don't have much—as Dickens has also said. Friendly, decent people. Had good news for Jette Wulff about her coming to Hastings.

Friday, July 10. I was moved when saying goodbye; tipped seven and a half shillings. Their son accompanied me to the omnibus; my baggage was put up on top. I drove up to Oxford Street and from there, home in a cab for a six pence. Met Dickens; we won't be going to the country until Monday; so I won't leave until Wednesday. Dickens will drive me to Maidstone. Called on Reventlow-Criminil, Mrs. Bushby and Miss Gipps—I didn't find her in. She was in the garden; I was shown out there and went by mistake into the Rothschilds'. After that, during my visit, the crown prince of Oudh[7] and his uncle (brother of the king of Oudh) were there; they stood up, greeted me. The interpreter and some sort of minister and someone else were with them. The uncle asked what kind of kingdom Denmark was, how far away, whether I'd traveled by sailing ship. He thought it was a wild country, more so than his own, said Mr. Kelly. At the Lyceum with Mrs. Dickens in the evening and saw Ristori as Lady Macbeth. The last act is the crowning glory. That wonderful, dry, deep voice, as if her thoughts were revealed from within; those anguished sobs are gripping and true. Macbeth himself was in the Italian style, not without truth, but the expression of intonation and gesture so intense that it exceeded reality. The Macbeth of Scotland, at least, never spoke like that.

Saturday, July 11. Said goodbye to Count Reventlow-Criminil and Christian Moltke. In the evening, at a performance for The Jerrold Fund with Mrs. Dickens. Got the center seat in the first row, right by the footlights. Now I could hear and understand almost every word. First *The Frozen Deep,* after that *Uncle John.* Dickens was masterful in the drama, true, natural and magnificent! I cried like a baby. Then he played Uncle John with remarkable humor. Mark Lemon, remarkable mime and comic. An older gentleman came to me and thanked me for *Picture Book.* The newspaper editors had their own box and left after the first play was over. The company gathered at the Dickenses' home. We drank champagne again. My neighbor . . . very cordial to me. It was after two o'clock before I slipped up to my room. (The scene painter, Stanfield, drank to my health.)

Sunday, July 12. Got up at 9:30; very warm. Sore throat and chest. Worried about tonsillitis. My left arm really red; I feared Saint An-

---

7. Oudh (Awadh) is a region in northern India, Uttar Pradesh (formerly United Provinces of Agra and Oudh).

thony's Fire, that I might need to stay on at the Dickenses' home and inconvenience them because I was sick. At 3 o'clock drove with the Dickens family out to Albert Smith's. It was a large, empty house with a garden. A tent had been raised on the green patch of lawn; champagne bottles, soda water bottles were lying around. Cheese, bread decorated with dolls were set out. Everyone was in a dress coat. The whole company from *The Frozen Deep* was here. I presented Collins with my most recent book. In the sitting room saw Lady Blessington's hands in wax. A scene from Switzerland; inside the courtyard lay bits and pieces of paper mountains. Smith's brother was walking around in his shirt sleeves wrapped in a flag. There was a lot of eating and drinking. Mark Lemon and Dickens were in the thick of it. Lemon was in fine fettle the whole time. I gave him a poppy seed box with a flower. "I understand, indeed," said he, "this is the bottle for me!"—There was a young singer, Miss Keeley, whose father was a famous comedian; she sang very beautifully. An author was there. . . , whose father was a famous actor; he could speak German. We lay on the grass. Claret with ice was passed around. It was so Danish in its light-heartedness, just the thing for Ingeborg. Young Walter Dickens asinine! I'm thinking of his father. In the evening the garden was illuminated with candles in bottles. It was warm and still like in Italy; the stars twinkled in the clear sky. We drove home at around 12 o'clock.

Monday, July 13. Very hot. From London at 2 o'clock. My little friend (the music genius) gave me a casual and unfriendly reception! I lounged around; got an idea for a story: "Without Love," which is to say, someone whose heart is full of it but finds none in his mother, none in the girl he loves. When Dickens arrived home late, everything was pleasant. It was a starry night. The red house with the four bay windows, the porch with its stone columns, the big window above, the gilded vane on the little turret, the cedar trees over on the other side of the road, the raven in the empty dog house, the dogs Dandy and Turk, Hogarth's pictures in the corridor, a richly pasted screen.—In the dining room a picture of Cromwell, one of a carriage in which the jockey steals a peek at the book (*Bleak House*) the lady is reading.—The box at the theater.—Birds in the cage. This evening the gypsies had a fire close to the road.

Tuesday, July 14. Dickens is suffering a bit from aches in his face. Today some friends came to play cricket on the field outside. I drove with Mrs. Dickens to Strood, where I had a shave, and then took from there a carriage home in oppressive heat.—Here were a number of friends playing cricket. Mrs. Beard got a ball in her eye, so that it turned black and blue.

Wednesday, July 15. Toothache. Up at 6 o'clock, off at 8:30. The painter . . . accompanied us as far as two and a half miles on the other side of Strood, where he wanted to catch the train. The area picturesque, as if we were in a balloon looking down over the woods. Dickens himself drove me to Maidstone. My heart was so full. I didn't speak very much, and at parting I said almost nothing. Tears choked my voice. I rode in oppressive heat to Patrick's Wood, was put into another coach and reached Folkestone, where I waited over two hours on board the ship before it sailed. The sea dead calm until we neared the French coast at 5 o'clock in the evening. There my passport visas and baggage were examined. A nice woman carried it to the Hôtel des Bains. First got a room facing out on the court-yard, then one out to the street. Sent my clothes to be washed and decided to stay until later in the day. My mood like my poor tailor's. I'm on the verge of morbid obsessions. View out over the sea.

Andersen continued his journey via Paris and Frankfurt to Dresden, where he spent the month with his friends the Serres before leaving for Weimar to participate on September 3 in the centennial celebration of the birth of the grand duke's grandfather. Because of the growing tensions between Denmark and Germany, this was the last time Andersen and Carl Alexander were to see each other. Andersen was back in Copenhagen on September 12, but left again two days later because of an outbreak of cholera. He spent ten days with the Ingemanns in Sorø and three weeks at Basnæs with the Scavenius family before returning to Copenhagen on October 19, the day after his last diary entry.

The spring of 1858 was an eventful one for Andersen. In March he was decorated with the silver cross of the Order of Dannebrog, and the first installment of New Tales and Stories *was published, to be followed by a second one in May. One month later, on June 15, he began a diary of his tour of Switzerland, this time with Harald Drewsen, Viggo, and Einar's younger brother. Andersen recorded in his diary a week later that Harald was as unpleasant a traveling companion as his brothers had been: "Harald is difficult to rouse in the morning and awkward to have around—he won't call on people, won't speak German, very ponderous like Viggo. . . ."*

The journey home from Switzerland included stops in Munich and Dresden, where Andersen received a letter from his close friend Henriette Wulff asking him to meet her in Eisenach before her departure for, and indeed emigration to, America. Andersen was unwilling to do so, claiming that he had promised Harald to travel home via Braunschweig and that, on account of the German Confederation's opposition to a joint constitution for Denmark and Holstein, he did not wish to call on Grand Duke Carl Alexander as etiquette would require should he find himself in Eisenach. He never saw Henriette Wulff again—her ship caught fire and sank.

In 1859 Andersen spent his summer touring Jutland instead of traveling abroad. He left Copenhagen on June 1 to visit the Ingemanns in Sorø and the Scavenius family at Basnæs, but he did not begin his diary for the trip until three weeks later, when he took the ferry from Korsør to Århus. After visiting a branch of the Drewsen family in Silkeborg, he headed for the West coast of Jutland to visit Titular Councillor Tang at Nørre Vosborg.

Monday, July 4 [1859]. Feeling really ill. A letter, probably from a madman—I had myself convinced that it was from a crazy smallpox patient and washed my hands.—At 12 o'clock drove in a rented coach to Herning (six rix-dollars and four marks in all). Most beautiful and wild near Silkeborg.—The higher elevations covered with heath and bouquets of scrub oak; the hills as if they were made of black peat with the white sand shining through.—In the distance houses and hills rose up as if from a glassy sea. The district got better and better: prosperous-looking farmhouses, even estatelike farms lay sown over the countryside hearth to hearth, like on Zealand, but with better farmlands. Fields of grain where the grain looked full of promise, the whole sky pulsating with the song of larks; and then I reached Herning, which could be seen from all around. The estate Herningsholm is located nearby (Wolff). A room had been reserved for me by the postmaster; it was the best in the house, new and facing out onto a small garden and a bowling green. Right across from the inn is the postmaster's house with white roses growing up the wall and encircling the king's name. Ate a good beefsteak and drank a very good red wine. I spoke with Postmaster Hansen's little children; I asked little Anna if she had any books, and she answered: "Andersen's tales!" Later, when I called on her father and the little one knew who I was, she brought me a bouquet of flowers, and I gave her my most recent tales in return. Her father said there had been a district meeting today, the farmers were drunk, there might easily be a rumpus at the inn. It was extremely upsetting for me. I closed my curtains and hung towels up. My room is off the garden—I worked out how I could get out in the event of an assault—for someone had told me that people here are hard up. I went to bed early but got almost no sleep; lay feverish, waiting to be attacked.

Hans Christian Andersen, 1860

Tuesday, July 5. Up before 7 o'clock. No carriage arrived from Nørre Vosborg. I was annoyed and went to order a rented coach. That would be about nine rix-dollars to get there; and yesterday, over six. This is an expensive business. I ordered a coach to Holstebro and went and packed. Then Postmaster Hansen came to say that *now* Tang's carriage had shown up. The rented coach was cancelled, but I had to wait there for two hours. Tang hadn't gotten home until late last night and then had sent a carriage immediately, since his wife had misunderstood my letter.—Jette Pedersen's house, where she used to live, is the second house from the post office; has a well and a pretty garden. The postmaster's wife is pregnant and has Saint Anthony's Fire on her feet. He was here this morning and entertained me for a good half hour.—At 10:30 drove with an inoffensive Jutlander who was not, however, entirely understandable. The land was better settled and cultivated than I thought. Here and there rose a column of smoke from heather being burned. At 3 o'clock we reached Holstebro, where a man was standing at the entrance to town and asked us to drive to Knudsen's inn; that's where Titular Councillor Tang was. He welcomed me with jubilation. His closed carriage awaited me there with its clock, lantern and lectern. We had our dinner, fried eel, and then departed. On the street a man greeted us; he had 100,000 rix-dollars, but had lost his mind from masturbating. We drove along a barren road to endless, fascinating anecdotes about the family. There was material for a whole novel.—His grandfather was the son of a rich farmer; he was sent to Lemvig and became a clerk there. Later he worked in Ringkøbing for a merchant—in his contract was written that every shilling found in the boy's pocket would be regarded as stolen from his employer's cash box. As a commission agent he had to travel by ship to Norway and, in particular, to Holland, where goods were shipped home. The merchant had a stock of wines. When the town sheriff had guests who wanted to leave before it suited him, he used to knock their hats out of their hands and stand on them. Once, as he left, Tang took the sheriff's own new beaver hat, which got the same treatment. There were wolves hereabouts: an old woman had told about how a horse kicked a wolf and trampled it, even though its legs were bitten and clawed at. The story about the eel: "The eel mother said to her daughters, 'Don't go too far, because then the evil eel catcher will come and get you'; but they went off anyway and of the eight daughters only four came back home to the eel mother, wailing, 'We only went a short way from the door and the evil eel catcher came and caught our four sisters!' 'They'll be coming back again,' said the eel mother. 'No,' said her daughters, 'because he skinned them!' 'They'll be coming back again,' said the eel mother. 'No, he cut them up into pieces, fried them and ate them.' 'They'll be coming back again,' said the eel mother. 'No, because he drank a big glass of schnaps afterwards!' 'Did he drink schnaps!' said the eel mother. 'Oh Lord a'mercy, then they'll never come back again, be-

Decorative papercut (made at Nørre Vosborg Manor, 1859)

cause schnaps is the death of you!' 'And that is why they say you
should drink a dram of schnaps with your eel,' said the man." When
we arrived at Nørre Vosborg, the flag was flying; the whole family
was standing on the balcony and then down in the doorway. There
was a clergyman on a visit . . . . , who had matriculated with me. A
Reverend Tang, who lives here. Climbed up onto the ramparts and
had a strong tea toddy in the evening. I'm to sleep in the chapel,
which is haunted by the White Lady.

Wednesday, July 6. Was still tired when I got up at 8 o'clock. My
face is chapped from the west wind, feeling coldy and haven't had

a real bowel movement in two days. Later on the problem worked itself out after a walk. Two young fellows from the university have arrived—a Repsdorph from Holstebro and a Pedersen from Copenhagen. The old ramparts rise up right outside the house; up on top there's a gazebo—"Breidablik."[8] We walked down to the garden, which is a veritable elfin thicket; old, as if it hadn't had an airing out; not a ray of light, not a breath of wind; scummy water in the moat; withered and dilapidated arbors covered with moss, a bowling lane in disrepair, reed huts overhung with spider webs and falling apart at the joints. An angry swan swam over toward the wattlework bridge. A large, flat view out to Nissum Fjord. We entered a garden that was better tended—fruit trees grew on espaliers. Here a lovely cottage has been built for the brother, Pastor Tang, who is a great follower of Grundtvig. We paid a call there. Back at home I read "The Wind Tells of Valdemar Daae and His Daughters" and "Anne Lisbeth." Today is the anniversary of the Battle of Fredericia,[9] and so six of the employees who had fought in the battle were invited to a celebration. One of them was the gardener and the other the house servant. Tang proposed a toast for Denmark and then one for her soldiers; the minister, for the Danish flag, which had been hung up in the parlor; I, for Danish womanhood. We had rather strong toddy in rather large quantities. Then at Tang's request I read the tale "Holger the Dane" for the farm hands. It was 1 o'clock before we got to bed.

After a visit to Skagen, the northernmost tip of Jutland, where he visited his letter-writing friend Anna Bjerring, Andersen followed a circuitous route back to Silkeborg and then to Kolding, where on September 10 he made his last diary entry of the trip.

The year 1859 was a rewarding one for Andersen. In March and December he had the satisfaction of seeing in print the third and fourth installments of New Tales and Stories, *both of which contained some of the best tales and stories of his later years, "The Wind Tells of Valdemar Daae and His Daughters" and "A Story from the Sand-Dunes." He also received two pieces of good news in December: King Maximilian II of Bavaria had decorated him with the Maximilian Order of Art and Science, and his annual stipend was to be increased from 600 to 1,000 rix-dollars.*

8. In Nordic mythology the name of Balder's dwelling known for its view.

9. During the Dano-German war (1848–50), the Danish army, besieged in the town of Fredericia, successfully undertook a counterattack on July 6, 1849, defeating the German forces.

In late May 1860 Andersen set out on a six-month tour of Germany and Switzerland. During the first of his three visits to Munich, he renewed his acquaintance with the writers Emanuel Geibel and Paul Heyse and the painter Wilhelm von Kaulbach. On an extended side trip to see the passion play at Oberammergau, he saw two familiar faces from home—the actor Lauritz Eckardt and the ballet dancer Harald Scharff—which he got to know much better in the coming years. Traveling via Brunnen, Le Locle, and Montreux, he arrived in Geneva, where he spent three weeks.

Saturday, September 1 [1860]. Want to go home. Wrote a letter in that frame of mind to Edvard and asked for his advice. Later in the day a Mr. Kertbeny, who'd sent me his translation of Petöfi, came and paid me a visit. He was very entertaining, mostly on the subject of Hungarian literature. There was a heavy rainstorm with thunder that lasted from 2 o'clock in the afternoon until 8:00 in the evening. I spent the evening at a party at Blanvalet's, where all of the guests spoke German; there was also a man there from Schleswig, Pastor Andersen, with whom I spoke Danish. I read them " 'Something,' " "The Pen and the Inkpot," " 'Lovely!' " and "It's Perfectly True!" Arrived home after 10 o'clock, my blood in a wild turmoil.

Sunday, September 2. Went up to the reading room; saw there in the *General News* that Heiberg died on the 25th. When I got to the post office, I found a letter from H. P. Holst with the same news. My spirits are down; want to go home and yet don't want to. Sent off a letter to Mrs. Henriques, and while on that errand found a letter from Miss Bjerring waiting for me. The Hungarian sent me a picture of himself by von Kaulbach and a page from his album to write something on. He seems to be an intelligent man and he admires me, but I don't know anything about him. It's discomforting for me to come into contact with people whose personal qualities and situation I'm unfamiliar with. I have a morbid feeling, a strange fear about going crazy. This evening I read a couple of stories to the German-American and his daughters.

Monday, September 3. It's as if there's a demon riding my spirit. Where does it come from? Why? I'm unusually tired of everything! But I don't dare ask You, God, for help. I don't deserve it. Why should everything always go well for me? No one knows from one moment to the next what his fate will be. Took a walk by the rushing Rhône; a demonic urge to throw myself in. I hurried away from there. Was called into the Hôtel d'Écu by Mr. Hoppe, who is here with the two Swedish ladies and will be leaving tomorrow. Found a nice letter from Thiele at the post office; then I was stopped outside a café by Petöfi's translator, who said he would come some day and take me out for a drive—I don't want to!—My mind is sick! My God have mercy on me!—At 5 o'clock Professor Humbert came and fetched me out to his country home, which was very elegant; he had his immediate family assembled. I made cutouts, which were greatly admired, for two nice little boys, Émile and Ernest. People were very attentive to me, and at 9 o'clock I was driven home. If only I could curb the demon riders that oppress my spirit. It reminds me of a dream I had about a bat that was grappling with me and almost choked me.

Tuesday, September 4. This morning warm. Upset. My spirit demon-ridden. Wished for sudden death; a frequent thought.—At 9 o'clock, a visit from Professor Briquet with an invitation to tea tomorrow. Received a letter from Hambro in London. At 1:30 the young attorney Binet came with his father to pick me up in the pouring rain to go and see the poet Petit-Senn, whom I presented with a copy of my *Picture Book* in French, and he read a few chapters aloud. An elegant dinner party, many kinds of wine, champagne. Petit-Senn proposed a toast to me; after that we sang several songs. The old man was extremely youthful and full of life: he sang and told stories. Finally, I also had to sing a few Danish songs. There were a couple of very charming older gentlemen there. The entire conversation was in French. I saw Petit-Senn's album, with letters from Lamartine, Eugène Sue, Émile Souvestre. What I had written was, on account of my name, the first thing in it. He presented me with his book *Literary Trifles and Trivialities.* I was home by 6:30.

Wednesday, September 5. This morning Professor Barrelet came with a beautiful, big bouquet—he had read that it was indeed the anniversary of my arrival in Copenhagen. Then he shared with me the manuscripts he had from Toepffer and presented me with a little book that one of his students had dedicated to him. That impoverished man gave generously of the treasures he had. I was moved. *He* had today thought about my arrival in Copenhagen, and I hadn't given a thought to the fact that God had guided and helped me for forty-one years. If He should abandon me, He would only let go because I've let go. Later in the day, I received an equally beautiful bouquet from Miss Achard with a few words about how she had read that the 5th of September was a special day for me and that she therefore was sending me this greeting. Then, from Wiedemann, I also got the English translation and, along with it, a copy in German of *From the Heart and World*. I've sent the latter to Mrs. Blanvalet. A visit from Plantamour, a professor of chemistry I know from Copenhagen.—At the post office there was a nice letter from Edvard and from Jette, but it couldn't yet provide a reply to my letter—it had been mailed the same day I mailed mine. The German-American woman helped me to write a letter to Bentley. The weather is cold; the lake is casting waves against the jetty. My spirits will not rise! God, make me happy! (I also got a letter from Bentley, who informs me that for Christmas he wants to publish an illustrated edition of "The Sand-Dunes.") This evening I went to tea at Pastor Briquet's. His son, who is married and living in Bex, was there with his wife. He played a few pieces on his violin, accompanied on the piano by his sister and on the organ by his mother. They were all extremely attentive to me. There was a lovely supper, but I was nervous, in a morbid mood and got to feeling worse and worse. At 9:30 I took my leave, and Mr. Briquet accompanied me home in lovely moonlight. My legs were shaking; I didn't feel well. Went to bed early.

Thursday, September 6. Cold weather! Desperate about having to go out to tea again this evening. Sent a letter to Bentley and Mrs. Bushby. Got a cordial letter from Otto Müller in Rome, which I replied to at once with one of my own.—My mood depressed. Sincere prayer to God. The lake is quite as green as glass and is beating against the jetty so that it splashes higher than a man is tall. No vessels outside the harbor; here inside they are rocking violently. The coast indigo blue; behind the green mountains in sunlight but as if behind a thin, white veil; the furthest mountains fading into the distance. At 6:30 went to see Cherbuliez, who was waiting for me at his bookstore. He lived far out on the other side of the city in a small, rural cottage. Only the family was there. I was favorably impressed by his wife. His sister, who is a writer, drove me home afterwards in a tiny, little carriage. I made cutouts for the grandchildren. Cherbuliez's brother spoke some German. People were extremely cordial to me, and I found it very pleasant.

Friday, September 7. Now I had to pay a visit to that well-mannered translator of Petöfi; was in a foul mood. I arrived, looked at his full album; many friends from Munich in there. He was awfully cheerful and friendly; read from a couple of older books in which I was named. Looked at some interesting pictures, and my dark mood brightened quite a bit. It was as if God had heard my prayer yesterday and was good to me. At home I found a couple of books from Cherbuliez and his sister that they were giving to me. In one I was mentioned in favorable terms. I read aloud in French; the Englishman Baron Fitzhamel burst into tears. An English woman translated for them from the English "The Pen and the Inkpot" and "The Child in the Grave." I really am having an incredibly good time; only I myself can ruin my enjoyment. Stayed at home the rest of the day.

Andersen left Geneva on September 16 and traveled via Basel and Stuttgart to Munich, where he stayed for a week before heading north for Leipzig and Dresden. After three weeks in Dresden, where he was invited to the castle to read for King Johann of Saxony, he set off for home. Stopping for the night in Odense on November 9, he mused: "I'm alone at the Post Inn, alone in my hometown, whereas in foreign lands I am surrounded by friends and admirers."

For the first time Andersen did not close his diary on one of the last days of his journey, but continued after his arrival in Copenhagen until the Christmas holiday and the last days of the old year, which he spent at Basnæs.

Sunday, December 30. Received a nice letter from Mathilde Ørsted, which gave me pause in the midst of my bad mood and my lack of faith in God. I wrote a tale, "The Dung Beetle" and read it—it seemed strangely to apply to so many things I hadn't thought about while I was writing it. The young folks from Espe came for dinner. Nelly is a strange, cold person who stands as if her hands were wet and she were saying: "Don't touch me!" I had to read aloud, and it was not at all entertaining—the gentlemen sneaked off to smoke tobacco. Saint-Aubain came with the people from Borreby and joined the dancing and games.

Monday, December 31. Spent the day writing letters—which weren't sent off anyway—to the grand duke of Weimar, Mrs. von Eisendecher and Jules Jürgensen in Le Locle. Cold, clear weather. Five rix-dollars were missing from my wallet. It upset me, but I don't want to dwell on that matter. The sole of my feet tingling with the cold. Lucie quite lively—she'd been setting up a lottery. I won a small, blue glass. As early as 10 o'clock we were served a toddy for toasting the New Year in, but at midnight we got nothing—it was a rather awkward way to begin the New Year, and it disturbed me. Today I wrote a tale—"The Snow Man."

Andersen continued his diary into the New Year as a terse record of his social activities and homely complaints, such as toothaches and troubles with his false teeth. However, throughout the winter he seemed first and foremost preoccupied with getting a new installment of New Tales and Stories *ready for publication, reading his tales aloud to friends, listening to their comments and then polishing and refining his work. The slender volume appeared on March 2 and it was reviewed favorably in all the newspapers, although Andersen was amused to note that the critics were determined to contradict each other's judgments of individual tales.*

On April 4, Andersen began the diary of his four-month trip to Italy with Edvard's son, the young Jonas Collin. They traveled by train via Frankfurt and Basel to Marseilles and from there by coach to Nice and Genoa. From Genoa they continued by boat to Civitavecchia, arriving in Rome on April 28.

Sunday, May 5 [1861]. Went with Jonas to the Capuchin Church and saw their graveyard with its chapels made of bones. There sat the dead monks in their cowls; one from 1848 still had his beard. Went over to see Isabella Knight in the Palazzo Braschi on Via Vasella with the letter from Miss Kestner. Jonas felt suddenly very still; I asked him what was wrong with him. His face turned red all over, as it does when he is upset, and he said nothing was wrong. I asked him if I had done anything to incur his displeasure; he said no, he wanted to go home to do some writing. I became dispirited—I live for him, do everything for him; and he said the other day that I have only "my egoism." I'm grieved by this. I am staying in Rome for his sake alone, may never leave here. I'm feeling despondent, unwell. Sat in tears on my bed. He said he was often in this mood at home— it had nothing to do with the trip! I don't believe him about this; he doesn't trust people, has a mistaken impression of me. I am only "egoism," and yet I live only for him!—Later in the day his mood, which he said he was to blame for, worked itself out, brightened. Drove out to the church of S. Pietro in Vincoli; it was closed. Walked to S. Maria Maggiore and passed the Quirinal Palace and the Trevi fountain to arrive home very tired. At 4:30, to the Alibert Theater. The performance began at 5 o'clock, a translation of a French drama by Paul Duport—*Reason Proposes, or a Diplomatic Marriage.* It was well acted. The first act we viewed by the light of day; then they lighted the lamps and, for the ballet, the chandelier. The house has six storeys and is owned by Torlonia. The ballet terrible, far worse than Casorti's pantomimes; the dancing miserable. We left there at 8 o'clock in the pouring rain and had dinner. Back at home Jonas and I sat and talked about Christ as God and human being. It was nearly 11 o'clock before I got to bed. (At the theater I composed the story about Psyche.)

Monday, May 6. Didn't get up until after 8 o'clock. Sent letters to Father Collin and Edvard. Kolberg stopped by while I was out. Bought a lottery ticket; if I win any extra money, I'm going to buy the big photograph of St. Peter's. Walked out to the Vatican, saw the *God of the Nile,* the *Torso (Perseus* and *The Pugilists* of Canova), *Laocoön, Apollo,* the porphyry sarcophagi, the *Biga,* and the Egyptian Museum, the Stanza and the Sistine Chapel; but both Raphael's and Michelangelo's frescos seemed to me older and sootier than the last time I saw them; the colors were so dark and worn.—Wrote a song for the party for Bravo. After dinner Bjørnstjerne came; we drank coffee together, and he went up to my room with me and stayed from 6 o'clock to 11 o'clock. During that time I told him a large part of the story of my youth. He was completely enthralled. Presented him with my photograph. Got to bed late.

Tuesday, May 7. Very cold, but sunny. Walked a long way out to S. Pietro in Vincoli and saw the powerful *Moses,* which didn't appeal to Jonas. After that we walked to the Palatine and saw Domitian's rooms and Livia's (wife of Augustus) bathrooms—there was still some gilt on the ceiling and frescowork. Saw Agrippina's room; a lovely view out over Rome—the Colosseum before us, the Peace Arch, and the Alban and Sabine Hills, where the snow lay high. The entire Palatine ruins consisted of a large vegetable garden with artichokes, beans and grapes. Big green lizards darted off across the stones. Up there lay the Palazzo Farnese, the Villa Mills (which is now a convent) and S. Bonaventura. We saw the old walls from the time of Romulus, the temple of Castor and Pollux, as well as the Tarpeian Rock and all of the Avertine Hill. What vanity! Birds sang in the laurel trees. We were very tired when we reached the Osteria Lepre and rested then. I didn't feel like taking any more walks; in the evening I started writing down the story about Psyche.

Wednesday, May 8. Very cold. Drove with Bravo over to see Küchler at the monastery, where his copy of a Perugino painting was just in the process of being packed for shipment home. He took me to see Brother Ignatius from Westphalia, who in his early years had read my *Improvisatore.* He was a young man, kind and happy in Christ; remarked that there was religious feeling in the North and that each approached God in his own way. He had of course been born a Catholic, he said. We all were in search of truth. He found he had so much in common with me, even though I was a Lutheran.

I told him about the passion play in Oberammergau and "The Angel" and "The World's Loveliest Rose." Then drove to see Galli, one of Thorvaldsen's students; there were some beautiful things in his atelier, but many pieces were sentimental and not correct. I was otherwise impressed by the Berlin sculptor Wolff; here were lovely things and a lot of them. Saw a bust of the duchess of Weimar, a lovely Venus and finally a statue of Thorvaldsen that he wanted to have displayed and was only waiting for contributions and permission concerning where in Rome it might stand. A letter from Mrs. Schwartz with a ticket to the Villa Ludovisi. Jonas tired today, lay sleeping on the sofa. In the evening Weilbach came—I had left out two lines in the third verse of the song; I had, of course, to supply them. We also had a visit from the sculptor Kolberg.

Thursday, May 9. Jonas slept restlessly last night, screamed once in his sleep so that I rushed out of bed and in to him. He had dreamt that his father had been killed. Jonas got a letter from his father; I, from his mother, who informs me that Pepita will appear in my folk comedy *Willie Winkie*. Sent letters to Mrs. Neergaard and Hartmann. At 11 o'clock I drove with Jonas out to the Lateran. Today is Ascension Day; there was a throng of people there and a great press within the church. I felt ill and left. Jonas stayed and saw the pope. A long time went by before Jonas came; I explained how ill I felt. He told me to pull myself together and then went off to watch. It was a long time before we found each other. I had the feeling and the hope that he would be concerned enough about me to stay, but he went. I was standing by the Holy Steps; it started to rain, and I took shelter in a doorway where a number of people were standing. The water was pouring down; people were pressing in; there was a great crowd; some farmers were pushing and shoving. I fell over a stool and wound up with some people on top of me and shouted "Jesus" out loud! It was awful. The papal blessing was given in the church on account of the rain. I didn't get to see him, and there were no carriages available. I was bothered by it all and irritated; Jonas had as refrain: "You must pull yourself together!" I was not pleased by this. There was no thought of sympathy; he looked cranky and irritated. Mrs. Schwartz sent me an admission ticket to the Villa Ludovisi for to-day—now it was too late to go. We got seats in an omnibus to Piazza Venezia. At 2:30, after a half hour's rest, we drove to Raphael's (the owner's name) trattoria, which lies between the Lateran and S. Maria Maggiore and where Danes, Norwegians and Swedes were gathered to welcome Bravo, who had recovered from an illness. I got a seat by his side. There were fourteen ladies, each of whom received a bouquet; toasts for the kings of the North, for Bravo (with a song by me), for H. C. Andersen (with a song by Bjørnson) and a speech by Waage, the candidate in theology, a toast for the Scandinavians by Weilbach (a timid, slobbering introduction—he seems to me to be wooden, self-conscious and thin, his words like dry splinters without a trace of any sap in them). I expressed my thanks for the toast and proposed a greeting from Denmark and a toast for my fatherland. Bjørnson said I had displayed my usual incomparable tact.—Later I proposed a toast for Bjørnstjerne as Norway's writer. It got to be 7:30; the carriage didn't come. We drank coffee down in the garden, where there were some old ruins and lemon trees. Jonas trotted to the Piazza Barberini with Kolberg for a carriage; then ours came and we got home. Later, Bjørnson showed up with Collin and wanted to take him along to the Club. I wasn't happy about it, but I didn't want any sulking. He went and I remained at home, stayed up until 10:30. When I woke up during the night, I thought he hadn't come back yet; went into his room, but he was already asleep.—There was some ringing on the door outside, noisy. I slept until 8:30.

Friday, May 10. Jonas is out with Bravo arranging to have his snails shipped home to Steenstrup. Called on Bissen. A visit from Bjørnson, who was in a melancholy mood. Worked on the story "The Psyche."—At a little past 8 o'clock Mrs. Schwartz's carriage came. It accommodates only two people, so that I, Jonas and Bravo had to cram ourselves together. We met a number of foreigners—the rich American painter Story, who lives in the Palazzo Barberini. They knew and loved my writings. Bjørnson and Miss Kierulff were here. I read aloud in German: "The Child in the Grave," "Children's Prattle" and "The Pen and the Inkpot." An Italian woman, the best alto here in Rome, sang works by Mendelssohn, Haydn and Ravnkilde, who accompanied her. Mrs. Schwartz also sang. We had tea, ice cream and, after that, sandwiches with good wine (sherry). It was past 11 o'clock when we drove home and nearly 12 o'clock by the time I got to bed.

Saturday, May 11. A visit from Miss Kierulff. Sent off a letter with a description of the celebration, along with Bjørnson's song dedicated to me—the letter was to Adolph Drewsen. Went with Bloch, Bissen and Jonas over to see the famous Belgian painter Galé (that's how it is pronounced [Gallait]) and saw a portrait of the pope. I didn't think it was good. A painter from Berlin who knows me—

Lindemann-Frömmel—lives in the same house; he invited us in to see his paintings of Potsdam, Lake Nemi, beautiful sketches from Nice in all their tropical fullness. Drove with Jonas out to the Villa Doria-Pamphili, from which there was a glorious view of Rome and the mountains, as well as of the pine forest by the villa. We drove over to Acqua Paola, where the water plunged down into the large basin. Rome lay bathed in sunlight below us; floating beautifully in the air above, the mountains. This morning, a visit from Weilbach, who has written about the celebration to *The Fatherland*. The sun is burning hot today; in my sitting room I was freezing. Ravnkilde promised to visit us this evening. I decorated as if for a salon—hung our blankets in front of the doors. He arrived a little past 8 o'clock; we chatted and drank red and white wine. I enclosed a letter to Vilhelmine Wanscher, who is leaving tomorrow, in the letter Jonas is sending off.

Sunday, May 12. A lot of blood; not feeling quite well. Hired a carriage and used up a whole *scudo* driving with Jonas out to the church of S. Paolo Fuori le Mura, which is grand, full of light and magnificent. Next to St. Peter's it is absolutely the most impressive church here in Rome. A lovely cloister with roses and marble columns that looked almost as if they had been turned on a lathe; in the church, portraits of all the popes and ancient frescoes. Drove to Monte Testaccio and the cemetery; found a couple of Swedish graves and one in which a man from Dresden was buried. Was inside the Cestio Pyramide, which was dripping with water. Drove past the Baths of Caracalla out to the Scipio family tomb and went down into it; it was cold and nocturnal in these catacombs. I turned back to the sunshine and roses. Drove home in the burning heat of the sun. It was 1 o'clock before we got any lunch. At the dinner table at the Lepre, where we ate with several Norwegian ladies. (Miss Ribbing looks like *Venus de Milo*, which I told her!) Bjørnstjerne said that he could give a dramatic rendition of the scene between me and Mrs. Collett. I gave a straightforward account of it, and the word I used about Wergeland was that he was "crude"! To this Bjørnstjerne said that he too would have taken offense, for Wergeland had produced some of the most perfect poetry with regard to form. Later he wanted to take me up to Piazza della SS. Trinità dei Monti, but I didn't want to go up to the steps on account of Beppo and left them, but turned back and went up the promenade, where it was teeming with vehicles and pedestrians. Rome lay in a lovely sunset. The grounds up here have been ornately landscaped—there are masses of roses and

Scala di Spagna in Rome

tropical plants, but the view down over the wasteland behind the Villa Borghese has now turned into one of a friendly field with a road and fence. Before it was like a still untrodden piece of Switzerland—barren and pernicious isolation. After having run into my dinner companions up there and walking a bit with Waage, it got to be almost 8 o'clock by the time I got home. Jonas was at SS. Trinità dei Monti.

Monday, May 13. Letter from Mrs. Thiele. Letter to Mrs. Scavenius. At 2 o'clock I went with Jonas to see the American sculptor Story, who is very rich and lives in the Palazzo Barberini—very sumptious. A lot of Americans, Englishmen and Frenchmen, too, came there. I made cutouts for the children; had to read the beginning of "The Ugly Duckling" *in English,* but this was too much for me and I got Story to read the rest. A brother of the poet Longfellow was there, also the poet Robert Browning, who sat in a circle of children and read two of his poems to them, the one of them about the Pied Piper of Hamelin. He was himself in costume and played the part of the Piper—the children followed him through the rooms in a troop. We played an English children's game involving a dance. Jonas, who was bored and chilly because he'd taken off his waistcoat in the sirocco, stood around looking pale. I got him to leave with Ravnkilde but stayed myself. The children of the house placed a jasmine wreath on my head; a young girl gave me some beautiful roses. I was introduced to a crowd of people and came home around 6 o'clock. The sculptor Hertzog came to say goodbye; he'll be traveling home over Perugia tomorrow.

Tuesday, May 14. Overcast and rain. Visit from Küchler and Brother Ignatius. Went with Jonas to the church of S. Agnese on the Piazza Navona; happened by chance on the beautiful fountain with the turtles. Was in several churches; walked up to S. Maria in Aracoeli, which has antique columns. In the Capitoline Palace we saw a number of interesting paintings as well as *The Boy Removing a Thorn from His Foot* in bronze, two mosaic tables from Hadrian's Villa in Tivoli, busts of Sappho and Diogenes. Went into the church in the Palazzo Venezia. After 1 o'clock, drove with Jonas and Bjørnson out to the Villa Albani. There were calla lilies growing beautifully in the canal; roses twined around the ancient statues; a large cypress; tall boxwood hedges. Opulent halls with statues, busts and paintings. Drawings by Domenichino; marble busts of the hunchbacked Aesop. On the way home I told Bjørnstjerne about my tale "The Rags"; he told me about the plot of his *Sigurd Slembe.* We ate together; he and Jonas debated about the poetic sensibility of certain artists, namely, the young Bissen. "He doesn't have enough to cover a fingernail!" said Bjørnstjerne. Jonas respected his reticent personality.—At home, a conversation with Jonas, who placed Viggo over Bjørnstjerne and Clemens Petersen: he worked on his development and had nothing to do with other people. This provided me the inspiration to write the story about the snail and the rosebush.—It's approaching 12 o'clock at night, and I'm still up! Jonas hasn't come home yet; I don't want to write down what I'm thinking and feeling.—Now it is 12:30, and he isn't here yet. Everyone all around is asleep; I am nervous. My legs are shaking under me; my head is burning hot. I'm not going to think any more!

Wednesday, May 15. He didn't come home until after 12:30. He'd been at the club and later with the others at the café. He seemed sorry that I was still up. I left him with a less fond heart than usual and went to bed; was very nervous and upset. Today it was around 9 o'clock when we got up; he, later than I. My mood is not pleasant. What will he do now? What will the day bring? It may well be me who gets unpleasant this time. At the breakfast table I forgave him: He probably hasn't given a thought to how angry I've been with him. Now he is at the Doria-Phamphili with Bissen until 5 o'clock. He came home earlier, since the Pamphili was only open to people who came in carriages. He had then gone to Monte Mario. I left a calling card at Princess Pignatelli-Ruffo's and visited Thorvaldsen's daughter, who seemed glad to see me. We talked about her father and my writings. Went for a walk on the Piazza della SS. Trinità dei Monti; there was a fragrance of acacia and orange blossoms. The soldiers were making music; lots of people. Very warm. Today I wore my summer trousers for the first time this year. Jonas came along; while we were out, Story left his calling card at our place.— This morning I was at Mrs. Schwartz's and arranged a trip to Albano for Saturday; visited Ravnkilde. Tomorrow Jonas will be going with the Weilbachs to Tivoli. Jonas quite confidential this evening; we were drinking Orvieto. He'd drunk some wine, he said, on the trip to Monte Mario.

Thursday, May 16. At 5:30 I called Jonas, who set off for Tivoli at around 7 o'clock. Went out to visit the poet Browning but lingered at Bjørnstjerne's, where I read a few tales and he, some poems for me. One, "Before and Now," was particularly good. Gave him the four installments of my tales, along with the verse:

You mighty tree of Norway, bearing fruit and flower,
You have taught me to love your home near the Northern Pole.
In Rome, where the past displays its glory and power,
There I learned to see into your poet's soul.

The weather is terrifically hot today. Visited Bissen and Fladager. It's too hot today for running around and paying calls on people. Already by 8:30 Jonas was home from Tivoli. Ravnkilde wanted to take him along to Princess Pignatelli-Ruffo's, but he stayed at home.— (We had terrible thunder and lightning on toward evening.)

Friday, May 17. Jonas a little cross; I don't know why. Finally a letter to me from his father enclosed in a letter from Ingeborg Drewsen; there was also a letter enclosed for Jonas. Sent letters to Mrs. Koch and Louise Lind. Visited the English poet Mrs. Browning, who graciously expressed her pleasure at the visit. She looked very sickly. Went into Story's atelier; Story was just working on Browning's bust. Saw a few good statues: *America, Cleopatra, Beethoven.* Jonas is alone at the Vatican. (Today I'm having a bad time with bleeding.) Drove over to S. Maria degli Angeli and viewed the cloister garden (the smaller one). Lovely, with lemon and orange trees; they are bearing fruit and flowers. The other large, with arcades and in it, a painting on a door by the Neapolitan painter Balbi depicting one of the popes' fathers when he became a Franciscan: there was a candle with a long wick, carrots and white turnips, ancient folios—the whole thing extremely lifelike. In the garden itself, mighty cypresses three centuries old. In this cloister, too, there were French soldiers quartered.— Jonas went home on account of a headache; I proceeded over around the Piazza del Quirinale, or whatever it's called. In the evening Bravo came up with a letter from Mrs. Schwartz about the trip to Albano tomorrow at 11 o'clock.

Saturday, May 18. Cloudy weather; bleeding again. Mrs. Schwartz came at 11 o'clock, and when we reached the railroad station, there wasn't any train scheduled to depart. She and Bravo had made a mistake about the time, so we had to wait there until 12 o'clock and drive to Frascati and hire a carriage from there. The otherwise beautiful trip to Ariccia past the Castel Gandolfo, through Marino, past Albano, over the beautiful, big new bridge. It was 3 o'clock before we got there. There was a cold wind; I was freezing. Great view over the Campagna, but cloudy. We passed through a beautiful forested landscape that was reminiscent of Denmark. Bravo claimed that Danish beech trees were small and never reached the height of the Italian ones, that there were no heights there like the hills here and that I exaggerated when I was abroad on account of patriotic feeling. When Jonas told how many feet high our Himmelbjerg is, Bravo said: "Well, what kind of feet?" He claimed that the lovely

An Italian peasant woman

vine with lilac flowers trailing up the walls was the same as maidenhair. I couldn't be bothered to discuss it with him. In Albano we went into a hotel and had a huge dinner with champagne. Later we drank coffee at Miss Kierulff's, but we had to be off right away. Bravo said the omnibus was leaving. I would have liked so much to have gone the way we came, but Bravo was in a hurry, and so we arrived over a half hour too early and had to sit and wait in the street. It was a bad trip and, to be sure, expensive. Jonas went around always brooding. He was sick, he said, but he attached himself to

Ravnkilde and was talkative. He has no consideration for me, just like Drewsen's sons; I was grieved and offended. At 7 o'clock we drove to the railroad station. Bravo started to smoke in first class; it irritated and annoyed me. "Will Mrs. Schwartz permit us to smoke?" I said. This was a great insult, Jonas tells me. When I later got sick from the tobacco, Bravo was impolite about it. We arrived in Rome in a bad humor. Mrs. Schwartz told about Kertbeny, who has put the touch on her for money, courted her, etc.—When we got home, Jonas took some Hoffmann's anodyne and rhubarb tincture and went to bed. I did, too, without supper, terribly depressed, spiteful and in tears, jumping out of bed and ranting, beside myself. Jonas, quiet.

Sunday, May 19. Got up early and went out. Came home just as unhappy, brooding; was irritable and upset. Looked for Jonas at Ravnkilde's; we missed each other. I expressed myself with bitterness. Drove with Jonas to St. Peter's, where I felt dull and despondent. In one of the chapels the castrati were singing. One of the voices was resonant and moving; it was a handsome, young man. The entire Pentecost celebration was held in the Sistine Chapel, but Jonas couldn't go in there in his jacket and sombrero. We then went out of the church and exchanged clothes. He looked funny in my big coat; I went home with his short-armed jacket and sombrero. Later, we ate together with Ravnkilde. When I took a walk alone with him and told him about my state of mind, he advised me to go off somewhere for the afternoon. Later, when Jonas came home, I put my arms around him, said a few kind words; and he was moved and agreeable. It made me happy. The heavy clouds had lifted; I was in a good mood again, and after the meal we went for a drive with Bjørnson and Ravnkilde out along Porta Pia, viewed the mountains in the evening light. Went into an osteria and had some wholesome white wine to drink. Later we had coffee at the Greco. Now Jonas and I are at home; my mood is light, but I haven't been able to pass a stool, just some blood.

On their way home after a month in Rome, Andersen and the young Collin toured Tuscany before heading north via Turin and Milan to Switzerland, where they spent some time in Bex and Montreux. There Andersen received a letter from Adolph Drewsen that the senior Jonas Collin was dying. They nevertheless continued northward at a leisurely pace, making lengthy stops in Brunnen, Munich, and Dresden. In Korsør they parted ways—the young Collin headed directly back to Copenhagen, but Andersen made a detour to Basnæs and Sorø.

Monday, August 26. Drove from Basnæs with Kalkar, who is leaving this place, now that Otto has gotten into Herlufsholm Academy. We arrived in Slagelse a little before 1 o'clock. Ten minutes after the clock struck, the train departed. I was in a coach with Thorald Læssøe. In Sorø I was at the Ingemann's before two o'clock. There I met Mrs. Holstein and Miss . . . . Sent a letter to Edvard Collin. Read "The Psyche" in the afternoon and then again in the evening. Ingemann wanted to know about his inner psyche—how it would turn out. "I'd like to, too!"

Tuesday, August 27. Letter from Mrs. Hartmann. Read "The Ice Maiden" for the Ingemanns and revised the ending or, rather, developed my idea about Babette's dream more clearly. It's very cold; I'm wearing winter clothes. Letter to Mrs. Serre.

Wednesday, August 28. Letter to Mrs. Scavenius and one to Mrs. Ortwed. Later on in the day read in the June issue of the *Danish Monthly Journal*, where the last installment of my tales is judged among my weakest. This depressed me somewhat—the first mortification since my return home. There are more to come! Later in the day the teacher Mr. Lange and his wife came to speak with me about their trip to Nice this winter. Since it seemed to them too expensive, I mentioned Montreux. On a stroll, I met the Heises. They will be traveling this winter to Rome. Due to a misunderstanding, the young Bissen was at home this June—he had misinterpreted a letter. It wouldn't be very clever of him to make that long trip before first sending a telegram. This evening Mrs. Wilster and her son were here, likewise the Bang family. I had to read aloud.

Thursday, August 29. Letter from Edvard: Old Collin died yesterday at around noon. Immediately wrote a letter to Edvard. Strange mood. Toward evening I had a physical reaction, and when I had to read a little for the Harders I felt faint and went to bed before 10 o'clock. Letter from Mrs. Ortwed.

Friday, August 30. Since I read in the newspaper that Collin will be buried on Monday, I've given up the visit to Roskilde. Wrote a letter to Mrs. Ortwed to cancel, together with a letter to Mrs. Anholm, saying that I would be arriving before noon on Sunday.— Staying, then, with the Ingemanns until Sunday morning. Worked on a fair copy of "The Ice Maiden."—The weather is quite autumn-like, windy and cold with rain showers. Took a walk in the cemetery and there visited the graves that contain Molbech, Wendelboe, Wilster, the Bredsdorffs and Holck. Ingemann read in the afternoon and evening from his autobiography—very interesting what it related about the poet Bredahl, who also, along with Rosenkilde, attended Slagelse School. Letter from Edvard Collin—the funeral on Monday at 10 o'clock.

Saturday, August 31. The whole night, a terrible whistling through the trees—that's how windy it's been. Next to me slept the maid's little nephew, a watchman's son from Copenhagen, who, now that they've generously taken to letting children from charity schools spend their vacation in the country, has been staying with some relatives and is now on his way home. He has been given new clothes and money. Tomorrow I'll be going to Copenhagen. It'll begin there with grief and Collin's funeral. What awaits me this winter? What in the coming year?

> What's in store for us?
> What will be coming next?
> The seed of hope, oft crushed!
> Yet all does happen for the best!

Sunday, September 1. When I got to the railroad station and into the first compartment, there was a gentleman smoking tobacco. He didn't want to stop, so then I got a seat in the next coach and there met Pepita, who was on her way to Copenhagen. She recognized me and told about her seasickness and the courtesy of the captain—indeed, he should have something to remember her by, she said! I wasn't in the right mood, and when we reached Ringsted I left the coach, saying I had happened upon a friend. I preferred getting back in with the fellow who was smoking tobacco, which he now, however, stopped doing. It wasn't until 11:30 that we arrived at the train station, where Jonas and Viggo met me and we drove into the heart of town. On Amalie Street they are still holding open house today and tomorrow. The atmosphere tolerable. Mrs. Drewsen stood ready to go to Jonna, who is expecting a baby. She'll have to drive all night. Saw Old Collin's body. He looked as if he were sleeping peacefully. His beard was very red.

Monday, September 2. Anxious about sitting in the church during the funeral. Got the gravedigger to open the pew and the door out to the cemetery. Bishop Bindesbøll's eulogy was not satisfactory—he spoke too much about Frederik VI and the political scene. Blædel delivered a handsome supplement out by the grave at Frederiksberg. I drove out there with Hornemann and Minister Fenger. In the afternoon, I ate at a restaurant and felt very alone.

Little did Andersen know, but the death of his friend and patron Jonas Collin was not the only loss he was to suffer that winter. Six months later, on February 24, his close friend and fellow author Bernhard Severin Ingemann died in Sorø.

During the autumn of 1861, Andersen devoted himself to putting the finishing touches on his most recent tales and stories. In late November his new installment of the second series of New Tales and Stories *appeared, just in time for the Christmas rush. It was reviewed well and sold well, so that on December 23 Edvard Collin, acting as Andersen's financial adviser, was able to write to his friend at Holsteinborg that he had 8,200 rix-dollars in assets and was in fine shape. At once Andersen began to make plans for an extended trip to Spain and France with Edvard's son Jonas. The financing of the trip was clinched when his Danish publisher Theodor Reitzel unexpectedly offered him an honorarium of 3,000 rix-dollars for a reissue of the illustrated edition of his collected tales and stories.*

On July 23, Andersen and the young Jonas Collin set off on an eight-month trip to Spain. First, they traveled to Switzerland, where they joined Jonas's parents and his sister Louise and, together, spent a month visiting Brunnen, Interlaken, Berne, and Montreux. On August 30, Andersen and Jonas Collin proceeded to the Spanish border via Lyon, crossed it and headed for Barcelona, where they were welcomed by the Danish businessman Herman Schierbeck.

Friday, September 12 [1862]. Don't feel so good. My blood racing; fiery Spanish temper! Moved from our apartment and got some rooms on the third floor facing out to the Rambla. Two street performers, one in tricot, were dancing outside and doing tricks. Jonas has gone up to the castle. The women carry themselves well, but many here wear French hats. Today I've seen a number of Andalusian farmers in sandals, corduroy suits and red sashes. At 5 o'clock, to Schierbeck's for dinner; the entire party consisted of him, his wife and Buchheister. We had Liebfrauenmilch, champagne, rare Spanish wines—an enjoyable meal—and, to top it off, Swedish punch. It was a little too much. Jonas was unusually lively and argufied. It was almost 11 o'clock when we strolled home; the others, off to play billiards. My blood boiling hot.

Saturday, September 13. Dreamt unpleasantly all night long about the trip. My blood turbulent, headache, pain in my neck. Warm weather. Took a walk up onto the walls by the sea. Visited by Mr. Scheller from the consulate and afterwards by Buchheister. We went to the coach dispatcher's, ran into Schierbeck and toured the grand opera, where there was a rehearsal going on. In the summertime the troupe gives operettas in the outlying towns, and they were working on one of these with jingling-jangling music. We walked across the stage into the elegant boxes; leading into each one of them there was a vestibule with elegant couches. Some telegraph wires had been run up into the director's boxes; pressure on each one of them gives a different command—up or down with the curtain, stage manager summoned, etc.—Grand, spacious and elegant, with a spectacular foyer for the opera-goers; in front of the beautiful stairway stood a bust of the queen. From the roof, a great view out over the city, sea and mountains. Went to the café; there we sat chatting for two whole hours. I related episodes from my life. Got a letter from Hartmann. Bought tickets for this evening to Teatro del Circo Barcelona (Butaca de Palio)—ten *reals* each. The theater had beautiful, big refreshment locales for the public; above them, two levels. They were doing a work by Scribe, I think—*Caesar, or the Watch Dog of the Castle*. The owner of the castle had been killed in the revolution, the son struck on the head so that he had become an idiot. He arrived in that state at the castle, where even the watch dog had been killed, and crawled into the doghouse. He had given his papers to an adventurer, who had been a barber, and received five francs for them. The adventurer then presented himself as the son of the house to a relative who was waiting and wanted to marry him, but he had no memory of the past. Then the son arrived, recognized his playthings and, in a more lucid moment, the portrait of his father and knew where his father's rapier was kept. And under the tutelage of the chambermaid, he regained his patrimony but not his reason. It was a piece for children and unthinking seamstresses. The leading part was rather much too naturally played. After that they did *A Gentleman and a Lady*, but Jonas and I left before it started. Lovely weather.

Sunday, September 14. With Schierbeck to the cathedral, which has a lovely entrance hall, a cloister around a small square-shaped garden with lemon trees, palms, etc. A fountain with a horseman— there's a stream of water spurting out of the rear end of the horse. Some live geese were penned up in there, and they formed a strange contrast to the numerous altars along the gothic walkway, which went all around the garden. The church is black, big and magnificent. Everyone was kneeling; I had to kneel along with them, but hurried, embarrassed, away from there. Came to the church of S. Maria del Mar, which has a beautiful facade and inside rises up on slender pillars. We walked there through the street of the gold-smiths, where there is one splendid shop after the next. I got sepa-rated from the others and ended up by the queen's palace, where the beautiful new fountain is. I was planning to stretch out on the bed when I received a visit from Scheller and his wife. They were very warm and attentive; she got a picture of me. (Yesterday a Ger-man, Engelhardt from Saxony, was sitting next to me at the table. When he heard I was Danish, he told about how he had had the good fortune to meet Thorvaldsen with his long, white hair. "Now you have Andersen, too" he said and told about how beloved and read Andersen was in his small town and in his home. When I told him I was Andersen, he was delighted, shook my hand and said that he would write about this to his wife—it was one of the most interesting experiences he had had during his trip.) At 3:30 Jonas and I drove with Schierbeck out to the arena. It was almost filled—some 16,000 people. Music was playing. We sat on the stone benches of the amphitheater. They did a comical scene with Moors and Spaniards. Then a buli came out. Its horns were wrapped so it couldn't do any harm. There was some running around and comical scenes, but before that the audience put on their own show, throwing flour at each other and, to my surprise, condoms filled with flour—they grazed some of the ladies. Then a bull came and the fight began, but the bull turned timid because of the wild screams around him. People shouted *ferro*, and burning arrows were stuck into it. Schier-beck said it was a more dangerous fight than one with courageous bulls—the animal was so agitated that it was impossible to give it the death blow. The toreador's first blow was all right, just not deep enough to be fatal. The animal ran around with the rapier in its neck; after a lot of goading and sparring, it was given the death blow and keeled over. Caparisoned horses dragged it away. The next bull started off more courageously but ended up timid. People de-manded fire for it, and fire-arrows with exploding fireworks were stuck into its neck. It was a long fight and often dangerous. Then came a Moorish scene in which some Moors tended an ailing Moor, and then a bull was let in. It had its horns wrapped. It was led out of the arena by tame bulls that were used to it all—when they came in the bull ran over to them right away, and they at once led it out of the arena. Then the audience, mostly boys and youths, jumped down into the arena, and a bull with its horns rendered harmless was let in. It jumped several times over the barrier into the first circular aisle and tried to get up to where the audience was, but there wasn't room enough to jump and the barrier was too high, but it did reach its head all the way up to the first row. It was here in the arena where the 1833 revolution broke out. People did some shooting and the soldiers shot back at them, and it spread throughout the country with fire and destruction. In the evening, hung around in the cafés, drank beer that tasted like near beer at home with water added. A letter to Mrs. Neergaard and Mrs. Kahrs.

Monday, September 15. Pouring rain all night long. Slept badly—felt feverish and hot. Went to see Ortenbach and withdrew 1,000 *reals.* Got letters of recommendation from him to Don Eleuterio Peñafiel of Murcia and Don Hilario Roux of Cartagena. It was a downpour! After I had come home and been sitting for a while, Jonas said the street was flooding and ran downstairs. I could see from the balcony that a torrent of brownish-yellow water was racing along both sides down toward the Rambla—it was like a waterfall. I became anxious about him and ran down and then saw that the street on both sides of the slightly raised walkway was a raging torrent that carried everything with it—a cart loaded with porcelain had been washed a short way, and the water was breaking high up over it. Display tables and counters that had been standing out in the open were floating in the water. It forced its way into the houses—gourds and beams were carried off. People were walking in water up over their hips. A woman was swept off her feet and taken by the current. There came a scream and three fellows managed to get her half conscious up on dry land. Then a horrible scream could be heard from the other side—there, too, was a woman who had been carried off from the doorway of her shop, where she had been putting up boards to keep the water out. Never have I seen the power of water like that! It coursed down two narrow streets that ran parallel to each other like a rushing millstream. People could be seen on all of the balconies, even on the rooftops. Gendarmes came to help and to keep order.—When the rain stopped and the sun came out, the water receded so that I could work my way through mud and debris down one of the side streets, where there had just been a raging torrent. People were zealously bailing out the shops. The other side street was all red mire. I went up to see Schierbeck, who hadn't been outside since he had never known such a thing to happen in Barcelona—but now he was extremely surprised. We walked across the Rambla, where the carriages could now make their way along the streets filled with water. A balustrade on the first story of a low building had been torn off and a man and two children drowned.

When some men were removing the large stones leading to the sewers in the middle of the street, a couple of people crossing the street sank into the sewer and disappeared. We continued on out of town. A small river had burst its banks, broken through the railroad embankment—where the whole yard was under water—and torn up trees and cactuses over four feet tall. The highway had been washed out, and there was still waterfall after waterfall—we had to jump down into deep holes and then scramble up out of the wet earth. Carriages from the rural districts had pulled up in a row, and people now had to continue on foot. A whole timberyard had been flooded, the large beams scattered all over. We balanced ourselves on them, walked through deep mire and thus reached the railroad depot where the breakthrough had occurred.—*Sent letter to Eckardt and Scharff.* A man and a child are said to have drowned; one person, to have sunk into a hole in the street where the sewer had been opened up. At a café this evening. Undecided whether to travel by steamship tomorrow or stagecoach.

Tuesday, September 16. Walked to the sea. It looked calm, but I was still very anxious about the dark night out there. Went to see Schierbeck and drank chocolate and ate figs, but was extremely depressed and anticipated a disaster at sea. He advised me not to go by stagecoach, which could take several days and might leave us stranded in some desolate spot along the way. In very low spirits, went with him and got a ticket for the *Catalan,* which was supposed to have the best engine, a capable, young captain and could sail the fastest. At 11:30 we went on board. Buchheister accompanied us to the harbor and Schierbeck, on board—he has been a good friend to us and very helpful. We didn't sail until 1:30. Far out from the coast the flood waters had made the sea brownish-yellow. Suddenly the water turned blue. The ship moved around a lot. We had eaten lunch, but it was unthinkable for me to go down for dinner. Jonas was still sleeping. At 6 o'clock I had some chicken, but I got seasick at my first mouthful of wine and didn't have anything more. Marx, a young German from Mannheim, was very attentive to me, lent me his woolen scarf and put his cape over my legs. Thus we sat during the starry-bright evening until 9 o'clock. Then I went down and stretched out on the sofa in the dining room. However, I'll never forget the sight of the dark blue water, the silver-white froth and the fish shining like jewels. The clouds formed shapes—it looked this evening as if the coast was near with its stone walls and some long houses. Around 12 o'clock I fell into a doze.

Wednesday, September 17. I slept in two-hour snatches. The sea was calm, really. I got up at 6 o'clock and saw the coast of Spain. (Yesterday I saw Monserrat looking like a fish with a spiny dorsal fin.) The coasts were naked. They were illuminated by the rising sun. Thick rain clouds hung over the sea up toward the Bay of Castellón de la Plana. We arrived at 8:30; after that our baggage brought ashore. Went over to customs, where there was trouble about the poisonous stuff Jonas has with him for his animals. It and they had to stay behind until a chemist could get there to make an inspection. A Spaniard whose acquaintance I had made on board looked after us. We drove with him and the German in a chaise—our baggage in a second one—to Valencia in about three-quarters of an hour. Along the way lay tidy houses with thatched roofs, like our farmhouses but taller, with more whitewash on them and a curtain instead of a door. At the city gate they wanted to do another inspection, but our Spaniard took care of us and we reached the Fonda del Cid, where we got two rooms and a good lunch (the wine strong, the grapes and melons incomparable). Then Jonas went out to the suburb and came home with his half-confiscated things. In the meantime I had walked around in town and been to the barber's. (From the sea this morning we saw the ancient Sagunto with its broken-down fortress walls.) An especially good dinner—the melons sweet, the grapes firm of flesh. Jonas declared today, when I jokingly said that Vilhelmine Wanscher would suit me very well as a wife, that it was disgusting and that he would lodge a protest for humanitarian reasons. Then he said that I might think she and I would get along, but that we were in disagreement about the most important things. He pays me more insults than compliments. The latter are supposed to be sentimental; rudeness is manly. I felt irritable, but kept silent for the sake of domestic peace. He is remarkably inconsiderate of me. If only I can keep my composure. It is difficult, for I have a need to love him like a brother.

Thursday, September 18. The streets, that is to say with the exception of the larger main street, are without paving. When it has rained, like now, it all turns into muck to be waded through. Went to our consul, not the one whose name I'd written down at home, but Mr. Brito, who was available not at 9 o'clock, but at the earliest at 10 o'clock. He received me graciously, stamped my passport with visas for all of Spain. The police informed me that their visa wasn't necessary. Sent letter to H. P. Holst and one to Mrs. Drewsen. Drove out into town, came to a plaza with palacelike courtyards and a park where cabbage roses were in bloom. The streets have tall buildings with balconies, where colorful floor coverings of linen or straw hang out over the railings, as if for a festival. On the other hand, the streets are unpaved, with one puddle after the other. The doorways take up the width of the store fronts, and there people sit working. I saw a couple of beautiful women—they were beautiful, but the majority are not, as in Barcelona. The paved streets had the appearance of great cleanliness. Ten men or so went around sweeping with brooms made from fresh, green myrtle branches. Inside the courtyards, big, broad stairs or glimpses of small gardens. The churches don't stand open all day, but only during certain hours. Beggars sitting outside, but not so overfilled as in Italy. We are living in a less frequented quarter, but here the dogs bark as I have only heard them in Copenhagen. In bed by 8 o'clock.

Friday, September 19. Jonas is determined to go to Sagunto. I, for economic reasons, did not go along, because we're going to be faced with many expenses here and I had thought I would get less out of it. He was off on the train at 8 o'clock, and I wandered around to find the café. Was at the barber's and the fruit market, where there were masses of big, green melons. There were snails for sale. They were your common variety, and yesterday at the hotel we had soup made from them. It looked like a yellowish rice gruel—they were in there with their shells and everything! Even Jonas, who is a snail enthusiast, couldn't eat any of it. Was inside a big building where yellow silk was sold. It was a magnificent, high hall; the columns twisted and so slender—as if they were the mighty trunks of palm trees. Two windows as gigantic as city gates gave ample light. Beggars with badges on their arms were sitting around by the churches. Several streets are very lively with their throngs of people. It is scorching hot today. Letters to Mrs. Serre in Dresden and Clara Heinke. It got to be 5 o'clock; Jonas had not yet come. I was very uneasy on his account. At the table I heard that the train didn't arrive until 4:15; a little later he showed up. He related that the town looked miserable—miserable huts, a half circle of a theater, and overlooking everything, the castle with a garrison, with a large cobbled courtyard, many cactuses, no trees. On the mountain slopes below, olive trees and palms. Letters to H. P. Holst and Ingeborg Drewsen.

Saturday, September 20. Up at 3 o'clock; called to Jonas and then rang for the house staff. At 4 o'clock a chaise pulled up outside the door. It was a starry night. We drove through the narrow, dark streets out to the railroad station. It dragged on until a little past 5 o'clock before we departed. The route was as if through a garden. A palm tree rose up against the red morning clouds. Small streams embraced fields of grapes and corn. We made protracted stops and came then to barren, burned-out stretches. There were some isolated farms, all of them surrounded by walls, sort of like fortresses; scorched, as if corrosive water had been poured over the land. Here and there a cowed stone pine. Cactuses along walls and ditches. On the roads drove small carts with six mules, hitched one in front of the other. We passed through a tunnel. Had, moreover, a good first class coach with a sofa in the middle. At 10 o'clock we reached Almansa, which is referred to in *Don Quixote*. Here, there was a well-equipped restaurant building—the owner, French. We had to wait here until 6 o'clock for the train from Madrid and therefore took a room (in a separate building) that was large, clean and rather comfortable. We walked into town. The houses low, white, a broad doorway, a window or hole in the wall, no windowpane, no paving. Behind each house, a sort of garden or something green. Farther into town were some better houses, several even with glass windowpanes, but the most considerable ones, with coats of arms over the doorways, stood deserted. The church was large and as white as the Cathedral of Our Lady [in Copenhagen]. At 6:45 the train departed. The barren, burned-out landscape was covered by darkness. Halfway there, we were joined by a handsome Spaniard. He was from Seville and spoke French. Later on came an officer in the gendarmery, who was very lively. He made every effort so that we might understand him. He heard we were from Denmark—I, a poet. He didn't like the Englishmen and mimicked their coldness and sullenness. Emanuele Solér was his name. When we arrived at the train station [in Alicante], he helped us greatly by getting out baggage and procuring a chaise for us. Two gendarmes, one of whom carried Jonas's suitcase, took us to our carriage. We were guided there through the crowd in such a way that people must have thought we were either very distinguished persons or prisoners. We were driven to the Fonda del Bossio, where we arrived at 9:30 in the evening and got a good room with two smaller bedrooms. Ate cheese and grapes and then went to bed. Splendid! Got this far without trouble.

Sunday, September 21. Our room looks out over the promenade; went down into the garden. Here, there is much more life than in Valencia. The houses flat; a castle towers over the town. At the fish market we saw octopuses and strange varieties of fish, some looking like big, flatbellied snakes. It's extremely hot; my bowels a little loose. Here in the hotel you must pay separately for shoe shines. Jonas boiled some snails, and the waiter pulled them out of their shells and consumed them. Went to see our consul Alexander Harmsen, but he was out in the country today. Isabella the Second's Plaza is adorned with a fountain, flowers and palms. Strolled the length and breadth of the town. Women sat picking lice off their children. Walked to the sea. There, long waves rolled toward shore. The fortress lies on a yellow-colored cliff; the whole coast, as if scorched—not a bush, not a tree. In the evening there was music at 8:30 on the public promenade. Mostly ladies, in a long row, sat fanning themselves. Little girls, tidied and dressed up, were dancing with each other. Gaslights were burning under the trees. In all of this southern hustle and bustle, there came to me thoughts of beech woods, Øresund, all of my Danish home—"Abroad and at Home," as I wanted to call *A Poet's Bazaar* at the time I was working on it.—We happened upon some Swedish sailors, spoke with them. One of them was drunk and said right away: "Let's find us some women!"—The music played on until late into the night.

The following day Andersen and Jonas Collin left for Malaga via Murcia and Cartagena. After a week there, they continued to Granada, where they were able to attend the festivities in honor of Queen Isabella II's visit to the city. They spent two weeks in Granada before returning to Malaga on their way to Gibraltar, where they made the crossing to Tangier. There they stayed for a week as the guests of the British Consul General Sir John Drummond Hay and his Danish-born wife.

Sunday, November 2. When the cannon shot sounded at 5:30, I got up. My stomach still ached. Drank some tea and went with the hired servant to buy a steamship ticket. The sea was a bit rough. At 7:30 Consul Mathiasen came aboard and said goodbye. This morning his wife bore him a son. We didn't sail until 8:30. The ship sailed smoothly. We didn't cross over to Tangier until after we had gone along the Spanish coast for a way. Some Moors were on board—our hired servant had recommended to us one of them, the Moorish second mate. The ship was rocking a bit. We didn't approach land until 1 o'clock. From Ceuta on, the African coast was magnificent—you could see three mountain chains, one in back of the other, one of them jagged like Monserrat. Then the mountains got lower and green. There was heavy surf. With its flat-roofed houses, Tangier is quite Moorish. The countryside close to the town was like a section of desert with African sand. Pounding surf on the other side of a reef. We got into a boat, and then some ten Moors ran out into the surf in water up to their chests in order to hold the boat and take our baggage. Each one had one piece with him when he ran back. We ourselves were snatched out of the boat by two men, set up on their shoulders and carried to shore, where there were throngs of people dressed like Moors. Outside the gates there sat some six men dressed in long kaftans and ponderous turbans, who were responsible for the inspection of our things. It was very superficial—they opened the luggage and nodded. And now, followed by a shrieking mass of half-naked children and the people who were carrying the baggage, we reached the English consul's residence. His secretary came to greet us, told us that no letter had come concerning my arrival, but that they were expecting me. The family was still at its newly built country house, Ravensrock, three miles away. We were given some hurried refreshment, and then a horse came for Jonas. The secretary and I each seated ourselves on a mule. All our baggage was put on a third, and then we set off through narrow streets filled with people in oriental dress. We saw a couple of Moorish women. Not far outside town it was like a whole desert encampment. Here, lying in the sand, were Arabs by the hundreds. We were headed along a road that the consul had had built—as well as it could be done—out to his country house, Ravensrock, which lies out toward the Atlantic Ocean. At times it was like a narrow, paved lane, at times, a moorland path. In between the tight fences, I could see an Arab farm. Its burial ground lay close to the house. Rattan palms grew to a great height; mighty cactuses. Soon we saw the town and the sea below us. A few years ago, a lion strayed up to here. It wasn't killed. None have been seen in recent years; the area is becoming more settled. After a three-mile ride, we came to the country house, which is located in the midst of a large garden established just a few years ago. We got a warm welcome. Mrs. Hay spoke Danish and Hay, English. I was given a room with a lovely view out to the strait and down toward the mountains by Ceuta and over to Tarifa and, incidentally, out to the Atlantic Ocean, which now could be seen only as a horizontal ribbon. We ate dinner at 3 o'clock and then went for a walk out on the moorland outside the garden, where, in broad daylight the day before, a meteor, shining bright as the sun, had fallen, but nothing of it had been found. Mrs. Hay and I sat on a high crag and looked down at Tangier, with its masses of white houses. The moorland was rich in lovely, large-flowered heather, flowering myrtle and small fan palms. Later, when the moon rose, it was shining so brightly that I could see the lighthouse at Tarifa. This morning I had diarrhea; I seemed over it now. In the garden three holes had been dug for doing your business. There squatted Jonas and I in the moonlight under the bayberry, doing what business we could. It was a strange privy. Later Hay showed me a place in the house for use during the night. At 9 o'clock I went to bed.

Monday, November 3. Slept restlessly; had some pain in my stomach; didn't dream at all. It was cold; I was freezing. Up at 7 o'clock; the sun was shining in at me. The sea is blue but a little misty, though.—My stomach still not quite right. As I was squatting, a yellow dog came—I thought it was a lion! We ate in the open air down in the garden under a cliff. It was very summerlike. Hay told me the former seventy-and-something year old emperor of Morocco had 800 wives and every ten days he got a fresh young girl, usually as a present from various *cadi*. The present emperor had only a few hundred. Here in the garden, there had recently been a wild boar. Here, there are jackals that howl at night; there are also mongooses here. We went for a long walk westward toward the Portuguese consul's villa. Everything was in its natural state—only a lightly trodden path, bayberry, live oaks, myrtle all around. Jonas stayed behind to catch an Egyptian mongoose. When we came into the garden, we saw there the tracks of one and found one of its long quills. Greenish-white clouds hung in the red evening sky. The moon is waxing in strength. The dew fell.

Tuesday, November 4. Here, the darkness turns quickly to day. Jonas rode to town with the secretary, Mr. Green. I went for a walk with Sir Hay to the iron-rich spring. Close by there is one with softer water. Only this small section of the garden had been cultivated before; it lay by the house where Mr. Hay's interpreter is living. The larger building is barely one year old; the villa itself, completely finished only three weeks ago. The weather is quite lovely and warm. The sea appears calm to the eye, but you can hear its rolling surf. Sent a letter to Thiele and one to Titular Councillor Drewsen. Letters to Bille and Mrs. Henriques. Walked around alone in the garden park. Outside there were some Moorish men working. They looked as if they only had their dirty shirts on. Here in the house, they have employed a young Moorish girl, the first around here to serve in a Christian household. Mr. Hay told me yesterday about his stay in Constantinople, that he had seen a lovely portrait of one of the sultans. This is how it had come to be painted: a dwarf had been entertaining the emperor (Mahmud, the father of Abdul-Mejid), and said, "What will you now give me?" "I'll give you whichever one of my wives that you kiss." "Yes, but I cannot reach that high—they will laugh at me." "That is your problem!" A little later, the sultan asked for his pipe, and one of the most beautiful women knelt and offered it to him. Then the dwarf sprang forward, took her around the neck and and kissed her. "I will give you money," the sultan said, "but not her." "The sultan is not going back on his word!" answered the dwarf. "She may well be yours now, but do not ever dare to enter the gates of the seraglio!"—And she had to go with the dwarf. "Now I, too, want to have what I want," she said. "I want to live like the Christian women! I want to go for drives! I shall torment you!" And that's what she did! And that is how a French painter came to paint her portrait.—Went alone on a walk for an hour in the impenetrable thicket leading up to the garden. Here, something like paths have been made. Looked down at Tangier. The sea was dead calm, and, even so, the surf was splashing up against the cliffs. All around there grew bayberry, myrtle and some tall bushes bearing flowers resembling most our wild lilies of the valley and bearing at the same time fruit like cherries but with the flesh and color of strawberries. Like yesterday, we ate in the garden under the cliff. Jonas went hunting; I went with Mr. Hay up on a cliff and saw a chain of the Atlas Mountains, which are about eighty-five miles from here.—We were at the farm of one of the servants; his Moorish wife in just her shift; a handsome little boy and a less pretty little girl were playing in the yard and spoke Berber to us. A lovely moon-lit night; many Portuguese fishing boats in the strait. I sketched the view. In bed around 10 o'clock.

On November 9, Andersen and Jonas Collin made the crossing from Tangier to Cadiz on their way to Seville and then Madrid, staying for three weeks before heading for France. They spent Christmas in Bayonne and celebrated the New Year in Bordeaux, where Andersen made his last, rather subdued entry for 1862: "Now I've put cakes and champagne out on the table to bid the old year farewell and to thank the Lord for what He has granted me this past year; the coming one won't bring as many new and interesting things but, God willing, just as much heartfelt joy."

On January 14, Andersen and Jonas Collin left Bordeaux and arrived one week later in Paris, where he was given a warm welcome by the Scandina-

vian community. Shortly before the end of his two-month stay there, a princely celebration at the Palais-Royal was arranged in his honor by Bjørnstjerne Bjørnson, who happened to be passing through the city on his way from Italy to Norway.

In late April, just one month after his return from Paris, Andersen left Copenhagen to spend the spring and summer at the estates of Holsteinborg, Basnæs, Glorup, and Frijsenborg reworking the notes from his trip to Spain into the travelogue In Spain. *On August 10, he made his way back to Copenhagen to prepare the manuscript of* In Spain *for publication and, inspired by several successful performances of his fairy tale play* Mother Elderberry, *to work on two comedies—*He Has Yet To Be Born *and* On Langebro.

Wednesday, October 14 [1863]. Dinner at the Ørsted's, where I read *He Has Yet To Be Born.* Mrs. Ørsted and Mathilde had never known such out-and-out ludicrous characters as the ones I had created. "Well, I know the author!" said Mrs. Ørsted. "It has so much of you in it!" We laughed about her naïveté.

Thursday, October 15. At Edvard's today there was a little of the Collin brand of unpleasantness. Jonas is really an insolent twerp on whom I have wasted the kindness of my heart, etc.

Friday, October 16. Took a hot bath. Went for a walk out through West Gate,[10] around past the new railroad station, where I've never been for a walk before. Everything was new; everything was strange. I ran into Jerichau's boys out there. Walked through the rooms of the station, after that across the lake and along the embankment, where there was a whole new street of row houses with small English-style gardens in front of them. Everything strange—it didn't seem to me I was at home. The dome of the new City Hospital rose above the trees. I walked up a suburban street and could see the church of Saint John in the distance. My picture was hanging in a bookstore window. At 4:30 we had dinner at Nicolai Ørsted's; the Forchhammers were there. Reverend Ipsen seemed to think himself superior to me. I read for them from my stay in Seville. When I went home—in through the gate, where the lighting is bad—I had the feeling I might lose my way. At the theater, *Guillaume Tell.* Letter from Hauch that my comedy has been accepted.

Saturday, October 17. Dinner at Professor Meldahl's; read "Seville." Meldahl suggested to the Committee for Ørsted's Monument that

---

10. The western entryway (Vesterport) to the city through the old ramparts.

they purchase the bells from Frederiksborg for Ørsted's statue. We could get the copper one mark per pound cheaper than usual.— *Henry of Navarre* for the first time.

Sunday, October 18. Letter from Bentley that "The Ice Maiden" had just been published. On my behalf, he had asked the princess of Wales that it be dedicated to her and had received permission. Was asking now that I compose it. I was furious that he had done anything on my behalf that I neither knew about nor desired. Thiele and Edvard Collin thought I should let things be. I cannot, will not, without at least making it clear to him that I'm not happy about the way he does things. I'm not at all pleased to have a story like "The Psyche" dedicated to a young woman. Jonas out in Lyngby today. I drove all the way through town out to Frederiksberg and walked through the park up to see Hauch. The trees were loosing their leaves. Had coffee with the widow Boye.

Monday, October 19. Not well. Wrote a letter to Bentley, which Henriques translated. I feel nervous, upset and tired. My thoughts, as if pinioned. Raw, wet weather. Dinner at the Hartmanns'.

Tuesday, October 20. Moving Day today.[11] Rain and slush. Sent letters to Bentley and Mrs. Bushby. Dinner at the Drewsen's in Rosenvænget Street. At the theater, a poor house for *Henry of Navarre* (third performance).

Wednesday, October 21. Nervous at the thought of reading this evening for the first time for the university students in their wonderful, new hall. I gave up the idea of eating at the Ørsteds' and went to a restaurant. At 8 o'clock, I was at the Student Association, which was jam-packed—probably five hundred people. I read well, though. First, "The World's Loveliest Rose," then "The Butterfly," "The Goblin at the Grocer's," "Valdemar Daae" and "The Snail and the Rosebush." Each tale was applauded loudly. When I got home, I found on my table printed invitations to dinner tomorrow and for this evening from a Mr. . . . and wife. I don't know them at all. No one has paid a call.

Thursday, October 22. When I, nervous and tired, went out today to visit . . .—Lieutenant Fugl had come this morning and said he was the streetcar contractor and that his daughters "love" me and know my works—I first stopped by to see Thiele. He said, "But did you see *Mother Elderberry* yesterday evening?" He was referring to

---

11. A customary day for tenants to move (on the third Tuesday of April or October).

yesterday evening's review by Clemens Petersen of the performance of *Mother Elderberry* at the Casino. It was extremely flattering for me, nice for Carl Price, too. Then I went over to the Hotel Phønix to see . . . and wrote in the album of the young lady, who was so well disposed toward me. It is the birthday of Jette Collin and H. P. Holst. I wished him a happy birthday at the Casino; I had dinner with her and later went to the theater to see *The Barber of Seville*. Høedt and His Excellency seemed contemptuous of me—*they* are the patrons of my new comedy. Christian Winther has made us Danes sound pitiable in a poem to the king of Sweden. Ploug has published it in his *Fatherland*. I'd like to call it "Christian Winther's Begging Poem."

Friday, October 23. Dinner together with Hamilton at the Kochs'. I read from *In Spain*. This evening Carl Hartmann set off for Rome. His father accompanied him to Berlin.

Saturday, October 24. Lovely sunny weather, but very cold. Read my new comedy at the Kochs'. Felt extremely well. Visited by the American Schaffner, who is laying a telegraph wire from Europe to America over Iceland and Greenland. Ate at a restaurant.

Sunday, October 25. Dinner with the Hartmanns at the Henriqueses'. Walked from there to the Casino and saw *A Sparrow among Hawks*.

Monday, October 26. At the Eckardts' read *"He Has Yet To Be Born"*; was there for dinner. Lovely moonlight the last few evenings, but cold. Was at the Royal Theater and the Casino.

Tuesday, October 27. Walked out to the Vesterbro district,[12] to Absalon Street, to see the Norwegian lady Mrs. Schumann, who brought me a greeting from the Norwegian Mrs. Lorck. Gave her my photograph. Saw the new trolleys for the first time.

Wednesday, October 28. Was at Mrs. Ørsted's; had sweet soup again, which always makes me nervous. The antidote is to eat a lot of it. At the Linds' this evening; read from *In Spain*.

Thursday, October 29. Letter from *Bentley*. He glided lightly over what he had done to me; wanted to have *In Spain* and, stupidly enough, also *In Sweden*, which he, of course, himself published a long time ago. Dinner at the Collins'. Jonas insolent and inconsiderate, as always. A young lady was there; she was supposed to be charming and modest. She was very overbearing! I got nervous from irritation, but read, however, when Louise asked me.

---

12. An outlying district of Copenhagen beyond West Gate (Vesterport); see note 10.

Friday, October 30. A bad case of hemorrhoids and feeling ill. Went anyway to read from *In Sweden* for the Tillisch ladies and their party. Dinner at Mrs. Koch's with a Norwegian lady from Norway. Met them later at the Casino.

Saturday, October 31. Sent twelve gatherings of *In Spain* to Bentley. Dinner at the Linds' together with Miss Fürst of Randers.

On November 15, King Frederik VII died, throwing the whole country into mourning. A few days later, his successor to the throne, Christian IX, signed a new constitution for Denmark and just one of the duchies—Schleswig. This created a de facto separation of Schleswig and Holstein in the face of strong German opposition. Disturbing rumors of unrest soon reached Copenhagen, and the troops were called up. Distressed by these events, Andersen ended his diary for 1863 on a somber note: "The year is over; the outlook is pitchblack, sorrowful, bloody—the New Year."

Andersen's prophecy came true. In 1864 war was resumed with Prussia—now under the leadership of Otto von Bismarck—over the duchies of Schleswig and Holstein. The new constitution took effect January 1; during the month that followed, Denmark looked anxiously southward.

Friday, January 1 [1864]. Bright and shining, frosty day—eighteen degrees below freezing in the early morning hours [here at Basnæs]. Our poor soldiers are lying in barracks over there. The freezing weather is building a bridge for the enemy across the waters. A whole flood of people is pouring toward us! Whatever will come of us! Sent a letter to Richard Bentley and Mrs. Bushby in London, a letter to Anna Bjerring in Ålborg, to Mrs. Jette Collin and one to Mr. Rimestad that I will be happy to do a reading at the Workmen's Association. Letter from Henriques; a letter from Mrs. Ingemann with a photograph of Ingemann and her house enclosed. Today I finished the first draft of *On Langebro* and read downstairs the remaining two last acts, which they hadn't heard. This evening we had apple dumplings and spiced red wine. I proposed a toast to the king—he is on his way this evening to the army over in Schleswig.

Saturday, January 2. Sunshine and frost. Dreamed last night about the Serres—they were less than cordial to me; I seemed to be planning a trip to Egypt in the coming fall and was looking forward to it. Sent a letter to Eckardt and Scharff. At 1:15 Rosing and his wife left for Sorø.—You can read on a stone over the entrance to Basnæs: "God bless this house and those who rest under its roof." A letter from Edvard with my accounts—I have about 10,000 rix-dollars. Otto

Pavilion (papercut made at Basnæs Manor)

and Wissing were out for a drive; it was past 6 o'clock before they finally showed up. Mrs. Scavenius anxious, sent someone after them, and then they came shuffling back. Every day those two boys arrive at the dinner table a half hour after we do and sleep incredibly late in the morning.

Sunday, January 3. Frost and sunshine. Letter to Mrs. Anholm that I expect to arrive on Tuesday on the noon train, which will get there close to 6 o'clock in the evening.—Letter from Mrs. Ingeborg Drewsen. At the Casino I am diligently copying my play. In the evening, read aloud "The Marsh King's Daughter."

Monday, January 4. Dead calm, lovely sunshine. The rays warmed me as I walked along the beach to the bath house. Toward evening the frozen beach is whitish blue and shining white. The horizon—the atmosphere, a red-orange that fades into yellow-green and after that turns pure blue. There is a play of colors and clarity like a summer evening in the south.

Tuesday, January 5. Up at 8 o'clock. Departed at 9:30 in ringing frost and bright sunshine. Arrived at the railroad station at 12 o'clock;

didn't depart until 1 o'clock. I was alone in a first class coach for the whole trip. It was so cold that I couldn't keep a peephole melted through the frost on the window. It was hard for me to pass through Sorø without visiting Mrs. Ingemann. It was 6 o'clock before we reached Copenhagen. Mrs. Anholm's eldest son was there to welcome me. My room was toasty warm. A cup of tea was my dinner. Walked over to Edvard Collin's—there was supposed to be a party there for Roed and his Swedish son-in-law, Nyblom, who arrived just as I was leaving. He brought me a greeting from Beskow. At the Royal Theater they were performing Runeberg's *Can't Do* and *Little Kirsten* with a new cast. It went extremely well—the audience was kindly disposed but not numerous. When I got home, I drank a great deal of wine to give me strength.

Wednesday, January 6. (Collin's birthday.) Headache from the wine. Was at the Student Association, at Eckardt's, Collin's and Hartmann's. Dinner at the Ørsteds'. At the Casino they were doing *A Sparrow among Hawks*. A very young fellow, Neumann, played Peter Raven extremely well, just like Schmidt. He exhibits a lot of talent, if he can do it in other roles. Phister was there and very satisfied.

Thursday, January 7. Went to see the Henriqueses. The eldest of their little daughters has scarlet fever. They didn't tell me about it until after I had been in the living room for awhile. I went to see the Kochs, and there little Jøn was down with scarlet fever. They didn't think it was contagious and invited me for dinner tomorrow. Ate at Edvard Collin's.

Friday, January 8. Theodor wasn't sure scarlet fever wasn't contagious. I wrote then to Mrs. Koch that I couldn't come. Received from Mrs. Recke a ticket to her benefit that evening—saw *The Hunt for Adventure* and heard her sing her "Ball Medley." Close by me in the box sat the magnetizer Hansen; he has very fascinating eyes. Walked from there to the Royal Theater and there saw the second and third acts of *The Valkyrie*.

Saturday, January 9. Ate at a restaurant. Made a fair copy of my singspiel *On Langebro*. The Italians were singing for the last time at the Casino. I took Louise Lind, and she, her daughter Ingeborg. We saw scenes from *The Barber*, *The Sleepwalker* and *The Daughter of the Regiment*. Désirée Artôt, from Belgium—rather ugly but an excellent coloratura soprano with spirit and some talent—was the high spot of the evening. The rest of it was far inferior. It was a long performance, full house.

Sunday, January 10. At the Henriqueses' the eldest daughter has scarlet fever. I stayed away and therefore ate at Edvard Collin's. At the Casino, *The Woman in White,* based on a novel by Wilkie Collins. I would have called it "A Serial in Eleven Acts." That's how many acts there were.—Letter to Mrs. Scavenius.

Monday, January 11. Dinner at a restaurant. Wrote diligently; felt ill all day. It was little Anna Anholm's birthday; so gave her a pair of castanettes from Malaga. Stayed at home all evening and early to bed. A meeting at the Casino with Holst.

Tuesday, January 12. Letter from Miss Bjerring. Felt well; received 250 rix-dollars from Reitzel's, of which 150 dollars went into the savings bank. Drove in the omnibus out to Drewsen's. His wife was ill. As a member of the Ancker Scholarship Committee, I had to leave the theater after the second act of *A Partition* to go to a meeting. Hertz, who has taken Christian Winther's place, is in agreement with me about voting for the most competent applicant without regard to age. We voted for Kaalund.

Wednesday, January 13. Dinner with the Ørsteds. Felt very well all day. Letter from Miss Bjerring. At the Workmen's Association, read "The Red Shoes," "Holger the Dane," "The Snow Man," "The Collar" and "What Dad Does Is Always Right." Was given a welcome and applauded after each tale. After that, was called back and then read "The Butterfly."

Thursday, January 14. Dinner at the Collins'. Only Augusta Collin was there. The weather is cold. Almost every evening at the Royal Theater, a poor house.

Friday, January 15. My lip—which I split on Tuesday—still hurts. Saw three acts of *Robert the Devil*—persistently poor houses. There is a piercing, cold wind. The streets are swarming with reserve soldiers that have been called up.

Saturday, January 16. A little sunshine today, but biting cold. At 12 o'clock, read tales at Mrs. Güldencrone's. In the evening I heard Professor Emil Hornemann's lecture on mental illness, in which he took special issue with Hansen, the magnetizer.

Sunday, January 17. Lovely, sunny weather and frost. Promised the pharmacologist Mr. Hoffmeyer to read next Saturday for the pharmacologists at Vincent's Restaurant. Delivered a bit more of *On Langebro* to Holst. At the Casino, *More than Pearls and Gold.* There was a crazy man sitting right behind me continually clapping, so that I got up and took a seat all the way to the rear of the amphitheater. Sitting next to me there was a crazy man who was shouting loudly. The play didn't go well. At home, Josephine had forgotten to bring me my beer.

Monday, January 18. Not well! Wasted the day. Bright sunshine and frost. The wind is raising dust on the streets. Dinner at a restaurant. At the Casino the Persian danseuse Calepoliti performed two dances—they were rather strange; she, beautiful. The audience hissed. In addition to this, I saw most of *Little Kirsten* at the Royal Theater.

Tuesday, January 19. Snowy weather. Since I missed the bus, I walked out to Rosenvænget Street but rode home. This evening the young Helga Rasmussen, the stage manager's daughter, made her debut at the Casino in the play *Cora, or Slavery.*

Wednesday, January 20. Letter from a lady, who wants to tour on foot with me the most beautiful parts of Zealand. In the evening, saw the Persian dancer. Thaw.

Thursday, January 21. Gray weather and slush. Dinner at E. Collin's. In the evening Mrs. Heiberg appeared for the first time since her illness—in *The Weathercock.*

Friday, January 22. Bought Louise Lind a ticket for the parquet at an increased price so she could hear Mr. Jastrau, who will make his debut at the Royal Theater in *Lucia di Lammermoor.* Dinner at the Thieles'. The music in *Lucia* sounded like what comes out of a barrel organ. Døcker sang so woodenly. Jastrau is a good, powerful tenor, but he didn't arouse any emotion in me at all. The audience enthusiastic. Einar seemed to be offended because I'd written him that I had to read tomorrow and couldn't go with him to see the magnetizer. Marie Nutzhorn's birthday—I was invited for the evening or, if I wanted, to dinner. I decided to pay a morning call. Irritable and in a bad mood this evening. Mad at the world. Jonas always makes his appearance in my bitter thoughts—that twerp!

Saturday, January 23. The streets are swarming with reserve soldiers who have been called up. In the evening read for the pharmacologists at Vincent's Restaurant. I read seven tales; there were a number of ladies there.

Sunday, January 24. Dinner at Edvard Collin's. I feel gloomy and depressed. Can't get anything done. Wish for an end to everything.

Monday, January 25. Dinner at Eckardt's. He and Scharff charming; Mrs. Eckardt dull and not much of a hostess. I don't want to go there any more for dinner. A nice letter from Princess Anna of Hesse asking me to write something for her album. Enclosed I found some pages from Emperor Napoléon and his wife, etc. At the Casino, *More Than Pearls and Gold.*

Tuesday, January 26. Walked in gray weather, in wind and rain, out to Rosenvænget Street. Rode back on the omnibus and saw *Don Juan of Austria*.

Wednesday, January 27. Sent a letter with the "box poem" to Councillor Glud. After the theater I was at the Workmen's Association to hear Professor Hornemann's lecture on mental illness.

Thursday, January 28. Brought to Princess Anna her album and presented her with the illustrated English edition of "The Ice Maiden." Miss Steuber was very upset about the war. On Thursday they'll be traveling from here to Vevey. I was at the Casino and saw the rehearsal for Holst's new play, *At Dannevirke*. When I saw it now this evening, it was more flat.

Friday, January 29. Lovely sunshine but frost, although it melted in the sun. Out at Amalienborg at 1 o'clock the king said farewell to some soldiers. At 10 o'clock I was at the Casino to read the fairy-tale play, *On Langebro*, for H. P. Holst. He liked it.—Visited the Næboes and lent them *In Spain*. Received an anonymous poem in the mail. At the Ørsteds' we dined on ham and kale. Called on the Gades. At 6:30 I was at the Thieles' and read *On Langebro*. Thiele had little to say. I could see already in the first act that his wife and her sister were interested in it. The children thanked me soberly for the pleasure. Thiele only said: "It is a nice story—I know it from Musäus, of course!"—I felt downcast, depressed. Went to the Casino and heard people cheering for everything in *At Dannevirke*. The present times oppressed me. Overwhelmed and bitterly aware of my forsakenness, I went home.

Saturday, January 30. Bright sunshine and frost. Each day soldiers are mobilized. Dinner with Lord-in-Waiting Scavenius—a sumptuous meal. But I feel very awkward and don't like that arrogant man. Went to the theater and saw Calderón's comedy, *A Partition*, which was jeered at and unanimously booed. This was its second time on stage.

Sunday, January 31. Cold but lovely sunshine. At 1:30 more soldiers embarked on the steamer *Dania*. Several were sitting in the rigging swinging their caps. I saw Rasmus Nielsen's son-in-law, Lieutenant [Edsberg]. He looked jubilant, as if off on a holiday. Dinner with the Collins; presented Jette with the elegant English edition of "The Ice Maiden." Went from there in to see the Hartmanns briefly, but am not in the mood to work on anything. Now I'm sitting at home all alone. The African cactus gets shifted every evening away from the cold windows, but I'm not expecting any flowers, not even that it will survive.

In the early weeks of February, Andersen reported the Austro-Prussian invasion and the Danish rout at Dannevirke. His gloom concerning the course of the war was punctuated by painful visits to the dentist to have a number of teeth extracted and new dentures fitted. In mid-March the island of Fehmarn was taken by the Prussians without a fight, and two weeks later, on the eve of his fifty-ninth birthday, Andersen lamented: "The past year of my life has been full of trials and tribulations. First, Jonas Collin was mean to me—he is now out of my heart. The king died. The war is threatening Denmark with destruction. I've gotten old. I have false teeth that torment me. I'm not in good health. I'm heading for death and the grave." The following day, the city of Sønderborg was bombarded.

Wednesday, April 13. Still haven't accomplished anything. Haven't even gotten around to sending the manuscripts to America, even though the auction is over and the papers have been ready for weeks. At Mrs. Ørsted's I had sweet soup again and got the jitters from it— I was standing by the window reading a telegram, when I glimpsed the words "Viggo Drewsen." I nearly fainted, but I could see on closer inspection that it was "Begge Depecher." Those two *g* 's and the big *D* made my fantasy run wild. Today I've been out at Rosenvænget Street to visit with Mrs. Drewsen.

Thursday, April 14. Yesterday evening I received a very friendly letter from the young English attaché Bulwer-Lytton, the son of the author, inviting me to dine with him today. I accepted. He lives on the first floor of the Thomsen residence, right by the Casino. There was another young English attaché there, along with Hamilton, who arrived while we were at the table. I had to speak English. Bulwer-Lytton speaks good German, but it was against my heart of hearts to speak that language, found it unpatriotic. So I said in bad English: "At present there is for me in that language the sound of cannons and the shouts of enemies; I would rather speak bad English." He showed *Last Poems* by Elizabeth Barrett Browning, who has spent a lot of time in Italy and recently died in Florence. I spoke with her when I was last in Rome. Her *last* poem is "The North and the South," which was extremely flattering of me. Bulwer-Lytton made a good impression on me.

Friday, April 15. I couldn't go to Koch's today, where there was also a party, since I was supposed to do a reading at the Student Association in aid of the victims of the fire in Sønderborg. I and Michael Wiehe were the mainstays. I was nervous and exhausted, not at all disposed to read. It was an agony to read the tales. "Five Peas from One Pod" went tolerably well. I wasn't in the mood for "The Emperor's New Clothes," and during the reading I stood thinking about how badly it was going. "The Collar" went better. Wiehe read Paludan-Müller's delightful *Abel's Death*. He read superbly, but too softly—more than a third of the people there could hardly hear him. There was no lack of a warm welcome and applause. The wording of the petition bothered me.[13] My imagination—filled with torments, agonies and death—is running away with me.

Saturday, April 16. No peace of mind, no work. Rode out to see Mrs. Drewsen. Sunshine and warm. The wind, though, icy cold. At the goldsmith Michelsen's I've placed an order for my medal, the Knight of Dannebrog, and had a piece of the gold chain to my watch cut and fashioned to hold it. Mrs. Michelsen said she didn't know what it cost. Then her husband came. He said he didn't have anything to do with that; it was his wife! And then, moreover, she came with a silver thermometer with Goethe's bust and wanted to give it to me—she was so fond of my last poem, "Denmark"! I couldn't accept all that, but did accept the Dannebrog medal in return for bringing her a memento when the occasion presented itself. Then she showed me the draft of a letter she, as a Danish woman, had written and intended to send to Napoléon. She wanted to know my opinion of it. I said it couldn't do any harm, but it probably wouldn't help. The latter, she said, was what the king said when he had recently been in their shop. Today I've really been tormented by the pressure of political events that are carrying me along—I feel each kindness people in Germany have shown me, acknowledge friends there but feel that I, as a Dane, must make a complete break with them all. They have been torn out of my heart; never will we meet again; a beautiful past cannot be renewed. My heart is breaking! I am in complete agreement with the basic thrust of the petition—that we have suffered a grievous injustice, that the war has been conducted without any humanitarian considerations. But there are

13. The petition mentioned by Andersen was initiated in April 1864 by Carl Steen Andersen Bille, editor of the influential newspaper *The Daily (Dagbladet)* (see index). It was addressed to the Swiss people in order to stir public sympathy for the Danish cause during the Dano-Prussian war.

expressions of bitterness in the petition to which I cannot ascribe and which can do us no good, which pain me. I am now going to take stock of my life. I no longer have a future, but God has indeed granted me infinite joy and happiness in times past. Yesterday Christian Voigt came to see me and asked with an incredible embarrassment and humility—as if he believed that I wouldn't—to be godfather for his first son. Riborg's brother hasn't forgotten his old feeling for me.

Sunday, April 17. In the Funen paper there was a negative piece about our petition to Switzerland.[14] Worsaae is said to have had reservations about signing and didn't do it. My mind is in a turmoil! I cannot support the wording of the document and think it could have consequences. My guess is that I—as the one best known—will be attacked by the Germans and reminded about the kindness they have shown me. My imagination is running away with me, and yet I have the feeling I've done my duty, as each Dane now must and *will* do. Lord, my God, give me the strength to be undaunted. Let me be able to bear my lot. I've received unending kindness and blessings— perhaps my heaviest days are now coming. Let me be worthy of Denmark and what is Danish! Lord, my God, do not forsake me!

Monday, April 18. What a night I've spent in self torture, in rehearsing fixed ideas, in half madness, envisioning myself at the bottom of a ship, cast into a dark cell, tortured and abused—I'm making a fool of myself by recording my fixed idea. I lay bathed in sweat, unsleeping in the early morning hours. I confided in Jette Collin, who could see how upset I was, and she joked and said I was crazy. Later in the day the message came that the storming of the Dybbøl entrenchments had begun. Two hours later word came that they had been taken and many of our officers had fallen. I was physically and mentally overcome. I staggered to the Student Association and the War Ministry. I ate at Scharling's. Christian Scharling is off to Als tomorrow to build barracks. We drank a toast to him. Went from there to the War Ministry. The army has arrived on Als, destroyed the bridges, but we have lost many officers. When I went down to Zinn's a little later, Miss Regitze came and said that the 2nd Regiment, the 22nd, along with the 9th and the 20th, had suffered injuries, fatalities and capture by the enemy. I was horrified at hearing the 2nd Regiment named, precisely the one Viggo is with. She had heard it from Mrs. Falkenskiold in her building, whose husband

14. See note 13.

commands the 22nd Regiment. She went up to them again and heard the same news, to be sure not from the lady of the house but the maid. I left overwhelmed, but then turned back again and went to see Hartmann, and he then went down to Mrs. Falkenskiold, who said that the four regiments named had suffered most—some injuries and captures—but the others (the rest) were safe on Als. I was relieved. I clung to the possibility of some comfort.

During the following weeks, Andersen grieved for the sons of friends and acquaintances slain at Dybbøl and for Viggo Drewsen, who had been wounded and captured by the Prussians. After another Danish defeat in late June and the news that both France and England would remain neutral, a cease-fire was declared on July 20. A peace treaty was drawn up on October 30, and Denmark was forced to cede both Schleswig and Holstein to Germany. The next day, Andersen reports a dream: "Last night I again dreamt my usual, hideous dream about a living child that I press up against my warm breast— this time, though, it was just in my sleeve; it breathed its last, and I was left with only the wet skin."

The Elderly Man
(1865–1872)

URING HIS LATER YEARS, *Andersen's life was comfortable. He may have had no family, but he still had his old friends and continued to see them at least once a week as their dinner guest, a tradition that stemmed from his early years in Copenhagen. He saw in this way Adolph and Ingeborg Drewsen on Tuesdays, Mrs. Ørsted and her daughter on Wednesdays, Edvard and Henriette Collin on Thursdays, and Mrs. Ida Koch, the widowed sister of Henriette Wulff, on Fridays.*

Although his relationship with the Collin family was no longer quite as close as when the elder Jonas Collin was alive, Andersen was made welcome in the homes of a number of new friends, such as the Henriques and the Melchiors. The two brothers-in-law Martin Henriques and Moritz Melchior were prominent members of the Jewish business aristocracy of Copenhagen and, not having known Andersen when he was struggling for recognition, did not make him feel indebted and insecure. Indeed, they admired and accepted him with all his oddities, testiness, and self-absorption. He often stayed at Peter's Hill and Tranquility, the country houses of the Henriques and Melchior families, but it was the Melchior home [Rolighed; see upper part of the map on page 362]—a rendezvous for Denmark's most outstanding artists and scientists—which came to mean most to him.

Andersen claimed the greatest honor ever done him was when he was granted honorary citizenship of his hometown, Odense, in 1867. However, he was in fact a citizen of the world, made famous by his tales and stories. He chose to travel abroad as often as he could—at least once a year between 1865 and 1874—frequenting European courts of nobility and making the acquaintance of the greatest artists of his time. When in Copenhagen, his footloose ways made it most convenient for him to live in various hotels and rented rooms, always in the vicinity of the Royal Theater, where he spent so many evenings. When he finally had to buy his own furniture in the fall of 1866, he did so grudgingly.

Andersen was well-off during his later years, earning royalties from reprintings of earlier works as well as from his new work. He was still quite creative: more than half his tales and stories were composed during the last two decades of his life, and among these are some of his finest. However, early in 1865 he was still feeling too unsettled from the war to be able to concentrate on writing tales. Instead, he worked on a romantic comedy, When the Spaniards Were Here.

Thursday, February 2 [1865]. Sat from 11 o'clock to past 1:00 for the portrait artist, Miss Wittusen, who has an atelier in Christiansborg Palace. Reworked some things in my play and afterwards gave it to Edvard Collin for him to make a fair copy.

Friday, February 3. Sat again for Miss Wittusen. Arrived cold and hungry at Mrs. Henriques's, where I warmed up with a glass of milk. This evening, for the first time, Hertz's comedy *The Attorney and His Ward.* It is competently contrived, but nonetheless *contrived.* This evening I felt heels under my boots for the first time; now I have fast footing on the slippery streets. Hjerrild, the drama critic for *The Daily News,* is said to have died today from St. Anthony's Fire and an anthrax infection in his nose.

Saturday, February 4. Especially cheerful and well. Today I've sat for six whole hours for the portrait artist, but she still hasn't gotten my contour. She was about to give it up, but I promised to sit one more time on Monday. Letter to Hansen, the cathedral organist in Ribe.—Lovely sunny weather and hard frost. Tomorrow, according to the English weather forecaster, it's supposed to be fifteen degrees below zero. Today it's eighteen to twenty degrees above. *The Sylphid,* with Miss Healey, performed at the theater.

Sunday, February 5. The trains are stuck. The snow is deep. I had promised to read my new comedy at the goldsmith Michelsen's, but had to postpone, since it's still at the copyist's. When I got home, Madame Anholm sent a message up that I had probably spilled water on the floor—it had leaked down to her. I went into my bedroom; the floor was awash; the bedspread was sopping wet. I touched it and was squirted in the face. The gutter outside had frozen, and the water had worked its way through the wall. The ceiling was soaked. There was no staying there that night, and I had to have my bed moved into the sitting room next door and the door brought down from the attic to keep out the raw air. Mrs. Anholm flew into a temper when I cordially brought the matter up with her. At Edvard Collin's, where I was staying while they were fixing things up, I asked about the copying and whether it would be finished tomorrow. *He* had himself done the fair copy of the entire piece so that it would be finished as quickly as possible! Now I must say, if he didn't say anything the other day after the reading to express his sympathy, he has now expressed it through his deeds.

Monday, February 6. Sat for Miss Wittusen. The contours are better. Before I looked like old Nathanson; now I look like old Goethe. That's always an improvement, and I promised to sit for her again. Got from Edvard the fair copy of the manuscript of my new comedy, *When the Spaniards Were Here,* and immediately brought it to Professor Høedt, who has promised to get Kranold and Hauch to read it through in the next few days. Dinner with Minister of Finance David. It was an engagement party for Münter, the naval officer, and Miss Johnson from Bornholm. Mrs. David accompanied me to the table and was very charming. When I related later at Edvard Collin's that Mrs. David had said she had thought I was forty years old and not, as I had said, sixty, Jonas became irritated about how insincere people were. And it got worse when I said that in his speech to the young people David had wished them luck in the future and regarded it as an omen that chance had arranged to seat them there, right across from a poet. This was also insincerity and flattery aimed at me. This time I only saw the ridiculous in the young sage, who wants to appear as the champion of truth, but it is certainly not pure truth he wishes to have the appearance of. I'm on the verge of calling him a hypocrite.

Tuesday, February 7. Beautiful weather. Today water from the melting snow leaked in to Carl Price and from him through the ceiling down into my front room, so that I am about to be banished from there, too. When out at the Drewsens' for dinner, I said to Einar that if I went to Paris I would invite him along as my guest. At the theater I heard one act of *Physician and Pharmacist.* In the morning read *When the Spaniards Were Here* for Hultmann. He was enthusiastic, expressed himself extravagantly, compared this work to my tales, prophesied a brilliant reception for it, etc.

Wednesday, February 8. Was at the singing school and there made some corrections in the choral parts to *The Raven.* Read the text of *The Raven* to Mrs. Hartmann. Mrs. Minna Müller, born Levetzau, was buried today. Saw about four acts of the opera *Faust.* The freezing temperatures persist—between eighteen and twenty degrees above zero, a few days ago a maximum of three degrees just outside of the city.

Thursday, February 9. Presented Edvard Collin with a number of Ingemann's holographs. This evening I wanted to take my bedroom into use again, but the smell of whitewash was still too strong, so I moved my bed right out again. These days I am aimless and lazy; can't even be bothered to write letters. Fenger's birthday.

Friday, February 10. Twenty degrees below freezing this morning. The windows covered with thick frost, lovely sunny weather. Paid a visit to Jastrau and after that Gade. At Mrs. Koch's there was a family visiting, and we drank champagne. Afterwards I went to see Fenger and read *When the Spaniards Were Here* for him and his wife. Sore throat.

Saturday, February 11. A big fire this morning on Broad Street. The school that Rovsing owns burned down, and one of his sons almost died in the fire. He had come home from a ball at 3 o'clock, and the fire broke out at six; he was hoisted unconscious by rope out a window before the roof collapsed. Hjerrild buried—I attended, but in Garrison Church became overwrought and had to leave during the eulogy. Read *When the Spaniards Were Here* at the Henriqueses'. Had a chat with Jastrau on the street about the two Spanish romances he's to sing in it. Anna Lind has a fever.

Sunday, February 12. Beautiful weather, persistent hard frost. In the morning read *When the Spaniards Were Here* at the goldsmith Michelsen's. During dinner at the Henriqueses' Høedt said aloud to me at the table that my comedy had been sent to the copyist to get that out of the way while Hauch was reading the piece and so that the run-through could take place on the 20th of February, as he himself had said it would. I felt deep down that he was treating Hauch as if he were superfluous. At the theater they were doing Hertz's *Svend Dyring's House* for the fiftieth time. Holst had written a prologue for it extolling Hertz's great importance. It was nice, but so uncustomary—that sort of thing is only done for a dead man. After the prologue, when the play had begun, Carl Price came and asked me to raise a cheer for Hertz. I said that that should have been done immediately following the prologue or at the end of the play. He asked me if Hartmann wouldn't be willing to do it. I assured him with conviction—which Hartmann later confirmed—that it wasn't at all his way to appear in public.

Andersen's When the Spaniards Were Here *was first performed at the Royal Theater in early April, followed two weeks later by a revival of a reworked version of his* The Raven *(1832), with music by J. P. E. Hartmann. When he left the city in late May on a three-week visit to Basnæs, he finally found the peace of mind to begin work on some tales and stories,*

*completing five by the end of the summer and publishing them in November
as the third installment of the second series of* New Tales and Stories.

*On September 14, Andersen left Copenhagen on a month-long trip to
Sweden. He spent three weeks in Stockholm seeing old friends and dining
on several occasions with members of the Swedish royal family. On his way
back to Copenhagen, he stopped for a few days in Lund, where he was feted
by the students of the university. Back in Copenhagen, he took two rooms
at the Hotel d'Angleterre, staying there until early December, when he left
the city to spend a week at Holsteinborg before heading for Basnæs for the
Christmas holidays. He returned to Copenhagen on January 12, staying
again at the Hotel d'Angleterre, where the Norwegian violinist Ole Bull had
also taken up residence. From October 1866 to June 1869 Andersen lived in
a two-room apartment at 1 Little King's Street across from the Royal Theater.*

Sunday, January 14 [1866]. Last night or, if you will, this morning
at 1:30, I was awakened by the sound outside of "hurrahs" shouted
nine times in Swedish. It was for Ole Bull, who had the room where
I'm now staying but moved up into the rooms I was in before my
excursion to the country. I slept until 9 o'clock; then went up to see
Bull at 11 o'clock. He was just about to leave, kissed me on both
cheeks and said: "I always get an ovation when I'm staying in the
same hotel as you! Do you remember Marseilles?"—Really, he gets
them many places! Had coffee with Theodor Collin, who assembles
the family for coffee every Sunday the way his father used to do.
His fingers are remarkably nimble—he's just modeled a lion devouring an antelope, and it's wonderfully full of life. When he dies, the
world, which is to say the town chitchat, will have it that he was a
nonentity, and yet there was a lot to him, and many can say likewise when the judgment of the world is passed. Dinner at the Thieles'.
I was seated next to Mrs. Lønborg, who paid me a visit today. Thiele
proposed a toast to me as one newly come home and about to depart. Was at the Casino and heard *Rigoletto*. Powerful voices—I particularly liked the baritone and the tenor; the primadonna has a pure,
high voice, but often left words out, didn't excite any feeling in me.
One of the women in the chorus, Miss Kruse, made a fine showing—looked good and sang well. People's enthusiasm, however,
wasn't so great.

Monday, January 15. Gray, wet, slushy. Depressed. Was at Mrs.
Tutein's for an afternoon of music; invited by Miss Deckner, who
was giving a concert there. Slipped away with a pain in my stom-

ach, aching muscles. Dinner at the Henriqueses' with the young poet Hansen, who had composed a poem to me on the occasion of my recent—if not to say last—birthday. Went to the Casino to see *Lucia di Lammermoor*. The tenor and baritone excellent; Lucia, too, for the most part, but she doesn't have a dramatic soul.—I sat next to the royal box. The queen dowager's lord-in-waiting, Wedel-Heinen, very forthcoming, likewise Mr. Lund, the crown prince's adjutant. Paid a visit to the Melchiors; Mr. Moritz Melchior stopped by to invite me to dinner tomorrow. Called on Count Frijs in vain—they were out.—I have the feeling that the light of my poetic inspiration is extinguished. My time has passed; gone and forgotten, except perhaps to be torn apart by the mob, but they can only get at the surface which bears the imprint of my reputation. Visited today by Viggo Drewsen—this was really something! He never calls on people.

Tuesday, January 16. Gray, wet—"Lovely weather for this time of year!" as Copenhageners say. Went in vain out to see Mrs. Koch. Visited the Collins. After all, Jette is the one I get along with best, even though she is always advising me to live extravagantly—as if I were rich! All I have is 1,200 rix-dollars, and now 900 of them will be going for this trip! Dinner at the Melchiors' together with a Mr. and Mrs. Heiberg. I'm supposed to have held her on my lap when she was a little girl at Mrs. Joelsson's institute in Elsinore. Dr. Heiberg is said to be very self-confident. They were, by the way, a handsome young couple. Why was I not granted such youthful happiness? But I've been granted it in another way. Was at the Royal Theater and gave the ushers three rix-dollars as a New Year's present. Overskou's *East Avenue and West Avenue* consists entirely of characters modeled on other old works and dressed up in Copenhagen dress coats. Before, when the dress coat was fashionable, it was a good show. Now it isn't natural. Went to the Casino to hear Ole Bull and took in the first one and a half numbers. It was a full house. The Italians applaud for Albrecht, who sings with their opera. Ole's playing didn't excite me; he is himself an old man, as supple as Lord Chamberlain Levetzau. I left before it was over. Sent a letter to Mrs. Scavenius.

Wednesday, January 17. Alternating sunshine and clouds. Picked up 200 rix-dollars at Reitzel's for the two installments of tales that were reprinted. He told me that, of the 5,000 copies of my new tales printed this year, 4,500 had already been sold. A visit from the singer Jastrau—I ran into him this evening at the theater, where he told me that one of my tales "La madre" had been translated and published in one of Madrid's most widely circulated—especially in the Americas—newspapers. That same composition that proved to be so very popular when translated to Hindi has been published in a word-for-word translation by a Spanish poet! Had a visit from Henrik Scharling—when I asked his advice about making travel plans, he suggested I see Holland, since I have no great desire to go to Paris for a long while. He mentioned our compatriot Brandt in Amsterdam and his considerable hospitality—he has himself stayed for six weeks at Brandt's, where I would also be welcome. "But he has invited me," I said, "invited me especially!" And I decided to write to Brandt about whether he would be in Amsterdam and whether there was any cholera there. So right then and there I made the decision—to spend a little time relaxing on the way [to Portugal]. I sent a letter off and can expect to receive an answer by next week if he is at all pleased about my coming. Dinner at the Collins' with the young Davids from Rungsted (the wife is from the West Indies) and the scientist Bergsøe, who now seems to want to get closer to me. At the Royal Theater, *The Newly Weds* and Ole Bull. He has gotten gray, carries himself like Lord Chamberlain Levetzau (the one who acted as if he could button up the pants on a king)! I was bored. I can't stand violin music—if I once was moved by Ole Bull, it must have been my imagination, or now I've lost my sensibility. Hartmann said artificiality wasn't a good thing in music; spirituality, on the other hand, was gripping. But it was the former that made the biggest hit.

Thursday, January 18. Rain and slush. Was at the Foreign Ministry, where Titular Councillor Vedel received me warmly, as if we were old friends. He promised to arrange everything for me in connection with my departure. Dinner with Hartmann. Was at the theater for a short while and saw a little of *The Daughter of the Regiment*. Mrs. Riise's singing doesn't measure up, and her attempts at acting are unfortunate, but she was a Jenny Lind in comparison to Mrs. Zinck's rendition of the countess. You could call people in from the street who could do just as good a job. Empty house, except for Riise's family. At 8:30 I set off for Christiansborg; met a number of acquaintances, got terribly tired and left at the beginning of the concert, so that I was home by around 11 o'clock.

Friday, January 19. Very tired and sleepy. Was awakened by the janitor, who informed me that a Mr. Rasmussen from Odense had come to see me. I couldn't see him, of course, and asked him to write to me. Called on the Henriqueses, the Collins, the Eckardts, etc.—Dinner at Mrs. Koch's; after dinner the young Mrs. Koch had labor pains, so I left in a hurry. At the theater, heard the first act of *The Marriage of Figaro.* Before I left for the theater, I ran into Mr. Rasmussen by my door; I gave him just one mark. Later, when I got home from the theater, I found a letter from him that the mailman had brought. If I had received it earlier, I would have given him more.—This disturbed me.

Saturday, January 20. Rasmussen was here again this morning, but was sent away by the janitor. I was sorry about it. Called on Countess Frijs; saw her and her daughters. Ran into Caroline Hanck there with the Læssøes's children. Rain and blustery weather. Sent a letter to the bookseller in Hjørring, Marinus Petersen. Dinner with Mrs. Lord-in-Waiting Neergaard; I received a lovely, fragrant bouquet of violets and Spanish jasmine, Christmas roses and maidenhair. I brought it to Jette Collin. At the theater, Ole Bull. He doesn't interest me. At home, found a book and a letter from the authoress of *Shadow of the Past.* She had brought it to the hotel herself and asked me to call on her. At Mrs. Neergaard's, received one of those German pictures produced in Neu-Ruppin [for export to Denmark] portraying all the famous men of the North, in which I had also been included. In this morning's *Children's News* there is a poem dedicated to me. I said to Eckardt: "Things must be going pretty well now at home." "Well," he said bitterly, "can you imagine, [my wife] wants to play the wife in *The Newly Weds*—it's our story, you see, except that the husband doesn't accept charity from his in-laws." This morning I got a message that the young Mrs. Koch gave birth to a daughter at 7 o'clock yesterday evening.

Sunday, January 21. Clear weather. Drove out to Rosenvænget Street to Titular Councillor Drewsen's. There were violets blooming in the garden, Christmas roses, daisies, and big, yellow spring flowers. Had lunch there. Went in to see Theodor Collin—had a pain in one side of my abdomen and chest. Called on Mrs. Ørsted and the Kochs. Dinner at the Henriqueses'. Here was the physically (not intellectually) attractive Carstensen, who was going on a trip to Holland, Paris and Germany with the young Holmblad. He was very excited about it. We'll run into each other for sure. Went to the theater to see *Faust,* about four acts. Home and drank some port for my stomach and sat in sweet indolence with regard to my trip. It seriously occurred to me to turn to God for mercy, for it would be my *last.*

Monday, January 22. Rainy weather. Didn't feel so well. Felt like an old man! Wrote with the old man's fear of traveling abroad, his pining for this and that from home and after that about the young person's expectations and view of everything as rosey-red. Went to see Bramsen since his false teeth were cutting a hole in my mouth. Sent a manuscript and letter to the teacher Knudsen near Århus. Letter to Mrs. Scavenius. Dinner at Hartmann's, where I showed up in my everyday clothes and it turned out to be a going-away party for the teacher Ottesen, who is traveling to Jutland, and several strangers were there, among them the minister and poet, Fibiger. At the theater, Hertz's piece *The Brother-in-Law from California*, which has been severely criticized, but I found it interesting.—Ole Bull played the violin—it struck me as his best evening; I usually don't have a good time listening to him. A letter from the Brandt brothers. I've written to the one who hasn't invited me, but now I've gotten an invitation from him.

Tuesday, January 23. Some sunshine. A letter from the unmarried woman in Køge. Walked out to see Louise Lind—there wasn't a streetcar to be seen. Then ate at the Drewsen's, who all drank a toast to me because of my departure. Drove in to the Casino and saw *Mr. Sørensen Has Fun*, a crude, bad piece of work. But the audience applauded, and Mr. Erik Bøgh has acknowledged it has a number of good points.

Wednesday, January 24. At the dentist's. More clear weather and somewhat cold. Dinner at E. Collin's—a going-away party for me, so-called, but there were people there who couldn't be counted among those who should be invited to such an occasion, for example, the attorney Mr. Buntzen and his wife, the former Minister of Finance Mr. David and his wife. Of *my* friends, there were actually only Hartmann and his wife, Drewsen and the Linds. Went to the theater to see Ole Bull. My usual reaction. Today I met him on the street. We are staying at the same hotel—I was prompt in calling on him, but he hasn't yet been to see me. "I'll be paying you one more visit before my departure," I said. "You overwhelm me!" he replied.

Thursday, January 25. I didn't receive my winter coat from the tailor by 9 o'clock; he gave me another new one to wear until later in the day, when I was to get my own. When I went out onto the street, it occurred to me that it belonged to someone else—if he were now to come along and say: "That is my coat you have on!" I thought people were looking at me. By 12 o'clock, I'd gotten my own back. Called on Mrs. Koch, the Berners, Watt and the Billes. Dinner at Mrs. Ørsted's; she'd fallen ill on Sunday after I'd been there, but now she was feeling better again. Since then I've been eating only with Mathilde and Mrs. Scharling. Went from there to Reitzel's to say goodbye. He told me they were now going to do a new reissue of *The Improvisatore, The Two Baronesses* and *Picture Book without Pictures*. Subsequently, he agreed to my arranging a selection of my poems for the coming New Year. Thus, my trip itself would seem to be covered for eight months. It put me into a good mood. I had to see Jette Collin to tell her about it. Then went to the Royal Theater to see Hedberg's drama, *The Wedding at Ulfåsa*. Hedberg had come from Stockholm and was at the performance. I liked the work, and it won increasingly loud applause, but when the curtain fell there were nonetheless some that booed.

Friday, January 26. Went out to Christian's Harbor to see Titular Councillor Broberg in order to ship my books to O'Neill in Lisbon with one of his ships, but there were none. Then, went to the Eckardt's a little after 12 o'clock to read for the author Magdalene Thoresen, as I had promised. The author Hedberg was also there, and he got a copy of my most recent installment of tales. The actress Miss Müller and her two sisters were there and many others. They were extremely delighted to hear me read. Most of them said it was only now that you could really understand my tales! When I arrived home, I received a visit from Mrs. Ida Koch.—This morning, a letter

Girls holding a wreath (papercut made for Mathilde Ørsted in the 1850s)

from Reverend Thisted. Went up to see Carl Andersen and delivered the manuscript sent to me by the teacher Knudsen. At 4:30, went from there to Councillor Berner's, but the invitation was for 5 o'clock. I was of course the first to arrive, but was warmly received. Later, the proprietor of the building came, my friend Master of the Royal Hunt Ernst Bilsted, with his wife and two daughters. A large, lavish dinner party. I was seated next to the lady of the house. Jastrau was there with his young German wife; Schram and Hultmann. Berner proposed a toast to the engaged couple Miss Bilsted and a naval officer [Fritz Uldall]. After that, one to me. Then there followed several more, and I proposed one to Mrs. Berner that I got Schram to accompany musically.—Afterwards I was requested by Schlegel, from Odense, to read a tale. *He* had never heard me read, and it was only when you heard me read that my works could be seen in the proper light. I read five tales. Schram, Jastrau (who has never heard me read before), along with Hultmann, in ecstasy. In the meantime, I'd gotten so tired and faint from the effort that I left at 9 o'clock. Drove home and after that kind of day, suffered all night from extreme exhaustion.

Saturday, January 27. I was so tired that I would have liked to sleep late, but around 9 o'clock there was a knock on the door, and it was the messenger from the Ministry of Foreign Affairs with a letter to the foreign consuls and, moreover, my passport stamped with visas. I, who only today had planned to go to the police department to retrieve it and bring it to the Ministry of Foreign Affairs! I checked it over and noticed that they have omitted Holland, Belgium and Portugal, precisely those places I will be staying. On the other hand, they have given me England and Italy, where I have no plans of going at all. Indeed, even Italy had its visas. I was upset and gave the passport back to the messenger. Afterwards, was at the Private Bank to arrange for a letter of credit. On the way to Mrs. Koch's, I met one of the young Koefoeds who works at the Foreign Ministry. He took upon himself to arrange matters regarding my passport. Said goodbye to Mrs. Koch. Dinner at Hammerich's, where the Swedish author Hedberg was a guest. I met totally Scandinavian-minded Danes there, such as the vapid, swaggering Pastor Helveg, Professor Flor, Professor Clausen, the poet Richardt, Privy Councillor Hall. With Hedberg was the Swedish composer Hedberg.[1] Watt

---

1. Probably writing error. Perhaps Andersen was thinking of another Swedish composer, August Söderman.

and Hartmann were there, etc.—Hedberg, Hartmann and I went to the theater to see the second performance of *The Wedding at Ulfåsa*. It went well and was applauded.

Sunday, January 28. Took the streetcar to say goodbye to the Linds; afterwards, at Titular Councillor Vedel's and, lastly, at the Drewsens', although I didn't find Viggo at home. Drove into town and was at the Hartmanns' at precisely 12 o'clock to do a reading, but since the young girl who was supposed to listen and who had been invited at 11:30 didn't show up until 12:30, I went without reading over to Theodor Collin's, where I said goodbye to several members of the Collin family over afternoon coffee. At home there was a Spanish newspaper from Rio de Janeiro lying there for me containing "The Emperor's New Clothes." Plagued by several letters asking me to do people favors. Went to the Melchiors', where I was supposed to eat dinner and promised to eat there on Tuesday. Said goodbye to Mrs. Ørsted and Mathilde. Dinner at the Henriqueses' with the Gades and the Erslevs. We had oysters and several kinds of wine. Toasts to me. Then went for a short while to the theater to see *Elfin Hill*.

Monday, January 29. Overcast and rain. Ran to Edvard Collin's twice before I found him at home and got the money for my letters of credit. Then went to the Private Bank and got a letter of credit for 1,000 francs and bought four hundred-rix-dollar certificates. Then was at photographer Hansen's. While I was sitting, Ole Bull came and right away began playing. It made my face change expression so that I had to do it over again after Ole Bull and company were removed.—Then went to see Countess Frijs and said goodbye to her and all the children and governesses. She urged me to say goodbye to the king. Then went to exchange some gold and Prussian bills, sewed the money into my clothes and dashed around town taking care of most of what needed to be done for the trip. Dinner with Mrs. Lord-in-Waiting Neergaard and afterwards to the Casino to see the Italians. I got a young gentleman who always says hello to me to switch seats so instead of sitting in the middle I was near the outside. The seat I got was next to the naval officer Count Scheel and the stable master Scheele, whom I like quite well.

Tuesday, January 30. Yesterday, before we sat down to dinner at Mrs. Lord-in-Waiting Neergaard's, there were brilliant flashes of lightning with a blue-green cast, and thunder crashed. It's supposed to have struck somewhere in Christian Harbor. Sleet and hail were falling. After midnight it turned into a fierce windstorm with snow and thunder.—I went at 10:30 in the morning to register my farewell visit with the king. Bardenfleth was on duty. He was, however, going to announce me, but Bishop Martensen was inside. The king wanted to see me, but over an hour and a half passed before Martensen left. In the meantime, I went up to see the queen, who conversed at length with me and said she would have been sorry had she not seen me before my departure. She talked about her children and King George and the princess of Wales and shook my hand twice. Then came Princess Dagmar too and shook my hand. I went over to see the queen dowager; she and her ladies had gone to Lyngby where Pastor Rørdam's wife was to be buried. Then went in to register my visit with the crown prince. When I returned to the king's ante-chamber, I found Lord Chamberlain Oxholm, Kauffmann and Trap; subsequently, Count Frijs, which gave me an opportunity to say goodbye to him. The king was very warm, pressed my hand and wished me a good trip. Dinner at Mr. Moritz Melchior's with the two brothers and the sisters. We had the renowned oyster soup. Then went to the theater to see Gluck's *Iphigenia in Aulis*. At home I found a letter to the effect that the crown prince wished to see me tomorrow at 12:30. So there's no hope of departing at 12 o'clock.

Wednesday, January 31. The beginning of my trip. At 12 o'clock I was with the crown prince. We sat for a long time and talked about many things. He has read *The Fairy Tale of My Life*. Then I took my things to the Collins'. Mr. Moritz Melchior called on me. His wife wanted me to have fur boots for my trip. He returned with a large selection—I got an excellent pair that came to up over my knees. Then he told me warmly and in confidence that should I need money he was always at my service. I replied that I hoped I wouldn't and told him about my modest assets. And he added then that should it ever happen that I didn't wish to touch them, if I just would turn to him, he would be so very pleased to be of service to me. I told Edvard about how nice he was. Went to the telegraph office and sent a telegram to Korsør to reserve a heated room. Ate at Edvard Collin's. At a little past 6 o'clock, I drove to the train station. There I met Miss Deckner, who was also leaving on a trip. Lose came to say goodbye to me. I gave him my hyacinths to give to Jette Collin. Was in a compartment with a Swede from Gothenburg who was on his way to London and Paris. The weather was good. I regretted having reserved rooms in Korsør. There at the station stood Petersen, the owner of the hotel, and welcomed me. He said the wind was picking up, and so I went up to my room to spend the night. But the weather stayed calm all night long. It would have taken less time had I taken the steamer.

Andersen's leisurely trip to Portugal was to last seven months. On his way there, he stayed for five weeks as the guest of the Brandts in Amsterdam, where he was wined and dined and met the most prominent writers in Holland, among them J. J. L. ten Kate, who published a translation of Andersen's tales in 1868. From Amsterdam he traveled to Paris, arriving March 29. There, he enjoyed himself as the guest of Crown Prince Frederik of Denmark at the races in Vincennes and visited the Italian composer Gioacchino Rossini and the Danish artist Lorenz Frølich, who was already at work on illustrations for Andersen's later tales and stories. From Paris, he traveled by way of Bordeaux and Madrid to Portugal.

Crossing the border from Spain to Portugal was for Andersen "like going from the Middle Ages into modern times" (May 5). He spent his first month in Portugal as the guest of the businessman Jorge (George) O'Neill, a friend of the Wulff family, at his country home, Quinta do Pinheiro, outside Lisbon. While there, he was introduced to the writer Antonio F. de Castilho and granted an audience by King Fernando. On June 8, Andersen traveled to Setubal to spend a month with Jorge's brother Carlos, after which he returned to spend another two weeks with Jorge. By now, Andersen had grown irritated with his hosts, especially Jorge, who continually put off an excursion to the medieval university town of Coimbra. They finally set off on July 20.

Friday, July 20. At 8 o'clock I drove to Lisbon with George; stayed over an hour at the office and then went with him and José to the railroad station, where we met a salesman, an unpretentious man who was to accompany us, I suppose, because he and George had some business to do in Evora. First we followed the Tajo, which is as wide as a lake. Later it turned into a river with broad sandbanks. On the other side of the Tajo, saw Salvaterra and Benevente, where they hold bullfights and where the Marquis of Mariava was killed by a bull at the time of the earthquake during the reign of José I. Between Santarem and Matta there was a lot of woodland with cork oaks—a number of the trees, even young ones, had had their bark stripped off. Near Pombal, the ruins of a Moorish castle. The landscape was at times flat like in Denmark; at other times, reminiscent of Sweden. Rice fields as green as a Danish field of young wheat. Corn and grapes. A little after 5 o'clock we reached Aveiro, which is located in an utterly flat district by the river Vouga. We took rooms at a hotel of the same name. Aveiro is called "the Portuguese Holland." It does, in fact, look more like that country than it does Portugal! People have also called it "Venice," but the only common feature is a kind of big, gondola-shaped boat that plies the canal dividing the town into two parts. Because of the sand, this fruitful region had become a morass and extremely unhealthful; then, in 1801, the count of Linharas began building a canal and completed it in 1808, returning the water to its course, and the noxious swamps disappeared. With its sailboats, the canal up to Aveiro is very reminiscent of Holland. The landscape itself took me back to western Jutland, and there were, moreover, heavy, gray skies. A wet fog sank down over the district with an aguish chill. We arrived right at ebbtide; the river looked filthy. We drove along a long, low aqueduct to get to the hotel. A young, barefoot girl and an old granny carried all our baggage in big baskets on their heads. The inn, so-so. We trudged around in that cramped town where everybody looked at us from their open doors and windows as if we were great novelties. The ladies wore big, broad men's hats and heavy, thick coachmen's cloaks with a cape—and with all that, they had bare legs. It looked distinctive, but unattractive. On the other hand, there were a lot of beautiful women to be seen in this town, the likes of which I have on the whole yet to see in Portugal. They are supposed to be of Greek descent.

Saturday, July 21. Wandered all morning in this boring town instead of taking the morning train to Coimbra. We didn't leave until around 12 o'clock and were in Coimbra at 2 o'clock. The cab drivers swarmed over our baggage—some of it in one carriage, some in another. George got furious and took a swing at one of them, and then they all swarmed over him. With his foot he kicked one of them in the rear end. They were like wild men, and if they had had knives on them, it would have ended badly. In the meantime, I was afraid they might come and get their revenge later. It was a bad beginning. José was angry about what had happened, and the brothers were brusque with each other. We arrived at the Hotel Mondego, close to a river of the same name. There wasn't much water in it. Large sandbanks with a few wooden stalls out on them for bathing. The women waded across, but, indeed, gathered their skirts all the way up around their thighs. A lot of students were strolling around here in their long, black gowns, almost all of them bareheaded, even in the streets. I only saw one with his big, floppy black cap on. A big bridge with many arches traverses the river. On the other side is the magnificently sprawling monastery of Santa Clara. In a garden nearby are the ruins of the house where Ines de Castro and her children were slain. Here is the spring that Camões celebrates in the *Lusiads*. The town is most picturesquely situated on a mountainside and is like the loveliest flower in this bouquet of natural beauty. One house rises up over the next, and up above everything else, the university. Narrow, winding streets, steep alleys like in Amalfi. Lichnowsky says about the students that they are like the disciples of Faust and Paracelsus. They put on comedies in the winter, although there also exist traveling troupes. On the corner I saw a sketchy rendition of the tragedy *Ines de Castro*. They perform once a month for the professors, young ladies and matrons and ride around the countryside playing music on their guitars. This is a true university town. During the reign of Don Miguel there were some that rioted, and then a few of them were hanged. Toward evening, a young doctor of divinity came—I think it was da Silva Pereira—and he took us to see the abandoned monastery of Santa Cruz and its extremely lovely cloister with the graceful, picturesque arches. In the beautiful church, two graves—Sancho I's and Affonso I Henriques's. There was a painting of Vasco da Gama, but it didn't look like the ones I saw in Setubal. When we got home, I received a visit from the professor of German literature, Herman Christian Dührssen, from Schleswig-Holstein, who had heard of my arrival and came to offer me his services. Right after dinner, I walked through town with José to the botanical garden, which had magnificent palm trees and flowering magnolias. He wanted to stay there for a couple of hours and marveled at the fact that I didn't. I wanted to see a bit more and went then with a guide for a walk around the periphery of town. Saw some huge cypresses, everywhere big trees in the gardens, gardens and forest everywhere. Everything romantic and beautiful. Encountered several young students. Gave some thought to a novel—"The Two Students of Coimbra"—in which one lived for science, the other for cavorting and riding around singing and chatting with the ladies, for enjoying life. After I had gone to bed, George came and was supposed to sleep in the same room. I was bothered by my teeth, which I hadn't been able to take out; it was hot and the bed was very hard. Late in the night, like yesterday, I finally fell asleep thinking about the cabbies' revenge tomorrow.

Sunday, July 22. Heavy skies! It turned to rain. Neither one of the O'Neill brothers wanted to get their feet wet by taking a walk. But I, too, only had my thin boots. There was a commencement going on at the university. I walked up there with a guide. It started raining harder. I looked down across the river to Ines de Castro's house. At the university, I met Professor Dührssen, who took me to see the librarian, and he admitted me to the library, which is in rococo style with magnificent arches, frescoes on the ceiling, many books. I was thus shown a rare edition of *The Lusiads* with good etchings, two Bible manuscripts in which several pages looked as if they were covered with curlicues and flourishes, but when examined with a magnifying glass, each line turned out to be something written in Hebrew executed with unbelievable industry and precision—it was an extremely rare work of art. I had to write my name in the visitors' book. Then went over to the university hall, where the various faculties sat in their distinctive robes and different colors—white and blue, red, yellow. The young man who was receiving his doctor's hat was on his knees on a raised platform near the royal throne. All the benches were filled with students; along the sidewalls of the hall were boxes with large numbers of ladies; an orchestra was playing down on the floor. Afterwards, I saw the university chapel, the throne room, etc., and was then invited to stay. But we were leaving the following morning, so Dührssen saw me home in the pouring rain. At one o'clock we left this interesting town without any fracasses and saw on the way home several swineherds and saw shepherds under the olive trees watching over black lambs. In Entroncamento, we had to gulp down our food in six minutes. During the entire trip, José was mischievous, disagreeable, so that I'm worried about staying with him in Cintra.—We drove to the office and didn't reach Pinheiro until around 9 o'clock. There I found my old room and fresh flowers from Mrs. O'Neill. Talked a bit about the trip and José. At Coimbra, peasants with straw cloaks.

Monday, July 23. Not well. All my joints ache. Went back to bed for an hour and thus got the entries for the past few days written. Mrs. O'Neill's sick sister is now here in the house. The day is ending gray and wet; everything is as if covered by wet fog. George has been lying sick in bed all day.

Tuesday, July 24. "A dear guest becomes a burden if he overstays his leave!" I always awoke with this thought in my head when I was a guest. Loose stools this morning; don't feel quite well. Hot, heavy air, but the sky full of clouds. Slept for a part of the day. Thought about home and the trip home. George told me at the dinner table that José wasn't entirely well and we wouldn't be leaving for Cintra until the day after tomorrow. This is a bit too much!

Andersen thoroughly enjoyed his two-week stay in Cintra as the guest of George and Carlos's brother José. Here he had a pleasant reunion with the British diplomat Edward Robert Bulwer-Lytton, whom he had met in Copenhagen in the spring of 1864, and took great pleasure in the landscape around him. In a letter to Edvard Collin he wrote on August 7: "It's as if all the natural beauty of the different countries of the world was gathered here on this spot—here are the mountain crags of the Alps; here are the medieval castles of the Rhine and the Moorish fortresses of Spain."

On August 14, Andersen left Lisbon by steamer to Bordeaux and then traveled home by railroad via Paris, Cologne and Hamburg. Mr. and Mrs. Melchior met him at the station in Copenhagen and brought him out to Tranquillity, where he spent the remaining three weeks of September. After another four weeks visiting Holsteinborg and Basnæs, he returned to Copenhagen in late October to his new lodgings at Miss Hallager's by the King's New Square, right across from the Royal Theater. There he worked on his fourth installment of New Tales and Stories, *which was published two weeks before Christmas.*

Andersen spent the early months of 1867 in Copenhagen caught up in his usual round of visits and letter writing, dinners and evenings at the theater. In February, he began to make plans to travel to Paris to see the World Exhibition. He arrived in Paris on April 15 and was fascinated by the exhibition, viewing it several times alone or in the company of his many acquaintances there—the young Robert Watt, Lorenz Frølich, Jules Jürgensen, and Michael Drewsen, to name a few. As in 1863, the Scandinavian colony held a dinner party in honor of the great writer.

Wednesday, May 1 [1867]. The sun is shining. I went out, but turned back and put my heavy coat on. Then went to the legation and told the servant that I would be staying here for a week and so would be coming for dinner on Friday. Went over and took a seat on the omnibus to the exhibition. When we were on our way, I discovered I'd left my watch at home. I paid my fare and got out; rushed home and, all in a sweat, found my watch, which I was afraid had been stolen. I was so tired that I lay down on the bed for a nap. Tired of Paris. It's cold. I went to dinner late and was at the Scandinavian Society in locale nr. 50 of the Palais-Royal by a little after 8 o'clock. It had been decorated with the flags of the Nordic countries and portraits of King Christian IX and King Karl. Mr. Soldin took me over to see his wife; there were some Danish ladies there, among them Miss Sønderup, who writes for the *Berlingske News.* Soldin gave a speech in my honor as Denmark's greatest writer, as he called me!

It was a little difficult to hear him; he nevertheless meant well, even though he made a mess of it. Afterwards, there was a song by a Mr. Hartvig and I thanked everyone. We drank Swedish punch. Lord-in-Waiting Wolfhagen proposed a toast to the kings of the North. Toasts to Denmark, to Sweden and to Norway followed, along with appropriate songs. I was asked to read, and I did "The Butterfly" and "It's Perfectly True!" I received thunderous applause and a toast with nine hurrahs! Watt came up with a toast to women—it was a little tame. Then I proposed one to poetry in the North; I've forgotten, though, the Swedish Secretary of Legation Staaf's toast to the poets of the North, which was tacked onto the one to me. It was a lovely poem he recited, composed by himself for the last celebration held for me here at the Palais-Royal. Around 11 o'clock I sneaked away.

Thursday, May 2. Beautiful weather. Went to see Jules Jürgensen and presented him with my most recent tales. There discovered I had taken the wrong hat yesterday evening. Didn't care to wear someone else's dirty hat and bought a new one for eighteen francs. Drove out to the exposition and there met Køppen, who is here with the king of Greece and will now be traveling to America. Spoke with the naval officer Funch, also here with the king, who is returning tomorrow from London and will be staying at the Hôtel de Reine on Vendôme Square, where I can expect to be received at 1 o'clock tomorrow. Entered the Chinese House—it cost a half franc, and there is nothing to see. I didn't even see any Chinese but ran into Dr. Leo from Berlin, who introduced me to his wife. Annoyed to read in *Figaro* that I've arrived in Paris after making a stopover in Hanover— I, who don't want to make any stopovers in Germany at all. Had a good look around the grounds out there, which are now beginning more and more to look like something. Heard the gospel in Danish at the Mission House, where it's handed out in all languages. Saw a diver demonstrating his equipment in a building erected for that purpose. Then, when I got back home, I met the son of the painter Tidemand, from Düsseldorf. After having eaten, I went to the Thé-âtre du Palais-Royal and saw *The Orphan from China*, none of which I understood at all. After that, the new singspiel *Life in Paris* with Offenbach's ever raucous cancan. Left when the third act was over. At home, a letter from Mr. and Mrs. Henriques.

Friday, May 3. Wrote to a Mrs. Münster—from whom I've had a letter and who wishes to visit me with her daughter between 1 and 2 o'clock—to tell her that I won't be home before around 3 o'clock.

Didn't feel well. Went out to see Watt, who was with his compatriots yesterday evening at the Mabille, all of them rather drunk. Some of them spent the night with some wenches—a wild life!— Around 1 o'clock went to the Hôtel de Reine to pay my respects to the king of Greece, who was, according to Funch, available at that time. They had, in the meantime, just left the hotel. When I'd eaten lunch and gotten back home, I received a visit from Mrs. Münster with her daughter. She is taking singing lessons from Wartel (43 Rue de la Chaussée d'Antin). The family itself lives in Hegnsholt near Fredensborg. They invited me to visit them. Dinner at Count Leon Moltke-Hvitfeldt's. His wife speaks quite good Danish; she learned it from P. L. Møller. Present there were Wolfhagen, Bille (who made excuses for not having been at the party for me by saying he hadn't received the invitation for Wednesday evening's party until Thursday morning), Grøn and wife, along with Mr. . . . and Staaf. Left there at 9:30. I have in me the feeling that I'm not a young man any more. Went home and pondered this in my room.

Saturday, May 4. Started off the day by climbing up to the fifth floor to see Henni Koch on Rue des Hautes Alpes. Then took the omnibus out to the exhibition, where I arrived at 11 o'clock to eat lunch with Grøn. He is a really fatuous fellow; wants to be a gentleman, his wife to be a lady. Was invited to lunch but it got to be so late that I gave up on it. I met Miss Bartholin there; she'd been invited by Mrs. Grøn. Since they were expecting the king of Greece, I spent the whole day wandering around out there. The passageway from the Greek part of the exhibit was decorated with Danish and Greek flags, along with my verse:

> Here, the Danish Flag and the crest of Greece
> Salute you and wish you nothing but peace.

I was constantly in and out, grew inutterably tired. Ran into Watt, who no longer displayed the same camaraderie as when we first met. Should I be happy about it and thank him—or the Lord? I still have a high regard for him, but it's with too much youthful abandon that he dives down into the muck. There were seven Danish ladies today waiting for Georg. I left at 5:30, about to collapse from exhaustion and couldn't find a carriage. They were asking three francs for the trip, so I walked the endlessly long way home and ate at the Palais-Royal. But I wasn't up to going anywhere in the evening as I would have liked to.

1867

Sunday, May 5. At 10 o'clock I took a seat in an omnibus at the Stock Exchange. It drove to the more remote railroad station south of the Seine, and by 11 o'clock I was in Versailles. It was lovely summer weather; the woods green; the lilacs, golden rain and hawthorne in bloom. At once I sought out Mr. Demouceaux at 8 Place Hoches. He welcomed me with pleasure, offered me gingerbread and wine, which I declined; showed me his translation of "The Ice Maiden," "The Psyche," "The Snail and the Rose Bush," "The Butterfly," "The Silver Shilling," " 'The Will-O-The-Wisps Are in Town,' Said the Bog Witch," and "The Gold Treasure." Went with me up to the palace. There were tremendous numbers of people there. Looked at some pictures and, afterwards, the theater. Went out on the terrace—a wide view over the orangeries, but nonetheless not structured like a Danish landscape. The fountains weren't flowing yet. Very hot. Was accompanied to the railroad station by my new friend, whose brother-in-law is a grain measurer living in Odense—his name is Henriksen. Arrived at 2:30 in Paris at the train station on Rue Saint-Lazare and went for lunch at 3 o'clock. At the Café de la Recange, ran into Watt, who told about new adventures with the ladies. I wonder whether they're true. He's youthfully high-spirited, but not so polished that the ladies, as he describes them, would throw themselves at him like that. After eating dinner, I paced back and forth in a sexual frenzy. Then went suddenly up into a meat market—one of them was covered with powder; a second, common; a third, quite the lady. I talked with her, paid twelve francs and left without having sinned in deed, though I dare say I did in my thoughts. She asked me to come back, said I was indeed very innocent for a man. I felt so happy and light when I left that house. Many might call me a twerp—have I been one here? In the evening, wandered around on the boulevard and saw painted ladies sitting in the cafés and playing cards, drinking beer and chartreuse.

On May 9, Andersen headed for Switzerland, where he spent two weeks visiting Jules Jürgensen in Le Locle. On May 26, the day before he left the Jürgensen family, he was awarded in absentia the title of titular councillor on the occasion of the silver wedding anniversary of King Christian IX and Queen Louise of Denmark. After his return home on June 7, he spent most of his summer at Tranquillity with the Melchiors and at Basnæs, Holsteinborg, and Glorup working on a fair copy of his Portuguese travelogue.

On September 1, Andersen returned to Paris for three weeks with the financial help of Moritz Melchior in order to develop an idea for a tale "The

331

At Le Locle in the Jura Mountains

Wood Nymph" that had occurred to him during his April visit. Back in Copenhagen, he worked on this tale and looked forward to the publication of a collected edition of his poetry, Familiar and Forgotten Poems (1823–1867), *and a collection of tales,* Fifteen Tales and Stories, *illustrated by Lorenz Frølich, both of which were scheduled for publication in mid-December. On December 3, Andersen traveled to his hometown, Odense, to attend the celebration of his honorary citizenship.*

Tuesday, December 3. Freezing weather and wind. Drove to the railroad station a little after 11 o'clock and was under way by twelve. Alone with me in the car was the son of an old schoolmate of mine—Schou from Slagelse. It was cold. In Korsør I spoke with the youngest Baron Wedell-Wedellsborg, who was leaving right away with the steamer over to Funen. The wind had died down. I ate dinner, took a heated room and am now sitting there. The innkeeper told me that according to *The Funen Bulletin* there were no more seats available for the banquet in my honor. I read about it in *The Funen Bulletin* and that the young people would be there in the evening.

Wednesday, December 4. I went to bed early last night, but my teeth were aching and the pain increased so that I didn't really get any sleep at all until between 6 and 8 o'clock. The weather was lovely—clear skies, sunshine and no wind. I felt as if my back and chest had taken a beating—the wind yesterday, the fierce drafts on the train have chilled me to the bone. I stayed down in the cabin until we were in Nyborg Fjord. Didn't speak with anyone; no one in with me except for one person traveling to the south of France for six weeks. Went first class from Nyborg to Odense, where I arrived at 12:30. Bishop Engelstoft and the shoemaker Gredsted were there to welcome me—it wasn't known in town that I would be coming with this train today. I drove over to the bishop's residence, where I was given a large sitting room facing out to the front yard and a small bedroom out to the garden. Ate lunch. Bothered by the stumps of my teeth, which are hurting, and by my false upper teeth, which are loose. Rested for about an hour. Here for dinner were His Excellency, County Magistrate Unsgaard, Dean Damgaard, Mayor Mourier, the teachers Kragh and Nielsen, Titular Councillor Schlegel and others. The bishop proposed a toast to me. I was having difficulty speaking because of my loose upper teeth. I still read a couple of tales anyway. Colonel Vaupell was an especially animated listener.

Thursday, December 5. Last night I slept restlessly. All at once, felt strong rheumatic pains in my chest; I became a little anxious. At 9 o'clock I got up. Right away a painter from Ålborg showed up with a portrait of Frederik VII that he wanted to have put on display here in the bishop's residence and me to arrange a collection—he needed 150 rix-dollars. I explained to him what an embarrassing position it put me in as guest to take up a collection, and it ended with my subscribing to a lithograph of the picture which would cost two rix-dollars. I paid half of it on the spot as all the others had done who had paid. Then an old cabinetmaker came—Haugsted (?)—who said he had gone to school with me at Carsten's. This was now fifty and some odd years ago. He nonetheless thought I should be able to remember him. I presented him with a picture of myself. When I was leaving the barber's this morning, I ran into Mayor Mourier, who accompanied me home. Later, I went with the bishop to Mourier's, where I found only his wife and her sister in. (Weilbach is their brother.) Then went to Police Chief Koch's, where Councilman Petersen and Mourier were; afterwards, to see His Excellency [County Magistrate] Unsgaard. At home there lay letters from a citizen of

Odense, who wanted a photograph of me, and from a photographer, who wanted to take one of me. We had a quiet dinner here at the bishop's residence. Some young girls, the Misses Hein, were here in the evening; I read a couple of tales for them. A letter to Mrs. Melchior.

Friday, December 6. Slept restlessly, but the swelling in my gums has gone down somewhat. Sent a letter to Jette Collin. I was up at 8:30—then the barber came and afterwards the hairdresser. I was rather self-conscious. The schools weren't in session today on account of the celebration for me. At around 11 o'clock, Mayor Mourier and Police Chief Koch came for me in a carriage. I had the seat of honor to myself. Flags were waving; townspeople were standing in uniform in front of City Hall; the band was playing my song "In Denmark I Was Born." There was a bust of me in the hall with greenery all around it; several hundred people were gathered there, both men and women. The city council welcomed me, and Mourier gave a speech and handed over to me the certificate of honorary citizenship. I expressed my gratitude, but nearly collapsed. I saw tears in the eyes of many; both beforehand and afterwards the entire assemblage cheered me with nine hurrahs. I was home by 12:30 and received visits from several members of the city council, among them a son of Peter Wich. A congratulatory note came for me from the Melchiors. After that, an issue of *The Daily* that described the celebration in flattering terms. I received two copies of my poems from Reitzel and one of my tales.—I am tired but in much better spirits than this morning. At 4 o'clock, Police Chief Koch took me to City Hall, where there were tables set up all over the main hall. My bust with a laurel wreath and the Danish flag and flowers. At the table, I was seated next to Mrs. Mourier with Mrs. Koch to my left, right across from Mourier, the bishop's wife and the elder Lord Holsten-Charisius of Langesø. Petersen proposed a toast to me, and I responded. The young catechist Møller spoke with a most marvelous youthful abandon; Henrichsen and Titular Councillor Schlegel proposed humorous toasts. (I've collected everything from the newspapers now.) Lots of telegrams came—from the Student Association, from the Workmen's Association in Slagelse, from Stege, Hjørring, Ålborg and friends in Copenhagen; and after dinner a telegram arrived from the king with congratulations from him and his family. It was received by the entire assemblage with great jubilation. Then came the children, and they danced around me. I read "What Dad Does" and after that "The Butterfly." While I was reading, there was a loud disturbance at the other end of the hall. A torchlight parade had arrived—a deputation from the Association of Labor and Industry was there to pay its respects, and now I had to stand by an open window to hear them singing. The banners of the craftsmen's associations looked handsome among the bright torches. I was given a cheer of nine hurrahs. I said a few words, and then the children began to dance again. There are flags all over town today. At 10 o'clock, tired; arrived home happy, however, but couldn't sleep. I didn't hear from the Collins or the Drewsens, the ones who are supposed to be my closest friends. It didn't occur to Bloch either, but, on the other hand, it did to Robert Watt.

Saturday, December 7. Sent letters to the king, to the Student Association and to the Craftmen's Association in Slagelse. (There was no remembrance from the one in Copenhagen.) There was a storm last night; the snow is drifting. A large number of beggars, the last one, a drunk. Called on the shoemaker Gredsted, who seems to be prosperous, the newspaper publishers Dreyer and Lauritsen, along with Miss Susanne Bunkeflod. Dinner at Titular Councillor Mourier's; I was seated next to his wife at the table. There was a toast to me; it was a lovely dinner. At 7:30 the president of the Music Association, the dentist Jensen and the businessman Christian Andersen arrived and took me to the elegantly illuminated main hall of City Hall, where there was a seat of honor for me. I was seated in the midst of all the ladies, and the only men in the vicinity were Unsgaard, Koch, Mourier and the bishop. The concert began with a song in my honor; later they did "In Denmark I Was Born" in four part harmony. Two young Poles, Julius and Henry Schloming, got up and played the violin. It was past 10 o'clock before the concert was over and past 12 o'clock before I was in bed.

Sunday, December 8. There's a hard frost outside and snow on the ground. Read in *The Fatherland* a telegram about my Odense celebration; yesterday evening there was a report of it in the two Funen papers. Sent a letter to Robert Watt and a Funen paper to the Henriques. Called on the widow Mrs. Rosenberg, W. Petersen, Scholten, the dentist Jensen, the tailor Wich (nice children—the son was in Paris with me at the celebration held for me there last spring). Went to see Schnakenburg, the merchant. Dinner at 4 o'clock with the bishop at Dean Damgaard's, whom I heard this morning at the church of St. Knud. (It was very cold there. I was sitting in the bishop's pew.) Before church, a visit from a fellow who had graduated with me—Sørensen, a Schleswig-Holsteiner in exile. He really wanted me to remember him; I couldn't, and I'll discard the vague recollection that I do have, because then he owes me for a copy of *Fantasies and Sketches*. After that, a visit from the widow Henrichsen—little Ane, who boarded with my parents and with whom I wouldn't share a cot. She was now at a charity home for old folks; looked quite well dressed and wept at the thought of how far I had gone in life. During the torchlight parade, she had been standing out on the street talking about me with some other old people, and they had shed tears because they could see that I was being treated like a king—the king and queen hadn't been made more of. Dinner at Dean Damgaard's with Mayor Mourier and wife. At 8 o'clock there was a big party here at the bishop's residence—a hundred people. I read five or six tales for them. Everyone stayed until 2 o'clock at night.

Monday, December 9. Got up late. Received a visit from an old fisherman. Sent a letter to Miss Hallager. Went to see Fire Chief Petersen, who had been in charge of the townpeople's torch parade. Then went to see the principal Mr. Møller; then, with the bishop, to the charity school, which I had myself attended as a boy. I heard the students being quizzed in geography. Then went to see various members of the city council—Urban Hansen, Jensen, Brummer and Bierfreund. Called on the two old Misses Wagners; after that at the miller Mr. Krag's.—A quiet dinner at the bishop's. A visit from Sick. In the evening read "Godfather's Picture Book." Stormy weather this evening.

Tuesday, December 10. A thaw. Visit from Gredsted. Drove with the bishop to the party at the Lahn Foundation. A particularly nice speech was given by the principal Mr. Møller; in it I was mentioned among Denmark's outstanding citizens. Afterwards, went out to pay farewell visits to Prøvensen, Unsgaard, Koch, Boesen, Dean Damgaard, Pharmacist Lotze, Reverend Steenbuch, Captain Helweg of the merchant marine, Titular Councillor Schlegel and Mayor Mourier (whose wife got a copy of my *Familiar and Forgotten Poems,* as Mrs. Koch did also). Afterwards, I went to see Mrs. Bertelsen, who is now old and deaf. I heard that Petersen, the merchant and Gerson's father-in-law, who is in the city council, was the only one of the members who did not support or participate in the festivities. His daughter was angry because no fuss had been made over her fiancé, Gerson, whom she thought to be such a great poet, and when Gerson was over here on a recent visit, he expressed his opposition here at the bishop's residence to the proposed grand doings, but was set straight by the bishop and then quickly held his tongue. Quiet dinner at home. This evening Dean Damgaard and wife were here, along with Principal Møller and his mother. Letter from Mrs. Melchior. Sent letters to Mrs. Melchior and Mrs. Collin.

Wednesday, December 11. Beautiful, sunny weather. Went to see Petersen, the master smith; Nielsen, the teacher; Kragh, the senior teacher; and Mr. Faber. Visited my childhood home, which is owned by Schmidt, the tailor. The yard was quite the same, only the shed in the rear had been placed in the middle of it. A couple of gooseberry bushes were probably still there from my childhood. The distiller Hagenau brought me a poem. I wrote one myself on the picture of me for Mrs. Engelstoft:

> So warm and sunny was your good home,
> That my thanks grow forth in a humble poem;
> But its root springs up from deep in my heart;
> It will grow for years in fertile loam!
> I leave my picture, as I depart.

Went with the bishop to see Professor Henrichsen; saw the Latin school and the gymnasium, where half of the senior class was. Paid a visit to the publisher Dreyer and the town's most elegant merchant, L. B. Jürgensen, whose store looks like they do in Paris with one, big glass window. At home the Kochs had stopped by and brought me a picture of themselves. Forgot to call on one member of the city council . . .[2] Wrote a note to him. Also forgot the director of the town chorus. At a little after 4 o'clock I left with the bishop and his wife. Beforehand, the mayor had brought me a lovely bouquet of roses from his wife. There were people at their windows when we left. A throng headed for the train station. It got very crowded. I walked around greeting many of my friends. When the train came and I entered the coach, with Titular Councillor Koch carrying my baggage, Mayor Mourier gave a farewell speech. I said goodbye and then I chugged off to the resounding shouts of hurrah. There was a Frenchman in the car with me. On the train in Nyborg I ran into Holger Stampe, who had gotten on at Middlefart and slept until he was awakened in Odense by the shouts of hurrah and thought then it was probably for me. Made the crossing on the new screw-propelled ship, which is to be used for breaking the ice. The

---

2. Either the attorney Th. Borch or the cloth manufacturer S. Hempel.

passengers were friendly and attentive, as if the hurrahs from Odense still filled the air. The sea was calm, and at 10:30 I reached Copenhagen, where Edvard Collin and Jonas welcomed me back with wide open arms and escorted me home. The sitting room was warm; letters and books lay there for me. It was around 1 o'clock before I got to bed. Thanks be to God and hallowed be His name!

Thursday, December 12. The whole thing is like a dream. When I went out to see Edvard, I ran into Professor H. P. Holst and Molbech. I stopped them and shook hands with them. "It's probably been an ordeal!" they said and talked about my toothache. Not a word followed to show they cared about the honor shown me. On the way home I met Brun, the author of *The Three Musketeers*. He spoke warmly and was happy for me; praised Odense and emphasized the pleasure and honor I had received which is so rare for anyone to get, even among thousands of people. Visited the Melchiors, who were endlessly happy; went to see the Henriqueses, Bloch, Hartmann and Mrs. Ørsted. A big dinner party at the Melchiors', which was also attended by the two Polish violinists I'd heard in Odense. (There they'd been staying at the same hotel as Israel Melchior.) Then went to the theater to see *The School for Wives*. Thiele, Watt, Gade and Scharff and Rosenkilde, too, were really happy for me. Gerson was sitting in front of me; didn't say a word to me and after the play moved to a seat further away. How silly and childish!

Friday, December 13. Hard frost. Adolph Recke was buried at 10 o'clock. I would have gone to the funeral, but the king was in town for a meeting of the ministers of state, and I had to go and see him. Brought my illustrated tales for the crown prince, Prince Valdemar and the king; for the queen, *Familiar and Forgotten Poems*. The king congratulated me; said that he and his family had been thinking and speaking about me on the day of the celebration. His telegram was private and to me alone and not for the public. I told him about the jubilation it had occasioned, and he looked pleased. I showed him the beautifully bound volumes and he said: "My wife will be looking forward to reading your book, but right now she's ill!" He took my hand and expressed the wish that I live a long life for the sake of my friends and the "honor of our fatherland." All the ministers of state, who were just coming from their meeting with him, congratulated me; Bishop Kierkegaard, most heartily. Dinner at Koch's, where they were really pleased on my account. Went to the Casino to see Brun's *The Three Musketeers;* afterwards to Thiele, whose birthday it is today. Now I am sitting in my warm room, with frostwork on the windows, enjoying my good fortune and reflecting on it, without proper words to express my gratitude to my Lord God!—Today visited my young friend Otto Scavenius of Basnæs; he was here yesterday.

Andersen spent the first three months of 1868 quietly in Copenhagen. During this period, the major cultural event was the mid-March series of three concerts given by the German singer Julius Stockhausen and the composer and pianist Johannes Brahms. Andersen applauded Stockhausen's singing but found Brahms' playing "dry and monotonous." During the following weeks, the city buzzed with confused rumors of Brahms' strong pro-German sentiments.

Wednesday, April 1 [1868]. Sunny but cold. At 12 o'clock I read some tales and stories at the home of Raasløff, the minister of war. Baroness Liliencron was talking about the fanaticism of Danes against everything German, and it was her opinion that the pianist Brahms had said they would be happy in Berlin to have something as superb as the Thorvaldsen Museum. She was perturbed—more German than she is Danish, to be sure. Heard Stockhausen; the applause more subdued—the result of the attack on Brahms in the *Daily Telegraph*. I noticed my wallet was missing but found it at home on my desk.

Thursday, April 2. God has granted me another birthday! It is beautiful, sunny weather. From 9:00 to 5:00 I've received visits, flowers and gifts. Along with some flowers, Mrs. Melchior sent me a comfortable chair for in front of my desk. Louise Melchior, an embroidered strap for the plaid blanket I take with me on trips. Sophie Melchior, a lovely case for newspapers. Flowers from Mrs. Puggaard. The little daughter of my neighbor Bruun was here. Sophie and Juliette Price, a bouquet with a large calla lilly. Anna Bille. A rosebush from Mrs. Lund. Three potted plants with flowers from Mrs. Scavenius. An incomparably lovely azalea from Scharff and Eckardt—it was white and looked as if it were covered with snow. Mrs. Raasløff, a red azalea. Several pots full of violets and stocks from Mrs. Melchior. Teacups with my name and the date on them from an anonymous person. A vase with a stork painted on it—in the vase itself, sprigs of laurel. Letters from Miss Bjerring, from Bournonville. A telegram from Countess Holstein of Holsteinborg. A telegram from Moses Melchior in England. A book with a translation of "The Porter's Son" also came from England. Visits from Mrs. Koch, Mrs. Sødring, Mrs. Eckardt, Mrs. Melchior and Sophie and Louise Melchior, Mrs. Collin, Mrs. Lind, Agnethe Lind and Rigmor Stampe, Mrs. Raasløff and daughter.—I went for the first time briefly to the exhibition. There Captain Nielsen from Svendborg related that a young, dissipated farmboy with the riflemen had received a copy of my tales as a prize for marksmanship; he read them, and the result was that he developed a taste for reading, and he is greatly changed for the better. Visits from the composer Gade, Hartmann, the singer Stockhausen, Brosbøll, with wife and daughter (he brought me the first part of his book *Mixed Company*). Mrs. Koch brought me an embroidered pillow. Neither Jonas Collin nor Bloch paid me a visit; I didn't see them until at the Melchiors'. There the dining room was decorated beautifully—a bust of me with a laurel wreath and greenery and Danish flags all around; beneath, a verse written by the editor Bille. The song was by Ploug, who was also a guest. Moritz Melchior gave the speech. I responded by telling about my life, which had begun with the Iron Age and ended with the Golden Age. When I got home at 9 o'clock, a lovely rose was there from Mrs. Recke. Little Anna, a daughter of the goldsmith Michelsen, had sent me a beautiful bouquet. From Mrs. Jerichau-Baumann, an oil painting—a mermaid rising from the water. What a lavish day! Telegram from Israel Melchior, who is at the moment in Hobro. Letter from Bishop Engelstoft.

Friday, April 3. Sunny. Many begging letters. Edvard Meyer came with a beautiful poem and a plea that I write an introduction for his translation of Florian; it was awkward for me to refuse, but I did and promised I would enlist subscribers. From the dinner table at Mrs. Koch's, where a toast to me was drunk, I went to the theater and saw the premier performance of H. P. Holst's comedy *"They've Got a Daughter."* I found it entertaining; it was well performed.

Saturday, April 4. Not at all well. My blood pressing, pounding; made myself take a walk. It was sunny and warm; I put away my scarf and galoshes. At 1 o'clock read tales at Lord-in-Waiting Wichfeld's. His wife invited me to visit them when I was on Lolland. This evening Stockhausen will be singing my poem "The Fiddler" set to music by Schumann, but I won't get to hear it since I've bought a ticket for Otto Zinck's student production in the big hall at the Casino. After dinner at Mrs. Scavenius's I went to the Casino and had a good time. Plough's student comedy *Mr. Sørensen Out for Adventure* has something in common with "The Galoshes of Fortune." *The Tourist in North Zealand* was a funny parody of the Royal Theater's rendition of "Gurre." The Arabian Company surprised me with its

Andersen and child

competence. The [parody of the] Italian opera *[La Masacrata]*, in which *The Lay of Thrym* was also parodied, was very funny. I left with two acts to go, but it was then already past 10:30.

Sunday, April 5. Sunny but the air cool. Drove out to Rosenvænget Street and said goodbye to Einar Drewsen, who is leaving for Paris this evening. At home, a visit from little Marie Henriques, who was carried by her nanny Sidse. A letter from Miss Heinke. Gave to Mrs. Jerichau-Baumann, who will be leaving the 10th of April, a letter to A. L. Brandt in Amsterdam. Dinner at the Henriqueses'. In the evening, a while at the theater. Early to bed.

Monday, April 6. Up earlier than usual. Beautiful sunshine right away, but cold; then it turned overcast, rainy and windy. Sent a letter to Countess Holstein and to her daughter Bodild. Letter to Bishop Engelstoft. A visit from Mrs. Henriques and her daughter Fernanda. Dinner at the Collins'. Theodor has returned too early from the hunt, which didn't go well, and on top of that, he had a toothache. At the theater, *The Lay of Thrym;* the house still sold out. This evening the trapdoor wouldn't go down with Loki and up with the snake—Loki-Scharff had to run off stage. During the performance I was at a meeting of the Ancker Scholarship Committee, where we, in place of Bissen, were to nominate to the minister of culture the sculptors he could choose from among. We suggested Conradsen, Peters, Stein and Hertzog, and outside the academy, another two: Freund and Saabye. The weather was stormy; I had to offer my arm to Hertz when we entered the theater. So the times change and we with them.

Tuesday, April 7. Sunny but very cold. I had put away my galoshes but soon had to put them on again. I'm freezing. Brought to Reitzel and Watt the list of the contents of volumes 25, 26, 27, and 28 of my collected works. At 1 o'clock read tales at the home of Mrs. Scavenius from Basnæs. Dinner for the first time at the home of William Tutein, who owns the sugar refinery on Elsinore Street. The children were so happy to see me. I was seated next to Mrs. Brun, née Bluhme. Titular Councillor Suhr was there with his wife, two daughters and son, who was here on a visit from Antwerp, Professor Reinhardt, the actor Holst, etc.—a big, sumptuous dinner party. I went home at 8 o'clock and for the first time burned the oil lamp I received on the 2nd of April from Mrs. Henriques. (At Tutein's the host proposed a toast to the 2nd of April.)

Wednesday, April 8. The king's birthday. Sunshine, lots of Danish flags waving. At 12 o'clock I went to the Christiansborg Palace, where there was a reception for the first three ranks—I, as titular councillor, have now been placed in the third and was present, but didn't get to go in until around 1:30 with the last ones, and since that was so, I wanted to be the very last of all the congratulators. We paraded past, but the king spoke with me as the last one and shook my hand. At home I found a letter from Bishop Engelstoft, who has now decided that I should do a reading on Thursday and Friday, the 23rd and 24th. Before I left for dinner at the Melchiors'—the Ørsteds were at the home of Bishop Martensen, whose wife's birthday is on the 8th of April—a summons came from the queen to come at 9 o'clock, if I had time, to read a little for them. Then I tried to find the tale "Peiter, Peter and Peer." Miss Hallager didn't have it, but promised to get it from one of her acquaintances nearby. It wasn't to be found there, and so she went over to see Watt, and since he wasn't at home, she got the maid to open up his living room, and just like that she took the issue out of the collection of *Figaro* he'd set aside. I was chagrined about it and right away wrote a few words to Watt. It was almost time for *The Lay of Thrym*, which they were doing instead of *Joseph*. At 9 o'clock I was at Amalienborg. The king was at the theater for a while; the queen was sitting alone at the piano. I entered the frontmost sitting room unannounced. A little later came first Oxholm, then Thyra and Valdemar. It was pleasant, and besides the king, queen, and Thyra and Valdemar, the heiress presumptive, the king's oldest and youngest brothers, along with Prince Bentheim-Steinfurth, present were only the ladies-in-waiting and the equerry Danneskiold-Samsøe and his wife, Chief Master-of-Ceremony Oxholm and wife, Lord Chamberlain Løvenskiold and wife and Lord-in-Waiting Castenskiold and wife. I read "Who Was the Happiest?," "The Days of the Week," "The Snow Man," "The Snail and the Rosebush," along with "Væn Isle and Glæn Isle." Spoke at length with the queen about the exhibition and about Stockhausen and Gade. The king related that he had received from his daughter in England some shirt buttons with portraits of her children on them; related about how it had happened that he said to Marstrand concerning his picture of Puggaard: "It's probably by a beginner." "It's by me," said Marstrand, and the king excused himself by saying he knew so little about that sort of thing. I found the evening jovial and was happy to be there in the bosom of the family on the king's birthday. It was 10:30 when I left.

Thursday, April 9. Cloudy and cold. Visited Watt, who had scolded his maid because she had allowed somebody to take any of his possessions. Sent a letter to Bishop Engelstoft. Stayed long after dinner at the Melchiors' and read tales to them.

Friday, April 10. Sent a letter to Georg Brandt and little Sara in Amsterdam. After dinner out at Mrs. Koch's, read. At 8 o'clock in the evening I was at a party at Scharff's, where I met Brodersen and

wife, Gade and wife, Hansen and his wife, besides Kolling, Hultmann, etc. and little Schnell, Miss Petersen and [Miss] Møller. I read
five tales—read well and made a great hit. Hultmann was especially
enthusiastic. Eckardt sang correctly and beautifully. The young Simonsen has a strong, resonant voice.—Went home around 10 o'clock.
Lost a lot of blood today. Rainy and windy.

Saturday, April 11. Sunny but cold. Went from the Melchior's up
to see Brandes, who wasn't at home. On the way home I was utterly
exhausted and jittery. At home, a visit from Mrs. Weidemann and
all of the Marstrand children; the eldest is learning to be a smith.
Then I received a visit from Lord-in-Waiting Castenskiold, who is
with the king. Both Their Majesties had really enjoyed themselves
at the reading. Then came a visit from Bjørnstjerne Bjørnson, who
arrived with Clemens Petersen and Mr. Schmidt. I told Mr. Petersen
that in his article he should have emphasized the Danish sense of
humor, which the Norwegians didn't have.

Bjørnstjerne pointed out that Holberg was from Norway and full
grown when he came down here—didn't therefore belong to Denmark. Wessel, too, was Norwegian. Large dinner party at the home
of Lord-in-Waiting Scavenius; he was elegantly boring. At 8 o'clock
at the painter Lund's, where I met the Collins, the Melchiors, etc. I
read three tales. Stormy weather this evening.

Sunday, April 12. Snowy weather this morning; later in the morning, rain and drizzle. A visit from the American governess from Holsteinborg concerning her manuscripts.

Monday, April 13. At the Henriqueses' for dinner; heard there from
Mrs. Erslev all about Brahms' effrontery. He had praised Bismarck's
great character. She had gotten up and said that he was Denmark's
misfortune and that she couldn't stand to hear him praised and that
he mustn't ever recover from his illness. Brahms got more vehement
and said that the Thorvaldsen Museum was going to Berlin and then
it would be over with Denmark. None of the men at the table had
spoken up. She'd only later heard from them what Brahms had said.
Blood had rushed to her head and she had asked what he had said
about *Berlin* and the *Thorvaldsen Museum*. Høedt had not, as he said,
spoken up, but had told the ladies in Danish about how in a compartment on a train to Paris he'd met some Frenchmen who had
been almost impolite to him, but when they were talking about the
sea and he'd said that his fatherland was surrounded by the sea,
they'd asked: "Aren't you a German?" and asked his forgiveness for
their discourtesy to him. Gade then said: "What is it you are saying?

Say it in German!" It wasn't until then that Høedt had come with his story. At the theater I saw the two first acts of *Jeppe of the Hill*. Sunny weather. Promised at 12 o'clock to read for the Lord-in-Waiting Castenskiolds' at the royal residence.

On April 21, Andersen set off on a ten-week tour of Holland, France, Switzerland, and Germany. On his way southward, he stayed for a week in Amsterdam with Georg Brandt and then another week in Paris, where he visited with Einar Drewsen and continued work on his tale "The Wood Nymph." In Switzerland, he stopped for a week in Geneva with Jules Jürgensen before heading northward to the German resort Ems and then on to Hamburg and home.

On July 7, three days after his return from Hamburg, Andersen received a letter from the editor of the American periodical Riverside Monthly Magazine for Young People, *Horace E. Scudder. Although this was not Andersen's first contact with a prominent American—the poet Henry Wadsworth Longfellow had corresponded with him in 1866—it did turn out to be his most important one. Between 1868 and 1870, Scudder arranged for the publication of ten of Andersen's tales and stories in* Riverside Monthly Magazine *in advance of their appearance in Denmark. He also worked for the publication in 1869–71 of Andersen's collected works in ten volumes and his autobiography, for which the author wrote an appendix covering the years 1855–67. Moreover, from 1871 to 1873, Scudder saw to the publication of three more of Andersen's tales and stories and his last novel* Lucky Peer *in* Scribner's Monthly Magazine.

During the fall of 1868, Andersen continued to work on his travelogue about Portugal, which was published in November in Travel Sketches and Pen Drawings. *In December, three thousand copies of his tale "The Wood Nymph" reached booksellers, and it sold out within ten days.*

Andersen spent the holiday season at home fretting about bad odors that seemed to permeate his rooms. First he thought there was the stench of something rotten coming from the tile stove, and he insisted it be torn apart— with no results. Then he was sure it was gas he smelled and had the landlady tear up the floor, where there were in fact some leaky pipes. He dined out on this story, spending Christmas and New Year's eves with the Melchiors and the Henriques.

Monday, January 11 [1869]. The same cloudy weather. Received thirty-six dollars in all from Thorkilsen as an honorarium for the little tale "The Days of the Week." I said it was too much according to Danish standards; I suggested fifteen rix-dollars. He then pressed me to take twenty (as the entire payment). Dinner at Edvard Collin's with Wanscher's daughters and Mrs. Ingeborg Drewsen. Received a letter from a widow from Erlangen. Once, when she was a bride, she had heard me read on Als at the home of the duchess; she asked me in her hour of need for a tale. On Saturday Just Thiele passed his exam with a top grade. Sent letters to Georg Brandt in Amsterdam, Wiedemann in Leipzig and Mrs. Serre in Dresden. Yesterday I presented the English secretary with a Danish edition of "The Wood Nymph" and Count Paar from Austria with a German translation. At the theater saw *Masquerades*. The interlude.

Tuesday, January 12. My clock was running an hour too slow, so I was just getting up when the king's footman stood at my door with a summons to come to Amalienborg at 12 o'clock to see the princess of Wales. I used the morning to spruce myself up and was at the palace fifteen minutes early. There I met Mrs. Bloch, née Trepka, who had been summoned for 11:30. I sat for a while and waited. Then came the composer Niels Gade, who had also been summoned. The door opened, and the queen and the princess of Wales entered. They were both extremely charming. The princess of Wales gave me her hand, said that she had seen me at the theater every evening. I said I had looked up at her, but had had to lower my eyes when she was looking at me. She graciously thanked me for "The Wood Nymph," and I mentioned it had just appeared in English in the last few days. I would have been very happy to bring her a copy, but hadn't yet gotten any. I asked about the children. They were out, "but I said they must be home again by 12 o'clock—they aren't here yet; what shall we do!" "It's good for them to be outside in the fresh air," said Gade. "Well, then I'll get to see them in London!" I said and told them that I had been invited there, likewise to America, "but I won't find Your Royal Highness there!" "Oh, we'll be back there again by late March," said the princess. The queen, too, extended her hand to me, and I kissed it, as I did the princess's. The queen mentioned that Prince Bentheim-Steinfurth had wanted to give Alexandra "The Wood Nymph," but since she had already received a copy from me, it had been sent to Dagmar in St. Petersburg.—As Gade and I were leaving the palace, we saw the carriage with the royal children. "Let's stand here," said Gade, "and watch them drive by." "Let's go back to the palace and watch them get out," I said. Inside the gate, the carriage came to a halt. The two oldest boys got out with a sort of governess. Then came a woman with the smallest child. I asked the governess in English which one was the oldest. She pointed to him. I then said: "I am Hans Christian Andersen." She became quite friendly and said to the oldest: "Give the gentleman your hand—he gave you the book with the nice stories." The little one and his brother each reached out his hand, and the smallest one on the arm of the nursemaid stretched out both hands. I squeezed them and would have liked to kiss the little thing, but didn't think it proper. The whole incident was more fun than if I'd gotten to see them at the audience.—Up at the castle little Valdemar came in and thanked me for the book (*Travel Sketches*) I'd given him. The queen said he was already familiar with it and preferred "The Wood Nymph," which he had read with great pleasure. At the theater saw two acts of *A Folk Legend*. Sent a letter to Mrs. Serre.

Wednesday, January 13. Colder today. Visited the Billes and Høedt. The latter wrapped up in writing against Ploug. At the theater, the premier performance of *In the Other World* by Goldschmidt. The first act diffuse and boring: the man loses his mind. The second act gruesome: the man goes around thinking he's dead. The audience laughed and clapped a lot. I wouldn't have accepted this piece for the Danish stage. If I'd written it, it would have been booed off the stage.

Thursday, January 14. The newspapers are showing signs of praising this work. I'm outraged at the unfairness of it. Received a letter from Scotland, from Livingstone's little daughter with her father's autograph and a small photograph of her. A letter to Miss Heinke, letter to Councillor Petersen. Today is the big drawing for 50,000 rixdollars. I won't get anything, of course, *No!* Nothing! I won't find my luck in the lottery, but somewhere else instead, from the Lord. Got a letter with a small photograph of a young child from Scotland. It was a letter from the daughter of the famous explorer Dr. Livingstone—she'd written a childish letter wishing me a happy New Year and sent me her father's autograph.—Dinner at the Melchiors'. Sent letters to Miss Clara Heinke and to Councillor Petersen in Odense. In the evening was at a meeting of the Ancker Scholarship Committee. This year eight authors made application: Hother Tolderlund, Henriette Nielsen, Ole Christian Lund (these last two are the ones I'm most in favor of), Topsøe, Gerson, Pauline Worm, Preetzmann, S. Schandorph.—Went to the theater. This evening the prince of Wales attended *Orpheus in the Underworld* for the second time at the Folk Theater. The weather is cold now; no ice, though, but a piercing wind. A letter from Claussen in Christiania.

Friday, January 15. Worked on the story of my later life. In a cranky mood. Cheated by a tarted up young beggar. Gave Jonas Collin a parquet ticket for the opera *The Jewess,* which they are doing this evening. Yesterday I received a visit from the singer Nyrop and his wife; presented his little boy Charles with the three most recent volumes of *New Tales and Stories.* Cloudy and cold weather. This evening the prince and princess of Wales will be departing for Egypt over Lübeck. From the Kochs', I went to the theater to see *The Jewess.* The opera was well performed. Miss Pfeil's fresh voice and nice appearance excellent, her diction better; Christophersen's voice smooth and powerful; Nyrop's voice broke on him, but it was expressive. I stayed until the opera was over at around 11 o'clock.

Saturday, January 16. Cloudy and an icy wind. A visit from the Russian attaché Ozeroff. I presented him with a German translation of "The Wood Nymph." Dinner at the Henriqueses'. Invitation to Count Frijs's for Wednesday evening.

Sunday, January 17. Since the Henriqueses had been invited out, I went to dinner at the Melchiors'. A letter from G. Brandt in Amsterdam. Yesterday I saw for the second time Goldschmidt's *In the Other World,* and since I now didn't expect much of it, I enjoyed the performance.

Monday, January 18. A letter from ten Kate with a verse translation of my tales bound in violet-colored velvet and embossed in gold—one copy for me and one for the king of Denmark. In the package lay a letter in Danish from him to the king. Dinner at the Collins' with the Billes (their first time there), Melchiors, Davids, Hornemanns, etc. Bille proposed a toast to the Collins, whose splendid qualities he had gotten to know during the summer. I added a few words—that I found them to be so splendid in the winter, when I stayed most with them, that I couldn't imagine they could be any more so in the summer, and for that reason I wanted to stay with them in Hellebæk this summer on my way up to Norway. Then came David with a rehash of what Bille and I had said, but it sounded almost as if I, "who had known them for so many years," had to be aware of the fact that they were charming in the summer as well as the winter. Went to the Casino and saw Hans Sachs's *The Lamentable Tragedy of Prince Concretus,* which was being performed for the first time. Then went over to the Collins' for a while.

Tuesday, January 19. Clear, freezing weather. Was over on Rosenvænget Street in the evening visiting Rasmus Nielsen. Walked back into town and spent a little time at the Collins'.

Wednesday, January 20. Mrs. Ørsted ill; went therefore to the Henriqueses'. In the evening the ball at Count Frijs's. The king, queen, crown prince, and Prince Hans were there. I talked with the Russian ambassador, who spoke about literature in Russia, etc.—It was very hot there. I walked home in a cold wind.

Thursday, January 21. Coldy and hoarse voice. I was given a promise by Colonel Holten that if I were to come to Amalienborg tomorrow at 11:30, I would probably get in to see the king. I went and got in right away. The king asked me for the time being to extend his thanks to ten Kate and mention that it had been a joy for him to see how well he wrote Danish. We discussed Alexandra—it hadn't been easy for her to travel over Berlin. Spoke about how nothing yet had happened regarding our cause. The king was, as always, gentle and kind; shook my hand when I arrived and took my leave. In the antechamber Holten and I talked about our hometown Odense. He remembered my mother; once when she'd been sick, he'd taken her some garden cress from his mother. Since the crown prince will be leaving on Monday to see his bride-to-be in Stockholm (where in February twenty-eight balls will be held), I stopped in; chatted a bit with the footman, a young fellow from the country, who told about what he'd seen on his travels with the prince—Athens and Constantinople. Then the prince's visitors left, and he announced me. I straightaway was received warmly. The crown prince led me into his small cabinet, and we sat and conversed for more than half an hour about various things—about his bride, about his sister Alexandra, about Goldschmidt's *In the Other World*, about Høedt's and Ploug's stubbornness, about Bille, the editor, etc. At home I found a letter from America, from Scudder. When I later let Melchior read it at dinner, he said that the letter was supposed to have contained a ten pound note. I hadn't seen any, but when I got home later, I found it on the floor. Sent Holst's monthly journal *[For Romanticism and History]* containing "In the Jura Mountains" to Jules Jürgensen in Le Locle. Letter to Livingstone's little daughter in Scotland, enclosed a photograph of myself and my calling card. Letter to Miss Plesner in London. Found an invitation from Count Frijs for dinner on Wednesday. I was at the Melchiors', where it was little Birgitte's birthday today, together with Ploug, the editor, and wife. I talked with her. At the theater, *The Dumb Girl of Portici.*

Friday, January 22. A letter to Miss Daugaard. visited Count Moltke-Hvitfeldt, who kissed me when I arrived and took my leave. Paid a call to Count Frijs. Called on Mrs. Scavenius. Cloudy weather. I am irritable and listless. Dinner at Titular Councillor Suhr's. I escorted

Miss Raasløff to the table and had the most beautiful of Suhr's daughters seated on my left. Bishop Martensen was there. After dinner I talked with Mrs. Heiberg and Professor Reinhardt. He talked about Goldschmidt's matchless style and said that, after all, in *this day and age* people had to appreciate his dramatic works, that *In the Other World* was entertaining. Mrs. Heiberg and I expressed our opposition to this, and she was bitterly opposed to Goldschmidt personally and to his conduct. He just about agreed with Goldschmidt that Offenbach was the greatest composer of our times; on the subject of Bjørnson he expressed a quite negative opinion when I said that he was always a true poet. He tore *The Newly Weds* apart, and about *A Happy Boy*, he said that it was mannered and stilted. Then I turned away from him and recalled how this same person had spoken in Forchhammer's house during the last war—that when the ship sank, the best thing for the crew to do was to abandon it; even the rats did that!—Denmark had gone under, and we should let her go.

Saturday, January 23. Sent a letter to ten Kate. A little snow today, but only like sugar sprinkled on a pancake. Dinner at the home of Mrs. Scavenius with Miss Brandis, Otto and Peer Scavenius. At the theater I saw the second and third acts of *Master and Apprentice*.

Sunday, January 24. Wrote a letter of recommendation for Waldemar Price, who is going to travel to Vienna, and took it to Edvard Collin so that it could be reworked into German style. Clear weather. A little sprinkling of snow from the night before. Spent the whole day organizing and arranging my books. A letter from Mrs. Anholm about whether I wouldn't like to have the old rooms I had before; they would be available by summer. At the theater for the first acts of *Faust*.

Monday, January 25. How strange it is that after a few days an entire day can vanish into oblivion. Today, Thursday, I am clear about nothing regarding this day. It has sailed by like in a dream. I didn't go to the theater; I didn't write letters; I only know what I didn't do!

Tuesday, January 26. Snowy weather. A letter from a young lady . . . in Vienna; she asked me for my autograph and picture. At the Collins' together with Jette Boye and her daughter. Gave Waldemar Price a letter of recommendation for Vienna. At home during the evening working on *The Story of My Life*. Recently Scharff has been visiting me regularly and often.

Wednesday, January 27. Worked on *The Story of My Life* and looked for letters. Among them I found one from Bentley that he had given me two hundred pounds for *The Two Baronesses*—not bad, as a matter of fact. Thinking about this, it occurred to me that I hardly had a right to authorize the issuing of this work in an American collected edition. It put me in an anxious and depressed frame of mind. I was invited to dinner today by Professor Ortwed and wife, who paid me a visit yesterday. It made me feel anxious to find a letter from Bentley in which I could see he had paid me two hundred pounds, that is, 1,800 rix-dollars for *The Two Baronesses*. Could I, then, even twenty-one years later, authorize an American edition of my collected works in which it had been included? Spoke to Edvard Collin about it. Large dinner party at 6 o'clock at Count Frijs's. Fourteen courses with appropriate *wines*. Present were all the Danish ministers of state, the brothers Danneskiold-Samsøe, Zytphen-Adeler, Bruun, the president of the Upper Chamber of Parliament, and Titular Councillor Bregendahl. I sat between Fonnesbech and Worsaae. Arrived at the theater at 9 o'clock for the last two acts of *The Magic Flute*, which was being performed for the first time in a Frenchified adaptation.

Thursday, January 28. Letter from an unbalanced peasant woman from around Skelskør. The Blochs and Lunds were at the Melchiors' for dinner.

Friday, January 29. Sent a letter to Scudder in New York. Letter from Miss Plesner that "The Wood Nymph" had been published in London. Today I was supposed to go to a large gentlemen's dinner party given by Jacobsen, the brewer, at the Carlsberg Brewery, but decided against it and went to Mrs. Koch's and from there to the theater and heard *The Magic Flute* from the beginning. Went home after the third act because at the theater I'd gotten the idea for the story "The Comet." I told it there to Thiele and went home and wrote half of it.

Saturday, January 30. Finished "The Comet." Beautiful, clear weather. In the sun, forty-five degrees. Visited Mrs. Ørsted. Dinner with Miss Brandis at Mrs. Scavenius's. Saw the first act of *Far from Denmark*. Ended the story about the comet. (Read it to Edvard and Jonas Collin.)

Sunday, January 31. Rainy weather. Made a fair copy of "The Comet." Read it to Thiele and his wife. They were moved. Thiele said it was perfectly delightful—beautiful like "The Wood Nymph" and full of serenity. Read it to Bloch, who was working on his painting *Christ as a Child in the Temple.* Dinner at the Henriqueses' with the Blochs, Jerichau and Frederik Bøgh. Went to the theater; heard *The Magic Flute*. Got into the mood, went home and wrote the tale "Sunshine Stories." It got to be late, and I was tired of writing, but stuck with it until it was on paper past midnight.

Monday, February 1. Rain and drizzle, but not at all winterlike. Read the tale to Thiele, who was pleased with it. I didn't have the peace of mind to do any work; needed to get out, wander around. Read the tale and "The Comet" to the writer Munch and his wife. He preferred the tale. Read it to Bloch and, after dinner at Edvard Collin's, to him and Jonas. Jette and Louise got to hear it this morning. Went to see the Melchiors. Only Louise, Harriet and Anna were there; they heard it. I read it to Mrs. and Miss Raasløff, who is now translating it for *Riverside Magazine*. Read the tale to Bournonville. He preferred "The Comet"; felt that the tale should also contain what the rain and wind had to tell. Didn't go to the theater, but home.

Tuesday, February 2. Cloudy morning, clear day. Received the February issue of *Aunt Judy's Magazine;* in it, the first half of "The Wood Nymph." Gave Jonas Collin a ticket to *The Magic Flute*. At the Casino, the skater and my comedy *Mother Elderberry*. At the Drewsens' on Rosenvænget Street read the two most recent tales. Drewsen liked these better than "The Wood Nymph"—he's never had any liking for that one. Took a carriage into town and was at the theater for the three first acts. When I got home, I found a ticket to Winding's concert lying there. His wife had brought it to me herself, but then it was too late.

Wednesday, February 3. Beautiful sunny weather. Made a fair copy of "Sunshine Stories." Dinner at the Ørsteds'. A concert for ladies and gentlemen at the Student Association. Before the intermission I read "The Goblin at the Grocer's" and "Heartbreak" to great applause. After the intermission, the two new ones in manuscript, "The Comet" and "Sunshine Stories." Was loudly applauded. The theater closed in the evening.

Thursday, February 4. For dinner at the Melchiors' were the Billes, Adlers, Henriqueses, and, from Hamburg, Simon Henriques. I proposed a couple of toasts. Brought Miss Raasløff "The Comet" for translation into English. At home in the evening and worked on *The Story of My Life*.

Friday, February 5. As early as today received the English translation of "The Comet" from Miss Raasløff. At the theater, the premier performance of *Three Days in Padua* by H. Hertz. It excited the audience, like *Twelfth Night* and *A Winter's Tale*. There was a whiff of poetry in it. It received a lot of applause. The ballet *Bellman* was performed for the hundredth time. In the mail received from America "The Wood Nymph" translated and published in *Riverside Magazine*.

Saturday, February 6. Visited Henrik Hertz. Presented him with some flowers. Sent a letter to Scudder in New York together with the English translation of "Sunshine Stories." The widow Mrs. Thusnelda Moltke was at Mrs. Scavenius's for dinner. I heard the second act of *The Magic Flute*. Went home and worked on my autobiography and on "Croak."

Sunday, February 7. Sunshine this morning, then cloudy weather, but mild. Worked on *The Story of My Life* for most of the day. Little Anna Bille paid a visit to me and brought the gloves I'd forgotten at her parents'. I was at the Henriqueses' for dinner together with the brother Simon Henriques from Hamburg, along with Høedt, etc. I went to the Casino and saw the skater and the young lady who skates with him. On the way home I bought a Shrovetide switch[3] for Miss Hallager's little foster daughter. I had to take the switch home with me. Decided then not to go to the theater to see *Jeppe of the Hill*, which will be performed again tomorrow. I stayed at home and worked on my autobiography.

Monday, February 8. Rainy weather. Read from my autobiography to Mrs. Melchior and her daughters. Worked on same. Today is Shrove Monday. From the Collins' went to the theater to see *Jeppe of the Hill*. There composed the tale "What People Do Think Up" and wrote it down at the end of the evening.

Tuesday, February 9. Spent the whole morning going over the tale I wrote yesterday evening and making a fair copy of it. Read it first to Mrs. Jette Collin. She was delighted and said it was the best of the three recent ones. The Melchiors found it quite entertaining. Dinner at Christian Thyberg's. It was the first time I've been at his home since he married for the second time. Pastor Rørdam was there, Pastor Monrad and the Collins. I read the three most recent tales. At the Casino, *Willie Winkie* and dancing on skates. I'd given Miss Hallager a ticket to the Casino. Moses Melchior was there.

On February 19, Andersen went to the University of Copenhagen to hear a lecture by Professor Rasmus Nielsen: "It was extremely interesting, but I was sort of embarrassed listening to it, since the entire lecture concerned

---

3. A decorated switch given to children at the beginning of Lent.

mainly me as a composer of tales. To be sure, he didn't mention me by name a single time. . . . He read all of the tale "The Snow Man" and analyzed it in detail, making it the heart of his lecture. I felt myself to be exalted by it all, as if I were dead and now witnessing one of the university's venerable professors holding a lecture about me at the University of Copenhagen." Five months later, Andersen found in The Illustrated News *the first installment of a long essay about his work by the promising young scholar Georg Brandes.*

On September 10, four days after celebrating the fiftieth anniversary of his arrival in Copenhagen and the beginning of his new life, Andersen departed on a six-month trip to Vienna and the Riviera. On his way to Vienna, he stayed at the estate Maxen to visit with Mrs. Serre and her houseguest, the painter Clara Heinke, both of whom he had not seen since his last trip to Germany in 1861. Once in Vienna, Andersen was disappointed with his hotel accommodations and the sharp increase in prices since he last was there and left at the end of three weeks for Munich and Nice. In Nice, where he stayed for all of December and January, he was prompted by persistent ill health and loneliness to write to Edvard Collin inviting Edvard's son Jonas to southern France. Jonas arrived January 18, and two weeks later the two of them headed for Paris and home.

Buoyed by the publication of his Three New Tales and Stories *in mid-December, Andersen was very productive during the spring of 1870. On March 20, a little more than a week after he had returned to Copenhagen from his trip, he wrote "What the Whole Family Said" in one sitting. Within the next five weeks, he wrote three more tales and started on* Lucky Peer, *which was to be the last of his novels. On May 21, he left Copenhagen to spend a month at Basnæs.*

Wednesday, June 1 [1870]. Gray weather; sunshine later in the morning. A letter to Miss Mathilde Ørsted. Began to write out some Danish legends for *Riverside Magazine.* Rainy weather most of the day. In the wet weather a lot of the big snails have crawled onto the walkways. In several places they were lying two by two against each other, but strangest of all were two that were clinging together. They had crawled all the way out of their shells and cleaved to each other belly to belly. With their shells lying on the ground they reared straight up against each other, and moved their feelers alternately toward each other—a small fly had crawled all the way out onto one of them, but the snail thought it was probably a part of the proceedings, because it did not pull in its feelers the way they otherwise do at a puff of air when someone walks by. They stayed in the same

Stealer of hearts (papercut made on the estate of Maxen, Saxony, in 1856)

position swaying back and forth and reared upwards again. They were probably mating. Up at the house, Miss Schumacher said to me: "You can see down in the garden that the snails are certainly having themselves a ball—it's probably a wedding."—A letter from Otto to his mother that he won't be coming home to Basnæs until after Whitsunday.

Thursday, June 2. Cloudy weather. A letter to Miss Bjerring in Ålborg, a letter to Jonas Collin. Went for a short stroll in the garden—it's been raining continuously. Contradictions, nothing but contradictions, but a good heart. Letter from Edgar Collin, letter from the poet Mads Hansen with a photograph of him, letter from little Marie

Geibel and her mother in Leipzig. A letter from Henriques. A beautifully bound copy of *From Nordic Poets*, probably from Thorkilsen. Read in it in the evening.

Friday, June 3. Wrote a greeting to send by telegram to General Christensen on the occasion of the banquet in his honor at Klampenborg. Was about to send it off but realized that it wasn't Thursday today, but Friday, and thus too late. Sent a letter to Edgar Collin from whom I received a letter yesterday. Sent a letter to Mrs. Koch. This morning one of the two small parrots died on Mrs. Scavenius.—The weather isn't quite clear, but pleasantly warm. Sent a letter to Mrs. Koch. Contradiction—irritable trying to understand me. A bit tired of it. A new moon shining and could see all of the blue sphere.

Saturday, June 4. Slept badly last night. (Yesterday my dream was again about being dependent: I ran away from Meisling, was afraid of Old Collin because everyone was dissatisfied with me at the new school.[4] Talked to Viggo about it and he exclaimed: "What would Grandfather say!" That I still can have such dreams! How it must have tormented me in my youth!) Sunshine.—A letter to Mrs. Geibel in Leipzig and to her little Marie. Sent Emil Wiinblad the manuscript of his tale and a letter.—Drove with Mrs. Scavenius and Miss Schumacher out into the forest to Herman's house. The woodruff was in bloom. Lots of people in the forest. At home a letter lying there for me from the City Rifle Club in Odense about coming to their celebration on the 14th of June. I got upset about it and went upstairs to write my regrets. Another letter from Viggo Rygaard in England with poems for me to look at. Letter from Thorkilsen. Went early to bed very tired.

Whitsunday, June 5. Warm sunshine. Mrs. Scavenius and Miss Schumacher drove to church at Holsteinborg. A letter to Countess Holstein. Letter to the officers of the City Rifle Club in Odense. Received a letter from Miss Mathilde Ørsted and the second volume of her father's letters. A letter from General Christensen, who will be leaving Copenhagen on Monday (tomorrow).—Large dinner party— Judge Schjørring with his wife and mother-in-law, Dr. Krebs and daughter, Fabricius and wife. At the table Mrs. Scavenius proposed a toast to the constitution and the king. (It's Constitution Day.) Schjørring toasted me. I showed him the view from the tower, the

4. Since 1857 Andersen had been writing in his diaries about dreams of his early days when he was dependent on Simon Meisling's and Jonas Collin's good opinion of him.

gravestone of the alderman in Skælskør and the monument for the late Scavenius of Basnæs. When I woke up this morning, I was suffering from arthritis and the feeling under my arm that I was developing a boil. I checked it, and it looked like an *I* burned on my side. I bathed it with a solution of tar in the belief that it was ringworm. Later I thought it might be several cuts from a pin that had gotten enflamed. I told Dr. Krebs. He didn't look at it, but advised me to bathe it with almond skins.

Monday, June 6. Warm and summerlike. It's still burning under my arm. Thought, as always, of death in various forms. Sent a letter to Mrs. Drewsen on Rosenvænget Street. Today Mrs. Scavenius had dinner at Espe with Mrs. Moltke. I and Miss Schumacher alone at home. Read aloud from the second volume of *Letters from and to Hans Christian Ørsted.* She knew several of the people named from Holstein. The air mild and filled with the fragrance of the lilacs. I lay in the grass.

Tuesday, June 7. Lovely weather. A letter to Professor Hartmann, to Theodor Collin. Letter to Henriques and little Marie. Received a letter from Countess Holstein. The sore is burning, but today I want to see if it will get better if I don't do anything to it. Read aloud until almost 11 o'clock from *Ørsted's Letters.*

Wednesday, June 8. Slept restlessly last night. The welts were burning, and I'm anxious about it. Mrs. Scavenius wants to have me driven to the doctor today, but I am a little embarrassed about it. Today I am bathing the sore only with cold water. Sent a letter to Viggo Rygaard in England with a few words about his poems. Mrs. Scavenius wanted me to go to Skelskør to show the welts on my chest to Dr. Møller. I left shortly after 2 o'clock, and it was lucky I got there because that was precisely when Mr. Nagel, the merchant, came from Korsør with the birds Mrs. Scavenius had been expecting on the train. I took them right home then. Dr. Møller looked at my side and said that they weren't cuts from a pin. It looked like shingles, but he didn't think it would spread all over like a belt. He prescribed that I rub it with almond oil.—It was extremely hot to drive in the burning sun on the dusty road. Got a letter from Georg Brandt, who is here on a visit with the Jacobsens at Falkensten. A letter from Mrs. Jette Collin. Early to bed. It was still light outside.

Thursday, June 9. Slept better than yesterday. The rash is burning today. Sent a letter to Harald Scharff and to Mrs. Collin. It's less warm today but sunny, though. Letter to Moltke-Hvitfeldt, whose birthday it is tomorrow. The widow Moltke with her two sisters

(Sehestedt Juul) here for dinner. Read to them "Danish Popular Legends." Cold weather. Rubbed the shingles for the first time with almond oil.

Friday, June 10. Cold. Lord-in-Waiting Grevenkop-Castenskiold with wife and daughter arrived here early in the morning. Around 12 o'clock a carriage came with our young friend. He was sound asleep when he arrived and was cranky when he woke up. After lunch I was asked to read for the young Mrs. Castenskiold (her husband, a gentleman-in-waiting with the king). She told me that portraits of Ingemann and me hung over her desk and that we were the two writers most dear to her. I presented her with a picture of myself. I was asked right away by her mother also to give one to her other daughter. I was reluctant to do it because it was one of the last I had. Carl Castenschiold and Lucie came for dinner. I really feel a little uprooted since Otto came home. We have so little grasp of one another and yet certain things in common. God knows whether this is the last time I'll be coming to Basnæs, where I otherwise feel so at home. Read again before dinner. A letter from Countess Holstein and from Henriques. Received the June issue of *For Romanticism and History* from H. P. Holst. Cold weather.

Saturday, June 11. Very cold. Sent a letter to Louise Collin. These shingles are still burning and seem to have spread further up under my arm. After dinner, Otto quite communicative and forthcoming. Letter from H. P. Holst, who left yesterday for Finland, St. Petersburg, Warsaw, etc.—Letter from Robert Henriques. Letter from Carl Bloch. I read in the paper this evening that Charles Dickens died on the evening of the 9th of April. So we'll never see each other again on earth, never tell each other our innermost thoughts. I won't get an explanation from him why he didn't respond to my last letters.— Stayed up until almost 11 o'clock talking with Otto and the two ladies. Pouring rain. Two storks in the garden.

Sunday, June 12. Very cold. I have a constant stinging sensation under my arm, and today it's been a week since it started. Sent a letter to countess Holstein that I'll be coming to Holsteinborg on the 25th of June. Letter to Mrs. Melchior that I'll be traveling in to Copenhagen on the 2nd of July. In his muddle-headed zeal, the postmaster returned my letter to Countess Holstein with the notation: "The countess is in Copenhagen." Then it was sent in along with Otto's servant Peter. Dinner at Borreby. Drove over there with Miss Schumacher. We were together with the two Misses Qvistgaard. After dinner I read several tales for them so that I got tired. The master of the house more lively and talkative than usual. At 8:30 I drove home alone. It was extremely cold weather. Letters from Theodor Collin and Mrs. Ida Koch, a package containing this week's issues of *The Daily News.* A letter from Horace Scudder in New York and the June issue of *Riverside Magazine,* in which my "Spring Song" had been translated into English. My shingles aren't any better.

Monday, June 13. Only forty-six degrees. I'm freezing, and it's burning under my arm. Sent a letter to Mrs. Collin in Hellebæk with a letter to Dr. Collin enclosed. (Always contradictions, always things misheard. I ask the question: "Is he the one who has planted so many fruit trees?" And the answer comes: "He's not a planter at all; he's a gentleman farmer." Today, concerning Christian II, that a remarkable lady who is delivering some lectures in Copenhagen (Miss Meinert) has discovered in Allen's book the most horrible secrets of Christian II.—Later, that if you didn't believe in a personified devil you couldn't believe in Christ, either, because then you didn't believe the creed.) One must constantly try to keep in mind the exceptionally kind heart of this opinionated woman in order to be able to put up with listening to such things. Another dispute about the trip. "You'll be leaving one of the first days in July." "No, the 23rd of June." "Yesterday morning you were saying the 28th." "At dinner someone said the races in Slagelse would be on one of the first days in July—we can look at the calendar. See, they're on the 3rd of July!" "Well, that's one of the first days in July!" "Yes, but not the first of July!" "That's not what I said; I said one of the first days of July!" "Well, then, there must have been a misunderstanding." That's how it goes without a break. I'm quite a nervous wreck. A letter from Robert Watt whether I wouldn't compose a poem in honor of Charles Dickens or a short prose piece about him. A letter from Louise Lind. Letters from Jonas Collin and from Mrs. Jette Collin. Finished *Letters from and to Hans Christian Ørsted.*

Tuesday, June 14. Cloudy weather. Last night the red bird died. This is now the fourth of Mrs. Scavenius's birds to die during the past two weeks. She thinks this one didn't get the food it needed and starved to death. I think it froze to death. A letter to Henriques and a letter to his son Robert. Letter to Robert Watt. Letter to French, the bookseller in Leipzig with enclosed copies of "The Comet," "Sunshine Stories" and "The Teapot."—A letter from Eckardt in Vienna. A big, unpleasant argument this evening involving all three women about Christ and religion. I said Christian dogma was from God and it was a blessing, but that although the circumstances of the birth and family were of interest, they were not necessary for me. Then the fur began to fly—if one didn't take His birth and death into account, then His teachings would be meaningless! This last point was necessary to affirm one's conviction in the truth, etc. Since I didn't believe in the Father, the Son and the Holy Ghost, I wasn't a Christian. I answered that I believed in them as concepts but not as people, corporeal beings. They almost gave up on me. However, when I left, Mrs. Scavenius squeezed my hand with warmth and sincerity. She is a dear soul *but* . . .

The disputes and bickering of the Scavenius household disturbed Andersen, and on a walk in the garden on June 18 he thought of his own mortality: "I don't have many years left to live. Why, then, spend my days where I feel so oppressed? I'd rather be *independent*—free to enjoy what I have left, to die before my fellow man forgets me and my work. What I have lived to see praised will be forgotten or belittled by a new generation. Good to sleep a dreamless sleep with no awareness of having been alive—and yet frightening, horrible to die, to disappear. That is my lament, who have been granted more happiness than millions." *A week later, Andersen left Basnæs to visit a few days at Holsteinborg before returning to spend the rest of the summer in Copenhagen staying with friends.*

At the Melchiors' one evening in mid-August, Andersen learned that the Norwegian playwright Henrik Ibsen was in town. That March he had seen Ibsen's play The League of Youth *at the Royal Theater and was interested in meeting him. This was arranged for the following week, and on August 18 Andersen did some reading to prepare himself for conversation with Ibsen that evening:* "Finished up *Peer Gynt*. It's as if it were written by a mad poet! You go crazy yourself trying to understand that book. The poetry isn't good either—there is something wild and unwholesome in it all. Regret having read it, since Ibsen will be coming here this evening for the first time. I have never seen him. He is supposed to be gloomy and taciturn. After dinner, he came with Bloch, and he made a good impression—we all liked him."

Andersen spent most of the summer finishing his novel Lucky Peer *and readying it for publication in early November. It was otherwise an unhappy summer for him. There was war in Europe—the French had declared war on Prussia in mid-July, and the Danish newspapers were filled with disturbing reports from the front. Moreover, he was distressed by news of the deaths of Signe Læssøe and Orla Lehmann, both of whom he had known since his earliest days in Copenhagen. On September 19, he moved into rooms in a boarding house on Tordenskjold Street run by the two Rossing sisters.*

Thursday, November 10. Received from Reitzel the first copies of *Lucky Peer* with a red binding and embossed in gold, but I'm not to hand them out until tomorrow—that's when the book will be appearing in the bookstores. The lottery drawing will also be held— maybe it'll be me now who's a Lucky Peer. Dinner at the Melchiors'. (Yesterday evening our other maid was at the theater—she got her ticket from me.) During dinner at the Melchiors' Carl Bloch told me that Orla Lehmann had not been fond of me, had spoken ill of me and hadn't understood how to appreciate me. "Everyone from your early years has stood too close to you and can't see how important you've become." It depressed me. I went to the theater, where Brosbøll and Gerson gave me an icy-cold look probably wishing I was six feet under. Outside the theater I ran into Peter Müller, who saw me to my door. I'm tired of life—for tonight!

Friday, November 11. Today is the drawing of the lottery. I want to have a look at the list of numbers. I probably haven't won. Received from Reitzel fifty-five copies of *Lucky Peer;* handed out twenty-two today. Felt depressed and tired of life.

Saturday, November 12. Extremely overcast and yet sunshine later in the day. Gave away a number of copies of *Lucky Peer.* Received a lovely letter of thanks from Rosenkilde, the actor. Ole Christian Lund, the writer, brought me his new book *Zitta, Daughter of the Cathedral* and, in addition, a lovely poem dedicated to me. The young beggar who was given a few of my clothes when I was living at Miss Hallager's and is now constantly pestering me, came again today, and when I went out he followed me the whole way in order to beseech me anew. I got frustrated and angry and asked him how he dared harass me like that.—Sent *Lucky Peer* to the queen and the crown prince.

Sunday, November 13. Sat for Moyel, the photographer. Lunch at the Melchiors' and heard a long letter from Mrs. Hänschell read aloud. Sent *Lucky Peer* to the queen dowager. Received a lovely note from Miss Reventlow expressing the ruling queen's thanks for the book and saying we'd be seeing each other in Copenhagen soon.

Monday, November 14. A letter from Mrs. Heiberg that she had confidence in her prophecy about the success of *Lucky Peer.* Everyone overwhelmed me with thanks for my book. Some liked the first

Map of Copenhagen from 1870

half best; others, the last. Theodor said: "How they all lie—I can't be bothered reading that crap!"—A visit from Louise Lind. Stayed home in the evening.

On November 19, Andersen attended the 100th anniversary celebration of the sculptor Thorvaldsen's birth. He was affected by the ceremony: "With bared heads, we walked around the grave. I was saddened, but felt free from the unhealthy despondency, the unending depression and even the total self-resignation that had engulfed me as a result of the awful, bloody course of the war, the omnipotence of the cannons, which had turned me into a blubbering idiot, turned me from God. It was as if I had awakened strong and healthy from a feverish dream. I need not hide on these pages—which will never be published but stem from my daily thoughts—that I felt I had so much in common with Thorvaldsen—our low birth and our struggle and our great world recognition. To be sure, I am as well known in the world as he, which our countrymen, however, don't see, but it is certainly true. But I think his name will live longer than mine. Indeed, I do believe my name is now more well known around the world than his, but mine will be forgotten and his will live. Is this vanity? Will I ever know?"

Wednesday, November 23. A letter from Miss Bjerring. My back and abdomen ache. Sent *Lucky Peer* to Krohn at Bregentved. Visited Jette Melchior, who was pleased with the book and said she'd heard people say that the choirmaster was her brother Moses, but he probably wasn't aware of it. Visited Bloch, who spoke with scorn of the arrogant nobility, who, indeed, also look down on us artists. The day before yesterday Mrs. Suhr came to visit me with Treschow, her son-in-law, and her daughter; I wasn't at home. Today I repaid the visit; they were likewise out. Mrs. Gade wrote to me yesterday about coming there this evening with the Hartmanns and the Henriques. I went over and said I didn't go out evenings. Mrs. Gade remonstrated, and Gade said: "It's quite natural; just let him be!" A warm, enthusiastic letter of thanks from Miss Bjerring for *Lucky Peer*. Visited Mrs. Melchior. She said people didn't feel it was right that Peer had to die and the beginning of the book was reminiscent of "The Porter's Son."—Saw two acts of the ballet *Naples*.

Thursday, November 24. In the review in *The Daily* of *New Danish Monthly Magazine* and Mads Hansen's *The New Almanac for 1871*, several contributions were singled out, but not one of my tales. Nor in

references to the Casino, the 25th anniversary of which is being celebrated, has sufficient note been made of me. The bust of me still
hasn't been set up again in the Student Association. I'm annoyed
and wish I were rich enough never again to have to undertake any
poetic task. I'll be quickly forgotten and flung to the winds by the
coming generation—" It's over! It's all over! And that's how it is
with all stories!"[5] Dinner at the Melchiors', where they wished to
keep me, but I wanted to go to the Casino to see the anniversary
performance. There it was jam-packed at elevated prices. The crown
prince and his consort, with them Nægler and Holten, such decent
fellows, to be sure, but hardly too bright. Miss Larsen, as the fairy
godmother of the Casino, recited a poem extremely well. A curtain
was lowered with the names of all of the Casino's celebrated virtuo-
sos, dancers and singers, its authors—my name, as the first in al-
phabetical order, first. In the revue of works that had enjoyed fifty
or more performances, the stork from *More than Pearls and Gold* came
and recited a lovely poem suggestive of me. The audience clapped
for it especially and for the little four-year-old Willie Winkie (who
made his debut in *Froufrou*). These two were the only performers of
all of the included works to be applauded by the audience. How
strange. *More than Pearls and Gold,* as well as *Willie Winkie,* was attacked by Erik Bøgh—he wrote *"More than Enough,"* or *Willie Winkie,*
which made a laughingstock of me and these works. And now I
behold here that he celebrates and performs them, and they turn
out to be the only ones the audience applauded at the opening performance. Went home after the second act, but a little detour up to
the Henriqueses', where two young ladies from the country wished
to be introduced to me. One of them sang beautifully. (How full of
meaning it seemed to me that Miss Larsen, who played the fairy
godmother of the Casino, paid special attention to Willie Winkie,
probably not on account of my work, but because of the little four-
year-old child. But I saw in this a poetic tribute to my work—chance
can be meaningful!) This day began with despondency and droop-
ing spirits. Ended with a sort of comfort and lifting up of my heart.

Friday, November 25. Letter from Vilhelm Boye in Haderslev. Sent
him a *Lucky Peer.* When I went out at dusk to let in the single Swedish lady who lives here, their little dog came and nipped me on my
pants leg. I got angry and nervous about being bitten. Arrived very
irritated at the Henriqueses'. Ate there with the Hartmanns, Wind-

---

5. Quotation from the conclusion of the tale "Grantraet" ("The Fir Tree," 1845).

ings and Wedels. Then went out to the Casino and saw the second act of *The Caliph Out for Adventure* again. When I got home, I found a potted plant with a verse from the little dog that had bitten me—he was never going to do it again.

Saturday, November 26. Two of the barberry branches I got at Tranquillity several months ago and put in water have sprouted green leaves and flowers while still bearing the old red berries. I took them to Mrs. Melchior. At the Student Association I saw that several of the other busts were removed yesterday and today. Consequently, it's not just my bust, and so there's nothing to be said. Sent Miss Plesner a *Lucky Peer*. The other day I sent a copy to Krohn at Bregentved. Was at Titular Councillor Thiele's for dinner. (The weather gray and wet.) Nicolai Bøgh told me that he'd been standing on Green Street during the celebration of Thorvaldsen's 100th birthday and overheard two ordinary folk talking: "That such a man was born in such a little house—and he was visited by kings! Andersen is also a great man, I suppose. Some say Oehlenschläger was greater, but I don't understand him so well. Andersen I can understand—there'll probably be a 100th birthday celebration for him, too. Yes, it'll be over in Odense, then, and illuminating the city will be cheaper—most of the houses are only one story high. But then we won't be able to go to his grave. Well, I suppose no one knows where that'll be."—Saw two acts of *Thunderstorm*.

Sunday, November 27. Cloudy weather. The Collins have gone to Hellebæk. The Henriques and Melchiors at a wedding. Today I'll have to resort to a restaurant. This evening, the first review of *Lucky Peer*. It was in *The Fatherland*, written by Winkel Horn—he counts it among my weaker works and says that the idea is flawed, since Lucky Peer shouldn't die precisely the moment he achieves success; dwelled in particular on what the reviewer didn't like and then paid me a few compliments as a great author of fairy tales, although without the power and genius of my youth—I've gotten older!—This was the first public acknowledgment and thanks for *Lucky Peer!* There were characters in the book, though, that indeed deserved mention, much that could've deserved favorable comment. To hell with it all!—*The Fatherland* was never any special friend or admirer of mine. It's cliquish!—Old Fabricius, whose broken rib has now mended, came into Vincent's, where I was having dinner; he was holding the issue of *The Illustrated News* with the article about Thorvaldsen's house. "His works," he said, "are to be found all over the world, but H. C. Andersen's writings are all over, too. I'm itching to see the continuation of your *Fairy Tale of My Life!*" In a sensual mood. Wandered around in the moist air; came home and felt tired. No desire to go to the theater. Stayed at home all evening. Discontented. +

Monday, November 28. Lovely, clear weather, sunny and mild. A letter from Vilhelm Boye in Haderslev. Received from Thomas Lange his story *The River and the Sea*; sent him *Lucky Peer* in return. I'm not happy and yet there is reason for me to exclaim: "Thank the good Lord for everything You've granted me." My writings usually come under immediate attack and later are highly praised. Now I'm being treated by *The Fatherland* like the Russian priest who's to have a whipping—first he's kissed on the hand, then they tear his robe off and give him a beating, and afterwards he gets his priestly robes back and a kiss on the hand. But he has had his whipping. At the Collins' for dinner—roast goose and peas. The meal was probably too heavy—I got a pain in my abdomen, and it didn't go away until late in the evening. Saw one act of *The Wiles of Scapin* and at the Casino, two acts of *The Caliph*.

Tuesday, November 29. Feel embittered and angry about *The Fatherland's* criticism of *Lucky Peer*. I feel like giving up writing. If I were young and rich, I would live to embrace life. "You've got to have a body!"[6]—Went out to Rosenvænget Street to see the Drewsens. Too late for the streetcar and had to take a carriage in to the theater. Saw the first three acts of *The League of Youth*. Reading Thomas Lange's *The River and the Sea*. Today a young girl came up to me on the street and asked: "Are you the poet H. C. Andersen! Would you write a story for me about a streetcar hack? It's an old, white horse. You can see it out in the Vesterbro district. It can't pull any more, but it still lifts up its head and follows along."

Wednesday, November 30. The first snow fell this morning. Was at Mrs. Ørsted's for dinner together with Mrs. Bech and her daughter—the latter a friend of Miss Brandis—who spoke in a harsh and unfriendly manner about Miss Brandis's *Triumph*. It was very cold when I left there for home—winter is coming. At the theater, saw *The Portrait*. It's long and dull according to the strict standards we set for original works. *The Elves* was also unimpressive—our stage production lacks imagination, and there's's too much prattle by children in this work. Miss Suhr and Treschow were married in the Cathedral of Our Lady.

6. Quotation from the tale "Springfyrene" ("The High Jumpers," 1845).

Thursday, December 1. My windows are frozen—it's like winter. Yesterday I finished Thomas Lange's *The River and the Sea.* It has convincing descriptions of nature and people. It has sensual fireworks, fireworks of passion, but you find yourself overwhelmed by the darkness that follows. There is truth in it, but nothing uplifting and no reconciliation.—Mrs. Henriques, who has been so emotional and neurotic since the birth of little Marie, unburdened herself to me today—she's afraid of going crazy. There's a buzzing in her head, and she feels so devoid of feeling. Dinner with her and her husband at the Melchior'. From there I went to the theater for one and a half acts of *Lohengrin.* Police Chief Crone told me he'd read *Lucky Peer* yesterday evening in one sitting. News about the war—it's going well for the French.

Friday, December 2. Cloudy weather. A letter from Krohn at Bregentved. Very fidgity and tired. I could hardly hold myself together at the Student Association and turned back on my way since I wished to visit the Collins'. Finally I forced myself to go there. Felt a little stronger afterwards and had dinner at Mrs. Koch's. Peter Koch thought Lucky Peer shouldn't have died but experienced adversity and yet remained Lucky Peer. Had the heat on in my bedroom.

Saturday, December 3. It's written in *Heimdal* that people smile and are touched by Lucky Peer, but there's no steel in him. He's weak, and our age has no use for weakness, but strength. People put the book aside and say it doesn't have anything to do with us.—Oehlenschläger's *Aladdin* came along at the right time and in the fullness of its beauty. That criticism didn't depress me, but it hardened me. The weather lovely. A visit from Jonas, who honorably repaid an insignificant outlay I had made for him. At the Henriqueses' dinner party Hägg, the young Swedish composer, played the music he'd written for my poem "Never to Return." It seems to render the mood, but since he can't sing, I couldn't hear how it sounded with voice. At the theater I saw the first two acts of the *The Fussy Man.*

Sunday, December 4. At Reitzel's read a very friendly review of *Lucky Peer* in today's number of *The Illustrated News.* My mood brightened a bit. Had wanted to have the notes to the illustrated tales in the back of each volume, but now it's too late because the book will appear at the end of this week. Attended a large dinner party at Israel Melchior's and saw at the theater Bournonville's *Dance Divertissement.* In the morning I was at Miss Zahle's to read tales and stories to 130 ladies. I was somewhat nervous and my hands were shaking.

Shortly before Christmas, the first volume of a new edition of New Tales and Stories *appeared, with illustrations by Lorenz Frølich. Both it and the month-old* Lucky Peer *were well received at the sales counter and in the newspapers. On New Year's Eve, Andersen counted his blessings: "Thank You, oh Lord, for the great good You have done me this past year—great quantities of money and a new literary work."*

Andersen spent the spring of 1871 in Copenhagen "lying around on the sofa doing nothing." He was suffering from rheumatism in his back and legs, and as he wrote on April 23: "I can feel the old man in me—this is his first year. I'm not really taking good care of myself—too much good food, different wines, not enough peace and quiet." In an effort to improve his situation, he decided at the end of April to move from the Rossings's establishment, which he had found to be cold, narrow, and noisy and much too expensive. He moved into the Hotel d'Angleterre with its sweeping view of the King's New Square and the Royal Theater and felt himself a new man.

In early May, Andersen left Copenhagen to spend a month in the country, at Espe and Basnæs. He resumed writing and began working on the tale "Auntie Toothache" before returning to the city to assist in the preparations for the Melchiors' silver wedding anniversary.

Thursday, June 1 [1871]. Cold and cloudy weather. Composed little Poul's speech in verse for the Melchiors' silver wedding anniversary. Sent it with a letter to his mother, Johanne Melchior. Felt in a poetic mood and compelled to work on the story about toothache. Perhaps the 1st of June will be the day of my first visit of the year from the muse! Welcome!—Today we were going to have another meal at 4:30—it was 5:45 before Otto appeared. The day before yesterday, when his sister was invited for 4:30, he was even later. Letters from Anna Henriques, Sophie Melchior and Countess Holstein. Very cold and windy.

Friday, June 2. Sunshine and good weather. Up before 7 o'clock. Otto left at 7:30 for Frijsenborg. He was very cordial at his departure, and I was asked to come here during the hunting season (October). Sent letters to Martin Henriques and Anna Henriques. Letter to Rambusch, the Danish vice-consul in Minneapolis in America. Read this evening to Mrs. Scavenius, Baron Düring-Rosenkrantz and Øllgaard. The dog Bob was making a constant racket. I got irritated and said to Mrs. Scavenius: "It's really a shame for the poor dogs that they have to sit and listen to me read!"—Then they were at last put out of the room! Got a package containing *The Daily News* from Wednesday of last week to Wednesday of this. A letter from an American in Boston with an enclosed photograph of Retzsch's *Flight to Egypt*, which I've mentioned in *The Fairy Tale of My Life* and which the American has a painting of.

Saturday, June 3. Sunshine and better weather but cold, though. I'm still using the stove.—Sent a letter to Mrs. Melchior that I'll be coming, God willing, on Tuesday the 6th. Yesterday got a package from New York containing *Scribner's Magazine*. Today I received from London *Aunt Judy's Magazine* with the continuation of *Lucky Peer*. A letter from a gentleman in New York who sent me a couple of extremely friendly reviews of my autobiography.

Sunday, June 4. Warm, sunny weather. This morning Baron Düring-Rosenkrantz left to attend the funeral of Rosenkrantz, who died in Paris. Sent a letter to Reitzel, the bookseller, and to Robert Watt. Here for dinner today were Carl and Lucie from Borreby with their little Bertha.

Monday, June 5. Cloudy, cold weather. Yesterday and today a buzzing and burning sensation in the pulse artery in my right wrist. Bodild Holstein's birthday—sent a letter to her. Letter to the post office in Copenhagen.—Here for dinner was a young daughter of Pastor Rønne and a friend of hers from the neighboring rectory. I read a couple of tales and, for the first time, the beginning of "Auntie Toothache."

Tuesday, June 6. Last night around 1 o'clock I woke up and heard a knocking at my door. Several people who have overnighted in this room have heard this knocking—Miss Dunlop, now Mrs. Rosing, didn't dare sleep here after having heard it a few times. Rainy weather. Got somewhat wet gathering flowers and boughs for Mrs. Melchior. A letter to the postmaster in Skelskør. Around 12 o'clock Countess Schulin and Miss . . . from Holsteinborg arrived on a visit. They ate lunch here and returned home so they could still make it to Copenhagen today over Sorø. At 3 o'clock I left Basnæs (Lars, four rix-dollars; the maid, three; the coachman, one and a half.) By 4:30 I was in Korsør. There, along came Mrs. Koch with little Jørgen—they had spent a week in Odense and were now returning home. In Sorø the Misses Schulin and . . . got into my car. It was 9 o'clock before I was in Copenhagen, where Moritz Melchior came in his carriage to pick me up. At Tranquillity I met the Baronesses Bretton, who were now leaving Denmark. Bloch and wife were there. I brought with me two big bouquets for Mrs. Melchior—lilies of the valley, beech boughs, woodruff, etc. Got the two rooms facing out over the lake. Cold, foggy weather.

Wednesday, June 7. Warm sunshine. A letter from Watt and one from Louise Collin sent to Skelskør. A letter and package from the feeble-minded Miss Svendsen sent from Fredensborg. Wrote to Mrs. Scavenius, who was supposed to have come here for a visit this evening, but Mrs. Melchior was not at home. Drove out to see Johanne. Lit a fire in the stove. Very cold.

Thursday, June 8. Sunshine, cold wind. Took a streetcar into town. Had a haircut, shave. Sent the letter and package back to Miss Svendsen in Skelskør.—A letter from Hägg about the cantata. Quite a solitary dinner with Mr. and Mrs. Melchior out here at Tranquillity.

Friday, June 9. A letter from Mrs. Jette Collin in Hellebæk. Letter from the editor Franz Hirsch in Königsberg. Letter from Jonna Stampe. Clear, warm and sunny weather. Planted here in the garden the forget-me-not I received from Drewsen. Sent a letter to His Excellency Moltke-Hvitfeldt, whose birthday it is tomorrow. Autographed the Baroness Bretton's fan. Yesterday and today visited the Drewsens two times each day. Today Israel Melchior let me in on the arrangements for the celebration of the silver wedding anniversary. Thought about how to end "Auntie Toothache."

Saturday, June 10. Sunshine, but a cold wind. A letter to Mrs. Henriques. Took the streetcar to town at 9 o'clock and was back again at Tranquillity by 12 o'clock. Yesterday was the drawing of the lottery—I didn't win this time either. Dinner at home alone. Not really in a good mood. Go regularly to see the Drewsens, about twice a day. Heard from Mrs. Grove about Svend Grundtvig's unkind statement about Bjørnstjerne that now he ought to join the ballet so he can bask in the glow of the Bengal lights.[7] Stopped in at Mrs. Eckardt's. She was in the country, in Øverød, where her mother, sister and sister's husband and children are staying with her. In the afternoon a really lovely rainbow, all of it intensely colored—it was visible for over an hour in all its splendor. A letter to Mrs. Henriques at Peter's Hill.

Sunday, June 11. Lovely, warm sunshine with a cold wind. Visited the Drewsens. Spent the whole day at home, by the way, and wrote the rhymed speech the children were to deliver in conjunction with

---

7. A type of firework that burns with a brilliant colored light.

the toast at the celebration this Saturday. Just as the Melchiors were about to go for a drive after dinner, Mrs. Scavenius came and was here having tea all evening. We went for a walk in the garden and over to Rosenvænget Street. The Melchiors liked her, and she, them. It got to be 11:30 before I made it to bed.

Monday, June 12. Gray, rainy, very cold weather. Walked along Nøjsomheds Way up toward Vibenshus to get a streetcar. It was full; so went over to see the Linds and arrived with the next car in Copenhagen in the rain. Stopped in to see Miss Levison; she hasn't found an apartment yet. Called on Mrs. Scavenius. Came back home at 11:30. Now the weather is clearing up. Jette Melchior here for dinner. First proofs for the second volume of the illustrated tales (the first two signatures). It won't be published until at Christmas-time.

Tuesday, June 13. It's cloudy and cold. Melchior and wife have driven to town. I read the newspaper, down at heart. Feel like flying off and feeling really young at heart, but it's not going to happen. Dinner at the Drewsens' with Mr. and Mrs. Grove, Stella Semb from Norway (who received a picture of me) and her daughter. Mrs. Drewsen her usual self in her insistence that Carl Price had been sitting at the front table (he sat close to it and right by the biggest table, but not at it) and that Louise Lind had been sitting on the side of the table facing the windows. (That wasn't the case. She was sitting at the front table on outermost side of it—which is to say, by the head table.) When I was unwilling to concede she was right, she got excited—she didn't care at all where people had been seated; it had been such a long time ago that she didn't want to talk about it. When I got home, Israel was parked outside. He had taken a carriage from Vedbæk in order to speak with me. "The troops are restless!" he said. "They don't want to sing the cantata if it isn't printed with a "k" instead of a "c." I replied that it was very insulting to me that they wanted to have their way like this, that it was unfair to Mr. Hägg, who had composed and rehearsed the piece, that I had handed over the piece two months ago and there had been plenty of time for them to talk with me about this matter, and that it would be wrong of me to accommodate them in something unreasonable. "Well," said Israel, "both P. Hansen and Bille have said that one could indeed spell "cantata" with a "k," but that they didn't."— There was no time now to be making changes, and so I said that I wasn't going to give them the answer they deserved and that I was offended. But in order not to disrupt the celebration, they could do what they wanted, since the cantata was referred to, as he'd said, in the other tableau verses. However, I would say to everyone that it had been against my will. I was irritated all evening long. At 11:30 Hägg and Louise came home. Hägg has now moved in here.

Wednesday, June 14. Warm sunshine. Bitter, irritated, cranky. Drove to town. Lunch with Mrs. Koch. Visited Edvard at the bank. (Yesterday Jonas stopped in with a greeting from Peter Müller, who will soon be paying me a call.) Today they are all in town. Not at all happy. If only I had enough money and were younger, I'd fly away or live my life independent of everybody! They're all egoists, weak sisters—like me.

On July 25, a week after the Melchiors' anniversary celebration, Andersen left on a five-week trip to Norway—his first to that country—at the express invitation of Bjørnstjerne Bjørnson. He enjoyed the trip immensely, especially the banquet held in his honor and attended by all the foremost people in Norwegian cultural life. On his return from Norway, he stayed at Tranquillity with the Melchiors until October 23, when he moved into new lodgings in Miss Hallager's boarding house at 18 Nyhavn Canal, just off King's New Square. In his front room he placed two busts, one of himself and one of Jenny Lind.

In the spring of 1871 Andersen had been encouraged by the American ambassador to visit the United States, and that fall he received a letter from a Danish-American editor, Louis Bagger, of Washington, D.C., begging him to do the same. Horace Scudder even offered to pay his travel expenses. Andersen was flattered by the invitation, but he decided against it: "I would like to go, but I can already feel the torments of the ocean voyage and fear that I don't have the physical resources for such an undertaking. I'd rather die in Denmark" (November 15). This was not the last of the invitations to visit America—the following February the poet Longfellow also urged Andersen to make the visit.

Thursday, February 22 [1872]. Cloudy weather. Gade's birthday, but didn't pay him a call since I'm feeling so tired. Jette Collin is in bed with typhus. Theodor spoke with concern about it. Edvard has been going to the bank daily since Tuesday and is feeling well. A visit from Scharff, who showed up alone with a walking stick. It's his first visit to me here in Nyhavn, where I'm now living. Foggy, but mild.—This Tuesday I had a visit from Watt, who is home from America. He was delighted with the reception my letter obtained for him from Longfellow, who has asked him to tell me that if I were to

From the apartment in Nyhavn, May 1874

read three of my tales in America, read them in English, which I probably, with only three, could manage to rehearse, then he could assure me a whole fortune. I could earn money over there the way Dickens did, and Longfellow and my other friends would arrange everything in advance.—Dinner at the widow Mrs. Salomonsen's. She escorted me to the table. On my other side I had Mrs. Phister. All us older folks were in one dining room. The younger people in the one next to us—that's where all the fun was. In where we were, so-so. The only toast was to me (Henriques). There I met the critic Brandes, who greeted me with youthful pleasure. I didn't go over to the theater, since I was tired and indisposed from all that light, sweet food we'd eaten.

Friday, February 23. Cloudy, wet weather. Wanted to go visiting, but kept running into hindrances. I simply must call on the Gedalias; it's not right of me to put it off so long. Annoyed about what Mrs. Melchior told me—that the translator . . . had said to Harriet that they'd been wondering over at the crown prince's why I hadn't been there to pay my respects, since I hadn't come that evening to read. I've been irritated about all the people who've come and said: "You weren't at the crown prince's to read!"—I replied that I was sick, that I'd get up from my sickbed and go out there myself so they could see it was so, but that it had been stupid of me not to have written. Dinner at Mrs. Koch's. When I got home there was a letter from Westrup, the bookseller, who wrote that he thought it was his duty to bring to my attention that it said in the coming issue of *The Illustrated Children's Magazine* that I had promised the publisher to contribute something, and he enclosed the issue. I was very annoyed, since I've said to Mr. Westrup that I have and insist on having the freedom to contribute to whomever I wish. I promised something to him early on, but later I also promised Mr. Bang. Agitated, I wrote several drafts of my reply and didn't sleep well.

Saturday, February 24. Felt decrepit, tired, old, sad about myself and my present life. Wrote a letter in English and took it to the American consul Griffin's wife, along with her poems and reviews of them. The family wasn't living any more at the Hotel Phønix, but out at 33 Great King's Street. Mrs. Collin still suffering. A visit from Rigmor and Astrid Stampe to get some verses for their ball this coming Saturday. Dinner at Titular Councillor Thiele's. I was seated next to the widow Mrs. Holm and on my left had Mrs. Gottschalk, née Rosing. Left there at 8 o'clock for the scholarship meeting at the Academy. The Ancker Scholarship—Paludan-Müller and I agreed this year to give the part reserved for an author to Erik Bøgh. When I got home, there was a letter from Anton Nielsen that he was expecting to get the scholarship, that because of his work as a popular writer he was more qualified than Erik Bøgh, who was a mere exhibitionist, etc.

Sunday, February 25. Felt depressed, dissatisfied with myself. Went to the Melchiors's. From there, finally over to pay a visit to Gedalia. His wife very nice; his daughter, son and the governess quite pleas-

1872

ant. Gedalia talked to me a little too much about medals of honor—that the writer Goldschmidt indeed hadn't received a single medal here at home or from other nations. When I was leaving and shaking hands with the family, their little dog dashed up and ripped my pants, luckily down by my bootlegs so there weren't any tooth marks on my leg. Took a streetcar out to see Johanne Melchior, whose birthday it is today. I gave her the English translation of *Only a Fiddler*, the New York edition. (It's also Mrs. Madsen's birthday—she's still sick in bed after she fell on stage and jabbed herself in the groin with a key ring.) Went to see Ambassador Due and family. Presented his wife with *Lucky Peer*; read to them the first three chapters. They were extremely charming and natural. When I arrived, Admiral Bille and wife were there—how arrogant that man is! It oozes from his pores, from what he says and how he looks at you. If only I were being unfair to him!—Called on Scavenius and Moltke of Bregentved. Dinner at the Henriqueses'. Present were Berner and wife (the brother of the theater director) and little Miss Harriet Salomonsen, pretty, mature for her age, which is to say a chatterbox.

Monday, February 26. A little sunshine, somewhat cold. I'm suffering from some sort of ennui. Depressed. Sent a letter and a copy of "The Gardener and the Lord and Lady" to Scudder in New York. Bournonville's *A Fairy Tale in Pictures* was packed and sent to Bagger in Washington. Went to the printer's with the last manuscript. Went up to see Møller, the editor the *New Danish Monthly Magazine*. Dinner at the Melchiors'. At the theater saw the first act of *Amanda*. Today I wrote a verse on each section of the fan Mrs. Scavenius sent me.

Tuesday, February 27. A visit from . . . , who is leaving for Sweden. We have beautiful, bright sunshine. A ball this evening at the crown prince's. I wasn't invited. Today they began tearing down the left driveway to the old theater. Count Moltke of Bregentved's birthday. Mrs. Collin is doing better; Mrs. Madsen, worse. Took a streetcar out to the Drewsens' on Rosenvænget Street. I spoke there with Captain Lund's wife, who'd been with him in China. I was going to stop by the Linds', but the weather was too cold. At 7 o'clock took a cab home and am now sitting and reading page proofs of the tales.

Wednesday, February 28. Brought Jonna Stampe the verses her daughters had requested for their ball on Saturday. We talked about how I hadn't been invited to the crown prince's ball, and she thought some members of the inner circle had maligned me because I hadn't come to read when I'd been summoned and was ill. She thought I

375

should go out and explain it to the crown prince. It went completely against my grain to do that, since I hadn't done anything wrong except to be ill. I gladly visited those people, and no one had been warmer and spoken more warmly about those two than I. What was I supposed to apologize for? In the meantime, it has saddened me, since I'm so fond of the young royal couple. Dinner at the Ørsteds'. Stopped by the Henriqueses' for a while and from there, home to read page proofs. I am in a bad mood.

Thursday, February 29. Gray, cold wind, snow! Woke up early. It was still dark, couldn't sleep. Worked myself into a froth. Couldn't get my mind off the incomprehensible fact that they were so displeased with me at the crown prince's.—I then went out to Danneskiold-Samsøe's to bring his wife the fan she had asked me to write verses on. Neither the count nor the countess was at home. Went with the other fan I had promised the young Mrs. Scavenius. She wasn't dressed. Went to the Collins'—Mrs. Collin is feeling better. I arrived home tired and listless, but immediately went in a strangely agitated state back out to see Danneskiold-Samsøe, who received me politely but coldly. Trap was with the crown prince, so I couldn't go in. He promised to say I had been there. When I left, I was very relieved. At home I fell asleep in the chair from exhaustion. Countess Holstein wasn't at home, either. Dinner at the Melchiors'. Bille was there—it was precisely the day he'd ended publication of *The Daily*. Mr. Melchior proposed a toast to him, an expression of appreciation for the work he had done in times past and good wishes for the new and different tasks he would be embarking upon. Bille gave his thanks for the toast and ended by saying he knew that no one wanted him to close here with a mere thanks but would rather have him propose a new toast, and it was addressed to one of the old writers who had far more significance for literature than all the recent emphasis on Taine, etc.—he was referring to Brandes—who were put above what we still had. He spoke so warmly and flatteringly about me that I became agitated, and just as we got up from the table, Mrs. Melchior took me into a side room and gave me a glass of cold water. Later, when I was talking with Bille, he said that I should go out to the crown prince's anyway—it was a matter of courtesy and customary to thank them because they'd wanted me to read for them and I was surely fond of the young royal couple. I decided right away to go out there tomorrow. It was raining cats and dogs when I had to leave at 9 o'clock to go to see the Russian ambassador. I wanted to stay at home but pulled myself together and went there and said at once that I wasn't well, that I would be leaving very soon but had felt compelled to come to thank them for the friendly invitation. Baron Mohrenheim thanked me very cordially and amiably for coming, showed me around in their rooms. I stayed there until the crown prince and crown princess had arrived. I was reluctant to meet them on the stairs. It got to be about 10 o'clock. I talked with Hall, Prince Hans, Trap, who is leaving for Rome this week and will be seeing the Prince of Wales and the royal family, as well. There was music by Balduin Dahl. When I left, the young Mrs. Scavenius offered me her carriage to get home, but I walked. A letter to Mrs. Scavenius at Basnæs.

Friday, March 1. Cloudy weather. Took a streetcar out to Frederik Street and then walked to the crown prince's palace. It was 10:30. My legs were tired, and I was sore in all my limbs. The footman admitted me at once to see Holten and right after that to see the crown prince. He extended his hand to me, asked me to be seated, and we talked for three quarters of an hour. He related how the little prince had gotten sixteen teeth without any discomfort. We talked about Watt in America, about Longfellow, about the royal family in Greece, about the tearing down of the theater, etc. Then took a streetcar up to the Melchiors' and ate lunch. When I got home, I received a visit from Miss Recke, who has come from Funen to visit her sick mother and will be staying here until her mother's birthday on the 18th of March. Called on H. P. Holst and returned his book to him. Visited the Bournonvilles, to whom I read "The Comet," "The Most Incredible Thing" and "Sunshine Stories." They were very delighted. Dinner at Mrs. Koch's. Henny showed me some of the things from China he'd brought back with him. Paid a visit to the Henriqueses'. Saw the second act of *By Right of Conquest,* but was tired and didn't get out of it what I'd wanted—the vocal numbers and the dancing. This evening is incidentally the first time I've been to the theater since they started tearing down the foundry.[8] The whole left side, where I used to sit, is as if paralyzed—all the exits there are locked. An invitation from our Minister of Foreign Affairs for Friday, the 8th.

Saturday, March 2. Spring weather. Lots of people out for a stroll. Lunch and dinner at the Henriqueses'. Paid a visit to Mrs. Collin,

8. The foundry was built in 1671 on the King's New Square for production of bells, cannons, and so forth. In 1773 the building became a cadet academy, from 1830 to 1866 a military college, and in 1872 it was torn down to make room for the new Royal Theater.

who is feeling better but bedridden. Was out at the Stampes' to excuse myself from their ball this evening. They were all abustle there—rugs on the stairs, flowers and greenery all around. Took a streetcar to Mrs. Koch's and made my excuses concerning dinner on Friday. At the theater, the first two acts of *The Fussy Man*. The acting wasn't especially good. Rosenkilde was awfully dull. When I got home, I got one of my nervous asthmatic attacks. Letter from an American authoress.

Sunday, March 3. Listless and not well this morning. Pains in my knees and across my loins. Didn't dare go to town; first a little walk all the way down to the harbor. It was only gradually that I began to feel any better. I didn't dare cross the square, but made my way along the buildings along Tordenskjold Street to where Heiberg Street had been blocked off. I had to make a detour along Holberg Street. Lunch at the Melchiors'. Paid a visit to the Collins and after that to Scharff. Warm sunshine all morning; cloudy and cold in the afternoon. Dinner at the Henriqueses' with the Price sisters and the Nerudas. At the theater, the opera *The Barber of Seville*.

Monday, March 4. Cloudy weather. Feel quite well. Visits to Miss Jette Melchior, the Collins and the Swedish-Norwegian ambassador, as well as to our foreign minister, Baron Rosenørn-Lehn. Dinner at the Melchiors'. When I left there, I felt tired and gave up going to the Casino to see Brossbøl's new play *Tordenskjold in Marstrand*. Went home. From Collin, an accounting of my assets—19,824 rix-dollars and 30 shillings. That's really something. I get 1,000 rix-dollars per year.

Tuesday, March 5. Clear, sunny air, quite springlike and warm. Strolled around in the sunshine. Took a streetcar out to the Linds', where I found only Harald at home with Ingeborg. They must certainly be engaged. Walked around in the Drewsens' garden, which is in bloom—yellow and white flowers (not crocuses), the ferns really fresh and green. Valdemar Drewsen from Norway is here; on the path his dog and both Theodor's and Viggo's dogs were running all over me, and again at the table I was bothered by Viggo's dog. Theodor thought it funny; I didn't and said it was so unusual where I was a guest that dogs were around during meals. Theodor and Valdemar dominated the conversation at the table—about dogs and snipes. It was extremely boring. I asked Mrs. Drewsen if I might get up from the table and was happy to leave and take a streetcar to the theater, where I saw *A Course of Therapy* by Hertz. This morning, when I came to the corner of East Street and Willow Lane, I saw two shabbily dressed women talking to a red-faced, shabbily dressed, fat man. The man ran over toward me and said: "Father is dead!" I thought it a little strange and said: "I don't know who you are!" "Father died yesterday in Rome!" he said. "I'm Hauch." It was William, the eldest of the author Hauch's sons. So there's one less in the ranks of old authors! I dare say he liked me and became my friend. Titular Privy Councillor Jonas Collin always denied it and thought I was naive. He's now dust and ashes, dead, extinguished, burned out like a light which is no more! My Lord God, can You let us vanish completely? I'm afraid of that, and I've gotten too clever— and unhappy.

On March 30, four days before his birthday, Andersen saw the publication of the first installment of the third series of New Tales and Stories, *containing thirteen tales and stories. A week later, he left on a nine-week tour of Vienna, Venice, and Munich with the young playwright William Bloch as traveling companion. On June 13, the opening day of the Nordic Industrial Exhibition, he returned to Copenhagen and went to stay with the Melchiors at Tranquillity.*

Friday, June 28. Awoke at 2:30 and looked out the window—the sea was smooth as glass. Like that all night long, so Marcus will have a smooth crossing. I wanted to stay home today, but Mr. Melchior came a little before 9 o'clock and said the queen and Thyra, just back from Greece, would at 9:30 be going ashore at the square by Garrison Church. I then hurried to the streetcar. A silly little girl came and wanted me to give her a few shillings and then asked whether I was "talking to myself." She made me feel uncomfortable. Reached the square by Garrison Church a few minutes before the royal family arrived. There were lots of people and fluttering flags. Saw the queen and Thyra, but wasn't noticed by them. The king, on the other hand, saw me and waved to me.—In . . .'s shop I met a Danish man from America who began the conversation with: "Well, I know you. I read you and am glad when I see your name in the newspapers over there." On King's New Square an unknown young woman came and thanked me for writing *Lucky Peer.* She was from Svendborg. Right at Broad Street Pastor Boye from Norway spoke to me.—Paid a visit to the Linds on Strand Way on my way home. On Rosenvænget Street I ran into the young Bournonville with his fiancée and her father, the capable Schleswigian Ahlmann. He hadn't walked along Rosenvænget Street before. I showed them around a little and then let them out by the strand, near Mrs. Heiberg's house. Called on the Beutners and was given a lovely rose, which I gave to Anna Melchior.

Saturday, June 29. Showers. Didn't go to town. The big leaves of the burdock I put in the ground yesterday are hanging as if they were the tattered remnants of green quarantine flags. Mrs. Drewsen isn't able to sleep, constantly taking opium. She is continually plagued by pains in her abdomen and some kind of intestinal infection that causes her tongue to be covered with sores.—I've been working on "Auntie Toothache" all day, so that I'm really tired. Read to the Melchiors some poems by Klaus Groth and, in the evening, the tale "The Garden of Paradise."

Sunday, June 30. Showers. Mrs. Drewsen still sick. Moses was here for lunch. (My impression of him.) Sent a letter to Hägg in London.—When I got up this morning, I had a nosebleed. That hasn't happened in many, many years. Feeling old and weary! God, give me an idea! Give me something I can do! It's awful to be idle.—The family went out to see Johanne in the evening. Mrs. Melchior's ailing brother came here and visited with me, Anna and Harriet. +

Monday, July 1. Dissatisfied with myself. My feeling of youthfulness is evaporating. I look forward to nothing. I'm irritable, discontented and lazy. If I could just lie down and sleep all the time. This morning I was going to go to town, but felt tired, in a bored frame of mind. Went anyway to Strand Way, where there was nary a streetcar to be seen. Went into the barber's, and just as I was finished it came, but I let it go, trudged home depressed and *weary of life*. An evening visit from W. Bloch and N. Bøgh.

Tuesday, July 2. Took a streetcar to town. The actress Miss Jensen was on it, and I talked with her. Went out to the exhibition. There weren't many people there and no excitement. Left for home in less than an hour. Later in the afternoon, when Mrs. Melchior and Anna accompanied Johanne to Elysium, I rode to Peter's Hill and paid a visit to Mrs. Henriques. Read the first act of *The White Roses*, which I received yesterday from the two authors.

Wednesday, July 3. A letter from Mrs. Scavenius and Miss Bernard. Lovely weather still. Stayed at home today.

Thursday, July 4. A letter from Lord-in-Waiting Tillisch. Rode into town and picked up several loose pieces of paper on which I've written drafts of "Auntie Toothache." Came home and worked on it diligently—organized it, gave it more clarity and unity. Mrs. Schousboe and her small son Hermann have moved in here at Tranquillity.

They've arrived from Sweden. My mood won't really settle down. (To live or not to live, that is the question!)

Friday, July 5. Very hot. For the first time had my light summer trousers on all day. Worked on "Auntie Toothache" from morning to evening. Wound it up, but feel tired. Today we had a visit from Mrs. Mannheimer, née Meyer. She had to leave again before 5 o'clock, so we had dinner at 4 o'clock with no appetite, etc.

Saturday, July 6. Hot like yesterday. Rode into town lightly clad. Was in the windmill on the ramparts and saw the pneumatic chamber where Anna sits in compressed air. The Industrial Exhibition was only open to the royal family. The queen and the queen dowager were there for the first time. Took the streetcar home at 12 o'clock and now have all the rest of the day been alone at home writing "The First Ride on the Streetcar." Finished reading *The White Roses.*

Sunday, July 7. Still lovely, hot weather. A big dinner party for a number of the members of the Nordic Economic Conference and the Exhibition Committee. I was seated between Sohlman, the Swedish editor, and the Norwegian Meinich. Melchior started off with several speeches; then asked me to propose a toast to Ploug as a member of the Economic Conference. I did so, and then Count Sponneck proposed a toast to me, who wasn't a Scandinavian, but belonged to the entire world. I expressed my thanks, but called attention to the fact that I had nonetheless been the first here in Denmark to write a Scandinavian song, "I am a Scandinavian!"—The American ambassador proposed in English a toast to me and my importance in America as the poet of Scandinavia. Privy Councillor David gave a speech for Mrs. Melchior. (Later I took him up into the tower, where he stayed for a long time, so I brought him my travel blanket so that he wouldn't catch a cold.) The waters of Øresund lay clear and shining. It was an especially lovely evening. Present were the Norwegian Faye, Daa from Bergen, Brock, Klein, the architect, and Professor Heinrich Hansen.

Monday, July 8. The heat continues. There was to be a meeting at 12 o'clock at Titular Councillor Suhr's concerning the Ørsted monument. Tillisch and I arrived first, then Suhr and Jacobsen, the brewer, last. There were more requests again for money from Jerichau, who has utterly neglected to put his work on display at the Industrial Exhibition, where it would then have been seen by people, and we could have used it for publicity and requested contributions. Went to the exhibition, where it was terribly hot in the main building and stank from the manufacturing of chocolate.—Saw Hansen's photograph of me. It has been hung with Høedt's above that of King Georg of Greece and on either side of Mrs. Melchior's. Down in the garden, ran into Bishop Engelstoft. Count Steen Lewenhaupt from Malmö asked me to visit him when I was over there. Sent a letter with Erik Bøgh's letter, on which there is now a spot, out to Paludan-Müller in Fredensborg. Early in the evening Moritz Melchior came home from Bernstorff Castle, where he had been to dinner with the king, who had talked a lot to him about me. Lady-in-Waiting Miss Reventlow had said: "Andersen is my passion!" and gave Melchior permission to repeat it to me.

Tuesday, July 9. Very hot. Almost can't walk to Rosenvænget Street because of the heat of the sun. Visited Mrs. Drewsen and read to her "Auntie Toothache." The day before yesterday Einar arrived in Vordingborg from Norway and is happy there.[9]—Read "Auntie Toothache" to Thorald Læssøe. Sent a letter to Mrs. Scavenius in Wildbad in Württemberg. Letter from Eckardt in Ems. Portrait photograph from an American lady in Canada.

Wednesday, July 10. Very hot. Took the streetcar to town. Rode with Wanscher, who said that Prior, the merchant, had been in Oringe near Vordingborg, just like Einar. Paid a visit to Mrs. Heiberg, who talked about the young poet Recke. He called on her in his military uniform and first off looked unimpressive, but she thought he looked more interesting as time passed. Sent a letter to Mrs. Collin in Hellebæk.

Thursday, July 11. Pouring rain and gray weather until late in the day, when it also got very hot again. After lunch young Mr. Marcus left for home. He insisted he'd seen Mrs. Heiberg in a comedy two years ago (which I don't believe) and couldn't remember anything about her except she was slender, had short skirts and spit curls. I was irritated by his assertion. Peter Hansen (Cabiro) was here for dinner. How fat he's getting! William Bloch, the Jøhnkes and Mrs. Lund. I read to them "Auntie Toothache," which is now finished and well-rounded. I've been writing out a fair copy of it all day. Later Nicolai Bøgh came.

Friday, July 12. Lovely, warm weather. Thought a lot last night about the story about the woodcutter and his wife and got the idea of using it. Therefore stayed at home all day working diligently. Likewise, finished the fair copy of "Auntie Toothache." Later in the day there were probably 300 sailboats to be seen from the win-

---

9. Here Andersen refers to Oringe Mental Hospital near Vordingborg.

dow.—Read to Privy Councillor Drewsen "Auntie Toothache," which he was delighted with and thought quite brilliant.—At noon ate in the garden (likewise yesterday evening).

Saturday, July 13. Anna rode into town to her pneumatic chamber. I rode with her and was back here again by lunch. Worked all day on "The Book of Fairy Tales." Rode out to Elysium and the Teglgaard House.

Sunday, July 14. Rainy weather. Finished "The Book of Fairy Tales," which I worked on all day, and felt tired. Read it to the Melchiors.— At home all day. Harriet in the forest and didn't get home before the violent thunderstorm that broke as I went into my room for the evening.—Big party. Mrs. Simonsen here from London, etc.

Monday, July 15. Lightning struck the four-foot-thick wall by School Hill near Klampenborg, where Bruun is building a house. A fortyfour foot section of the wall collapsed onto the roadway. There were six to eight inches of rainwater covering the railroad tracks.—I stayed at home in this cold weather. Worked on "The Flea and the Professor." Late in the day, received a letter from Countess Holstein about having dinner there with the Count Lewenhaupts from Sweden, but I'd promised Jonas Collin to stay home at Tranquillity after 7 o'clock, when he was coming with a young Swede Dr. Stolpe, who had once stayed with the Collins while on a student visit. Stolpe sang beautifully for us.

Wednesday, July 17. This morning they said the little deer that had been shut up had gotten out. It had worked a slat loose and squeezed out, but had gotten a bloody cut down to the cheek bone. It was probably far away by now—early this morning somebody had seen it walking in the garden; dogs had been barking, etc. Later on it came back again and ate strawberries out of Mrs. Melchior's hand. I saw it later. Thea offered it milk, which it drank and then ran. In the evening I read to Titular Privy Councillor Drewsen and family "The Book of Fairy Tales." He was very appreciative. At home all day. A letter from Hägg in London.

Tuesday, July 16. Worked on the fair copy of "The Book of Fairy Tales." Finished "The Flea and the Professor."—(N.B. Got mixed up when writing this down.)

Thursday, July 18. Very strong wind and some rain. Yesterday, fifty degrees; today, fifty-three degrees; and just recently we had over sixty-eight degrees. Took the streetcar to town, but was back out here again for lunch. Finished the fair copy of "The Book of Fairy Tales."—Found a full house here at home—Anna and Fernanda

Henriques. Their mother and father hadn't come—they'd had a visit from "Høed-Mørk-Magnus."[10] Dr. Stolpe sang beautifully. I read "The Book of Fairy Tales" for them.

Friday, July 19. Cold weather—the last two days, only fifty degrees. Read "The Flea and the Professor" for Privy Councillor Drewsen. In it I have the professor shoot his wife. He said the entire story resembled something he'd experienced. A Miss Møller had married a similar sideshow performer and had sat selling tickets at the entrance, and he had been careless and shot his wife. Drewsen had known her brother; he was a minister. It would certainly upset her family to read my tale. I changed it then so that *she* was put in the drawer and disappeared. This morning I ran into the painter Frølich at Læssøe's. He said he hadn't gotten any books from Reitzel for him to illustrate, let alone several, as Reitzel had constantly been assuring me. I then gave him a copy of "The Wood Nymph," etc., and read to him the last three tales, including "Auntie Toothache," which really fascinated him. I felt like reading these to Mrs. Heiberg, but have been on my way to see her several times now and turned back. I don't really believe what she says. She is so hard on most people—I suspect she isn't kind to me when my back is turned.

Andersen spent most of the summer and early autumn staying with the Melchiors at Tranquillity. During the first week of November, however, he fell seriously ill, exhibiting a variety of symptoms—severe abdominal pains, tarry stools, nausea, and alternating bouts of constipation and diarrhea. His doctor, Theodor Collin, first made a diagnosis of bleeding hemorrhoids, but a few days later he advised Andersen to move back into his rooms in Copenhagen because of a "stomach illness" that was making the rounds in the suburbs where the Melchiors lived. Andersen was dissatisfied with Collin's treatment, finding him cold and unsympathetic, and asked Dr. Emil Hornemann for a second opinion. Both doctors saw to the patient during his illness, which began to subside during the Christmas holidays.

Two weeks after the onset of his illness, Andersen read in the paper that his comedy More Than Pearls and Gold *would have its one hundredth performance on November 18, with a special prologue dedicated to its author, and he was very upset that he couldn't be there. Indeed, Dr. Collin advised against his going, but Dr. Hornemann thought it might do him good and offered to accompany him in case there was need for him. Andersen*

10. Unclear reference. Perhaps Andersen refers to the actor and stage director Frederik Ludvig Høedt (1820–85) or Consul Johannes Magnus Mørk (1827–89), member of the city council of Århus (see index).

accepted his kind offer and, leaning on Dr. Hornemann and William Bloch, managed to attend the performance. Five days later, the second installment of the third series of New Tales and Stories *was published and enthusiastically received by critics and reading public alike. It was to be Andersen's last work.*

The Last Years
1873–75

A LTHOUGH HIS CONDITION IMPROVED *after the New Year of 1873, Andersen never regained his health and he continued to suffer severe attacks like the one in November 1872. On his good days, he would go for a drive in the carriage sent by Mrs. Melchior and eat dinner at the home of one or another of his close friends, as he had always done. Because of his general weakness and shortness of breath, however, he seldom went out without someone to accompany him, such as the attentive Nicolai Bøgh or one of the university students—Erik Oksen or Matthias Weber—living on the floor above. On his bad days, he was confined to his rooms, often choosing to lie on a comfortable couch in his study and dining on food sent to him by Mrs. Melchior.*

Throughout the winter of 1873, Andersen was troubled by his teeth—his last four real ones were loose and painful and had to be extracted, and then his new dentures did not fit properly. Despite these additional discomforts and the insomnia caused in part by a persistent phlegmy cough, he was nonetheless determined to follow his doctors' advice to take the cure at a spa. After all, travel had always been his best restorative.

Sunday, January 19 [1873]. Wind and rain. Regrets sent that the weather was too bad for a drive. A visit from the sculptor Jerichau. Dr. Voss came at about 3 o'clock and pulled out my last tooth. It was anesthetized, but I could still clearly feel the wrenching. He stayed with me for a good half hour. I was lighthearted at the thought that I was now rid of all my teeth, but not quite as jubilant as the other day, when he extracted the first of the four loose ones. Well, now I am completely toothless. (On Sunday, the 19th of January, 1873, I lost the last one. When was it I lost the first one? Wasn't it done at school in Slagelse by Dr. Hundrup?) The two young students from Odense and from the Duchy of Schleswig were down to visit me this morning. Fernanda Henriques and her brother Robert have also been here today. Dr. Collin comes here *daily*. When I probe my gums, I can feel that I still have the bony protuberance on my jaw that I discovered the other day right under my last tooth. Now

I'm worried about any new occurrences and operations. A visit from Henriques and Consul Mørk. Edvard Collin and wife came between 8 o'clock and 9 and stayed for about an hour. It cheered me up. Before bedtime, when I spoke to Miss Hallager about fetching a trunk down from the storeroom so I could go through various things in it, she answered that I had given Miss Bang permission to sleep there and that all her things had been moved in. It seemed strange to me that the room was put to that sort of use when it was mine. And when I went to bed, I couldn't get my mind off it—was it Miss Hallager's intention that I should pay for the room each month even though someone else was using it? I didn't get to sleep before around 4 or 5 o'clock and felt unwell.

Monday, January 20. As soon as I got up, I got hold of Miss Hallager, and when I asked for an explanation concerning this arrangement with the room, she admitted that little Thora had been sick with the measles and had therefore been put in Miss Bang's room. They'd been, along with Mrs. Melchior and Mrs. Collin, in agreement about keeping me in the dark about the illness, which I'm very upset about now, because people are saying that Zeuthen-Schulin has died of it within the last few days. The bony lump on my jaw also has me worried. Dr. Collin and Hornemann have been reassuring me with regard to that. I wrote a letter about it to Dr. Voss.— Lovely, sunny weather, but Mrs. Melchior didn't arrive until after 1:30. (Charlotte and Poul were along.) We drove to Tranquillity, where the maid was outside dusting the furniture. I walked in the garden for several minutes. Then it began to rain. I had to go inside and then home. A visit from Dr. Hornemann and a little before that, from the nursing sister, Miss Anna Buch, who thanked me for the books I'd given her.—Felt tired and sleepy.—This evening Henriques failed to visit me for the first time during my illness because his wife is sick in bed. The kitchen maid came and brought me the message. Moritz Melchior, on the other hand, came at about 9 o'clock and stayed for half an hour. I'm nauseated, besides, and dreading a sleepless night.

Tuesday, January 21. A visit this morning from the writer Munch, who arrived with Louise Melchior's fan on which he's written some verses. Then Mr. Eckardt came and after that, Privy Councillor Drewsen, who talked about the many flowers he had already blooming out in the open air. Afterward I rode with Harriet Melchior out to see Mrs. Drewsen, where there were lots of people: Miss Bielke, Mrs. Lind and Agnethe, Miss Thoresen, who is now staying there at the house. The sun was shining in the garden, where there's a dwarf Japanese apple tree in bloom. We drove home through West Gate. Before I left home, the poet Mr. Recke arrived and delivered a copy of his work, but didn't want to come in. He said he didn't have time to Miss Hallager, whom he'd impressed as quite a briskly confident kind of fellow. The inscription to me on the book is as thin as it can be. A visit from Dr. Voss, who reassured me with regard to the bony lump on my jaw. Got Baedeker's *Switzerland*. It did away with my desire to visit the spa Tarasp, which Hornemann has recommended. The climate there is like in Finland or northern Sweden. You have to wear winter clothes, and snow can come at any time during the summer.—This evening he came here with the student Weber, and we conversed a little. I'm in a very depressed mood, besides, with all this tedious sitting around inside, and I don't feel, moreover, that I'm really getting any better. (Before dinner-time, a visit from Mrs. Koch.)

Wednesday, January 22. Lovely, sunny weather. Last night when I'd gone to bed and was falling asleep, I noticed the night lamp was burning more dimly, and at last there was only the glowing-red wick left. I got up and extinguished it, but it was so early in the night that I rang, and Miss Hallager got up and came in with a fresh, lighted wick. It was only 12:30.—This morning Hornemann didn't come (not this evening either), and I really want to talk to him about the spa Tarasp in Graubünden. He has recommended it, but I can see from Baedeker that it has a climate like Finland's, that you have to wear winter clothes and that there is rain and snow. That is, indeed, not at all for me, who has a cough and catches cold so easily.—A visit from Miss Brandis. Letter from Mrs. Scavenius. Mrs. Melchior didn't arrive with the carriage today until after 2:45. In an hour I hurried home to meet Hornemann, but he hadn't been there and didn't come. After eating dinner while it was still light, a visit from Scharff and, later, Jonas Collin. A little earlier Countess Holstein came with Bodild to say goodbye to me. Her young daughter is to be married at Holsteinborg on the 1st of February and will leave for Altona that evening. When we parted, I was agitated and burst into tears. Henriques didn't come in the evening—it's the first time during my illness that he has failed to come without letting me know. The evening slow, my spirits low.

Thursday, January 23. Beautiful sunshine. Looked forward to getting out for a drive. Then I got a letter from Mrs. Melchior that the coachman had said the horses were overexerted and they had to

Stork and dancer (papercut made for Axelline Lund in the 1860s)

have a rest today, and so the carriage wouldn't be coming. This is the only carriage that's warm and comfortable for me. I always have a companion when I'm in it. So I'll have to stay at home, since no other carriage is comfortable enough for me. The letter announced next that they were giving a dinner party and so the kitchen maid couldn't bring me my food today, since I ate much earlier. I had to let Miss Hallager take care of it. Everything depressed me. I didn't expect to see any of the Melchiors today, although Moritz Melchior came with Thea after lunch and a little later Mrs. Melchior came. My mood picked up. Sent a letter to Scudder in New York.—Spoke with Professor Hornemann and gave up going to the spa Tarasp, which I'm afraid is too cold for me and too far from all the railways. He checked my backbone, but didn't find any weakness in it. After dinner, a visit from Henriques, Miss Jette Melchior (who said she had plenty of room for all my things this summer). Then Eckardt came and after that, Oksen and Weber, the students who have the rooms above me. I was tired and soon had to send them away. Afraid of not being able to sleep at night. In bed at 11:30.

Friday, January 24. The weather cloudy. Drove with Mrs. Melchior out to Tranquillity and walked for almost a half hour. It was nearly 3:30 when I got home. Then received a visit from Mrs. Lund. Afterward Paludan-Müller came to talk with me about the Ancker Scholarship, and we agreed to give it to Anton Nielsen this year. In the evening, a visit from Titular Councillor E. Collin and wife. She stayed and had tea with me. I slept badly last night. It got to be around 4 o'clock before I got any kind of rest, I think. I was terribly impatient and even though I thought about the agonies that can torment a sick person during the night and how I should be glad to escape with just insomnia, I was upset and tired of life—it seemed to me that now I was indeed finished, and how little have I then accomplished!—Then, in the early morning, a letter came from western America. I was afraid to read it, expecting to find something in it that might bother me, but quite the opposite! It was like a sign that I, with the help of God, had accomplished something! A young compatriot who, according to what he wrote, had cast shame on his whole family because of a youthful folly. He had been over there for three years and had a job with the telegraph company, but this Christmas he had been especially homesick for Denmark and his parents. He had recently been reading my story "The Comet" and had also thought about the past and the future. My writings were an inspiration and comfort to him. He thanked me and asked for a letter from me.

Except for drives in the Melchior carriage, Andersen was housebound and unable to make his usual round of social calls. His friends and acquaintances had to come to him—even the royal family paid him several visits to show him their concern. On April 12, he moved out of his rooms in Nyhavn and took his first walk of the year to the Melchiors' city residence on Højbro Square. Two days later he and Nicolai Bøgh left on a fourteen-week trip that would take them to the spa Glion in Switzerland for a whey-cure. On their way there, they followed Dr. Hornemann's advice and stopped in Berne to seek a consultation with Dr. Henri Dor, who first thought the problem was with Andersen's lungs but found nothing and then decided he was afflicted with "excessive excitability." Dor's prescription was for quiet, hearty food, and good wine.

Exhausted from the trip, Andersen returned to Copenhagen on July 28 and was met at the station by the Melchiors, at whose country home he was a guest until new accommodations in the city could be found for him. Unfortunately, he was unsuccessful in locating a suitable place and moved on September 9 back into his "old sickroom" in the boarding house in Nyhavn. It was now managed by Miss Ballin, who proved to be a better landlady than Miss Hallager, and Andersen soon felt at home.

Wednesday, October 1. Mr. Moritz Melchior brought me the French translation of my letter to Mr. Grégoire in Paris. At 11:30 Mathilde Ørsted came with old Mrs. Ørsted. They both thought my rooms very comfortable, poetic and lovely. I had wine, cakes and grapes served. They stayed over half an hour and seemed to enjoy themselves. I was deeply moved to see the old lady. We talked about Ørsted, and tears came to my eyes when it was said that people abroad often mentioned my name in conjunction with his. Afterward I received a visit from Dr. Collin and after him, from Mrs. Melchior, who'd brought the carriage and wanted to take me out for drive, but I didn't feel like it. Paid Miss Ballin forty rix-dollars for the rent for October. Tired and lazy, unproductive. The day frittered away.

Thursday, October 2. Today, like yesterday. Sick and tired. Rainy weather. Home again today. Paid little Emilius his monthly salary in advance—two rix-dollars. A letter to Frølich and one to Reitzel. A visit from Collin-Lund, who brought me a second-hand greeting from Jenny Lind, who'd been staying with her husband and children at Lake Zug three weeks ago. Spent the evening reading several back issues of H. P. Holst's *For Romanticism and History*. Received from London the monthly issue of *Aunt Judy's Magazine*, which is sent to me punctiliously.

Friday, October 3. Sunny weather. Sent letter to Grégoire in Paris along with a package containing my biography and picture. A letter to Mrs. Collin, who has, I assume, moved back to town with her husband yesterday or today. Drove in an open cab out to Tranquillity, but there was no one at home. A visit, when I got home, from Theodor Reitzel, the bookseller. This evening a Norwegian came who introduced himself as a nephew of Welhaven, my childhood teacher in Odense. He wanted to borrow ten rix-dollars. I wasn't sure whether it was true or whether I was only being hoodwinked. I referred him to Titular Councillor E. Collin, as the person who has assumed responsibility for my financial affairs during my illness. When he had left, I was somewhat upset and wrote a long letter about this to Collin, about how I was reluctant to lend him money, but would probably give him one or two rix-dollars. Before it was sent off, Collin himself arrived. He and his wife moved back into town yesterday evening.

Saturday, October 4. Bad weather—rain and drizzle. A visit from Dr. Collin, later from Professor Hornemann. Sent a letter to Mrs. Scavenius, whose birthday it is tomorrow. Later in the afternoon Miss Sophie Melchior came; gave her the edition of my tales illustrated by Pedersen. In the morning Privy Councillor Drewsen arrived here dripping wet. Martin Henriques was the last to come.

Sunday, October 5. A letter from Mrs. Melchior about coming to Tranquillity for lunch, but I couldn't. I was expecting the artist Frølich. He came and we discussed in particular the drawings for "Godfather's Picture Book." I wanted one for each of its pages. A visit from Jonas Collin, to whom I assigned the transfer to Titular Councillor Suhr of the letter signed "S. T." containing twenty-five rix-dollars, which had been sent to me the other day for the H. C. Ørsted Monument. Dinner at the Henriqueses', who have now moved back to town. Lund, the musician, and Juliette and Sophie Price were there. At 6:30 I drove home, but had trouble going up the stairs— extremely tired in my legs and short of breath to boot. A letter to Countess Frijs.

Monday, October 6. Plagued today by tiredness and shortness of breath. In addition, my bowels are rather loose. Unsure about whether I can make it up the Melchiors' stair to watch from their windows the unveiling of the monument for Frederik VII today at 2 o'clock.— A letter from Mrs. Scavenius that Otto is engaged to Countess Scheel of Gammel Estrup.—Wrote a letter right away, just a few words, to Mrs. Scavenius promising to write soon to Otto. A visit from Mr. Fugl, who wanted to get something I'd written in order to identify himself to Mr. Poles, who is Wilkie Collins' agent. Mr. Fugl wished to have part of this in manuscript form so it could be translated. I don't know this "Fugl," and Mr. Poles I rebuffed once this winter, when he wrote to me himself about publishing the letters of Fredrika Bremer. I contrived for the time being to put off doing anything, but was very upset. I wanted so much to go to the Melchiors', but Miss Ballin advised me not to go out. She thought I was too weak to go. It was a hard struggle for me, but then I gave it up and sent a messenger with a letter to Mrs. Melchior that I wasn't coming. When he was gone, Harriet and Anna came with the carriage to fetch me. It was a great temptation, and I was in tears having to give it up. Tomorrow I'll probably feel worse—it's all downhill.—At 4 o'clock, when I'd eaten half of my meal, Mrs. Melchior arrived full of excitement about the celebration. She stayed until 5 o'clock. Mrs. Collin came early in the evening. I got started on my plaint about how old Collin could often be so harsh and exasperated with me. She agreed with me, but in addition reminded me graciously of all the kindness and friendship the old man had shown me. A letter from Miss Brandis asking me to write a few words to Topsøe about accepting her novel for serialization in *The Daily*.

Tuesday, October 7. A visit from Nicolai Bøgh; after that, from Miss Jette Melchior. Then Carl Reitzel came and finally the writer Bauditz with some lovely roses for me. In the meantime, Mrs. Melchior had sent more flowers to dress up my rooms. Last night I slept from 11 o'clock to almost 9 o'clock with only five interruptions. I felt quite a bit stronger, but I'm weak in the legs, and when I walk from room to room, I get short of breath. I didn't make it outside today either. Sat alone all evening.

Wednesday, October 8. Lovely weather. Legs heavy, short of breath, anxious thoughts about my livelihood if I live for another ten years or lose the money I've saved. Everything is more expensive now; my requirements are greater; I get older and older and am so weak now—what will happen if I lose my small capital! At 2 o'clock I rode out to Tranquillity. On the avenue by the square, I met Miss Anna and Louise on a stroll. They then rode with me home, where Mrs. Melchior proved to be out (in Copenhagen). So Mrs. Trier drove home with me and saw my apartment. Mrs. Koch had been here while I was out. At about 6 o'clock, after I'd eaten my dinner and lain down for a rest, Mr. and Mrs. Melchior came. I was awakened and felt not at all well when they had left again! There's a heaviness and tiredness weighing upon me. I had tea with milk for my evening repast and felt drowsy and unwell. Took Hoffman's anodyne and went to bed before 10 o'clock, but sleep wouldn't come right away and the night was a restless one.

Thursday, October 9. Cloudy, wet weather. No desire to go out. Feeling better than yesterday, but drowsy right after lunch. Wrote a letter to Dr. Hornemann, whom I haven't seen for a week as of tomorrow. The last time he was here was on Friday. Theodor Collin has been out at the Stampes' hunting all week. Received a letter from Countess Frijs on the occasion of Clara's wedding this past Tuesday.—Hornemann arrived just as the letter was sent off. He has more confidence concerning me than I have. A visit this evening from Titular Councillor E. Collin, likewise from Martin Henriques with his youngest son.

Friday, October 10. For my lunch Mrs. Melchior sent me some morsels of the "beast" that was devoured yesterday at Tranquillity—a gift to them from Moltke-Hvitfeldt. Wrote a letter to the editor Topsøe recommending he accept Miss Brandis' newest story for serialization in *The Daily*. Rode over to Mrs. Koch's. Henny is a captain now. Young Mrs. Koch had dinner with us after her confinement. Peter Koch drove home with me. At every other step on the stairs I rested and thus reached my sitting room less short of breath than usual.

Saturday, October 11. Cloudy, rainy weather. My feet—especially the left one—are quite swollen. I've been at home all day. Mrs. Melchior paid me a visit. Right after that my physician, Dr. Hornemann, came. He reassured me about my legs. This evening, after I'd bought some cake and wine thinking that Mrs. Henriques might possibly come, I received a visit, not from her, but from her oldest daughter, Anna, and Edmond. When they left, Bøgh and Bloch showed up. Well, they ate the cakes and drank the white port. As they were leaving and I was walking across the floor over to the door, I had a bad neural attack, as if my limbs were about to fall off. There was no chair near me, so I had to hold onto the doorknob in order not to collapse. I could feel my hand trembling. It was as if the doorknob were swelling in my hand. It lasted only a moment, but there was something apoplectical about it.—To bed and up again. The lamp didn't quite want to shine.

Sunday, October 12. Slept restlessly last night. Lovely weather all morning. At 2 o'clock it turned cloudy. Sent a letter to Eckardt, who hasn't visited me in a long time. Letter to Otto Scavenius with congratulations concerning his engagement to Countess Scheel of Gammel Estrup. Received yesterday the second delivery of *New Tales and Stories*. Drove out to Tranquillity at 2 o'clock and from there to the Henriqueses', where I had dinner. When I got home, I went up the stairs very slowly, resting on every other step, and thus reached my sitting room not so short of breath. Letter from Eckardt.

Monday, October 13. At home all day. A visit from Fernanda Henriques in the pouring rain. Been reading every evening Berlepsch's *The Alps,* which has been translated by Jonas Collin. This evening I read so long that it was almost 12 o'clock before I made it to bed.

Tuesday, October 14. Alternating cloudiness and sunshine. Sent a letter to Reitzel and one to Miss Raasløff. Received a letter from Topsøe regarding what I wrote to him about Miss Brandis. Went for a drive at 1:30. Dr. Hornemann went with me as far as Assistens Cemetery, where he visited the grave of his son Johannes. He remained there. I drove home along Bülow Road and Old King's Road. Drove in a circle around Frederik VII's statue in front of the palace. The figure is wrong. Here we have a big, strong, well-built fellow. He was himself, indeed, short and stocky. In the meantime Rigmor Stampe had been here to pay a call, likewise Gredsted, a student from Odense. He was going to come back in the evening. Bournonville came before dinner. A little later Hartmann came; his daughter-in-law, Carl Hartmann's wife, has been spitting up blood, and they're leaving this evening for a spa in Switzerland near Chur. They wanted to travel the shortest route and assumed it was via Frankfurt and Basel. I showed them this would be a detour; they shouldn't head west from Cassel to Frankfurt, but east over Eisenach, Bamberg and Augsburg to Lindau. I felt quite emotionally drained, even more so since it all was repeated to Miss Jette Melchior during the following visit, when she also suggested the route over Basel in our conversation on this subject. After she'd left, the student Gredsted arrived. He had nothing on his mind, as I'd thought, but the conveyance of a greeting from his father.

Wednesday, October 15. Louise and Thea Melchior arrived as early as 9 o'clock, just as I'd gotten out of bed, in order to tell me that I wouldn't find anyone at home today at Tranquillity. I wasn't at all presentable, so I only opened the door a crack and talked with them through it. Then came Mrs. Wulff with lovely flowers from Rosenvænget Street, afterwards Dr. Collin. Molard, a Frenchman who'll be staying here for the winter, came with a letter of recommendation from Asbjørnsen in Norway. At 2:30 drove out to the Frederiksberg Circle and home. (Collin brought me a number of letters requesting my autograph, likewise magazines and newspapers.) Stine, the maid, has gotten a new position. Now it's going to be the same as it was with Miss Hallager—new help will have to be broken in. When I woke up this morning, my left arm was almost useless because of arthritis pain. Th. Collin prescribed oil of chloroform. I applied it this evening before I went to bed.

Thursday, October 16. Feeling in better shape! I can move my arm better without great pain. Yesterday evening walked fifteen steps back and forth across my room and today, twenty steps, and feel on the whole a good deal better. Another fan letter from America just arrived in the mail. It would be better if they got together over there and sent me a sum of money to help me in my impecunious old age. Also from Stuttgart, Leipzig, etc., letters requesting autographs. At 2 o'clock I drove out to Tranquillity. Mrs. Melchior had driven into town a few minutes before. As I got home, Mrs. Melchior arrived and right afterward Mrs. Koch. It's always after dinner that I feel tired and weak. Today, precisely during this low period, Mr. and Mrs. Henriques came. I wasn't feeling quite well and wasn't a lively host. In bed after 10 o'clock.

Friday, October 17. Beautiful weather. I'd hardly gotten out of bed before Mr. Melchior came with a letter the mailman had delivered to Tranquillity. It was wrapped in a piece of paper that looked like what you might find used as an envelope for a begging letter. In it were two documents—one from Grégoire to the effect that he, and he alone, must have the rights to translate and publish my tales and stories in France; and one from my publisher to the effect that I must protect my rights. I didn't wish to obligate myself regarding Grégoire. I was also put off by the way it had been handled—no letter from Grégoire or his agent had been enclosed. Dinner at Mrs. Koch's with young Mrs. Rørdam, the sister of young Mrs. Koch. Letter to Edgar Collin.

Saturday, October 18. A visit from Edgar Collin. Neither he nor Watt have sent me the Grégoire papers. Gave Edgar the idea of doing an "Album of Danish Literature" with photographs of thirty-eight Danish authors that I suggested to him.—He could certainly earn something with it around Christmastime. Wrote a letter to Grégoire.

Sunday, October 19. Lovely, sunny weather. Reminded more than once by my landlady to go out for a drive in this weather. I wasn't ready and didn't want to go until after lunch. Annoyed, like yesterday evening, when I also got a lot of good advice. So I cordially said I didn't want advice like this, that I wasn't accustomed to it and wanted what I wanted. Afterwards I regretted having said it.—Drove out to Tranquillity at 1 o'clock. Bille was out there; I was very lively. Arrived home by 4 o'clock, made it up the stairs rather well, and left right away for the Henriqueses', where I was seated at dinner between Mrs. Neruda and Juliette Price. I proposed a toast to the two ladies!—When I got home in the evening, I had a lot of trouble getting up the stairs again. A visit from Weber. Read this evening the entire first volume of Overskou's *History of the Royal Danish Theater*.

During the winter of 1873–74, Andersen continued to suffer from respiratory problems, abdominal pain, rheumatism, and fatigue. When he was able to leave his rooms, it was always with the help of a friend or servant; and although he still tried to maintain his old dining schedule at the homes of friends, he now found himself sending his regrets more often than not. But that winter had its pleasures, too. In November, his number was drawn in the lottery and, much to his delight, brought him five hundred rix-dollars. He also became immersed in a new project—the decoration of the panels of a screen with a collage of cutouts from books, magazines, and photographs—and he spent months happily cutting and pasting. Moreover, on his birthday on April 2, he was made privy councillor.

By late spring, Andersen's diary entries seem to indicate that he was feeling somewhat stronger. He even assayed two visits to the Royal Theater—his first since his health began to deteriorate in the fall of 1872—where he saw the opening act of Adolphe Adam's opera The Postilion of Longjumeau *and, on his second visit a few weeks later, two acts of Christoph Willibald von Gluck's* Iphigenia in Tauris. *He also had energy enough to compose two poems—one for a celebration in honor of the composer J. P. E. Hartmann and the other, "The Old Man," the first verse of which seems almost prophetic:*

> Before that great portal I now stand,
> Near death and grave.
> Three score and ten is the age God gave
> The time He planned.

Despite the improved sense of well-being reported in his diary entries for April and May, Andersen was nonetheless a very sick man. An account of the visit to Andersen by the English man of letters Edmund Gosse in the middle of May reminds us of that fact: "As I entered the bright, pretty sitting-room, Hans Christian Andersen was coming in from an opposite door. He leaned against a chair, and could not proceed. I was infinitely shocked to see how extremely he had changed since I had found him so blithe and communicative, only two years before. He was wearing a close-fitting,

The English section of Andersen's screen

snuff-coloured coat, down to his heels, such a burnt-sienna coat as I remember to have seen Lord Beaconsfield wear as he went walking slowly up Whitehall, on Mr. Corry's arm, in the later 'sixties. This garment, besides being very old-fashioned, accentuated the extreme thinness of Andersen's tall figure, which was wasted, as people say, to a shadow. He was so afflicted by asthma that he could not utter a word, and between sorrow, embarrassment and helplessness, I wished myself miles away."

Nonetheless, by the latter part of May Andersen felt well enough to leave Copenhagen to spend the summer visiting friends in the country—the Holsteins of Holsteinborg, the Melchiors at Tranquillity, and the Moltkes of Bregentved, where he had not been in almost thirty years. In July, while at Bregentved, he received a letter from America from a little girl who had enclosed a dollar bill and a newspaper article exhorting American children to repay the debt they owed to their Hans Christian Andersen and thus secure for the elderly man a comfortable old age. Two weeks later, when he had returned to Tranquillity, Moritz Melchior told him the American ambassador had come to see him with a gift of two hundred rix-dollars from children in Washington, D.C. Andersen was outraged and asked the ambassador to inform the senders that he had a pension and was not indigent. Only Georg Brandes's book from 1873, The Romantic School in Germany, with its new morality could distract him, at least temporarily, from fretting about the American children's gift.

Saturday, August 1 [1874]. Stomach bad. Up last night at 1:30. Sharp pains in my abdomen, bad diarrhea. Cold and rainy weather. Letter from Countess Moltke of Bregentved. Felt irritable and unwell.— Sent to Miss Clara Ballin forty-five rix-dollars for rent for the month of August. Annoyed that I got a plain receipt back and no thanks for the friendly letter I'd enclosed with the money.—Reading the Brandes book. He doesn't say anything pernicious himself, but sows poison in other works by his use of quotations. He is working for free love and the abolition of marriage, and he does it in lectures mainly for young girls. A letter from Miss Bjerring.

Sunday, August 2. Sent a letter to Mrs. Koch that I'm here [at Tranquillity]. Letter to Count Moltke of Bregentved. At 7:30 saw the captain of the air balloons, Mr. Sivel, rise up in the air with his five balloons: Europe (the largest), Asia, Africa, America and Oceania. The wind was strong and blew him at great speed across the sound to Sweden.

Monday, August 3. Pains in my abdomen still. A letter from Fernanda Henriques in Modum [Norway]. A letter from Jonas Collin.

Drove to town with Mrs. Melchior. The new theater looks good; the old one is a gaping hole. I was at the hairdresser's and had a haircut. Then drove with Mrs. Melchior over to see the Misses Ballin. The elder sister was out. The rooms comfortable. I felt rather well while there and returned home over Langelinie with less of a stomach ache, too. Chagrined about the Brandes book. Miss Harriet was in favor of it and of him.

Tuesday, August 4. Sunshine, but a cold wind. A visit from Miss Clara Ballin, who was glistening from her walk from the streetcar. When she went home, I accompanied her down along Rosenvænget Street. Finished the Brandes book. In it there's a German poem—it lies between the pages like a flower, an obscene flower. A lustful young woman longs to be embraced by "ein süsser Knabe" and is angry with her mother because she is not allowed to display the beauty nature has endowed her with. Moritz Melchior to dinner over in Gentofte. We are therefore going to eat at 5 o'clock. I was looking forward to eating at a decent hour, but then Mrs. Melchior waited for Commander Jøhnke to come, and so we didn't sit down at the table until 6 o'clock. He didn't arrive until almost 8 o'clock. A visit from Carl Reitzel. Anna Henriques' birthday.

Wednesday, August 5. I'm not getting anything done—idle, irritated. This morning the cream stank and tasted so bad that I sent it back downstairs. Miss Harriet came with a pencil sketch. It was supposed to be of their croquet field. It was impossible to figure out, and when I made her go downstairs to show me where she'd drawn it from, I could see she'd gotten it all wrong. What was supposed to be a triangle was a circle—the entire thing was as if drawn by a child. And since she has been praised by Professor Buntzen for her great drawing talent, I demonstrated and described for her how devoid of talent it was, how she revealed here her utter lack of an artistic eye. I then led her to a spot where she would have a picturesque view of the scene. I was annoyed at her, but also at myself for asking for trouble.—That impertinent little Jeanina Stampe was playing a game with the Læssøe children in which they had to greet each other. It worked out that Jeanina had to greet the Læssøes's little girl (whose mother, after all, is the sister of Count Frijs). Then that stuck-up little Jeanina, who *didn't want to greet her*, said: "An aristocrat never greets a commoner first!" Called on Mrs. Drewsen. To begin with she wasn't going to see anybody, and then, later in the day, I was admitted. I was informed that Jonas Collin was in town. "That's great!" I said. "Then I'll surely be seeing him, because

Mrs. Melchior will have invited him to dinner!" Then Mrs. Drewsen flew into a violent temper: "He won't be coming! *I* have invited him!"—"It's none of my business," I said calmly.—I asked Drewsen how it could be that the police punished a poor woman if she told fortunes with cards and coffee grounds, while, on the other hand, they gave the clairvoyant Guloton permission to make her prophecies, whether it was because she was dressed in silk, stayed at one of the best hotels and commanded higher prices? His answer was that there wasn't anything to be said, since she had permission from the police. They probably regarded her as a performer on tour. Viggo, the smart one, the philosopher, observed that one presumed those who could pay the higher prices to be better educated than common folk and therefore that it was only a joke for them. (What a knowledge of human nature!) Then Jonna showed up. She asked me about an answer to her letter about whether I would be coming to visit her. I asked if I might take a rain check for another year, and she likewise passed lightly over the matter. I didn't want to say to her that I don't want to be beholden to her husband for the stay since it's obvious he doesn't care about me. During my entire illness this year he didn't visit me until the very last days when I joked with Jonna about his "loyalty." I couldn't say to her either that I was afraid of losing my peace of mind out of irritation with those two singularly liberally raised, as they say, daughters and that rude little Jeanina. That one, I am certain, I would give a tongue-lashing to at the first sign of incivility, and then there would be no peace in the house. I'm only interested in Jonna, and she's also a strange character.—Moses came home today.

Thursday, August 6. Moltke-Huitfeldt of Glorup sent a deer. It had to be eaten, so various people were invited. I liked P. Hansen the best. It's Carl Melchior's birthday today. I proposed a toast to him, likewise to the Icelandic celebration tomorrow. We Danes have sent up there the best we have—one of the hearts on Denmark's coat of arms—our king himself was present there. Present here was a Dr. Zachariae, whose son is a naval officer and with the king on board the *Jylland*. The father wanted to send my toast to the king. I toasted the *university-bound* Emil Melchior and the physician Brandes, who was here. Later on in the evening I was very chatty until it got to be 11 o'clock. There is a strange, febrile resentment within me. I'm irritated by almost everything and sort of look right into people's hearts and say to myself: I don't like them. Sent a letter to Carl Bloch in Hellebæk with the pages of Miss Heinke's letter concerning him enclosed. I received a letter from Dr. Hornemann, who said nothing at all regarding any kind of evaluation of my condition.

Friday, August 7. I was bothered a lot last night by arthritis. The weather is turbulent—yesterday we had hail, thunder and lightning. My arthritis grew terribly worse—after dinner I took such a chill that my hands were shaking and my teeth chattering. Mrs. Melchior had my bed warmed up. I went to bed and lay there for a long time before the warmth penetrated my bones, but I got no sleep all night long.—Now, as the day wears on, I'm feeling better. A letter from the theological candidates Oksen and Weber. They have already returned from Switzerland. They got only as far as Lucerne and—via Munich, where they met Mrs. Kaulbach—returned to see Oksen's father in Schleswig. Letter from Anna Henriques about prices at the Klampenborg Spa. Letter from Countess Frijs.

Saturday, August 8. A letter from Count Fritz Moltke of Bregentved. Time passes without my accomplishing anything, and I'm getting terribly sluggish. Mrs. Melchior is kind and considerate, despite the fact that I often feel I'm a cranky and dull guest that can't tolerate open windows and doors. A visit from Jonas Collin here for dinner.

Sunday, August 9. Lots of people for dinner. I was seated next to little Miss Meyer, who seems so vivacious. She has been infected by Brandes's teachings and accused Harriet of being even more so. I had arranged sixteen bouquets for the dinner table, probably the loveliest I've ever done. Melchior spoke with me about Carl and Emil and the dangerous, young time of life they were in! It's my opinion that you have to leave them alone and let them do what they want. William Bloch was here for dinner; he spoke about the subject of his new work. It sounded promising to me—I felt like doing something similiar myself. Brandes is a superb character with his seductive teachings. At 7:30 the balloon with Mr. Sivel and his four fellow travelers appeared headed over toward Landskrona. A letter from Nicolai Bøgh.

Monday, August 10. A visit from the composer Professor Hartmann. He said his son Emil had been sent to [the insane asylum at] Vordingborg a year too late, according to what Dr. Jensen had said. I heard from Læssøe that a son of the writer Thomas Lange has also been sent there. This year he was supposed to have sat for the entrance exams to the university. He believes himself to be a very great poet and painter and in exchange for his works wants the whole world and his own railroad. Melchior home late. We never make it

Papercut (made for Dorothea Melchior in 1874)

to the dinner table until after 7:30. Visited Læssøe. Sent a portrait photograph with my autograph and a letter to H . . . in Sweden. A letter to Nicolai Bøgh and enclosed the letters from Mrs. Kaulbach and Oksen. Letter to Schmidt, a school teacher in Odense. Letter from Carl Bloch.—Kidded around a bit with little Charlotte, who is staying here. A visit from His Excellency Holstein of Holsteinborg. He was also angry about Rosenberg.

Tuesday, August 11. Sore throat. Mrs. Melchior's blind sister, Mrs. Eva Henriques, is here today. I walked with her in the garden and brought her a bouquet with dill from the vegetable garden and fragrant flowers from the flower garden. Later I read for her three tales: "The Little Matchgirl," "The Butterfly" and "It's Perfectly True!" Little Charlotte tore two buds off the red carnations she'd been given. I said that it was a pity for the carnations' mother to tear her children from her and that the sandman was coming tonight with the carnation mother, who would cry: "What have you done with my children?"—Little Charlotte was of the opinion that flowers couldn't talk and wished to ask her governess about the matter. Charlotte left this afternoon to go home to Elysium, where there will be great doings tomorrow, since it is her sister Augusta's birthday. I've composed a poem for the occasion to be recited by little Poul dressed up like a sprite:

> I'm one of the wee ones, the household sprite;
> My sister Charlotte dressed me up just right!
> I swing the Danish flag up to the sky!
> It's Augusta's birthday! Swing it high!
> We'll put on a show so fine and dandy!
> And then eat our fill of cake and candy
> And toast our Augusta, skol on her birthday!
> A lemonade toast! Hurray! Hurray!

Received a letter today from Mrs. Henriette Collin in Hellebæk.

Wednesday, August 12. Aching pains around my middle last night. Turbulent weather. It's Augusta Melchior's birthday out at Elysium. That's where everybody here is, so that I am completely alone. Mrs. Melchior wanted to invite Peter Hansen to dinner, but I prefer solitude. My spirits are low. Sent a letter to Weber in Odense. A letter and page proofs to Mr. Møller at Reitzel's. Letter and two photographs of my sitting room in Nyhavn along with a picture of Tranquillity. I've also sent a letter to Mrs. Privy Councillor Koch. Alternating rain and sunshine today. At 4 o'clock the whole household drove out to Elysium, where the birthday party was held. Poul and Otto were supposed to play roles in a Punch and Judy show. I sat down to eat, and the servant placed in front of me the bottle of red

wine that Melchior yesterday had said didn't taste good and was
sour. I requested another, but the servant didn't have any. He came
back with a carafe with a few drops in it—it was flat. I asked for
some port, but the housekeeper was out and had the key with her.
So I had to drink beer and *sherry*, which I can't stand. At last the
coffee came. It was undrinkable. Then I got very annoyed and bored
and felt ill at ease. I told the servant that no one but the housekeeper was to prepare my evening tea for me. And so went to bed
before 10 o'clock. Around 11 o'clock the servant came with my tea—
the cook had made it, since the housekeeper hadn't come home yet.
Then I boiled over but couldn't rant and rave and so was infinitely
spiteful and told him to go and not bother about me. I thrashed
around in my bed, cursed and was completely beside myself. The
housekeeper didn't come home at all—she was in town putting up
preserves. Their "Nibs" came at around 12 o'clock. Anna had gone
along with the rest of them and in the morning had gone for a swim
at the beach. Now that's a strange consumptive! I had an urge to
move back to town right away. Was feeling miserable out here—one
day limping along after the other.

Thursday, August 13. Glad I had no chance to speak to anyone last
night. I might have said too much. Mrs. Melchior regretted the incident and said the sewing maid had the key to the wine cellar. It
would have been better to give it to the servant. Received a letter
from Schmidt, the school teacher in Odense. A letter from Mrs. Koch.
Responded to Mrs. Koch's letter. Arranged sixteen bouquets for the
party today. Deep down inside I don't feel at all kindly, grateful or
patient. Present here were Mrs. Levy with a governess from England, Mrs. Nathan Melchior and her daughter Sophie, and a boy
(the son of Strochi, who is in charge of the opera troupe at Tivoli).
Moses Melchior came up to me to say hello before we sat down to
eat and told me how famous I was abroad. He repeated the same
thing at the dinner table. Before all this I'd proposed a toast to him,
and Moritz Melchior, who will be leaving for London tomorrow,
also got a toast from me. I read "What Dad Does Is Always Right"
for little Strochi, who had asked me to. Then did a good job of translating "The Butterfly" into German so the lady from Hamburg—I
was seated next to her at dinner—could follow it. Then read "The
Rags."

Friday, August 14. Warm sunshine but windy. Received this morning a newspaper from New York with an account of the two little
girls who had given their "tribute" to the "old storyteller Hans

Christian Andersen." This put me in an irritable mood. Lazing around aimlessly, killing time and, along with it, myself. Eating and sleeping are my most important activities. It's enough to drive me to despair. At 6 o'clock Moritz Melchior drove to the railroad station. Mrs. Melchior, their daughters with their two young girl friends, together with Emil, went with him. They were going to go to Tivoli. Melchior was on his way to London. Today we had a visit from Mrs. Cerillo from Naples, along with her sister Miss Knudsen, who is a friend of the Collins. Her brother, Dr. Knudsen from the West Indies, and his wife came with them. We'd met in 1829 at a ball at the home of Dr. Colsmann (of the hospital's autopsy department) on Broad Street. I recall that I was there the evening of the day I had taken my second examination. Sent a long letter to Mrs. Collin at Ellekilde. The Moltkes left for Switzerland.

Saturday, August 15. A letter from a young American in Copenhagen with several clippings from the newspapers over there about the children's collection for me. Another letter about this came from Asger Hammerich. Beside myself again. Mrs. Melchior and her daughters then translated everything that had been published about this, and I got a different impression. It was all so beautiful, so moving, that I regretted having expressed my distress so vehemently to the American ambassador, Cramer, when he was here. I am now, for the moment, in a more tranquil mood. Mrs. Trier arrived after dinner with her husband and son. There was another big discussion about the dangers of letting Emil join the Student Association. There was someone who had alarmed Mrs. Melchior about the tone there— about Brandes' influence with regard to free love. I spoke much too vociferously against such defamation of the association, and the young university student Trier and his mother agreed with me.—How much there is to be said about this matter!—Hold your tongue!—A visit from Mrs. Koch.

Sunday, August 16. Heavy, gray weather. Boring out here. My task is to eat, drink and sleep. (Louise and Harriet are out in the country today for dinner at the Hirschsprungs.) A very solitary dinner. Nothing is getting done—just that I'm dying of boredom during the time I have left.

Monday, August 17. Emil Melchior's birthday. I wanted to go into town by 12 o'clock at the latest, but by then Christian, the coachman, had left for town without telling anyone. I was annoyed. I wasted the morning dragged on with hawking and coughing—it's an incredible amount of phlegm that I cough up. I'm extremely hoarse today. At 3 o'clock I drove in, circling the new theater. You can still see how the smoke from the fire has licked the wall above the topmost window. Oehlenschläger's statue is standing ready in front of the theater, waiting to be put into place. The old theater is now almost down. After having my hair done, I drove over to Lose and Delbanco and bought the piano arrangement for the ballet *Waldemar* for Emil. I arrived home in a somewhat more serene frame of mind. The young student Boysen was here for dinner. I proposed a toast to Emil and was very talkative during the evening, but extremely hoarse. In *The Daily News* today there was something about the collection in America.

Tuesday, August 18. Lovely sunshine. Mrs. Melchior offered me the carriage for a drive out to see the queen dowager, but I was too hoarse to make such a visit. Commander Jøhnke came to say goodbye; he'll be leaving on a business trip to London on Saturday. Today is his son's birthday. A letter from Miss Ballin. The barber didn't come until after 12 o'clock. He said the band of gypsies that had crossed over from Sweden to Elsinore on Saturday and driven along Strand Way had now set up their camp by the Triangle Square. The two leaders with their silver scepters were in town at the police station—two or three wagons with dirty children and girls with gold coins in their hair were milling around there. Since I was just about to go for a drive with Anna, we went there first and saw a woman asleep with a little, golden-brown infant at her breast and dirty children. I had eleven copper shillings, and I gave them to two children. I'd brought a colorful shawl, but since none of the young girls showed themselves I kept it and put it to good use, since there was a strong wind blowing out along Strand Way. Mrs. Collin on a visit from Ellekilde. Mrs. Lund came late in the evening from Viborg. She'll be staying here until September and then will travel to Italy with her husband. He wanted to stay here overnight and then early tomorrow head for Korsør, where he has some restoration work to do in the church. A letter from a man who wants an office job. Letter from Mr. Frost and at last one from Reitzel with page proofs.

Wednesday, August 19. Sluggish, dull, cranky. A visit from Mrs. Louise Lind just as we were about to go for a drive. It dragged on, as always, past the time we were supposed to leave. I was very annoyed. At Teglgaard House, which looks as if it had been tossed out in the middle of a field by a duck pond, there were lots of visitors, among them young Mr. Marcus and his wife. He looked boring and right away began his conversation with me by talking about the collection in America, and I got angry and immediately cut him off. At the home of the Henriques, who have just returned from Modum, I saw the enlarged garden for the first time. Miss Anna Falbe was there, old and toothless and with her hair hanging in wisps over her forehead like you see on prisoners when they are released from jail or ladies of the night in Paris before they have their hair curled.

Thursday, August 20. Beautiful weather. Went into town before lunch and paid a visit to Mrs. Lind. Young Mr. Marcus was here for dinner with his wife from Hamburg. I was again tiresomely out of sorts and bored with life.

Friday, August 21. Nicolai Bøgh, a dinner guest. I'm idling and languishing.

Saturday, August 22. One day like the next. I'm agitated and regret what I've said and told about. Drove into town and had my hair cut and curled. When I went to see the heiress presumptive, to whom I wished to pay my respects, she had already left to pay her respects to the queen, who arrived home from Rumpenheim today. Called on Dr. Studsgaard to hear a little about the Collins. I told him about how I was feeling, my itching penis. He looked at it, had me wash it and dried it rather roughly and put some lint on it. I got instructions to bathe it. Felt febrile and out of sorts.

Sunday, August 23. Strong wind. This morning fourteen ships from the United Steamship Company passed by headed up into the sound to welcome the king. We heard later he had reached Vedbæk as early as yesterday evening, but had had to spend the night there, since his arrival had not been announced until Sunday at 1 o'clock. Mrs. Melchior drove to the Customs House. I didn't want to go with her and walked over to the Triangle Square. The coachman Christian, finally came shuffling up from town. He was supposed to be fetching Miss Anna now—that took its time. I sat with Mrs. Lund and Thea in two different omnibuses on account of the rain squalls. Then the carriage came. A little later Mrs. Melchior came and right after that, the royal family. Christian got rattled rotating and turning the carriage. He wanted it closed on account of a few drops of rain. I was annoyed. "Don't make a scene!" said Mrs. Lund. Finally we were on the right-hand side of the road facing away from town. The royal family was looking out in the opposite direction, but then Princess Thyra cried: "There's Andersen!" And then the king saw me, greeted me and waved several times with his hand, but neither the queen nor Alexandra did I see. Then came Prince Valdemar, chubby and fat. His greeting to me was rather distant and cold, whereas

Prince Hans's was not like that. The crown princess also recognized me right away and greeted me, and the crown prince followed her example. Among the attendants were Captain von der Maase and Miss Reventlow—I was seen by them. I was otherwise in low spirits, and then, at home, I had a visit from Mrs. Lund, who wished to read for me her novella "Veronica's Sorrow." I was in no mood to hear it. She advised me to give notice to the Misses Ballin and travel instead to Rome, where she and her husband were going to go, or perhaps to Florence. She enlivened me, but didn't cheer me up. In the meantime I wrote a letter to Jonas Collin about paying me a visit as soon as he could. (I wanted to speak with him about an itinerary and about whether he could accompany me.) I wrote a letter to Bille asking him to designate some time during the week when I could speak with him. The letters were sent off, and shortly afterwards Bille came. We talked about the money from America, and about my itinerary. He gladly fell in with everything and promised to help and advise me. I was in a good mood again. In the evening Carl Bloch came with his wife. He was again grumbling about earning money and wasn't favorably disposed toward Moltke of Bregentved, who had invited him home, but when he'd gotten there it was only for hanging up his pictures. If it had been now, he would have sent him a bill for his travel expenses there and back, as well as for the two days wasted.

Monday, August 24. Sunny, but a strong wind. At 10:30 Moritz Melchior arrived from London. He left there in the evening of the day before yesterday. With him he's brought some presents—for me a little bookcase. My penis is still sensitive, but it looks much better. Yesterday a letter from Miss Bjerring. Received a new vest and gray summer coat from Lund, the tailor. At 2 o'clock, drove into town in the Melchiors' carriage and stopped by my residence in Nyhavn. When I couldn't find the copy of *The Improvisatore* for Mrs. Lund, who wants to translate it when she gets to Italy, I wrote to Reitzel for one.

Tuesday, August 25. A visit from Carl Reitzel, who brought a copy of *The Improvisatore*. Low spirits. My penis constantly sore. Late in the evening Dr. Hornemann came and looked at it. He declared it to be all right now. Sent a letter to Mrs. von der Maase at Bregentved. A letter from. . . .

Wednesday, August 26. Cold and windy, rain squalls. A letter from Weber in Odense. At 11 o'clock I drove out to Sorgenfri Castle to visit the queen dowager. I stopped off at Miss Rosen's. She was in the middle of getting dressed, and in order not to waste a half hour waiting for her, I then drove over to see Gade, the composer, who lives in the late Dr. Mürer's house. Gade was in town, but I found his wife and parents-in-law at home. When I went back to see Miss Rosen, she was at the queen's, but would be returning soon. She had some open-faced sandwiches and port brought in to me, but I didn't partake of them until after I had been at the queen dowager's where the lady-in-waiting Miss Paulsen received me. The old queen was looking extremely lovely and well; gave me her hand. We sat down and talked about all sorts of things—about the king's trip, about the American children's gift to me. She found it very touching. She was so sympathetic and told me that she hadn't expected me to recover from my last illness, that now God had surely granted me several more years to live. She promised to extend my greetings to the royal family, since I wasn't expecting to get an audience today. Then I called on Miss Rosen and afterwards drove over to Bernstorff Castle. The doorman told me Captain von der Maase was in royal attendance, adding that I always had access to the royal family. Von der Maase came down from his room to welcome me, announcing soon afterwards that the king was awaiting me in the queen's chamber. All the English children were there (two young princes and three little princesses), as well as the crown prince's son, little Christian, Thyra, Valdemar, Prince Hans and the king. Then the queen arrived and, soon after, the princess of Wales, who has gotten very thin but looked just as young as Thyra. On her face was a very happy, childlike expression. She took both my hands. Everyone shook my hand. The crown prince was there with his consort, so I didn't have to drive over to Charlottenlund to see them. They received me with such warmth and such friendliness, as if I were visiting the family of any of my good friends. We talked about the king's trip to Iceland, and he was excited about it and praised Carl Andersen and said he had conveyed my greetings when at Geysir and likewise informed him about the toast to the king that I had proposed at the Melchiors' (the day before the celebration of Iceland's thousandth anniversary) and about which Zachariae had written to his son, the lieutenant. I told about the American children's gift. The king thought it was a shame (for the sake of the children) to send the money back—I should rather give it to destitute children here at home. I told the princess of Wales about Miss Burdett-Coutts, in whose home I had stayed in London and to whom I had turned concerning my bed, which hadn't been made well. I told the crown prince how happy I was that people in Jutland had gotten to know him and thus get really fond of him. The king wanted me to have some thing to eat and a little port. He also suggested some "red fruit pudding" and junket. I replied that I didn't feel like anything and that Mrs. Melchior had given me a lunch basket. "It's not proper," said the king, "to take along a lunch basket when visiting the royal family." I replied that I hadn't expected to get to see any of them. How warm and open they all were! I clapped the king on the shoulder, and when I spoke about my stay at Holsteinborg and Bregentved the queen said: "The ladies are spoiling Andersen!" When I left, the princess of Wales asked me for a picture of myself and Princess Thyra came with the same request. It was a lovely visit. We've had rain squalls, sunshine, rain and hail. At 3:30 I came home very tired, especially of sitting—my anus hurt. Visited the painter Læssøe. He told me that during the war a peasant woman had gone to the queen dowager and said that she could surely see that the queen had suffered greatly because of her two brothers and the plight of the nation, and she wanted to do something nice for her. She'd brought her little son as a gift for the queen dowager. He was such a good boy, and the queen would enjoy him. The dowager queen was dumbfounded. The woman insisted on her keeping the boy, and she took care of him. He is now a fine first mate.

Thursday, August 27. Extremely lovely weather. The sea shining and blue. The Swedish coast lay so clear and close. I wrote my letter to America, which Bille has promised to translate. Sent a letter to Hansen, the photographer, about getting some portrait photographs of myself and gave him one of my room. A large dinner party. I arranged sixteen bouquets. The American ambassador, Mr. Cramer, and wife were here, the youngest sister of President Grant, Bille and wife, Carl Andersen and wife and her niece, who sings well, the author Bergsøe, etc.—I proposed a toast to America: "Once England was our distant neighbor, but now time has made everything closer, and now America is closer to us than England once was. People from the North visited and knew about America before Columbus knew about it. Now it has been made manifest and familiar to us through the great lifeworks from over there—through Washington Irving's *History of the Life and Voyages of Christopher Columbus* and Cooper's picturesque stories. We have sensed a kinship with the North in Longfellow's *Song of Hiawatha*. And it has become precious to me because of the love flowing out to me from the hearts of its young people. The children of America have broken open their piggy

banks to share what they have with the old Danish writer they believe to be living in need. It has been a whole page in the fairy tale
of my live. I raise a toast to that great, dear nation; and since one of
its representatives is present here, along with a close relative of the
able leader of the union, they can convey our greetings!" Later, when
Bille proposed a toast to me—that I was used to going on journeys,
but that he had made the most recent one with me (he was referring
to the fact that he had gone up the stairs with me today when I had
climbed them two at a time)—he prophesied that I would now be
making many, long journeys in good health and spirits. I responded
by saying that if I weren't to be granted many or long ones, the
longest one in store for me was nevertheless into that great, unknown realm, and then I would wish I could use the force of elec-
tromagnetism to send a ray of light down to clarify things in this
foggy chaos that envelops so many here.—N. Bøgh was also here.

Friday, August 28. Cold, gray and wet. A letter from Mrs. Scavenius in Hellebæk. Went in to visit Miss Brandis, who was lying on
the sofa. Two of her male relatives were there; one of them has been
exiled from Schleswig with his wife.—Mrs. Lund read for me a little
Italian story she has written, "Veronica's Sorrow." It was very nice
and different from the novella Bergsøe read yesterday evening, "My
First Dream in Rome," which was sort of a fantastic story reminiscent of Hoffmann. A visit from Jonas Collin. We talked about the
possibility of a little trip abroad to refresh ourselves. We talked about
lots of other trends and ways of life. He has developed quite a sound
and loyal character.—Harriet has gone out to Teglgaard House. Out
at Christinelund Mrs. Drewsen has a case of the three-day flu. In
the evening Mrs. Lund read one of Turgenev's stories—the one about
the naval officer who goes to a brothel and is robbed and assaulted.
I declared it to be disgusting and not for young ladies to read aloud.
Before that I had myself read "Hen-Grethe's Family."

Saturday, August 29. I was tormented by that horrid dream I often
have about a child who sickens at my breast and turns into just a
wet rag, but in the early morning hours I dreamt a lovely dream.
I've only dreamt the like once before—I had an infinitely beautiful
singing voice and could pour out every thought in song. A sister of
General Christensen in New York was here. She gave me her brother's address. I visited Mrs. Lind, who was delighted about my letter
to America. I then walked down the street to see Admiral Peter Wulff.
He thought what I had written wasn't cordial enough toward the
Americans. Ran into Eckardt, who wished to call on me. Sent page

proofs and a letter to Møller. Copied the English translation Bille has sent me of my letter to the editor in Philadelphia regarding the collection for me. The weather lovely. Sunshine.

Sunday, August 30. Heavy rain showers. Yesterday the painter Lund from Korsør arrived and will be staying here until Monday. Mrs. Lund's "A Pen-and-Ink Drawing" appeared today in *The Illustrated News.* I'd said it was very cute, but that was about as much as anyone could say. Then she came with the issue in which it appeared and asked me to read it myself and then I might perhaps like it better. I got annoyed because I'd said as much as could be said, and she wouldn't hear anything better from me. I reread it and said that now I would come with my criticisms. The style was all right, as everyone wrote when they were writing well. But the way you wrote when you were narrating was one thing, and direct speech, another. When she let her characters speak, it was in the same style as her narration. I demonstrated in almost every line that people weren't so stilted when they were speaking. She thought they were and said it was my style that was different from the way others wrote. I replied that indeed it was when I was narrating, but not when I was rendering the speech of others—that was the way people spoke. She looked disgruntled. Johanne Melchior came with the children today for dinner. I got neither my letter off to America nor my package out to Bernstorff Castle.

Andersen's letter to America was addressed to the editor of The Evening Bulletin *in Philadelphia: "My sympathetic friends must not, therefore, think of me as a poor, old, forsaken writer, who worries about his daily bread and cannot tend his sick body. God has also been good to me in this regard—I am surrounded by dear friends. I've been blessed with endless happiness, if not a great fortune; and not the least of my joys is the experience that many dear children in America have broken open their piggy banks to share what they have with their old Andersen, whom they believe in great need."*

Andersen was quite active during the following months. In mid-September, he moved back into his rooms and occupied himself with social calls, dinners with friends, and the gala opening of the new Royal Theater on October 15 and, a week later, a performance of his Little Kirsten. *During this period, he also worked on explanatory notes and proofs for the third volume of the illustrated edition of his tales and stories.*

On November 15, Andersen was enormously gratified to find himself mentioned in The Fatherland—*along with Ørsted, Thorvaldsen, and Oehlenschläger—as one of Denmark's most prominent men. The next day, a committee headed by Mrs. Melchior, Mrs. Bille, and Mrs. Meldahl called on Andersen to discuss raising a statue of him in the King's Garden on his seventieth birthday. A week later, he began sorting through papers for a continuation of his autobiography.*

During the fall, Andersen's phlegmy cough grew worse, and he began taking morphine to help him sleep at night. On the evening of December 8, after he had been reading the last volume of the author Knud Lyhne Rahbek's Memories of My Life *(1829), he took his morphine and dreamed about his youth: "The morphine must have worked well—I had lovely dreams and one that was especially comforting, about how I coolly and confidently went up for my exams. Meisling came in the room, and I declared that he couldn't listen while I was being examined because I would feel such pressure that I would give stupid answers, which is exactly what I did. A little while later I was walking with Meisling, and he came with his brand of humor. I felt cheerful and confident, and we soon started to talk about art and everything beautiful and ended up very firm friends. He seemed to respect me and I, him."*

The Christmas holidays were full of activity for Andersen. The third volume of the illustrated edition of his New Tales and Stories *appeared, and he was kept busy reading all the enthusiastic reviews it occasioned and sending copies to all his friends. In early January, he was approached by the composer Axel Liebmann and asked to rework the dated language of his previous libretto for C. E. F. Weyse's singspiel* The Celebration at Kenilworth. *Nevertheless, he was distracted from these happy occupations by his correspondence with the American ambassador concerning the money being collected from children in the United States.*

Thursday, January 14 [1875]. A heavy fog. *The Daily* has a report about the "children's gift" from *The New York Tribune* that for Christmas I've been sent over two hundred dollars along with a two-volume deluxe edition of a book about America purchased with the rest of the money. Furthermore, in the New Year issue of *Harper's Magazine* there was a poem "The Children's Christmas Eve" that ends with the children's exclaiming when they see Andersen's image in a magic mirror:

> Ah, do we know him! dearest men!
> God bless our Hans Christian Andersen!

(Yesterday evening I felt as if I'd been stung by an insect on two of my fingers—they're itching. The curtain in the bedroom fell down and the rod hit me on the head.) A visit from Miss Marie Neergaard and a cousin Neergaard(?). I was in the middle of changing my clothes, and when I was informed that two ladies were waiting for me, I got out of breath hurrying to finish and couldn't quite speak with them to begin with. They stayed for over a half hour and saw my folding screen. We talked a lot; I got tired. Then Mrs. Henriques' housekeeper came with an invitation to dinner there on Saturday. Then came Liebmann, whom I told about my idea of rewriting the dialogue in *The Celebration at Kenilworth* and reworking it as recitative, and since he was so familiar with Weyse's music he could do just as Berlioz had done for Weber's *Freeshooter* when he turned its dialogue into recitative—he could compose the music for the dialogue in *Kenilworth*, which I promised to shorten and versify. He was eager to do it, and I advised him to speak with Paulli and, after that, with Linde. Then came a visit from Moses Melchior and, after that, from Krohn. I was completely exhausted. A little after 4 o'clock Melchior's carriage came to fetch me to dinner. Only Ploug, the editor, and his wife were there. She and I conversed at length. I became very talkative and carried on at length. The letter with the bank draft from America turned out now to be in *crowns* and not in rix-dollars and, furthermore, it was reported that they had spent money on a telegram to me from America—it had cost thirty-five rix-dollars. (There was no reason at all to sent me that telegram—I could easily have waited two weeks for the letter, especially since I still haven't received the promised package of books the telegram proclaims.)

Friday, January 15. Another gray, foggy day. A letter from America asking for an autograph. No visits. Dinner at Mrs. Koch's. There, got to borrow the first volume of *The Oldenburg Line in Denmark. A Cycle of Plays* by Benedicte Arnesen Kall. This evening I read *Christian the Father of Kings* and started on *King Hans*. What a close relationship to the recently rejected drama *King Waldemar and Bishop Absalon*, especially the rendering of *King Hans* in prose! It is no doubt the same author.

Saturday, January 16. Cloudy weather. Another letter from America about an autograph. Didn't win in the lottery. Paid for a load of kindling, cut and delivered for twenty rix-dollars, two marks and eight shillings. Visits from Professor Hartmann and from Johan Krohn. Dinner at the Henriqueses' with a Norwegian Miss Knutzon, whom the family knows from Modum. They couldn't guess my riddle at all—the name of two Danish writers. It got to be past 7 o'clock before I left. I was thinking about going to the theater to see *The White Lady*, but gave it up and went home. A visit this afternoon from Mrs. Karen Scharling. Not well after the evening meal.

Sunday, January 17. Dreamt continuously and restlessly. Cloudy weather. For the first time this year walked a short way down the street, not further, though, than around the corner and past the Royal Mint. Stood looking at the new bridge over the canal, which is in place but still under construction. Arrived home tired from this extremely short excursion. Read this morning "To Grundtvig's Friends: A Letter in Verse from F. L. Grundtvig." A visit from Moritz Melchior, who wrote a letter for me to the banking house of Duncan, Shermann and Co. in New York. Dinner at the Collins' with Miss Reimer, Dr. Studsgaard, Viggo Drewsen and wife. Viggo is becoming more and more like a stranger to me. There is something so withdrawn about him. Read my riddle about names, which was of interest. Theodor quite an ignoramus. Later on in the evening, a visit from Dr. Hornemann. He asked me if Viggo weren't a complete atheist. He's the one who has been working on his wife and on Rigmor and Astrid Stampe, who have now lost their faith. "It's a sin to slay the body, but worse to slay the soul."

Monday, January 18. Sent a letter to the banker in New York. Cloudy weather. Tired and in no shape to go for a walk. A visit from Mrs. Melchior, to whom I gave Jochumsson's letter to me about the Ancker Scholarship. Asked her to let Ploug read the letter. While she was here, Mr. Frost, a foreign correspondent, came with an article for *The Standard* about the American children's gift to me. In it he called me a Danish Aesop. I asked him rather to call me a Danish Perrault! He asked if he might encourage the children of England also to send me money. I asked him to spare me such questions—it had been embarrassing for me to receive money from America; I wasn't in need, etc.—Liebmann came and had spoken with Paulli, who looked favorably upon receiving *Kenilworth* with recitatives, but said that it couldn't appear on stage this season. I therefore promised to get started on the recitatives right away. Today I've been working on my autobiography. Lots of talk in town about the houses that collapsed.

Tuesday, January 19. Rainy weather. I can't go out today either. A visit from the young xylographer Lauritsen from Odense, who wanted a recommendation from me for Germany or Sweden so that he could find employment there. It wasn't clear to me how I would be able to do that and referred him to Titular Councillor Collin to see if he might know what was to be done about this matter. Busy all day long working on the recitatives for the opera *Kenilworth*.

Wednesday, January 20. Sunshine this morning. Soon cloudy again, though quite springlike—45 degrees, but windy so that I wouldn't be able to stand on the street, people told me. Dinner at the Henriqueses' together with J. P. E. Hartmann and wife along with Pastor Wedel and wife. I was lively, read my riddle and then the entire first act of *The Celebration at Kenilworth*. In *The Berlingske News* this evening, an enumeration of the initial contributions to my statue—3,743 crowns. Miss Clara Ballin's birthday—I gave her a portrait photograph of myself.

Thursday, January 21. Today took a walk to the broad canal over by the harbor. A visit from Count Frederik Moltke of Bregentved. While he was here, little Charlotte Melchior came, the three-year-old child so ready with an answer. He asked what her name was. She said Charlotte. He persisted: "Don't you have any other names?" and she said all five of them. "You do have a lot of names!" he said. "A sweet child has lots!" she replied.—Then came Mr. Barnekow with the piano arrangement for *Kenilworth* so that he could go through the text with me. I got so tired that I had to ask him to continue tomorrow. Dinner at the Melchiors', where there were some twenty people. I chatted and told about a lot of things. Read for Peter Hanpsen my riddle and promised he could have it for *Near and Far*. (A visit from theater manager Andersen!)

Friday, January 22. From thirteen degrees above freezing yesterday it got down to nine degrees below today. I went for a walk around the corner, almost over to Heiberg Street, but was so cold that my eyes were watering.—This evening at the Casino a "benefit performance for the monument for H. C. Andersen. The overture to *Little Kirsten*. A prologue with Miss Lerche. "Gurre" sung by Mr. Albrecht and the fairy tale comedy *Willie Winkie*." I sent a letter to Mr. Andersen that I wasn't well enough to accept his cordial invitation to be there and that I was also shy about being present at a performance in my honor. Gave two children's tickets to my little errand boy Emilius and his sister. I also wanted the Misses Ballin to attend and around 3 o'clock got three more tickets for the fourth row in the orchestra. Drove in snowy weather over to see Mrs. Koch. It turned into quite a snowstorm, so that the servant couldn't get a carriage before he'd reached Old Square, and I then had to pay for two trips—one over to Mrs. Koch's and one home, accordingly four marks and four shillings plus the trip there costing two marks and four shillings. So I've paid one rix-dollar and eight shillings in all to get there and home. When the Misses Ballin and Mrs. Koppel arrived home, they said there was a very full house despite the harsh weather, loud applause and a prologue that had moved them to tears. This afternoon I went through the first act of the *Kenilworth* score with Mr. Barnekow, and in the evening composed a whole new verse in Leicester's and Emmy's first duet.

Saturday, January 23. Heavy snow. Nine degrees below freezing. Wrote a letter to Barnekow. Wrote on the flyleaf of a book for Miss Zahle and cut out pictures at Mrs. Melchior's request. At the performance yesterday at the Casino, eight hundred crowns were collected.

Despite severe pain from arthritis during the cold of the winter months, Andersen finished reworking the libretto for The Celebration at Kenilworth *and composed six poems. Toward the middle of March, however, his condition began to worsen—he was plagued by sharp abdominal pains and a debilitating cough, and he hardly had strength for anything but sitting at home.*

It became obvious to Andersen's many friends that his seventieth birthday might be his last, and they were anxious to make the occasion as festive as possible. On the day before, he was summoned to the royal palace and was made commander of the Order of Dannebrog, first grade. On the morning of his birthday, Henriette Collin and Dorothea Melchior came early to help him with all the gifts and flowers that arrived and to serve as hostesses for the many congratulators that kept knocking on his door. Later, there was a banquet in his honor at the Melchiors'; and in the evening two of his works, The New Lying-in Room *and* Little Kirsten, *were performed at the Royal Theater.*

On May 5, Andersen attended the dress rehearsal of a ballet by his friend August Bournonville, but he was too weak to enjoy it and this turned out to be his last visit to the Royal Theater. Nonetheless, despite his poor health, his thoughts turned to travel, as they did every spring.

Friday, May 21. Made the decision to travel to Menton and stay there for the winter. Edvard Collin went along with the plan, likewise Hornemann and Theodor Collin. Krohn promised to accompany me down there. I was very pleased, but after he'd gone it occurred to me that since we'd have to be leaving here before the 1st of August, it would then be too hot for me to travel down there at that time of year. Then I had the idea of going with him down to

Montreux and staying there until the end of September. So Jonas Collin promised me to come at that time and take me to Menton. This trip will surely be a big expense for me—two companions each way, down and back. I won't get away for less than 3,000 rix-dollars.

Saturday, May 22. Constipation. I was in a bad way in the early morning—my bowels wouldn't move at all. Sent right away, then, for Dr. Collin. I was given a big spoonful of oil. It didn't seem to have any effect, and then to my horror, I could feel that I couldn't pass any water. I sent for Hornemann. He arrived at 2 o'clock and said that my water would have to be removed from me (through a tube in my penis) by this evening at the latest. I was terrified. He had me go to bed. He went himself to see Dr. Collin—they both would then come this evening to see how it was going with my water. The only effect the oil had was that a kind of diarrhea was continually seeping out and soiling my bed and clothing. That's the effect the oil had had even before I'd gone to bed. I had to have a clean sheet and yet was continually lying in a mess. The pains were intolerable. The constipation was pressing on my bladder. It was impossible for me to pass any water, and I was dreading the procedure that might possibly be necessary to remove it. At 3 o'clock I sent for the barber. He was out. It was 5:30 before he came, and the preparations took a whole quarter of an hour. I only had a small portion squirted in. The diarrhea seeped out, but the obstruction remained and was even worse. I had to have it out even if my rectum went with it. I strained until it hurt, and two big, hard turds came out and more right after that. I felt as if my anus had been torn apart. My bed was an awful mess. I then had one more enema without its bringing about any new evacuation; but I was relieved, although I still didn't venture to see whether I could pass any water. It wasn't until after a quarter of an hour that I gave it a try. It worked. God, how happy I was! In the meanwhile I was lying uncomfortably in half-soaked clothes, but I was resting easy. Mrs. Melchior had arrived here at 3:30. I couldn't stand having her or anyone else in with me, and she stayed at Miss Caroline's until 7 o'clock when the barber left me and the doctors had gone. She was profoundly happy and wouldn't leave the house before she knew how it was with me. Hartmann had also been here, and he was very sad when he left. With great difficulty the maid got the wet sheet out from under me, but the dry one proved difficult to put on. I was extremely exhausted and uncomfortable, but it was bliss to be lying there as I was. Then came Jonas Collin and helped me to put on clean, dry clothes. I lay back down exhausted. Jonas Collin stayed here overnight, resting in the front room.

Sunday, May 23. Didn't get to sleep before the morning hours, and when I awoke I felt as if I'd been through a beating. During the night I did some coughing. Now it's much better today—until now I've been able to pass my water. I've only been drinking tea and had gruel and half a roast chicken from the restaurant for my dinner. I'm very tired, but can't sleep, can't rest. Today Mrs. Koch and Hartmann have both paid me such a comforting visit; also Dr. Hornemann and Theodor Collin, three times. J. Krohn spent the night in the front sitting room, but all night long I had a bad cough and didn't fall asleep before 7 o'clock in the morning and had in the hour that followed the most horrible dreams. Melchior came in the evening straight from Miss Meyer and Mr. Magnus's (from Gothenburg) wedding. The young pair left for Århus this evening and from there to Gothenburg.

Monday, May 24. I was very tired and sleepy this morning. After Th. Collin was here at 11 o'clock, I could feel that I wasn't going to be able to pass any water today either. I was quite horrified then. Sent a messenger to Professor Emil Hornemann about having the barber give me an enema again. If I didn't have the strength to pass any water, it would *have* to be removed from me this evening by Dr. Collin. Nielsen, the barber, came at 4:30. It was awfully painful to have the tube inserted into my anus. I was given a full dose—it stung the inside of my anus because of the salt in the enema. The purge worked for a half hour, but I couldn't piss, and therefore, when I first felt this, my hands and legs shook so that I couldn't even hold myself upright. Then I sent for Theodor, but since I had already squeezed out as much as a glass of urine in several tries between 11:00 and 7:30 before he arrived, he was of the same opinion, likewise Jonas Collin, who had been with me a little earlier. Emil came and quickly changed his mind, but when he then saw how great my anxiety was and had his instrument with him, he felt I should try it in order to see that it wasn't as painful as I thought, and I wouldn't live in fear of it. I declined that sort of rehearsal. In the meantime Miss Ballin had come home. Her sister, Caroline, had telegraphed to her in Gothenburg, where her family lives. She had then taken the train the long way home from Gothenburg to Malmö. I received a visit from Mrs. Koch and Baroness Jonna Stampe, who was now home from her trip south. Krohn spent the night here again. The maid was incredibly stupid about everything and so slow to boot that I was annoyed. She sulked. Earlier today Th. Reitzel was here. He talked about the new, bargain edition of all of my tales. A letter from a Paul Apfelstedt in Frankfurt about autographs.

Tuesday, May 25. Sunshine and a strong wind. Last night, after having taken some morphine, I fell asleep—or into a pleasant dreaming state—and was almost completely untroubled by my phlegmy cough. While I was still in bed, Dr. Collin came; and when he saw how much water I had passed since yesterday evening (even though it wasn't much), he assured me that it was enough. I was out of danger—this time. Later in the day, Dr. Hornemann came and was of the same opinion. Wrote a letter to Oksen at Bregentved concerning my health and to find out whether or not I could come there or not. I got quite tired and worn out from writing. This evening Munch's *Mountain Lake* will be performed at the Royal Theater for the first time. My comedy *The New Lying-In Room* was supposed to have been performed, but last Sunday Miss Nielsen got the mumps and can't appear, so my work won't be performed any more this season. At around 3:30 I heard shooting—the Swedish Royal family had arrived at the Customs House, received a very festive welcome and proceeded to Christiansborg Palace along a flag-draped Broad Street, across the square and over Holmen Bridge to the palace. This evening, a special performance for King Oscar and Queen Sophie. It began at 8 o'clock and wasn't over until almost midnight. The second act of Holberg's *The Lying-In Room* was done. Yesterday *The Mountain Lake* was performed for the first time and was booed. The newspapers are critical of this work. Krohn sent word he wouldn't be sleeping down here, so I was completely alone and managed everything as best I could. In bed before 11 o'clock.—I had a better night than recently. Began, moreover, but in a very small way, to arrange things this afternoon.

During the week following his attack, Andersen seemed to swing between apathetic listlessness and nervous excitability, which was exacerbated by misunderstandings with Miss Ballin's maid and displeasure with sculptors' conceptualizations of him for the statue destined for the King's Garden. He also experienced trouble with his two doctors—on the one hand, Hornemann wanted to send him to the hospital; and, on the other, Collin was leaving the city to spend the summer at his cottage in Hellebæk. Andersen accepted

Collin's departure with good grace, but fiercely resisted Hornemann's suggestion, believing he would receive adequate care at the Bregentved estate, where he was planning to spend the early summer.

Friday, June 4. Lovely, hot summer weather. Took a carriage at 11:30 and drove out through West Gate and in through East Gate. The sun was burning hot. I got so drowsy along Farimag Street that I fell asleep.—At home a visit from the sculptor Saabye, to whom I said loud and clear that I was dissatisfied with his statue of me, that neither he nor any of the sculptors knew me, that they hadn't seen me read, that I didn't tolerate anyone standing behind me and never had children on my back, on my lap or between my legs, that my tales were just as much for older people as for children, who only understood the outer trappings and did not comprehend and take in the whole work until they were mature—that naïveté was only a part of my tales, that humor was really what gave them their flavor. Asked him to talk to Vermehren, who was his friend, after all. He could tell him everything I had stated. When he was gone, Moritz Melchior came with two copies of *The New York Tribune* containing my letter to the editor thanking American children for the lavish illustrated work they had sent me *[Picturesque America]*, which had arrived punctually on my 70th birthday. My letter was referred to in cordial, friendly terms. Dissatisfied with myself because I'd expressed myself so harshly and vociferously to Carl Bloch. Inclined to write to him, but I gave *that* up! It is light every evening until 10:30. Four letters requesting *autographs*.

Saturday, June 5. Very hot weather. I couldn't sleep last night because of a phlegmy cough. So around 3 o'clock I took another little teaspoonful of morphine, but it didn't work until it was light outside, and I was half asleep when I got up after 9 o'clock. As I was sitting there without any clothes on, the maid (Marie) came and said that a Mr. Melsen was here and that he wished to speak with me. I replied that I didn't know anyone by that name and that I couldn't see him now. "Yes, but he said he would wait." Then I got annoyed: "I can't have people waiting for me—let me have a peek through the door at what kind of fellow this is." And it was Emil Melchior, who just wanted to say good morning, and he was on his way in no time. "That was Mr. Melchior, you know, and not Melsen," I said to the maid. "Yes, that's what I said—Melchior!" she maintained. "But I told you I didn't know any person by the name 'Melsen,' didn't I?" and she had to acknowledge that I can't under-

Statue in the King's Garden by A. V. Saabye

stand what she says. "Yes, but you haven't said anything about it!" Then I got upset and angry again. At that point Hornemann came. After lunch I drove in a carriage out through West Gate and in through East Gate. It was over 70 degrees! The whole town was waving flags. I passed the socialists with their banners, and on the way home I couldn't get through a procession of guilds marching with banners. Sent a letter to Jonas Collin in Hellebæk and to the theological candidate, Oksen, at Bregentved. When I retired late in the evening, the bed was badly made—the entire upper part of it with pillows in terraces. Annoyed, I had to get up to remake it.

Sunday, June 6. Didn't get any regular sleep before 6 o'clock. I rang at 4 o'clock. Miss Clara didn't hear it. I rang at 5 o'clock. No one came. It wasn't until my third ring, when the clock sounded six, that Miss Clara came and soon after, the maid who had of course, so she said, made my bed as always. She remarked that Miss Clara had gone in to me during the night with a glass of seltzer water. I replied that it wasn't during the night; it was just ten minutes ago. "Well, that's what Miss Clara said," and to my speech about how it might be possible that she had made still another mistake with regard to the bed she replied: "After all, anyone can make an occasional mistake." Mrs. Melchior came later on. She saw that I was occupied arranging several little things. She was adamantly opposed to this and thought I should rather pay Miss Clara for an extra month so that there would be plenty of time for other people to do my packing when I was away in the country. I replied that since I was leaving on the 10th, there would be twenty days left for organizing and moving my few things, which wouldn't take four weeks, that I had furthermore paid for all of the month of July, which is to say, an extra 31 days. If I were now to pay for August too, my things wouldn't be any closer to being taken care of—people would say that there was plenty of time for that. I couldn't understand that suggestion at all. The boy Emilius was a great help tying up with cord newspaper-wrapped bundles of letters and documents. A visit from Peter Koch. No appetite at all for dinner. All day yesterday I had nothing at all to burn in the stove. Today, however, they put a little in. The morphine syrup that Hornemann has prescribed doesn't seem to be strong enough. If I take it in the evening at 11 o'clock, then I don't fall asleep until 6 o'clock in the morning, and I'm very sleepy all morning long.

Monday, June 7. It's getting cloudy and cold again. I have a little tile fuel in the stove. Daily torments because of these stupid people. A letter from a poet in Odense regarding a response to some poems he sent me. These must have arrived when I was at my sickest. If they're here, they've been put somewhere and probably packed away. I can't have all the bundles opened up again—irritated. A letter from the encyclopedia author in Geneva who is writing biographies of famous men. He wants a complete record of everything—I don't have the strength to do it, and here he comes with his third unstamped letter. No letter from the countess or from the theological candidate Oksen. Went to bed early this evening and had what I could call a good night. A visit from Mrs. Koch and Mrs. Melchior.

Tuesday, June 8. Cloudy and cold. Mrs. Melchior down at Mrs. Johanne's in Køge. A letter from Oksen that he doesn't quite have time to pick me up on Thursday, so now I'll be leaving on Friday and will get Emil Melchior to accompany me to the station in Haslev. Found the letters and poems from that Mr. Lefevre of 38 Castle Street in Odense. I'm wearing myself out with this packing. No one who promised has come to help me. A letter to Oksen. Rested well last night. Daily visit from Mrs. Koch. J. Krohn also looks in on me regularly. At 2 o'clock today Bloch's son will be christened "Jørgen Andersen Bloch"—Jørgen after his grandfather and Andersen after me, since he was born on April 2nd of this year, on my 70th birthday.

Wednesday, June 9. Now the weather has turned cloudy and rainy, and I who need the warmth of summer! Mrs. Melchior is in Køge. Toward evening Jonas Collin came into town to help me with my packing. He'd rather come tomorrow morning at 11 o'clock and then eat lunch, and we can see how much of the packing we can do. Went to bed before it got dark.

Thursday, June 10. A letter from Oksen that he would be at the Haslev station tomorrow with a carriage. Jonas came twice and helped with the packing. By 4 o'clock we were almost finished. Then Johan Krohn came with a message from Count Moltke of Bregentved that the change of ministers would require his presence in town. Tomorrow the countess would be coming in, accompanied by all of the estate's servants. There would be no one out there to take care of or provide for me. They won't be coming home until Saturday, the 17th, and then they will be expecting me. I was utterly put out about this sudden, new arrangement and, regarding it, wrote to Mrs. Melchior about whether she and her husband wanted to have me the day after tomorrow (Saturday, the 12th). I was infinitely tired.

Friday, June 11. Cloudy, cold, rainy weather. Moritz Melchior was here—I would be welcome, but he was hiring a servant for me during the visit. He insisted on it because otherwise I wouldn't be looked after and tended there the way he and his wife might wish. Delbanco received my poem "Difficult Hours" yesterday. Wrote a list of what I wanted done with all of my things, and turned it over to J. Collin, Mrs. Melchior, Mrs. Koch and Salomon, the upholsterer.

Saturday, June 12. In bed yesterday evening at 9 o'clock. Soon fell into a deep sleep, so that when I awoke, I thought it was 2 o'clock—

and it really was only 2 o'clock! I didn't do any coughing, felt miraculously well! All that was lacking was a morning bowel movement. It would come, was Dr. Hornemann's opinion, but it didn't come. When I got up, I soon tired of all the organizing I had to do. It was 3 o'clock before Miss Harriet arrived with her parents' carriage to take me to Tranquillity. It was very cold. The rooms very cold. There was smoke right away when a fire was lighted. Melchior brought me a letter from the lady painter from Munich about returning her pictures. A few days ago I also received a note from the publisher Hartknoch about this matter. A former servant who had gotten water on the knee was hired by Moritz Melchior to take care of me. Rested well and slept not too badly even though I went to bed so early in the evening. So, the 12th of June is the date of my entrance into my out-of-town residence, and it is at Tranquillity!

Sunday, June 13. Very cold. Thick smoke from the tile stove—it wasn't until later on that the stove began to draw the way it was supposed to. Felt quite a bit better, especially in that my mind is not in a distraught state, but getting something done is completely out of the question. All of the Melchiors at the Bille's, where there was a large dinner party. They have not yet left town.

Monday, June 14. Somewhat better weather. A fire burning, almost too vigorously, in the tile stove. All day long, no bowel movement. (It wasn't until late in the evening yesterday that I had a movement, but nothing at all today.) I was discouraged. They are definitely tired of me out here—I'm too much trouble, to be sure. Yesterday I had too little morphine and had a cough all night long. Last night went better. Yesterday my latest poem, "Difficult Hours" was in *The Illustrated News*. Today I haven't had a bowel movement, even though I took some castor oil a few hours ago. My spirits are very low today! Lord! Lord! What will become of this miserable invalid!

Tuesday, June 15. A visit from Dr. Meyer and wife, who live over at the Krause House. I told him I wasn't well served with a doctor who lives thirty miles from Copenhagen and never comes to town. Professor Hornemann lives in town but has no carriage. I asked Meyer to be my doctor. He refused and declared it would distress Theodor Collin, who was fond of me. He would in the meantime look in on me, etc.

Wednesday, June 16. Last night I had three to four full hours of sleep. During the whole day, however, I've been suffering from a phlegmy cough, especially in the morning and evening, whenever I have anything to drink. Out in the fresh air for the first time in a long while. Jens walked with me down in the garden—I could hardly move my legs. The sun was hot. I made a pitiable tour around the garden and thus stayed out in the fresh air for almost three hours. It was a little too much. While I was eating in my room, in came the chambermaid, who otherwise never comes in here, and brought with her a lady from Jutland to see me. I thought it was Miss Anna Bjerring and said that she should do no more than look in, but that I was too ill to speak with her. (On my table were several serving dishes from which I hadn't taken a thing, along with two kinds of wine.) The lady was dressed in saffron yellow and black. She wanted to have a response to a letter from a lady in Horsens or Århus—I didn't understand, but what came straight to mind was the long letter sent to me, I think, with some poems enclosed. I flew into an awful temper and said that I didn't know her, that no one was supposed to come in to see me, that it was the result of a misunderstanding. She again said something about getting a response to the letter and extended a greeting from a Councillor, or something, Black. I could recall a Dr. Black in Sorø over twenty years ago, but didn't know whether it was him. Finally I got rid of her and was highly overwrought.

Thursday, June 17. Today Jens unpacked the two bags that Miss Clara Ballin took care of on the Saturday when I came out here. God have mercy! Dirty clothes and clean shirts helter-skelter; my clean, white scarves crumpled. Bille and wife, the Blochs, P. Hansen here for dinner (Melchior and his wife's silver wedding anniversary). It was only on Wednesday, yesterday, that I didn't have a fire in the tile stove—I'm constantly cold, and it needs warming up here. The nights pass rather comfortably; the days are difficult and painful.

Friday, June 18. Yesterday sent a letter to Dr. Black. Mrs. Melchior wrote it for me. Sent a letter to Countess Moltke of Bregentved. On Wednesday, to Jonas Collin. I'm not up to doing anything, keep nodding off. A visit from Nicolai Bøgh. Already in bed by 8 o'clock.

Saturday, June 19. Today is when I thought I'd be arriving at Bregentved, but I'm not on my feet yet and I'll be extremely happy if I can make it there a week from today. This morning a letter from Robert Henriques, likewise one from Miss Mathilde Ørsted, who is leaving today with her mother for Fredensborg to stay with Bournonville. Jonas Collin has come into town and promised to take care of all my affairs. A visit from the theological candidate Krohn. This afternoon I've recorded the events of just about the entire week on my own, but am a piteous fellow for all that. The sun is shining, but I'm cold anyway and have a fire in the tile stove.

Andersen allowed several days to elapse without making any entries in his diary. When he resumed his nearly life-long practice, he no longer did his own writing but dictated his thoughts to Mrs. Melchior or to one of her two daughters, Harriet and Louise, with an occasional word or phrase written in by Nicolai Bøgh. From July 28 to August 4, Mrs. Melchior herself composed the entries.

June 20. Mrs. Collin has come in to visit me. Twelve days ago Edvard wrote a letter to me. It's been sitting in the pocket of the fellow at the bank all this time.

Thursday, July 1. The days are passing in a blur. It's the bronchitis that's bothering me and the neuralgia in my right leg. Not getting any rest, no appetite, no sleep. Dr. Meyer comes every evening. Today Mrs. Collin came from Hellebæk to visit me. Over twelve days ago Edvard sent me a letter. It's been sitting all this time in the pocket of the messenger at the bank.

Friday, July 2. Titular Councillor Collin came in today to see me. I was so tired from the barber, tailor and hairdresser. Got my will written. Determined several small sums to be distributed at once. Miss Harriet wrote for me today, and in recent days she has written to Weber and Miss Bjerring. Earlier Miss Louise and Mrs. Melchior wrote for me to Miss Clara Heinke.

Saturday, July 3. (In the evening on Friday the servant Jens and the kitchen maid Caroline were at Tivoli. When they got home at around 1 o'clock, I was very sick. I had spilled water all over myself and had to be changed into dry clothes.) Many letters requesting autographs have arrived during the course of the week. One has my name with my address as "King Christian IX." A visit from Krohn. Didn't see him. Ate today and yesterday with little appetite. Dr. Meyer very satisfied. Dr. Hornemann comes too late in the evening—it's tiring for me. Lay awake last night dreaming pleasant dreams.

Sunday, July 4. Lovely summery weather. My condition to begin with quite good; on the other hand, less good right after a little sleep. (Yesterday a letter from Weber.) A sailing race at Klampenborg. Sat for an hour and a half on the veranda. Felt happy and well. After lunch, tired, sleepy, unwell. A visit from Oksen who had

Portrait of Andersen as an old man

a greeting from Bregentved. (The countess's birthday is the 23rd of July.) No sailing race because there was no wind. Feeling fine.

Monday, July 5. A visit from Jonas Collin. Visit from Viggo Drewsen. Dr. Meyer says I am making good progress. A letter to Nicolai

Bøgh. Last evening I couldn't sleep because of a poem about Funen and Switzerland. Mrs. Melchior wrote it down about 11 o'clock. Gade, his wife, Count Moltke of Bregentved on a visit this evening. Lovely weather. Didn't set foot outdoors.

Tuesday, July 6. Up early. Lovely weather. A letter from Edvard Collin. For the last few days my phlegmy cough hasn't been starting up until around 4 o'clock.

Wednesday, July 7. About the same unchanging state of health, but almost always good nights.

Thursday, July 8. Hornemann, late in the evening. He'll be leaving soon for the country. He'll come only once beforehand.

Friday, July 9. Mrs. Melchior wrote for me to Dr. Leerbeck in Clarens. A visit from Hartmann. Received from Paris my new tales in French with beautiful illustrations. Extremely pleased. Letter from Eckardt.

Saturday, July 10. A little rain. Stayed indoors. Ate rather well. (Yesterday evening a severe, debilitating bout involving an entire change of clothes, followed by a bad phlegmy cough.) A visit from Mr. Martin Henriques. Little Charlotte has gone home to Køge with Sophie Melchior's mother. A visit from Peter Müller. Two bad bouts with phlegm. Meyer assures me there is absolutely nothing wrong with my back.

Sunday, July 11. A lovely, pious, blissful night. Awakened suddenly last night, it seemed, by my own scream. All the joy and forgiveness that I thought lay before me suddenly sank so horribly. Early this morning a thick phlegmy cough. Later in the morning one just like it, long and severe. The family left for Køge.

Sunday. Seems on the whole to be my most trying day.

Monday, July 12. Slept only a little last night. Letter and flowers from Countess Moltke of Bregentved. Letter from Miss Bjerring in Ålborg. Letter from the editor of the *Odense Folk Calendar*. Sent a letter to Weber about whether the shoemaker Gredsted had received the money for the foundation in Odense. Received flowers from Mrs. Meyer.

Tuesday, July 13. Up early. Began with rain, now sunshine. Sent a letter to Mrs. Collin. Letter to Grégoire. "The Story of a Mother" to Moland. Letter to Reitzel. To bed around 9 o'clock. (Hornemann is leaving for the country tomorrow.) Felt well. Dr. Meyer said I had a fever, though.

Wednesday, July 14. Lay all night long without closing my eyes. As with the word "nadar" in Erik Bøgh's *The Caliph Out for Adventure*, there was a word tormenting me, and I couldn't find out what it was. I wanted to, though. It got to be a bright day. The sun was shining into my rooms. It was around 9 o'clock. I felt the way I can imagine a poor crazy person might. Finally, I found the word and slept without a break from 9:00 until almost 1:00. I seem to have undergone a great change: my swollen legs have gone down, and I'm feeling good and infinitely happy. Sent a letter to Countess Moltke. Meyer says there's still a little fever. Jonas Collin was here.

Thursday, July 15. Have figured out how to avoid the incessant expectoration of phlegm when I'm in bed in the evening by continuously allowing drop after drop of gruel to pass through my mouth. Fell asleep around 12:00. Slept without a break until 6:00. Lovely sunshine. A visit from Nicolai Bøgh. Feeling good. After lunch sat on the veranda. Bøgh is leaving for Funen tomorrow. A visit from Jonas Collin. He is leaving tomorrow for Jutland, where I'll write him. Sophie Melchior paid me a visit.

Friday, July 16. Around 12 o'clock last night I was wishing for that rare delight—to be able to sleep without interruption until 6 o'clock in the morning—and it happened. A lovely rest without dreams. A letter from the shoemaker Gredsted; responded right away. Warm, incomparably lovely summer weather.

Saturday, July 17. Nice weather. The never-ending, daily desperation when the servant can't understand me and I can't understand him. A visit from Jürgensen from Switzerland. Sent him away. Regretted it and immediately sent him a letter. Krohn has gone to Funen, from there to Bregentved.

Sunday, July 18. Last night, everything of no importance. Quite a "Miss Bremerish" feeling. A letter from Dr. Leerbeck in Switzerland. Very pleasing and enjoyable. Mrs. van Herwerden has come from Utrecht to Teglgaard House. The boy from the West Indies disturbed my morning. A letter to the actor Eckardt. Mrs. Bloch here with her two delightful eldest children and those lovely twins that I hadn't yet seen. The most recent baby, which bears the name Jørgen Andersen Bloch, was carried by his nursemaid. I kissed the child—it was on a cheek soft as a newly baked little bun. Dr. Meyer was here very early. Went to bed and was feeling good.

Monday, July 19. A miraculous, lovely sleep—slept actually for fourteen hours, from roughly 8:00 in the evening until 10:00 in the morning. The first time I woke up, the most lovely sunshine. Feeling so well that it was impossible for me to want to sleep through it. Fell asleep at once. Woke up again one and a half hours later.

Felt just as healthy, strong and happy. My attention absorbed by two things in particular: the one, an incident at the Hotel du Nord. I was interested in recording it in my autobiography. I'll ask Mrs. Melchior about doing it right away today.—A letter from von Lüt-gendorff-Leinburg in Munich, who, along with his daughter, it seems to me, has shown a great interest in me. He sent me a package of books very painstakingly sewn into a canvas bag, including his latest translations of *Hroar's Saga, Helge, Yrsa* and *Frithiof's Saga*. Plagued me moreover with his long letter from Munich to Copenhagen. Kept repeating the same thing. It was about immediately obtaining authorization for reprinting *Picture Book without Pictures* for the impending publication of the new edition he has prepared. He furthermore wished to use my name and motto as a signature in front of the book. A visit from Anna. Hornemann came in to see to the Marquise de Bonnay in Copenhagen and to me.—The Hotel du Nord under the management of Rasmus Jørgensen was a strange place. One of our socially prominent, now married, young gentlemen had a young danceuse in to pour his tea every evening. On several occasions he had stag parties, and she poured the tea. Later a young friend of mine arrived, and she poured tea for him then. One evening he invited me. I went, and he opened the door, stepped out into the hall and told me about her, that she was reluctant to see me since I probably had funny ideas about such things—besides, they had been out for a lovely sail that day. A young nobleman fell in love with her and married her. His family was enchanted with her personality. Old Collin, who was especially fond of her mother-in-law, declared he was terribly surprised that anyone would speak ill of her, even though Dr. Collin reminded him of the fact that several times during his management of the theater the old man had asked him about what really was ailing her—he had had to sign so many strange prescriptions for the pharmacy. When Doctor Theodor kept on assuring him, the old man said: "This he couldn't remember at all!" She became a baroness. I never heard anything else bad about her. She is dead; he is, too.

Tuesday, July 20. Sunshine this morning. Later on, cloudy and rain. Didn't go out on the veranda today, either. In the newspaper appeared: "To A.: L. did not receive any information before his departure about when and where the requirement will be met. After the experiences of two years ago, a conversation wouldn't be any more likely to lead to anything now than it did then. A. had not been willing to meet the requirement, and thus we will not be responsible for the consequences. We insist that the things be sent to us at once without fail." This put me in a very crazy frame of mind. It has to be nonsense, of course.—My watch sent to the watchmaker. My morning coat delivered.—A visit from Robert and Edmond Henriques. Always this silliness about the newspaper. The doctor, however, was of no help to me in clearing it up.

Wednesday, July 21. How full of riches the hours are! Like billions of scents, billions of thoughts! Explainable, though, on account of my peculiar turn of mind. What fear earlier of each letter brought by the postman—rude remarks one wouldn't dare or care to print in any paper! Comical infatuations! One day during Christian VIII's coronation (the philosopher Steffens with wife and daughter invited to be there by the king), when I was living at the Hotel du Nord, a silk-clad young girl with a crooked back came and asked me to write a poem for her for her mother's birthday. I told her she had to come upstairs, where I had my rooms. She came a little later, rushed right over and sat down on the sofa, jumped up and onto the raised floor by the window facing out toward the stage manager's room in the theater. "What exceptionally lovely rooms you have!" she exclaimed. "You are *my* poet; I adore you!" She leapt back over to the sofa and stretched. "Embrace me!" she said. "Good Lord! What is wrong with you?" I exclaimed. She got terribly aggressive. "But don't you have a mother?" I said. "Whatever would she think and say if she could see and hear you like this? You must be quiet mad! Really, you must leave—you're frightening me! You're asking me to . . . ! Go away!" Then her whole personality changed. "You are a disgusting person!" she said. "I used to love you; now I hate you. Are you a poet? You don't even know what a poet is!" "Go!" I said, shaking. She ran off. I hurried to get dressed, ran over to Titular Councillor Collin's. Old Madam Thyberg was there: "But what has happened?" "God, there was a female up in my rooms!" She laughed when she heard the explanation. One day later Dr. Andreas Buntzen paid a visit to me, and I told him the story. "What was her name?" he asked. I mentioned the name she had given me. "Oh, that's that hysterical young girl out at the hospital, of course, who's in love with you and constantly quoting indecently from your *The Mulatto.*" He gave me a couple of strange examples. "She got out by accident and slipped up to see you. We will certainly be holding on to her." Several years later, I think I met her on the street a little more crooked than before. It looked as if she didn't recognize me at all. In the meantime someone has mentioned to me some of her family ties—

she's distantly related to the old Collins.—One day I received a letter: "A young girl requests an interview." She asked me to go out to Amager and gave me the address—I was to be treated to apples and cherries—but nevertheless she thought it would be more convenient at that time tomorrow to meet at a certain place on Farimag Street. She began the letter with "Professor" and ended it with "eternally beloved Hans Christian." Naturally, I didn't answer her at all. Then she sent letter after letter. "I must and will speak with you. I will pursue you. I know which homes you visit, for example, old Mrs. Ørsted's." I told them about it there. Each time someone rang the doorbell when I was there, the family said: "There's Andrea!" That was her name, which they had seen in the letter.—One day at Madam Anholm's I received a letter signed "Adelgunde": "I love you as a writer and a person, have never seen you, am leaving the city today. I must see you and press your hand." She named a time somewhere between 12:00 and 1:00—during the day, of course— at which I could meet her walking from Gother Street along the North Rampart. I would at that time encounter a young lady dressed in black silk carrying a folding parasol. At once I told everyone about it during lunch at Titular Councillor Collin's. The present Admiral Sommer, who could hear that I didn't want to show up, said: "Then, I'll do it, by Jove!" My thought was that the young students who lived right there by the rampart would see me come rushing up. I was soon informed that there hadn't been a trace of such a lady to be seen. I went out, returned. Madam Anholm welcomed me with a greeting from Adelgunde, who was sorry I hadn't shown up at the established time and place. "What did she look like?" I asked. "Pretty, in black silk with a folding parasol." "Wasn't she odd?" I asked. "She looked indecent, didn't she?" I asked. "Not at all!" What am I to make of all these stories!

Thursday, July 22. A fine night! Last evening and almost all day yesterday free from coughing phlegm. Three hours out on the balcony. Dr. Meyer was here long before Anna's and my dinnertime. Professor van Herwerden and wife came for dinner. Sophie Melchior, Mrs. Koch and Anna were here. She has her children here from Randers and even the Norwegian lady-in-waiting. Very early to bed. Wrote to Countess Moltke, whose birthday it is today.

Friday, July 23. Up suddenly three times last night. Poor Jens! Sat on the balcony for more than four hours in very fine weather.— Baron Rosenkrantz talented, very proud of his high birth. Mrs. Zahrtmann gave a ball and asked me to compose some short verses for the dances. After I'd written them, I asked her if there was a chance that any of them might offend someone. I had written: "Here am I with my baronial stance, but my heart and soul are devoted to dance." From that moment Rosenkrantz ignored me completely and wouldn't greet me. If he was the one who got that verse, he would have been extremely offended. I asked Mrs. Zahrtmann what could have caused this. She replied: "I told him I'd removed a verse that would surely have offended him." "Who composed it?" "Andersen," she replied. That explained things.—Once I left Basnæs on a visit to Holsteinborg. Rosenkrantz, who was an official in Korsør, was there. I found him to be lively and amusing with no hint of the slightest nag. He liked me, and we became good friends. When he was working at the supply depot on Als during the war, I heard that he had stood in his shirt sleeves on the town square cutting up meat for the populace. I rushed over to him when I saw him one day in Copenhagen outside the entrance to the Hotel Royal to thank him for his extraordinary kindness. During the war I ate dinner at Titular Councillor Collin's with Admiral Sommer. We talked about what the newspapers had to report about the duke of Augustenborg, who was in Bremen with his family ready to depart for America. I went to see Mrs. Zahrtmann. "It's indeed very interesting," she said. "You've received a letter from the duchess that they are now all traveling to America, haven't you?" I replied: "Good heavens! I don't correspond with the duke's family." These were my words, and they were understood.—I went to see Moltke of Nütschau, the minister at that time. His wife asked me at once to tell her what was in the duchess's letter. "God have mercy! Where did Your Grace hear that?" From Mrs. Zahrtmann, who expressly heard that at the Collins', since they had the letter there.—Prince Ferdinand sent me a good paper copy of an oil tinted engraving of his brother. I went out there to express my thanks and was received by his consort Caroline. The preceeding evening Jetsmark had run "Danes Have Taken Rendsburg" in *The Berlingske News*. The princess asked: "What's new?" I replied: "Yesterday's news from Jetsmark had unfortunately to be retracted immediately by means of a handbill—'Rendsburg Not Taken!' " "That's awfully interesting! I must tell Ferdinand right away!" And she rushed out of the room, then came back and asked me at once to tell her how we had taken the town. "But God have mercy!" I exclaimed. "Jetsmark reports that it has *not* been taken!" "Oh, you've made me so happy!" she said. When I got down to the street, General Hegermann-Lindencrone shouted to me: "Do tell me the interesting news you brought the princess about the taking of Rendsburg!" "It's just hearsay and a misunderstanding!" I said. "Oh," he exclaimed, "the prince was just saying, 'Andersen has been to see my wife and informed us of the capture!' "—Often so little strength as we lie dying that it utterly vanishes through the smallest of our nerves. It brings a clarity that has a light of its own.

Saturday, July 24. Every sixth wave from the sea must diminish, though still a wave. Thus, too, thoughts.—Slept well last night. A visit from Dr. Meyer in the morning. Had results four times. Worked out an itinerary for Emil Melchior's trip to Switzerland. A visit from him and his father.

Sunday, July 25. A letter from Countess Moltke about her birthday, one from Miss van Braam from Holland, who has gotten married.— Likewise a letter from Jonas Collin and Jules Jürgensen. The master tailor—paid my entire bill. I'd say I'm losing my mind, since I can't understand anything about rix-dollars and crowns. The tailor, the servant, Professor Hartmann couldn't get me on the right track at all. A visit from Jules Jürgensen, who is leaving for Switzerland this evening. Today, again, results four times. Wrote to Jonas, to Frederikshavn.

Monday, July 26. No sign of a result. Slept well last night. A very early visit today from Dr. Meyer. A visit from Anna and Louise. Out on the veranda for a couple of hours. A visit from Hornemann. Emil has left.

Tuesday, July 27. A good night and yet extremely tired. A result. Clear but windy weather. A letter with an illustrated magazine enclosed from Miss Clara Heinke. Sat on the balcony for almost three hours.

Wednesday, July 28. Andersen was still up. Sat for a while on the veranda. Said he was feeling all right, but wasn't in the mood for writing.

Thursday, July 29. He felt very tired and wished to stay in bed. This morning as usual I brought him a lovely white rose, which he kissed. He took my hand and kissed it repeatedly, pressed my hand warmly as he gazed at me with a blissful smile: "Thank you and God bless you," he said as he again closed his eyes and dozed off again. He is growing visibly weaker, and his face is shrunken and looks just like a mummy's. Poor Andersen!

Friday, July 30. Today he lies there. I have tried to refresh him by feeding him alternately a little gruel and some wine soup that might possibly strengthen him a bit. His mind is beginning to wander a little—he repeats the same thing over and over. Now at 11 o'clock he has dozed off again. After you have been sitting in with him for a short while, he asks: "May I be alone?"

Saturday, July 31. Andersen stayed in bed again today. He is a little less lethargic than yesterday. Ate a little and drank unbelievable quantities of gruel, but that is also the only thing that is keeping him alive. He says: "Don't ask me how I feel—I don't understand a thing now." Martin Henriques and Privy Councillor Drewsen have said hello to him from the other room.

Sunday, August 1. He looks awfully bad. He was extremely surprised that it is already the 1st of August. "How tired you must be of me!" he said in a weak voice. I assured him quite the reverse and said that, on the contrary, I was glad to be able to take care of him. Thank God he is not among strangers!

Monday, August 2. He slept all night long lying motionless in the same position until 10 o'clock in the morning. I rattled the doorknob a little to see if he would wake up because I thought it might be necessary for him to have something to fortify him. Finally he opened his eyes, saying: "Oh! How blessed, how beautiful! Good morning, everyone!" And he reached out both his hands at once to the servant and me. "Well, what have we here? I don't understand anything. I can't hold a thing in my head. I won't be getting up any more, then." A few days ago he asked me if I would promise him to have his veins cut when he died. "But what if I were still on the way? Oh, well, then I could leave a note." I said jokingly to him that he could of course do just as he'd done earlier—written: "I just look dead" on a piece of paper and left it by him on the table.—A little smile spread across his sunken features. All day he had been repeating: "I don't understand a thing. I'm better today, aren't I? How strange everything is!" Oddly enough, he could get out of bed and sit in a chair while the bed was being made. Dr. Meyer hasn't been here today—he has been called to Slagelse, but, fortunately, Professor Hornemann came in from Hornbæk and looked in on him. He found him greatly changed since he saw him a week ago. Since he'd been dozing a lot today, Hornemann advised we give him a smaller dose of chloral hydrate.

Tuesday, August 3. Andersen got almost no sleep at all last night. To my question about how he felt, he still replied: "I don't know anything at all." His eyes look as if they have a veil over them. He is not very pleased that the servant has gone upstairs to sleep. He has been up and down all night, and he can use a little rest.

Wednesday, August 4. Andersen has been sleeping since 10 o'clock yesterday evening. Now, at 10 o'clock in the morning, he is still sound asleep with what is apparently a high fever. The servant heard him cough once last night, and when he came in later he was lying there with a cup of gruel in his hand, most of the contents of which had spilled out onto the blanket. He hadn't had the strength to reach over and put it down.—After Dr. Meyer was here yesterday, he said to me: "The doctor will be coming back this evening—it's not a good sign." I reminded him that he had been visiting him twice a day for the last two weeks—he took comfort in that.—Now the light is out! What a happy death! At 11:05 our dear friend breathed his last.

Bibliography

T HIS SELECTIVE BIBLIOGRAPHY *includes only works in English translation. For a more extensive bibliography see Elias Bredsdorff. "A Critical Guide to the Literature on Hans Christian Andersen."* Scandinavica 6, no. 2 (1967): 108–25 *and* Tales and Stories by Hans Christian Andersen. *Translated by Patricia L. Conroy and Sven H. Rossel. Seattle and London: University of Washington Press, 1980: 273–79.*

Andersen's Works

AUTOBIOGRAPHIES AND OTHER WORKS

The True Story of My Life. Translated from the German editions by Mary Howitt. London: Longman and Co.; Boston: J. Munroe, 1847.

The Story of My Life. Translated by D. Spillan. London: G. Routledge and Co., 1852.

The Story of My Life. Translated by Horace E. Scudder. New York: Hurd and Houghton, 1871.

The Fairy Tale of My Life. Translated by W. Glyn Jones. New York: British Book Centre, 1954.

Tales the Moon Can Tell. Translated by R. P. Keigwin. Copenhagen: Berlingske Forlag, 1955.

Seven Poems. Translated by R. P. Keigwin. Odense: Hans Christian Andersen's House, 1955.

TRAVEL BOOKS

A Poet's Bazaar. Translated by Charles Beckwith. 3 vols. London: Richard Bentley, 1846.

Rambles in the Romantic Regions of the Hartz Mountains, Saxon Switzerland, Etc. Translated by Charles Beckwith. London: Richard Bentley, 1848.

Pictures of Sweden. Translated by Charles Beckwith. London: Richard Bentley, 1851.

In Sweden. Translated by K. R. K. MacKenzie. London: G. Routledge and Co., 1852.

In Spain. Translated by Mrs. Bushby. London: Richard Bentley, 1864.

A Poet's Bazaar: Pictures of Travel in Germany, Italy, Greece, and the Orient. New York: Hurd and Houghton, 1871.

Pictures of Travel in Sweden, among the Hartz Mountains, and in Switzerland, with a Visit at Charles Dickens' House. New York: Hurd and Houghton, 1871.

In Spain, and A Visit to Portugal. New York: Hurd and Houghton, 1870.

A Visit to Portugal 1866. Translated and edited by Grace Thornton. London: Peter Owen, 1972.

A Visit to Spain. Translated and edited by Grace Thornton. London: Peter Owen, 1975.

A Poet's Bazaar. Translated by Grace Thornton. New York: M. Kesend Publishing, 1986.

CORRESPONDENCE

Hans Christian Andersen's Correspondence with the Late Grand-Duke of Saxe-Weimar, Charles Dickens, Etc., Etc. Edited by Frederick Crawford. London: Dean and Son, 1891.

Hans Christian Andersen's Visits to Charles Dickens, As Described in His Letters, Published with Six of Dickens' Letters in Facsimile. Published by Ejnar Munksgaard. Copenhagen: Levin and Munksgaard, 1937.

The Andersen-Scudder Letters: Hans Christian Andersen's Correspondence with Horace Elisha Scudder. Edited and translated by Jean Hersholt and Waldemar Westergaard, with an essay by H. Topsøe-Jensen. Berkeley and Los Angeles: University of California Press, 1949.

Secondary Literature

A Book on the Danish Writer Hans Christian Andersen: His Life and Work. Copenhagen: The Committee for Danish Cultural Activities Abroad, 1955.

Bredsdorff, Elias. *Hans Andersen and Charles Dickens: A Friendship and Its Dissolution.* Anglistica, no. 7. Copenhagen: Rosenkilde and Bagger, 1956.

——. *Hans Christian Andersen: The Story of His Life and Work 1805–75.* London: Phaidon; New York: Charles Scribner's Sons, 1975.

Clausen, Julius. "Hans Christian Andersen Abroad and at Home." *American-Scandinavian Review,* 18, no. 4(1930): 228–34.

Dal, Erik. "Hans Christian Andersen's Tales and America." *Scandinavian Studies,* 40(1968): 1–25.

Heltoft, Kjeld. *Hans Christian Andersen as an Artist.* Translated by Reginald

Spink. Copenhagen: Royal Danish Ministry of Foreign Affairs, 1977.

Marker, Frederick J. *Hans Christian Andersen and the Romantic Theatre.* Toronto: University of Toronto Press, 1971.

Rossel, Sven H. "Hans Christian Andersen: Writer for All Ages and Nations." *Scandinavian Review.* 74, no. 2(1986): 88–97.

Spink, Reginald. *Hans Christian Andersen and His World.* London: Thames and Hudson, 1972.

Index

A LL LITERARY WORKS are by Hans Christian Andersen (HCA) unless otherwise indicated. Only those by HCA have been given a publication date. A work that has been published in English translation is listed under the English title. Fictional and legendary names have not been included in this index, which is based on the indexes prepared by Helge Topsøe-Jensen for the Danish edition of the diaries.

Ansgar (801-65), Benedictine monk and missionary, called the "Apostle of the North," archbishop of Hamburg-Bremen, 98

Apollo, sculpture in the Vatican, 63, 274

Apollo Citharoedus, sculpture in the Glyptothek, Munich, 87

Apollo Musagetes, sculpture, Berlin, 157

April Fools (Aprilsnarrene), play by J. L. Heiberg, 154n

Ariel, sculpture by John Graham Lough, 187

Arndt, Ernst Moritz (1769-1860), German author, 138

Arnesen, Anton Ludvig (1808-60), government official and author, 128

Arnim, Bettina von (née Brentano) (1785-1859), German author, 152

Arnim, Gisela von (1827-89), daughter of Bettina; German author, 152

Artôt, Désirée (1835-1907), French opera singer, 303

Asbjørnsen, Peter Christen (1812-85), Norwegian folklorist and author, 395

The Ascent of Mont Blanc, travelogue by Albert Smith, 251

Asschenfeldt, C. C. J. (1792-1856), German hymn writer, pastor, and bishop, 141

At Dannevirke (Ved Dannekirke), play by Hans Peter Holst, 306

The Athenaeum, journal, 178, 179, 253, 254, 258

"Atta Troll," poem by Heinrich Heine, 131

The Attorney and His Ward (Advokaten og hans Myndling), play by Henrik Hertz, 312

Auerbach, Berthold (1812-82), German author, 180, 238, 239

August (1783-1853), grand duke of Oldenburg 1829-53, 150, 152, 158

Augusta (1811-90), empress of Prussia (née princess of Saxony-Weimar-Eisenach), daughter of Carl F., wife of Wilhelm I, 152, 154, 155

Aunt Judy's Magazine, 352, 369, 391

"Auntie Toothache" ("Tante Tandpine"), tale, xiv, 368, 369, 370, 380, 381, 382, 383, 384

"Axel and Valborg" ("Axel og Valborg"), Danish medieval ballad, 71

Axel and Valborg (Axel og Valborg), play by Adam Gottlob Oehlenschläger, 11, 71

Baedeker, Karl (1801-1859), German author and publisher of travel guides, 388

Bagger, Louis, Danish-American journalist, editor of *The Patriot* in Washington D.C., 372, 375

Baggesen, Jens (1764-1826), Danish author, 71, 169, 217

Balbi, Felippo, Neapolitan painter of the nineteenth century, 281

Balbus, Marcus Nonius, Roman proconsul, 81

Ballin, Caroline (1838-1901), sister of Clara, 400, 409, 417, 418, 419, 420

Ballin, Clara (1824-87), HCA's landlady at 18 Nyhavn Canal, 391, 393, 399, 400, 407, 409, 417, 418, 420, 421, 424, 427

Balling, Helene (née Næboe) (1799-1893); wife of Jonathan, 17, 18, 20, 21, 156, 177, 238, 243, 251, 260

Balling, Jonathan (1773-1829), warehouse manager at the Royal Greenland Trade Department, 11, 17, 18, 20, 21

Balzac, Honoré de (1799-1850), French author, 130

Bang, Caroline Amalie (née Ibsen) (1815-93), wife of Frederik S., 167

Bang, Frederik Siegfred (1810-89), banker in London and Copenhagen, court official and art collector, 167, 185, 193

The Barber of Seville (Il barbiere di Siviglia), opera by Gioacchino Rossini, 66, 112, 188, 300, 303, 378

Barck, Nils Ludvig Ferdinand (1820-87), count, Swedish cavalry officer and businessman in London, 170, 171, 177, 181, 182, 186, 188, 193, 206

Barnekow, Christian (1837-1913), Danish composer, 417, 418

INDEX

Jerichau-Baumann, Elisabeth (née
Baumann) (1819-81), wife of Jens
A.; Danish painter, 340, 342
Jerrold, Mary Ann (née Swann) (1804-
59), widow of Douglas, 251
Jespersen, Jacob Vilhelm (1805-60),
physician, 35, 37
Jetsmark, J. (1781-1853), editor in
Copenhagen, 435
Jette. See Collin, Henriette or Wulff,
Henriette
The Jewess (La juive), opera by
Fromental Halévy, 348
Jochumsson, Matthias (1835-1920),
Icelandic author and minister, 416
Joelsson, Julie (née Cantor) (1801-77),
principal, 316
Jøhnke, Ferdinand (1837-1908),
husband of Julie Sophie Andrea
(née Reitzel); naval officer, admiral,
and minister of naval affairs, 382,
400, 407
Jøn. See Koch, Jørgen Hansen (1861-
1935)
Jørgensen, Bendt Søborg (1815-88),
agronomist and professor at the
Royal Veterinary and Agricultural
School, 152, 153
Johann (1801-73), king of Saxony
1854-73, author and translator, 272
Johann (Hans), prince of Schleswig-
Holstein-Sønderborg-Glücksborg,
brother of King Christian IX, 343,
349, 377, 409, 410
Johannes. See Oehlenschläger,
Johannes
Johanne, Mrs. See Melchior, Johanne
Johansson, Louise (?-1894), Jenny
Lind's companion and friend, 151,
167
Johnson, Johanne. See Münter,
Johanne
Johnson, Samuel (1709-84), English
lexicographer and author, 172, 197
Jomtou, Johan Jørgensen (1791-1866),
Danish author, 147
Jongh, John de (?-1855), Danish
consul in Smyrna, 114
Jonna. See Stampe, Jonna
Jordan, Miss. See Sarmento, Caroline
Wilhelmine
Jordan, Rudolf (1810-87), German
painter, 101

José I (1714-77), king of Portugal 1750-
77, 324
Joseph, opera by Étienne-Nicolas
Méhul, 343
Joseph Rushbrook, novel by Frederick
Marryat, 126
Josephine, maid at Joachime
Anholm's, 305
Journal for the Elegant World (Zeitung
für die elegante Welt), newspaper,
88
Journey Through a Part of Germany,
France, England and Italy in the Years
1819 and 1820 (Reise giennem en Deel
af Tydskland, Frankrige, England og
Italien i Aarene 1819 og 1820),
travelogue by Christian Molbech, 11
A Journey Told in Letters to My Home,
(En Reise fortalt i Breve til mit Hiem),
travelogue by Adam Gottlob
Oehlenschläger, 10
Jürgensen, Anne Leth (née Bruun)
(1755-1828), widow of royal
watchmaker Jørgen, 12
Jürgensen, Jules (1808-77), son of
Urban; watchmaker in Le Locle,
272, 328, 329, 331, 345, 349, 431, 436
Jürgensen, L. B. (1812-72),
businessman, dry-goods dealer, 337
Jürgensen, Louis Urban (1806-67), son
of Urban; watchmaker, 48
Jürgensen, Sophie Henriette (née
Houriet) (1780-1852), sister of Jules
Houriet, widow of Urban, 40
Jürgensen, Urban (1776-1830), son of
Anne Leth; watchmaker, 19
Judith, painting by William Etty, 197
Juul, Christian Sehestedt (1806-61),
captain and court official, 134

Kaalund, Hans Vilhelm (1818-85),
Danish author, 304
Kahrs, Anna Henriette (née
Neergaard) (1835-91), daughter of
Louise N., 289
Kalkar, Otto (1837-1926), pastor and
lexicographer, 284
Kall, Benedicte Arnesen (1813-95),
Danish author and translator, 415
Karl X (1622-60), king of Sweden
1654-60, 223n
Karl XIV Johan (née Jean Baptiste
Bernadotte) (1763-1844), king of

470

INDEX

Koch, Johan (*cont.*)
Frederiksen (1827–1914), politician, police chief, mayor, and court official, 333, 334, 335, 336, 337
Koch, Jørgen Hansen (father) (1787-1860), architect, professor, and court official, 211
Koch, Jørgen Hansen (son) (1829-1919), son of Jørgen H. (father); teacher, 177, 195, 197, 300
Koch, Jørgen Hansen (Jon) (1861-1935), son of Peter; president of the Maritime and Commerce Court, 303, 369
Koch, Mathilde (née Hauch) (1831-1910), daughter of Carsten J., wife of Peter, 317, 318, 394, 396
Koch, Peter (1832-1907), son of Jørgen H. (father), civil servant in the Ministry of Justice, police chief, and judge, 367, 394, 424
Koefoed, Jens Laasbye Rottbøl (1832-1913), archivist in the Ministry of Foreign Affairs and diplomat, 321
Køppen, Adolph Ludvig (1804-ca. 1873), professor of history, geography, archaeology, and German in Athens and the United States, 87, 110, 111, 112, 329
Køppen, Lovise (1803-76), sister of Adolph Ludvig; teacher at a girls' school in Copenhagen, 110
Koës, Georg (1782-1811), classical philologist resident in Paris, 131
Kolberg, Andreas (1817-69), Danish sculptor, 225, 274, 275, 276
Kolling, Harald (1835-1904), actor, 344
Koop, Andreas Ludvig (1792-1849), Danish painter, 65, 106
Koppel, Frederikke (Rikke) (née Goldschmidt) (1802-89), boarder with the Misses Ballin, 418
Koreff, Mrs., wife of Johan Ferdinand, 131
Koreff, Johan Ferdinand (1783-1851), German physician in Paris, author, 131
Koren, Wilhelm Frimann (1842-1913), student in Christiania (Oslo), pastor and dean, 252
Koss, Joseph Albrecht von (1787-1858), Danish diplomat in Paris, 37, 165

Krag, Frederik Carl (1829-1915), owner of Munke Mill, bank manager, and member of the city council of Odense, 336
Kragh, P. H. (1820-90), senior teacher at Odense Cathedral School and member of the city council, 333, 337
Kranold, Rudolph Heinrich Carl Conrad (1819-89), civil servant in the Ministry of Schleswig and managing director of the Royal Theater, revenue officer, 313
Krarup, Nicolai Edinger (1813-67), director of conscription and member of the Upper Chamber of parliament, 133, 134
Krebs, Frederik Christian (1814-81), physician, editor at *Berlingske News* (*Berlingske Tidende*), medical officer, 356, 357
Krefling, Emilius (1862-?), HCA's messenger boy, 391, 417, 424
Kretzschmer, Johann Hermann (1811-90), German painter, 121
Kreysig, Friedrich Ludwig (1770-1839), professor of pathology in Dresden, 25
Krieger, Andreas Frederik (1817-93), Danish politician and minister of finance, 132, 133, 134
Krogh, Georg Frederik von (1787-1853), postmaster, officer, and court official, 98
Krogh, Juliane Marie von (1818-85), lady-in-waiting to Louise Sophie, 146
Krohn, Johan (1841-1925), teacher and author, 363, 365, 367, 415, 420, 421, 425, 427, 428, 431
Kruse, Fanny (1847-1925), chorus singer and actress, 315
Kruse, Laurids (1778-1839), Danish author and translator, 131
Küchler, Albert (1803-86), Danish painter and Franciscan monk, 50, 52, 54, 58, 61, 67, 68, 69, 71, 103, 274, 279
Kuhlau, Friedrich (1786-1832), Danish composer, 19, 135
Kuhlau, Georg Frederik (?-1878), nephew of Friedrich; pianist and member of the Royal Orchestra, 19

472

Palin, Gustaf (1765-1842), Swedish
diplomat and egyptologist, 63
Pallesen, Hans Carl Christian (1812-
50), actor, 100
Palmerston, Lady Emily Mary (née
Lamb) (1787-1869), wife of Henry J.
T., 169, 170, 178
Palmerston, Henry John Temple
(1784-1865), viscount, English
minister of foreign affairs, and
prime minister, 169, 175, 178
Paludan-Müller, Frederik (1809-76),
Danish author, 72, 308, 374, 382,
390
Paracelcus, Aureolus Philippus
Theophrastus Bombastus von
Hohenheim (1493-1541), German
physician, 326
Pardoe, Julia (1806-62), English
author, 255, 260
Parmigianino, Francesco Maria
Mazzola, called P. (1503-40), Italian
painter, 77
A Partition, play by Pedro Calderón
de la Barca adapted by Benedicte
Arnesen Kall, 304, 306
Patriotic Poems and Songs from the War
(Fædrelandske Vers og Sange under
Krigen), 1851, poetry collection,
227
Paulli, Holger Simon (1810-91),
Danish composer and conductor,
415, 416
Paulsen, Elisa (née Thorvaldsen)
(1813-70), daughter of Bertel, 280
Pechlin, Elise von (1792-1858),
baroness, lady-in-waiting, 170, 195
Peder Paars, comic epic by Ludvig
Holberg, 60n
Pedersen, Henriette (Jette) Sophie
(née Boye) (1821-95), daughter of
Caspar J., 130, 266, 350
Pedersen, Ole [Sr.] (1767-1826),
distiller in Slagelse, 10
Pedersen, Ole [Jr.] (1807-54), son of
Ole [sr.]; student at Slagelse School,
distiller, 8, 9, 10, 11, 14
Pedersen, Vilhelm (1820-59), officer,
painter, and illustrator of HCA's
tales and stories, 158, 235, 392
"Pedestrian Journey to Amager." See
A Walking Tour
Peer Gynt, play by Henrik Ibsen, 360

"Peiter, Peter and Peer" ("Peiter,
Peter og Peer"), tale, 343
Pellegrini, Giulio (1806-58), Italian
opera singer, 89
"A Pen-and-Ink Drawing" ("En
Pennetegning"), short story by
Axelline Lund, 413
"The Pen and the Inkpot" ("Pen og
Blækhuus"), tale, 269, 272, 276
Pepita. See Olivá, Pepita de
Périer, Casimir-Pierre (1777-1832),
French politician, 134
Perrault, Charles (1628-1703), French
author, 416
Perrot, Jules-Joseph (1810-92), French
ballet master, 175
Perseus, sculpture by Antonio Canova,
274
Perugino, Pietro di Cristoforo
Vanucci, called P. (1446-1524),
Italian painter, 274
Peter Schlemihl's Strange Story (Peter
Schlemihl's wundersame Geschichte),
tale by Adelbert von Chamisso;
translated as The Marvellous History
of the Shadowless Man, 33
Peters, Carl (1822-99), Danish
sculptor, 342
Petersen, Clemens (1834-1918),
Danish literary critic and emigrant
to the United States, 279, 300,
344
Petersen, Johanne (1844-1934), ballet
dancer, 344
Petersen, Marinus (1825-67),
bookseller in Hørring, 318
Petersen, P. Holger (1813-83),
businessman and member of the
city council of Odense, 336
Petersen, Peter E. (1805-72), attorney
and councillor, a fellow student of
HCA's in Odense, 347
Petersen, Poul (1815-91), master smith
and member of the city council of
Odense, 333, 337
Petersen, Rasmus (1823-97), master
carpenter and fire chief in Odense,
336
Petersen, Wilhelm (1817-95),
businessman, president of the city
council of Odense, and member of
the Upper Chamber of the Danish
parliament, 334, 335

Worm, Pauline (1825-83), Danish author, 347

Worsaae, Jens Jacob Asmussen (1821-85), archaeologist, curator of the Rosenborg Collection, director of the Museum of Northern Antiquities and Ethnography, and minister of cultural affairs, 309, 351

Wulff, Antoinette Christiane (née Birch) (1823-92), wife of Peter, 395

Wulff, Christian (1810-56), son of Peter Frederik; naval officer, 19, 218

Wulff, Henriette (née Weinholdt) (1784-1836), wife of Peter Frederik, 6, 12, 15, 16, 19, 21, 23, 93, 324

Wulff, Henriette (Jette) (1804-54), daughter of Peter Frederik, 15, 30, 31, 35, 59, 71, 84, 93, 94, 97, 111, 128, 130, 137, 185, 195, 197, 204, 206, 212, 219, 238, 242, 250, 259, 260, 261, 263, 264, 311

Wulff, Ida. See Koch, Ida

Wulff, Ida (1808-76), opera singer, 16, 17

Wulff, Peter (1808-81), son of Peter Frederik; naval officer and admiral, 144, 412

Wulff, Peter Frederik (1774-1842), naval officer and admiral, author and translator of Shakespeare, 5, 12, 15, 16, 17, 19, 21, 23, 93, 132, 324

Wynn, Sir Henry (1783-1856), English diplomat, ambassador in Copenhagen, 171

Youthful Attempts (*Ungdoms-Forsøg*), 1822, work; published under the pseudonym Villiam Christian Walter, 5

Yrsa, play by Adam Gottlob Oehlenschläger, 432

Zachariae, Georg (1850-1937), son of Georg J. Z.; naval officer and admiral, 410

Zachariae, Georg James (1818-88), father of Georg; port medical officer, 401, 410

Zahle, Natalie (1827-1913), founder and principal of several girls' schools in Copenhagen, 242, 367, 418

Zahrtmann, Christian Christopher (1793-1853), naval officer and minister of naval affairs, 144

Zahrtmann, Elisabeth (née Donner) (1805-58), daughter of C. H. Donner, wife of Christian C., 200, 434, 435

Zahrtmann, Peter Tetens (1808-78), brother of Christian C.; teacher and civil servant, 180

Zahrtmann, Wanda. See Danneskiold-Samsøe, Wanda

Zanoni, novel by Edward Bulwer-Lytton, 126

Zeise, Frederik (1754-1836), pharmacist in Slagelse, 11

Zeise, Heinrich (1822-1914), Holstein author, translator of HCA's work, and pharmacist, 149, 193, 228

Zeuthen, Frederik Ludvig Bang (1805-74), pastor, 54, 56, 59, 63, 66, 79, 80, 82, 92, 93

Ziegesar, Marie von (1824-1901), lady-in-waiting to Grand Duchess Sophie of Saxony-Weimar-Eisenach, 169

Zimmermann, Johanne, acquaintance in Berlin, 152, 153, 154, 155, 156

Zinck, Johan Georg (1788-1828), opera singer, 16

Zinck, Josephine Amalie (née Lund) (1829-1919), opera singer, 317

Zinck, Otto (1824-1908), actor and author, 340

Zitta, Daughter of the Cathedral (*Zitta, Domkirkens Datter*), novel by Ole Christian Lund, 361

Zöllner, Karolione von (née Grape) (1795-1868), German author (Karoline von Göhren), 244, 245, 246

Zytphen-Adeler, Georg Frederik Otto (1810-78), baron, politician, court official, and member of the upper chamber of parliament, 351